DISCOVERING MORE BEHIND THE BLUE LAMP

Policing central north and south west London

by

Peter Kennison

David Swinden

Alan Moss

Printed and published by
Coppermill Press
Unit 5 Fanton Hall Farm,
Wickford
Essex
Ss12 9JF
Tel: 01268 768080
Fax: 01268 768484

© The authors

All rights reserved; no part of this publication may be reproduced, stored in a retrieval system, or transmitted in any form or by any means, electronic, mechanical, photocopying, recording or otherwise without prior written permission of the publisher or a licence permitting copying in the UK issued by the Copyright Licensing Agency Ltd., 90 Tottenham Court Road, London W1P9HE

First published 2014

ISBN 978-0-9546534-5-3

British Library Cataloguing-in-Publication data.
A catalogue record for this book is available from the British Library.

All photographs and illustrations are reproduced by kind courtesy of the Metropolitan Police Historic Collection with the exception of the following;

Peter Kennison xii, xiv (2), xv (2), xvii (3), xviii(1and2), 2 (2), 13, 15, 17, 18(1) 18(2), 20(1), 20(2), 27, 28, 36, 46, 47, 49, 51-53, 55, 60,63, 65, 67, 72(1), 75(2), 83,84,101,102, 104, 111(1), 111(2), 112, 113(1), 113(2), 114, 122, 133, 134, 135(2), 136, 143-145, 152, 158, 203, 222, 226, 231, 233, 234, 235(1), 251, 300, 302(1), 316, 327, 328, 333, 334, 345, 346, 350, 352, 353, 354, 372, 375, 377, 385, 386(1), 386(2), 400, 405, 406, 415, 421, 428, 429, 435, 480, 482, 493-496,
David Swinden vii, x, xiii, xiv, xvi, xxix(2), 138, 173, 174, 176, 180, 186, 191, 195, 239, 271, 290, 293, 298, 302(2), 303(1) 303(2), 307
Alan Moss 7, 45,
Julian Jephcote 153, 156, 157, 159, 164, 181, 188, 198, 201, 202, 208, 209, 215(1), 241, 275, 294, 295, 296, 306, 308-400, 311, 326, 358, 379, 380, 381, 412, 427(1)
George Plumb xiii, xvii(4)
Mrs T. Reed 417,
Neil Watson 254, 258, 259, 261, 262, 265, 266(1), 266(2), 267, 269, 272, 273(1), 273(2), 278, 280(2), 283,
D. Collett 166
Jeff Cowdell, xvii(2), xxii (1 and 2), xxv (1 and 2), xxvi (1 and 2), 322, 335,

The late Mike Fountain 175,
The London Borough of Ealing, 203, 205, 207, 215
The London Borough of Hillingdon 301,
The National Archives, 29 (MEPO9/39), 409 (MEPO 9/122),
Westminster Archives 30.
Janice Horne 73, 74(1), 74(2), 75
The Metropolitan and City Police Orphans Fund 491-496

Every attempt has been made to credit the source of the photographs used in this book. Any omission's brought to our attention will be corrected in any future publications.

This book is dedicated to the men and women of the Metropolitan Police (past and present) who risk their lives daily in the protection of the public.

Acknowledgements.

The authors are particularly indebted to friends and colleagues, who advised, directed and discussed the research, yet still remained interested. Particular gratitude and thanks are also extended to;

Mr Julian **Jephcote** (retired police officer and historian) whose knowledge and pictures were invaluable. Phillip **Barnes-Warden** with Paul **Dew** and Neil **Paterson** all from the Metropolitan Police Historical Collection provided essential assistance and reliable information including pictures - often at short notice.

Bernard **Brown** – (Sergeant Metropolitan Police retired) again deserves an extra mention also because it has been the consistent historical research and work of Bernie that has made our task easier - thank-you.

The Metropolitan and City Police Orphans Fund formally The Metropolitan and City Police Orphange who kindly allowed us to reprint material from their website.

Also requiring special mention is the late John **Back**- whose research from 1970's in the Metropolitan Archives provided us with valuable material.

Dave **Allen**- Friend of Bow Street Police Station
Phil **Anderson** – Metropolitan Police Officer retired.
Helen **Barnard** - Friend of the Metropolitan Police Collection
Ken **Butler** - Friend of the Metropolitan Police Collection
David **Capus** – Records Management Branch
Sioban **Clark** - Friend of the Metropolitan Police Historical Collection
David **Collett** – Historian and police medal collector

Jeff **Cowdell**, - ex Police officer Staffordshire Police and badge collector
Chris **Forester** – Retired police officer and Friend of the Metropolitan Police Collection
Anna **Gardiner** - MPS Historic Collection
Alex **Hart**- serving Metropolitan police officer and police history enthusiast
Janice **Horne** – Family historian who gave details about Inspector Charles Brown.
Neville (Spike) **Hughes**, -Metropolitan Police retired (who sadly passed away in 2008)
Trefor **Jones** – Epsom Historical Society
Dr Jonathan **Oates**, Archivist - London Borough of Ealing.
Ken **Moxley** – Metropolitan Police Officer retired.
Dick **Kirby**- Retired Metropolitan Police Detective Sergeant
Hazel **Ogilvie** – Harrow Central Librarian (who gave permission to use Harrow pictures)
Camilla **O'Hare**- Head of income generation, Metropolitan Police
Simon **Ovens**- Chief Superintendent and police medal collector
Barnaby **Palmer** - Police history researcher
George **Plumb** – Specialist Police badge collector
Peter **Reed** - Webmaster of the Epsom and Ewell Historical Explorer
T. **Reed** (Mrs) – for kind permission to use a copy of her painting relating to the Horse Patrol
Keith **Skinner** – Police History Society
Jude **Swinden** – Title Contributor.
Roger **Vaughn** – Specialist photograph collector
Neil **Watson** - For researching and writing the chapter on Harrow
Dave **Wilkinson** - historian and helmet plate/badge collector
The staff of Brent Central Library
The staff of Hillingdon Central library
The staff of Hammersmith and Fulham libraries

List of Illustrations

No	Description	Page
1.	A pre 1844 Metropolitan police button with oak leaves and crown	viii
2.	Metropolitan Police Constable circa 1860's	ix
3.	Victorian button issued for senior officers tunics.	x
4.	Victorian Metropolitan Police silvered button	x
5.	A pre 1863 constable's tunic	xi
6.	The new helmet and uniform introduced from 1864	xii
7.	The 1864 wreath type helmet plate	xii
8.	Inspectors helmet plate for Dockyards	xiii
9.	The black Victorian button with garter	xiii
10.	Taits advertising picture showing Maltese crown plate	xiv
11.	The Tipstaff of an Inspector	xiv
12.	Victorian Tipstaff and belt holder	xv
13.	Chief Inspector with Tipstave.	xv
14.	Chrome button with Kings crown produced between 1935 and 1953	xvi

15.	Taits original drawings for the senior officers helmet	xvii
16.	Taits design for the constables and sergeants helmet plate	xvii
17.	The 1870 new conical helmet and plate	xvii
18.	The new 1870 plate	xvii
19.	Constable 465 'Y' with new helmet and plate	xiii
20.	Superintendent Thomas Butt 'P' Division and ceremonial helmet	xiii
21.	Superintendent's Ceremonial helmet and plate as worn by Butt above	xix
22.	Superintendent Smith Chatham Dockyard	xix
23.	The Brunswick star issued in about 1880 to dockyards	xx
24.	The new Brunswick star for divisional wear	xx
25.	Superintendent James Thomson 'E' Division in ceremonial uniform circa 1880	xxi
26.	Metropolitan Police helmet Plate 1901 (1906) - 1935	xxi
27.	Superintendents cap badge 1935	xxii
28.	Inspectors cap badge 1935	xxii
29.	Metropolitan Police War reserve cap badge	xxiii
30.	George V Metropolitan police helmet plate with rope effect	xxiii
31.	Inspectors WW2 steel helmet	xxiv
32.	A Special constables WW2 steel helmet	xxiv
33.	Womens Auxiliary Police Corps badge	xxiv
34.	Edward VIII Helmet plate (mock-up)	xxv
35.	Flat cap badge for constables and sergeants	xxv
36.	Flat hat badge for Inspectors	xxvi
37.	George VI Helmet plate with cypher in the centre	xxvi
38.	Annie Matthews in Bather uniform	xxvii
39.	The two styles of uniform 1920 and 1956	xxviii
40.	The new EIIR helmet plate issued in chrome in 1965	xxviii
41.	Cape number	xxix
42.	Cape chrome number for a sergeant	xxix
43.	The 1980/1 EIIR helmet plate.	xxix
44.	Black resin Greatcoat button	xxx
45.	A Division Band Circa 1864	2
46.	A Division Band Circa 1907	2
47.	The 1911 Coronation Medal	3
48.	The back entrance of 4 Whitehall Place	5
49.	Central London Divisions in 1837	6
50.	Site locations of Metropolitan Police telephone boxes on 'A' Div.	4
51.	Scotland Yard, designed by Norman Shaw	7
52.	Ariel view of Scotland Yard and Cannon Row Police Station	8
53.	King Street Police Station. 1847 – 1899. 22 King Street, Westminster	10
54.	King Street Mascot. Topper the dog	12

55.	Metropolitan Police Minstrel Troupe.	13
56.	Cannon Row Police Station 1902 – 1985. 1 Cannon Row, Westminster	14
57.	Superintendent 'A' Division Creswell Wells 1912	15
58.	Senior Officers of 'A' Division	16
59.	Mrs Pankhurst being arrested in Victoria Street	17
60.	Superintendent Wells at Goodwood stables	18
61.	Lying in state of Edward VII	18
62.	Cannon Row Police Station. 1985 – 1992. Curtis Green BuildingSW1	19
63.	Kings Police and Fire Service medal and George Cross	20
64.	Rear aspect of Hyde Park Police Station	21
65.	Hyde Park Police Station opened in 1902	22
66.	Rear Yard of Hyde Park Police Station	23
67.	Hyde Park Police Observation box, erected 1902	24
68.	Wellington Arch Hyde Park Corner SW1 used as a police station 1831 to 1992	25
69.	Wellington Arch Police contingent 1906	26
70.	Marble Arch 1851 – 1950 Tyburn Way W1.	27
71.	1863 map showing the location of Clarks Buildings Police Station	28
72.	Side elevation plans of Clarks buildings police station	29
73.	Bow Street, the first police station 1831 – 1881. 33-34 Bow Street Covent Garden, London	30
74.	Bow Street Police Station and Court. 1881 – 1992. 28 Bow Street, W1.	31
75.	Charing Cross Police Station. 1992 – present day. Agar Street, London WC2 4JP	34
76.	Waterloo Pier from 1873	35
77.	Map of 1863 showing Marlborough Street Police Station	36
78.	Great Marlborough Street Police Station in 1910. 19 -20 Great Marlborough Street, SW1	37
79.	West End Central Police Station. 1940 – present day. 27 Savile Row W1.	39
80.	Beak Street Section House. 1910 – 1999. 40 Beak Street, London W1	41
81.	Greek Street (watch) Station house in 1830	42
82.	Vine Street Police Station. 1868 – 1997. 10 Vine Street, Piccadilly W1	44
83.	Trenchard Police Section House. 19 – 25 Broadwick Street, Westminster W1F 0DF.	45
84.	Rochester Row Police Station. 1901 – 1993. 63 Rochester Row SW1	46
85.	Ambrosden Police Section House. 1886 – 1973. 1 Ambrosden Avenue, Westminster.	47
86.	Metropolitan Police Training school, Peel House, SW1 circa	49

	1910	
87.	A class of recruits at Pell House in the 1920's	50
88.	A final practical before passing out from Peel House circa 1920's	50
89.	The dining hall at Peel House.	51
90.	Peel House Training school staff in 1911	52
91.	H. W. Mallin	53
92.	A boxing class at Peel House.	54
93.	The official funeral of Ex sergeant Harry Mallin in 1969	54
94.	Assistant Commissioner Georg Abbiss	55
95.	Aybrook Street Police Section House, circa 1923	56
96.	Women Police tug of war circa 1920's	57
97.	Gerald Road Police Station. 1885 – 1993. 5 Gerald Road, Pimlico SW1	59
98.	Ex Inspector John Syme on an advertising postcard explaining his plight	60
99.	Belgravia Police Station. 1993 – present day. 202-206 Buckingham Palace, SW1W 9SX	61
100.	1863 map showing the location of Marylebone Lane Police Station.	63
101.	Marylebone Lane Police Station. 1892 – 1977. 59 Marylebone Lane, W2	64
102.	1863 map showing the location of Molyneux Street Police Station	65
103.	John Street Police Station.1904 – 1933. 26 Crawford Place, Edgware Road W1.	66
104.	1863 map showing Hermitage Street Police station, Paddington	67
105.	Paddington Police Station. 1864 – 1971. 62 Harrow Road, W2	68
106.	The rear yard of the police station showing married quarters and prisoner transport	69
107.	Paddington Police Station 1864 – 1971 after alterations. 62 Harrow Road, W2	70
108.	Paddington Green. 1971 – present day. 2-4 Harrow Road, London W2 1XJ.	71
109.	1863 map showing Carlton Crescent Police Station (Harrow Road)	72
110.	Harrow Road Police Station. 1859 – 1912. 22 Carlton Crescent, Kensal New Town (Kensal Green) Paddington	72
111.	Inspector Charles Brown	73
112.	Inspector Charles Brown with King Edward VII at the Derby in 1909	74
113.	Inspector Brown on Ceremonial duty	74
114.	Brown in Masonic outfit	75
115.	Constable William Harper	75
116.	Harrow Road Police Station. 1912 – present day. 325 Harrow Road, London W9	76

117.	Tottenham Court Road Police Station. 1900 – 1940. 56 Tottenham Court Road, W1	77
118.	Tottenham Court Road Police Station. 1942 to present day. 58 Tottenham Court Road, W1	78
119.	A group of police officers pose at the Barnet fair with a donkey in about 1908	83
120.	Map showing the location of Aldenham police station	84
121.	Superintendent Loxton 'S' Division circa 1865	85
122.	Barnet Police Station. 1863 -1915. High Street, Chipping Barnet	86
123.	Superintendent Williams, Inspector Wilkinson and men at Barnet in 1910	90
124.	Barnet Police Station. 1915 – 1977. High Street, Chipping Barnet, Hertfordshire.	91
125.	Barnet Police Station. 1977 to present day. 26 High Street, Barnet, Hertfordshire EN5 5RU.	93
126.	Borehamwood Police Station. (1965) Elstree Way Borehamwood, Hertfordshire.	94
127.	Officers of Borehamwood pose outside their police station in 1956	95
128.	Construction of the Borehamwood Police Station in Elstree Way.	95
129.	Borehamwood Police Station. 1959 to present day. Elstree Way, Borehamwood, Hertfordshire.	96
130.	Bushey Police Station. 1840 – 1884. High Street, Bushey, Hertfordshire.	96
131.	Bushey Police officers taken in the yard in around 1900.	97
132.	Bushey Police Station. 1884 – 2000. 43 Clay Hill, Bushey, Hertfordshire	98
133.	Colindale Police Station. 1997 to present day. Grahame Park Way, Colindale, NW9 5TW	100
134.	East Barnet Police Station. 1884 – 1932. 2 Edward Road, East Barnet, Hertfordshire.	101
135.	November 1919 setting off the maroons in celebration for World War One ending	102
136.	A topographical view of Elstree High street circa 1910.	104
137.	Elstree Police Station. 1893 – 1971. Barnet Lane, Elstree, Hertfordshire.	105
138.	Finchley Police Station. 1893 – 1967. Ballards Lane, Finchley	109
139.	Special Inspector Scott- Finchley 1917	111
140.	Special Inspector Alderton, Finchley 1917	111
141.	Willow Lodge- Finchley Special Constabulary HQ, 1915	112
142.	Finchley Special Constabulary 1926	113
143.	Sub Divisional Inspector Trott	113
144.	A group of 'S' Division who sounded the all clear after an air raid	114
145.	Finchley Police Station. 1967 to present day. 193 Ballards Lane,	115

	Finchley NW3 1LZ	
146.	Golders Green Police Station. 1913 to present day. 1069 Finchley Road, NW110QB	118
147.	Hendon Police Station. 1884 – 1998. 26 High Street, Barnet, EN5 5RU	121
148.	Chief Inspector Fitt and his 'capture' Grahame White	122
149.	Constable Jock Cobban and Rinty 2	125
150.	Father Christmas arriving at the children's party – Constable Whyte on his 'noddy' motor cycle	126
151.	Constable Whyte with his national hammer throwing prize	127
152.	The winning first aid team with the divisional superintendent	128
153.	The rear yard of Hendon in 1977 after renovation	129
154.	The new Metropolitan Police Training school- The Peel centre, Hendon circa 1974	131
155.	A sergeant takes the wheel of one of the first car simulators	132
156.	One of the first driving courses of 1935	133
157.	The formal class photograph taken at the front of the Driving school	134
158.	Students receive instruction on traffic flow	135
159.	A dummy is catapulted in front of a driver to test reactions	135
160.	Metropolitan Police Driving school 1961	136
161.	Chief Superintendent Hinxman and his deputy discuss driving arrangements.	137
162.	A Metropolitan Police Driving certificate for the Lightweight motor cycle course.	138
163.	Officers on the Lightweight motor (noddy) cycle course in the 1960's	138
164.	Car pursuit on the skid pans	139
165.	Motor cycles lined up before going out on the streets.	139
166.	Sergeant Matthews teaching the Traffic Patrol Wing Advanced Course 50 in 1966 about car braking systems	140
167.	Teaching a class about lighting systems in 1960s	141
168.	A modern day traffic officer on his solo motor cycle	141
169.	Metropolitan Police Detective Training School, Hendon	143
170.	A class of cadets passing out from Hendon in October 1958 with their instructors	144
171.	William Blackwell shown with his cadet wrestling team in 1971	145
172.	A drill class of 'B' course cadets in 1976	146
173.	Mill Hill Police Office. 1965 – 1977. 11-12 Deans Drive Edgware, Middlesex.	147
174.	Potters Bar Police Station. 1871 – 1886. The High Road, Potters Bar Hertfordshire.	148
175.	Potters Bar Police Station. 1886 – 2011. The Causeway, Potters Bar, Hertfordshire.	149
176.	Radlett Police Office. 1967 – 1980. 77 The Oakways, Watling Street, Radlett, Hertfordshire.	151

177.	Shenley – the old cage taken in about 1905	152
178.	A modern photograph of the old police station as it is today	153
179.	A picture taken in the rear yard of Shenley Police station in about 1902	155
180.	Constable Neil walks past the Shenley Police Office in 1967	156
181.	South Mimms Police station. 1871 – 2000. Old St. Albans Road South Mimms.	157
182.	Station Sergeant William Baker circa 1919	158
183.	A picture of South Mimms station strength taken in 1894	159
184.	West Hendon Police Station. West Hendon Broadway, Edgware Road, Hendon Middlesex.	160
185.	Whetstone Police station. 1889 – 1965. 1230 High Road, Whetstone N20	164
186.	The 1887 Jubilee medal, the 1897 Jubilee (bar) medal and the 1902 Coronation medal awarded to Inspector Bissett	166
187.	Whetstone Police Station. 1960 to present day. 170 High Road, Whetstone London N20 0LW	167
188.	Chief Superintendent Matthew Gardner Borough Commander	173
189.	Willlesden Police Station. 1860 – 1913. Craven Park Road, Harlesden	174
190.	Inspector George Robert Hodder	175
191.	Harlesden Police Station. 1913 to present day. 76 Craven Park, Harlesden	176
192.	Kilburn Police Station. 1891 – 1940. Salusbury Road, Kilburn, NW	180
193.	Inspector Charles Taylor and his station sergeant in the yard at Kilburn	181
194.	Kilburn Police Station (temporary) 1965 – 1967. 36 Salusbury Road, NW6	183
195.	Kilburn Police Station. 1967 – 1977. 2 Harvist Road, NW6	184
196.	Kilburn Police Station. 1980 to present day. 38 Salusbury Road, Kilburn NW6 6NN	184
197.	Kingsbury Police Station. 1973 – 1977. The Mall, Kingsbury Middlesex.	185
198.	Kingsbury Police Station. 1977 – 2012. 5 The Mall, Kingsbury, Kenton	186
199.	Wembley Police Station. 1910 – 1971. 167 Harrow Road Wembley.	187
200.	Sergeant Walter Weaton	188
201.	Wembley Police Station. 1971 to present day. 603 Harrow Road, Wembley Middlesex, HA0 2HH	189
202.	Willesden Green Police Station. 1896 to present day. 96, High Road, Willesden Green NW10 2PP	191
203.	Chief Superintendent Andy Rowell Borough Commander	195
204.	Acton Police Station. 1894 – 1977. 250 High Street, Acton.	197
205.	The front door of Acton Police Station.	198

206.	Acton Police Station. 1972 to present day. 250 High Street, Acton, W3	199
207.	Ealing Police Station. 1877 – 1966. 5 The High Street, Ealing W5	201
208.	The rear yard and front gate of Ealing Police Station 1966.	202
209.	The Ju Jitsu class of Capt. Leopold McLagen circa 1922	203
210.	Ealing Police Station. 1966 to present day. 67 – 69 Uxbridge Road, Uxbridge W5	204
211.	Police Constable Piara Singh Kenth a Sikh, was the first Indian officer appointed in the Metropolitan Police.	205
212.	Greenford Police Station. 1896 to present day. 21 Oldfield Road Greenford, Middlesex. UB6 9QL	206
213.	Greenford Police Station garden being tended by Constable Norman Chatland	207
214.	Hanwell Police Station. 1868 – 1886. High Street, Hanwell.	208
215.	A police funeral procession at Hanwell in the 1920s	209
216.	Hanwell Police Station. 1886 – 2012. 169 Uxbridge Road, Hanwell.	210
217.	Norwood Green Police circa 1890s	212
218.	Norwood Green Police Station. 1890 – 2008. Norwood Road, Southall	213
219.	Southall Police Station. 1908 – 1927. North Road, Southall, Middlesex.	215
220.	Southall Police Station. 1927 – 1975. 250 High Street, Southall Middlesex.	215
221.	Southall Police Station. 1975 to present day. 67 High Street, Southall, UB1 3HG	216
222.	Map of Walham Green, Fulham circa 1861	222
223.	Fulham (Walham Green) Police Station. 1914 - 1992. Heckfield Place, Fulham SW6	222
224.	South Fulham contingent taken with SDI May in the centre in 1912.	224
225.	Line-up of officers from South Fulham in greatcoats	225
226.	Superintendent Bacchus 'B' Division	226
227.	Fulham Police Station. Built 1914 extended 1992 still in use today. Heckfield Place, Fulham SW6 5NL	228
228.	The 'F' Division contingent at Earls Court for the 1904 Italian Exhibition.	231
229.	The Navy and Military Tournament Olympia circa 1907	233
230.	Children from the Orphanage together with SDI Littlejohns (seated 2nd left), Chief Inspector Shervington (centre) and others in the yard at Hammersmith Police Station	234
231.	SDI Littlejohns	235
232.	Hammersmith Police Station. 1940 - to present day. 226, Shepherds Bush Road, Hammersmith.	235
233.	The front entrance to Hammersmith Police Station.	236

234.	Shepherds Bush Police Station. 1884 – 1963. 87 Askew Road, Shepherds Bush W6	239
235.	Shepherds Bush Police Station. 1963 – Present day. 253 – 258 Uxbridge Road, London W12 7JB	241
236.	Front entrance of the earlier, now demolished Edgware Police Station in Whitchurch Lane	247
237.	The building on the right is the court house in High Street, Edgware and to the left is the Chandos Arms Public House. The photo is thought to be a Victorian wedding party.	248
238.	Edgware Police Station. 1848 – 1892. Whitchurch Lane, Edgware	249
239.	Plan of the 1931 Edgware Police Station by Architect G. MacKenzie French Esq., OBE, FRI, BA, FSI	250
240.	Edgware police line up circa 1920's	251
241.	Edgware Police Station. 1932 – present day. Whitchurch Lane, Edgware, Middlesex HA8 6LB.	252
242.	Group outside Pinner Police Station circa 1902	253
243.	The 13 Mile post next to the 'police pub' the Oddfellows Arms opposite Pinner Police Station in 2012.	254
244.	Pinner Police Station 1899- Waxwell Rise (later Waxwell Lane), High Road, Pinner, Middlesex	256
245.	Station Sergeant John Moore 68 'X'	257
246.	Pinner police station lamp	258
247.	Police Constable 469 'X' Thomas Piner	259
248.	Waxwell Lane entrance to the station c 1908. The scene is little changed today except that the lamps, the dog kennel and the washing have all been removed.	260
249.	Pinner Specials in 1918	261
250.	An affectionate artist's impression of Pinner Police Station	262
251.	West Street Police Station, 76 West Street, Harrow on the Hill, Middlesex	263
252.	Yorkshire Herald 27 February 1899	265
253.	Signpost in Grove Hill, Harrow where the fatality took place	266
254.	The wheel's come off! A West Street policeman surveys the damage and controls the crowds at Britain's first 'FATACC' involving a motor car passenger death.	266
255.	Constable Potter was involved in the arrest of the four defendants. Harriet had been starved to death by the four accomplices	267
256.	West Street Police Station C 1960's. Note the 'police' inscription above the main entrance which has now been removed.	268
257.	An artist's impressions of the forlorn looking Constable Cooke at West London Police Court	269
258.	Harrow Division Tug of War team winners 1920	271
259.	West Street as it looked in November 2011 following its sale to	272

	Harrow School	
260.	Station Sergeant Charles Potter and Acting Sergeant James Walter Pearce both retired on Coronation day 1902	273
261.	Picture taken in 2003 outside West street Police Station	273
262.	Harrow Police Station under construction	275
263.	Harrow Police Station 1963 – Present day. 74 Northolt Road, Harrow, Middlesex.	276
264.	Wealdstone and Stanmore Police Pay Parade (S Division) 1907	277
265.	Map taken from the Met Police Property records	277
266.	Front elevation plans for Wealdstone Police station	278
267.	Site of the Wealdstone police station in 1907	279
268.	Wealdstone Police Station and Court Circa 1910	280
269.	The Police station lamp	280
270.	Wealdstone Police Station in 2012.	282
271.	Acting Sergeant 713 'X' Eddie Phillips	283
272.	Harlington Police Station. 1890 – 1973. 75 Bath Road, Harlington	288
273.	The rear entrance and yard of Harlington Police Station	289
274.	Victorian map of Harefield	290
275.	Harefield Police Station (cottages). 1862 – 1932. Rickmansworth Road, Harefield, Middlesex	291
276.	Harefield police cycle patrol circa 1908	291
277.	Harefield Police Office. The Gate Office, Harefield Hospital, Hill End Road, Harefield.	292
278.	Early Victorian Map of Goulds Green	293
279.	Hayes Police Station. 1870 - 1938. High Road, Hayes.	294
280.	A rare view of the front office to Hayes Police Station	295
281.	Hayes Police Station. 1938 – present day. 755 Uxbridge Road, Hayes. Middlesex UB4	296
282.	The horse patrol station at Stratford Bridge in 1854	298
283.	Uxbridge Police Station. 1871 - 1988. 49 Windsor Street, Uxbridge.	299
284.	Sub Divisional Inspector Wade	300
285.	Uxbridge police station yard showing the old hand ambulance and new mode of transport the station van	301
286.	Sub Divisional Inspector Brownscombe	302
287.	The old police station now a public House – The Fig Tree	302
288.	Uxbridge Police Station. 1988 – until present day. Warwick place, Uxbridge.	303
289.	The plaque outside the old Uxbridge Police Station	303
290.	Northwood Police Station. 1911 – to present day. 2 Murray Road, Northwood.	305
291.	Special constables leaving the station on patrol in the 1920's	306
292.	Victorian map showing the Ruislip horse patrol station now King Edward Road, Ruislip	307

293.	Ruislip Police Station. 1869 – 1961. 17 High Street, Ruislip.	308
294.	The police station sandbagged up during the 2nd World War.	309
295.	Ruislip station following judging for the garden competition	310
296.	Ruislip Police Station. 1961 – present day. The Oaks, Manor Road, Ruislip	310
297.	Silver Jubilee celebrations at Ruislip in 1977	311
298.	Staines Police Station. 1872 – 1999. London Road, Staines, Surrey.	313
299.	Staines Police Station Yard and rear entrance to the building	314
300.	The rear yard of Staines Police station circa 1908 showing gardening plot	315
301.	Staines Police Station celebrations for the 1911 Coronation	316
302.	Awards ceremony at Staines circa early 1930's	317
303.	Staines Police Station 1998 to present day. 22 Kingston Road, Staines Middlesex.	320
304.	Shepperton Lock Police Office. 1965 - 1992	321
305.	Sunbury Police Station. 1880 -. 189 Staines Road Sunbury, Surrey	324
306.	A building in the rear yard of the station	325
307.	The well and parade shed in the yard at Sunbury	325
308.	Sunbury Police Station strength celebrating the end of the War in 1919	326
309.	Sunbury Police Tug of War team	327
310.	A retirement group at Sunbury circa 1910	328
311.	West Drayton Police Station. 1965 – 2011. Station Road West Drayton, Middlesex UB7 7JQ.	329
312.	Ministry of Civil Aviation Constabulary Helmet Plate Badge	332
313.	Ministry of Civil Aviation Constabulary Inspector cap badge	334
314.	British Airports Authority Constabulary Cap badge	334
315.	General Roys ordnance survey baseline	334
316.	British Airports Authority Constabulary Helmet Plate Badge	335
317.	Heathrow Police Station 1974 -2011. East Ramp, Heathrow Airport, Hounslow TW6 2DJ	336
318.	Both Police and Military at Heathrow Airport in 2003	338
319.	Heathrow Police Station 2011 – present day. Polar Park, West Drayton	340
320.	Edward Fitt Superintendent. 'T' Division	345
321.	The signature of William Fitt when he signed the Police attestation registers on joining the regular police.	346
322.	Commander George Gentry OBE	346
323.	The pair of cottages of the Bedfont horse patrol station	348
324.	A line up of the Bedfont police in the 1880's	349
325.	Inspector Barrett of Bedfont from 1881 – 1894 on his horse patrol	350
326.	Bedfont Police Station. 1868 – 1932. Staines Road, Bedfont.	351
327.	Coronation celebrations at Bedfont Police Station in 1902	352

328.	Sub Divisional Inspector Herwin	353
329.	Sub Divisional Inspector Smith	354
330.	Brentford Market square circa early 1800s	357
331.	Brentford Police Station. 1813 – 1830 (1897) 60 High Street (previously front Street), Old Brentford, Middlesex.	358
332.	Brentford Police Station. 1830 – 1869. 60 High Street, Brentford, Middlesex.	361
333.	Brentford Magistrates Court. 1850 – 2011. Market Place, Brentford, Middlesex.	362
334.	Brentford Police Station. 1869 – 1966. 42 High Street, Brentford, Middlesex.	364
335.	Brentford police station yard and a retirement celebration circa 1906	366
336.	Special constable Fredrick Tickner	367
337.	A 1940's map of Brentford showing clusters and single bombs dropped.	368
338.	The station lamp	369
339.	Brentford Police Station. 1967 – present day. The Half Acre, St. Pauls Road, Brentford Middlesex TW8 8BH.	369
340.	Sub Divisional Inspector David Rawlings	372
341.	The rear of Chiswick Police station taken in about 1908	374
342.	Chiswick Police Station in 1919 dressed up in celebration of the ending of WW1.	375
343.	Chiswick Police Station. 1884 – 1963. 210 High Road, Chiswick, Middlesex	376
344.	Police Box in Chiswick Road circa 1950's	377
345.	Chiswick police station. 1963 – present day. 205 -211 High Road, Chiswick.	378
346.	Feltham Police Station. 1952 -1971. 34 Hanworth Road, Feltham, Middlesex.	379
347.	The garden at the front of the temporary Feltham police station being lovingly tended	380
348.	Felthams' Chief Inspector prepares himself with the task of moving to the new station.	381
349.	Feltham Police Station 1971- present day. 34 Hanworth Road, Feltham, TW13 5BD.	382
350.	Hounslow Police Station. 1887 – 1965. Montague Road, Hounslow.	383
351.	The rear yard of the station in circa 1908	384
352.	The senior officers and sergeants of 'T' Division receive their Coronation medals and certificates at Hounslow in 1937	385
353.	Staff Officer Sub Inspector Percy Fitt (shown right) at Hammersmith	386
354.	George V MSC Long Service Medal	386
355.	Hounslow Police Station. 1965 – present day. 5, Montague Road, Hounslow, TW3 1LB	387

356.	The local police gather outside Isleworth Police Station circa 1887	388
357.	Isleworth Police Station. 1873 - 1931 . Worple Road, Isleworth.	389
358.	Side aspect of Isleworth Police station circa 1906	390
359.	Chelsea Police Station. 1852 – 1897 (added to). Milmans Row j/w Kings Road, Chelsea.	395
360.	Chelsea police station. 1897 – 1939. 385 Kings Road, SW10 (demolished 1984)	397
361.	Chelsea Police Station, 1939 – present day. 2 Lucan Place, SW3 3PB	398
362.	The location of Kensington Police Station in 1863	400
363.	Kensington police station 1873 – 1956. 78 Kensington High Street, London	402
364.	Constable Riseboro receives his Distinguished Flying Medal at Kensington Police Station from the Commissioner in 1920	405
365.	The Distinguished Flying medal	406
366.	Kensington Police Station, 1956 – present day. 72 Earls Court Road, Kensington W8.	407
367.	The architect's plan of Notting Dale, opened 1868	409
368.	Notting Dale Police Station, 1968 – present day. 58 Sirdar Road, Notting Hill.	410
369.	Notting Hill Police Station 1854 – 1906. Ladbroke Road j/w Ladbrooke Grove W11	412
370.	Notting Hill Police Station. 1906 – present day. 101 Ladbroke Road W11.	413
371.	Yeoman's Row, showing the rear of Walton Street (left background)	414
372.	Walton Street Police Station. 1894 – 2009. 60-62 Walton Street, Brompton SW3.	415
373.	Bow Street Horse Patrol circa 1812	417
374.	An early Kingston Police officer taken in 1868	421
375.	Kingston Police Station. 1864 - 1968 . London Road Kingston, Surrey	422
376.	Rear Yard aspect of Kingston Police station	423
377.	The rear entrance to the station taken in 1906	424
378.	Retirement through injury at Kingston circa 1908	425
379.	Motor Car accident on Kingston Hill in 1903	427
380.	Rear aspect of Kingston Police Station in 1908	427
381.	Sergeant 5 VR Brooks stationed at Kingston	428
382.	Kingston Police Station (VD) 1968 – present day. 5-7 High Street, Kingston, Surrey.	432
383.	Surbiton Police Station. 1888 – 1974. 1 Ditton Road, Tolworth, Surrey.	435
384.	Rear aspect of Tolworth (Surbiton) Police Station circa 1908	436
385.	Surbiton Police Station. 1977 – 2012. 299 Ewell Road, Surbiton, Surrey.	439

386.	New Malden Police Station. 1881 – 1998 . 128 Malden Road, New Malden Surrey.	440
387.	Rear aspect to New Malden Police station circa 1908	441
388.	Barnes Police Station. 1892 – 1976. 371 Lonsdale Road, Barnes SW13	447
389.	Rear access to Barnes Police station circa 1908	448
390.	Barnes Police station yard showing the dog kennel and parade room circa 1908	449
391.	Barnes Police Station. 1976 – present day. 92- 102 Station Road, Barnes SW13 0NG	450
392.	Cobham Police station. 1947 – 2000. 91-93 Portsmouth Road, Cobham, Surrey, KT11 1JJ.	452
393.	Thames Ditton Police Station. 1855 -1933. Ferry Road, Thames Ditton	455
394.	The rear yard and dog kennels at Thames Ditton in 1908	456
395.	Thames Ditton Police Station Garden in 1908	457
396.	East Molesey Police Station . 1902 – 2000. 1 Walton Road, East Molesey, Surrey.	458
397.	Esher Police Station. 1960 – 2000. 113 High Street, Esher, Surrey.	461
398.	Ham Police Office. 1972 – 1999. 18, Ashburnham Road, Ham, Richmond, Surrey	463
399.	Hampton Police Station. 1848 – 1901. 1 New Street (now 12 Station Road) Hampton, Middlesex	464
400.	Hampton Police Station. 1901 – 2013. Station Road, Hampton Middlesex.	467
401.	Hampton Police Station dressed for the 1911 Coronation	468
402.	Rear aspect and stable views circa 1908	469
403.	Hampton Police Station yard circa 1970's	470
404.	Kew Police Station. 1914 – 1933. 96 North Road, Kew	471
405.	Richmond Police Station. 1871 – 1912. 35 George Street, Richmond, Surrey	475
406.	Rear aspect of Richmond Police Station with officers by the scullery	476
407.	The rear gate and yard of Richmond Police station.	476
408.	Mrs Thomas the murder victim	477
409.	Webster the murderess	478
410.	Constable James Frank Dellar (wt. no. 78885) who was constable 1169 'V'	480
411.	Royal Flying Corps verses Richmond Police station teams raise money for the British Sportsman's Ambulance Fund	481
412.	Map of the Richmond area dated 1960	482
413.	Richmond Police Station. 1912 – present day. 8 Red Lion Street, Richmond, Surrey.	483
414.	Teddington Police Station. 1881 – 1998. Church Road, Teddington. Surrey	485

415.	Teddington Police station rear aspect taken in about 1908	486
416.	Teddington's protective wall against bombs	486
417.	Teddington Police station retirement celebrations circa 1910	487
418.	Teddington Police Station. 1998 – present day. 18 Park Road, Teddington TW11 0AQ	488
419.	Twickenham Police Station. 1858 – 1947 (demolished and rebuilt) 41 (previously 45) London Road, Twickenham, Surrey	489
420.	Rear aspect to the station circa 1908	490
421.	Parade shed and station year circa 1908	490
422.	Twickenham Police station rear yard circa 1908	491
423.	Twickenham Police Station 1947 – present day. 41 London Road Twickenham TW1 3SY	492
424.	Metropolitan and City Police Orphanage	493
425.	Metropolitan and City Police Orphanage- Group of children	494
426.	Metropolitan and City Police Orphanage- The Dining Hall	495
427.	Metropolitan and City Police Orphanage – A Dormatory	496
428.	An early mounted police officer	497
429.	The opening of the Clubhouse at Imber Court in June 1929	498
430.	Final rehearsal at Imber Court of the combined Mounted Branch and Traffic patrol display for the international Horse show	499
431.	The Clubhouse in 2013 at Imber Court originally designed by G. Mackenzie Trench	501

Discovering More Behind the Blue Lamp

Index   i - iv

Introduction   v - vi

Badges of Office, Top Hats   vii - xxxi

The City of Westminster   pages 1 - 80

Scotland Yard	5
Gardiners Lane	8
King Street	9
Cannon Row	12
Hyde Park	21
Wellington Arch	25
Clarks Buildings	27
Bow Street	29
Charing Cross	32
Waterloo Pier	34
Great Marlborough Street	36
West End Central	38
Beak Street	40
Dean Street	41
Greek Street	42
Vine Street	43
Rochester Row	45
Ambrosden Avenue	47
Peel House	48
Gerald Road	58
Belgravia	61
Marylebone Lane	63
Molyneux Street and John Street	64
Paddington and Paddington Green	66
Harrow Road	71
Tottenham Court Road	77

London Borough of Barnet   pages 81 - 172

Aldenham	84
Chipping Barnet	85
Borehamwood	94
Bushey	96
Colindale	99
East (New) Barnet	100
Elstree	102
Finchley	106
Golders Green	116
Hendon	119

Hendon (Peel Centre)	130
Mill Hill	146
Potters Bar	147
Radlett	150
Shenley	152
South Mimms	157
West Hendon	159
Whetstone	162

London Borough of Brent   pages 173 - 193

Harlesden	173
Kilburn	179
Brent	185
Kingsbury	185
Wembley	186
Chalkhill	190
Wlleseden	191

London Borough of Ealing   pages 195 - 219

Acton	195
Ealing	200
Greenford	205
Hanwell	208
Norwood Green	211
Southall	214

London Borough of Hammersmith and Fulham   pages 220 - 234

Fulham	220
Fulham (Walham Green and South Fulham)	221
North Fulham	229
Hammersmith	229
Shepherds Bush	231

London Borough of Harrow   pages 245 – 285

Edgware	246
Pinner	252
Harrow (West Street)	263
Harrow (Northolt Road)	273
Wealdstone	275

London Borough of Hillingdon   pages 286 – 344

Ashford and Ashford Cottages	287

Harlington	287
Harefield	289
Hayes and Goulds Green	292
Hillingdon and Uxbridge	297
Northwood	304
Ruislip	306
Staines and Spelthorne	311
Shepperton Lock	320
Stanwell	322
Sunbury	323
West Drayton	328
Heathrow Airport Division (SO18)	330
Heathrow Airport	334
Heathrow (Polar Park)	339

London Borough of Hounslow   pages 345 - 393

Bedfont	347
Brentford	358
Chiswick	371
Feltham	380
Houslow	384
Isleworth	390

The Royal Borough of Kensington and Chelsea   pages 394 - 416

Chelsea	395
Kensington	399
Adam and Eve Mews	404
Notting Dale	408
Notting Hill	411
Walton Street	413

The Royal Borough of Kingston on Thames   pages 417 - 444

Ewell	419
Kingston	419
Surbiton (Tolworth)	433
New Malden	439

London Borough of Richmond upon Thames and Elmbridge   pages 445 - 504

Barnes	446
Cobham	450
Ditton (Thames Ditton and Long Ditton)	454

East Molesey	457
Esher	459
Ham	462
Hampton	463
Kew	470
Richmond	471
Teddington	485
Twickenham	488
Metropolitan and City Police Orphanage Strawberry Hill	493
Imber Court	497

Appendices

1. List of Police Officers mention in this book   pages 505 – 526
2. Omission from Book 2   pages 527 – 529

DISCOVERING MORE BEHIND THE BLUE LAMP

INTRODUCTION

This is the third book in this series and completes the station histories of central, north and south west London. Book one was sub titled 'Policing North and North East London' (ISBN 978-0-9546534-0-8) whilst book two focussed on 'Policing South and South East London' (ISBN 978-0-9546534-3-9).

In 1829 the Metropolitan Police were established in London to control the streets of the Metropolis. They were one of the largest employers, at the time, and later they became one of the largest landlords in the country. Today the Metropolitan Police is still the largest London employer. They had highly regulated and disciplined work practices, which led to distinct work patterns that changed the nature of employment. This had far reaching repercussions for society at large mainly because of daily contact between the police and public[1]. Since that time much has been written about the police in terms of enforcement, however little has been done to tackle the institutional [2] nature of policing and to show the social side of the police organisation. These books help to fill that void.

A large number of local topographical histories have been written and many forget to tell the story of the local police. Other more general histories have been written which tell the story of how the police evolved from early times, yet they omitted the day to day functions and duties of constables apart from riots, murders, and the strange or outrageous. The histories of the stations, section houses and other police buildings, which housed our police in London were also left out. We aim to put this right and tell the individual station histories known.

A great deal of the recent comment on the police has been critical, but it is easily forgotten that the British police represent an admirable balance between liberal and authoritarian control. The increase in the pace of life, improvements in communication and advances in technology are all issues of the moment, and are matters which the police must consider in their daily tasks. Yet in many quarters we seem to expect more from our police than we do from any other profession. Many people, these days, only see the police when a uniformed police officer attends an incident out on the streets, or when a police vehicle passes them either on patrol or answering an emergency call. Lack of resources have always kept the police 'low on numbers' a fact which led to the old adage that 'you can never find a copper when you want one'. This, together with the fact that the majority of people never see the inside of a police station except perhaps when portrayed on television, attracts accusations from some quarters that the police are a secretive, covert and biased organisation. This book looks at the London police from its very beginning through its organisation, buildings, equipment, work practices and social groups. It portrays the police at work and play.

Many of the older police stations have disappeared or have been sold and new ones have been built to keep pace with the increases in population and new technology. Police stations, like hospitals and schools, add to our sense of community, and it threatens our security when police decide to close them for ever and this also generates a sense of loss for those living nearby.

The gradual increase in manpower, changing work patterns and the implementation of new technology have all created demands for more space. Although many of today's police stations have been rebuilt on the same original sites, many details, photographs and plans of the original buildings have long since disappeared. Our original research started in 1998 and has involved collecting material from a variety of sources including the archives of the Metropolitan Police (Historical Collection) Museum, the National Archives (formerly the Public Records Office) and many Local Authority Libraries.

In this book we have examined and documented details from existing records in central, north and south west London, and have included stations which have at some time either been within, or are no longer in, the Metropolitan Police Area. The book plots the changing face of London police stations and the closures of famous landmarks many of which will soon disappear. We hope the book will be of interest to a wide variety of people, and particularly those who enjoy police history and also those serving and retired police officers, special constables and civilian support staff, who want to remember some of the police stations where they once served or were posted to. This book may also be useful to those who have an interest in family history and want to add more detail to their family tree of ancestors who were, and may still be, police officers. A list of the named officers mentioned in this book, are shown in the Appendix 1.

This book is an opportunity to look behind the 'blue lamp' in a socio/historical way, and reveals how police culture developed historically, socially and institutionally. The book is organised so that the police history is set within each of the borough boundaries. The social aspects of policing have been introduced throughout the text.

Badges of Office, Top hats, Helmets, plates and uniform of the Metropolitan Police 1829 – 2013.
by Peter Kennison

In books one and two [3] we dealt with badges of office from constable to commissioner and it is not intended to repeat any information on ranks in this chapter which therefore deals generally with police uniforms and accoutrements. Many subjects like tipstave's, whistles, buttons and helmets etc. deserve individual books in their own right.

Over the course of time there have been many experiments carried out to find suitable garments for police officers which would stand the test of time in all types of weather. In the beginning the only real precedent was the army and many commissioners turned to military outfitters to fulfill their requirements. Police Orders issued to stations would inform the officers and men regarding changes of uniform including equipment, helmets, plates and so forth. Because there were no illustrations included in the published orders, much of what we know now has to be gleaned - not only from the detail of these instructions - but also from rare photographs taken at the time. Other documentation, for example from the Home Office also exists from which we can draw useful information. In the end much is open to debate and interpretation. For example there is a commonly held misconception that the second helmet plate, issued between 1870 - 1875[4] with laurel wreath removed, was only issued to dockyards and not to divisions. The evidence, taken from old and dated photographs, although contested and presented below, tends to dismiss this claim. The research into uniforms etc. cannot be exhaustive as new information from archives on this subject is surfacing online regularly.

1829 – 1864.

On Tuesday 29th September 1829 at 6 p.m. the first Metropolitan Police officers took to the streets clothed in a uniform based very much on civilian attire of the period. Initially, Home Secretary Sir Robert Peel favoured a military-style jacket of red, like those of the Horse Patrol but it was eventually decided that a non-military style of uniform should be provided and the first men were fitted in the grounds of the Foundling Hospital in Bloomsbury. A clothing return of 1830 established what should be worn and when it would be replaced. This instruction was for sergeants and constables only and consisted of;

> '1 greatcoat, 1 cape, 1 badge, 1 coat, 2 pairs of trousers, 2 pairs of boots, 1 hat cover, 1 stock (neckware), 1 embroidered collar, 1 number to hat cover, 1 button brush and stick. The coat, trousers, boots and hat were to be changed every second year. The pay

was stated to be £1.2s.6d.(£1.13p) per week for a Sergeant and 19/- (95p) for a Constable'[5].

Before the formation of the Metropolitan Police in September 1829 police (watchmen) buttons were made of pewter. By the mid-19th Century nickel buttons were introduced. This was followed by brass with the front dipped in chrome – known as dipped silver. Some buttons were made of chrome on nickel silver but this proved too costly.

A pre 1844 Metropolitan Police button with oak leaves and crown

The first police officers were issued with a uniform which was meant to be more civilian than military although later the military influence especially regarding the helmet prevailed.

The tunic (issued in 1844 featured eight gilt buttons) with a crown in the centre and the words 'POLICE FORCE' in the centre, on a dark blue swallow tail coat. Inside the coat tail was a pocket for the rattle and truncheon. To guard against being strangled a four inch leather stock was worn inside the stand collar. The trousers and coat were of blue felt cloth. The trousers were so thick that it was said they could stand up of their own accord. **The greatcoat** was also of dark blue cloth, double-breasted with stand-up collar and detachable cloth cape[6].

The stove pipe **top hat** was six and three quarters inches tall with a two inch wide brim. Black three quarter inch braid was stitched around the base with a knot worn over the left ear. The **top hat** was 7 inches wide and 7½ inches front to back. The brim was 2 inches wide and was piped in black braid. Hat covers were issued for use in bad weather. The top consisted of black leather which had a half inch overlap onto black beaver skin[7]. The inside was reinforced with cane side stays to protect the wearer from head injuries. Following complaints from the public that it was impossible to tell whether a policeman was on or off duty, a **duty armlet** was issued in 1830. This was two inches wide with eight horizontal blue and white alternating stripes and was to be worn on the left arm above the cuff.

In the picture below the constable is wearing the new white metal divisional numbers and single divisional letter which indicates that this was a later photograph taken around the early 1860s.

Almost immediately the officers and men were unhappy at the inferior quality of the garments which they said were sold to them at exorbitant prices. These concerns were immediately raised with the Commissioners because each man was required to pay for his clothing. His dress coat cost £1.7s.6d.(£1.38p), greatcoat £1.15s.(£1.75p), trousers 12s. 9d.(64p), hat 12s.(60p), and boots 12s. (60p), thus payment for his entire uniform was £4.19s.3d. (£4.93p), for which two shillings (10p) per week was deducted from his wages[8] making it nearly one year before the monies due had been paid.

Metropolitan Police Constable circa 1860's

As a matter of urgency the Commissioners examined the clothing which was supplied and were determined to placate their own men's concerns. They set about to alter the arrangements about uniforms, and instructions were given to the clothing contractors, Charles Hebbert military clothiers of 8 Pall Mall East, Westminster, to supply them with new and better quality clothing forthwith. Founded in 1815 the firm was originally known as Hebbert & Hume in Leicester Square, London and from 1826 had moved to Pall Mall. From 1830 the company was known as Charles Hebbert, and then in 1852 Charles Hebbert & Co. In 1843 they were described as 'Army clothiers' and by 1863 'Army clothiers, cap, & accoutrement maker'[9] although by this time Hebbert had lost the Metropolitan police contract. Hebbert was a very enterprising man[10] who outwitted his competitors by offering the police a made-to-measure service and even set up a store to accept returns of uniforms etc. from men who had resigned. This enterprise involved Hebbert in losses at first but eventually provided a very lucrative business[11].

The replacement of defective clothing was undertaken before Christmas 1830. These instructions to Hebbert and Co. included that:

> 'The private men are to have cloth of a better quality, the Serjeants are to wear the same description of costume as at present worn by Inspectors, the Inspectors are to wear a pattern the Superintendents now possess, the

Superintendents' clothes are to be decorated with the acorn and laurel leaf embroidered in silver on the collar, and the collar and cuffs are to be edged with a narrow silver lace; all to wear chin straps to their hats, 'a la militaire', The inscription upon the button is to be altered; instead of 'Police Force' it is to be 'Metropolitan Police'. The total number of men now in the service amounts to 3,540, and about Christmas two more divisions are to be added'[12].

After 1841 the hats of superintendents and inspectors were made one inch taller for constables and sergeants. **A tunic** was issued to superintendents in 1843 and an example of their button is shown below.

Victorian button issued for inspectors and above.

In the 1850s constables began altering their top hats in a number of ways. Some filled the hat with old clothing or newspaper because in their experience the hat offered little protection when attempting to quell a riot or demonstration. Others altered their hats by cutting the brims or even resorting to wearing their own private better quality top hats. Instructions were issued forbidding the altering of any hats and the wearing of non-issue hats with leather tops was also forbidden. As can be seen from the photograph on the previous page the hat was stitched down the side and officers were reminded to wear the hat straight so that this stitching together with the knot was over the left ear. It was often popular fashion at the time with men wearing top hats to tilt them slightly: hence the commissioner's instructions. The top hat also was fitted with a wide chin strap although none survive to be seen today with it still attached.

Victorian Metropolitan Police silvered button

In 1838 constables, sergeants and inspectors were permitted to wear suitable tunic **belts.** These were 2½ inches wide with a brass buckle. Belts had been originally issued for use with a greatcoat so as to carry a lantern however not with a tunic. The Victorian button at left was introduced in 1830 and shows the Metropolitan Police within a garter belt. This is consistent with the pre-1844 but shown earlier – a response to the commissioners directions to change the button designs.

x

Senior officers wore braided tunics which did not require crested (eg. raised) **buttons**. It is clear that in some forces they adopted black buttons for their jackets as a distinction from the lower ranks. The most common use of **black buttons** was on greatcoats and raincoats[13]. In 1843 superintendents tunics were made single-breasted with a hook-and-eye front that had a stand collar. There were no shoulder straps although later uniforms showed a twisted braid on each shoulder (see later pictures of Superintendent Butt). The front was edged with two rows of plain black braid and the cuffs were embellished with the Austrian knot[14].

Many officers, sergeants, inspectors and superintendents needed to patrol their divisions on horseback and no special riding clothes were provided until 1839 when the mounted branch was formed.

In 1853, sergeants were issued with **armlets** with two narrow blue lines which were to be worn on the right arm.

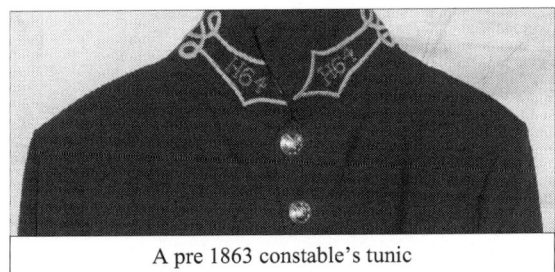

A pre 1863 constable's tunic

Greatcoats were issued to all police officers. They were dark blue double breasted frock coat pattern with straight fronts and a stand up collar. Down either side of the front were four black Victorian Crown buttons. There was also one small Victorian Crown button underneath each side of the collar so as to attach the cape. Instructions were given in 1853 that the coats were to be buttoned uniformly on one side and sides changed once a month.

The badge of office for constable which was worn on the coat collar consisted of a white embroidered crow's toe containing the divisional letter and number (shown above). These were later replaced with metal numbers and a letter (see picture on page ix).

In 1859 the uncomfortable stock collar was reduced to two inches. During the summer, (and until 1861) white trousers were worn, but they were not standard issue and were purchased by the police officers at their own expense. Sergeants were distinguished through the numbers on their collars from one to sixteen and the fact they wore the duty armlet on their right cuff. **Duty armlets** were withdrawn on 1st July 1968.

Changes to the old uniform began at the end of 1863 and the new issues were not completed until 1865 meaning that some officers were wearing both types of clothing whilst others had completely new uniforms.

1864 – 1870

Police officers were obliged to wear their uniform at all times and were even, on occasions, required to sleep in them during an emergency. The **top hat** was heavy, uncomfortable and cumbersome. The hat also afforded no ventilation, a factor made worse in hotter weather.

Superintendents, inspectors and sergeants could not easily be distinguished from constables. Those officers, many of whom were from military backgrounds, soon became conscious of their ranks, and pressed for their uniforms to be distinguished from more junior officers[15]. A coxcomb **helmet** modelled on the German (Prussian) military 'pickelhaube', and standard issue for the British army, replaced the by now unserviceable top hat in 1864. The military-style helmet described by *Punch* as an, 'Upturned escutcheon urn',

The new helmet and uniform introduced from 1864

The 1864 wreath type helmet plate

was introduced probably because many of the senior officers were ex-military and the Army and various militias had copied the Prussian helmet in 1854. The helmet with its ventilation tab at the front allowed cooler air to circulate inside making it more comfortable to wear. The coxcomb helmet was issued only to constables, sergeants and Inspectors. These were made of dark blue pressed felt. They had an overall length of eleven and half inches, height of eight inches with the width surmounted by a comb. The brim was two inches wide front and back which was slightly turned down. A three quarter inch black leather band was fitted around the base. There was a similar but wider band inside the helmet for the head to rest against.

Weighing eleven and a half ounces it was fitted with a black leather chin strap two and a half inches wide which was worn to the point of the chin[16].

The 1864 **helmet**[17] **plate** (shown above left) consisted of a laurel wreath type in japanned black, bearing a Victoria crown and garter ribbon. The ribbon contained the words METROPOLITAN POLICE in raised letters and a square buckle. The centre was made of black leather. Constables' and sergeants' helmet plates bore the divisional letter above the number which was fastened through the black leather centre. In the case of inspectors a much larger divisional letter was shown. Introduced first into the dockyards the distribution was phased into the London land divisions gradually (from 1st February 1865). Inspectors and superintendent's wore the same helmet plate except it was silvered as the example below shows. The dockyard was recognised by its 'fouled anchor' which was worn in the centre of the plate by inspectors and superintendents (as shown below) whilst their divisional 'town' colleagues had a large divisional letter instead.

Inspectors helmet plate for Dockyards

Superintendents and inspectors were each issued with a **kepi**. This was the standard pill box type with ventilation holes on both sides. The peak was made of patent leather. The superintendents wore an embroidered button surrounded by black scroll embroidery on the crown of the kepi. An embroidered black oak-leaf braid was fitted around the kepi with the peak being kept horizontal. Inspectors wore something similar with a knitted button to the crown plus a band made of embroidered black braid around the kepi with a peak at 45 degree angle. Initially there was no badge to the front but later a knitted crown was added to the front.

In 1864 acting sergeants were also introduced, and together with sergeants' were given a distinctive badge of office. This was for sergeants, three bar silver lace (Russia Braid) chevron, whilst acting sergeants had two bar silver lace chevron, both to be worn on the upper arm. Worsted chevrons were worn on great coats however whilst initially the chevrons were worn on the upper right arm within a few months they were worn on both arms.

The black Victorian button with garter

Truncheons for inspectors, sergeants and constables were carried in a leather case which consisted of a black leather tube sewn with a single seam. These were convex shaped with a bucket-style bottom to accommodate the rounded end of the truncheon. There was a loop strap for attachment to the belt and a clip down leather lid with a spring inside the tube[18]. These were withdrawn in 1887 when a truncheon pocket was fitted in the trouser leg.

Taits advertising with Maltese crown plate

A double breasted great coat with a stand collar and blunted ends was issued to all ranks in 1864. This was made of dark blue cloth and was made to button both sides. There were five composition black **buttons** on either side in parallel rows and the rear of the coat had two pleats sewn in.

An instruction was issued regarding leather belts to Constables and sergeants in 1860. Recommendations on a police issued leather belt to help carry a police cape were made by the Commissioners stating that these could be supplied by Messrs. Bramston and Co. of Kings Cross at a cost of 2/6d (13p)[19]. A double thickness **belt** was issued for the first time in 1864 (until 1973) to Inspectors, sergeants and constables for wear with a tunic. This was made of leather with a snake clasp although belts had been issued for use with a greatcoat as far back as 1847. **Tunics** were of dark blue cloth for inspectors to constables similar to the old swallow tail except the tail was shortened and the front lengthened to correspond.

There were eight metal buttons to the front, and to the rear one button over each of the two slits. Instructions were issued in 1864 that armlets issued to sergeants should be worn on the left arm. Inspectors were instructed to have a small piece of silver lace on the collar whilst constables and sergeants wore white metal numerals and a letter(s) on each collar replacing the crow's toes with embroidered numerals and divisional letter.

The suppliers of uniform and equipment to the Metropolitan Police in 1864 were R. T. Tait and Co of 10 Essex Street, Strand, WC London and they had been the contractors since 1859[20]. The advertising picture from Taits of the same year

The Tipstaff of an Inspector

above shows a constable wearing a coxcomb helmet with wide brim front and back together with a Maltese Cross helmet plate badge[21]. He is wearing an eight button jacket with snake buckle belt from which hangs a truncheon case. This obviously was a preliminary design by Taits as it is uncertain whether a Maltese cross plate was ever issued by them for use by the police. In the same year an instruction was issued regarding chin straps on helmets which stated that they should be worn at all times. Also that the strap, should not be worn beneath the under lip but on the extreme point of the chin and is not to be worn in the crown of the helmet[22].

Swords were also worn by some police officers (dismounted horse patrol) but usually these were originally the horse patrol and later the mounted police. Suppliers of swords, rattles and truncheons were often military suppliers first, and included Charles Hebbert of Pall Mall, William Mills 120 High Holborn, R. S. Garden of 29 Piccadilly and William Parker founded in 1790 based at 233 Holborn (this business was taken over by the son-in-law in 1886 when Field was added to the title.

The picture at left and below shows a Victorian gilded brass tipstaff with a pouch or

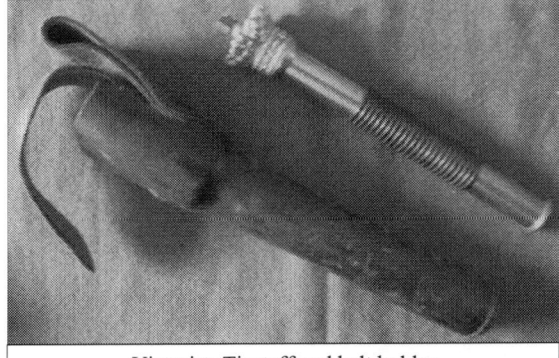

Victorian Tipstaff and belt holder

holster, sometimes also referred to as a frog. The holster has a loop where it is threaded onto the officer's/official's belt. **The Tipstaff** was the badge or insignia of office of a customs official, police officer, magistrate or other official working on behalf of the crown. It represented the ancient symbol of authority under the crown. For police these were carried before the days of warrant cards which eventually replaced them.

The expression 'I'll crown you' is derived from arrests made by police officers in plain clothes or on detective duties, who on production of the tipstaff would say 'I crown you' to validate an arrest. The

Chief Inspector with tipstaff in 1880s.

tipstaff was made of hollow gilded brass, with an un-screwable gilded brass crown finial. To enable it to be held in the hand an ebony (or even perhaps lignum vitae) grip was fixed to the tubular shank. The item shown is dated to around the 1860s and was made by Tait & Co, Southwark Street London, which ceased to trade when in 1870 it became insolvent. The **tipstaff** measures 18.5 centimetres long, and weighs 159.8 grams and fits into the pouch or holster which is spring-loaded to enable it to be quickly drawn to show proof of office. Originally issued to the Bow Street Runners, superintendents and inspectors purchased their own tipstaffs until 1867 when they became part of the official uniform. Parish Constables did have tipstaves but after 1829 constables of the new police did not. Tipstaves were withdrawn in 1887. Even today tipstaves are represented on the badges of office for Chief Officers, which consist of crossed tipstaves within a laurel wreath.

First mentioned in 1845 an experiment to trial **whistles** for police use was abandoned and only in 1869 was the naval flute pattern whistle introduced into dockyards. In 1873 Thames division adopted the whistle. In 1884 whistles were introduced for outer divisions during the daytime although rattles remained in use for night duty until 1886 when they were withdrawn. Matters remained the same until recently when whistles have been withdrawn completely.

Chrome button with king's crown produced between 1935 and 1953

Early police **buttons** issued during the mid 19th century were originally made of pewter. These replaced by brass versions with the front dipped in chrome known as 'dipped silver'. Some other buttons were produced made in chrome on nickel silver but these proved costly and were abandoned. This chrome Kings crown button at left has the garter belt and buckle removed in favour of two concentric circles within which Metropolitan Police is displayed. This denotes that this button is pre 1953 but post 1935.

1870-1880(?)

Tait's original drawings for the senior officers helmet

In 1870 the helmet was again remodelled to a design which is recognisable today and the coxcomb was discarded. Companies such as J. R. Gaunt of Birmingham (who made military headgear) were asked to present designs for police helmets and their plates. Their instructions included helmet plates for constables and sergeants whilst inspectors and superintendents were to be afforded a different plate completely.

Tait's design for the constable's and sergeant's helmet plate

Gaunt's designs, taken from their pattern book, show that their original artwork was accepted with some modifications. The 'VR' (Victoria Regina) cypher or more correctly the Guelphic crown shown in the centre was removed in favour of the divisional letter and number. Gaunts originally suggested a (Brunswick) star pattern of white plate, again with 'VR' cypher and filled in Victoria crown for Inspectors and sergeants however this pattern was rejected for inspectors and issued instead to Superintendents in 1875. Instead of Metropolitan Police written in the garter the French 'HONI SOIT QUI MALY PENSE' is shown which literally means 'shamed be he who thinks evil of it' and is the motto of the English chivalric Order of the Garter[23]. This design of helmet plate for superintendents continued for many years.

The 1870 new conical helmet and plate

The new 1870 plate

The coxcomb helmet was withdrawn in 1870 and replaced with a more conical six panel helmet (although the number of panels is subject to speculation- see below) without comb. The crown of the new helmet was strengthened by inserting twelve overlapping segments of cork which were glued into place. There were six panels of blue cloth with raised seams with two attached to each panel. The peak and brim were lowered (as can be seen at left) with the back enlarged to prevent rainwater dripping down the neck. The rim was finished in black patent leather trim. The crown was affixed with a metal rose on the top of the ventilation holes. Two similar holes were made on either side of the helmet near the crown top. An ornamental black leather band three tenths of an inch deep was pinned around the base. Inside the helmet American cloth and a leather band was fixed together with a soft felt inner band[24] for comfort. There were similar holes fitted near the crown to provide additional ventilation.

Constable 465 'Y' with new helmet and plate circa 1870

The helmet plate badge was also changed in 1870 although another change occurred in 1880/1 when the star pattern plate was introduced.

The laurel wreath on either side of the badge had been removed and instead of a Victoria crown which was filled in, it was replaced with a hollowed one in japanned black instead. The number and divisional letter was retained in the helmet plate although the helmet itself has no discernible panels and appears to be made in at least one or more probably two sections. The helmet band masks the joins in the helmet. In the example above what can also be clearly

Superintendent Thomas Butt 'P' Division and ceremonial helmet

seen is the divisional number and letter 'Y 465' in the centre of the helmet plate.

The plain belt buckle was removed and a more ornate buckle was introduced as can be seen by Gaunts designs. Whilst station sergeants (and clerk sergeants) were recognised in 1871 they were not issued with a badge of office until 1875 when four Russia braid (silver lace) chevrons were introduced.

In 1870 the superintendent's uniform tunic of 1843 was amended and 4 rows of black cord with drop loops and eyes, knitted buttons and olivets were added across the chest[25]. At the rear an Austrian knot was added to the back seams Crow's toes with two knitted buttons were sewn into the skirts. In 1875 two sets of eye braiding were added to the back seam embroidery with shoulder cords being added in 1906[26].

Superintendent's ceremonial helmet and plate as worn by Butt

The photograph on the previous page shows **Superintendent Thomas Butt** of 'P' Division, probably taken on promotion in his fitted dress uniform dated circa 1881. Butt is wearing his duty helmet with plate as shown later with chain mail embellishments, riding breeches, riding boots, and sword. The collar of the tunic shows oak leaves either side together with knotted shoulder cords. The cuffs of the tunic show an upturned 'V' formation which later changed to a more elaborate design as can be seen from the uniform jacket below.

Superintendent Smith Chatham Dockyard

The picture at left for comparison shows how the uniforms changed. Superintendent (wt. no. 52797) **William Smith** of Chatham dockyard is shown in a similar jacket with more embellished forearms. He is also wearing the kepi with obvious 'slashed' peak rather than a helmet. Smith retired in 1910 after 40 years' service.

1880/1 – 1901/6)

The Brunswick star issued in about 1880 to dockyards

In 1880/1 the helmet and plate were modified again to a shape and design that we would recognise today. In fact this particular plate remained in use until about 1906 even though Queen Victoria had died in 1901. The new headwear comprised of six panels and a seven pointed Brunswick star type badge with Victoria crown, introduced to replace the garter type. Again this was japanned black and had METROPOLITAN POLICE in raised letters around the circumference within the garter ribbon together with silvered divisional letter and numbers in the centre.

Gaunts also quoted the Metropolitan Police for inspectors and superintendents to have chain mail as helmet furniture together with a rose top that provided ventilation but it appears that inspectors wearing the 'Prussian' helmet except for ceremonial occasions. This helmet pattern remains the same today.

The 1864 greatcoat was also modified for chief constables to inspectors to include the latest design called a Lancer front - top buttons which are 2½ inches to the point of shoulders and the bottom ones 5 inches apart. The coat had one rear pleat with four small composition buttons.

In 1871 the rank of Chief Inspector was introduced although it had been used before this date for the CID. In 1886 the chief constables to superintendents uniform was modified. The collar was edged with a ½ inch black braid with bullet eye embroidery within. The cuffs were made with black braid to a point with one row of eyes and one fan below, together with eight rows of tracing with small crows toes.

The new Brunswick star for divisional wear

Truncheon cases were withdrawn in 1887 when trousers included a pocket in which to place the truncheon out of sight. In the same year a number of senior inspectors were re-designated to the new rank of Sub Divisional Inspector (SDI).

Superintendent James Thomson 'E' Division in ceremonial uniform circa 1880

Armlet loops were sewn into the left sleeve of the jacket in 1895.

In 1897 a five buttoned blue serge patrol jacket was introduced which had two breast pockets. This jacket was for summer wear between May and September. In the same year a waist slit for a shoulder belt was added to the tunic. Epaulettes were added to the jacket in 1960. In the picture at left shows Thomson the famous ex-detective who was later promoted to superintendent. Here he is shown in his superintendents dress uniform with oak leaf collars and cuffs. The front has crows foot edging vertically on both sides. He has a stripe down the outside of each leg.

1901/6 - 1935

Following the death of Queen Victoria in 1901 the Edward VII helmet plate was introduced. A slightly smaller plate was introduced featuring Imperial crown. Everything else remained the same.

Prior to 1906 embroidered badges of rank for chief constables (silver Victoria crown from 1886) and superintendents (Silver Victoria crown from 1875) were worn on collars but after 1906 they were changed to their epaulettes. In 1901 the crown was altered to an imperial crown and for superintendents in 1908 an embroidered star was added to the crown.

Metropolitan Police helmet plate 1901 - 1935

The Home Office recommendations of 1934 included standardisation of buttons for all English and Welsh police forces. The most obvious effect was that chromium-plated buttons (which do not require polishing) began to be introduced. The report also recommended that forces should adopt a common basic design of button showing the royal crown and the title of the force[27].

The five button tunic was replaced by a seven button tunic in 1934[28]. During the 1930s the Royal College of Heralds informed the Metropolitan Police that its garter ribbon within the star and buttons had not been given proper authorisation to be worn on helmets. This caused some concern at the time, but led to quick and significant changes, not only relating to police headgear. In terms of the helmet plate, one change placed the 'Royal Cypher' of the reigning monarch in the centre of the badge (see below on page xxiii).

Superintendents cap badge 1935

At the same time the Home Office established a panel of inquiry to standardise the police uniform. In 1935 the pattern of plate changed because even though the George V plate had been in use for some 34 years the garter was removed. This was replaced by two plain rope effect circles which still retained the words METROPOLITAN POLICE. This also afforded an opportunity to remove the divisional letter and numbers from the plate and transfer them to the collar of the new 'dog collar' style tunic, the jacket being made of a lighter serge material. The cap badge at left is for a superintendent whilst the one below is for inspectors.

The belt was discarded for this uniform as the design had a more draped appearance. The five buttoned summer wear serge patrol jacket was fixed with metal letters 'MP' on the epaulettes in 1932 although the collar still showed the officers divisional letter and number on both sides. However the jacket was replaced in 1934 with a seven button version instead but it was not until 1937 that all these replacements had been carried out. The letters 'MP' were stitched down all around probably from fear of injuring a prisoner during an altercation. The two breast pockets had a three pointed flap with a central external pleat

Inspector's cap badge 1935

The eight-buttoned tunic was altered in 1934 when two extra buttons were added to the back of the coat and the inverted 'V' on each sleeve was removed leaving plain sleeves.

With the start of the WW2, three types of auxiliaries joined the police family to aid the war effort. These were categorised with titles of Reserves. The 1st Reserve were re-engaged (previously retired Metropolitan Police) pensioners from all ranks. The 2nd Reserve were members of the Special Constabulary who volunteered for duty on a full time basis although existing members of the MSC could remain on their part time basis. Lastly, the 3rd reserve were men recruited for war service only and they were referred to as War Reserves.

Metropolitan Police War reserve cap badge

The helmet badge below shows the 'G V R' cypher within the double circle centre having had the garter ribbon removed. Such was the pressure to clothe and equip these reserves it soon became clear that no strict adherence to established patterns of distribution could be achieved. Those who were given clothing and equipment, whether or not they were officially entitled to have them soon exchanged them with others and cooperated in times of need. This often occurred following damage and destruction of clothing after bombing or during rescue work. Helmets and helmet plates were only issued to 1st reserves, whilst 2nd and 3rd reserves were supplied with caps and cap badges. The reserve forces were also given patrol jackets, trousers, greatcoats, shoes, gloves and black woollen armlets (to denote they were on war service). In terms of letters and numerals 1st and 3rd reserves were supplied with those as for the regular service. Meanwhile all officers of the regular force were issued with steel helmets which

George V Metropolitan police helmet plate with rope effect circles

clearly showed the word 'POLICE' in white at the front. The regular force also had badges of office on the helmet front as well. The 2nd reserve had the letters 'SC' and the 3rd reserve had 'WR' above the word 'POLICE'[29]. On the 15th October 1940 the Secretary of State deemed it necessary to issue instructions relating to the wearing of steel helmets. He stipulated;

'It has accordingly been decided that the helmets of officers of, and above, the rank of Inspector shall be painted white, with the word POLICE painted in blue in the front, and above, it the appropriate badge of rank. The blue helmets of Sergeant will be marked by two horizontal white bands ½ wide and ½ apart, the lower band commencing at the base of the crown of the helmet and both bands encircling the helmet from the extremities of the word POLICE'[30].

Inspectors WW2 steel helmet

This instruction shows that the steel helmet below is that of a sergeant in the Special Constabulary whilst the helmet left is one for a regular Inspector.

Wartime shortages meant that there were sometimes differences in for example the weight, colour and make up of certain materials for capes, belts and greatcoats. Each regular and reserve officer was issued with a haversack containing a respirator and another rucksack containing special protective anti gas clothing. These included a coat, trousers, galoshes and a hat cover[31].

A Special constables WW2 steel helmet

Between 1944 and 1946 wound stripes and War service chevrons were authorised for members of the uniform branch and reserves. Wound stripes were made up of narrow braid one and a half inches long either in gold or red in colour. Gold marked each occasion in the current war when the holder was wounded whilst red (one only to be worn) denoted injury to a member of the armed services in earlier wars. Inspectors and above wore their stripe above the inverted 'V' and sleeve embroidery on their respective tunics on their right side whilst constables and sergeants wore theirs some six inches above the start of the same side sleeve[32].

Womens Auxiliary Police Corps badge

In 1942 members of the Women's Auxiliary Police Corps (WAPC) were attested and their wound stripe was worn four inches above the bottom of the right sleeve. Its members were afforded no police powers, but employed to take on clerical and driving duties. When the Corps was disbanded in 1946 many of its members applied to join the regular police force[33]. As Critchley asserts;

> A Women's Auxiliary Police Corps, instituted in August 1939, for women between the ages of eighteen and fifty five. In the early part of the war the women were allowed to carry out only a restricted range of police duties which typically included the driving and maintenance of motor transport, and clerical, telephone, radio, and canteen work, but many were later attested as constables, so that their duties expanded over the whole range of law enforcement (Critchley, 1978:224-225).

War service chevrons were issued for the same period as wound stripes.

1936

Edward VIII Helmet plate (mock-up)

With the assent of Edward VIII to the throne in 1936 a new japanned helmet plate, again based on the seven pointed star was designed for police wear. The plate appears to have been made in brass before being blackened and designed to include the raised words 'METROPOLITAN' occupying the top section and 'POLICE' being reversed around the bottom of the double circle.

Those who were issued with them needed to return the old, 1935 George V helmet plate. It would appear that helmet plates were only issued to 'A' and 'D' Divisions before they were withdrawn. The helmet plate, above, however is not authentic as the badge should be bigger as the cypher overlaps the double circle which should have had the rope effect.

The same situation occurred with police cap badges where three were designed for use. Firstly for constables and sergeants, secondly for inspectors, and lastly for superintendents. No special helmet

Flat cap badge for constables and sergeants

plate was issued to officers of inspector and superintendent.

Flat cap badge for inspectors

The helmet plates were withdrawn when King Edward decided to abdicate from the throne given his wish to marry Mrs Wallis Simpson.

Very few survive in the correct form as the illustration above shows. Instead the title passed onto his younger brother George VI. The Metropolitan police then retained the 'GV' helmet plate badge until stocks of 'GVI' plates became available. The Edward VIII helmet plate is rare and very few have been seen or are in private hands. The stocks belonging to the Metropolitan Police were disposed of and probably melted down.

The flat cap badge shown above was produced for superintendents whilst the badge above that was for wear by constables and sergeants.

1938 – 1954

When George VI came to the throne the helmet plate changed again although retaining many of the features of previous plates. Again the seven pointed star pattern of japanned plate (black) and chromium (silver) plate with METROPOLITAN POLICE around the circumference and Kings crown remained but the centre which had contained the divisional letter and number was replaced by the George VI Royal Cypher. These two helmet plates were of the same size. The black plates were meant for night duty and silver plates for day duty. It was felt that it would be easier to detect and arrest offenders at night with a darkened helmet plate. As well as constables

George VI Helmet plate with cypher in the centre

and sergeants, the chromium plates were also worn by inspectors upwards as ceremonial dress helmet plates from 1937 – 1953/4. The plate seems not to have been replaced immediately in some divisions and it took the authorities nearly a year after the coronation to design, make and issue it to officers. Whilst the japanned version of the helmet plate was worn by constables and sergeants, a chromium version appears to have been worn by Inspectors and above for ceremonial dress helmet plate use from 1937 until 1954.

Police officers had been issued with two 'dog collar' eight button tunics however in September 1948 one was retained only for ceremonial purposes and finally withdrawn in March 1973 after 109 years use by the Metropolitan Police. White **gloves** were worn with the ceremonial tunic. In 1949 a further change to the closed neck seven button jacket was authorised when it was replaced by a five button version with open neck which was to be worn for the first time by constables and sergeants. The entire replacement programme again took several years to complete, finally being finished in 1952. The open neck jacket with five buttons was worn with a blue shirt which initially had detachable collars. Black ties were also issued for wear with the shirts. The jacket had two breast pockets that had three-pointed flaps and an external pleat. The serge jacket was also made up for summer wear using a light-weight serge material. The issue of this jacket saw the removal of 'MP' from the epaulettes and was in use until 1959/60 when a four pocket version was introduced. Numbers and divisional letter previously worn on each side of the collar were transferred to the epaulettes. In 1950 station sergeants and sergeants were issued with chromium-plated badges of rank for epaulettes of mackintoshes.

Annie Matthews in Bather uniform

Perhaps one of the most famous women police of our time was Annie Matthews (1890-1966) who joined the Women Police Service in 1918 and remained for 30 years. Annie became a Women's Police Patrol no. 17 (wt. no. 64). In 1920 she was highly commended for her part in working under cover and infiltrating a gang responsible for distributing cocaine in Piccadilly. Her role in the discovery of evidence against the gang was very brave and highly dangerous.

She was described later on her retirement in 1950, by Lilian Wyles as 'the perfect police woman' demonstrating 'strength, wisdom and immense charity in a rugged exterior'.

Annie is shown wearing the 'Bather uniform' after its originator Elizabeth Bather which was issued to women police from 1946 until 1960. The new uniform was first modelled on the Women Auxiliary Air Force uniform worn during WW2. The four buttoned open neck jacket with epaulettes and tie had two small upper (button down) pockets and below the belt two larger pockets. It was accompanied by a tailored skirt and was an altogether smarter uniform. The cumbersome wide-brimmed bowler type helmet gave way to a more armed service style – a lighter weight peaked hat. The hat shows the George VI cypher cap badge. The picture above contrasts the two styles of women police uniform.

The two styles of uniform 1920 and 1956

1952 – 2013

On the accession of Queen Elizabeth II to the throne two specific changes took place to the design of the helmet plate. The St. Edward's crown was replaced by the Tudor crown and the 'E II R' cypher was introduced. The original plate issued in 1952 was of japanned black and it wasn't until 26th February 1965 that a chromium plate replaced it.

In the same year of the Queen's accession new badges of rank were issued. Chief Superintendents were issued with a new St. Edwards crown to accompany two stars. Superintendent's grade one were also issued with the same crown until 1959 when a star was added to their badge of rank. Superintendents grade two were issued with the St. Edward's crown from 1953 until

The new EIIR helmet plate issued in chrome in 1965

1959. Likewise station sergeants were issued with the new crown in the same year. Cap badges, with the new St. Edwards crown with royal cypher was issued to the ranks of commissioner down to inspectors. New St. Edward's buttons were also issued to the commissioner down to deputy commander. In 1959 the first police reserve was disbanded.

Cape number

A belt was designed to be worn with the new open-neck four-button jacket in 1959 which had had a further two button down pockets added to the lower part. This was fitted with a cloth belt with a two pronged white metal buckle. The new jacket had four buttons to the front. Inspectors' and above tunic jackets differed from those of constables and sergeants only in that they had an inverted 'V' with button on each cuff. They also had bellows-style pockets with three pointed flaps rather than 'inpatch' pockets with three pointed flaps[34]. Shirt sleeve order (SSO) was introduced for the first time in 1960. All sergeants and constables were allowed to wear SSO for certain duties without jackets during warm weather.

Cape chrome number for a sergeant

In 1968 Inspectors and above were issued with a lightweight office jacket for wear whilst performing office duties. These light blue terylene cotton jackets were nicknamed 'ice-cream jackets' and displayed the badge of rank on dark blue epaulettes but these were later removed to either side of the lapels. These single breasted jackets had three front St. Edward's crown buttons, two open-waist patch pockets and an open left breast pocket. Lightweight jackets were issued for summer wear in 1960. In the same year open neck greatcoats and Mackintoshes were issued to constables and sergeants and the old 'oilskin' cape was replaced by the mackintosh cape. Cloth capes were retained by chief superintendents down to station police sergeants. Lightweight patrol jackets were issued to the ranks of and between chief superintendent and constable in 1960 for summer wear. Issued trousers until 1960 had been self-supporting

The 1980/1 EIIR helmet plate.

meaning that braces could be worn to hold them up but in 1967 a leather belt was issued. The chromium badges were permitted for wear for bush type shirts in 1961 and raincoats in 1962. In 1965 Traffic Division officers were issued with 'TD' as part of their shoulder number instead of divisional codes.

The duty armlet worn for about 100 years, was discarded in 1968 and later versions of the tunic saw the armlet loops removed. In January 1970 the first British police officer to wear a turban was Kenya-born Special Constable Harbans Singh Jabbal at East Ham. White shirts replaced the original blue style with detachable collars in 1977.

Black resin greatcoat button

In 1980 a new style tunic with no epaulettes or waist belt was introduced including two breast pockets each with button and flap that had four silver buttons down front[35].

In 1980/1 a new helmet plate (shown on the previous page) was designed and issued. The new plate continued use of the seven pointed star but adopted the blue circle from the flat cap badge making the surround of the 'E II R' coloured in blue off-setting the silver of the surrounding star.

The design of the black resin great coat button is shown above. It shows the EIIR crown within a double circle showing Metropolitan Police.

---

[1] Shpayer-Makopv, H. (2002) The making of a Policeman. Ashgate Press, Aldershot
[2] Ibid p7.
[3] Behind the Blue Lamp (2003) and More Behind the Blue Lamp (2011)
[4] Even this 2nd plate is open to debate since there is evidence to suggest that the coxcomb helmet was fitted with a Maltese Cross badge at some stage.
[5] The Standard dated 16th August 1830
[6] Taylor, M. B. and Wilkinson, V. (1989) Badges of Office. Hazel and Co. Henley on Thames.
[7] ibid
[8] The Standard dated 30th August 1830
[9] Burt, D. (2008) Hebbert and Co. info http://www.authentic-campaigner.com/forum/showthread.php?14899-24-October-1864-Invoice-from-Hebbert-%28sic%29-Pall-Mall-East&s=0c9c5060555563c5a2994b2ae34b4254 accessed on 24.7.13
[10] Hebbert also supplied military clothing and equipment to the confederate forces together with Tait and Co.
[11] Howard, G. (1953) Guardians of the Queens Peace. Oldmans London. p 129
[12] ibid
[13] Ripley H Police Buttons. R.Hazell & Co 1983
[14] Fairfax, N. and Wilkinson, V. L. (undated) History of Metropolitan Police Uniforms and Equipment. Vol. 2. P24

xxx

[15] Ibid p23
[16] Ibid.
[17] There is an image of this helmet in Appendix 1 of the Official Encyclopedia of Scotland Yard
[18] Ibid p31
[19] Metropolitan Police Orders dated 12th June 1860
[20] The Police and Constabulary Almanac 1864
[21] Whilst it is uncertain whether this plate was issued generally to officers it is known that a picture exists of a mounted Metropolitan police officer wearing one.
[22] Metropolitan Police Orders dated 5th July 1864
[23] http://en.wikipedia.org/wiki/Honi_soit_qui_mal_y_pense accessed on 17.8.13
[24] Fairfax, N. and Wilkinson, V. L. (undated) History of Metropolitan Police Uniforms and Equipment. Vol. 2. p33
[25] Ibid p34
[26] Ibid p35
[27] Ripley H Police Buttons. R.Hazell & Co 1983
[28] Met Police Heritage Collection
[29] Fairfax, N. and Wilkinson, V. L. (undated) History of Metropolitan Police Uniforms and Equipment. Vol. 2. p57
[30] Supts instructions from the Home Secretary dated 15th October 1940
[31] Fairfax, N. and Wilkinson, V. L. (undated) History of Metropolitan Police Uniforms and Equipment. Vol. 2 p57-58
[32] Ibid p 58
[33] http://www.peoplescollectionwales.co.uk/Item/7743-lapel-badge-womens-auxiliary-police-corps-193#sthash.EIgJNR4D.dpuf visited on 28.7.13
[34] Fairfax, N. and Wilkinson, V. L. (undated) History of Metropolitan Police Uniforms and Equipment. Vol. 2 p64
[35] Metropolitan Police Orders dated 22nd August 1980.

Chapter 1

The City of Westminster

by Alan Moss

Introduction

The city of Westminster holds within its boundaries many institutions, arms of government and organisations that play a central role in our national life. Events in Trafalgar Square, Parliament Square and other famous locations often have a national impact, so Westminster is rather more than a local authority within Greater London. There are some famous police stations in Westminster, but also a number of other prominent Metropolitan Police buildings.

The Metropolitan Police Act that established the Service received its royal assent on 19th June 1829. At the time, policing in London consisted of a number of local watchmen, sometimes operating from watch houses, supplemented by the magistrates at seven police offices which had been established under the Middlesex Justices Act 1792. Each of these, the forerunners of our modern magistrates courts, had three stipendiary magistrates and six constables. The offices outside Westminster were at Hatton Garden, Worship Street (Finsbury), Lambeth Street (Whitechapel), Shadwell (later at Marylebone High Street) and Southwark, whilst Westminster had Great Marlborough Street and Queen's Square. The most famous additional and eighth office was at Bow Street, from where the Bow Street officers and patrols operated. There was a Receiver appointed to raise money from parishes to fund these offices.

The first ever appointment to the Metropolitan Police was also a Receiver when the Home Secretary, Sir Robert Peel, appointed John Wray on 7 July 1829 to perform a similar function for the new police. It was John Wray's job to finance, accommodate and supply the new organisation, and the fact that over 1,100 new police officers were recruited, fitted with uniforms and then started to patrol London's streets by 25 September that year, 10 weeks after his appointment, was an enormous achievement.

The 'A' or Whitehall (later Westminster) Division Band

'A' Division were renowned for their band perhaps influenced by the example of military bands performing in central London. The picture below shows the 'A' Division police band in 1864 just as the new cox comb helmets were introduced replacing the stove pipe hat.

The 'A' Division Police Band circa 1864

Several Divisions formed their own bands from 1840 onwards, often employing civilian bandsmen. Senior officers encouraged officers to take up playing instruments and practising in their spare time for band duty at the station since it afforded them a group of reserve officers who were on standby in the event of disturbances etc. Bands were used to entertain

The 'A' Division Band circa 1907

walkers and visiting crowds on a Sunday at bandstands set up in the royal parks, especially Hyde Park. In the early days normal uniforms were used by the bandsmen but later they introduced distinctive and specially produced flat hats or kepis like the 'A' Division Band of 1907 pictured above, with their own dedicated divisional badge. In the centre behind the drum are two 'A' Division senior officers. Superintendent Creswell Wells is in the white hat.

Divisional bands were also called to duty to play at retirement celebrations attended by the officers at the station when pictures were taken commemorating the event. They also played for the police officers and their families at social events, award ceremonies, weddings or attended police funerals.

Constable Ernest Heasman 'A' Division

Westminster officers undertook their share of gallantry and good police work. The coronation medal below was awarded to constable 94405 Ernest Edward Heasman born Richmond Surrey in March 1881. Heasman applied to join the Metropolitan Police in January 1907 aged 25 years. He was 5ft 9 inches tall, weighed just over 12 stone, his complexion fresh, eyes brown and hair black. He was married with one child and his previous trade was that of fireman for Croydon Corporation. He was interviewed and seen by the Police surgeon who passed him fit for the police service. He went to the newly built Peel House Regency Street for training. He passed all his exams and was posted to 'S' Division as Constable 169.

Late one night Heasman was on patrol in St. Johns Wood (Portland Town) when he was involved in a shooting which left him injured and very lucky to be alive. Whilst he went through the gateway of the All Souls Church, Hampstead he walked along the gravel path and after hearing a noise he flashed his lamp, saw two men who appeared to be up to no good and noticed marks consistent with someone trying to force the church door.

One man decamped and Heasman took hold of the other man who had a chisel and two pairs of pliers on him. After arresting him he walked him to the police station by restraining his left arm, but Francis Bett used his free hand to reach into his pocket, pull out a revolver and fire at the officers head. The bullet grazed his head and passed straight through his helmet. Heasman seized the prisoner and kicked him in the

The 1911 Coronation medal

stomach in order to restrain him whereupon Bett on steadying himself fired four more shots at the constable, all making holes in his thick uniform great coat but inexplicably not causing any severe injury but making the officer faint. Bett ran off but it was not until the end of the year and Bett was found to be serving a sentence of imprisonment for another crime in Wormwood scrubs prison. After the trial which was held at the Old Bailey, Bett was found guilty and, once his list of previous convictions had been read out, he was sentenced to 7 years imprisonment to be added to his current sentence of 18 months hard labour. Heasman was off duty on the sick list for two weeks and deaf for three weeks. He resumed duty after that with no long-lasting injuries. Strangely there was no verbal appreciation or judges commendation before the court as was often usual as to the officers bravery in trying to arrest an armed and dangerous criminal.

In November 1910 Heasman was transferred to 'A' or Westminster Division (posted to Cannon Row Police Station) and clearly quite satisfied with his posting because he spent the next 22 years there retiring in April 1932 aged 51 years old. In 1911 Heasman was part of the Royal celebrations that were the Coronation of George V and received the medal as thanks. When the Second World War started Heasman re-joined the police again as a re-engaged pensioner from September 1939 until February 1940 as constable 147 of 'T' or Hammersmith Division. He died aged 81 in 1963 having drawn a pension for 29 years.

Telephone Boxes.

There were telephone call boxes on 'A' Division and the list below shows the site of each, their number, the date they were erected and removed.

SITE LOCATIONS OF METROPOLITAN POLICE TELEPHONE BOXES AND TELEPHONE POSTS
A DIVISION

No.	INST. TYPE	A.R.W SIREN	OPERATIVE/ REMOVAL DATES	SITE LOCATION	SUB-DIV	REMARKS
A51	Police Call Post		24 Jan 38 Feb 79	Junction of Strand, north side and Trafalgar Square, east side - Charing Cross	Cannon Row	Sited on E division
A52	Police Call Box		24 Jan 38 15 Dec 70	Victoria Embankment, west side 8 yards north of Charing Cross underground station entrance - Charing Cross	Cannon Row	Sited on E division
A53	Police Call Post		24 Jan 38 15 Dec 70	Buckingham Gate, north side 100 yards west of Birdcage Walk - Westminster	Cannon Row	
A54	Police Call Post		24 Jan 38 09 Dec 70	Junction of Millbank, east side and foot of Lambeth Bridge, south side - Westminster	Rochester Row	
A55	Police Call Post		24 Jan 38 09 Dec 70	Victoria Street, north side 25 yards west of Broadway - Westminster	Rochester Row	
A56	Police Call Post		24 Jan 38 09 Dec 70	Piccadilly, north side outside Apsley House - Mayfair	Rochester Row	
A57	Police Call Post		04 Aug 65 15 Dec 70	Belgrave Square, southern corner at junction of Belgrave Place - Belgravia	Rochester Row	

Scotland Yard

In 1829 the existing police offices run by magistrates continued to operate as courts under the new arrangements, so a Metropolitan Police headquarters had to be found for the new police. Wray purchased a vacant house at 4 Whitehall Place, off Whitehall, and had it converted to offices for the first joint Commissioners Colonel Rowan and Richard Mayne, bachelor quarters for Colonel Rowan, and offices for himself, the Chief Clerk and two others who assisted him. The former servant quarters at the back, towards the north, were converted into a police station for 'A' Division and a recruiting centre[1]. The route by which the public gained access to this part of the premises was through an archway from Whitehall and into Great Scotland Yard, which soon lent its name to the Metropolitan Police headquarters.

The back entrance of 4 Whitehall Place, looking West towards Whitehall

Many streets around Whitehall had changed over the years. Whitehall Palace, built by Cardinal Wolsey, once stood at the southern end of what is now Whitehall and Parliament Street until it burnt down in 1698. Some houses stood to the West as the land rapidly gave way to St James's Park. To the north of Whitehall Palace once stood a palace for the Kings of Scotland, but this building later fell into disuse and gave way to Great, Middle and Little Scotland Yards, of which only Great Scotland Yard exists today. Whitehall Place ran parallel to and between Great and Middle Scotland Yards[2]. The association with the Kings of Scotland is probably the basis of how the Scotland Yard name arose. Alternative theories are that a nearby farm, once owned by an Adam Scott, could have become known as 'Scottes Land', then shortened to 'Scotland'; or that the land was connected with the old English word 'scotte', meaning rent[3].

Rowan and Mayne were not the first Commissioners of Scotland Yard. By coincidence the Hackney Coach Office, which licensed all cab drivers and their vehicles taking the public for a fee, had been headed by Commissioners since 1654, and this office was also based in Scotland Yard. In 1850 some of their duties were taken over by the Metropolitan Police, and the Public Carriage Office was born. This department of the Metropolitan Police was transferred to Lambeth in 1927, sharing premises with the Lost Property Office, and in 1966 it moved to Penton Street, Islington[4]. The responsibility for licensing cabs and drivers transferred to Transport for London in 2000.

As well as policing its own territory, 'A' or Whitehall Division was intended to act in support of Scotland Yard in the early days of the Metropolitan Police. The first Superintendent, John May, had served as a Sergeant Major with Rowan in the army, and undertook direct

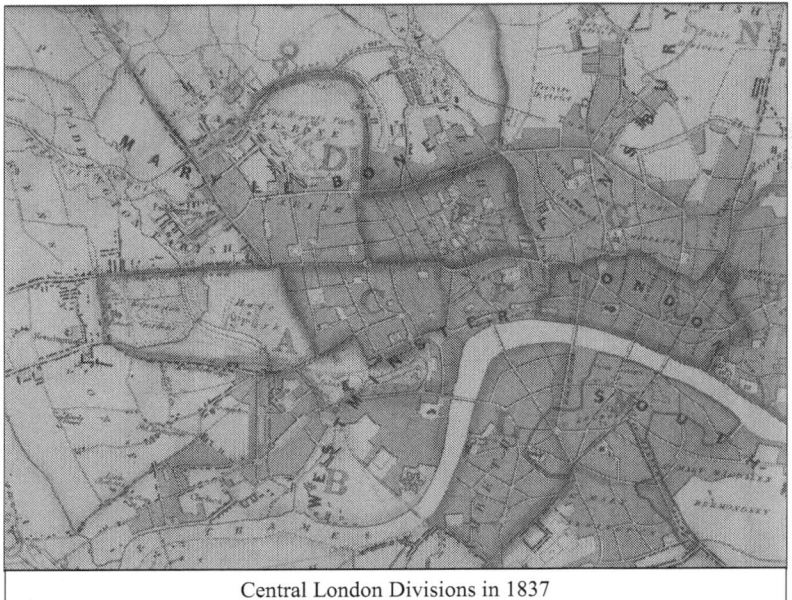

Central London Divisions in 1837

responsibilities on behalf of the Commissioners to a far greater extent than his counterparts on other Divisions. He was Superintendent of 'A' Division for 22 years.

Running a rapidly expanding organisation from a relatively small house soon became difficult. *The Times* commented;

> 'Innumerable books are piled up on staircases so that they are almost impassable, piles of clothing, saddles and horse furniture, blankets and all manner of things are piled up in little garrets in a state of what outside Scotland Yard would be called hopeless confusion'[5]

So it was not surprising that more buildings in the vicinity were taken into use. By 1887 the police were using numbers 3, 4, 5, 21 and 22 Whitehall Place, and numbers 8 and 9 Great Scotland Yard. Within the yard itself, the police used numbers 1-2 Palace Place as a prisoners' property store and Surveyor's offices. There was a freestanding building that had variously been used to hold stores, the Public Carriage Office, and CID offices. In due course a police station, and then a set of stables, was built on the opposite, north side of Great Scotland Yard and the stables still exist today.

From 1870, the search began for a new headquarters. The completion of Victoria Embankment had created a stretch of land reclaimed from the River Thames, and when a project to build the Grand National Opera House on part of this ground collapsed through lack of funds, the building was then completed in the form of the now famous New Scotland Yard, designed by architect Norman Shaw.

The building provided 140 offices, of which 40 were for the Criminal Investigation Department, with the

New Scotland Yard, designed by Norman Shaw

Commissioner enjoying a turret office overlooking the river. The police took over the building in 1890. The old headquarters 4 Whitehall Place was eventually sub-let before being sold.

Five years later, the police built another building in matching style, known as Scotland House, with a connecting bridge to the original Shaw building. An extension of the north part of the Norman Shaw building was completed in 1940 and was first used by Combined Operations in World War Two under Lord Louis Mountbatten, before eventually reverting to Metropolitan Police use, and becoming known as the Curtis Green building, after the architect, William Curtis Green. Cannon Row police station completed the complex.

Aerial view of New Scotland Yard and Cannon Row police station

Gardiner's Lane Police Station

Probably the first police station on 'A' or Whitehall Division that was not part of the Scotland Yard complex was at 2 Gardiner's Lane, a short road that ran west from King Street towards St James's Park, perhaps a few yards south from where the modern King Charles Street runs.

Gardiner's Lane was a brick and tile building, without a yard, leased by Receiver John Wray from midsummer 1830. It was vacated by the police in 1850, by which time King Street police station had been taken into use. Gardiner's Lane had five rooms, and, on the ground floor, an office and charge room, two unventilated cells and stabling for three horses. At one point it was used by the detective branch, which was formed in 1842. A note in the property register states;

> 'Dustbins and men's cupboards wanting ... with other conveniences for the detective force'.

Modern police officers would probably recognise equivalent shortfalls in accommodation when a squad has to be set up urgently, but at least they would have had the consolation implicit in another note;

> 'Drain to sewer clean and healthy. Ventilation good'.

The 1841 census shows six police officers living in Gardiner's Lane, three of whom were married and parents of young children.

In May 1842, Queen Victoria was riding down Constitution Hill in her carriage when she was shot at by John Francis. Constable 53 William Trounce of 'A' Division was on the scene and arrested him, but not without some additional intervention from Colonel Charles Arbuthnot, the Queen's equerry, who ordered that the prisoner be taken to Buckingham Palace. From there, more conventional police procedures followed, and it was to Gardiner's Lane police station that the prisoner was later taken and charged with high treason. This incident was one of a series of attacks on the Queen, and formed part of the arguments for the establishment of a detective branch. Nicholas Pearce, the first Detective Inspector, had his office at this police station. King Street no longer exists as a thoroughfare, but it once ran south from the junction of Whitehall and Downing Street, and parallel to Parliament Street.

King Street Police Station

In 1847 a police station was built at 22 King Street, on the corner of Gardiner's Lane, with the police taking up possession at Christmas that year. It was a substantial police station, costing £7246 10s 10d (£7246.54), with 13 rooms, including a charge room, offices for a Superintendent and two Inspectors, a library, and living accommodation for two Inspectors and four Sergeants. A section house for 104 single officers fronted on to Gardiner's Lane. There were stables for 16 horses with rooms for the grooms, and two sheds for horse-drawn vans. By 1894, a scheme to

King Street police station, 1847 – 1899. 22, King Street, Westminster.

widen Parliament Street meant that the police station had to be demolished, and the station was replaced by Cannon Row.

The officers at the front of the station were from left to right, Sub. Div. Inspector Cousins, Reserve Inspector Pashley, Chief Inspector Winkler (Marlborough Street Court) Chief Inspector Horsley (House of Commons) Superintendent Beard, Chief Inspector Rose, Chief Inspector Robinson, Inspector Hobden, Inspector German, Inspector Scantlebury, Inspector Stratton, Inspector Lowe and Local Inspector Baldock (in doorway).

King Street police station was notified as vacated in Police Orders of 23rd March 1899 when officers transferred to the new Cannon Row. Great Scotland Yard and King Street were the only two stations on 'A' division in 1849 however by the 1880s other stations like Rochester Row and Hyde Park had been absorbed. By 1891 New Scotland Yard had become so big that it was removed from 'A' or Whitehall Division and became Commissioner's Office (CO) under three Superintendents who shared differing responsibilities.

The policing of Whitehall and Parliament Square often takes place under the gaze of politicians and people of influence. State occasions and processions pass through the ground with world-famous pomp and pageantry, and incidents that might not be publicised had they occurred elsewhere in London sometimes become magnified because of the location where they occurred. Officers often had a good view of historic events.

In March 1863 police sergeant 57 'A' (wt. no. 20847) James Swinden[6], stationed at King Street Police Station, was selected to be in charge of eleven Police Constables and sent to Windsor. They were there to control the crowds outside the castle on the occasion of the wedding of H.R.H. the Prince of Wales to Princess Alexandra of Demark[7]. They were complimented on their work during the time they were there[8].

Sergeant Swinden had joined the Metropolitan Police in 1843 at the age of 21 years, having previously been a gardener in his home village of Speen in Berkshire. By 1851, James was a young constable living in the Police Barracks at 18, Northumberland Street, Westminster. On the night of the national census on 30th March 1851, he was one of thirty nine single Police Constables living there[9] in the section house.

In May 1857 he married Fanny Rounswell, and by 1863 was promoted to sergeant and posted to King Street Police Station.

He lived with his wife at 10, Barton Street, Westminster, but unfortunately by 1867 he had died of bronchitis[10]. He was one of 61 serving police officers who died that year. At that time London was not a very healthy place to live. In those days authority was given, within the Force, for a subscription to be held for his widow[11]. His wife, Fanny, originally from Sudbury went on to marry Police Sergeant John Measures from Huntingdon who later became a Police Inspector.

One officer who was familiar with policing in Westminster was Inspector Daniel Bradstock (warrant number 20585). He was appointed in charge of the Division for a period when Superintendent Walker was on sick leave in January 1864. By that time the Inspector had 21 years' service and had clearly risen to a position where he exercised great responsibility. On 2nd June 1868, he was tragically murdered on duty by an insane prisoner who had been detained at the police station.

King Street mascot –Topper the dog

Some police stations acquired pets as a form of mascot. In a cemetery for cats and dogs off Bayswater Road is the grave of Topper, a mongrel who appears to have inhabited King Street police station. According to the *Strand* magazine of 1893, the dog was 'of thoroughly dissipated habits' and eventually ate himself to death, perhaps because he was spoiled by the officers at the station[12]. Topper is seen (reproduced left) in the picture of King Street above being held by a sergeant on the first floor.

Cannon Row Police Station

This small street off Bridge Street, opposite the Houses of Parliament and sometimes spelled Canon Row, was once the place where the canons of St Stephen's chapel in the Palace of Westminster had their lodgings. The Police station was built between1898-1902 and designed by J. Dixon Butler with R. Norman Shaw as consultant, as part of the New Scotland Yard extension (1896-1906). The redevelopment of King Street provided the opportunity for the police to acquire a site in Cannon Row, backing on to New Scotland Yard. A new station was duly built by Messrs E Lawrence and Sons at a cost of £36,468, and taken into use on 21st July 1902. This convenient location adjacent to Scotland Yard brought fame to Cannon Row, not only because of its central location but also because the famous Scotland Yard detective squads would tend to bring their high profile prisoners there. The building contained married quarters for two inspectors and two constables, with accommodation for a further 96 single officers.

The building was constructed from granite, Portland stone and red brick, with a slate roof. The style was an amalgam of Flemish and English Baroque sources continuing Shaw's original New Scotland Yard theme. The design included an L-shaped plan with screen wall to courtyard. There were 4 storeys and attic main block with 2 storey range in parallel fronting Cannon Row and 5 storey east wing. The main range was one window deep and 7 windows wide. The ground and first floors were built with granite facings with large rusticated doorway under cornice and blocking course in north gable end. Segmental arched casement windows those in upper brick and stone banded floors in stone architraves; rusticated Venetian windows to north gable end. The east wing had pairs of narrower segmental arched windows. Stone eaves cornice and stone dressed gables to main block with tall coupled banded chimney stacks. The granite masonry of north gable end ground and first floors is continued at slightly lower level as the screen wall to courtyard with pedestrian doorway and segmental stop-moulded and keyed arch carriage entrance; 4 storeys added above in similar style to east wing[13]. This is now a listed building.

The Metropolitan Police Minstrels

The troupe was founded by ten police officers from 'A' or Whitehall Division (Whitehall Division) which included James Olive (later Sir James

Metropolitan Police Minstrel Troupe at Fulham Military Hospital, Wednesday, September 8th, 1915.

and Deputy Commissioner) who became associated with it for over 50 years. They were set up to raise money for police charities including the

Orphanage and Convalescent Home and in their 60 year time span (1872 until 1933) they raised £250,000. The minstrel troupe gave standard 'Nigger Minstrel' entertainment with singers and musicians in black evening dress and blacked up faces (now considered to be offensive to black people) giving performances involving banjo's, guitars, trumpets, tambourines, and ensembles who sang popular ballads, songs, and negro spirituals. In the picture above a selection of the minstrels entertain the troops at Fulham's Military Hospital during WW1. Clearly they helped cheer up the injured troops. Here they are not in performance dress and there was a chance to raise much needed funds for their charities. Postcards were prepared for sale to mark such occasions.

In 1935, the section house at Cannon Row was closed and the accommodation converted for use as offices. Cannon Row was used by the Metropolitan Police until May 1985 when the police moved to a new Cannon Row police station converted from the Curtis Green building, which later became a base for the Diplomatic Protection Group when

Cannon Row Police Station. 1902 – 1985. 1 Cannon Row Westminster SW1

Charing Cross police station replaced both Bow Street and Cannon Row police stations in 1992.

The officer in charge of Cannon Row had the privilege and responsibility of having Buckingham Palace and the Houses of Parliament on the Division. Until the establishment of specialist branches to undertake these roles in the 1980s, Cannon Row's remit extended to maintaining the policing presence for the Palace of Westminster and the royal residences.

Modern policing tends to bring stories of security scares every so often, but there has not been anything recently to compare with the action of John Bellingham on 11th May 1812. Spencer Perceval, the Tory Prime Minister, was walking through the lobby of the House of Commons to attend a Committee examining the problem of the recession when he was accosted by Bellingham who had fallen into debt after having been imprisoned in Russia. The security of the Houses of Parliament was far less strict in those days, and Bellingham had been able to lay in wait, armed with a pistol, and murder the Prime Minister, whom Bellingham appeared to blame for his personal situation. Bellingham was detained by unarmed bystanders and given into custody.

Superintendent Creswell Wells

Superintendent of 'A' Division
Creswell Wells 1912

A famous member of the Metropolitan Police was Superintendent Creswell Wells who spent 46 years in the police. He joined in February 1871 as wt. no. 52767 and retired in November 1916 during the First World War which must have been a very difficult decision for him to take especially at time of hostilities. He left on a high as holding the prestigious position as the senior officer in charge of 'A' or Whitehall Division and was decorated a number of times for his exemplary service by the King.

It would appear that Wells from Bosham in West Sussex was posted to 'D' Division and lived in the police section house in Wellbeck street, Marylebone in 1871 as a single man aged 20 years old. In March 1877 whilst having been posted to

'V' Division he was made a 1st class constable. Later when he was an Inspector at Wandsworth Police station in 1881 as he resided in West Hill, Wandsworth with his wife Fanny and their 4 children. Wells had got his experience as a senior officer in the East end of London on 'K' or Stepney Division firstly as an Inspector in 1885. By 1891 as Chief inspector of 'E' or Holborn Division only to return to 'K' or Stepney division by 1893 as the Superintendent in charge. He stayed there until 1908 when he was transferred to 'A' or Whitehall Division. Wells presided over the militant suffragette demonstrations and was instrumental in ensuring that sufficient officers were on duty to cope with the disturbances. Wells was particularly upset by suffragettes stabbing his officers' horses with hat pins which meant that many were arrested and brought before the courts. Wells monitored all the suffragette marches, incidents, demonstrations and protests. He was present at court to ensure they were prosecuted and to feedback anything important to his superiors.

In January 1911 he was awarded an MVO for his contribution and safe keeping of King Edward VII. Appointment to the Royal Victorian Order recognises distinguished personal service to the Sovereign, the reigning monarch of the Commonwealth realms, any members of their family, or

Senior Officers of the 'A' Division with Creswell Wells in helmet.

any of their viceroys.

Established in 1896 its motto is *Victoria*, alluding to the order founder, Queen Victoria and admission remains the personal gift of the monarch and one medal to denote the order has five grades of service[14].

Wells was always regarded 'as a first rate officer, a well-known and popular figure, and a very nice man'. When a prosecuting solicitor reported to Wells that he had left his wristwatch in the men's wash room at Bow Street Court and that the attendant had denied any knowledge of the item, Wells immediately left their lunch table at the Gaiety restaurant and

Mrs Pankhurst being arrested in Victoria Street

returned the lawyers wrist watch without disclosing how he had managed avert an embarrassing incident[15].

Wells held his responsibilities of protecting Buckingham Palace, Parliament, the House of Lords and the Prime Minister's residence 10 Downing Street very seriously indeed. Anyone attempting to over-run any of these was subject of arrest and prosecution on his orders. In 1909 three suffragettes who wished to speak with the Prime Minister outside his residence refused to move when Wells had asked them to. There were a further 150 members of the League who supported them. Wells was left with little choice but to have the three arrested and the 150 supporters moved on. This caused some disquiet amongst the gathering crowd but was ably dealt with by Wells and his men. Again in 1910 his officers arrested suffragettes again in Downing Street for obstruction and he appeared before the court to explain himself and justify their arrests. Wells was accustomed to court proceedings (See London Borough of Richmond for another case by this officer).

Wells was an accomplished horse rider and had a groom at Cannon Row who was responsible for the good health of all the horses in his charge.

Wells would also be present for the visits of the monarch outside London and responsible for attending Royal events and particularly also for various race meetings at Goodwood, Ascot and Kempton Park which were his own responsibility. For example attending on the King at Goodwood required use of his horse which would be transferred to the stables at Goodwood as shown above. Wells would always be seen at royal

Superintendent Creswell Wells on horseback at Goodwood stables

The lying in State of King Edward VII at Westminster Hall

ceremonial events like Trooping the Colour in his full ceremonial uniform.

Wells would also be responsible for the arrangements for the state funeral of Edward VII in May 1910. The king was laid in state in Westminster

Hall and thousands of people were shepherded into the hall to file past the coffin. Wells was responsible for the good order of the people wishing to pay their respects and police arrangements. The picture above shows a police inspector from 'A' Division (under the statue at left of the main door) with his men on duty regulating the queues.

Superintendent Wells resigned on pension with an exemplary certificate in

Cannon Row Police Station 1985 – 1992. The former Curtis Green Building, Whitehall, SW1

1916 but his health was failing and he took very badly the news that one of his sons had been killed in action. He retired to Clapham and within a few short months at the start of 1917 he was found dead at home. There was a full service funeral held at Tooting cemetery which was attended by representatives of the Metropolitan Police, Sir Edward Henry the

Commissioner and Officers and men from 'A' Division with whom he had served. This was a sad end to such an exemplary career.

However on a happier note his son Sidney George Wells, who had joined the police at Bow Street in 1914 was doing well with his new police career becoming a sergeant by 1919, Station sergeant at Albany Street in 1925 and three years later Inspector at Kentish town. Soon he became Sub Divisional Inspector at Marylebone Lane in 1933, Chief Inspector and then superintendent at the new Traffic Branch, New Scotland Yard in 1945. Like his father he excelled at organisation and management which was recognised by the King and other foreign royals on state visits by the award of a number of important medals including the MBE in 1949 and the Kings Police and Fire Service Medal for distinguished service in the 1953 Coronation awards.

Kings Police and Fire service medal

Chief Inspector Fredrick Rivett had been transferred to Cannon Row on promotion in 1916 when he preplaced Chief Inspector Joseph Short. This rising star, who was set for higher rank three years later came off his horse in similar fashion as Sir Robert Peel on Constitution Hill and broke his neck. The recently promoted James Powell, who had replaced Wells as Superintendent, soon had to arrange a full service funeral for his unfortunate deputy.

The Houses of Parliament were the scene of great gallantry in 1885, when constable William Cole became the only Metropolitan Police officer ever to have been awarded the Albert Medal in gold (later to be equivalent to the George Cross). He removed a Sinn Fein bomb from Westminster Hall, and was badly injured when it exploded. The practice of militant Irish republicans of leaving bombs in London has been frequently repeated over the years. The famous Detective Inspector Robert Fabian was awarded a King's Police Medal for dismantling an IRA bomb in Piccadilly in wartime 1940, but the increasing sophistication of these lethal devices led to the deployment from Cannon Row of a distinguished and brave group of Explosives Officers.

The George Cross

Originally recruited to deal with the paraphernalia of criminals intent on blowing open the doors of safes, their role became intimately bound up with counter terrorism operations from the 1970s. Roger Goad, awarded a posthumous George Cross, was killed whilst defusing a bomb in Kensington Church Street in 1976. Kenneth Howorth, a recipient of the George Medal, was killed whilst dealing with an IRA bomb in Oxford Street in 1981. Donald Henderson, Geoffrey Biddle and Peter Gurney were all awarded George Medals, and Derek Pickford a Queen's Gallantry Medal for their outstanding courage in defusing bombs designed to kill and maim innocent Londoners. Their courage, and that of other explosive officers, has been an awe-inspiring contribution to the safety of London and the conviction of terrorists.

Hyde Park Police Station

Within 'A' Division's boundaries were the central London royal parks, including Hyde Park up to Kensington Palace. Originally part of Henry VIII's hunting forests, there was a treeless area to the east of the park that was used for military reviews and other events, and it became a venue for public leisure and sporting events. It was the scene of Oliver Cromwell becoming entangled with the harness of his bolting horse. The social scene of horse riding by day was contrasted with the situation at night

Hyde Park Police Station

when crime became prevalent. One of the hunting parties of King George II (1683 –1760) was robbed. It was the location of the Great Exhibition in 1851.

It was shopkeepers who first had the idea of holding an organised public meeting in the park. In July 1855 they applied to the Commissioner, Sir Richard Mayne, for permission hold a protest about a Sunday Trading Bill. Mayne refused, but a few months later, in October 1855, a carpenter gathered a small crowd interested in hearing him expressing his opinions. He had not asked permission, and no official notice was taken, so he returned the following Sunday, again without incident.

The following three weeks saw speakers, and crowds, escalating, and a strong police presence was then deployed to prevent them recurring. In 1859 there was a large meeting that expressed sympathy for Napoleon's invasion of Italy, and then another meeting in 1862 to pledge loyalty to

Rear Aspect to Hyde Park Police Station, opened 1902

Garibaldi, but Speakers' Corner really became established in 1866.

In that year the Reform League unsuccessfully applied to hold a meeting at the park. There was serious rioting when police tried to stop the meeting from taking place and a tree was set on fire, reducing it to a stump, but forever giving the name of the location, the starting point of many later protest marches and demonstrations, as 'Reformer's Tree'. When the Reform League applied again for permission to hold a meeting, permission was granted for the location known as The Meeting Ground at the North East corner of the park, 150 yards away from Reformer's Tree. This then became 'Speakers' Corner'.

In August 1866 it was proposed that 'the system of appointing Constables for special service in the Parks under the charge of the Board of Works should be forthwith abolished and that, in future, the protection of the parks should be confined exclusively to the Metropolitan Police Force'[16] The Metropolitan Police started formally to patrol inside the park in 1867, operating from a part of the Magazine Barracks of the Household Cavalry.

Rear Yard to the police station

In 1889 an iron shelter was provided for the protection of police officers on duty at meetings. This was located in the kitchen garden of the Ranger's Lodge, approximately where the hallway of the current police station is situated. In 1899 approval was given for the building of a new police station.

The land for the new station had been leased from 31 December 1898 with a condition that the agreement would lapse if the police were no longer to be employed by the Commissioners of Hyde Park. The Receiver was obliged to build a station, which would be the property of the Crown, within 5 years. A temporary station was erected in 1900, and a new station opened on 10th March 1902[17].

In the early years of World War Two, Hyde Park was among many police stations to form a pig club. This was intended to help the nation's food shortages during the war. Constable G. R. Plumb described how he returned from war service with the RAF in 1949, was posted to Hyde Park, and took up one share in the pig club for £80. The club owned 50 pigs, housed in four sties made available by the Ministry of Works. Constables Huxley and Plumb drove around the West End collecting swill in a converted 1933 Austin 16 truck, purchased pigs and straw from markets, and took pigs for slaughter to Islington. The club was wound up in 1954[18].

Hyde Park's police observation box, erected 1902

Park keepers were employed in the Royal Parks in 1872 and were given police powers within the parks themselves, but the Metropolitan Police retained overall responsibility for Hyde Park. The Royal Park keepers became the Royal Parks Constabulary (RPC) in 1974 and in April 2004 the Metropolitan Police took over the duties of the RPC for policing the 17 royal parks within the Metropolitan Police District and instituted a Royal Parks Operational Command Unit.

Wellington Arch, Marble Arch and Trafalgar Square Police Stations

In the middle of Hyde Park Corner stands Wellington Arch, built in 1828 at the same time as Buckingham Palace, and, since the 1960s, surrounded

Wellington Arch (circa 1980), Hyde Park Corner SW1. Erected in 1828. Used as Police Station 1831 - 1992

by a busy one-way traffic scheme. Inside the arch is a small police station, used primarily as a base for observing and controlling traffic, particularly before the advent of computer-controlled traffic management schemes. Wellington Arch was at one time referred to as the Triumphal Arch, the landlord being shown as Her Majesty's Commissioners of

Woods and Forests. It was described as a section house and had 4 box rooms, a kitchen and boot cleaning room.

Marble Arch, at the north end of Park Lane, had a similar set of accommodation and was first used in 1851. There was a gap some time prior to 1886 when the upper rooms were not used, but in 1887 officers were again allowed to reside there. It was transferred to 'D' Division on 18 September 1908. The police became more overtly responsible for controlling the traffic flow through London from 1841, when the Commissioners rather reluctantly took on the responsibility for fixing the location of cab ranks. In 1869 the police had been given licensing

Wellington Arch Police contingent circa 1906

responsibilities, and by the 1880s and 1890s the streets were as congested with horse-drawn traffic as they are by motor vehicles today.

The first traffic signal was a gas-lit device in Bridge Street near the Houses of Parliament, inspired by a railway signal, but when it exploded the system of using police officers on point duty regained support until more efficient electric system were introduced.

Marble Arch Police Station. 1851 – 1950.Tyburn Way, W1.

The introduction of computer-coordinated traffic lights has been assisting London's traffic flow since the 1970s. GATSO cameras, named after a Dutch rally driver Maurice Gatsoides who invented automatic cameras to improve his driving performance, have been introduced to enforce speed limits and compliance with traffic signals progressively since 1988. Another use of technology has been the widespread use of CCTV. All of these developments have transformed the way in which London's traffic is controlled and some traffic laws enforced.

A small unit is built into a pillar at the North-East corner of Trafalgar Square and is a variation of the blue police box, once a common sight in London.

Clarks Buildings Police Station, St Giles

Clarks Buildings situated in the area of St. Giles was south-west of Bloomsbury, in the Rookeries; it ran north from High Street towards, but not quite reaching, Church Lane, running parallel with and west of Dyot Street. It was too far south to be immediately affected by the development of New Oxford Street in the 1840s, although it had become more overcrowded as displaced residents of streets cleared for this development flooded into the area[19]. It came up for auction in 1845.

The original watch house at George Street, St Giles was replaced, in 1843 by 4 separate brick and slate buildings at 9 – 12 Clark's Buildings, leased from 25th March 1843 and enjoying a large yard at the back. There were 4 cells, warmed and ventilated, and 34 rooms, without a scullery, a charge room and offices.

In April 1893 it was announced that the tenancy had been relinquished, but a new section house for an Inspector and 45 Constables was announced in orders of 9th March 1896, apparently replacing the accommodation at 33-4

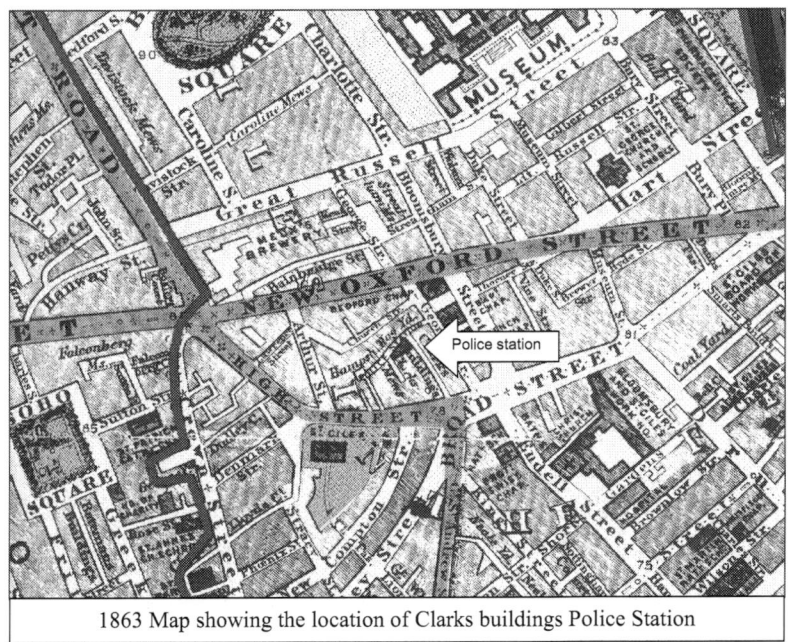

1863 Map showing the location of Clarks buildings Police Station

Bow Street[20]. The building was sold to Charing Cross Hospital for £14,000 on 31st January 1939.

Henry Mayhew described, in 1860, a visit to St Giles' rookery[21] which acquired infamy for its cramped, insanitary slum dwellings where crime and poverty, villains and prostitution were prevalent. Locations like these (sometimes also known as 'stews') were called rookeries by analogy to the untidy, multiple, noisy nests of rooks. Slum clearance schemes transformed the area.

The picture below taken from plan drawings shows the side elevation plans for the police station of Clarks buildings. It shows a substantial three storey 'L'- shaped purpose built police station with basement.

Side elevation plans of Clarks Buildings Police station

Bow Street Police Station

This street started its road to fame in the history of maintaining law and order in 1739 when Thomas de Veil occupied a house at No 4, on the west side, and began work as London's first notably honest magistrate. In 1749 the Police Office was opened[22] when Henry and Robert Fielding later took over as magistrates and established permanent officers employed as Constables by the court to investigate complaints of crime and to execute warrants. In 1803 no.3 was acquired to extend no. 4[23]. Later there were uniform foot patrols organised from the court, and in 1763 the Bow Street Horse patrol was commenced although it only lasted a year through lack of funding[24]. Later in 1805 these patrols were re-introduced and they extended their operations throughout what is now Greater London.

But this was not the first station for this area as the watch house in Covent Garden by St. Pauls Church was originally chosen and adapted at an early date but went on to cause John Wray much consternation. The watch house stood in an empty space near to the church and according to Superintendent Thomas 'F' Division this was an ideal site for his headquarters. Yet he came into conflict with the parishioners who complained about the drunks 'recovering from drunken orgies' who abused them from the basement on their way to church on Sundays. A furious row broke out between the two parties and Thomas begged Rowan to ignore the complaints but the Bishop of London was dragged into the argument. A temporary (but unsightly) wooden annex was erected on the side of the watch house which added to the parishioners concerns. It was stated that the watch house was situated on consecrated ground and as a result the Commissioner asked Wray to investigate. Wray reported that the parishioners' calls were appropriate and that a new station in Bow Street should be sought in the vicinity[25]. It was then that Bow Street became the centre of policing for the area.

In 1832[26] the police therefore moved to opposite the court, on the East side of the road to 33-4 Bow Street, into a brick and slate built house leased from the Duke of Bedford by the Receiver, John Wray for 61 years from midsummer 1831[27]. There was a yard at the rear, nine cells, a charge room, a mess, and a kitchen in the basement. The advent of the new police made it unnecessary to keep the old watchman's booth by the portico of St Paul's church, Covent Garden. Bow Street became the headquarters of the first 'F' Division of the Metropolitan Police, with the station taking responsibility for policing Covent Garden, from the City of London boundary down to Trafalgar Square, and up to St Giles.

Bow Street Police Station, 1831 - 1881. 33-4 Bow Street, Covent Garden. London

In 1866 Bow Street became the Divisional headquarters of 'E' Division, when a new 'F' (Paddington) Division was formed. Bow Street became part of 'C' Division in 1965.

The current Bow Street police building and court is further North at number 27-8. Plans were first discussed in 1876 and a new building, designed by Sir John Taylor of the

Office of Works, was completed towards the end of 1880 with the house at 33-4 being retained for a period as a section house. The fine stone façade, opposite the Opera House, has led to the building being Listed (Grade 2). It is one of the few examples in London of a police station and court being built together, and was famous for its lamps not being in the traditional police station blue colour. The story is that when police station blue lamps were introduced in 1861, Queen Victoria objected to this reminder of the blue room, in which Prince Albert died, confronting her each time she went to the Royal Opera House[28].

A section house at 7 Ricketts Place, Strand had 22 rooms and was given up in 1845. 82 Charing Cross Road was also a section house from 30 November 1886. In 1901 it housed 129 unmarried constables, 7 single sergeants and a married Sub Divisional Inspector by the name of Hayers who lived there with his wife and son[29]. By July 1916 it was occupied by the Victoria League Soldiers Club at a nominal rent.

In 1920 the station accommodated temporary buildings for an Aliens Registration Office (ARO), which moved to the station's basement in 1925

Bow Street police station and court. 1881 – 1992. 28 Bow Street, WC1

when the section house was closed. Later in 1965 the ARO moved to Vine Street, then premises above Holborn police station, and from 1999 to Borough High Street with a new name of Overseas Visitors Records

Office. In 1961 'identikit' was used for the first time at Bow Street in the murder of Elsie Batten at 22 Cecil Court WC2[30]. In 1965 there were boundary changes between Albany Street (ED) and Bow Street (CB)[31]. In October of the same year a W. H. Smith Van caught fire and constable Cawdwell ran and saved the driver from burning to death[32]. In 1967 Bow Street won their section of the sub divisional football league but were beaten in the final by Hammersmith. At the same time Norwell Roberts became the first black police officer in the Metropolitan police was transferred to Bow Street[33]. In 1973 constable Michael Whiting was killed in Oxford Street on cup final day[34]. In 1984 constable Yvonne Fletcher was killed in St. James's Square by shots fired from the Libyan Embassy during a demonstration[35]. In 1989 Bow Street and Cannon Row were amalgamated to form Charing Cross Division (CX). On 5th October 1992 at 6am Bow Street police station was closed.

In 1985 although Bow Street was replaced by the new Charing Cross police station, the magistrates court continued to be used until its last case was heard on 14th July 2006. In 2012 planning consent was obtained granted for the building into a hotel with the cell block used as a museum to be created on the site, but the Property Service Department (PSD) of the Metropolitan Police declined to support the scheme, quoting legal reasons. The long term future of the building, no longer in police ownership but owned by a Hotel chain, was still unclear in 2013 but plans to create a police museum in the cellar alongside the hotel are currently being considered.

Charing Cross Police Station

The former Charing Cross hospital in Agar Street, WC2N 4JP, designed by Decimus Burton, was refurbished for use as a police station and officially opened by the Queen in December 1992. It replaced both Bow Street and Cannon Row police stations. It was designed with a large number of cells so that it could cope with arrests arising from demonstrations in central London and also became a base for part of the Diplomatic Protection Group.

Charing Cross is, of course, famous for its railway station, where many thousands of people arrive into central London each day without any problem or controversy. Every so often, however, something extraordinary happens. On 6th May 1927, a man, looking as if he might have been a soldier, arrived in a taxi, and deposited a trunk at the station's left luggage office, leaving in the same taxi. After a while, the trunk began to smell, and a police officer was called before the trunk was opened. The contents turned out to be various parts of a murdered woman. Over the years we have become used to calling in the CID to make sense of these distasteful and perplexing situations like these. Their professionalism and skill are great assets for the life and safety of London, and Detective Chief Inspector George Cornish started a murder enquiry.

Some items of clothing had laundry marks, perhaps more common then than nowadays, and the police traced them to a Mrs Holt, who was found to be alive, well, and living in Chelsea. Mrs Holt had had ten female servants in the previous two years, and all but one was accounted for, a Mrs Rolls. The detectives then traced a Mr Rolls and established that the victim had once been living with him, her real name being Minnie Bonati, a prostitute. A shoeblack had picked up the left luggage receipt after it had been thrown from the taxi window, and the taxi driver was then traced. The taxi had taken his fare to 86 Rochester Row, where a John Robinson had a second floor office, working as an estate agent. At his lodgings, a telegram was found that led to a Mrs Robinson, who had believed that she was John Robinson's legal wife, unaware that he had committed bigamy at their wedding. Mrs Robinson became just as anxious to trace him as the police, and took George Cornish to meet him at a pub in Walworth, where John Robinson was arrested. Robinson denied any knowledge of the crime, was not picked out at an identification parade, and the murder enquiry was in danger of stalling. But George Cornish asked for a grimy duster found in the trunk to be washed and examined more carefully – it revealed the word 'Greyhound', creating a link with the hotel where Robinson had been staying. A renewed search of his offices also revealed a blood-stained match, and this led Robinson to confess.

This case occurred before the Metropolitan Police Forensic Science laboratory had been established in April 1935, but the case did enjoy the expert attentions of pathologist Sir Bernard Spilsbury who had first come to public attention with the Dr Crippen investigation in 1910.

Another forensic science connection to Charing Cross was the gun shop in nearby Agar Street owned by Edwin Churchill, where detectives would often call for an opinion about firearms. Edwin, assisted by his nephew Robert Churchill, gave expert evidence in the 1903 Moat Farm murder case where Samuel Dougal had shot Camille Holland, demonstrating the distance from which a gun would need to have been fired to have inflicted a head injury.

Charing Cross Police Station, 1992 to present day. Agar Street, London WC2N 4JP

Robert Churchill helped his uncle by test-firing bullets into sheep heads, and eventually developed an encyclopaedic knowledge of firearms. In later years he regularly gave evidence as an expert witness alongside Bernard Spilsbury, and was one of the first people to use a comparison microscope to confirm or disprove, from tiny rifling marks, that bullets had been fired from the same gun barrel.

Waterloo Pier Police Station

The Marine Police on the Thames was established in 1798, before the Metropolitan Police, and installed a floating police station, the former warship *Port Mahon* alongside Somerset House to become its upstream station (the middle station being Wapping and the lower station at Blackwall). Waterloo pier was rented in 1873 to replace the old warship, and the location covered not only the incidents that might occur in the river near Westminster, but also the unfortunate trend for depressed people to throw themselves into the river from Waterloo Bridge.

The spectacular reduction in crime from the London docks when the Marine Police was first established gave way to a steadier pace of patrolling the river, but the dangers of the river are sometimes seen when boats collide.

In 1878 the *Princess Alice,* a paddle steamer, was near Woolwich on a

Waterloo Pier, from 1873

'moonlight trip' back to London Bridge from Gravesend when she collided with the *Bywell Castle*, a much larger vessel used for carrying coal that was being accompanied by a Thames river pilot. Confusion over how they should pass each other led to the *Princess Alice* being cut in two and rapidly sunk, with the loss of over 650 lives.

The river police had only been using rowing boats at the time, but the Inquiry into the disaster recommended their being supplied with steam launches so that they could be more effective at dealing with such rescue emergencies in the future.

In August 1989 the *Marchioness* pleasure boat was sunk by the dredger *Bowbelle* near Cannon Street railway bridge with the loss of 51 lives, providing another example of the importance of careful seamanship when small boats use the same river as much larger vessels.

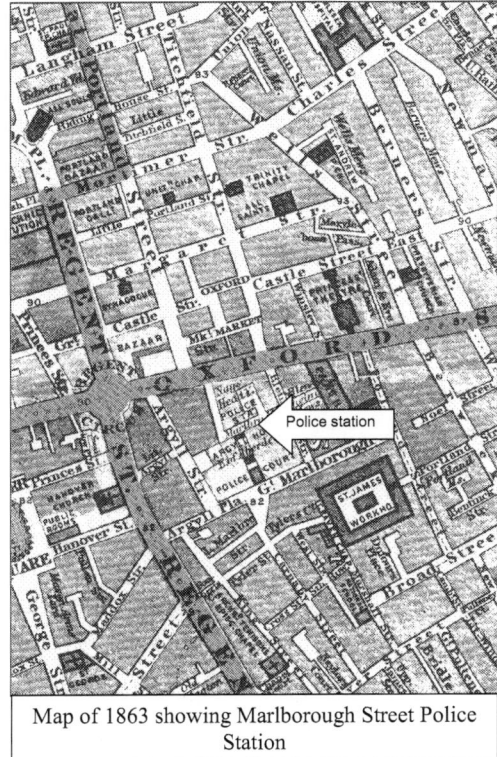

In 2011, the Royal National Lifeboat Institution, who have now largely taken over lifesaving duties from the Metropolitan Police, launched their lifeboats 919 times and assisted 245 people from their bases at Teddington, Chiswick and Tower (the new RNLI name for Waterloo pier where conversion work was completed in 2006).

This was the first time that the RNLI had been asked to cover lifesaving duties on a river rather than on a coastline.

Map of 1863 showing Marlborough Street Police Station

Great Marlborough Street Police Station

The court began its famous role in dispensing justice in London's West End under the 1792 Middlesex Justices Act when in 1793 21 Great Marlborough Street was adapted for use as one of the public or police offices created by the Act. The premises also covered ground to the rear, in Marlborough Mews (now Ramillies Place).

In 1856 the Receiver took a lease on the house at No 20, let it out, but used the ground at the rear to extend the police station.

The freeholds were purchased in 1892 and a new police station was built at No 20. No. 19 was bought from the Elwes family in 1912 and a new building, replacing numbers 19, 20 and 21 was designed by JD Butler and built by Patman and Fotheringham in the following year.

The new building enjoyed, like Bow Street, a distinguished stone frontage shared by the court and police station, and continued as a bustling, busy court until its final closure.

The court heard many cases involving famous people, including John

Great Marlborough Street Police Station in 1910. 19 – 20 Great Marlborough Street W1

Lennon and Yoko Ono (cannabis possession, 1968), Mick Jagger and Marianne Faithfull (cannabis possession 1969) and Keith Richards (drugs possession and unlicensed firearms 1973). Early in his career, Charles Dickens reported on the stream of characters that passed through the court, and it was here that Oscar Wilde began his infamous case against the Marquess Of Queensbury that ended in Wilde's downfall.

According to a London newspaper, one of the court's famous magistrates, Mr St John Harmsworth, once acquitted a political demonstrator on the basis that his egg throwing was 'a time honoured tradition of British political life'. Many call girls marked the occasion of his retirement by sending him cards, acknowledging his fair sense of justice; he responded by writing off many of their fines!

On Jubilee night 1887, Elizabeth Cass, a 23-year-old seamstress new to London, went out to watch the celebrations, but became separated from her companions, and started to wander a rather circuitous route around the Oxford Circus area. Constable Bowden Endicott started to observe her movements, including apparently approaching three different gentlemen, and then arrested her for disorderly conduct. She was duly charged for behaviour amounting to soliciting for prostitution, and was let off with a warning by the magistrate. Mme Bowman, Elizabeth Cass's employer, wrote furious letters of protest to the Commissioner, Sir Charles Warren, who then held a formal inquiry to determine whether any action should be taken against constable Endacott, but the case continued to cause controversy, even to the extent of being debated in Parliament. The evidence of Endacott and the character of Elizabeth Cass were both put under great scrutiny, with the case encapsulating the fears of Victorian police critics who feared that police officers would either blackmail prostitutes or harass innocent, respectable women[36].

West End Central Police Station

A famously busy station, West End Central, 27 Savile Row W1S 2EX built of steel and concrete, was opened on 14th July 1940 as a purpose-built police station to replace Great Marlborough Street and Vine Street stations. The new station's location was the subject of comment, and there was some resistance to the idea that Savile Row would be associated with something other than the purchase of gentlemen's fine suits. It was pointed out that 'The Commissioner too has paid for a Savile Row address', and the controversy may have contributed to the station becoming known not by the name of the street in which it is located but as 'West End Central'.

West End Central Police Station, 1940 to present day. 27 Savile Row, W1

Just over two months after its occupation on 14th July 1940, a Second World War parachute mine fell on its front doorstep, killed three officers, injured 22, and reduced the brand new station to a shell. It was re-occupied in December 1940, and was counted amongst the ten Metropolitan Police stations 'knocked out', as distinct from being heavily damaged, during World War Two[37].

On 15th December 1941 King George VI and Queen Elizabeth paid a morale-boosting visit to the station. Ralph Kirker, a West End Central officer, misjudged the timing of his meal in the canteen, and contrary to carefully-laid plans, was eating his meal when he was interrupted by the Royal Party's arrival. The officer described the kindly comments from the Queen but noted that the faces of the senior officers looked distinctly less gracious. He waited with some trepidation for repercussions about this unplanned incident, but was relieved not to hear any more about it[38]!

Always at the centre of policing the vice-related crime of the West End, the station dealt with many street prostitutes, particularly before the Street Offences Act of 1959 changed the system from routine but ineffective fining, to a system of cautioning and then liability for imprisonment.

Temptations to corruption can only be combatted by eternal vigilance, preferably in the context of a legal framework that is effective and practical in matching public morality. In 1921, sergeant Horace Josling accused a fellow sergeant, George Goddard, of taking bribes from illegal bookmakers. Later there were anonymous letters that also accused Goddard of taking bribes from club and restaurant owners who permitted gaming, erotic cabarets and prostitution on their premises, including a notorious Kate Meyrick of the Cecil Club in Gerrard Street, Soho. Horace

Josling's case was not accepted and it was he, rather than Goddard who ended up being dismissed. Chief Constable Frederick Wensley later used the Flying Squad to raid the Cecil Club and prosecuted Kate Meyrick. He also prosecuted Goddard, using Goddard's assistant as a witness against him. When Goddard was sent to prison, Horace Josling, an honourable man, was thoroughly vindicated.[39]

During the Second World War the vice scene in Soho thrived. 'Bottle parties' where patrons brought their own alcohol to otherwise unlicensed clubs, became havens for prostitutes and organised crime, and the Clubs Office was introduced to focus policing operations to control them. 'Near beer' joints (selling malt liquor with insufficient alcohol to need licensing) and brothels proliferated, and card games were often organised to fleece visitors to Soho who rarely realised that the other members of the card game were collaborating against them.

By the late 1940s the Messina brothers were organising marriages of convenience for French prostitutes and had started to organise a thriving vice trade, some of the proceeds of which were channelled back to Malta, the country to which Guiseppe Messina had moved from Sicily. The 1950s saw Bernard Silver charging exorbitant rents for prostitutes to use to ply their trade. He and eight others were prosecuted for living on the earnings of prostitution in 1956 on the basis that the rents they charged were eight times the normal market rent, but were acquitted on legal grounds by direction of the trial judge. Silver was, however, eventually convicted in 1974 at the beginning of a sustained effort from the Metropolitan Police which saw convictions for James Humphreys, a prominent pornography merchant, a reorganisation of responsibility for policing pornography away from a central CID branch at Scotland Yard, and a drive against police corruption. Since then, changes to licensing laws and close collaboration with Westminster City Council have significantly reduced the various manifestations of Soho's vice trade.[40] The reduction of police corruption in the 1970s and 1980s, both in this area and more generally, has been one of the significant unsung achievements of the Metropolitan Police Service.

Beak Street Section House

A new section house, designed by J Dixon Butler, was built at 40 Beak Street W1 in 1909-10 and taken into use on 22nd August 1910 for 88 unmarried officers from Great Marlborough Street and Vine Street police stations, with the rent being assessed at 1 shilling (5p) per week. It was at

Beak Street shortly after Christmas 1918 where the first group of Metropolitan Police women police officers began their training.

Many officers will have remembered the small cubicles, with partitions stopping well short of ceiling height, that comprised the personal living space here and in many other section houses of the period. The building also accommodated offices and other functions at various times.

Beak Street Section House 1910 – 1999. 40 Beak Street. London W1

Recruitment candidates were interviewed here, including after the Second World War. Records state that the building re-opened as a section house on 16th December 1957 with room for 75 officers and 13 junior cadets. Offices for the administration of central traffic process functions were located here for a period, and the newly-formed Diplomatic Protection Group had a temporary base here. When the section house had closed because of the standard of accommodation for single officers being raised, officers attended Beak Street for assessment centres and resettlement courses. The building was put up for sale at the end of 1998.

Dean Street Police Station

At number 6 Dean Street was a police station in operation in 1830, its location being central to the parish of St Anne's, Soho[41]. A 'List of Police

Stations where Charges are taken in the Metropolitan Police District where police constables are at all times' was published in 1836 showing that 'C' or St. James's Division had two police stations, at Little Vine Street, Piccadilly; and Dean Street, Soho. By 1838 the station was no longer in use[42]. Dean Street was occupied by 'B' Division in 1832[43] but the premises were later relinquished by the police.

It was, however, a good site for a police station, especially as Soho developed as a vibrant and diverse centre. The Admiral Duncan public house in Old Compton Street, a few doors down from the junction with Dean Street, became the centre of a bomb outrage in April 1999 when David Copeland, an English neo-Nazi militant, planted a number of nail bombs in various parts of London aimed against gay, Bangladeshi and black communities. His nail bombs killed 3 people and injured 129. A paranoid schizophrenic working alone, Copeland was sentenced to life imprisonment with a recommendation that he serve at least 50 years, a reminder that bombs are not always the weapon of organised terrorist groups.

Greek Street Police (watch) Station house in 1830

Greek Street Police Station

Greek street runs north south from Tottenham Court Road towards Leicester Square and Chinatown. Number 58 Greek Street was occupied by 'C' Division in 1829 had been turned over to the police from the parochial authorities for use as a police station. Originally erected in 1733, the station house was situated in front of the local water pump where people would gather. The premises were subject of much alteration over the years, and its ground floor, like many premises in the area, is now a restaurant. The station was no longer in use by 1832[44] as other more suitable premises were found.

Vine Street Police Station

The original St James's parish watch house was at 10 Little Vine Street, later Piccadilly Place, and 10 Vine Street was taken over in 1829 as the original 'C' Division headquarters. It was rebuilt in 1868-9, enlarged in 1897 and extended into the former 'Man in the Moon' public house to accommodate administrative functions in 1931. When West End central was opened in 1940, Vine Street became the Aliens Registration Office. The merging of the two Divisions of Vine Street and Great Marlborough Street into West End Central caused much work for the one station, and Vine Street re-opened in 1971 to overcome the anomaly where two Divisions, CD1 and CD2, had been created for West End Central, each with its own command structure. A small back street near Piccadilly Circus, Vine Street was the centre for the policing of Boat Race celebrations in the 1930s and, with Marlborough Street and Bow Street, achieved the fame of featuring in the famous Monopoly board game. Its final closure in November 1997 brought to an end the premises' long association with policing.

In 1914, Constable 356 'C' Foreman, a single man who had been a police officer for seven years, was stopped by pickets on his way to Vine Street from Bow Street section house. It was the day of a police strike that had been called to protest against police pay and conditions. Constable Foreman defied the pickets and went on parade at Vine Street where 13 of 35 officers due to parade were absent. The Superintendent took the parade and warned the officers that they could expect opposition from pickets.

The first officer in the file being marched out refused to lead the others on to the street, but Constable Foreman saw that the pickets were from 'B' rather than 'C' Division, and, using his high opinion of his own Division, threatened the pickets with his truncheon saying 'No one from 'B' Division is going to tell me what to do!'

The dispute was settled by a pay increase of 13 shillings (65p) per week and the grant of widows' pensions of 10 shillings (50p) per week, but the First World War intervened[45]. There were further police strikes in 1918 and 1919, the year that the Police Federation was formed (See Inspector Syme later in this chapter for further information).

'C' Division held Trenchard House section house, Broadwick Street within

Vine Street Police Station 1868 – 1997. 10 Vine Street, Piccadilly, W1

its territory, and the Division's Social and Athletic Club held a concert there on 10th March 1949, featuring Tommy Trinder, Edmundo Ros and his Rumba band, Jon Pertwee, the magician George Braund, Len Marten, Arthur Haynes & Frederick Ferrari from the BBC show 'Stand Easy', and various other accomplished entertainers. This was a reflection, perhaps, of a form of police social life that has largely disappeared, and of a good relationship between the police of the West End and the entertainers in London's theatres.

Trenchard Section House was purpose built in the 1930s to provide individuals with single rooms for 214 persons, with shared bathroom/shower facilities. Ancillary facilities to the building included catering, bar and common room areas, squash courts and gymnasium facilities, as well as laundry facilities.

In 2004 the Metropolitan Police announced that it had sold the section house to the national regeneration agency English Partnerships who provide affordable homes for sale, for groups such as key workers and first time buyers. The premises had been unoccupied since 1999 and were considered no longer fit for its original purpose of housing single police officers. Day-to-day management of the police estate is delegated by the MPA to the Metropolitan Police Service's Property Services Department.

Trenchard House Police Section House
19-25 Broadwick Street, Westminster W1F 0DF.

The estate comprises over 600 operational buildings and 1116 residential properties, used by 42,000 police officers and staff, and is valued at c£1.7billion. The MPA Estates Strategy is detailed in the strategy documents *'Building Towards the Safest City'*[46] and the Metropolitan Police had been under pressure for some time to part with the property. Plans were submitted in 2012 to Westminster council for the unlisted section house to be demolished in favour of a nine floor single building, with underground car parking, with 78 residential units and commercial floor space[47].

Rochester Row Police Station

In the first days of the Metropolitan Police, the new 'B' Division took over the watch house at New Way, off Tothill Street Westminster. This had a reserve room, three cells, a parish engine house, charge room, Superintendent's office and a small yard used for parading officers. The Property Register noted that

'the whole premises need thorough repair, and [it is] intended for demolition for Westminster Improvement Schemes[48]'.

Rochester Row Police Station 1901 – 1993. 63 Rochester Row, SW1

In 1845, a new police court (at number 69), station and section house (numbers 63-7) was built in Rochester Row, this new building replacing the old watch house, the section houses in Cowley Street and Great Smith Street, and the old Westminster police court at Queen's Square, Pimlico.[49] Originally the part of Westminster lying to the South and West of Buckingham Palace and Knightsbridge had been part of 'B' Division before 'B' Division became co-terminous with the boroughs of Kensington and Chelsea.

A Superintendent's residence for the 'A' Division and three sets of living quarters were established in 1906 at 68 Vincent Square that backed on to Rochester Row. Clues about the duties of Superintendents appear in Police Orders. On 29th January 1835 an Order directed that Superintendents should sign the Occurrence Book in red ink for the date and time they had visited stations, a later Order on 14th January 1850 clarifying that this procedure was not required more than once in 24 hours. Superintendents had to deal with the cases of discipline defaulters no later than 7am each morning, and an Order for 11th November 1848 dictated that any Superintendent arriving late at the Commissioner's office with his morning report would miss his turn and wait until the last Division had been dismissed[50].

Two sets of annuity charges, representing the money spent on erecting the buildings, were payable to the University Life Assurance Society based at 25 Pall Mall, this being John Wray's – the Receiver's address. The Receiver had in fact been a founder member of the Society, and used its investment capacity to fund several police buildings[51].

Ambrosden Avenue (Westminster Section House)

Ambrosden House (also referred to on occasions as Westminster section house) accommodated single and married officers under one roof providing the area with police officers who could walk to work at nearby Rochester Row. Purpose built, it was an imposing building situated at the corner of Ambrosden Avenue and Francis Street and is still there today. The section house was purchased freehold in 1886 and its address was 1 Ambrosden Avenue, Westminster SW1. In December 1927 it was closed

Ambrosden Police Section House. 1886 – 1973. 1 Ambrosden Avenue, Westminster

and the residents moved out whilst the building underwent substantial refurbishment. The Metropolitan Police sold the block of flats and they are now in private ownership. This was a building over six floors and was located near to the Roman Catholic Cathedral. Originally it had rather spartan sleeping arrangements with occupants residing in cubicles which were small, noisy and draughty.

During the 1927 refurbishment those large rooms with cubicles had the partitions removed and furnished single bedrooms were developed in their place. The section house was not far away from the Windsor Castle public house which meant a change of scenery and time to relax for many residents when off duty. The building had drying rooms, a canteen, snooker room and darts board so there was always recreational activity. The section house employed a number of wardens who maintained the security and also were responsible for the Book 92 to record times when officers were absent from their duties and the booking in an out of visitors. Also these wardens were responsible for early morning calls to residents so they paraded a quarter of an hour before 6am on early turn, for late turn at 2pm and 10pm for night duty. In the early 1950s an elderly ex-serviceman was the night duty warden and he had to trudge up the five floors to wake those who had signed in the book at reception for a call.

There were periodic inspections by the local inspector and section sergeant who would call at the section house and sign the occurrence book held in the reception office. They would then check the visitors book to ensure that non-resident police officers were not hiding away perhaps in the canteen or snooker room when they should have been on duty patrolling. Ambrosden had few facilities for parking motor cars;

> '…except outside on the street. However whilst car ownership by single officers was limited a number did have motor cycles which were kept safely near the kerb outside. The section house also had fire escape facilities and exited at the rear gate that led onto the pavement. It was always claimed that female giggles were never to be heard in this all male environment'[52]!

The section house was shut and sold in 1973 as part of a review into section house accommodation[53].

The Metropolitan Police Training School Peel House. (For Hendon and the Peel Centre see The London Borough of Barnet)

Training of recruits also took place not far from Scotland Yard. Freeholds were purchased to land in 1904 and 1910 in Regency Street and Causton Street SW1 on which was built a recruit training establishment for men which was called Peel House. The block also had married quarters for police officers who found it difficult to obtain affordable housing in central London. The five blocks of flats were Gladston House, Harcourt House, Douglas House, Matthews House and Ridley House provided accommodation for 54 families. When built the Training School consisted of class rooms, entertainment hall, section house and six sets of married quarters for teaching staff and their families.

Between 1829 and 1907 recruits had been posted to division after two weeks' foot drill, followed by a period of accompanying an experienced constable and then armed with an Instruction Book learning on the beat as they went along.

The Commissioner Sir Edward Henry decided to improve this system and Peel House became the centre for much improved training. After passing a revamped selection procedure including an educational test, recruits undertook a residential course of instruction at Peel House. This included

Metropolitan Police Training School, Peel House SW1 circa 1910

lessons in police duty but also general education, physical training, self-defence (added in 1908) and first aid.

In the picture below recruits are being given practical instruction in stopping a member of the public, questioning and arrest. In this scenario a man has been stopped and detained for suspected unlawful possession of a bicycle.

Notice all the potential police officers are required to provide their own clothes as they did not get fitted for uniforms until the end of training. Here the Station Sergeant is restraining his suspect using a hold which reduces chance of escape or assault on the officer by the person detained.

In the picture below a class of recruits are being tested on licensing matters at the end of their course as part of their final asessment before being posted to Division. There were a variety of scenarios that recruits would be put through as part of their final test. In the example shown a constable has

A class of recruits at Peel House in the 1920s

A final practical prior to passing out from Peel House circa 1920s

been called into licensed premises probably by the licensee who has a drunk and incapable male on his premises. Notice the Inspector to the right with his clip board assessing not only the constable but also the instruction given by the Station Sergeant.

The picture below shows the dining hall at the Peel House in about the 1920s and recruits probably sat at the tables in alphabetical order according to the class they were in.

By 1909 Peel House was given an extension as it was already too small. During World War One part of the complex was handed over Dominion troops to use as a club for the duration but by 1918 some sections of the

The dining hall at Peel House

building were reclaimed for training Metropolitan Women Police Patrols. Post-war expansion saw a site taken into service in Aldwych called 'Eagle Hut' where Bush House now stands. In 1923 Peel House started to run Staff College courses for senior overseas police officers as well.

By 1927 the basic training course was lengthened to ten weeks and the following year pre-promotion courses for constables and sergeants aspiring for higher rank were introduced. On its temporary closure in 1939 it soon re-opened to help train the 12,000 War Reserve volunteers who had enlisted.

In 1937 Superintendent F. Smith was in charge of the training school with Sub Divisional Inspectors S. M. Ogden and H.S. Glasby in support.

For a short period in 1940 additional premises were used for War Reserve officers at the Holy trinity Church School Mayfield Road, Dalston. Later in the war, in 1941, training also took place at Grey Coat School, Grey Coat

Peel House Training School Staff 1911

Place SW1[54].

In 1946 Hendon or 'Peel House II' as it was termed at the time was opened again for basic training and operated together with Peel House in Regency Street. With the running of both training schools (and its satellites) a little gentle rivalry occurred with competitions in all aspects of sport, first aid and other games between the two. After World War Two, Peel House also provided senior officer non-residential training courses.

A Training School Magazine was started in January 1963 under the editorship of Chief Superintendent J. J. Miller MBE. This magazine was produced to inform interested parties of what was happening in the training environment, and had a very wide circulation considering that many Commonwealth countries sent their more senior police officers on the Overseas Police Course and CID for Training at Hendon. As such many of these found their way into police libraries around the world.

In the 1960s other courses were run at Peel House. These included courses for probationer constables, Traffic Wardens and also promotion courses for uniform branch constables. The Royal Park Keepers course trained 16 men and women in 1963. This course was designed to assist them in their daily duties in the Parks where they could exercise the legal powers of a constable.

The Metropolitan Police organised many sporting activities (arranged within the rules of the Metropolitan Police Athletic Association MPAA). The clubs would enter competitions including cross country, table tennis, rugby and lifesaving. In fact sport has until lately been positively encouraged by senior officers so as to maintain general fitness but also focus on group participation and teamwork. Senior officers would take a personal interest, would select and encourage officers of particular sporting prowess in their divisions. Being good at sport at the Training School could become an advantage.

Sergeant Henry William Mallin

The signed picture at right shows one of the Metropolitan Police heroes and premier sportsman, Sergeant Henry William Mallin. Mallin joined the police in 1915 (he had been a store keeper) initially on 'E' Division and then within two years posted to the 6th Division or Roysth Dockyard where he was allowed to train as a boxer. Otherwise, during his service he spent time in the Training school and in Administration at Commissioners Office (CO) having passed the sergeants examination in 1924. He trained constantly often in duty time and is pictured with all his cups, and prizes in boxing. He opened his account as a 28-year-old (he was ABA champion of 1919 and 1920) and opened his bid for the Olympic middleweight title at
Antwerp in 1920 by out-pointing Lt. Joseph Cranston of the US army. In a hard fought final Mallin won on points to take the Gold medal. Mallin successfully (and with much controversy) defended his Gold medal in Paris four years later. Sergeant Mallin is also seen as a referee in the gymnasium at Peel House. The boxing group would meet up regularly, most evenings and go through their fitness and training regimes. Whilst he was perhaps the greatest athlete the Metropolitan Police has had he was beset with injury worries which were probably the reason he never turned professional. His left leg had been injured badly during the 1st world war and was always a source of aggravation to him which perhaps explains

A boxing class at Peel House

why he was often photographed wearing leg coverings or trousers. His leg was amputated in later life[55].

Mallin stayed single all his life and he remained in the service for a very long time until on age limit, aged 60 years in 1952 having completed 37 ½ years he retired. Whilst his police service was untypical, as he only gained experience on 'J' Division in 1945 his impressive display of medals, cups and prizes for boxing made him an ideal role model for aspiring police officers. As such he was a recruiting sensation for the police. After his retirement Mallin lived until 1969 and

The official police funeral of ex sergeant Harry Mallin in 1969

died at Lewisham.

Sir George Abbiss Assistant Commissioner

Sir George Abbiss was an English policeman and had much to do with Peel House. He was born in 1884 at Hitchin and died in 1966. He was the second officer to rise through the ranks to become Assistant Commissioner of Scotland Yard. Originally a gardener, he joined the Metropolitan Police in 1905 and was an ordinary constable, later a Sergeant and Station Sergeant before being promoted to Inspector in 1919. In 1920 he was awarded the MBE and in 1932 the OBE in 1933 being appointed Assistant Commissioner before retiring in 1946[56]. In 1936 George Abbiss OBE (later knighted) became the Assistant Commissioner 'D' Department with a responsibility for the Training of recruits in which he actively participated.

Assistant Commissioner George Abbiss

In the picture at right Abbiss is shown in a light suit at the front centre of a class of recruits who have successfully completed their training prior to being posted to division.

Abbiss was an approachable person who had risen up the ranks from constable and understood the nature of being a well-balanced police officer. He had a nice nature, possessed a good sense of humour which was absent in most senior officers of the time and would even autograph the class photographs for the students. The class photographs (of which Abbiss is often sat front centre), are in fact taken by T. H. Everitts of Annerley Road SE19 – the official police Metropolitan Police photographer, who were even taking pictures up until the 1990s.

Male and female officers did not mix in those days. The women's social study course was carried out at Aybrook Street Section House in Paddington where single women were later resident.

Aybrook Street Police Section House circa 1923

The picture above shows the section house building in 1923. Introduced in 1922 following disbanding of the Women Police Volunteers – (a Geddes Committee recommendation following economies of police expenditure), such was the outrage in Parliament that a compromise was reached to retain some 20 Women police as a nucleus, but with full powers of arrest. In 1948 Peto House in Aybrook Street, was named after Miss Dorothy Peto, an early senior female officer, and replaced Wandsworth Section House as the training school for women[57].

In 1918 women were initially housed in Beak Street Section house where they commenced training for the first time. Aybrook Street section house was erected between 1908-9 for the Metropolitan Police, and was designed by J. Dixon Butler. It is an austere building reflecting something of the influence of C. R. Mackintosh. The walls are of grey brick above a base of brown glazed bricks, and there are plain stone surrounds with cyma-moulded labels to the arched doorway and the three-light windows of the ground storey. A large segmental bowed window, divided by stone mullions and transoms, lights the staircase[58]. In later years Aybrook Street accommodated Management Services Department. Women police were notably supportive of First Aid competitions.

The National First Aid competition very often took place in London at Central Hall, Westminster SW1 in early February each year and the Training School always provided a team. The trophy was the Parsons Shield. The Metropolitan Police First Aid competition challenged for the 'Vivian Rogers' First Aid Trophy and eliminations took place within the four districts. The top two teams in each district were selected to compete in April each year, competitors were not allowed to take part in 'service time' and each team paid one shilling to enter[59].

In the picture below women police are involved in a tug of war with

Women police tug of war circa 1920's

another women police team (probably in Hyde park) showing if the men can do it then so can they.

In 1955 Superintendent (wt. no. 118329) 'Tommy' Wall joined the police in April 1929 and posted to 'N' Division. He was a real character, tough and uncompromising and feared by recruits when he later took charge at Peel House. Thomas George Wall was born the son of a Gas Inspector, in Cardiff on 16th August 1909 and was formerly a transport worker. He soon came to attention after making notable arrests and was commended by the Commissioner on no less than five occasions. He passed the promotion examination to sergeant in 1938 and transferred to 'G' Division and within a short time was transferred as Station Sergeant 16 to 'N' Division in 1945. He was married and had a son. Some five years later, as Inspector, he was sent for the first time to the Training School. Whilst 'Tommy' Wall was a stern disciplinarian there was also a compassionate side to him for those who asked his help. He was a member of the Salvation Army and was often seen in his Army uniform in his spare time, giving his services for the greater good. Such was his talents he became a staff officer on 'A' Division in September 1954 and three months later as chief inspector moved to staff officer on 'C' Division. Sadly in the interim his wife died. Between 1955 and 1963 he rose through the superintending ranks to Chief Superintendent and was awarded a Queen's Police Medal for distinguished service in 1961. Whilst still serving aged 57 years old and of pensionable age, he developed stomach cancer and died in service after 38 years. His not unsubstantial pension was never paid as his wife had pre-deceased him. His rival and opposite number at Hendon was Superintendent A. Buchanan. Training schools came under the heading of D3 Department whilst Buildings, Cadets and Dogs were the responsibility of Chief Superintendent P. R. Broad in D2.

In 1974 Peel House closed for Training purposes and the staff were transferred to Hendon.

Gerald Road Police Station

The first police station known variously as Roberts Buildings, Ebury Square, or Elizabeth Place, comprised a house leased on a yearly tenancy, with two cells, a charge room a reserve room, mess, kitchen and two bedrooms. It was noted that it as 'in need of thorough repair. The men have no lockers. Drainage very imperfect.' Nos 1 and 2 Roberts Buildings were two small cottages used as section houses.

In 1845, the station was replaced by new premises at 5 Cottage Road, re-named as Gerald Road forty years later in 1885. The building was rented on a 78-year lease at an annual rent of £170 12s 9d (£170.64) from Miss Minnis who apparently lived at number 14. In 1848 it was described as 'new and substantially brick and slate built with charge and reserve rooms, four cells and a section house'. It was later described as having 7 cells, an association cell and an ambulance shed. This would have housed a hand ambulance, a common means of conveying ill or injured people to hospital before the advent of the London Ambulance Service and the later general introduction of motor ambulances.

The station telegraph code was originally CR, then BG, and later, when it became part of 'A' Division in 1965, AL. In 1891 the Metropolitan Police purchased the next door premises, at number 3, from Canon Fleming, the vicar of St Michael's church, Chester Square and the freehold of both premises. Extension work was undertaken between 1892 and 1894 and the whole building was extensively reconstructed in 1925. An annexe in adjoining first floor premises of Elizabeth Street was acquired in 1981 and the station eventually closed, replaced by Belgravia police station in 1993.

One famous Gerald Road incident occurred in August 1909 when two officers arrested two drunken men for disturbing the residents, particularly a Mrs Costa, in Warwick Street Pimlico. It later transpired that the prisoners were Mrs Costa's husband and their lodger who had, noisily, been trying to persuade her to let them in to the house by 'knocking at the door and pulling the doorbell without lawful excuse' (then an offence under the Metropolitan Police Act).

Gerald Road Police Station. 1885 – 1993. 5 Gerald Road, Pimlico SW1

The case of Inspector Syme and the refused charges.

The inspector on duty was Inspector (wt. no. 79972) John Syme who joined the Metropolitan police in October 1894 and had risen rapidly through the ranks. In 1896, he was appointed to clerical duty in the offices of the Commissioner, and was promoted in 1899 and 1901, becoming a clerk sergeant- a very responsible position. In 1907, he had been transferred to the 'V' or Wandsworth Division and not long after, in 1908, he was promoted to Inspector and transferred to 'B' Division. John Syme investigated the circumstances of the arrest, and decided not to charge the men. This then required an entry to be made in the Refused Charge book, at a time when officers were very likely to be formally disciplined if they had made an arrest which did not justify a charge. The Sub Divisional Inspector berated the two Constables and then Inspector Syme, who had defended the two Constables by arguing that they should not be disciplined because the two drunks had not revealed the true facts to the officers before their arrest. Syme was fair, but very pedantic. His senior officers thought that he was too close to his junior officers, and transferred him to another station. Syme complained. Matters escalated. Syme was suspended, reduced in rank to Station Sergeant, appealed to the Home Office, threatened to write to his MP, but was then treated as 'impossibly insubordinate' and was dismissed.

What was originally a trivial matter became far worse as Symes' obsession increased and the situation escalated out of control. Syme was dismissed for approaching the Home Secretary, Winston Churchill, to appeal against his reduction to sergeant and compulsory transfer for alleged insubordination. On 28th June 1911, the Central Criminal Court tried Syme for sending a threatening letter to murder Alfred Reed. On 4th July 1911, Syme was sentenced to six months' imprisonment without hard labour[60].

From this 'The Police Union' was founded in 1913 by the now ex-Inspector John Syme, although from the outset, Sir Edward Henry made it clear that the Union was an illegal body, and warned that any man found to belong to it, would be dismissed. During World War 1, Special Branch officers and military police raided Union meetings and any policemen caught in the net were promptly sacked and drafted into the army[61].

Ex Inspector John Syme on an advertising postcard explaining his plight.

And so it continued that in March 1914, Syme was again charged with publishing a defamatory libel, entitled *'Fighting Officialdom: A three years' battle against Police and Home Office Persecution'*, concerning the Commissioner of the Metropolitan Police, Sir Edward Henry. The trial King vs. John Syme took place before the High Court of Justice, King's Bench Division, from 9th to the 16th July 1914. He was sentenced to eight months' imprisonment, and on 29th July, the Court of Criminal Appeal dismissed his appeal. Syme continued campaigning for an inquiry into his dismissal.

Syme gave up his quest in 1940 when he informed the Home Office he had finished his campaign and he died in 1945. In the meantime the Police Union became a recognised body as the Police Federation Staff Association.

The Union's biggest obstacle to progress was actually John Syme himself who had become so obsessed with his fight that he was becoming more unwell. Twice during the war he went to prison, for threatening to kill the Prince of Wales, and for criminally libelling Henry in a *Police Review* article. John Syme pursued his grievance for many years afterwards, including throwing stones at 10 Downing Street and organising a prototype police union.

When it was known in 1977 that Gerald Road police station might close, (it was shut in 1993) the vicar of St Peter's church, Eaton Square composed the following special prayer in verse:

Visit, we beseech thee, Lord
The station down at Gerald Road.
Drive far, we pray, the hostile snares
That come from Scotland Yard (upstairs)
And let thine angels dwell therein,
To keep the manor free from sin.
Accept each detainee's contrition
And guard it, Lord, from demolition.
Thus blest, it may yet with us stick;
Our very own, Saint Peter's nick!

Belgravia Police Station

Opened in 1993 as newly-built police station at 202-206 Buckingham Palace Road SW1W 9SX, Belgravia is now the headquarters of the policing of South Westminster, covering the areas of the former Bow Street, Cannon Row, Charing Cross, Rochester Row and Gerald Road stations. Gerald Road and Rochester Row Divisions had amalgamated on 1st October 1989. The station was built in just over two years and cost about £7m [62].

It was to Belgravia police station that Eric Joyce, Labour MP for Falkirk, was taken after a disturbance in the Strangers Bar in the Houses of

Parliament in February 2012. Mr Joyce later pleaded guilty to assault and provides an example of how junior police officers are sometimes called to arrest and deal with offenders regardless of their position in life.

Members of Parliament have been found indulging in dishonourable behaviour a number of times. Horatio Bottomley MP was the Liberal member for Hackney South from 1906 to 1912. He commenced publication of *John Bull*, a patriotic journal. He started the John Bull Victory Bond Club, a forerunner of premium bonds, and had a great talent in persuading people to spend their money on the bonds. A mixture of fraud and mismanagement resulted in the collapse of the scheme, his conviction for fraud, a sentence of 7 years imprisonment, and his expulsion from Parliament. In 1972 Reginald Maudling, the Conservative Home Secretary resigned when the Metropolitan Police commenced fraud investigations against John Poulson, a bankrupted property developer and architect whom Maudling had assisted to win contracts.

Belgravia Police Station. 1993 to present day. 202-206 Buckingham Palace Road, SW1W 9SX

Officers in the nearest operational police station to the Houses of Parliament are likely to reflect, more than most, upon the importance of separating politics from the operation of the criminal law. This principle, perhaps set out most explicitly in the Police Act 1964 that dealt with the separate roles of Chief Officers, Police Authorities and the Home

Secretary, will no doubt continue to give food for thought, particularly since 2012 when elected Police Commissioners have taken over the role of Police Authorities outside of London.

Marylebone Lane Police Station

The original 'D' Division in 1829 was centred on Marylebone, with its boundaries comprising, in modern terms, the area north of Oxford Street, West of Portland Place, East of Edgware Road, and encompassing Regent's Park.

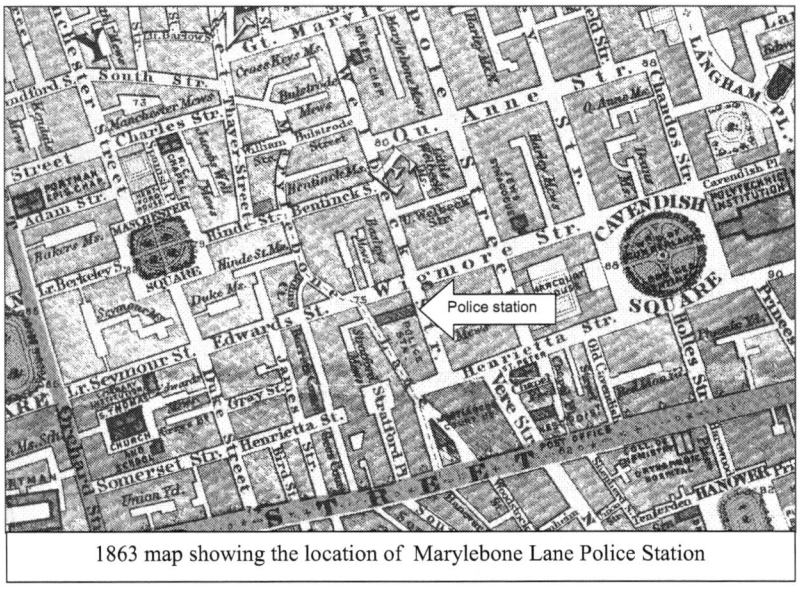

1863 map showing the location of Marylebone Lane Police Station

Marylebone Lane was one of the two original watch houses on 'D' Division taken over by the Metropolitan Police in 1829, and referred to as being 'vested in the Receiver by Act of Parliament'[63]. There was also a separate Marylebone Police Office in Marylebone High Street that had been established under the Middlesex Justices Act of 1792, which we would refer to nowadays as a magistrates court.[64] This office opened after the office at Shadwell had closed.[65]

Number 69 Welbeck Street was leased for 60 years from Michaelmas 1857, and a station built in 1859. The ground floor had a Superintendent's office, an Inspector's room, a charge room and 12 cells. The 69 Welbeck Street frontage was to maintain the appearance of a private residence with a private entrance 'for the superior officers only'. A new police station was erected in 1892 at 50 Marylebone Lane W1 in 1892 at a cost of £6935. This was, in turn, replaced by a more modern building at 19 Seymour Street W1 in 1977.

Marylebone Lane Police Station. 1892 – 1977. 59 Marylebone Lane W2.

The policing of Lord's cricket ground is part of the Division's responsibility, and indeed the demands of coping with those who steal from Oxford Street, one of the busiest shopping centres in the world.

Molyneux Street and John Street (Crawford Place) Police Stations

The second station listed for 'D' Division in 1836 was 5 Little Harcourt Street, Marylebone, and, perhaps as a replacement for these premises, John Street police station and section house was built and occupied in 1848. The John Street site (called Molyneux Street, Edgware Road) was eventually the result of amalgamated freehold purchases at 1 Molyneux Street, 8 - 10 John Street, 41 – 3 Horace Street, 1, 3 and 5 Molyneux Street and the Horse and Groom public house. The station came into use in 1849 and an Inspector was in charge. The building occupied the corner plot and was situated opposite the Union Almshouse and a short distance from Edgware Road as we see in the map below.

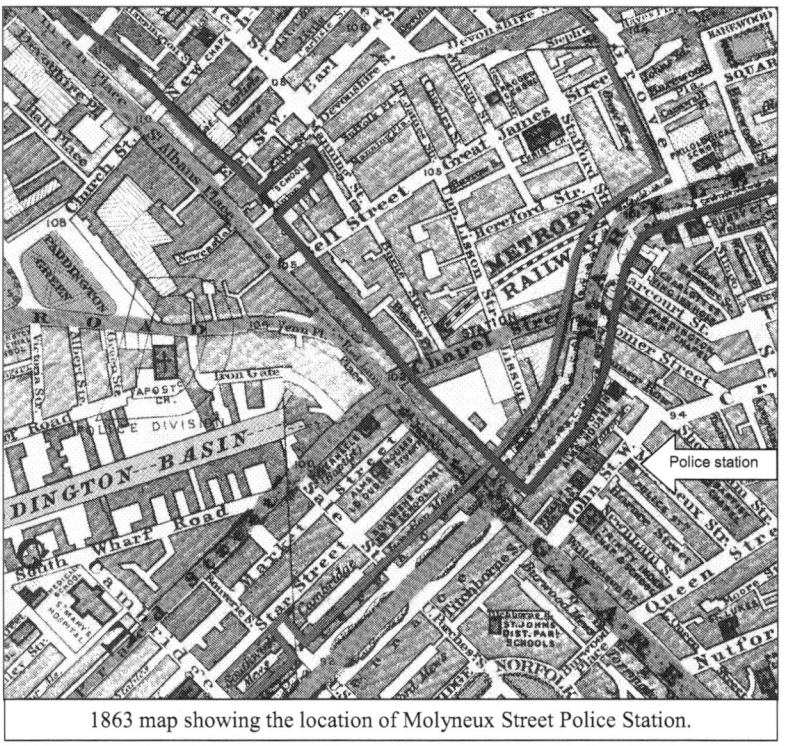

1863 map showing the location of Molyneux Street Police Station.

A new police station was then built and its opening announced in Police Orders of 4th July 1904. It was re-named Crawford Place in Police Orders of 8th February 1913, and was closed on 28th November 1933.

John Street housed, at no 32, the Shaftesbury Society and Ragged School Union from 1914. The Society (now known as Livability) is a large Christian based charity that works with disabled people and communities to achieve social inclusion, empowerment and justice.

The Ragged School Union was formed by Lord Shaftesbury in 1844 and was a great force for establishing free education for poor children. As the police stations, and officers in them, upheld the law in London during and after Victorian times, it must have been apparent to many of them that poverty, lack of educational opportunities and the state of local communities would often be the background from which offenders launched into a life of crime.

John Street Police Station. 1904 – 1933. 26 Crawford Place, Edgware Road, W1

It is a reminder that the police service does not uphold the law in isolation from other features of society.

Paddington and Paddington Green Police Stations

An early Paddington police station existed, vested with the Receiver by Act of Parliament, and was probably the station referred to in about 1832[66] as 'T' Division's Church Place, Paddington which was given up in 1840. The Property Register recorded this building as substantial with 3 cells, a coal cellar, a charge room, a WC and a small yard, but noted that 'the cells are not warmed and the floors are decaying'. There is confusion between identifying some early stations, especially Paddington and what later became Harrow Road as both had addresses in the same road but at differing ends. In 1841 a station at Hermitage Street (called Hermitage Street, Paddington) was situated at the junction with Bishops Row, Paddington with Inspector William Wiggins in charge as a station of 'D' or Marylebone Division[67].

This substantial station backed on to the alms-houses and was right opposite the Paddington vestry hall. The station was given up in 1865 when the replacement at 6 Harrow Road became available[68].

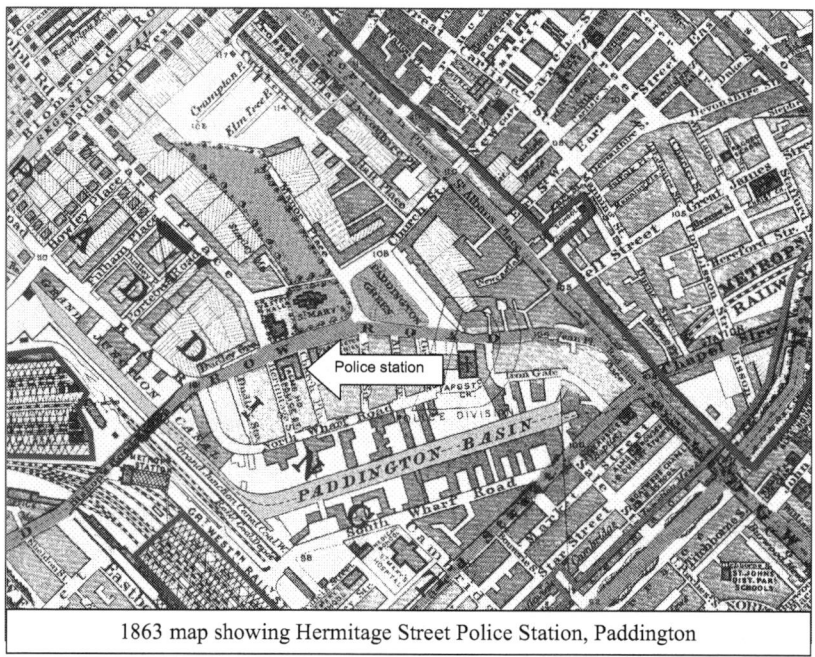

1863 map showing Hermitage Street Police Station, Paddington

A police station was built in Dudley Grove immediately opposite the old station in the stretch of Harrow Road west of the hall, in 1864. There were 88 rooms, 17 WCs, 16 coal cellars, 12 pantries, 12 sculleries 5 cells and 3 dust shafts. Both the vestry hall, which later became the town hall, and the police station were afterwards substantially enlarged, giving some dignity to an already run-down neighbourhood at the price of being separated from many of Paddington's later public buildings nearer Bayswater.

Business was transferred to the new police station in 1865 - to 6 Harrow Road W2, the address being referred to as no 62 in 1924[69] including 31 Dudley Grove. It was built as a station, section house and a complex of 66 model dwellings, at a cost of £8,617 after the land had been purchased for £2875.

Alterations to remove the triangular-shaped gables on its roof were made and it closed in 1971, being replaced by the current large, modern complex we see today.

Paddington Police Station, 1864 – 1971. 62 Harrow Road W2.

Paddington had become part of 'F' Division in 1909 and reverted back to 'D' Division in 1933. In the picture below one can see the police station to the right and the section house and model dwellings to the left. There was a separate door into the accommodation part and these buildings were essentially separate.

The most striking change was the construction in the mid-1960s of the flyover across Edgware Road and its linking in 1970 with the elevated Westway, which ran parallel to a widened and realigned Harrow Road

The rear yard of the station showing married quarters and the station prisoner transport

along the southern edge of Paddington Green. Buildings at the junction of Harrow and Edgware roads, including the Metropolitan Theatre of Varieties, were partly replaced by the large Paddington Green police station at the north corner and the towering London Metropole hotel at the south.

The old town hall, police station, and houses of Dudley Grove were also demolished, to allow Harrow Road to pass closer to the church. Modern road building has reinforced the separation of Paddington Green from the south part of the parish, where Edgware Road, except near Praed Street, is much more imposing and uniform than it is between the flyover and Maida Vale[70]. The stark new concrete police station and yellow-brick blocks of

Gilbert Sheldon House contrast with many converted mid-19th-century houses, those of the old Devonshire Terrace having shop fronts built over their gardens, and with J. Turner & Son's former boot factory of *c.* 1865 at the corner of Cuthbert Street. Similarly the shopping parade and towers of Hall Place contrast with a late 19th-century red-brick range near Maida Avenue[71].

On 23rd March 1971 the new Paddington Green station was opened on a site that included the former Metropolitan Palace of Varieties. The new building, which cost £1.4m, was hailed at the time as the most modern in the world.

Paddington Police Station 1864 – 1971 after alterations. 62 Harrow Road, W2

Dominated by the A40 Marylebone flyover, it was at the time by far the largest station complex ever built by the Metropolitan Police. It accommodated a section house, but more significantly the recruits selection and careers information centre, and became the first police building entered by many officers during their service.

Building work had started in January 1968 on the new Paddington Green Police station situated at 2-4 Harrow Road. Designed to be defensible against attack, the station also accommodated a secure custody area set aside for terrorist prisoners and high risk suspects.

The cells are described as;

> 'The walls are a cheery yellow, a colour designed to give an illusion of space. The chair and the thick mattress are an equally bright blue. Daylight filters in through a perspex domed window in the ceiling; there's air-conditioning, a private WC and basin, a desk, storage for clothes and books and even access to music and films. It could be any superior budget hotel, and it's in a great location - just ten minutes from London's Oxford Street'[72].

There are 2in-thick steel doors, with sound-deadening materials in the walls, and a CCTV camera monitoring system that follows your every move (except perhaps those using the en suite facilities)[73]. They've been refurbished at a reported cost of £490,000. Suspects could potentially stay for up to 28 days although in reality they stay less than 6 hours in the main. For the longer stay customers this is reflected in that beds have a thick mattress and, instead of a police blanket, detainees get a soft duvet.

Paddington Green, 1971- present day. 2 – 4 Harrow Road, London W2 1XJ

Harrow Road Police Station

Harrow Road became one of the stations of 'D' or Marylebone Division in 1859 however it was transferred to the new 'X' or Kilburn Division under Superintendent Samuel Hughes in 1865 where it remained until it returned to 'D' Division in 1965. The address 22 Carlton Crescent later Terrace

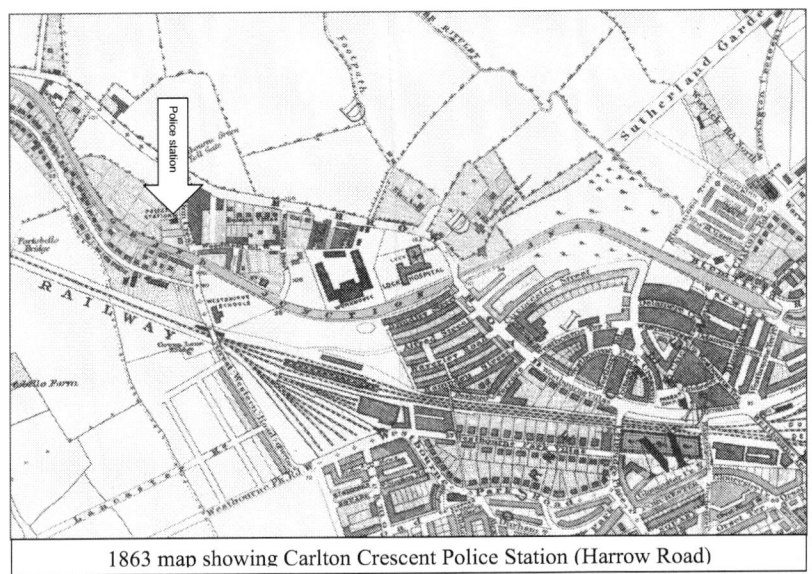

1863 map showing Carlton Crescent Police Station (Harrow Road)

was leased in 1873, and then additional premises acquired over the years at 6, 12, 14 and 16 Woodfield Road.

Inspector John Mobley was one of the officers promoted to fill the void in supervisors in 1885 when he was posted to Harrow Road. Inspector Frederick Mitchell was the Sub Divisional Inspector at Harrow Road in 1893. Also with him was Scotsman Reserve Inspector Hugh Newlands who was responsible for the mounted officers on reserve for 'X' Division. Harrow Road was the principle station for the division and housed the many horses needed by the mounted reserve.

Mitchell remained until 1895 when he retired and

Harrow Road Police Station, 1859 – 1912. 22 Carlton Crescent, Kensal New Town, Paddington

was replaced by Inspector William Bell[74].

It was important to have a police presence in the area as the fields either side of the newly built toll road were being converted to dwellings and more people were moving into the area. Land at 22 Carlton Crescent (later Terrace) situated between the Harrow Road and the Grand Junction Canal was obtained on lease from 1856 from Mr Charles Woodrooffe of Harrow Road for an annual rent of £30. The lease was for 100 years. A station was erected on the site which was convenient for the Westborne Green Road Toll gate in the Harrow Road, the Lock Hospital and the Paddington Workhouse at the bottom of Woodfield Road. Additional premises were acquired over the years at 6, 12, 14 and 16 Woodfield Road opposite the station. This was a substantial station with ground floor and three further floors. The station also contained a basement. By the 1900s the station was no longer suitable for policing purposes and new premises were sought on which to build a modern purpose-built station. Land situated at the corner of Woodfield Road and Harrow was purchased. It was important that there should be access to the rear of the station and that the station should be built on the main thoroughfare. A new police station and a section house for 60 officers was then built and opened on 4th March 1912, with a postal address of 325 Harrow Road.

One famous officer located at the old Harrow Road Police Station was Inspector Charles Brown (wt. no. 71791) who was born in 1863 and joined the Metropolitan Police in 1888 when there was a recruiting drive. He lived until 1933 and died in Canada where he moved after he retired from the police. During his service he rubbed shoulders with royalty and saw service at race meetings, fairs, strikes and unrest. In 1905 Brown was earning 63 shillings (£3.15p) a week as an Inspector of 'X' Division, Kilburn.

Inspector Charles Brown

In the picture below he is seen at Epsom Downs in 1909 when Minoru won the Epsom Derby. Here shown with his Kepi on he is providing protection for King Edward VII as part of his duty as a reserve Inspector. He was there as part of a large contingent of police officers drawn from all over the Metropolitan Police.

Charles Brown and King Edward VII at the Derby 1909

The Derby was a popular venue to visit for lots of ordinary people however there were also teams of thieves who would prey on the race goers either through illegal gaming or just simple crime such as stealing or pickpocketing. The police were there to prevent offences from taking place.

In 1908 Inspector Brown was photographed (as shown below) in uniform with an 'XR' helmet plate. The 'XR' helmet plate indicates that he was a Divisional Reserve Inspector although there is little to indicate his rank as an Inspector.

His pension records show that he was paid an extra 4s (20p) per week for being a reserve officer. These officers were on call to deal with ceremonial and public order duties, usually in central London, and were rewarded for their additional bearing and efficiency. They also wore a slightly better grade of uniform and were all trained to ride horses in case they were needed quickly.

A new police station and a section house for 60 officers was then built and opened on 4th March

Inspector Brown on ceremonial duty

Brown in Masonic outfit

1912, with a postal address of 325 Harrow Road. In July 1912 just as he would have been moving to the new station in the Harrow Road, Brown retired on pension of £121. 15s and left the police service at the age of 48 years with an exemplary record. Later that month he set sail and settle in Calgary in Canada with his wife Rose Ada. Brown had been a life long mason during his police service and membership was seen by many officers as offering opportunities for self-improvement and companionship. Here he is shown in his masonic costume at his lodge in Calgary. Charles passed away on 10th January 1933, in a Calgary hospital after a period of ill- health having drawn his pension for over 21 years and buried in Union Cemetery Calgary. He was accorded a Masonic Funeral Service on 16th January 1933. He had joined Ashlar Lodge No. 28 on 25th March, 1920 and served as Tyler from 1922 to 1932. He was re-elected in the Autumn of 1932. Rose Ada passed away 10th June 1933 in Epsom, England and is buried there. She and Maggie Rose had returned for a visit. She had an accident on board as the ship was nearing Southampton and during her treatment it was discovered that she had cancer with little chance of survival. She was transferred to London and then to Epsom Cottage Hospital where she died.

In 1900 constable William John Harper (wt. no. 86240) joined the 'K' Division but by November he had been transferred to 'X' Division residing at 28 Charlton Terrace, Paddington in the police section house situated upstairs. Harper was 21 years old when he

Constable William Harper

joined, born in Rotherhithe, height 5' 10" and weighing 10st 10lbs. He had been in the 1st Middlesex Volunteer Engineers for 2½ years probably fighting in South Africa.

The character of Harrow Road patch has been transformed by development since 1960 and the Westway overhead motorway, but its streets featured in the iconic film *The Blue Lamp,* 1950 which led on to the famous TV series *Dixon of Dock Green* in which constable George Dixon, played by Jack Warner, played an archetypal police officer character relating to the community in a manner which has come to symbolise a traditional and respectful excellence of public relations in British policing.

The origin of *The Blue Lamp* came from a letter to Commissioner Sir Harold Scott dated 6th May 1948 where Jan Read, who worked for J. Arthur Rank, sought the assistance of Scotland Yard in making an authentic film about policing. The plot that ended in the death of the police officer was based on the story of constable Nat Edgar who was murdered on duty in February 1948. It was during the search for constable Edgar's killer that the phrase 'helping police with their enquiries' was first used[75].

Harrow Road Police station, 1912 – present day. 325 Harrow Road, London W9

Tottenham Court Road Police Station

At various times part of 'C', 'D' or 'E' Divisions, Tottenham Court Road is located just within the boundary of the London Borough of Camden. The remainder of the police stations within Camden are dealt with in a companion volume *Behind the Blue Lamp – policing North and East London (2003)*.

Tottenham Court Road police station replaced George Street in about 1876. A station at 56 and 58 Tottenham Court Road was built in 1900 and demolished in 1940. The premises comprised a police station, section house and three sets of married quarters. The replacement station was built on the site and opened in 1940. The oral history project of the Friends of the Metropolitan Police Historical Collection contains an interview with an officer who had served at this station in 1919, during a police strike,

Tottenham Court Road 1900 – 1940. 56 Tottenham Court Road, W1.

when the branch secretary of the police union (as it then was) told officers coming to the police station for early turn duty that all officers at Tottenham Court Road were already out on strike. The officers then returned to their homes and were dismissed, along with hundreds of other officers.

The harsh treatment was a reflection of the discipline of the times, but their grievance was exacerbated by the fact that the branch secretary's information about other officers being on strike was false. One sergeant, Fred Hillier, kept his officers at the police station and would not let them return to their homes because he feared that they would be dismissed as strikers. At that time police officers often had part-time jobs acting as doormen at night clubs and theatres, but this practice was stopped by the Commissioner Lord Trenchard.

Tottenham Court Road Police Station, 1942 – Present day. 58 Tottenham Court Road W1

The officer remembered 142 officers on the strength at the police station, with sometimes up to 50 officers parading for night duty. Every crossing along Oxford Street was controlled by a police officer, and it would not be surprising that level of police cover has led to reminiscences of how frequently officers were seen on the beat.

In 1941 there was a change of Sub Divisional Inspector (SDI) at Tottenham Court Road. SDI (wt. no. 113487) Gavin who had been at the station when it was bombed was transferred to West End Central and SDI (wt. no. 113848) Osborne replaced him.

Today the police station has a front office to deal with enquiries but is no longer used for charging and housing of prisoners.

---

[1] Weinreb, B. and Hibbert, C. (1983) The London Encyclopedia, Macmillan, London
[2] Ordnance Survey map of 1871.
[3] Waddell, B. (1993) The Black Museum,
[4] Fido, M. and Skinner, K (1999) The Official Encyclopedia of Scotland Yard. Virgin London.
[5] Weinreb & Hibbert, as above.
[6] Metropolitan Police Divisional Records 'A' Division. Met Heritage Collection.
[7] Swinden, D.R. (1992) Police in London during the early 19th Century, University of London (Unpublished)
[8] Letter sent by the Clerk to the Justices, Guildhall Windsor to Sir Richard Mayne, Commissioner, Metropolitan Police dated 16 March 1963. National Archives, MEPO 3/37
[9] National Archives Census 1851
[10] Register of Deaths of Serving Metropolitan Police Officers (1829-1889) – National Archives MEPO4/2
[11] Metropolitan Police Orders dated 26th March 1867
[12] Sunday Express 17th July 1994.
[13] http://www.britishlistedbuildings.co.uk/en-208954-canon-row-police-station-greater-london- accessed on 9th October 2012
[14] http://en.wikipedia.org/wiki/Royal_Victorian_Order accessed on 5th August 2012
[15] Dornford Yates (2001) 'As Berry and I were saying' House of Stratus.UK
[16] Hyde Park Police Centenary Booklet 1967.
[17] Metropolitan Police Surveyor's Property Register
[18] Hyde Park Police Centenary as above.
[19] Journal of the Statistical Society of London, vol. XI, March 1848
[20] Metropolitan Police Orders dated 7th April 1893
[21] Henry Mayhew A Visit to St Giles Rookery and Its Neighbourhood
[22] Bow Street Police Station timeline (Dave Allen)
[23] ibid
[24] ibid
[25] Browne, Douglas, C. (1956) The Rise of Scotland Yard. Harrap and Co, London p88
[26] Bow Street Police Station timeline (Dave Allen)
[27] The Property Register also refers to a lease from Christmas 1832 for 41 years.
[28] Fido, M. and Skinner, K (1999) The Official Encyclopedia of Scotland Yard. Virgin London.
[29] Census records 1901
[30] Bow Street Police Station timeline (Dave Allen)
[31] ibid
[32] ibid
[33] ibid
[34] ibid
[35] ibid
[36] Fido, M. and Skinner, K (1999) The Official Encyclopedia of Scotland Yard. Virgin London.
[37] The Metropolitan Police at War H. M. Howgrave-Graham. HMSO 1947.
[38] West End Central- Commemorating the Official Opening (after refurbishment, 2007) Metropolitan Police.
[39] Fido, M. and Skinner, K (1999) The Official Encyclopedia of Scotland Yard. Virgin London.
[40] Eight Area Clubs and Vice Unit – A Brief History. Metropolitan Police.
[41] From a picture donated by Bernard Brown.
[42] Kellys Directory 1838
[43] Private correspondence with Mr Ken Butler

[44] Return of Mops (1832) Metropolitan Police. ESB
[45] Best, C. F.(undated) 'C' or St James's – A History of Policing in the West End of London. ESB London .
[46] http://www.gov-news.org/gov/uk/news/trenchard_house_soho_sale_announced/80326.html accessed on 3rd December 2012
[47] http://transact.westminster.gov.uk/CSU/Planning%20Applications%20Committees/2008%20onwards/2012/30%20-%208%20August/ITEM%2002%20-%20Trenchard%20House,%2019-25%20Broadwick%20St,%20W1.PDF accessed on 3rd December 2012
[48] Metropolitan Police Property Registers, ESB London
[49] Following in Footsteps, in The Job newspaper 15th May 1987 by Bernard Brown
[50] Best, C. F.(undated) 'C' or St James's – A History of Policing in the West End of London. ESB London .
[51] Reynolds, J. (undated) The Receiver for the Metropolitan Police District: A Short History
[52] Stoner, M. (2011) 'Home Service' London Police Pensioner 141-June p17
[53] The Commissioners Annual Report 1973
[54] Metropolitan Police Orders dated 24th November 1941
[55] Private correspondence 21st November 2012
[56] http://www.flickr.com/photos/hillview7/2957298019/in/photostream/#comments accessed 18th November 2012
[57] http://www.metpolicehistory.co.uk/1946-to-date.html accessed on 27th November 2012
[58] http://www.british-history.ac.uk/report.aspx?compid=41469#s5 accessed on 16th November 2012
[59] Metropolitan Police Orders dated 18th February 1949.
[60] ibid
[61] http://policecommunitysupportofficer.com/phpBB2/viewtopic.php?t=12389 accessed on 15th August 2012
[62] Belgravia Police Station – Commemorating the Official Opening. Metropolitan Police.
[63] Property Registers ESB London
[64] Bernard Brown (undated) A Short History of 'D' Division.
[65] International Centre for the History of Policing, Crime and Justice, The Open University.
[66] Return of Mops (1832) Metropolitan Police. ESB London
[67] The Police and Constabulary List 1844
[68] Kellys Directory 1865
[69] Metropolitan Police Property Schedule, February 1924
[70] 'Paddington: Paddington Green', A History of the County of Middlesex: Volume 9: Hampstead, Paddington (1989), pp. 185-190. URL: http://www.british-history.ac.uk/report.aspx?compid=22663&strquery=police accessed: 03rd December 2012
[71] ibid
[72] http://www.dailymail.co.uk/home/moslive/article-1287132/Inside-terror-cell-The-London-police-station-housed-failed-July-21-bombers-Guantanamo-Bay-prisoners.html#ixzz2E1oOEUki accessed on 3rd December 2012
[73] ibid
[74] Kellys Directories 1880 - 1900
[75] Moss, A. and Skinner, K. (2006) The Scotland Yard Files. National Archives, Kew.

Chapter 2

The London Borough of Barnet

by Peter Kennison

Introduction

The policing of the Barnet area before 1840 was carried out and supervised by the various vestries and Parish authorities. There was a fairly efficient police within the Parishes and these consisted of sworn constables (including those of the Bow Street horse patrol), beadles and headboroughs who would patrol during the day and night by rota.

When the Metropolitan Police boundary was extended to cover the Barnet area in 1840 the responsibility for supervision fell to the senior officers of Metropolitan Police of 'S' or Hampstead Division. The divisional headquarters and administration moved from Albany Street police station to High Street, Highgate during 1840 when 'S or Hampstead division as it was now known became the largest police division in terms of area covered. From this time on the other 'S' Division stations were Stone Bridge, Willesden; Edgware Road, 8 mile stone; 52 Albany Street, Regents Park; Junction Place, Kentish Town 1 Heath Street, Hampstead; 52 Salisbury Street, Portman Market; Pheonix Street, Somers Town; High Street, Chipping Barnet; High Street, Bushey and South Mimms[1]. The 'S' or Hampstead Division was shaped rather like a wedge with its apex located in the centre of the metropolis and its outer edges bordering the county of Hertfordshire. The policing of the division has evolved, expanded and become more complex as greater numbers of people moved into the suburbs to find work. Gradually, as travel and transport became easier, cheaper, sleepy villages soon became overwhelmed with traffic, people and crime.

Administratively, Barnet borough was created in 1965 from the former urban districts of Chipping Barnet and East Barnet, both previously in Hertfordshire the urban district of Friern Barnet, and the boroughs of Finchley and Hendon, previously in Middlesex[2]. These changes in local authority boundaries caused police borders to be re-aligned with them, and changes to police areas and divisions resulted.

Barnet Borough in 2011 has become one of the larger boroughs of the Metropolitan Police with a population of over 331,000 people and 157,000 households covering some 34 square miles. Within Barnet there are inner city and town centre areas as well as leafy suburbs and swathes of countryside. Barnet enjoys a diverse multi cultural population spread across the borough. The London Borough of Barnet is presently served by four police stations; Barnet, Colindale, Golders Green and Whetstone. There are also twenty-one Safer Neighbourhood Teams who help prevent crime and deal with community problems. Response teams operate on a 24 hours a day basis and deal with the emergency calls; Criminal Investigation Department (CID) officers and forensic teams investigate crimes and bring criminals before the court. All this work is undertaken for the Barnet community with the express aim of keeping Barnet Borough one of the safest in London[3].

Transport in the borough of Barnet

It is crossed by three main roads from London to the north. On the western boundary, the Edgware Road, Watling Street, or A5, is part of a major Roman route. The main medieval route was put through further east and runs through Finchley, Whetstone, Chipping Barnet and Hadley. It was once the Great North Road, or A1, but after a bypass was built in the 1920s it became the A1000. The M1, the next generation of main roads, also opened through the borough in 1966.

The first railway through the borough was the Great Northern main line, running up through Friern and (New) Barnet, which opened in 1850. New Barnet began to develop as a new suburb near the station during the 1860s.

Railways arrived in Barnet in the 1860s: the Midland mainline through Hendon and Mill Hill and Great Northern Railway (GNR) suburban lines through Finchley to Barnet and to Edgware via Mill Hill. London had always expanded in rings, and since areas closer to London were not yet developed, these lines stimulated very little change. By the end of the century the inner rings were full and it was this area's turn. A new underground line to Golders Green opened in 1907 and a brand new suburb developed simultaneously.

Development stopped during the First World War, but in the 1920s the line was extended through Hendon to Edgware and again the building of new housing spread concurrently[4].

Chipping Barnet Fair

Chipping Barnet was founded around 1100 to take advantage of the new main road. It was granted a market in 1199 (chipping means market) and a fair in 1588. The fair became so famous that 'Barnet' became cockney rhyming slang for hair (Barnet Fair = Hair). Having the fair in Barnet became a very lucrative for business and provided opportunities for making money. This brought the benefits of employment but it also drew in crime, disorderly conduct and drunkenness as well.

In 1758 John Tomlinson, the Lord of the Manor of Barnet was granted permission to change the dates of the fairs from June to April for the first one and from October to September for the second due to it being better for business. Animals were driven from all over the country to the Barnet fairs, with cattle from Scotland, cows from Devon and ponies from Wales. The September cattle fair was held in fields near Wood Street (until 1909) and various fields around the town were used for herding

A group of police officers pose at the Barnet Fair with a donkey in about 1908

and displaying the livestock. In September 1834 it was reported in *The Times* that the Barnet Fair was the largest cattle market in all of England with up to 40,000 animals on offer and £100,000 being taken in trade on the first day. It was necessary from the early days of the fair to ensure order was kept and police officers were posted each year to keep the peace.

The picture above shows eight police officers posing before a crowd and a donkey at the Barnet horse fair in about 1908. Notice how the police officers are in the habit of carrying walking sticks.

By the mid-18th century Barnet fair had become associated with horse racing and races were held on the last three days of the event. The course they ran on was where the present High Barnet station now is and the last race held there was "The Barnet Stakes" on 6th September 1870. But the fair carried on and the animals kept coming, usually to the land opposite High Barnet station[5]. In the 17th century there was a briefly famous spa near Chipping Barnet, which was visited by Pepys[6].

Aldenham Police Station

The District of Aldenham is situated at the outer extremity of the Metropolitan Police situated between Watford junction and Radlett. Col. W. Stuart of Aldenham Abbey, Watford, local land owner and lord of the manor owned a small cottage in the village near Roundbush. The cottage was situated on the east side of the road (now called Summerhouse Lane, Watford) south of the triangle and not far from the almshouses situated across the road.

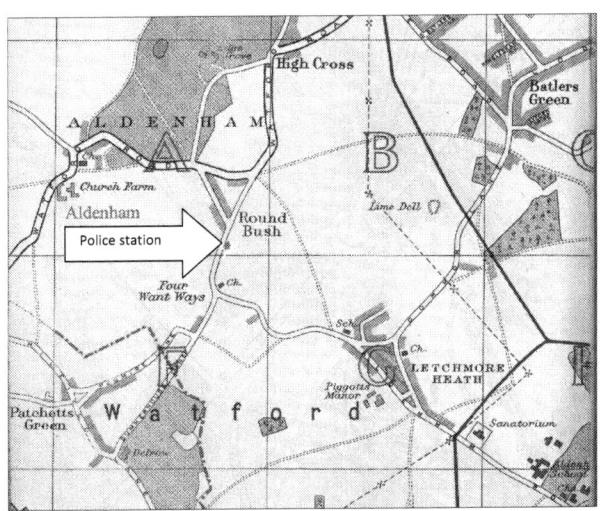

The Metropolitan Police rented the cottage, originally paying £10 per year rent but rising to £15. 10s (£15.50p) in 1912 and £23.18s (£23.90p) in 1922.

The accommodation consisted of a two-stall stable, a wood and coal shed and a privy. This was not a police station for the purposes of taking and holding prisoners as there were no cells or a charge room for these purposes. This was a station where a constable was in charge. It appears to have been formerly a Bow Street horse patrol station. Any prisoners would have been taken to Barnet police station by the arresting officer. When the constable was out on his patrol it was common for his wife to take messages on police business for her husband from people who would call at the cottage.

The owner was required to pay the rates and carry out repairs. On the 1st floor were three rooms whilst the ground floor had two rooms. The accommodation was used to house a married constable and his family. The cottage was still occupied in the 1930s.

(Chipping) Barnet Police Station

Evidence of a police presence in the village of Chipping Barnet, (now called High Barnet) on the Great North Road, can be traced back to 1841 when a station situated in the High Street was occupied for police purposes as part of 'S' or Hampstead Division with Divisional Superintendent John Carter in charge[7].

Annual rental for two cottages at 47 and 48 Barnet Road (later Barnet Lane), originally the Bow Street horse patrol cottages, were taken over by the Metropolitan Police in 1845. These consisted of standard brick and tile cottages with a small garden and stable in each. Each had four rooms and a coal cellar. The cottage was rented from Mr. Anderson of Anderson cottages, Finchley for £10 per year with the cost of the stable being an additional £5. When taken over by the Metropolitan Police they were in a sad state of repair and needed renovation which were immediately carried out, but the premises were given back to the landlord in 1849[8] and vacated by police.

It was felt that because of its position Chipping Barnet police station was an important enough station for an inspector to be in charge. Accordingly the first senior officer in charge was Inspector Samuel Evans between 1841- 5 (having been promoted to Inspector on 30th March 1832) residing there with his wife and six children. Also billeted at the station was 34-year-old constable Thomas Webb. Evans joined the Metropolitan Police as one of the very first police officers (warrant number 784) to be attested on 21st September 1829.

Superintendent Loxton 'S' Division circa 1865

Because of the exceptional leadership skills displayed by Evans (including the supervision of the Barnet horse fairs) he was recommended for promotion to Superintendent and was transferred to 'M' Division in

June 1845. Such was the exacting role of a superintendent that Evans retired on pension as 'worn out' just four years later in October 1849[9].

The Divisional Superintendent would make unannounced visits to each station on the Division on horseback. Above is a picture of Superintendent Loxton of 'S' Division 1855 -1867 taken in about 1865 seated on his dappled grey mount on Hampstead Heath. The Superintendent is wearing the new uniform and helmet introduced in 1865 although it changed again in 1870.

Loxton's predecessor in 1845 was Inspector George Billers, who was well known to Evans as they had both joined the police together on the same day in 1829. Billers, a Londoner from Kentish Town, took charge of the station[10] and stayed in post until 1855 when he retired on pension[11]. Billers had been promoted to Inspector in 1840 and then posted to Somers Town Police Station before being transferred to leafy Barnet.

Barnet Police Station, 1863 – 1915, High Street, Chipping Barnet.

In 1863 a new police station was brought into service (shown left). Barnet Police Station and section house for single police officers was occupied in June 1863 as a station on 'S' or Hampstead Division[12]. The station, which was designed over four floors cost £2,084 and consisted of an Inspector's office, waiting room, 4 cells, water closets and urinals. In the yard were stables and a hay loft together with a free standing parade shed where the constables would muster for parade before being posted to their patrols. Also downstairs in the basement was a library, mess room, kitchen, food locker, drying room and three coal cellars. Upstairs on the first floor was a bathroom and residential accommodation.

The section house accommodation for single police officers comprised space for six constables who paid 1 shilling (5p) each per week whilst the married quarters were charged at 5/6d (28p) per week[13]. The station was allocated the call sign of Bravo Alpha (BA) for telegraphic purposes in 1871[14]. The police station at Barnet was purposely situated on the main route north which saw a rise in traffic heading in and out of London as methods of transport evolved and horse-drawn vehicles were gradually replaced by motorised and mechanical vehicles.

Gradually, as more people came into London to find work from the countryside, the suburbs began to expand in terms of transport with the building of new roads and houses. This expansion also increased the need for more police officers and stations. The consequences of this were the need on occasions to re-balance police station and divisional boundaries. Such a re-organisation occurred in 1889 when a new sub-division was formed. The boundaries of Hampstead, Barnet and Edgware were altered and a new sub division of Finchley was formed, which Barnet was a part[15]. Sergeant Alfred Tuckwell was shown at residing at 163 South Mimms Road with his wife and child in 1871[16]. He was the Station Sergeant at the local Barnet Police station in 1875[17]. One married Inspector resided there with his family whilst a further six single constables also lived above the station. The inspector and constables contributed towards their living accommodation with the inspector paying 5/6d (28p) and the constables 1/- (5p) per week[18].

In 1871 a review was undertaken of police accommodation as there was a lack of affordable and clean housing in London. Apart from the Metropolitan Police being the largest London employer at this time, it was soon to become the largest landlord. And so began an audit of police buildings and living areas which considered housing conditions, cleanliness, sanitation and disease.

The duties of the inspector were clearly set out with strict instructions that he should patrol the area on horseback and was not to be posted to duty at the station itself. Because Barnet was an outlying station supervision of the constables fell to the patrolling inspector. Sergeant Tuckwell was to remain at the station at Barnet dealing with day-to-day inquiries and processing of prisoners for court. Tuckwell was one of two sergeants attached to Barnet, each working a 12 hour shift (one by day and the other by night). The sergeants would rotate their duties to ensure neither was permanent days or nights but there was also an acting sergeant who would cover for the substantive sergeant for 12 hours in every 24 hours whilst he was away from the station. The inspector was responsible for patrolling the sectional stations of (South) Mimms, Shenley and Whetstone. Shenley had no cell space so prisoners were transferred to Barnet either by trap or accompanied by the arresting officer on foot. There were no cells at Mimms although Whetsone did have cells for prisoners[19]. There were two horses stabled at Barnet.

The Barnet Fair

The Barnet Fair or Costermongers Fair as it was colloquially known was policed from Barnet Police Station and by the 1870s it had become as the most popular fair in the country with great opportunities to make money both legally and illegally. Large numbers of people meant that there were great opportunities to have a good time especially with betting and drinking. In 1859 the horse fair was held on land to the east of the railway, between Potters Lane and the Meadway and by 1929 development saw the fair move across Barnet Hill to fields to the south of Bedford Avenue. Two years later it moved to a field adjoining Pricklers Hill[20]. In 1874 *The Barnet Press* reported that 20 plain-clothes detectives, four sergeants and 44 constables from London were brought in to be on duty at the fair. This probably did not work very well as in 1888 there was a serious attempt to close down the fair on the grounds that it had become a nuisance. Serious disorder had been narrowly avoided by the strong presence of police but local businessmen got together a petition that stated;

> 'It has been ascertained that an average of over 20,000 persons attend Barnet on each fair day and expenditure in the town and neighbourhood alone is estimated at upwards from £10,000 to £12,000 among tradesmen and farmers'[21].

The April fair had ceased in 1881 which left the September fair and this took place in the area around Wood Street. Later this became part of Barnet Common. The matter of rowdiness was referred to the Home Secretary who decided that there were insufficient reasons to close the fair and the local people were pleased with the outcome. So the fair continued at High Barnet.

The code signal for Barnet for the telegraph was published as Bravo Alpha (BA) in 1871 although during the 1930s this was altered under the new Trenchard re-organisation[22].

In 1873 Barnet police station was one of five Inspector Stations on 'S' or Hampstead Division with Albany Street (at 104 Albany Street, Regents Park) being the headquarters station[23]. The other stations were Portland Town (St Johns Wood),

Hampstead, and Edgware (Whitchurch Lane). In 1881 Thomas Cole aged 36 years from Farnham in Surrey was the Inspector in charge at Barnet and he lived above the station with his wife and family. There were nine single constables also living there in what was termed the section house.

By the 1880s space at the station was becoming cramped as the Divisional Superintendent indicated in 1888 when he requested the need of an additional three cells to be added to the four already in existence[24]. Sub Divisional Inspector Robert Nutt took over from Cole took charge in 1890, with three sub inspectors, five sergeants and 38 constables[25]. Nutt from Ollerton in Yorkshire lived at the police station at 23 High Street, Barnet with his wife and five children in 1891. In the section house at the time were single constables William Turner, Tom Webber, Ernest Randall, Albert Holmes, William Todd, Truman Ellis, Arthur Woolmore, John Houndsome (who married and moved to Shenley by 1901) and Edwin Robbins.

Instructions were issued that land should be purchased in Barnet and a police station built there for a sum not exceeding £1,200. Messrs.E. Ryde and Sons (surveyors) reported that on 23rd December 1898 that they had settled negotiations for the purchase of land at £1,150 plus costs. Messrs. Ellis and Ellis (solicitors) completed the purchase of land at Chipping Barnet and as a result the freehold title to land located at 26 High Street, Chipping Barnet was purchased by the Receiver in May 1899[26]. The continued increase in the local population raised concerns that the station and its facilities were already becoming too small and further negotiations commenced to acquire an adjacent piece of land (No.s 28, 30 and 32 High Street, Barnet) to be added to the station. Negotiations with the owners the Leather-sellers Company were slow and eventually the purchase of this land was finalised in 1908[27] for the sum of £1,800[28]. Plans were re-drawn and builders obtained but the start of the war delayed the progress of the station. As a result, the police station and three sets of married quarters were re-built on the site and opened in February 1916[29]. The cost of renting the two married quarters was set at 10s (50p) per week. Inspector Thomas Browning and his family were living at the station in 1901. He lived there with his wife Clara and five daughters[30].

Resident at the old station in 1911 was the Sub Divisional Inspector 74035 Albert Tom Wilkinson from Pickering in Yorkshire who resided at the station with his wife and three teenage children. Also resident in the section house above the station in a dormitory were nine single constables, Charles Jenkins, Arthur Meadon, Henry Racey, William Artherton, Ellis Cooper, Thomas Jasper, Gray Herbert, Charles Yallop and (wt. no. 97854) Arthur Cloughton[31].

The photograph below shows Inspector Wilkinson (with flat cap) seated to the right of Superintendent Thomas Williams (in plain clothes centre, front) was taken in the yard at Barnet Police station in 1910.

Superintendent Williams, Inspector Wilkinson and men at Barnet in 1910

In the meantime and given the increased tensions in Europe with the impending arms race with Germany arrangements were made to give police officers practice in shooting firearms. By July 1912 the Receiver agreed with the War Office to lease the miniature rifle range located at the Barracks, Barnet on an annual rental of £2[32]. By 1914 Sub Divisional Inspector Herbert Grace was in charge of the station and he was supported by Inspector Arthur Smitheram. There was also one station sergeant, nine section sergeants, 45 constables and one officer from the Criminal Investigation Department[33].

In 1926 there was a further re-organisation of station and divisional boundaries. In 1925 the Sub Divisional Inspector was O. Webb and the divisional code was changed to Sierra Bravo (SB)[34].

The Barnet Fair continued to be the challenging for police due to the large crowds and transport problems. Whilst clearing a path through the crowds to allow a

Barnet Police Station 1915 – 1977 26 High Street, Chipping Barnet, Hertfordshire

heavily laden lorry out of the fair late on Saturday night, Constable 112399 James Warrender Thomson KPM of 37 Mays Lane, Barnet was struck and killed by a lorry[35] . There were three other fatalities all from the same family together with four people who were injured and taken to hospital.

The accident happened when the lorry, heavily laden with cement bags, was about to pass a stationary tramcar just as a motor car drew out from an open space. A collision occurred and the lorry mounted the footpath, which was crowded with people. Police constable Thompson, who was directing traffic nearby, saw the danger. He rushed to the footpath, and flinging out his arms, pressed the crowd back from the path of the lorry. Many people were saved from death or injury by the policeman's action. He himself was struck down and received multiple injuries, from which he died soon afterwards in hospital. Thomson won the Kings Police Medal for gallantry posthumously in 1936 and the medal was received from the

Prince of Wales by Mrs Thompson. Police Constable Thompson, who was married, with three children, had been in the police force about 15 years[36].

In 1965 local authority boundary changes occurred and the station code was changed again, this time to Sierra Alpha (SA). In due course the officer in charge became a Sub Divisional Inspector but this rank was abolished in favour of a sub divisional superintendent by the 1950s.

In 1926 the sub divisions of Finchley, Golders Green, Hendon and Barnet Sub Divisions were policed from the stations of Barnet, Whetstone, South Mimms and Shenley[37]. Further re-organisation took place north of the Thames in 1933 when Barnet sub division was re-shaped to absorb Potters Bar as well. This was part of re modelling of the larger Divisional boundaries which saw Potters Bar move into S Division from 'Y' Division. Because of tensions in Europe precautions were taken to ensure that the country was prepared in the event of war. Air raid warning centres were set up and dedicated telephone lines were laid between police stations. The dedicated line between Potters Bar and Barnet police stations was laid in 1936 with the local authority being responsible for damage during installation and for removal after when it was no longer needed[38].

Concerns were raised in the 1960s that the station was no longer suitable for policing purposes as it was too small. Estates Branch with Surveyors Department considered that the station should be re-built and enlarged, so a programme of work was instituted to commence in 1967/1968 but this was postponed in favour of a compromise. A nearby house at 2 Park Road was purchased for £8,000 in January 1969 to act as additional accommodation for administrative functions and to act as a temporary police station whilst renovation and refurbishment took place at the old station[39].

Police boundaries were revised again following the change of boundaries relating to Local Authorities under the Local Government Act 1964. Barnet was now designated as being located on 'S' Division within the London Borough of Barnet (SA) together with Whetstone, South Mimms, Potters Bar (losing Shenley).

Chief Inspector F. Brokenshire and Superintendent A. M.F. Bundock were in charge in 1966[40].

The station was eventually re-built in 1972 when the sub divisional office moved its functions to Whetstone (ST) but during the building works station reverted to sectional station status[41]. The re-building works took four years to complete with the station being brought back into service in 1976 when it reverted back to sub divisional status with Whetstone again becoming a sectional station.

Within a year the local police were inviting members of the public to attend two open days when the station at Barnet threw its doors open to people who were

Barnet Police Station, 1977 – Present day. 26 High Street, Barnet, Hertfordshire EN5 5RU

interested to see the daily workings of a busy re-built police station.

On 15th and 16th April 1977 the station was open from 6pm daily for a display of equipment. Commander 'S' Division Stan Squire held a reception for the mayor of Barnet and local dignitaries including the new Police Commissioner Sir David McNee. Other police branches were represented including Mounted Branch, Dog Section, Careers Section, the CID and Thames Division[42].

In 2002 Barnet was a station within Barnet Borough and was open to the public from 6am until 10pm daily. This was a station where prisoners were detained and charged for court until 2007. In 2012 the station opening hours were 0700 to 2200 daily, except public holidays and would be closed between 1000 - 1045 and 1800 - 1845 each day[43].

Borehamwood police station

The population increased in the Borehamwood area from 9,000 in 1945 to an estimated 22,000 in 1955. The Commissioner first started to consider locating a police station there in 1949. The London County Council encouraged the Commissioner to increase the police presence and in 1955 it was decided that a temporary prefabricated police station be erected on a site purchased from the British and Dominions Film Co-operation Ltd.

Borehamwood Police Station (1956) Elstree Way, Borehamwood, Hertfordshire

This station was given the station code (SR) and was occupied for police purposes. In March 1957 the station was occupied for police purposes[44]. Contractors tendered for the building of the more permanent station and the winning builders were Yeomans.

Between 1957-8 the new Police Station situated also at Elstree Way, Borehamwood Hertfordshire was erected[45]. The station at Shenley was closed on the same day in 1959 as this new station was opened and the staff and business were transferred to Borehamwood which became a sectional station attached to Barnet sub division.

The station at Borehamwood was still located at Elstree Way, Borehamwood within the borough of Aldenham, Hertfordshire in 1967 but this time it had been removed from Barnet and was a sectional station of West Hendon sub division instead[46]. In the

Officers of Borehamwood pose outside their temporary police station in 1956

meantime a much bigger new station was built in Elstree way Borehamwood replaced the temporary pre-fabricated station which was closed[47].

The picture at left shows the station under construction from the rear and shows the extent of the building with its rear yard. In 1965 Borehamwood was a sectional station of the sub divisional station at Barnet.

The station code changed from (SR) to (SD) in July 1971 when the

The construction of the Borehamwood Police station in Elstree Way.

divisional headquarters at Golders Green was moved to Borehamwood whilst

Borehamwood Police station 1959 – Present Day. Elstree Way, Borehamwood

extensive building work was undertaken[48].

In 2000 the station and its area was transferred to Hertfordshire Police.

Bushey Police Station

Bushey Police Station 1840 – 1884. High Street, Bushey, Hertfordshire.

The Metropolitan Police extended its boundary to encompass the parish of Bushey in 1840. A police station was shown in the High Street, Bushey, Hertfordshire in 1841 when a suitable building was purchased[49]. The station was considered a suitable station for a sergeant to be in charge and in 1855 the sergeant in charge was Zachariah Hollier[50].

There was sufficient room above the station to house a married officer (most likely the sergeant and his family) costing the occupant 5/- (25p) per week[51]. During the 1860s the station manpower consisted of one sergeant, one acting sergeant and fifteen constables. Four constables were posted to day beats and ten constables to the night shift each week. There was a floating constable who would fill in for absences, sickness or would be used as reserve officer and retained at the station for prisoner transport etc.[52]. The picture on the previous page shows the original police station now called 'Church View House' the first police station in Bushey opened in 1840, which remained in service until 1884 when the building was given up.

Bushey Police officers taken in the yard of the station in around 1900

The station call sign for the telegraph published in Police orders in 1893 was Bravo Hotel (BH) but by the 1926 it changed[53] to Sierra Uniform (SU) and its status was that of a sectional station of Edgware.

The picture above shows the station strength at Bushey Police Station taken in the yard at the rear in about 1900. The two police officers in charge were station sergeants who wore four chevrons on each forearm rather than the three worn by sergeants. Notice there is not one clean shaven officer amongst them perhaps a help when getting ready for the day shift.

The freehold title to land located at 43 Clay Hill, Bushey, Hertfordshire was purchased by the Receiver in 1876[54] on which to build a replacement police station[55]. By 1884 the new station was completed with 2 sets of married quarters and opened.

This new substantial station is shown below. By 1881 an Inspector had taken charge of the station as large numbers of police officers were recruited. Up until 1881 a sergeant had been in charge.

A police fixed point box was located on land owned by the London and North West Railway outside New Bushey Railway station in 1912. A police (hand) ambulance shelter was also situated there[56].

In 1914 the station at Bushey was located at Sparrows Herne area of the village, with one Station Sergeant Tom Allinson in charge. He was supported by one other station sergeant, two sergeants, two acting sergeants and 22 constables[57]. In 1929 Bushey was a sectional station to Barnet police station.

Bushey Police Station. 1884 – 2000. 43 Clay Hill, Bushey, Hertfordshire.

In 1947 the station was shown to have one set of married quarters above the station where the Inspector would mostly reside.

In 2000 Bushey Police station was transferred to Hertfordshire Constabulary following government decisions to make the boundaries of the Metropolitan Police coincide with the Greater London Authority and institute the Metropolitan Police Authority to replace the Receiver. In 2010 the residents of Bushey were informed by the Hertfordshire Police that their station was likely to close due to the high maintenance costs and the need to save money.

Colindale Police Station.

In about 1990 plans were laid to co-ordinate the policing arrangements in Barnet and to replace some worn out stations. This would allow for a much larger modern multi-functioning state-of-the-art station that could also act as an Area Headquarters. The intention was to replace Hendon, West Hendon and Mill Hill with a 'super station' to be named Colindale[58] situated between all those stations.

The site for the new Colindale police station and No. 2 Area Headquarters was purchased from the Ministry of Defence on the 25th April 1991. The police station design was suggested as being in keeping with its surroundings such as the former Hendon airfield, the adjacent Battle of Britain museum and the listed control tower[59].

Tenders were requested from a number of building companies and the winning bidder commenced construction in March 1995 and the building being completed in January 1997 and costing £8.8 million. It consists of a 6,500sq. metre building with four storeys of accommodation broken down into two wings with a rotunda in the middle to house both the station office and reception area[60].

The building was meant to offer staff all the benefits of a safe and efficient working environment while providing accommodation that was to establish 'the image of a modern police building'. The rotunda was extensively glazed at ground and third floor levels to 'reinforce the building's prominence during the day and night'. The ground floor contains the custody suite and offices associated with day to day policing. The station has the largest custody suite of any station in the borough with 17 cells and four detention rooms.

The building also houses an Area control room which can be used to control major incidents including large scale public order events anywhere in north-west London. The rest of the building is made up of large open-plan and cellular offices. The building has been designed to give it a great degree of flexibility and to cater for changes in operational and legislative needs. Provision for staff and visitors with special needs and disabilities has also been included throughout[61].

The station at Colindale opened in 1997 however the front office counter responsibilities for West Hendon were undertaken from Simpson Hall, Aerodrome Road (the old cadet centre less than half a mile away) until the new front office was completed.

Colindale Police Station, 1997 – present day. Grahame Park Way, Colindale NW9 5TW.

East (New) Barnet Police station

The freehold to a piece of land was purchased in East Barnet in 1874 by the Receiver. A station was built on the site in 1883 and opened a year later. The accommodation included housing for two families, one married inspector and a married constable[62]. The station included one inspector, three sergeants and fifteen constables. The station remained an inspector designated one until it shut.

During WW1 East Barnet was allocated a squad of special constables to make up for the call up of regular officers to the colours[63].

The station call sign for the telegraph published in Police Orders in 1893 was Echo Bravo (EB) but by the 1920s these were changed[64].

East Barnet, because of its position, was a sectional station together with Potters Bar and Southgate to the sub divisional station of Enfield. Unlike most other stations in Barnet who were situated on 'S' or Hampstead Division, East Barnet was located on

East Barnet Police Station. 1884 – 1932. 2 Edward Road, East Barnet, Hertfordshire.

'Y' or Highgate Division. In 1890 there was station strength of one Inspector, three sergeants and 15 constables[65].

In charge of the station was Station Sergeant George Jewell who was assisted by two section sergeants and 15 constables[66]. In 1899 the officer in charge of the Division was flamboyant Superintendent Louis Vedy who paid periodic visits.

The station address was shown as 2 Edward Road, East Barnet and was a station on 'Y' Division[67] taking up a large plot of land that bordered Margaret Road, New Barnet. There was a confusion over the title of the station whilst it was called East Barnet because it was in fact closer to New Barnet with the train station being under a quarter of a mile away.

In 1914 Station Sergeant Joseph Thompson of 'Y' Division Section Sergeant William Norris, detective constable Ernest Milner, two acting sergeants George Sharplin and Henry Barton and 18 constables were attached to the station[68].

The end of World War one was marked every year by ceremonies which included the police setting off maroons or small explosions in the station yard at the 11th hour, on the eleventh day of the eleventh month.

The photograph below shows this happening in the yard at East Barnet being supervised by the Station sergeant in charge.

November 1919 setting off the maroons in celebration of World War One ending.

The constable on the cycle displayed the 'take cover' signs that were used during the war itself.

The building remained in service as a police station up until 1932[69]. Its future was discussed and as a result during the Trenchard re-structuring programme the old station became residential accommodation for three families until at least 1947[70] although it was sold later.

By 1985 East Barnet was in a sad state of repair having been vacated and left in a derelict state. Today the building has long since been demolished and the plot has a new building on it, a service station called 'the Barnet Service and Tuning Centre'[71].

Elstree Police Station

Several of the roads in Elstree have interesting histories. Deacons Hill Road was created in the 19th century by the owner of Deacons Hill House in Barnet Lane, to provide easier access to the railway station, which was opened in 1868. Other roads, including Barnet Lane, Furzehill Road, Shenley Road, Allum Lane and Theobald Street, were created as a result of the Enclosure Act of 1776, whereby the 684 acres of Borehamwood Common were divided up amongst various landowners, including the Church, and in return new roads were laid out which were to be sixty feet wide including verges[72].

Originally a small cottage (possibly a gatehouse) on the Aldenham Abbey Estate (now Aldenham Park) was used as a police station in 1853. It was situated near the main road now known as Elstree Hill immediately opposite Allum Lane[73].

A cottage was rented by the Metropolitan Police in High Street, Elstree in 1869 from Mrs Cornelia Willis who lived near the Green Dragon Public House in Elstree. The building was surveyed by the Receiver and considered to be well constructed and agreement was reached that the annual rent should be £15[74]. To defray the costs of the station the Receiver rented out rooms above the station to a serving officer and his family. Calculated at a rate of 6d (3p) per 50 square feet this cost the occupant 3/3d (16p) per week[75]. Whilst the cottage was adequate enough for the purposes of policing it was essential in these outlying areas for the constables to have access to transport. As a result stables were rented from Alderman John Bailey of Elstree Hall, Elstree at an annual cost of £10[76]. The station was opened in November 1869 and was designated a station on ' S' Division[77]. The station was given up in June 1892.

The freehold was purchased to an address in Barnet Lane, Elstree and a new station was brought into service on 24th June 1893[78]. The station was situated on the north side of Barnet lane between Sumner Grove and Fortune Lane, Elstree. The building consisted of a new station with one set of married quarters above. There were also two sets of married quarters behind the station[79].

In 1914 the officer in charge of the station was Station Sergeant Henry Lewis and he was assisted by two sergeants, one acting sergeant and 12 constables[80].

The telephone exchange at Elstree had just 97 subscribers in 1924! The police were even reluctant to be connected in the early days, in case it encouraged the public to 'phone in crime reports'! (a feeling some older policemen shared about the 999 system)[81].

The station call sign for the telegraph published in Police Orders in 1893 was Echo Echo (EE) but by the 1926 this was changed[82] to Sierra Lima (SL) when it was a sectional station of Edgware.

During WW1 Elstree police station was an Air Raid observation post along with Barnet Police Station due to their elevated position. Special constables would be posted to the roof and made observations regarding any bombing by German planes or zeppelins and report their positions via telephone to Scotland House (located in another building at Scotland Yard) where the reports were collated and action taken to send the alert to anti-aircraft batteries and search light stations, or the fire brigade or police units for their attendance.

A topographical view of Elstree High Street circa 1910.

Also these observation posts were there to see if the population were complying with the 'Blackout' and keeping their curtains closed so as not to alert a passing foreign plane. to a likely target. On seeing a light in any house a police unit, normally on a cycle, would be dispatched and call attention to the light by paying the owner a visit and getting the light hidden.

In 1965 when the local authority boundaries were altered it retained the same station code but moved to being a sectional station of West Hendon (SW).

As few members of the public were using the station, it closed at night from 10pm on 31st July 1960 for an experimental period of six months and the station officer, usually a constable, was posted to outside duties on night duty. In a pillar at the front of the station a telephone was installed which had a dedicated line to the divisional station. Incoming telephone calls to the station were diverted to Edgware police station[83]. Following a revision of local authority boundaries Elstree (SL) was designated a sectional station of West Hendon (SW)[84] in October 1964.

The photograph below taken in the 1960's shows Constable Ivan Bracey tending to the garden at the front of the station.

Elstree Police Station. 1893 – 1971. Barnet Lane, Elstree, Hertfordshire.

By 1968 the status of the station was down-graded further when it became a police office with limited opening hours and incorporated into Borehamwood (SB)[85].

The station closed on the 30th August 1971 but Elstree Rural District Council became interested in the building for providing residential accommodation for four families. The long term future for the building was for it to be demolished to provide higher density housing[86].

Finchley Police Station

The Constable or Headborough, was a duty performed for a period of twelve months without payment from the 16th century onwards in Finchley, the Vestry records show that 3 Headborough and 3 Constables were elected for the East End, and 3 Headborough and 3 Constables were elected for the North End of Finchley Parish, making twelve men in all[87]. Between 1801 and 1861 the population of Finchley rose threefold from 1,500 to 4,900 people.

The Bow Street horse patrol patrolled the Great North Road, adjoining common land, woods and the leas of Finchley between 1805 and 1851.

The Metropolitan Police did not extend its boundaries to take in Finchley until 1840. The Hampstead or 'S' division came into being on 12th February 1830 and its strength was recorded as one Superintendent, four Inspectors 12 Sergeants and 190 constables but as far as is known they did not patrol the Finchley district until much later[88].

Bow Street Horse Patrol

Two cottages with stabling from the original horse patrol were transferred to the Metropolitan Police in 1845. These were located at 49 and 50 Whetstone Road, Finchley Common. They were the property of Mr. Joseph Bourton of Willesden who rented them out for £15 each per year. These buildings consisted of brick and slate and were in a good state of repair having been renovated in 1844. There was a large garden to the rear with good stabling, a four room wash house and a large water closet. There was also good clean water supply which was important in those days in order to maintain health and keep infection away[89].

The 3rd Division of the Bow Street Horse Patrol comprised Handwell, Hillingdon, Harrow Road, Hendon, Highgate, Edgware and Whetstone[90], its officers included No. 45 Joseph Higgs, No 46 Robert Broffam, No. 47 Thomas North and No. 48 Samuel Collard who resided at the Finchley station. Joseph Higgs' patrol was a routine carried out each day. He either patrolled, rode or walked the New Finchley Road for a distance of five and a half miles, Barnet Road to Grand Junction gate twice a day and the fourth and fifth mile stone four times. Broffams beat overlapped that of Higgs in that he patrolled, walked or rode Finchley New Road, Barnet Road, to Grand junction gate for a distance of five and a half miles twice per day whilst patrolling from the 2nd to the 4th milestone four times per day. Patrol No. 47 North walked, rode or patrolled the Barnet Road from Wellington bar to Whetstone Gate for four miles twice a day and from the 6th to the 8th milestone four times a shift.

Patrol 48 Collard was required to ride, walk or patrol the Barnet Road from Wellington Bar to Barnet Gate a distance of a distance of five and a half miles and between the 8th and 9th milestone four times per day[91]. The cottages were given up in Christmas 1851[92]. Police numbers were small in Finchley during the 1840s and whilst no accurate figures exist they were probably one sergeant and three constables.

The vestry, concerned with crime in their area, often requested the Commissioners for more police officers (1860, 1865) to patrol the area however these were declined due to lack a available numbers[93]. In 1866 the vestry even sought to sweeten their request by offering Sir Richard Mayne land free of charge next to Holy Trinity Church, in Church Lane N2 but this was turned down as unsuitable land to build a police station.

There were also a pair of stocks in Finchley which originated in 1575. They remained there until 1815 and stood on a site near the Church and the village cage or lockup built nearby in 1815, in a position near the new public library. This was near to the reputed position of a plague pit.

In the period 1854 to 1859, 143 people had been arrested and placed in the village cage or lockup. In February 1860 Sir Richard Mayne wrote a letter to the Clerk of the vestry saying;

> 'That the Supt. of the Division reported that the Finchley Cage was required by police, it being the only lockup within 3 miles, and that in the last 5yrs 143 persons had been locked up, and that it was required more than ever' [94].

During this period the local police sergeant resided in a cottage opposite the Manor Cottage Tavern, and he had constructed a special coal bunker into which he would fling the drunken men to sober up before being taken to court[95]. The village cage situated to the east side of the council offices in Hendon Lane continued to be used until 1906,because it was a perpetual cause of annoyance to the local population who were always complaining of the foul language used by its inmates. There was evidence to suggest that the cage was also a secure place to locate dead and unclaimed bodies prior to post mortem and burial.

After 1866 one of the lower rooms of a tall brick house in the Broadway was used as a police office, and this would appear to be 355, Regents Park Road. The building was later turned into shops, and was occupied by Messrs Williams, Sportswear. It was pulled down in 1964, and the site is now occupied by Winston

House, built by Tersons Ltd. and in the 1970s number 355 Ballards Lane, was occupied by estate agents.

There is evidence to suggest that a police station existed in Hendon Lane, and may have been known as Ballards Lane, as it was often the case to name the station after the road, lane or highway it was situated on. The station was located between the old King of Prussia public house and the Post Office, this being next to St Mary's School, known then as the National School, and it appears to be facing Lichfield Grove, from 1874 onwards, until it moved to its present site in Ballards Lane in 1888.

In 1872 a new cottage was leased from Mrs Ann Woods of Church End, Finchley for £26 per year until 1893. This was located at 7 or 9 Regents Park Road, Church End and consisted of a charge room on the ground floor and three rooms on the 1st floor which served as the Inspector's married quarters. (Regents Park Road was the main road that stretched from Ballards Lane and Finchley station in the north to Temple Fortune in the south).

By the early 1880s the cottage/station was described as modern but it had cramped conditions, no place to accommodate prisoners and cell space was urgently required. It did house a married inspector and his family but was considered no longer fit for purpose. Recommendations were made to the Home Department (later called the Home Office) for a new station to be found elsewhere when funds were available[96]. The occupant appears to be Inspector Bejamin Ellis, his wife Sophia and their four children[97]. In 1885 Finchley was designated an Inspector's station[98]. The old station was given up in 1889 together with the old cage which was given back to the parochial authorities[99].

The sum of £2,400 was paid for the freehold purchase of land formally called Wentworth Lodge in Ballards Lane, Church End, Finchley N3 in 1886.

Arrangements were made by surveyors for builders to tender for a contract to build the new station. The planners had to be mindful of the chapel next door whose trustees were rather concerned that the newly-built station would block out light through the main window. The trustees argued that they had a right to light and wished to enforce this right on the Receiver. The same right to light was expressed by the owner of the photographic shop with a glass roof on the other side of the station site.

A new station costing £3,759 was erected and included two cells, association cell (later known colloquially as the drunk tank), inspector's office, waiting room, store, and two sets of married quarters. In the yard there was an ambulance shed, parade shed, and a three stall stable with hay loft. To ensure the boiler fires were working in colder weather there were three coal sheds and a coke shed. Also on the ground floor were urinals and a toilet whilst on the first floor there was a bathroom[100]. The married inspector had six rooms at the station which cost him £14. 6 s (£14.30p) to rent yearly, whilst the married constable paid half that, with one less room. These amounts, calculated weekly, would be deducted from their pay which they would receive at 2pm on a Wednesday. The new station was occupied in 1889[101].

Finchley Police Station 1893 – 1967. Ballards Lane, Finchley.

The following is an entry from the *Finchley Brochure* of June 1905;

'The parish is exceptionally well policed and forms part of 'S' Division, under Supt. Dodd of Albany Street, and S.D.I. Leech and at Finchley there are 2 S.P.S.s J. Warne and A. Sutherland and 120 men. There are several mounted patrols in the district and the C.I.D. is represented by D.S. Francis PIKE'[102].

The use of cycles was gradually being introduced to travel around the division and were taking over from horses which required greater maintenance. So in 1910 there were alterations to the station that increased the accommodation at a cost of £274 whilst a cycle shed was erected in the yard at a cost of £20. 5s (£20.25p). Next to the station was a car show-room in 1914 which had previously been a chapel but later converted. When Detective Constable George Knell retired in 1914 he took over the show rooms, altered the layout and converted it into a billiard hall[103].

Surplus land was sold to Mr. S. L. Day for £1900 in 1924 and negotiations with Mr. R. Payne for additional land adjacent to the station at a cost of £50 were completed in the same year[104]. The police took possession of the land purchased.

An elder of Finchley recalled that there was a constable named GRAY, (most likely to be Constable William Gray (wt. no. 64393) of 'S' Division 1880 -1901) who was portly and unable to give chase because of his size. As a boy he would stand with his mates on the opposite side of the road, and sing the popular tune of the day, and wave as well, 'Good Bye Dolly Gray', and would run off when the good officer gave chase. But Gray always got them in the end, with a clump round the ear[105], often with his gloves which were weighted in the ends with something heavy like thimbles or three penny coins. Often the police officers would wait near the schools for the children to be released and those unsuspecting pranksters would receive their come-uppance with a flick that could not be reported back to their parents for fear of another thick ear from them.

The station call sign for the telegraph published in Police orders in 1893 was Foxtrot Yankee (FY) but by the 1920s these were changed[106] to Sierra Foxtrot (SF). In 1907 Finchley Police Station was an important station with a Sub Divisional Inspector in charge as part of 'S' or Hampstead Division[107] remaining so until the 1930s.

Inspector Robert Ruff was stationed at Finchley from 1907 until he retired on pension in 1910. He retired with an exemplary record and a first class certificate for good service. Born at Maldon in Essex he was educated at Billericay leaving school to work in the building industry in his native town. Joining the Metropolitan Police in 1885 he was first posted to Hunter Street on 'E' Division. Becoming Superintendent's clerk within two years of joining earned him recognition and on the resignation of his Superintendent his skills as clerk were required at Blackheath Road – still a constable. In the meantime he studied for his sergeant's exam which he passed very quickly. On promotion to Inspector in 1901 he discovered he was not a well man and also needed to care for his ailing wife who needed country air away from the smog of London. On application to his Superintendent he was transferred to a healthier location. Ruff had commendations for good arrests of thieves and restraining runaway horses. Sport was a central feature of the police and encouraged by senior officers. Ruff was also a good athlete and won prizes at cricket, cycling rowing and punting. He also played cricket to a good standard for the Metropolitan Police central cricket club against outside teams[108]. Ruff supported his 45-year-old Sub Divisional Inspector John Cundell from Cambridgeshire who resided at the station with his wife and three teenage children.

Special Inspector Scott - Finchley 1917

In 1924 surplus land from the site was sold to Mr. S. L. Day for the sum of £1900 but in the same year adjacent land was purchased from Mr. R. W. T. Payne for £50. Next to the station were married quarters located at Wentworth Lodge, Wentworth Park, Finchley NW3 a building originally purchased in 1886.

WW1 and The Finchley Special Constabulary

During the 1914-1918 war the Specials who helped our local police in their duties were without a headquarters and it was decided to use a large house opposite the police station of the name of 'Willow Lodge'. The ground today is used by the Victoria Bowling Club and part of the grounds and garden of Willow Lodge is now 'The Ridgeway'. A drawing of Willow lodge as the Special constabulary headquarters is shown below.

Special Inspector Alderton, Finchley 1917

Willow Lodge - Finchley Special Constabulary HQ 1915

Experience in World War one made people vigilant to the dangers of fascist aggression in Europe. In the late 1930's arrangements were put in place in the event of war and a number of publications had been prepared and published by His Majesty's Stationery Office (HMSO) to aid the public, police and other agencies. All constables and reserve staff including special constables were issued with certain additional publications in order to make them conversant with special arrangements. Metropolitan Police Special Constabulary (MPSC) were well organised in Finchley during the war. Large numbers of men who did not qualify for war service and stayed at home volunteered to be special constables such was the enthusiasm for joining the war effort.

These volunteers were supervised in the by main ex-military gentlemen, especially at Finchley and 'S' Division in general. Each special constable was required initially to attend the station each evening once they had returned from work then to complete four hours duty.

However it was soon realised that this was too much to ask and the norm became three times a week. Many of the WW1 specials stayed on until the 1920s as camaraderie had been built up amongst the men and officers. Central to the leadership was Chief Inspector Cross who is shown in the front centre of the picture above. Cross remained until he became Acting Assistant Commander in the same period.

In 1936 Air Raid Precautions Handbook No. 1 on Personal Protection against Gas was issued. This was not a confidential document as it was also for general public use.

Finchley Special Constabulary 1926

Sub Divisional Inspector Trott

However by 1939 the Metropolitan Police issued War Duty Hints which was confidential. On receipt of the orange coloured booklet the recipient wrote their name, division, divisional number and station in the front and then familiarised themselves with the contents. It contained the general instructions in wartime in terms of police organisation and equipment. Arrangements for air raid precautions, anti-gas safeguards, air raid warnings and police action in the event of an air attack are only some of the contents[109].

The Sub Divisional Inspector at the time was Thomas George Trott (wt. no. 87731) shown at left. Trott had joined the police in August 1901 and retired in 1927 a year after this picture was taken.

In 1937 the station code was Sierra Foxtrot (SF) and its importance had been reduced to that of sectional station to Golders Green.

The Police and Fireman (War Service) Act 1939 suspended the right to retire on pension other than through medical retirement or with the Commissioner's consent. In the meantime the ranks of the police were swelled by the police reserve (retired police pensioners under 58 years old) who volunteered to return because of a national emergency, special constables, Women's Auxiliary Police Corps and War Reserves (full time paid or part time unpaid) consisting of selected and suitably qualified members of the public. The 'WAR RESERVE' joined or re-joined the force whilst their colleagues and younger police officers went to the armed forces. All the War Reserve wore the same uniform as the ordinary personnel, but with 'W.R.' on their epaulettes. Their duties were the same as their colleagues and they were senior to special constables who only did specific duties.

A group of 'S' Division officers who sounded the all clear after an air raid.

In 1930 the divisions and sub divisions were revised. The status of Finchley was reduced in favour of Golders Green when the sub divisional administration and Sub Divisional Inspector were transferred. The following order was issued;

'Finchley will, from 1st September, be known as Golders Green Sub-Division and Sub-Divisional Inspector SPRUCES will be transferred to Golders Green Station, which will be the Sub-Divisional Station'[110].

There were many incidents of brave conduct by serving police officers. In 1943 Tom Alec Page, a War Reserve Constable, whilst on his patrol in Lyndhurst Gardens, Finchley challenged an armed soldier whom he came across breaking into a house. The soldier tried to escape by running away but the constable chased after him and when the soldier was in danger of capture he turned and aimed his rifle at the constable then shot him in the leg. Whilst on the floor injured the soldier hit the officer in the face with the rifle butt causing further injury. Later the soldier was apprehended and the constable was rewarded for his bravery. He was awarded the King's Police and Fire Service Medal by the King at Buckingham Palace[111].

There were concerns that the old station was too small and inadequate for the policing of the area. WW1 had seen that special constables had to be housed away from the station in a house opposite so even then the squeeze on space was problematic. The outside toilets with their exposed pipes would freeze up and often burst causing police officers to use the facilities in the park opposite.

Finchley Police Station 1967 – Present day. 193 Ballards Lane, Finchley NW3 1LZ

The flats above the station were empty and cell space was given over to the CID so when the pipes in the living space burst in the bad winter of 1963 the detectives would walk around inside with umbrellas up – a very inadequate situation. Moves were being made in Surveyor's department to upgrade the station.

In October 1965 a pre- fabricated building had been erected in the yard with access from Grunieson Road and the Finchley staff were transferred there. The divisional staff had been moved to Golders Green in the meantime during the refurbishment period and, once completed, the staff would return. The old station was then demolished and a new more modern one erected in its place. The new station now comprised luxury centrally-heated inside space with plush offices billiard and darts room, modern restaurant, a briefing rather than a parade room, writing room and at the back a block of married quarters. Also inside was a CID office, women police office and a dedicated room for the special constabulary. In the yard was a purpose-built cycle shed with a rack for at least 12 cycles[112].

Due to the building works the address of the station was altered to 5 Gruneison Road, N3 and was a shown as sectional station of Golders Green (SD). Gruneison Road NW3 was the next left turning past the old police station (being demolished) indicating that the entrance had been removed from the High Road for reconstruction and refurbishment of the old station. By 1967 the address had reverted back to Ballards Lane, Finchley when the new station had been completed and staff returned.

In the 1960s Chief Inspector Clelland was in charge here whilst Superintendent M. J. Byrne was in overall charge of the Sub-Division[113]. Superintendent Byrne supervised the transition from the old to the new station and ensured the smooth running of the division. Finchley was a sectional station of Golders Green in the 1960s.

The Youth and Communities section was housed at Finchley police station and covered the area of Barnet and Hertsmere. In charge was Chief Inspector John Oliver and Inspector Good. Superintendent Simon Humphrey was in charge of the sub division in 1998. In 2012 Finchley Police station was open to the public from 0700 to 2200 daily except public holidays[114].

Golders Green Police Station

On 21st July 1910 Superintendent Williams of 'S' Division reported on the availability of a plot of land suitable as a site for a new police station in the main (Finchley) road at Golders Green. The site could be obtained freehold for £1,080. The Receiver decided against this site but purchased a larger site opposite the one suggested by Superintendent Williams for £1,330 on 9th March 1911[115].

On 25th March 1911 the Receiver wrote a memorandum to the Commissioner on whether it was prudent to erect a (cottage station) at Golders Green bearing in mind the phenomenal rate at which the neighbourhood was growing. He recommended a much larger station should be built then rather than later and that work should commence by the summer of 1912. On 3rd June 1911 The Secretary of State for the Home Department agreed to this proposal and approved the building of a large first class town station with a section house for not less than 25 officers instead of a (cottage) type station.

On 12th August 1912 Home Office authorised the acceptance of the tender submitted by Messrs J. Grover and Sons for the building of the police station. A station, section house and married accommodation for one family was built on the site and on 24th September 1913 the Receiver notified the Commissioner that the station at Golders Green would be ready for occupation on 27th October 1913.

The new police station at Golders Green was taken into service on 3rd November when the lodging assessment was fixed as follows:-

> 'Married quarters (1 set) at 10s. 6d (55p) per week and 27 unmarried men paying at one shilling (5p) each per week'.

Consequent upon the opening of the new police station at Golders Green, the boundaries of Finchley and Hampstead sub divisions were revised[116]. There was a change in status for the station when in August Finchley sub-division was altered from 1st September, to be known as Golders Green sub-division and Golders Green enhanced its status to become the sub-divisional station[117].

Upon re-organisation of the divisions north of the Thames which took place on Friday 1st December 1933, Golders Green remained a sub-divisional Station of 'S' on Hampstead Division with Finchley as its Sectional Station[118].

In 1924 the location of the station was 7 St. Georges Parade Finchley Road, NW11 however this was later changed to 1069 Finchley Road, Golders Green, NW3 (Temple Fortune) in 1930 when it was a sectional station of Finchley.

In 1933 it was given divisional status after a re-organisation of the divisions (part of the Trenchard re-structuring) which saw Albany Street transfer to 'D' Division. Offices had been converted and a garage built as the building was made ready for the transfer of Superintendent Arthur Annis and his divisional support staff[119]. The station code was then Sierra Delta (SD). Finchley remained 'S' Division

Headquarters until 1962 when Superintendent C. J. Dace was in charge of the sub division[120] until 1966 when Dace moved to the Divisional office.

Taking over from Dace in 1966 was Superintendent M. J. Byrne with Chief Inspector D. Clelland as deputy whilst the Divisional Superintendent was Chief Superintendent L. R. Balm [121].

A further re-organisation, this time involving the whole Force occurred. This was designed to make the 'police boundaries co-terminous with those of the new local

Golders Green Police Station 1913 - present day. 1069 Finchley Road, London NW11 0QB

authorities. This was a direct result of the passing of the London Government Act 1963. Golders Green which was now the divisional headquarters of 'S' Division remained a sub-divisional station still with Finchley as its Sectional Station in the new London Borough of Barnet[122]. The division was also part of No. 2 District under the command of Commander R. E. Rogers MBE.

By the 1970s the 60-year-old station was in serious need of updating given the advances in technology and the need for computerisation. This meant that from 9 am on 12th July, the divisional suite and staff which included the senior officers as well were moved into temporary accommodation at Borehamwood Police Station whilst extensive building work was carried out at Golders Green. Whilst the divisional suite was accommodated at Borehamwood the station code was changed to (SD) whilst the new code for Golders Green became (SG)[123].

The Finchley Press reported that this massive and costly facelift to the station at Temple Fortune would extend its life by a further 15 years with improvements being made to the office areas and cell accommodation. It was reported that this was a far cheaper option than building a new station[124].

In 1990 the system of policing was changed at Golders Green and Finchley. Out went the four relief system with the traditional Inspector, 3 sergeants and up to 30 constables and in came beat based teams that became a forerunner to Safer neighbourhood teams which exist today[125]. Inspector Terrence Matthews, the author of an evaluation into beat policing at Golders Green (SF) was placed in charge of the four beats of Cricklewood, Golders Green, Garden Suburb, East Finchley and the station itself. Each beat had four dedicated constables attached to it.

In November 2010 a new safer neighbourhoods base was opened at 61 Golders Green Road N11 which formed the base for the safer neighbourhood Teams (SNTs) of Golders Green and Childs Hill[126].

Hendon Police Station

Parish cages, pounds and lock up had been known in Hendon since the 13th century. In 1796 a cage for detaining prisoners was located at the junction of Bell Lane and Brent Street, Hendon[127].

By 1829 a watch house and stocks had been built at the same site. In 1888 a pound existed in the middle of Burroughs Lane and Church Lane[128] (today The Burroughs and the Watford Way). The locally appointed parish constable was responsible for Hendon up until 1840 when the Metropolitan Police District (MPD) was extended. The boundary stretched to a radius of 12 miles from Charing Cross taking in Edgware, Whitchurch, Finchley, Harrow, Great Stanmore and Hendon. The original watch house would have been transferred from the parish authorities to the control of the Metropolitan Police. It was not until 1844 that a station or house was taken into service for police purposes by the Metropolitan Police although this was a small station being placed in the charge of a sergeant. It is likely that this was a horse patrol station. Hendon was a station on 'S' or Hampstead Division and it remained a sergeant designated station until 1881 when its status was upgraded and an Inspector placed in charge. In 1864 No. 4 Cowley Cottages, New Brent Street (opposite the Congregational Schools and the junction with Bell Lane) was rented by the police[129] and they were still there in 1880. The cottages stood until 1959 when they were pulled down to make way for the Foster Estate[130].

In 1869 the station strength was one Sergeant and one Acting Sergeant with four constables on the days beats. During the night there was one sergeant and seven night constables. There were four day beats and six night beats and 1 constable on reserve. Hendon was the sectional station to Hampstead and had no cells to house any prisoners so they were transported to Hampstead often on foot or by horse and trap for processing. The two inspectors at Hampstead were instructed to supervise Hendon on horseback in rotation 12 hours on duty and 12 hours off. This also worked for the horse because it would be rested following 12 hours away from the station[131].

The Inspector at Hampstead police station provided supervision and a horse was his mode of transport in order that he would patrol the district and call in at the stations like Hendon.

Times were hard with tours of duty lasting from 14-17 hours, seven days a week. On Sundays police officers were required to attend church in uniform. In 1868 respite came in the form of one day off a week but this was later revised down a year later with this privilege being only two days per month instead. Great unrest amongst the police developed in 1872 with the police going on strike. This caused a very hard-nosed approach by the government who arrested three of the ringleaders and imprisoned them, whilst dismissing 100 men from the service. Two weeks later the men was re-instated and punished by being transferred to other divisions.

The area was changing though with the influx of people and the development of transport and amenities. Modernisation had arrived with the arrival of the Midland Railway in 1868 followed by horse busses a year later on a route from Brent Street to Praed Street, Paddington. In the meantime the parish vestry were in discussions regarding the sale of the lock and cage which was currently in the possession of the Metropolitan Police.

In October 1882 it was sold to Mr. Smart for £47. 10s (£47.50p). The site was not forgotten as a plaque was erected by the local authority to ensure its place in history.

A new station was erected in 1884 north of the junction of Brent Street with Brampton Grove[132].The station call sign for the telegraph published in Police orders in 1893 was Hotel Bravo (HB) but by the 1920s this was changed[133] to Sierra November (SN).

Permission was given in 1915 for a fire escape shed to be erected in the station yard for use by the fire brigade and annual rental of 5 shillings (25p) was paid by the local authority for this facility. The station address was changed to 133 Brent Street

Hendon Police Station 1884 – 1998. 26 High Street, Barnet EN5 5RU.

in 1921 which was notified to the police by the local authority.

Travelling to and from work for police officers working long hours was often hazardous. In 1928 constable (wt. no.96525) Samuel Henry Luscombe with 19 years service was killed while cycling home after late turn duty at Hendon[134].

The birth of aviation in Hendon

Hendon was also one of the most important pioneering centres of aviation. Claude Grahame-White (engineer, aircraft manufacturer and flying record holder) founded his airport there in 1910 and brought work to the area when he designed and built aeroplanes (and later motor cars) for the war effort like the successful XV. This caused the greatest impact to the station in the whole of its history. White created many of the buildings (like those of the current driving school and the old Hendon Training school) and workshops which housed many of the workers he employed. He also staged spectacular, crowd-pulling air displays. The airfield was requisitioned from him during WW1 and was finally purchased for the RAF, which held annual pageants there until 1937. With the requisitioning of the airport and factories without compensation White sued the War Department, finally winning his action and receiving compensation in the early 1920s. Sadly, so disillusioned was White he shut his factories and sacked 400 workers which caused severe unemployment in the area. White is remembered in the area because the Grahame Park Estate and Road are named after him. In the picture above White is shown together with Chief Inspector William Edward Fitt of the 'S' Division (later Superintendent 'J' Division see book 1) in about 1912. White is dressed in driving or flying attire. During this time there were air shows, exhibitions, air races, illuminated flights and the construction of aeroplanes which drew huge crowds. For the police at Hendon there was extra duty and aid to the Aerodrome every week.

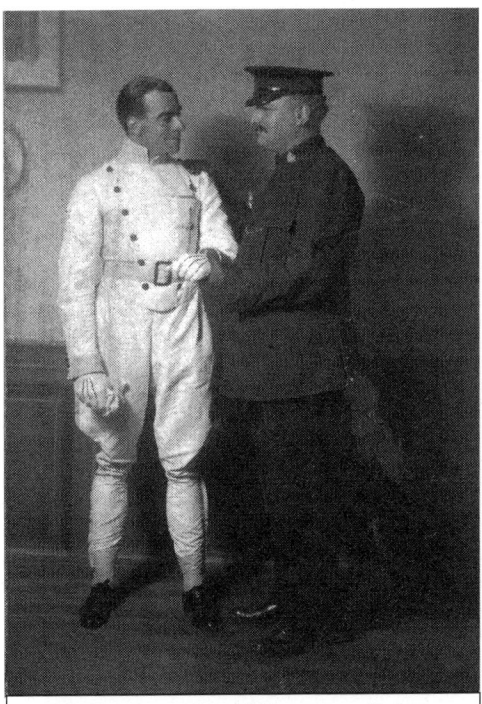

Chief Inspector Fitt and his capture Grahame White

Fitt lived in south Hampstead in 1911 with his wife and son Percy William Fitt who later was a prominent senior officer of the Metropolitan Special Constabulary[135].

Other nearby airfields and factories, at Cricklewood just across the Edgware Road, also lasted from the earliest pioneering days until the spread of housing. Apart from the early aircraft industry, the borough has never been heavily industrialised, but at the end of the 19th century significant concentrations of factories developed along the Edgware Road and at Barnet. Birt Acres was working for Elliot's photographic printing works in Barnet when he shot Britain's first moving picture there in 1895[136].

War Time 1939 - 45

Hendon Aerodrome ceased its spectacular displays and aerobatics, instead the planes over-head were more likely to be flown by the Royal Air Force (RAF) in practice for combat. Such was the case on 3rd September 1939 just as Neville Chamberlain was announcing that Britain was at war with Germany. A loud explosion was heard in Hendon and the residents thought that Germany had started bombing raids. This later turned out to be untrue. In fact an RAF bomber was circling Hendon Aerodrome intending to land when it ran into difficulties and plunged to earth crashing in Heading Street. Constable 928 'S' Len Fry saw it disappear over Greyhound Hill before it exploded killing all the crew in what were the first fatalities of World War Two[137]. The Metropolitan Police Driving School and Police College both shut for the duration. In the meantime Hendon was overwhelmed with applications for Aliens (non-Commonwealth citizens) to remain in the UK. The station could not cope with long queues forming the length of the pavement outside. A temporary office was established in the CID office, but confiscated property was a problem as all aliens were required to give up their cameras. Spalding Hall in Victoria was taken over where all the confiscated and labelled cameras were stacked from floor to ceiling[138]. Over 13,900 cases of aliens wishing to stay in the UK were heard by a special court in Hendon. Suddenly applicants joined His Majesty's Forces or signed up for air raid precaution duties so few turned up for court hearings on the 4th September. In preparation for war the station was fitted with air raid protection shutters and an air raid siren was placed on the roof.

Many local people joined the auxiliary police so larger numbers of police were coming on duty, usually averaging about 30 per shift. By 1942 the force had become so inflated that the Commissioner instructed that he was prepared to release men for service in the armed forces. Regular officers under 25-years old and auxiliary officers under 30 years were told they may apply. Instructions were also issued that the regular Police officers under 25-years old were no longer considered part of a reserved occupation[139]. The age for volunteers for the armed services was raised to 26 years and there was no shortage of applications, which caused the

Commissioner in May 1942 to stop any further applications except for pilot or radio observer[140].

On the 19th/20th September 1940 Hendon police station suffered bomb damage when a high incendiary (HE) bomb demolished the south-east corner of Victoria Street and Brent Street smashing all the front windows and damaging the window frames[141].

By far the largest explosion occurred on 13th February 1941 when a 2,500 kilo land mine destroyed Ramsey Road, Borthwick Road, Ravenstone Road, York Road and Argyle Road. Eighty people were killed and 520 people injured (148 seriously). It made 1,500 people homeless. Many police officers were commended for their tireless work and organization that day. SDI G. F. Payne and Sub Inspector Orr were awarded the British Empire Medal. Special Inspector Gore (SN) and Special Constable Hite were awarded the George Medal[142].

Further more personal tragedy struck Hendon when on 21st February 1941 Constable 603 'S' Whellams (aid from Golders Green) was killed by an HE bomb which fell in Brent View Rise. V1 and V2 rockets fell in Barnet and Hendon with the first one falling in Southfield Gardens on 27th July 1944[143].

Residential accommodation was being taken over in stations for essential administrative support as space became short. Following the war there was cause for celebration and street parties following both VE and VJ day. Police and public relations were good, and police attended the celebratory firework display in Hendon Park on 8th June 1946.

The Police Training School re-opened in 1947 and the nearby driving School started training police drivers again. It was at the latter part of the war that Hendon received its first solo motor cycle – a Royal Enfield which was well used.

Officers who had signed up for war service started returning to the station. Constable Jim Baldry drove the khaki-coloured Royal Enfield which was affectionately known as 'Bomber Brown'. Two riders per month per relief were deputed to ride 'Bomber Brown' and Constable Baldry's relief colleague 'Stormy' Winterflood was the other rider. The winter of 1947 was one of the severest of the century and riding the solo, officers wore peaked caps, riding breeches, leather gaiters, leggings and an apron something 'like a baby's' nappy'.

In 1948 the Enfield was exchanged for a big machine – a 500cc Triumph. Constable Baldry had a lucky escape one day when he was answering an emergency call and travelling past Bell Lane and into Brent Street when he collided with a traffic patrol officer riding another solo motor cycle. His leather gaiters saved him from serious injury.

Constable Jock Cobban and Rinty 2

Building alterations occurred at Hendon with the married quarters being reduced to one unit of three bedrooms on the first floor and a living room on the top floor. A bathroom was added in 1952. Station Sergeant Oliver and his family occupied those quarters. The CID were moved from the small room in the front hallway on the ground floor upstairs to the first floor. CID officers in those days worked split tours of duty 9am – 1pm and 6pm – 10pm and every other Sunday was taken as leave if duties permitted[144].

Police dogs were now being taken seriously as an aid to policing. The first two handlers at Hendon were constable Jock Cobban and 'Rinty 2' followed by Constable 'Taff' Lindburn and 'Joe'.

The station general purpose (GP) car was issued in 1948 which was garaged in the old shed in Brampton Grove near the rear entrance to the station. The same year saw the introduction of the National Health Service and people were much rielived because during the war there had been serious outbreaks of poliomyelitis.

On 9th February 1948 an Avro Anson taking off from Hendon crashed in the Edgware Road on top of a tram killing the occupants of the plane and injuring nine people on the tram. Four hundred gallons of petrol cascaded down the Edgware Road and there were calls at the time for flying out of Hendon to cease. Coupled with the difficulties of re-adjustment after the war, high inflation and low wages the strength of the Metropolitan police dropped from 18,600 in 1939 to 14,200 in

1946[145]. Despite a 15% pay rise even more officers left the service and life became very tough for those who remained. On 28th April 1949 another plane taking off from Hendon crashed in the grounds of the Metropolitan Police Training school, narrowly missing the main buildings and killing all three people on board. This was not the worst plane crash to beset the Hendon section as on 17th October 1950 a BEA Dakota on its way to Glasgow from Northolt crashed in Highwood Hill in a blazing inferno killing 27 adults and a baby. The town hall was used as a mortuary and officers from the station were faced with the difficulties of identification.

An individual and personal tragedy struck the station when in April 1954 Constable John Wren who just completed a double tour on Sierra 7 'WT' (wireless telegraphy Morse code) car felt ill at work and went home to his bed. Once at home he collapsed suffering from a heart attack and died. He was 44 years old. A service funeral followed. Tragedy struck again when ex Station Sergeant Raishbrook who had retired from Hendon just three years before was killed on a pedestrian crossing in October 1958[146].

Mrs Dangerfield's (who lived in Dorberic house next to the station) campaigned to have women police officers at Hendon (undertaken since 1936) finally bore fruit in 1954 when women police constables (WPCs) Beryl Sewell and Eleanor Wilson (as they were called at the time) were posted to the station as the first women police[147].

Father Christmas arriving at the childrens christmas party in the form of Constable Whyte on his 'Noddy' motor cycle.

Mrs Dangerfield sold her house to the police in 1955 and Chapel Walk married quarters were soon constructed. Police Sergeant 79 'S' Alfred Corden and his wife became the last residents to live above the station and when they vacated their quarters in 1957 their quarters were converted into a police canteen.

One Hendon police officer who should be acknowledged was Constable 304 'S' Jock

Cobban who was said to have been the 3rd officer since the formation of the force to not have had a single day's sick leave in 26 years service.

Police officers, who often socialized with colleagues rather than with friends outside the police service, formed local social and athletic clubs. These clubs arranged children's parties at Christmas for the police children where one of the police officers (with white beard if possible) would act as Father Christmas. In the case of Hendon it was John Whyte who would arrive at the station in full Father Christmas outfit on his 'Noddy' police solo motor cycle – rather than using his reindeer. The children (those not frightened off of course) would sit on his knee and get a present from him. There were organised coach outings to the sea-side and other places like the races. One such trip from Hendon to Fowley Refinery (in the New Forest) saw the bus stop at every pub on the way back just to top up the radiator with water – a trip said by Constable 155 'S' Johnny Howard (social secretary) 'to have been the best ever'[148]. The cricket team flourished during the post-war years when the sub divisional cup was won by Hendon who scored 239 against Lewisham Traffic Garage and then skittled out the opposition for 38. Often senior officers and sometimes even divisional superintendents would come to the ground to watch the matches because it was great kudos for them to have a winning divisional team[149].

Constable Whyte with his national hammer throwing prize

When there are errant police officers at stations and offences occur which defy explanation, then often the tight community of the police family becomes strained and many look at their neighbour with deep suspicion. During the late 1950s a police officer at Hendon was arrested and jailed for housebreaking offences, something which he admitted had lasted for over ten years. A collective sigh of relief came from the police family in what was described by some at

Hendon police station as the blackest period in their history. It took some years to return to normality after this.

One incident at Hendon was notable for its audaciousness. Constable 'Bunny' Warren (yes, the nicknames were a predictable as that) lost a prisoner (often a severe discipline offence) at court when he asked to the use the toilet. When Bunny went to find his prisoner who had been absent some time, he saw that the bars of the toilet had been sawn through (the night before by an accomplice) and the prisoner was long gone.

Cowley Cottage, the scene for the first Hendon horse patrol station, was finally demolished in 1959 when the Foster Estate was built.

At that time there were four foot beat and three motor cycle beats at Hendon. The foot beats were Brent Street, Hendon Central, West Hendon and the Hyde. Time off would not be granted unless the four foot beats could be covered from the ten police officers available per shift.

The national hammer throwing champion for 1959 (and the following year 1960) was Constable 710 'S' Jock Whyte (shown above with his trophy) at Hendon, and the first aid team won the Ralph Trophy twice as well mirroring Jock's achievements. Constable Lindenbern's dog did earn notoriety with 125 arrests to date but also won the prestigious Black Knight Trophy in 1957 as best police dog of the year. In 1963 saw the demise of the station library which passed into oblivion unnoticed except the librarians (who were police officers doing it as part of their duties) lost their jobs.

Another major air crash occurred on the section in 1965 when a DC4 Air Liner mistook Hendon for Heathrow and actually landed there to the concern of those on the

The winning First Aid Team with Divisional Superintendent

ground.

Hendon was always being beset with problems relating to traffic accidents especially since a number of main road carrying vast numbers of vehicles converge in the borough. In the same year a lorry carrying 2,760 eggs crashed on the Great North Road shedding its load. Men were 'scrambled' from the station to attend. Another accident two months later occurred on the North Circular Road when a heavy lifting jib from a crane buckled and fell on a passing coach, killing seven people and injuring eight[150].

Imminent boundary changes in 1965 caused concern for many at Hendon at a time when the all black helmet plate was changed to silver or chrome. The boundary changes saw Hendon become a sectional station of the newly-built West Hendon sub-division, which now comprised West Hendon, Mill Hill, Borehamwood, and Hendon. Hendon could not compare with the new spacious stations like West Hendon and some felt that the closure of Hendon was near. Some officers put in for a transfer rather than be forced to move to another station. One such was the remaining female officer Constable Curl who transferred off the division.

The rear yard of Hendon in 1977 after renovation work.

The first collator at Hendon was constable 'Ginger' Marshall whose office was on the first floor. The section was now divided into five home beats and in 1973 during the blackout because of power cuts the station reverted to candle power. Clip on ties, to prevent officers being strangled were issued to all officers in 1971.

In July 1977 the Queen Mother visited the station whose front garden won a certificate in the London garden Competition with the credit going to Constable 219 'S' Gordon.

A station modernisation programme to upgrade the station was planned for Hendon in 1981. The cost was £50,000 and work was carried out by Linbrook and Sons of Enfield commencing in 1982 in time for the centenary in 1984. The work was only just completed in time for the Open day on 1st April 1984. Amongst the 2000 visitors on that bitterly cold day, was the Metropolitan Police Surveyor, Mr. David Ratcliffe, who oversaw the work. All were pleased with the finished product. Gone were the outside toilets and the canteen upstairs was converted into a self-service catering unit. New toilets and a shower were also built, with central heating being provided to all floors. The fireplaces were all bricked up. Improvements were made to the communications suite, the front office and rear lobby[151].

In 1998 the station was closed after 110 year's service when the Metropolitan Police concentrated on occupying more modern stations. The building with its car park was sold at auction for £665,000. The occupants moved to the recently-built state of the art Colindale Police Station situated near the old Hendon Aerodrome site adjacent to the estate[152].

Hendon – The Peel Centre

In 1946 Hendon, or 'Peel House II' as it was termed at the time, was opened again after WW2 for basic training, and operated together with Peel House in Regency Street. With the running of both training schools (and their satellites) a little gentle rivalry occurred, with competitions in all aspects of sport, first aid and other games between the two. After World War Two, Peel House apart from recruit training, also continued to offer senior officer non-residential training courses.

A Training School magazine was started in January 1963 under an operating committee from both schools. In 1963 the editorship was under Chief Superintendent J. J. Miller MBE. This magazine was produced to inform interested parties of what was happening in the training environment, had a very wide circulation considering that many Commonwealth countries sent their more senior police officers on the Overseas Police Course and for CID training. As such, many of these magazines found their way into police libraries around the world. Also at Hendon was the Criminal Investigation Department (CID) Training School, a cadet school for young men aged 16 years (with an annex at Ashford in Kent called Kennington Hall) a wireless training school (later called the Communications School), a driving school and a forensic science laboratory, all located at the Hendon complex.

In the 1960s other courses were run at Peel House. These included courses for probationer constables, traffic wardens and also promotion courses for uniform branch sergeants. The Royal Park 'keepers' course trained 16 men and women in 1963 from the Royal Parks Constabulary. This course was designed to assist them in their daily duties in the parks where they enjoyed similar powers to a constable. The Cadet School also contributed to the magazine and were keen competitors in sport taking part in boxing, wrestling (under SPS Blackwell), cross country and canoeing competitions.

If there was a sport or activity, there was a force level organised club (arranged within the rules of the Metropolitan Police Athletic Association-MPAA). The clubs would enter competitions in sport organised for the Metropolitan Police and these included cross country, table tennis, rugby and lifesaving. In fact sport has until lately been positively encouraged by senior officers so as to maintain general fitness and to encourage participation and teamwork. Senior officers of divisions often, in banter between themselves would make remarks about their own sporting prowess amongst their colleagues. Team captains would go to Peel House and Hendon in order to ensure certain highly regarded sports men and women were posted to their

The new Metropolitan Police Training School – The Peel Centre, Hendon circa 1974

divisions.

In 1968 Peel House, Regency Street 105 Regency Street SW1 4AN was shut for training purposes and training was moved to Hendon. Extensive work was undertaken to modernise the site at Hendon which included building a completely new training establishment with sufficient classrooms, purpose built court room, training roads, canteen facilities, sports facilities, residential accommodation, medical facilities, library and parking.

Today the future of the Peel Centre is in doubt as the three tall residential blocks shown above are uninhabitable and have been sealed. In 2011 Farrow House the Telecommunications School came up for sale in Colindeep Lane and will be disposed of and vacated by the Police[153].

The Driving School, Hendon

To say that you were trained to drive police vehicles at Hendon is a high accolade indeed as the name is now established as synonymous with the best police driver training experience and as the premier driver training establishment, perhaps in the world certainly in the UK.

In 1930 mobile police were introduced in London known as Traffic Patrols originating from the introduction of the Road Traffic Act 1930.

In order to ensure that drivers on the road were suitably qualified and as such a compulsory driving test was planned to come into operation in 1935 with voluntary testing (introduced by the Road Traffic Act, 1934), to avoid a rush of candidates when the test became compulsory a year later.

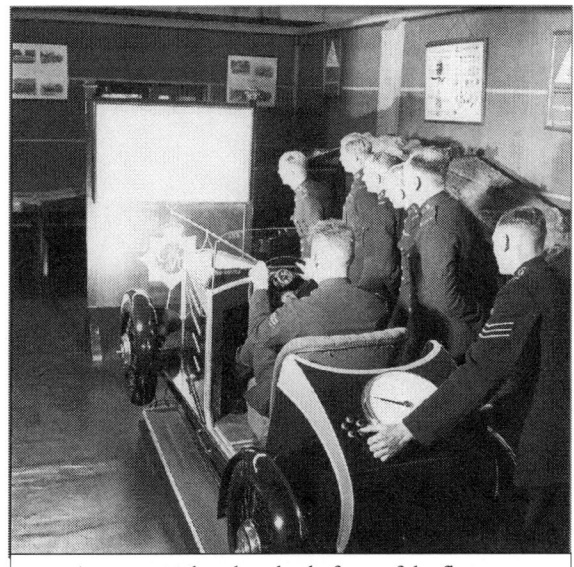

A sergeant takes the wheel of one of the first car simulators

Mr J. Beene was the first person to pass his driving test, at a cost of 7s/6d (37.5p)[154].

By 1st June 1935 compulsory testing (brought in for all drivers who had started driving on or after 1 April 1934) saw around 246,000 candidates applying to be tested. The pass rate was 63%, with 250 examiners (originally trained at Hendon Police Driving School) taking at least nine, and up to sixteen, half-hour driving tests a day. Examining staff also made all test bookings. Originally there were no test centres, examiners met candidates at a pre-arranged spot such as a car park or railway station. Anyone buying a driving licence was required to put 'L' plates on the car and eventually to take a driving test to get their full licence. Driving tests were suspended in September 1939 for the duration of World War Two and resumed once more on 1st November 1946. During the war, examiners, who were also designated traffic officers, remained on their respective divisions and some of their responsibilities included the supervision of fuel rationing.

As far as police officers abilities were concerned the Police Driving School was established in 1935 by the then Commissioner, Lord Trenchard who was concerned that many of his police drivers had no driving licence and that if they were to give evidence in court later about driving matters, they ought to be able to show that they were suitably qualified as drivers to the required standard. The school was established on a site (converted aircraft hangars) in Aerodrome Road, Hendon NW9

One of the first advanced driving courses in 1935

on 'S' Division a Training School, sports ground, motor repair garages, a district garage and also included five sets of married quarters[155].

Previously the buildings had formed part of Hendon Country Club, a section of Hendon aerodromes club house and albeit briefly, laboratories of Standard Cable and wireless. By the end of 1933 the number of vehicles in use by the Metropolitan Police had risen to 585. Unfortunately, as the fleet grew in size, so the number of accidents in which police were involved grew correspondingly. In the first few months of 1934 the accident mileage ratio rose to one accident for every 8,000

The formal class photograph taken at the front of the Driving school.

miles.

The high accident rate resulted in considerable adverse comment both in the press and motoring journals and, as a result of this criticism, the Commissioner, Lord Trenchard, arranged for the famous racing motorist, Sir Malcolm Campbell, to test a number of drivers from divisions. This difficult and strenuous test consisted of driving a squad or "Q" car on normal patrol and on an emergency (999) call, both in heavy traffic and on the open road. Campbell also advised on necessary vehicles, garaging and equipment.

Despite the severity of the test and the high standard demanded, all the police drivers passed with flying colours and such was Sir Malcolm Campbell's praise that the ill-founded criticism was silenced. It could not, however, be denied that lack of experience and in particular, inadequate training facilities were great handicaps in raising the standard of driving. For these reasons in 1934 the setting up of the Metropolitan Police Driving School at Hendon was ordered[156].

Students receive instruction on traffic movement

The introduction of the driving school caused very little comment, either locally or nationally. Few could have foreseen the impact which the teaching of the School would have on driving technique, not only in this country, but in other countries.

Nevertheless, 'tall oaks from little acorns grow', and this is especially true of the Driving School, for the seed so firmly planted in 1934 has today grown into a strong tree, the branches of which stretch far and wide[157].

The first course for instructors was held in November 1934, attended by Inspector King, Police Constables Steele, Fowles, Jordon, Skeggs, McCullock

A dummy is catapulted in front of a driver to test reactions

and Thomas. Many of these instructors remained for the rest of their service and some re-joined as civilian instructors when they retired from the service. These men were the foundation stones on which the driving school was built and their teaching has been perpetuated through the years by the current staff being responsible for the selection and training of future instructors[158].

The first Course for students began on 7th January, 1935, and on that day 21 young men, the forerunners of thousands, presented themselves for four weeks of

Metropolitan Police Driving school, 1961

instruction that included elementary motor mechanics and practical maintenance, in addition to driving. Eighteen instructional cars, including the Hillman "16", the Ford 14.9 and the Hillman 10 horse-power touring cars were allocated to the school. At the end of the first four days, which were spent in the classroom, the students were introduced to the principles of driving. All students were tested by the senior instructor before being allowed to drive on the public roads, and a system of routes was built up so that students graduated progressively from quiet country and suburban roads, through areas of heavier traffic, to the dense and crowded streets of inner London.

At the end of the first week, a second Course of 21 students commenced training, and thus was founded the Elementary or Standard Car Wing, which to this day provides the basic training for all students. So outstanding were the results achieved from the training given to the students who attended the initial courses that the pattern of future instruction was made clear[159].

The first officer in charge of the driving school stayed for 10 years and established a firm grounding to the driving courses and set the standard for years to come. He was Chief Inspector A. T. King who commenced on the 7th January 1935 and remained until 17th September 1945. After the war, the level of authority and the changes in the rank structure meant that a Chief Superintendent was the head of the driving school. Kings place was taken by Chief Superintendent. W. M. Taylor MM from the 18th September 1945 until 31st December 1952.

Supporting the driving school as advisor for the Commissioner was Captain J. C. Byrne who started on 7th January 1935 and remained in post until 19th December 1957.

In 1936 an Advanced Course of driving for Flying Squad, "Q" Car and traffic patrol Car drivers were introduced and early in 1937, the Commissioner appointed as his Civilian Advisor for the training of police drivers one of the most famous racing drivers of the day, Mark Everard Pepys, the sixth earl of Cottenham who had written widely on motoring.

Chief Superintendent Hinxman and his deputy discuss Driving School arrangements

Lord Cottenham, who in

earlier years had been a member of both the Alvis and Sunbeam racing teams,

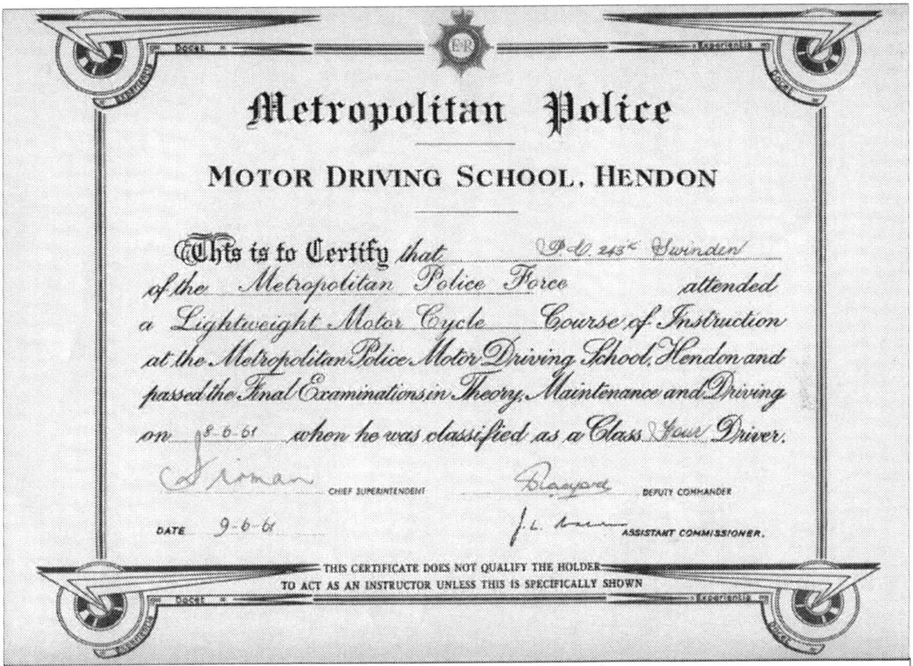

Metropolitan Police

MOTOR DRIVING SCHOOL, HENDON

This is to Certify that P.C. 243K Swinden of the Metropolitan Police Force attended a Lightweight Motor Cycle Course of Instruction at the Metropolitan Police Motor Driving School, Hendon and passed the Final Examinations in Theory, Maintenance and Driving on 8-6-61 when he was classified as a Class Four Driver.

CHIEF SUPERINTENDENT DEPUTY COMMANDER

DATE 9-6-61 ASSISTANT COMMISSIONER.

THIS CERTIFICATE DOES NOT QUALIFY THE HOLDER TO ACT AS AN INSTRUCTOR UNLESS THIS IS SPECIFICALLY SHOWN

A Metropolitan Police Driving certificate for the Lightweight motor cycle course

approached his task with rare zest. His aim was simple - to bring to the technique of advanced driving a new standard of perfection.

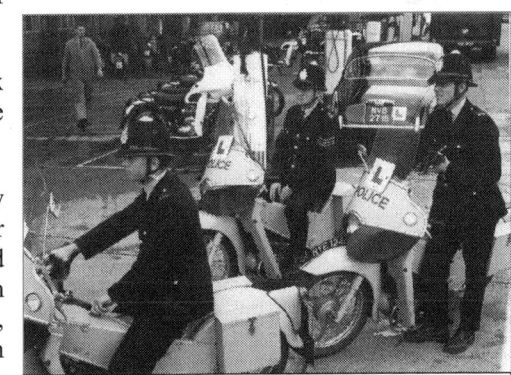

Officers on the lightweight motor (noddy) cycle course in the 1960's

To this end he personally trained six specially selected Instructors to give this training.

Briefly his system was that by implementing a simple "drill" or sequence of events, a driver would ensure that his vehicle was always in the right place at the right time, travelling at the right speed and in the correct gear. Thus, it was

reasoned, a driver would be in complete control of any situation with which he might be faced[160]. The success of Lord Cottenham's teaching can best be judged by results, for, whilst in 1934 the police vehicle accident rate was one accident to every 8,000 miles, by 1938 it had dropped to one accident to every 27,000 miles.

Lord Cottenham's stay with the Metropolitan Police was brief, as he left in 1938, however he developed new and improved standards of advanced driving based on 'defensive driving', and devised training programmes which still today lie at the heart of Hendon's courses. The impact of his teaching remains and the system of driving which he initiated has resulted in a police vehicle mileage for each blameworthy accident in 1982 of 26,108 miles for cars, 86,842 miles for motor cycles, proof, if proof were ever needed, that good driving pays handsome dividends in safety on the road.

Car pursuit on the skid pans

In 1946 Chief Superintendent Taylor and the Metropolitan Police driving school (MDS) took part in annual driving competitions, particularly with the Bentley Drivers Club (BDC) although occasionally other teams were invited. In 1964 Deputy Commander D. C. Macdonald was president of the MDS and the BDC president was Stanley Sedgwick. This was a prestigious annual event held on the training roads at Hendon where a purpose-

Motor cycles lined up before going out on the street

built section was used. Held on a Sunday and on occasions in conjunction with a gymkhana – it became a family day out, not only for police officers and their families, but also for invited guests, much needed entertainment especially after the recent long and costly war. In this competition of driving skills the best drivers of both clubs would be put forward to enter. The competition was for the Flying Wheel Trophy with the club gaining the lowest number of points retaining the trophy. The best individual driver in event six won the Harold Radford Trophy. Only members of the car clubs could enter. There were six events with six drivers taking part in each team. Up until 1963 honours were even with both clubs having won on 8 occasions each (one event cancelled in 1955 due to the rail strike). This was a well organised event with the No. 2 District Sports Club at Hendon organising refreshments and involving some other organisations such as the Royal Automobile Club, The Ministry of Transport, The Ministry of Works and local business and dignitaries. The prizes were presented in 1964 by the Assistant Commissioner who was Andrew Way CMG.

In the mid-1950s the system of driving was published in *Roadcraft* - The Police Drivers Manual published by HMSO at 3s and 6d (18p) to help the driver realise;

Sergeant Matthews teaching the Traffic Patrol Wing Advanced course 50 in 1966 about car braking systems

'the need for a high degree of physical and mental fitness in order to drive the car with a highest of standards of skill, safety and considerations for other user of the road ' (Roadcraft 1960 p1)

'The System', as it was called, was used whenever a hazard required a manoeuvre. A hazard is something which requires a change in speed, direction or both. The benefit of applying a systematic approach to driving was to reduce the simultaneous demands on the vehicle, and the driver's mental and physical ability. The system seeks to separate out the phases of a manoeuvre into a logical sequence of events so that the vehicle and the driver avoid being overwhelmed by having to do too much at the same time. For example, braking and steering at the same time places greater demands on the vehicle's available grip and in the worst case, can lead to a skid[161].

Teaching a class about lighting systems in the 1960's

The driving school also developed a traffic patrol wing to educate road users and reduce accidents. This included training for dealing with thoughtless parking, negligent driving, defective vehicles, and disregard for road signs because all these contributed to traffic accidents. This meant that 'TrafPols' could help prevent accidents and keep Londons traffic flowing freely.

Included in the courses were lectures on traffic law, covering diverse matters as Road Traffic Acts, Construction and Use Regulations, registration, licensing, driving licences, insurance, goods vehicles (and later Tachographs) steam rollers, street traders, road works, pedestrian crossings, road signs etc. Standard level courses were of 4 weeks duration, whilst the advanced course lasted three weeks with examinations on vehicle examination, report writing on a fatal accident investigation (later accident reconstruction), general technical knowledge and traffic law[162].

In 1953 the Special Escort Group (SEG) of motor cyclists were formed in preparation for the visit of Marshal Tito, President of Yugoslavia. The group escorted the Queen at her Coronation and has played regular and important roles during all State Visits.

A modern day traffic officer on his solo motor cycle

Members of the SEG are trained to a very high standard including riding formations headed by 'Red Diamond' so called because of the large red diamond affixed to the handlebars of the motor cycle.

In mid 1960s the programme included refresher, reclassification, instructors and special courses held as necessary. Approximately 2,000 students were trained each year and 1,000 drivers were tested.

The training track at Hendon was called Cottenham Drive as a mark of respect for the Lord Cottenham legacy. In 1970 the Hendon Training Centre acquired the premises of an old sign manufacturing business in Aerodrome Road, adjacent to the estate in front of Cottenham Drive and built a skid pan. This site was converted into a fully multi-functional driving school with its own petrol supply, washing bays, and garages as well as classrooms, workshops, canteen and assembly hall[163].

The driving school offered in 1999, a comprehensive range of courses from basic driving instruction for cars and light and heavy motor cycles for provisional licence holders, through to advanced vehicle inspection and accident investigation. They maintained a range of vehicles from motor cycles to rigid HGV's and the 'Z' Wagon (a lorry that can hoist up illegally parked cars). There were also a range of courses for instructors on the workings and inspection of lorries and HGVs including their tachographs. Bespoke courses are also included for students particular work environment. Today the school still retains its reputation for driving excellence and remains open except for the skid pan which is no longer used[164].

The Detective Training School

By 1958 Hendon housed the Detective Training School then C7 Branch with Detective Chief Superintendent. T. Barrett M.B.E in charge. In the 1960s it was decided to enlarge the site at Hendon with new classrooms, living accommodation, nursing home, library and cadet school.

At the front the Peel Centre is the statue of Robert Peel originally sited in Cheapside in the City of London. It was moved to Hendon in 1974. By 1974 the named changed on the opening of the Peel Centre when the old buildings were demolished and a purpose built complex was built.

The old Peel House in Regency Street then later housed the Personnel Department (later Human Resources) and continued to provide training for Civil Staff.

When the Empress State Building in Earls Court was taken over from the Ministry of Defence the old Peel House in Regency Street was vacated and then sold to Bowater House of Knightsbridge in 2006. Bowater have applied to redevelop the site for affordable housing and high end owner occupancy[165]. The sites outward appearance is unchanged because the company who sought permission was attempting to transfer the affordable housing element to another building although

METROPOLITAN POLICE DETECTIVE TRAINING SCHOOL, HENDON.

negotiation's were still in hand. The building works were completed by 2010 when properties started coming onto the market.

The picture above shows the intake of the Detective Training School including students from Commonwealth countries police forces.

The Metropolitan Police Cadet Corps.

In 1948 the idea to introduce a police cadet system was accepted and buildings were planned on the Hendon Complex for a cadet school under the then Commissioner of the Metropolis, Sir Joseph Simpson. During the 1950's the Metropolitan Police had two types of police cadet. There was a junior cadet who joined at 16½ yrs. These cadets received some initial training and were then posted to a division. They spent a part of their week at college on academic studies. The rest of the time they worked within the station. When they reached 18½ they became senior cadets and joined with direct entrants to the service at that stage. The senior cadets spent 12 weeks at

Hendon Training School on a course identical to the Constables joining course. The senior cadets at the end of their training were posted to a police station and attached to court, traffic patrol, beat duties, etc. At the age of 19 years they changed their uniform and were sworn in as constables. Normally they were then posted to a different police station. The new cadet corps was formed in 1960 at its own school located at the junction with Aerodrome Road and Colindale Avenue being entirely separate from the Metropolitan Police Training school. These cadets were fulltime paid members of the Metropolitan Police until they were old enough to join the regular force.

The buildings consisted of four low level accommodation blocks, an administrative

A class of cadets passing out from Hendon in October 1958 with their instructors

building with class rooms, the Simpson Hall and a gymnasium.

It was set up and run by the much loved and respected Colonel Andrew Croft the explorer, and as early as 1951 he was brought in to advise and head the new Metropolitan Police Cadet Corps. His aims were to promote citizenship, introduce the cadets to how the Police Service functioned as well as develop leadership skills in young men (and later women). This saw young men aged between 16 and 17 years old which in the first instance was meant as a career prior to National Service that could be rescued to policing afterwards.

Initially spending four weeks at Hendon the cadets were posted to a division to undertake varying low key roles. They did however take part in the Coronation in 1953 when their numbers totalled 300. After 1968, a more rigorous programme of training commenced, heavily reliant on lectures on improving their educational qualifications in addition to preparing them for police duty.

There were many characters in the Metropolitan Police Cadets Corps. They included Sergeant Bill Bailey the drill instructor at Hendon whose legendary voice could be heard on the parade square. Another character was Station Sergeant (wt. no. 125768) William Henry Blackwell who joined the Training School in July 1951 and moved to the Cadet Corps in April 1966. Born in 1917 in Sheffield and being 6 ft. tall he was a strong, powerful man who had been a miner before he joined the Metropolitan Police in 1937. He was originally posted to 'H' Division, and during

William Blackwell shown with his cadet wrestling team in 1971

the war became a corporal in the RAF between February 1942 and November 1945. Married with one child he was seconded to the Home Office in July 1949 having passed all the examinations to Station Sergeant. When he retired from the force after 30 years' service in 1967 he accepted a civilian job at the Cadet School. He later became head of Physical Training at the Cadets centre Grosvenor Hall, Ashford in Kent where cadets under-took their 2nd phase training. He was a wrestling champion, and taught the sport always being on hand to demonstrate moves and holds. Even at 55 years of age he was a strong and fit man. The picture above shows Blackwell in the centre of the Grosvenor Hall Cadet wrestling team in 1971. Ex-Sergeant Blackwell died in July 2003 aged 86 years.

Once the phase one was completed at Hendon cadets moved to phase two and were posted to Grosvenor Hall, Ashford, Kent for one year. The Hall consisted of nearly 200,000 sq. ft. and 50 acres of educational, adventure, sports and recreational facilities within a fully secure 50 acre site. The site was later given up for training of police officers from the southern counties. In 2010 it was sold to provide educational facilities for children and young people. The cadets were disbanded in the late 1980s and the cadet school at Hendon was shut in 1993.

A drill class of 'B' course cadets in 1976

The picture at left shows a drill class of the 'B' Course in 1976[166]. In June 1987 a Volunteer Cadet Corps was formed as a link between police and local communities in South Norwood as a pilot scheme. It was successful and it was gradually introduced on to other Divisions. Now, after the introduction of borough policing, all of the 32 Boroughs have at least one Voluntary Police Cadet unit.

Mill Hill Police Station

The Freehold of a vacant site at 11-12 Deans Drive, Edgware NW7 was purchased by the Receiver in 1910. Adjacent property fronting Victoria Road was for use as dwelling houses only[167].

The building was a temporary structure or prefabricated sections with sloping roof. It was principally made of wood and glass and finished off with a bitumen roof. The station was erected in about 1965 as a temporary police office.

In 1966 Mill Hill (SH) was a sectional station to West Hendon (SW) sub divisional station.

The station was shut in 1997 and the functions and police officers transferred to the newly completed Colindale Police Station[168].

Mill Hill Police Office. 1965 – 1997. 11 – 12 Deans Drive, Edgware, Middlesex.

Potters Bar Police Station

The 1825 Census shows a William Parish living at Potters Bar Police Station. His occupation was shown as 'Metropolitan Police Constable'[169] but this is somewhat strange as the Metropolitan Police were not formed until 1829 and it is more likely he was a member of the Bow Street horse patrol instead. When the Bow Street horse patrols were absorbed into the Metropolitan Police the houses and stables occupied or rented were also taken over and responsibility then fell to the Receiver to ensure their upkeep.

In 1851 Constable James Harrod, with his wife and family of seven children resided at 95 High Road Potters Bar village. Harrod would patrol on foot or by horse the High Road, by day and night. It was likely that this cottage was an old horse patrol

Potters Bar Police Station. 1871 – 1886. 90 The High Road, Potters Bar, Hertfordshire

station which had a separate stable in the garden. In 1871 constable George Fossket, his wife and family occupied a police house in Potters Bar at 90, The High Road[170]. William Parish, his wife and family also resided nearby in Potters Bar in Holly Bank Cottage at the same time as Fossket[171].

By 1881 a married Inspector, his wife and family occupied Holly Bank cottage at Potters Bar. Also a married constable occupied another part of the cottage in cramped conditions. The cottage was described as having no running water and the well in the garden was polluted. The cesspool had been sited near the well into which it seeped. A stable had been erected in the garden and a suggestion was made that a cell should be constructed as it was needed to house prisoners. There was no waiting area for people wishing to see the constable or report matters. There was also an administrative office where the inspector would make his daily reports. The station was designated as being on 'Y' or Highgate Division at the time[172].

In 1891 the officer in charge at Potters Bar was 45-year old Inspector John Geater from Glemham in Suffolk who resided there with his wife Sophie and their four children[173]. A short distance away in Laurel Cottage lived Constable Charles Moore, his wife and five children resided[174].

The 1901 Census shows Constable William Chandler living in the High Street, Potters Bar.

As a matter of interest, the boundary marks of the Metropolitan Police area (denoted by white posts erected with a City of London crest on) can be seen at Potters Bar in Hatfield Road, and in Church Road and also at Colney Heath Lane, South Mimms; and London Road, London Colney Hertfordshire. Potters Bar police station was situated very close to the boundary[175].

A cottage in Southgate Road, Potters Bar had been leased from Mr. C. Woodward the licensee of the White Swan Inn, Bell Bar Hatfield on an annual rental of £30. It was occupied for police purposes in 1871 and a stable was erected in the garden. In

Potters Bar Police Station. 1886 – 2011. The Causeway, Potters Bar, Hertfordshire.

1880 it was reported that the cottage had no cell space and there had been calls for some to be provided. The cottage housed a married inspector with his family and a married constable as-well, but the married constable and his family were moved out to make way for more space for the workings of the station.

The vestry, the parish based fore runner of the local authority did not confine itself to church affairs after 1835. It often discussed the water supply and in 1887 it complained about the increased police rate and questioned the necessity of having 22 policemen at Potters Bar[176].

Freehold to a site situated at the Causeway, Potters Bar was purchased in 1886 which at this time showed the station as situated on 'Y' or Highgate Division but a station and one set of married quarters were not erected until 1897. The station call sign for the telegraph published in Police Orders in 1893 was Papa Bravo PB but by the 1920s these were changed[177] to Sierra Papa SP. Potters Bar was a sectional station to the sub divisional station at Enfield on 'Y' or Highgate Division in 1899. It remained there until about 1937 when it transferred to 'S' or Hampstead Division as a sectional station on Barnet Sub Division. Potters Bar was allocated a squad of special constables to make up for the call up of regular officers to the colours[178] in WW1.

The address of the police station was shown as The Causeway, Potters Bar, Hertfordshire. In 1925 The Station Sergeant was David Partner assisted by Sergeants Hubert Porter and Phillip Phillips. James Cryan and Stephen Church were Acting Sergeants assisted by 14 Constables[179].

The station was renovated in 1938. In 1947 the station was still part of 'S' Division with the station code of SP and a sectional station of Barnet Sub Division[180].

After divisional boundary changes in 2000, Potters Bar transferred from 'S' Division. The Hertsmere area of the Metropolitan Police covering Potters Bar, South Mimms, Borehamwood, Bushey and its surrounding villages were transferred to the Hertfordshire Constabulary and Potters Bar is now part of 'J' Division', station code 'J3' within Hertfordshire. The station was sold in 2011.

The Hertfordshire Officers who patrol the Potters Bar area now parade out of Boreham Wood Police Station. Officers from the Potters Bar Community Team and Probationer Training Unit are the only officers now based at Potters Bar[181].

Radlett Police Station.

Radlett is a small village situated between St. Albans and Boreham Wood in Hertfordshire and currently has about 8,000 inhabitants. Records show that in 1932 a police station existed in Radlett village as a station of 'S' or Hampstead Division[182] although there are no firm details of where and for how long the station remained open. After World War 2 a police station was opened by the Metropolitan Police in Radlett in 1946 although again its exact location is also unknown. By the 1960's the Commissioner considered establishing a police office in Watling Street, Radlett which would serve as a base for officers who were responsible for the area and would be open at certain times of the day to cater for local enquiries. A shop front that previously was an electrical shop was leased initially for seven years and in November 1967 a new police office opened at 77 The Oakway, Watling Street, Radlett. The front clear glass to the building was replaced with obscured panes and bill boards for recruiting and local information when the station opened.

Radlett Police Office. 1967 – 1980. 77, The Oakways, Watling Street, Radlett Hertfordshire

The call sign of the station at that time was Sierra Echo SE and it was a sectional office as part of West Hendon sub division. In 1973 the lease expired and it was renewed for a further another seven years.

In the 1980's Radlett Police station was situated opposite Park Road next to the fire station at 193 Watling Street, Radlett, Hertfordshire, WD2 7NQ. The call sign had changed to SR prior to 1998. The station was transferred to Hertfordshire Police in 2000 and in 2012 no police station existed in Radlett.

Shenley Police Station

Evidence of the village cage or lockup can still be seen at the village of Shenley, by the village pond, at the junction of London Road, and Cage Bond Road. This was a brick or stone construction, and was used for a long time. Finchley cage was made of wood and brick and was still in use in the 1860s, but prior to 1815 the cage or lockup was used at Highgate instead, as it appears to have been the nearest[183]. In the picture below the old cage can be seen behind the three children in the foreground.

Shenley – The Old Cage taken about 1905

A police station has been recorded on Shenley Hill (now Harris Lane), Hertfordshire since 1849[184] and until the present day two stations have remained very close to each other. Buildings were rented in Shenley from Mr. Edward Osman, a local builder for £15 per year. The buildings, located in Harris Lane consisted of 4 rooms, an outhouse, and a four stall stable were converted into a police station and section house which was in use between 1852 and Christmas 1858[185]. Sergeant William Floyd was located there with his wife and four children in 1851[186].

This cottage became no longer suitable for use as a station and section house and was probably too small, so the police looked around the local area for further accommodation. They found suitable buildings of brick and slate locally which were then converted into a police station and section house for single officers,

Accommodation was rented in 1859 on an annual rent of £15. The owner Mr Rainsford, a barrister of 36 Lincolns Inn Fields provided the building with five rooms, a scullery, fuel house, kitchen and a one-stall stable. Surveyors reported that it was in a good state of repair and had good water supply[187].

Supervision of Shenley occurred by the patrolling inspector from Barnet riding out on horse-back from his station and visit South Mimms, Whetstone and Shenley. He

A modern photograph of the old police station as it is today.

would record his visit in the occurrence book so that the divisional superintendent could be assured that supervision of the constables and sergeants was strictly carried out. Whilst Shenley was a station where prisoners were taken and charged, they could not remain there in custody as there were no facilities to detain them. They were transferred by station transport to Barnet instead after charging and the Barnet station officer would be responsible for detention and transfer to the local magistrates court[188]. Another cottage and stabling was purchased for £400 in 1871 from Mr. Cordell of Shenley and this remained operational until 1892[189].

Land was purchased in Harris Lane (a cottage and stabling) including ground at the rear in 1885 and 1892[190] and to extend the station which was on 'S' Division. Shenley had no cell space so prisoners were transferred to Barnet by trap or accompanied by the arresting officer on foot[191]. Sub Inspector (wt. no. 56536) William Girling was the inspector who was resident with his family in 1891. His wife Jessie Girling and five children also lived above the station. Girling had joined the police in 1873, stayed at Shenley until 1899 when he retired on pension with 26 years service.

There was one substantive sergeant and one acting sergeant attached to the station. There were two day-time constables patrolling the vicinity and four night beats who would be supervised by the sergeant patrolling on horse-back[192]. The station call sign for the telegraph, published in Police orders in 1893 was Sierra Echo SE but by the 1920's this changed to[193] Sierra Yankey SY.

In 1901 42 year old Station Sergeant Richmond Young resided there with his family, his wife Mary and daughters Eliza and Angeline. Constable William Lancaster also resided in Harris Lane not far from the station he worked at with his wife Ellen and two sons and three daughters[194]. Constable Reuben Fordham and his family lived in New Road, Shenley, Constable Sackville Bobyer with his family in lived next door to Constable John Houndsome and family in Grove Place, and Constable Daniel Murphy in Bay Cottages[195]. Scotsman constable William Jones, his wife and seven children could not find accommodation sufficiently large enough in the village and the farmer at Limes Farm rented a house to them[196].

The picture below was taken in 1902 and shows the station strength with the Inspector shown with flat kepi (chin strap down) and riding boots flanked to the right with the station sergeant (four stripes) Richmond Young and to the left the section sergeant.

Note also the two acting sergeants at each end with two stripes on their arms. There were also eight constables plus two men in plain clothes. The man in the flat straw hat appears to be a detective whilst the man in cloth cap probably was the groom and tended the horses. He also was the reserve constable able to fill in any vacancy where necessary. The picture was likely to have been taken on coronation day in 1902 as a mark of celebration for the new king.

A picture taken in the rear yard at Shenley Police Station in about 1902

In 1914 Sergeant Thomas Henry Harris was in charge of the station and he was assisted by two acting sergeants and 12 constables[197].

The station at Shenley was shut on the 6th March 1957 when the staff and business was transferred to the newly built pre-fabricated buildings at Borehamwood[198].

The picture below shows the last police officer at Shenley, Constable Neal, walking past the station when it became a police office in 1967.

Constable Neal walks past the Shenley Police Office in 1967

(South) Mimms Police Station

The parish of South Mimms was added to the Metropolitan Police in 1840. A police station which consisted of a brick and tile house with stable was initially rented from Mr. Edward Whalley for £11 per year and was brought into service in 1844 on 'S' Division. This was located near to the toll gate in South Mimms and a sergeant was placed in charge. It was prudent to situate stations near turnpikes and toll houses since patrolling constables could obtain useful information and intelligence on crime which may have been committed on passersby. The toll house keepers would also inform the police of people who evaded paying the toll. Local residents resented paying the toll and often got into trouble.

South Mimms Police Station. 1871 – 2000. Old St. Albans Road, South Mimms, Hertfordshire

Prior to occupation, repairs were made as the accommodation was in a sad state. The freehold to the building and land in Old St. Albans Road was purchased in 1846. The station (now called Blackhorse Lane) consisted of four rooms with charge room, coal shed, a little garden and small stable[199] and opened in 1847. As was the norm, there was one substantive sergeant and one acting sergeant posted to the station. The sergeant would be attached to the night duty where he would supervise the seven night duty constables on horse-back. There were two horses attached to the station with the other horse being used by the reserve constable[200].

The station was small and so there was only sufficient space for one set of married quarters when it was rebuilt in 1870. Rent of 3/3d (16p) per week was charged to the married officer in 1871[201].

Sub Inspector (wt. no. 48679) Lewis Skeats and his wife Mary resided at the station in 1891. Skeats had joined the police in 1867 and by 1885 was an inspector on the 'S' or Hampstead division. He retired in 1892 on pension. In 1899 James Wheller was the station sergeant in charge, two acting sergeants one section sergeant and 11 constables[202]. Inspector Fredrick Leggatt aged 45 years his wife, son and three daughters lived at the station in 1901[203].

In 1905 a further set of 4 cottages were purchased for accommodation in the High Road, South Mimms in 1905. In the 1920s the station call sign changed to Sierra Mike (SM) and was a sectional station of Barnet.

The picture at left shows a rather stern looking Station Sergeant 84'S' William Baker (wt. no. 77760) posing in the garden of the station. Baker was the officer who was in charge of South Mimms Police station between 1912 and 1919. Baker, from Woodford in Essex had joined as constable 226 'W' division in June 1892 and by 1901 Baker was still a constable located in Southwark. He had decided to take promotion to better himself, Baker soon progressed to sergeant and then to station sergeant at South Mimms. By 1911, Baker then aged 43 years, his wife Mary and his son John William Baker occupied four rooms at the station[204]. It was likely that there were about seven constables attached to the station for whom he had responsibility.

Station Sergeant William Baker circa 1919

He retired with an exemplary record aged 51 years in January 1919 (once the war had finished) with 27 years' service and annual pension of £121 15 shillings. He was long lived to a ripe old age and died, aged 79 years, in 1948.

A picture of South Mimms station strength taken in 1894.

In 1925 sergeants Leonard Worth, Frederick Jardine and Charles Haines were shown to be based at South Mimms assisted by nine constables. South Mimms Police Station still exists today as a residential premises[205]. The station was further renovated in 1938. Records show that the station was situated in the Old St. Albans Road, South Mimms, Hertfordshire in 1947.

The station was transferred in 2000 to Hertfordshire Police who decided to shut it down and put it up for sale. In the meantime the buildings of this famous old station deteriorated into a very sad state of repair.

West Hendon Police Station

It was decided to include in the 1963-64 Metropolitan Police Building Programme a new station took place the current one at Willesden Green at the junction of High Road, Willesden Green, and Huddlestone Road, as it was considered no longer adequate for the functions of a modern police service. A site was sought in the Hendon area as proposed by the Dixon Committee Report, roughly doubling its area in size, and that it should serve as a sub-divisional station[206].

A suitable plot of land known as Beach's Fairground, West Hendon Broadway, by

West Hendon Police Station. West Hendon Broadway, Edgware Road, Hendon Middlesex NW9.

Brent Park Road, opposite the 'Old Welsh Harp (Public House) came on to the market. This freehold piece of land was purchased at auction by the Metropolitan Police in 1961 for the sum of £92,500. It had a frontage to Brent Park Road. It was previously used as part of the winter quarters of a fairground and of a permanent caravan site.

The planning stage was slow and a number of restrictions were imposed by the planning officer and the local authority to specify the height of the building fronting West Hendon Broadway to be four-storey, to allow sufficient space at the frontage. This was to allow for future road development in the Broadway by the Ministry of Transport, and to provide for a 20 feet deep area to Brent Park Road to be landscaped[207].

Police stations were designed to ensure that the public entrance was well defined and visible from a reasonable distance along a public transport route. The station yard needed to provide for the security of prisoners in transit, good vehicular access and direct access, from the yard into the charge room. Provision was also made to ensure that catering delivery and refuse collection could be facilitated easily. A 45 feet frontage to West Hendon Broadway was to provide a landscaped forecourt to ensure a pleasant introduction to the main entrance and thereby to encourage the public to use the police service. Suitable parking for visitors' and police private cars was also to be made. The entrance to the station yard was located at the back of the station site to ensure ease of vehicular access and the avoidance of congestion at the road junction. The boiler house, refuse collection areas, garage and stores were dealt with by ensuring that single out-buildings were built surrounding the yard space. The building was designed on a modular basis[208].

Permission was necessary from the Home Office to sell off the surplus land on the site to Hendon Borough Council and this was received on 8th February 1963. The sale was completed on 12th November 1963 and the £55,000 realised from the sale saved on costs for the future building work. In the meantime, tenders were requested from suitable building companies to erect the new station. Prospectuses were sent out outlining the planning requirements and expectations regarding the final form of the building. In February 1964 Home Office approved the acceptance of the tender of Messrs H. Fairweather & Co. Ltd. for £153,557. 4s. 8d (£153,557 53p) for the construction of the new station.

Police Orders of 1st August 1964 stated that;

> "Under the boundary changes to be implemented on 1st April 1965, a new sub-division comprising West Hendon, Hendon, Mill Hill, Elstree and Borehamwood Police Stations, is to be formed and the new station at West Hendon is to be the sub-divisional headquarters. The station will be situated in the new London Borough of Barnet."

The new West Hendon (SW) police station, part of 'S' Division with the postal address of West Hendon Broadway, Edgware Road, Hendon, NW9 was opened and taken into operational use at 6 am on 1st April 1964[209].

Willesden Green Police Station did not in fact close and was not replaced when West Hendon was opened. It remained functioning long afterwards as a station on 'Q' Division, with station code QL.

In 1966 there were three stations which were sub divisional stations with superintendents in charge and these were Golders Green, West Hendon and Barnet[210]. The first officer in charge was Superintendent G. H. K. Woolard who was succeeded by Superintendent W. L Rees. Chief Inspectors T. B. Hunt and J. F. Marriott supported the supervisory staff[211].

In the original designs they failed to ensure that there was space for the mounted section and the housing of police horses necessary for public order events and other functions. As a result Metropolitan Police surveyors arranged for the building of a set of stables on the site. Once constructed a police order was issued that stated;

> 'New stabling accommodation for Mounted Branch at West Hendon Police Station (SW) will be taken into operational use at 6 am on Monday, 29th February, at which time the stables at Harlesden Police Station (QH) will be closed'[212].

The station was shut in 1997 and the functions and police officers transferred to the newly completed Colindale Police Station[213] although for a time Simpson Hall, Aerodrome Road, Colindale was used for front counter enquiries until the new station was finalised.

Whetstone Police Station

In 1815 the vestry asserted that a place of confinement was absolutely necessary and planned for cages to be erected at Whetstone and near the stocks at Church End, suggesting that the earlier cage was no longer in use. There was still no agreement with Friern Barnet but a brick cage was built at Church End close to the Queen's Head[214]. Pupils of the National school had to pass the cage and in 1860 the prisoners' behaviour then led the vestry to demand its closure, but the Metropolitan Police insisted on keeping it: 143 persons had been confined there during the last five years. The cage was eventually removed in 1880[215].

Three police forces operated in the mid-19th century: the parish constable, the Metropolitan Police, and the Bow Street horse patrol. The patrol, revived in 1805 to safeguard the turnpike roads out of London,[216] was first recorded in Finchley in 1818. By 1828 its third division operated as far as Whetstone and in 1836 four constables worked from Finchley (Highgate) and two from Whetstone.

The two patrols at Whetstone were No. 49 Bow Street Horse Patrol Smith whose beat included patrolling, walking or riding from Barnet to Archway - Highgate a distance of six miles twice a day and from the 8th mile stone to the 9th mile stone four times a day. No 50 Davis patrolled in the opposite direction either riding walking or patrolling the Finchley New Road, from the police station to Grand Junction Gate also a distance of six miles and from the 3rd to 4th mile stone 4 times a day[217]. The distance travelled each day by each patrol was 20 miles on average and they would look out for coaches, carts and riders travelling from the north down the main highway towards London looking for crime, criminals or victim of robbery and violence. Their duty was to prevent and deter highway robberies. Their greeting was 'Bow Street Horse Patrol' which was reassuring to travellers. The patrol would seek information from the toll gate keepers who would provide intelligence on the movements of individuals. When the two patrols met up on patrol or back at the station they would exchange the information which would also be passed onto other patrols at Finchley (Highgate).

There was also still a Bow Street horse patrol station on the Great North Road in 1851, which was occupied by four men. There were then eleven other policemen from the Metropolitan Police residing in the parish[218].

From 1840 Finchley was included in the Metropolitan Police District[219]. The freehold to a building and land at Whetstone, High Street was purchased in 1851[220]. A substantial brick with slate roof police station was built at Whetstone, on the east side of the main road on land purchased for £72, in 1851. The station included one set of married quarters had been developed for occupation in the same year. The station also had three cells space for prisoners who were dealt with by one sergeant and a further acting sergeant. The other accommodation consisted of eight rooms with scullery and mess room on the first floor. Outside, there were two coal pens, two water closets, a two stall stable, with dung and dust pens[221]. In 1855 Sergeant Ralph Norman was shown in charge of the police and horse patrol station[222].

There was a total of 12 constables posted to the station with four on the day shift and seven on night duty together with a floating constable on double relief duties[223]. This relief officer would cover for an officer who was absent or remain at the station ready to collect prisoners from another station with the trap and convey them to Barnet or to the court. The weekly rent for the two married men's accommodation was 3/4d (17p) whilst the two single constables paid 1s (5p) each[224].

In 1865[225] the vestry requested more police[226] and in 1873 a police station was opened in Church End, in a rented house. In 1871 two married officers and their families resided at Whetstone respectively paying 3/- (15p) and 2/9d (14p) per week rent[227]. By 1881 Constable (wt. no. 59752) William Chennell, his wife and daughter lived in married quarters above the station until 1900 when they had to vacate their lodgings on retirement.

Wentworth Lodge in Ballards Lane was bought in 1886 and a station was opened on

Whetstone Police Station. 1889 – 1965. 1230 High Road, Whetstone N20.

the site in 1889, closed in 1965, and rebuilt shortly afterwards.

Drill Practice

Officers and constables (including new recruits) of each division were to be instructed in drill formations and for 'S' and 'Y' Divisions the drill ground was located at Finchley. This took place regularly each week on Wednesdays between 12.30 – 2pm. Each police officer was issued with a drill manual which showed the drill formations in which they were to be instructed. There was mounted and foot drill although Superintendents were excluded from both. The officer appointed for taking charge of drill was normally and inspector. No drill classes were taken in inclement weather, during very hot periods or during the winter. Drill classes which were postponed would be notified to stations by the drill instructor using the telegraph system. The inspector provided a return to the superintendent of those attending drill including the dates and hours involved. In turn the superintendent was required to notify the Commissioner quarterly giving the numbers attending drill. The Superintendent of No. 3 District oversaw the general riding drill to ensure that all sergeants and inspectors were suitably trained. Even those recommended for promotion would not be advanced until they had passed the necessary examination in foot drill. For riding lessons police officers would be relieved of their normal duties and be taught by the inspector of the 'B' Division Reserve although no expenses or allowances would be granted[228].

A drill training ground was needed by the local superintendent in order to drill his men as part of their training and in order to ensure that police officers remained a disciplined group. The training consisted of not only foot drill or marching of groups of men but of horsemanship, where mounted police officers of all ranks would be put through their paces on horseback. At Whetstone a drill ground was found owned by Mr. G. R. Hey of Blue House Farm Whetstone N. Commencing from May 1880 the annual rent was £30 however by 1885 this had been dropped to £10 per annum. Mounted drill sessions numbering more than 5 annually would cost £2 extra for each occasion.

Whetstone station which also housed a married inspector and his family was in a lamentable state. The well in the garden had become polluted from a nearby leaking sewer pipe and was in need of connection to mains water supply immediately. Conditions were cramped with the married constable and his family being moved out and these rooms reallocated[229]. The three cells were no longer enough to house prisoners at the station and a further additional cell was required[230].

Burglary at North Finchley.

From 1888 until 1891 the inspector at Whetstone was Thomas Bissett who was sub inspector when he came to 'S' or Hampstead division in 1888. He was initially based at Albany Street, Regents Park but later moved to Whetstone. Whilst at Whestone, Bissett was summoned to a burglary which took place at the jeweler's shop of Mr John Walker of High Road, North Finchley. At about 4am the owner was disturbed by a noise in his shop and, going down stairs, he found the shutters broken open and a portion of the window cut or broken out. The glass appeared to have been cut with a diamond glass cutter. Missing from the display, were several pocket watch's which also bore the owners private mark, and several pins with a total value of £80. The police were called and the inspector arrived soon after where a search of the local area was made for suspects without any trace. The inspector recorded the details and immediately, through the telegraph, at the station sent the details to Scotland Yard and the various divisions for circulation. From there constable 196 'M' Division Albert Hatton at Stones End Police Station duly recorded the details in his note book during parade before leaving the station on his beat. Once in Blackfriars Road he was passing Mr. Hyams shop on the same day and saw a man offering to pledge (pawn) a watch to the shop owner. The constable decided to inquire about the watch and immediately, on inspecting it, found that it corresponded with the description that had been circulated. The constable asked a man now identified as George Baker to account for the possession of the watch and immediately, the suspect offered to take the constable back to his lodging and show him a receipt. Once outside the shop the suspect ran off, quickly followed by the police officer. The chase lasted some distance when the officer caught Baker who struggled ferociously for about 20 minutes. Supported by a passing car man and an officer of the 'L' Division, Baker was subdued and arrested. The property was identified by Inspector Bissett who visited Stones End Police Station as that stolen from the shop that day. The prisoner was released into the charge of the inspector and handcuffed to be taken back to Whetstone for charging. There were commendations for Inspector Bissett, and Constable Hatton from the chairman of the bench for their prompt action and vigilance which resulted in the arrest of Baker.

The 1887 Jubilee medal, the 1897 Jubilee (bar) and the 1902 Coronation medal awarded to Inspector Bissett

Bissett retired from the police in May 1891 and moved to Whitstable in Kent. He had received the 1887 Jubilee medal because he was part of the Queens celebrations. Unusually, he was able to return twice more as a re-joiner for brief periods and take part in the 1897 Jubilee celebrations and the 1902 coronation for which he was allowed a clasp in 1897 and a coronation medal in 1902. Because he was part of the reserve he was allowed a seven day re-joiner in 1897 and a 28 day re-joiner in 1902 despite being 60 years old at the time[231]. Copies of the medals are shown above.

The station call sign for the telegraph published in Police orders in 1893 was Whiskey Echo (WE) but by the 1920s this was changed[232] to Sierra Tango ST. In 1911 however the local council wanted to widen the road and compulsorily purchased a strip of land approximately 20ft x 20ft from the frontage in Friern Barnet lane[233]. By 1911, a new site for the police station had been purchased in Friern Barnet Lane but this was considered too small for use and was rebuilt in 1938. Ten years later in 1948, adjoining premises at the corner of High Road and Friern Barnet Lane were bought, and in 1960 a new station opened there and the old

Whetstone Police Station. 1960 – present day. 170 High Road, Whetstone London N20 0LW

one closed[234].

The address of the station was 170 High Road, N20 0LW. In 2012 the station was open from 0700 to 2200 daily, except Public Holidays and closed between 1000 - 1045 and 1800 - 1845 each day (to allow for refreshments of the staff).

---

[1]Kellys Directory 1840
[2]http://www.barnet.gov.uk/index/leisure-culture/local-history-heritage.htm#chip accessed on 2nd November 2011

[3] met.police.uk/Site/barnetaboutus?scope_id=1257246650510 accessed on 29th December 2011
[4] http://www.barnet.gov.uk/index/leisure-culture/local-history-heritage.htm#chip accessed on 2nd November 2011
[5] http://www.barnet4u.co.uk/barnet%20history/barnetfair.html accessed on 4th November 2011
[6] http://www.barnet.gov.uk/index/leisure-culture/local-history-heritage.htm#chip accessed on 2nd November 2011
[7] Kellys Law Directory 1841
[8] Metropolitan Police Surveyors Records
[9] List of Superintendents of Divisions 1829 - 1953
[10] Kellys law Directory 1855
[11] ibid
[12] Metropolitan Police Orders dated 20th June 1863
[13] Metropolitan Police Orders dated 4th February 1871
[14] Metropolitan Police Orders dated 12th December 1871
[15] Metropolitan Police Orders dated 6th December 1889
[16] Census records 1871
[17] Kellys Directory 1875
[18] Metropolitan Police Orders dated 4th February 1871
[19] Metropolitan Police Special Police Orders 1869
[20] ibid
[21] http://www.barnet4u.co.uk/barnet%20history/barnetfair.html accessed on 4th November 2011
[22] Metropolitan Police Orders dated 19th December 1871
[23] Metropolitan Police Special Orders 1873
[24] Metropolitan Police Surveyors Records 1899
[25] Kellys Directory 1890
[26] Copyhold of the Manor of Chipping Barnet and East Barnet cited in Back, J. (1975) 'Barnet Police Station' The Metropolitan Police Museum, Charlton, London.
[27] Metropolitan Police Surveyors Records 1912
[28] Back, J. (1975) 'Barnet Police Station' The Metropolitan Police Museum, Charlton, London.
[29] Metropolitan Police Surveyors records 1912
[30] Census Records 1901
[31] Census Records 1911
[32] Metropolitan Police Surveyors Records 1924
[33] Kellys Directory 1914 and 1915
[34] Metropolitan Police Divisional Map 1926
[35] Metropolitan Police Roll of Honour
[36] The Times 9th September 1935
[37] Metropolitan Police General Orders dated 31st May 1926
[38] Metropolitan Police Surveyors Book Folio 152
[39] Back, J. (1975) 'Barnet Police Station' The Metropolitan Police Museum, Charlton, London.
[40] Metropolitan Police List 1966
[41] Metropolitan Police General Orders dated 13th October 1972
[42] Metropolitan Police Press Release 7th April 1977
[43] http://content.met.police.uk/PoliceStation/barnet accessed on 25.4.12
[44] Metropolitan Police Orders dated 26th February 1957
[45] Metropolitan Police Orders dated 26th February 1957
[46] Metropolitan Police Orders dated 6th August 1964
[47] Metropolitan Police Orders dated 5th July 1968
[48] Metropolitan Police Orders dated 9th July 1971
[49] Kelly's Law Directory 1841 p877
[50] Kellys Directory 1855
[51] Metropolitan Police Orders dated 4th February 1871
[52] Metropolitan Police Special Police Orders 1869
[53] Metropolitan Police General Orders 1893
[54] Metropolitan Police Surveyors Records 1912
[55] Metropolitan Police Surveyors Records 1912 p28
[56] Metropolitan Police Surveyors Records 1912 p30

[57] Kellys Directory 1914
[58] MPS Station closures Reduced Opening 1997 - 2000
[59] Colindale – A modern building for the 21st Century – The Job
[60] ibid
[61] ibid
[62] Metropolitan Police hygiene Inspection report of Police Premises 1880
[63] Col. W. T. Reay (1919) The Specials – How they served London
[64] Metropolitan Police General Orders 1893
[65] Kellys Directory 1890
[66] Kellys Directory 1894
[67] Metropolitan Police Surveyors Records 1912 and 1924
[68] Kellys directory 1914
[69] The Police and Constabulary Almanac 1919, 1929 and 1932
[70] The Police Property List 1947 MEPO4/133
[71] Google earth accessed on 22nd November 2011
[72] http://www.elstreeborehamwood-tc.gov.uk/joomla15/town-history.html accessed on 6th January 2012
[73] Metropolitan Police Map 1853
[74] Metropolitan Police Surveyors Records
[75] Metropolitan Police Orders dated 4th February 1871
[76] Metropolitan Police Surveyors Records
[77] Metropolitan Police Orders dated 15th November 1869
[78] Metropolitan Police Orders dated 23rd June 1893
[79] The Police Property list 1947 MEPO 4/133
[80] Kellys Directory 1914
[81] http://www.elstreeborehamwood-tc.gov.uk/joomla15/town-history.html acccessed 6th January 2012
[82] Metropolitan Police General Orders 1893
[83] Metropolitan Police Orders dated 29th July 1960
[84] Metropolitan Police Orders dated 6th August 1964
[85] Metropolitan Police Orders dated 1st November 1911
[86] Barnet Times dated 4th Jan 1973
[87] Martin, S (1970) The Policing of Finchley through the ages.
[88] ibid
[89] Metropolitan Police Surveyors Records
[90] Martin, S. (1970) The policing of Finchley through the ages. MPS Historic Collection ESB
[91] ibid
[92] ibid
[93] ibid
[94] The History of Ballards Lane by C.O. Banks, printed in the Finchley Press of 1927/8 C/603/LF*vol.1.pages 20/21).
[95] Ibid bk.1 folio 9264.
[96] Metropolitan Police hygiene Inspection report of Police Premises 1880 p70
[97] Census records 1881
[98] Kelly's Directory 1885
[99] Metropolitan Police Surveyors Records, Historic collection Empress State Building.
[100] Metropolitan Police Surveyors Records Historic collection Empress State Building
[101] Fletcher, J. (1972) Briefing note. Metropolitan Police Estates Management Department
[102] The Finchley Brochure 1905
[103] The History of Ballards Lane by C.O. Banks, printed in the Finchley Press of 1927/8 L942/191 LM402
[104] Metropolitan Police Surveyors Records 1924
[105] Martin, S. (1970) The policing of Finchley through the ages. MPS Historic Collection ESB
[106] Metropolitan Police General Orders 1893
[107] Kirchners Police Almanac 1907
[108] The Police Review and Parade Gossip 5th Aug 1910
[109] Metropolitan Police War Duty Hints March 1939
[110] Metropolitan Police Orders dated 29th August 1930

[111] London Gazette 1943
[112] The Job 19th January 1968 p2
[113] Metropolitan Police List 1965
[114] http://content.met.police.uk/PoliceStation/goldersgreen accessed on 3rd January 2012
[115] John Back Archive. The Metropolitan Police Collection ESB
[116] Metropolitan Police Orders dated 31st October 1913
[117] Metropolitan Police Orders dated 29th August 1930
[118] Metropolitan Police Orders dated 28th November 1933
[119] Metropolitan Police Surveyors records 1924
[120] The Police List 1962
[121] Metropolitan Police List 1966
[122] Metropolitan Police Orders dated 6th August 1964
[123] Metropolitan Police Orders dated 9th July 1971
[124] Finchley Press 7th January 1972
[125] The Annual report of the Golders Green and Finchley division 1990
[126] http://intranet.aware.mps/corporate/newarchive2010/11november210/sntbases
[127] French, I. (1984) Hendon Police. Local police charity publication in aid of 2 Area Widows and Orphans.
[128] Bacon, G. W.(1888) London and Suburbs
[129] French, I. (1984) Hendon Police. Local police charity publication in aid of 2 Area Widows and Orphans (p7)
[130] French, I. (1984) Hendon Police. Local police charity publication in aid of 2 Area Widows and Orphans (p91)
[131] Metropolitan Police Special Orders 1869
[132] Ex inf. Hendon Libr
[133] General Orders 1893
[134] Metropolitan Police Role of Honour
[135] Census records 1911
[136] http://www.barnet.gov.uk/index/leisure-culture/local-history-heritage.htm#chip accessed on 2nd November 2011
[137] French, I. (1984) Hendon Police. Local police charity publication in aid of 2 Area Widows and Orphans (p73)
[138] Ibid (p74)
[139] Metropolitan Police Orders dated 29th April 1942
[140] French, I. (1984) Hendon Police. Local police charity publication in aid of 2 Area Widows and Orphans (p76)
[141] Ibid (p77)
[142] Ibid (pp77-78)
[143] French, I. (1984) Hendon Police. Local police charity publication in aid of 2 Area Widows and Orphans (p78)
[144] Ibid (p83)
[145] ibid (p84)
[146] ibid
[147] Ibid (p87)
[148] ibid
[149] Ibid (p87)
[150] Ibid (p95)
[151] Ibid (p137)
[152] (1998) Daly Mail, May 22nd p62
[153] http://policeauthority.org/metropolitan/committees/finres/2011/1215/10/index.html accessed on 8.12.12
[154] http://uk.answers.yahoo.com/question/index?qid=20071010084856AAeTJVH accessed on 4.11.12
[155] Metropolitan Police property List 1947
[156] Chief Inspector WWR Fleming (196??) Police Driving School- A history of Police Transport and Driver Training with additions by J Kirby
[157] ibid
[158] ibid
[159] ibid
[160] http://content.met.police.uk/Site/drivingschoolhistory accessed on 4.11.12
[161] http://en.wikipedia.org/wiki/Roadcraf accessed on 4.11.12
[162] Chief Inspector WWR Fleming (196??) Police Driving School- A history of Police Transport and Driver Training p39
[163] Fido, M.. and Skinner, K. (1999) The Official Encyclopaedia of Scotland yard Virgin, London

[164] Private communication with author
[165] lhttp://transact.westminster.gov.uk/CSU/Planning%20Applications%20Committees/Pre%202008/Planning_and_City_Development_Committee/2006/09%20-%205%20October/ITEM%2001%20-%20Peel%20House,%20105%20Regency%20Street,%20SW1.pdf accessed on 18.11.12
[166] http://www.friendsreunited.co.uk/drill-lesson-b-course-1976/Memory/7a599a97-892b-4bce-81a1-a0f000d9c0a4 accessed on 27.11.12
[167] Metropolitan Police Surveyors Records 1912
[168] MPS Station Closures and Reduced Opening Hours 1997 - 2000
[169] http://www.pbhistory.co.uk/buildings/police.html accessed on 2.2.12
[170] Census Records 1871
[171] ibid
[172] Condition of Stations (1881) The Home Department. London
[173] Census Records 1891
[174] bid
[175] Martin, S. (1970) The Policing of Finchley through the ages.
[176] http://www.british-history.ac.uk/report.aspx accessed on 9th November 2011
[177] Metropolitan Police General Orders 1893
[178] Col. W. T. Reay (1919) The Specials – How they served London
[179] http://www.pbhistory.co.uk/buildings/police.html accessed on 2.2.12
[180] Police Property List 1947
[181] ibid
[182] Police and Constabulary Almanac 1932
[183] The History of Ballards Lane by C.O. Banks, printed in the Finchley Press of 1927/8 C/603/LF
[184] Post Office Directory 1849 p1528
[185] Metropolitan Police Surveyors Records
[186] Census Records 1851
[187] Metropolitan Police Surveyors Records
[188] Metropolitan Police Special Police Order 1869
[189] Metropolitan Police Surveyors Records
[190] Metropolitan Police Surveyors Records 1912 p29
[191] Metropolitan Police Special Orders 1869
[192] ibid
[193] Metropolitan Police General Orders 1893
[194] Census records 1901
[195] ibid
[196] Census records 1901
[197] Kellys Directory 1914
[198] Metropolitan Police Orders dated 4th March 1957
[199] Metropolitan Police Surveyors Records
[200] Metropolitan Police Special Orders 1869
[201] Metropolitan Police Orders dated 4th February 1871
[202] Kelly's directory 1899
[203] Census records 1901
[204] Census records 1911
[205] http://www.pbhistory.co.uk/buildings/police.html accessed on 2.2.12
[206] Metropolitan Police Surveyors memo and Back .J. (1975) West Hendon Police Station. Metropolitan Police Collection, ESB
[207] Metropolitan Police Surveyors memo and Back .J. (1975) West Hendon Police Station. Metropolitan Police Collection, ESB
[208] Metropolitan Police Surveyors memo and Back .J. (1975) West Hendon Police Station. Metropolitan Police Collection, ESB
[209] Metropolitan Police Orders dated 26th March 1965
[210] Metropolitan Police List 1966
[211] ibid

[212] Metropolitan Police Orders dated 6th February 1970
[213] MPS Station Closures and Reduced Opening Hours 1997 - 2000
[214] http://www.british-history.ac.uk/report.aspx?compid=22507&strquery=police accessed on 9th November 2011
[215] ibid
[216] A. Babington, *A House in Bow St.* 194
[217] Martin, S. (1970) The policing of Finchley through the ages. MPS Historic Collection ESB
[218] http://www.british-history.ac.uk/report.aspx?compid=22507&strquery=police accessed on 9th November 2011
[219] London. Gaz. 13 Oct. 1840, p. 2250
[220] Metropolitan Police Surveyors Records 1912
[221] Metropolitan Police Surveyors Records
[222] Kellys Directory of Herts, Essex and Middlesex 1855
[223] Metropolitan Police Special Police Order 1869
[224] Metropolitan Police Surveyors Records
[225] O.S. Map 6", Mdx. VI. SE. (1867-73 edn.); ex inf. New Scotland Yd. rec. officer.
[226] B.L.H.L., P.A.F. 1/9
[227] Metropolitan Police Orders dated 4th February 1871
[228] Metropolitan Police Instruction Manual 1873
[229] Metropolitan Police hygiene Inspection report of Police Premises 1880 p70
[230] ibid
[231] Private correspondence from David Collett
[232] General Orders 1893
[233] Metropolitan Police Surveyors Records 1912 and 1924
[234] http://www.british-history.ac.uk/report.aspx?compid=22507&strquery=police accessed on 9th November 2011

Chapter 3

The London Borough of Brent

by David Swinden

Introduction

The London Borough of Brent is divided by the river Brent into two major parts, Willesden and Wembley. In 1965 these two separate districts were joined to form a new London borough. It covers an area of 17 square miles (44 square kms) with a population of 263,464 people[1].

The Borough started as a collection of villages and farms surrounded by fields and woods. It was transformed into a London suburb by the arrival of the railways and extensive house building in the 19th and early 20th centuries.

Chief Superintendent Matthew Gardner
Borough Commander

Brent takes in much of Kilburn. The main thoroughfare running northwest –southeast is Kilburn High Road, part of the modern A5 road which forms the boundary between the boroughs of Brent and Camden.

In 2013 the Borough was under the command of Chief Superintendent Matthew Gardner. The four main police stations in the London Borough of Brent are Harlesden , Kilburn, Wembley and Willesden Green. In addition there are 21 Safer Neighbourhood teams situated across the borough. Mention is also made of Kingsbury Police Station which is now closed. Currently (2013) both Kilburn and Wembley Police stations are open 24 hours per day.

Harlesden Police Station (formerly named Willesden until 1896)

The first Police Station in the area was established in 1840 in a small house in Stonebridge. It was a one of a terrace of properties known as 'Ivy Cottages' and in 1911, long after police vacated this building, it was being used as a greengrocer's shop. There were only two constables and they covered an area from Kilburn Lane to Harrow including Kilburn, Willesden Green, Cricklewood, Hendon and Kingsbury [2].

In 1841 there were three policemen residing in Willesden according to the 1841 Census, but one was living at 'Railway Cottage' and may have been a railway policeman. The census in 1841 also shows there were two policemen living at Wood Lodge, Wembley [3].

In 1860 a police station was opened in Craven Park Road, at the junction of St. Mary's Road, Harlesden, with three Police Sergeants and four Police Constables. The cost of erecting the Police Station was £1132.

Willesden Police Station 1860 – 1913   Craven Park Road, Harlesden

The land was leased from James Wright of Willesden, Middlesex, from Lady Day, 1860 for 99 years. Rental for the land was £10 per year with the Receiver paying the rates, taxes, repairs and the insurance[4]. The police station had a charge room, inspector's office, store, three cells, two stalls, an ambulance shed, water closets, a cleaning shed and a stove. The freehold of the land was purchased by the Receiver in August 1899 for £440[5]. Eventually it was sold to Middlesex Standing Joint Committee for £1350 on 31st July 1913.

Willesden was shown as being a police station on 'S' or Hampstead Division in 1864[6], and was transferred to 'X' Paddington Division in 1865[7]. The station was called Willesden Police Station up until July 1896 when the new Willesden Green Station was opened and Willesden was renamed Harlesden Police Station[8].

Meanwhile, in 1879 Willesden was a Sectional Station on 'X' Division under the command of Superintendent Hugh Eccles and Chief Inspector George Browning. They were assisted by ten Inspectors. 'X' or Kilburn Division at this time covered a total of thirteen police stations[9].

In 1881 a report on the condition of all London police stations was critical of a number of issues. One in particular was that there were married quarters within the Station which were occupied by a married Police Inspector and a married Constable. The Inspector's kitchen was the Constable's wash-house [10].

Inspector George Robert Hodder

In November 1900 an Inspector George Robert Hodder, (wt. no. 62839), who joined the Metropolitan Police in 1878, retired from the Force whilst serving at Harlesden. He came to Harlesden in 1896 to assist a Sub-Divisional Inspector Joseph Cooper whose workload had increased considerably[11]. Inspector Sydney Smith was also stationed at Harlesden in 1899. Cooper moved to Harlesden as Sub-Divisional Inspector where he resided in 1891[12]. When Cooper retired, aged 48 years old in 1901, he remained in Willesden living at 4, Leighton Gardens with his wife and four children who were all employed by then[13].

On the retirement of Inspector Hodder there was a glowing tribute to his contribution to the community in the local press, which said,

> '…….Inspector Hodder will be a great loss to the district. During his service locally he had won the esteem of his fellow officers and men, but the regard of very many of the civil residents with whom his public work on the religious and temperance platform, as well as his professional duties, had brought him in contact. Mr Hodder was shrewd and capable in his office as second in command in the sub district and his qualities of tact and strict justice, tempered with good humour, made him many friends and few enemies. His Post Office service proceeding his Police duty rendered his retirement an earlier one than would otherwise have occurred, but whilst in the Police Service he won hearty praise from his superiors and more than one public commendation for saving life from fire in circumstances demanding great bravery and readiness of action'[14].

On retirement Inspector Hodder became involved with the Police Pensioners Executive, the forerunner of the National Association of Retired Police

Officers (N.A.R.P.O.). He was a founder member of the Retired Police Officers Association in 1910 and was elected its first Chairman. When this group became N.A.R.P.O. he was elected Chairman of that organisation. He was also actively involved with the Baptist Church and the Temperance Movement. He died in October 1932[15].

In the early 1900s plans were made to erect a new police station at Harlesden. A site was eventually found on the "West Ella" estate. In June 1909 a freehold parcel of land on this estate was purchased for £1,650 by Messrs Ryde and Sons acting for the Receiver at an auction of surplus properties owned by the Middlesex County Council. The site was situated on the south-east corner of the estate, i.e. Craven Park junction with Ella Road. The Home Office approved the purchase of the site, known as 'Fortune Gate', and returned the conveyance in October 1909[16].

Harlesden Police Station 1913 – present day. 76, Craven Park, Harlesden.

There was a delay in developing the site because of restrictive covenants in the deeds which dated back to 1894. One of the covenants stated that 'no building or lot shall be used for any purpose which may be a nuisance or annoyance'. Counsel's opinion was sought and advised the Receiver to go ahead and build the police station. The erection of the station was authorised by the Metropolitan Police Act of 1886 which incorporated the Land Clauses Consolidation Act of 1845[17].

In 1894 the station was still called Willesden when Constable (wt. no. 48245) James W. Swaine, retired on pension as the oldest serving mounted police officer in the Metropolitan Police, having served 24 years of his 27 year's service at Willesden[18].

By 1911 the strength had increased to one Sub-Divisional Inspector, three Inspectors, 15 Sergeants, and 78 Constables. On the night of the census in 1911 Inspector William Perry his wife Esther and family together with a large number of single Constables were all shown as residing at the police station[19]. When the new station was opened in July 1913 the old police station was closed down and eventually demolished. Later, Willesden Magistrates Court was erected on the site[20]. In 1911 Inspector William Dingle, (wt. no. 75042), then aged 44 years from Harlesden Police Station, resided at 4, Elynfield Road, Harlesden with his wife and five children in a 6-room house with two lodgers[21]. Dingle had joined the police in 1889.

The new station, designed John Dixon Butler, the Metropolitan Police Surveyor, was built and opened for business in July 1913[22]. Harlesden then took over the responsibilities of the Sub-Division and old Kilburn Police Station became a 'section house' and storage facility. The old building was reduced to rubble after an air raid in 1940 which killed a number of police staff – see under Kilburn Police Station.

During World War 1, the war effort intensified, the fields of the Royal Agricultural Show Ground at Park Royal were taken over for war use, and munitions factories were built. The largest of these, in Acton Lane, employed seven thousand people, mainly women, including many mothers[23]. Mrs S. Chambers of Winchelsea Road, Harlesden was a special war worker who worked in munitions during World War 1. She was employed at the National Filling Factory No. 3 at Park Royal, Willesden and later as a packer of fuses for bombs and grenades. She was a good worker and also became a police woman at the filling factory. Tragically she met her death during an accident at the plant.

The women police were established by Margaret Damer Dawson and Mary Allen, and Mrs Chambers was one of the early police women who were needed by the Munitions Minister and the War effort. Chambers' work initially was to fill shells with gun cotton and nitro-glycerine (cordite)[24]. Both men and women on essential war work were issued with an "on war service" badge. The men wore it on their lapel, so that they would not be accused of being cowards because they were not in uniform. Women also wore it with pride, but as a brooch or hat pin[25]. There were 140 men and 345 women employed at Park Royal. The workers were not pressed hard to do their work as the management wanted them to be slow and careful when handling the munitions so as to avoid accidents.

Sub Divisional Inspector William Macmillan, (wt. no. 95809), (who had transferred from 'H' or Whitechapel Division in 1909) was in charge of Harlesden up until 1915 when he was promoted to Chief Inspector and sent to 'F' or Paddington Division. Macmillan, a Scotsman from Perthshire, was destined for higher office, became Superintendent of 'K' or Bow Division in 1920[26] and retired in July 1929.

By 1915 the police station was under the command of Sub-Divisional Inspector (wt. no. 79509) William Gilbert Grimmett and in addition to Inspector (wt. no. 75042) William Dingle, there were also George Barnett (wt. no. 85719) and later in 1916 (wt. no. 78770) Oliver Millard[27]. Life at Harlesden must have suited Dingle since he remained there until January 1919 when he retired on pension after 30 years' service with an annual pension of £151. 6s 5d (£151.32). Grimmett later retired on pension from Harlesden in November 1921.

By 1928 Harlesden was designated a sub-divisional station of 'X' or Kilburn Division with Willesden Green and Wembley as its sectional stations.

In the reorganisation of the Divisions north of the Thames in December 1933 Harlesden remained a sub-divisional station[28]. The address, in 1938, of Harlesden Police Station was 76, Craven Park at the junction of High Road[29].

William George Gane, born 21st January 1911 in Harlesden, joined the War Reserve and was posted to Harlesden until October 1943 when he joined the Royal Navy. As a result of his police experience, he transferred to the Regulating Branch (naval police) in October 1944 as an acting Regulating Petty Officer (Master at Arms). He was discharged in August 1946 from service on the battleship HMS Rodney[30].

By 1955 Superintendent R. Linge was in charge of Harlesden Police Sub-Division.[31].

In 1965 the Local Authority boundaries changed and Harlesden found itself as a Sub-Division on the newly formed 'Q' Division. Its station code became 'QH' and its sectional stations were Willesden Green 'QL' and Kilburn 'QK'[32].

Harlesden was now part of the London Borough of Brent. In 2012 the station address was 76, Craven Park, NW10 8RJ and its opening hours 07:00 to 21:00, closed for breaks between 10:00 to 11:00 and 17:00 to 1800[33].

Kilburn Police Station

By 1851 there was a police station at Kilburn Lane[34]. Kilburn was also served by successive stations at 11-13 High Road (1870-1891), and Salusbury Road from 1891 until it closed in 1938[35]. Salusbury Road Police Station existed before other public buildings were erected next to it in 1894[36].

Kilburn Police Section House, at 5 & 6 Kempshall Terrace Kilburn, was a brick and slate building which had been repaired and adapted for occupation. The premises were leased from Henry and John Childs from December 1870 until December 1891. On the ground floor of one of buildings there was a reserve room, a charge room and 2 cells, and a kitchen in the basement. In the other building the ground floor consisted of a mess room and a brushing room. The basement had a washing room and a kitchen[37].

Police also rented a coach house and stable at 23, Bridge Street, Kilburn from June 1871 until June 1892, from Peter Mudie, Esq of Bridge Crescent, Kilburn[38].

At 11-13 High Road, Kilburn a portion of land and the houses thereon were leased from Mrs Jane Roy of Marl Hill, Carisbrooke, Isle of Wight at an annual rental of £107. The lease was from 1870 until Christmas 1891. The houses were converted for use by Police and this new police station was taken into use on 12th February 1872[39].

In June 1889, a freehold plot of land was purchased from the Ecclesiastical Commissioners for England for the sum of £960 for the erection of a new police station. It had a frontage of 80 feet in Salusbury Road, Kilburn, at the junction of Mortimer Road. The land then extended for a length of 160 feet along Mortimer Road. In December 1889 the conveyance for the site was received from the Home Office[40]. The conditions imposed were that if the Receiver wished to dispose of this property at any time, or make use of land other than for police, county or municipal purposes, six months notice must be given to the Ecclesiastical Commissioners who had the right to re-purchase.

In order to provide for the more efficient performance of the duties at Ealing, Acton and Hanwell, portions of Brentford, Shepherds Bush and Chiswick sub-divisions of 'T' or Hammersmith Division, were transferred to 'X' or Kilburn Division. The boundaries were then revised accordingly[41], and Harrow Road became the headquarters station from 1888.

The new police station and the section house were completed in 1891/2 at a cost of £5,905[42], and the station was opened in December 1891[43]. The single men's quarters at the new station were ready for occupation in March 1892.

The lodging assessment was at 1s (5p) each per week for the 20 single Constables[44].

In 1890 'X' Division was under the command of Superintendent George Carr, and at Kilburn were Inspectors Joseph W. Cooper, (wt. no. 52151), W. Redstone, N. Mansfield and A. McDonald[45]. Cooper joined the police in 1869 and was shown on 'X' Division located at Kilburn in 1891, where he resided in the married quarters with his wife and five children in the newly-opened police station. He had to move from the premises when he retired in 1899 after 30 years service. By 1893 Cooper had been promoted to Sub Divisional Inspector. In 1893 'X' Division was now under the command of Superintendent James Cuthbert, and at Kilburn were Inspectors N. Mansfield, A. McDonald and George Hodder[46].

Kilburn Police Station. 1891 – 1940 Salusbury Road, Kilburn, NW.

In September 1893 Constable 196 Craney, 'X' Division, was patrolling his beat in Victoria Road, Kilburn when his attention was drawn to a woman outside no. 18 who stated the house was on fire. The officer entered the building and went to the top floor where the occupant was desperately trying to put out a fire which had started when a paraffin stove had been accidentally knocked over. The officer put out the fire and rendered first aid to the occupant who had sustained burns to his hands. The occupant was not insured so was unlikely to have been compensated for any damage to the property[47].

Superintendent Cuthbert was still in charge of 'X' or Kilburn Division in 1895, and assisted by Sub-Divisional Inspector George Bridgen[48]. In 1898 Inspector

William Bell, taking over from Cooper, was the officer in charge of Kilburn Police Station and its area which was a sectional station to Harrow Road. Between 1895 - 98 Harlesden Sub Division was created and Willesden became a sectional station with Harrow.

The picture below shows Inspector Charles Taylor of Kilburn with his cycle

Inspector Charles Taylor with his Station Sergeant in the yard at Kilburn

together with the Station Sergeant in about 1910. Taylor stayed at Kilburn until about 1917[49]. The Secretary of State sanctioned the use of pedal cycles for patrol duty especially in outer lying stations in 1904, and an allowance was paid to police officers who supplied and maintained their own machines. The sum of 10d (4p) per day was paid to chief inspectors and sub divisional inspectors who were authorised by the divisional superintendent. Cleaning and maintaining the cycle was the responsibility of the officer concerned and was to be carried out in their own time. Each wednesday cycles would be inspected by the sub-divisional inspector or station officer (at the same time as pay parade), and the details were recorded in the station Occurrence Book (OB). Inspectors and station sergeants were paid 8d (3p) per day whilst for sergeants and constables the daily rate was 6d (2.5p). Supervision using a cycle was made easier although Inspectors still had their horses. Serious damage to a cycle which was caused in the normal course of daily police work was paid for from official funds, but if the damage was due to neglect then no compensation would be allowed[50].

Kilburn was a sectional station to Harrow Road in 1903. Taylor stayed at Kilburn until about 1917[51].

By 1918 the Superintendent of 'X' Division was James William Olive[52], (see chapter endnote 52) and at that time there were just four stations at Kilburn, Harrow Road, Willesden Green and Harlesden. At Kilburn there were three Inspectors Charles Taylor, Arthur Macer and Thomas Brain[53]. The address of Kilburn Police Station in 1924 was shown as 38 Salusbury Road [54].

The boundaries of Divisions north of the Thames were revised again in effect from 1st December 1933[55].

Kilburn Station was closed at 6am 1st March 1938, and all business was transferred to Harrow Road[56]. The station was converted into a section house, and on the outbreak of the war in 1939 it became a Group Reserve Centre.

On the 6th November 1940 the station received a direct hit by three high incendiary bombs and it was completely demolished. Fourteen out of the eighteen people on duty were killed. Kilburn continued to be policed from Harrow Road which was the Divisional Headquarters of 'X' Division until 31st March 1965[57].

Constable Don Light was on duty at Kilburn Station Police that night in 1940 when the station was destroyed. Describing in 1971 what happened that night he said,

> 'I was returning to the station having dealt with a fire. It was a terrible night, with bombs falling all over the place. The whole ground seemed to be alight. When we were about twenty yards from the station, which was the Group Reserve Centre, we heard a couple of 'crumps' and threw ourselves flat. I looked up to see what was like a million red-hot coals flying into the air. There were blokes from all over London who came to help, but it was no good. The bomb fell directly on the station. There was only one person alive when I went in and he died within minutes. There were 14 killed out of 18 on duty' [58].

Among those who died on that day were Constables 119605 John Brown, 124990 Clifford Davies, 094375 Charlie Summers (Re-engaged pensioner) and

Kilburn Police Station (temporary) 1965 -1967. 36, Salusbury Road, NW6

124285 Charles MacInnes, and War Reserve Constables (wt. no. 07717) George Borham, (wt. no. 23425) Leonard Bowes, (wt. no. 07737 Thomas Coe, (wt. no. 22374) Thomas Craven, (wt. no. 07753) Llewellyn Davies, (wt. no. 07787) Gerard Harvey, (wt. no. 07859) George Smith and (wt. no. 22586) George Wallis[59]. In addition Mr Robert Vose, station cleaner, also died that night[60]

A new police station, a prefabricated building at 36, Salusbury Road, NW6, was used from 1st April 1965[61]. Kilburn then became a sectional station of Harlesden (QH) Sub-Division in the newly-formed London Borough of Brent.

The freehold of a house at 2, Harvist Road was obtained in 1967. The CID moved from the temporary station into this house in 1969. The Receiver purchased the premises of the fire station and the mortuary which were next to the Kilburn site in 1970 with a view to erecting a new police station on the now enlarged site at Harvist Road[62].

In May 1977 Kilburn Police moved to a building in Albert Road, NW6 and the pre-fabricated building was vacated and shut for police purposes. This was a quarter of a mile from the one at 2, Harvist Road. The Albert Road premises were to be used for about two years until a permanent police station was rebuilt at the site of Harvist Road junction with Salusbury Road[63].

On 20th March 1980 the new Kilburn Police Station was opened by the Home Secretary, William Whitelaw, before an invited audience of local dignitaries. The Commissioner, Sir David McNee, invited the Home Secretary to unveil a plaque commemorating the event[64]. Another guest at the opening was retired Station Sergeant William Watson who was on duty in 1940 in Harrow Road when the bomb fell on Kilburn. A number of his friends were amongst those persons killed on that night.

Kilburn Police Station. 1967-1977. 2, Harvist Road, NW6

In 1980 the new station became the divisional headquarters and Harlesden Division was renamed Kilburn Division under the command of Chief Superintendent George Wise. The new station cost £1,000,000 and took three years to build[65].

Kilburn Police Station 1980 – present day. 38, Salusbury Road, Kilburn, NW6 6NN

In 2001 Kilburn was located at 38, Salusbury

Road, London, NW6 6NN with the station code (QK). The station was open 24 hours a day every day of the year and was also a station for the detaining and charging of prisoners.

Brent Police Office

The front counter service at Carey Way opened on 7th May 2001, (Mondays to Saturdays). There were also plans for police 'shops' or 'safety shops' under two regeneration plans in the borough. These would be in Kilburn High Road and on the South Kilburn Estate, although both were dependent on external funding[66].

Kingsbury Police Station

A temporary police office was established on this site during the petrol strike in the 1970s. The official date of the opening of the building was 23rd July 1973

Kingsbury Police Station. 1973 - 1977. 5 The Mall, Kingsbury, Middlesex.

and it took the code 'QY'. The address was 5, The Mall, Kingsbury and it was situated by the side of the cadet training centre. The permanent police station was built, and became fully operational and opened in 1977. Superintendent Ken Wright said at the time:

> 'There has been a long felt need to provide the people of Kingsbury with a better service. It's a long way to Wembley and this arrangement is obviously more convenient' [67].

By 2000 the Metropolitan Police had left the cadet training centre and the local authority planning committee agreed to a change of use for the site, and for the 106 separate rooms to be turned into a hostel for the homeless. It had also become prime land for further building. In December 2009 the local authority received a further application to demolish the existing buildings. This was approved and in 2012 the area of 1-3, The Mall was a large building site[68].

Kingsbury Police Station. 1973 – 2012. 5, The Mall, Kenton.

Meanwhile the small area, at the edge of the building site on which the Kingsbury Police Station was sited remained untouched although by 2012 it was closed to the public.

In 2012 a police office was built in Kingsbury which housed the Safer Neighbourhoods team located at Unit 19, Kingsbury Trading Estate, Barningham Way, Kingsbury, NW9 8AU[69].

Wembley Police Station

In December 1893 the occupant of Newton Villa, East Lane, Wembley, Middlesex wrote a letter to Willesden police station drawing attention to the need for adequate police protection in the Wembley area. Wembley Urban District Council had also been asking for better police coverage. The various new railways were bringing large numbers of vagrants to the area.[70]

In April 1900, the Home Office sanctioned an increase in the Force of two Constables for fixed point duty at the bridge on the main road at Sudbury and

Wembley railway station. This had been suggested by the Sub-Divisional Inspector at Harlesden and supported by the Superintendent 'X' Division. The fixed point was to be manned from 9am to 3pm daily, and it marked the boundary between Harlesden and Harrow police sections[71].

Wembley Urban District Council made a further request in 1902 for more

Wembley Police Station. 1910 – 1971. 167, Harrow Road, Wembley.
In 1950 re-named 551, High Street, Wembley

Police in the area, especially as they were contributing nearly £1000 a year to the police rate. The police then installed a 'fixed point box' with telephonic communication with the police station at Harlesden. This replaced the two fixed point men on the railway bridge at Sudbury and Wembley Railway Station. The box was erected in 1903 and was manned continuously until the new Wembley Police Station was opened in 1910[72].

Early in 1904 a search was made in the Wembley area for a site for a new police station. Some land, with a frontage to the Harrow Road junction of Ranelagh Road, was purchased in February 1905, by the Receiver, with the authority of the Home Office, for £1200[73]. This freehold piece of land formed part of the Curtis Estate. The police station was built and opened for business in February 1910.

In 1923 the Football Association Cup Final was held at the then newly opened Wembley Stadium. The organisers had not planned for such an overwhelming interest in the venue. Whilst the venue could accommodate up to 120,000 persons an additional 150,000 people turned up to watch the game. Fans stormed the gates and eventually there were about 200,000 persons on the pitch. A number of mounted police officers were on the pitch trying to move the crowds back but one police horse stood out from the crowd. A large grey horse named 'Billy', with its rider Constable George Scorey, became known as the 'White Horse' when shown on black and white film of the event. The crowd were eventually forced back to the touchline by the police horses. 'Billy' died in 1930, and one of his hooves was polished, mounted and presented to Constable Scorey. When the newly rebuilt Wembley Stadium was opened in 2007 fans poured into the venue via a footbridge named 'White Horse' a lasting tribute to 'Billy'[74].

Sergeant Walter Wheaton

The picture shows Sergeant Walter Wheaton, (warrant no. 99308), of Wembley at the British Empire Exhibition in 1924. A temporary police station was opened within the grounds at Wembley. There were plenty of opportunities for officers at Wembley Police Station to take part in special events at Wembley. This not only included football matches but exhibitions to showcase British and Commonwealth products. Wheaton retired from 'X' Division in 1935.

Wembley District Garage was built and the police station was reconstructed during the years 1935/36. The postal address at the time was 167, High Road, Wembley but later, in 1951, it was renumbered 551, High Road, Wembley. A freehold strip of land was purchased in July 1958 between the police station and 6, Ranelagh Road for £905 with a view to extending Wembley Police Station in the future.

The Home Office gave its authority in 1960 to purchase land to provide headquarters offices for the proposed new 'Q' Division. It was thought that the new Harrow Police Station could be enlarged to accommodate a divisional station. A site at Sudbury Hall, Harrow Road, Wembley was offered for sale by auction in May 1961. The proposed 'Q' Division covered most of Harrow and Uxbridge Divisions, on which Wembley was the innermost section. The site of Wembley Police Station and the district garage in 1960 was too small for a divisional station so the Sudbury Hall site was purchased in June 1961 for £90,000. This was large enough for the erection of a new Divisional Headquarters Station with room at the rear for a section house to accommodate 100 single police officers[75].

The reorganisation of the Force took place on the 1st April 1965[76], with the new London Borough of Brent coming into existence. Wembley was designated the Divisional Headquarters, but pending the completion of the new Station the Divisional Headquarters was accommodated at Harrow Old Police Station, 76, West Street, Harrow-on-the-Hill.

Wembley Police Station 1971 – present day.
603. Harrow Road. Wemblev. Middlesex. HAO 2HH

Stage one was completed at the Wembley site when the new section house opened in February 1965[77]. The address was 603, Harrow Road, Wembley.

Stage two, the new Wembley Police Station, was completed and opened in June 1971[78].

On the opening of the new Wembley Police Station the old station became a traffic warden centre. The Police Headquarters for 'Q' Division, moved into the two top floors of the new Wembley Police Station in 1971.

In 2001 a review of the whole estate was undertaken by the Metropolitan Police Authority (MPA) in conjunction with the Property Services Department. It stipulated that substantial renovation was required at Wembley Police Station costing in the region of £9,788,000 which included £740,000 for a new communications infrastructure and also included central charging facilities and headquarters functions at the station. Other functions carried out at Kilburn were also added to the new plans[79]. In 2003 work commenced which included converting the old police section house which was then to be re-named Sudbury House after an old building situated nearby in the 1880s. The new accommodation provided five floors of office space and catering facilities for police officers and support staff, but new demands increased the costs of the project which also needed to reflect diversity and disabilities policies[80].

In 2004 Wembley Constable Pirthi Ralpal Singh Bedi aged 24 was killed in a traffic accident and the conference room at Wembley Police Station was dedicated to his memory[81]

In 2010 Wembley became one of the stations to be a pilot, along with Kilburn and Acton, for the introduction of video conferencing along with Kilburn and Acton as a result of many different languages being spoken in Brent. The police team wished to change the policy in respect of linguistic matters and needed to collaborate with the Ministry of Justice, the Legal Services Commission, the Law Society, the Criminal Law Committee and the Crown Prosecution Service with a view to gaining wide acceptance on the principle of interpreters through video conferencing and to removing any possible legal obstacles[82].

In 2012 the old Wembley Police station had become an Indian restaurant.

Chalkhill Police Station

In 1997 plans were passed by Brent Council for a 'community police station' to be built on the land to the north-west side of Ken Way, Chalkhill Estate, Wembley, Middlesex, HA9 9DS. This building was eventually built, and owned, by the local authority. It became known as the 'police station' and was responsible for policing the Chalkhill Estate. In more recent times it has become one of the twenty one Safer Neighbourhood Teams offices in the borough .and officers there are known as the Welsh Harp Team.

Willesden Green Police Station

The arrival of the Metropolitan railway to the area in 1879 at Willesden Green, and then onward to Harrow the following year, increased the population, and so additional new police stations were needed. The old Willesden police station was renamed Harlesden to avoid any confusion.

The new Willesden Green Police Station was built by Messrs Higgs and Hill for the sum of £3,444, and was designed by the Metropolitan Police Surveyor, John Dixon Butler. It was built on waste land by the High Road, Willesden Green, at the corner of Huddlestone Road and opposite St Andrew's Church[83].The freehold for the site had been purchased in 1893. The new police station was opened for business at Willesden Green on 'X' Division in July 1896[84]. The staff at the station consisted of one Sergeant and two Constables. This meant a twice-daily cycle ride to Harlesden Police Station to receive orders from the divisional inspector.

Willesden Green Police Station 1896 – present day.
96, High Road, Willesden Green, NW10 2PP

By 1918 Willesden Green Police Station was under the command of Superintendent James Olive (see endnote note 52) stationed at Harrow Road Police Station. Inspector William George Cole was responsible for Willesden Green[85].

In the 1930s it was said that a local fishmonger used to drive his van into the station yard every week where local residents used to queue up to buy their fish[86].

In October 1956 the town clerk of the borough of Willesden wrote to New Scotland Yard asking whether police would be interested in erecting a new police station in a proposed civic centre at the High Road junction of Brondesbury Park, Willesden. (This new civic centre was built and comprises a library, cinema and a restaurant). The offer was declined as it would not be sufficiently central location for a new police station, and that a site at Staples Corner would be better placed in relation to adjoining police stations[87].

In 1965, when the new local authority boundaries were created Willesden Green Police Station formed part of the new 'Q' Division. It became a sectional station to Harlesden in the new London Borough of Brent[88].

In 1978 the station was slimmed down when the Metropolitan Police restructured the divisions, but in April 1985 the station was upgraded into a fully operational station[89].

In 1995 Willesden Green police were presented with the Vicountess Byng of Vimy Perpetual Trophy for winning the large garden category in the Metropolitan Police gardens competition.

In October 1995 the station closed leaving only a portakabin in the rear yard as a station office. A temporary office site was opened for police business in Neasden Lane, on the old 'McNichols' site. Meanwhile, the police station was completely renovated and staff then moved back into the premises which remain open for business.

---

[1] National Archives Census 2001
[2] Willesden Chronicle 17th March 1911 p.5
[3] National Archives Census 1841
[4] Metropolitan Police List of Police Stations 1873
[5] MEPO 4/484
[6] Metropolitan Police Orders dated 11th January 1864
[7] Metropolitan Police Orders dated 28th October 1865
[8] J. Back Archives circa 1965
[9] Post Office Directory 1879
[10] Report on Condition of Police Stations 1881
[11] Willesden Chronicle 29th May 1896
[12] Kellys Directory 1893
[13] Nation Archives Census 1901
[14] Willesden Chronicle 2nd November 1900
[15] The Late Mike Fountain (Police historian and active member of the Friends of the Metropolitan Police Historical Collection) supplied all the information on his great grandfather, Police Inspector George Robert Hodder. 2011
[16] J. Back Archives circa 1965
[17] J. Back Archives circa 1965
[18] The Police Review and Parade Gossip 19th January 1894

[19] National Archives Census 1911
[20] J. Back Archives circa 1965
[21] National Archive Census 1911
[22] Metropolitan Police Orders dated 8th July 1913.
[23] www.brent.gov.uk/museumarchive. Accessed on 19th June 2012
[24] www.military-genealogy.com/viewRecord?product=nr&q. accessed on 19th June 2012.
[25] www.brent.gov.uk/museumarchive. Accessed on 19th June 2012
[26] Kellys Directory 1920
[27] Kelly's Kilburn, Willesden and Cricklewood Directory 1918-1919.
[28] Metropolitan Police Orders dated 28th November 1933
[29] Kelly's Kilburn and Willesden Directory 1938.
[30] http://www.clanjackson.co.uk/genealogy/p14617.htm accessed on 19th June 2012
[31] Metropolian Police List 1955
[32] Metropolitan Police Orders dated 6th August 1964.
[33] http://content.met.police.uk/PoliceStation/harlesden accessed on 13th June 20.12
[34] PRO HO 107/1700/135/3, pp332 sqq.,404 as cited www.british- history.ac.uk 29th August 2011
[35] Kilburn and Willesden Directory (1872 – 1940) as cited above
[36] ibid
[37] Metropolitan Police Surveyors Book 1845
[38] ibid
[39] Metropolitan Police Orders dated 10th February 1872
[40] J. Back Archives circa 1965
[41] Metropolitan Police Orders dated 28th December 1889
[42] J. Back Archives circa 1965
[43] Metropolitan Police Orders dated 18th December 1891
[44] Metropolitan Police Orders dated 24th February 1892
[45] Kilburn and Willesden Directory 1890
[46] Kilburn and Willesden Directory 1893
[47] The Police Review and Parade Gossip 18th September 1893
[48] Kilburn and Willesden Directory 1895
[49] Kellys Directory 1910 - 1917
[50] The Police Review and Parade Gossip 9th September 1904
[51] Kellys Directory 1910 - 1917
[52] James William Olive was the first officer to join as Constable and attain the rank of Deputy Commissioner. He served a total of nearly 53 years. He was probably one of the longest serving officers. He was one of the founder members of the 'Police Minstrels' which raised money to support the Police Orphanage.
[53] Kilburn, Willesden and Cricklewood Directory 1918-1919
[54] Metropolitan List of Police Stations 1924
[55] Metropolitan Police Orders dated 28th November 1933
[56] Metropolitan Police Orders dated 23rd February 1938
[57] J. Back Archives circa 1965
[58] The Job 29th January 1971
[59] Metropolitan Police Orders dated 7th November 1940
[60] Listed on the Memorial Plaque at Kilburn Police station. Unveiled 21st May 2010
[61] Metropolitan Police Orders dated 26th March 1965
[62] J. Back Archives circa 1965
[63] NSY Press Release 18th May 1977
[64] NSY Press Release 20th March 1980
[65] Kilburn Times 28thMarch 1980
[66] http://www.mpa.gov.uk/news/press/2001/01-020/?qu=police%20stations&sc=2&ht=1 accessed on 21st June 2012
[67] New Scotland Yard Press Release 5th August 1977
[68] London Borough of Brent, Committee Report. Planning, Agenda Item 5 16th March 2010
[69] http://content.met.police.uk/Team/Brent/Kenton accessed on 3rd July 2012
[70] Wembley History Society Journal. Vol V No1 1980 p8.
[71] ibid
[72] ibid
[73] ibid

[74] http://www.news.bbc.co.uk/dna/place-lancashire/plain/A31655757 accessed on 18th March 2013
[75] Wembley History Society Journal. Vol V No1 1980 p10
[76] Metropolitan Police Orders dated 6th August 1964
[77] Metropolitan Police Orders dated 19th February 1965
[78] Metropolitan Police Orders dated 4th June 1971
[79] http://www.mpa.gov.uk/committees/x-f/2001/010619/25/ accessed on 21st June 2012
[80] http://www.mpa.gov.uk/committees/x-f/2003/030710/17/?qu=wembley&sc=2&ht=1 accessed on 21st June 2012
[81] Harrow Times 20th January 2005
[82] http://www.mpa.gov.uk/committees/x-resources/2009/091105/07/?qu=wembley&sc=2&ht=1 accessed on 21st June 2012
[83] Willesden Chronicle April 1895
[84] Metropolitan Police Orders dated 11th July 1896
[85] Kilburn, Willesden and Cricklewood Directory – 1918-1919
[86] Centenary Document MPHC Archive – Retired Police Officer 1984
[87] J. Back Archives circa 1965
[88] Metropolitan Police Orders dated 6th August 1964
[89] Kilburn Times 22nd March 1985

Chapter 4

The London Borough of Ealing

by David Swinden

Introduction

Ealing, the fourth largest London Borough borders Hillingdon to the west, Harrow and Brent to the north, Hammersmith and Fulham to the east, and Hounslow to the south.

The London Borough of Ealing was created in 1965 with the reorganisation to the structure of London Boroughs. It merged the municipal boroughs of Ealing, Southall and Acton.

Chief Superintendent Andy Rowell Borough Commander

The borough has a population of over 300,000 and is divided into seven districts. They are Ealing, Hanwell, Acton, Southall, Greenford, Perivale and Northolt. There are four main police stations – Greenford, Southall, Ealing and Acton. Ealing Police also has 23 Safer Neighbourhood Teams and 13 sector bases across the Borough. Andy Rowell was appointed Borough Commander in July 2011[1].

Over 40% of the local population are from a non-white ethnic group, 16.5% have origins in India. 31.0% of the population of Ealing was born outside the European Union (EU), compared to 6.9% nationally and 21.8% across London. Only Newham and Brent have a greater proportion of residents born outside the EU[2].

Acton Police Station

In 1815 a cage, or round house, was built beside the church to incorporate the new school room. Burglaries induced residents to subscribe in 1818 to a watch; three watchmen were employed from the town and one for East Acton, supervised nightly by the parish constable and others. Only two watchmen patrolled the town in 1828 after a fall in subscriptions but it was claimed that crime had been greatly reduced[3]. Then by 1831 Acton had no parochial watch according to the parish statement of accounts.

Acton was included in the new Metropolitan Police district in 1829. The expense of the new Police force was defrayed by private contribution. . In 1832 Samuel Lloyd is described as the Sergeant at Acton[4]. The next reference to policing in Acton is that police broke up a riot at the Kings Arms in 1837. By 1845 there was a police station in Acton at or near a site in High Road. The building was described as a station house owned by Mr Clewo of Acton. Police had a yearly tenancy that was given up after a notice to quit on Lady Day 1853. The building was described as a very old brick and tile house with a small yard, and workhouse with copper and sink[5]. Police may then have renegotiated the lease for a further three years from 24th June 1853.

In Acton in the 1870s lived many of the poorer people. Land owned by the British Land company provided houses which did not sufficiently attract the middle classes. Instead by 1872 there were sixty laundries on the South Acton estate which was an essential Victorian service, but these were often run by women with a reputation for hard drinking. Otherwise there was a slaughterhouse and a number of factories for the manufacture of fertiliser from bone crushing[6]. Such was the nature of the area to be policed.

The next police station in Acton was on Acton Hill in 1862[7], was another converted house. The existence a Police Station in Acton prior to 1864 was shown in the 'Distribution of the Force' published in Police Orders in 1864[8].

In 1863 Police Constable William John Davey was shot in the head and killed at his home in Avenue Road, Acton by a man he was investigating for theft of wood[9].

Acton formed part of 'T' or Kensington Division with a total strength of one Police Sergeant and eleven Police Constables. The Inspectors and station Sergeants on duty at Hammersmith police station were detailed to patrol Acton, Ealing and Chiswick on horseback[10].

Three new divisions were formed in 1865, 'W' or Clapham, 'X' or Paddington and 'Y' or Highgate[11]. Acton then came under the jurisdiction of 'X' Exterior Districts with Hanwell, Hillingdon, Harefield, Harrow and Willesden, Greenford and Ruislip. The Inner Districts were Paddington, Notting Hill and Harrow Road. Inspector Eccles was placed in charge of the Division as an acting Superintendent[12].

In May 1872 there was an enquiry from Henry George Briggs of Brighton asking whether the Commissioner intended to renew the lease of Acton police station. Home Office approval was given to renew the lease for 14 years at £50 p.a. In 1878 there were two Sergeants, Frederick Savage and Jesse Smith and 10 Police Constables shown as based at Acton Police Station[13].

Approval was granted by the Home Office in 1879 for the purchase of property at a sum not exceeding £1,500 and the freehold for the land was purchased for the sum of £1400[14].

In 1881 a Metropolitan Police report on the station described it as an ordinary dwelling-house with cells built in the yard. It was entirely occupied by married people. The quarters were too small. Occupied by a married Police Inspector and three married Police Constables. Urgent work was recommended such as sorting out the cess pool and adopting a 'dry earth' system for cells and privies; also to provide heating and providing oil lamps to the cells. There was no communication bell from the cells. Improved ventilation and daylight within the cells was needed.

It was also recommended the married quarter's part of the station be separated

Acton Police Station. 1894 – 1972. 250 High Street, Acton.

from the administrative areas. Finally there should be a supply of purer water to the police station[15].

By 1886 there were two Inspectors William Ellison and Thomas Mules and three Police Constables recorded at Acton Station[16] and by 1890 the station strength had grown to having two inspectors, two sergeants and 37

Constables[17]. The new Acton police station, designed by John Butler, the Metropolitan Police Surveyor, was built at a cost of £3,225 in 1894.

The address was shown as 250 High Street[18]. It was described locally as being 'plain to the verge of ugliness'[19]. The new station was handed over and married quarters occupied on 2nd July 1894[20]. There were also stables for horses which in the 1920s were converted into spaces for motor vehicles whilst some of the married quarters were converted into a CID Office[21].

In that year the station was under the command of Sub-Inspector Alfred Newnham assisted by two sergeant's and 30 constables[22].

By 1911 the Police Inspectors were Fredrick Instance and Archibald Watson. They were assisted by Station Police Sergeants Percy McCullock and Charles Butt[23].

In 1911 Sergeant Thomas King Cheeseman was living in three rooms in the Police Station at 250 High Street, Acton with his wife Laura and four children[24]

The front door into Acton Police station

Six years later in 1917 Inspector Instance, who had been stationed at Acton retired from the Police Service and he was presented with a canteen of cutlery by his Superintendent, James Olive. He was thanked for his service to the people of Acton. Among those colleagues present were Police Inspectors Watson and Brennan and Station Police Sergeants Hutchins and Brown[25]

In 1920 Police Constable James Kelly was shot three times and fatally wounded while pursuing an armed burglar he disturbed at Acton[26].

In 1933 the reorganisation of divisions north of the Thames resulted in Acton becoming a sub-divisional Station of 'T' or Ealing division, with Brentford as the sectional station[27].

Another piece of land was purchased in 1949 on the west side of the Station at a price of £400; this was an extension for the C.I.D and Metropolitan Police Special Constabulary (M.S.C.).

Yet more land was needed and in 1955 a site was purchased at 2, Lexden Road from London Transport for the sum of £35,000. This site had originally been used by the London General Omnibus Company for stabling horses for the horse-trams, and had been taken over by the London Transport Tram company and used as a tram depot[28].

The London Government Act 1963 caused a revision of boundaries aligning police and local authority boundaries. Acton became a sectional station with Ealing Sub-Division as part of 'X' Division[29].

Acton Police Station 1972 – present day. 250 High Street, Acton, London W3.

In 1972 a new sectional police station for Acton (XA) was taken into operational use at 6am Monday 10th July. The postal address 250 High Street, W3 and telephone numbers remained unchanged[30]. The cost of the new station was approximately £175,000[31].

The new Acton police station was built behind the old 1894 station. The old station was pulled down and a car park and gardens replaced it. It was hoped at the time that the old blue police lamp from outside the old station would be transferred to the new station[32]. Whilst clearing the rubble in front of the new police station an old brick well was discovered. It was still filled with water and situated underneath the CID office in the old station. It appears to have been covered up when the old police station was built in 1894. It is thought a large house previously built on this site in the early 18th century was occupied by a Miss Margaret Gainsborough, daughter of the famous painter[33].

In 1990 Police Constable Ashley Day was killed when the area car in which he was operator crashed responding to an alarm at Acton[34].

Ealing Police Station

There had been an earlier police presence in Ealing when in 1806 Lord Sidmouth set up mounted horse patrols[35].

The Ealing cage adjoined the engine house near the church in Ealing. There was a need for a police station in the town. On 27th July 1836, a letter was received from the Home Office authorising the police force to take on premises in Ealing near to the Uxbridge Road. The premises belonged to a Mr Samuel Grinsdell who leased them to the Receiver at a rent of £52. 10s (£52.50p) per annum[36]. The lease was for 21 years from Christmas 1837. It was described as an old brick and tiled house, with a large scullery with copper sink and convenience and two comfortable cells. It had rooms in the basement together with a coal cellar. There was stabling for two horses and it had a small garden at the rear[37]

In Police Orders of 11th January 1864 Ealing was designated as a Station on 'T' or Kensington Division[38]. In October 1865 the formation of 'X' Division was announced and many stations were transferred to the new Division[39]. It was not until December of that year that Ealing became part of 'X' or Paddington Division, the boundaries between 'T' and 'X' Division having been altered[40].

Prior to 1865 when 'X' Division was formed, in February 1862 an 'X' Division was specially created to police the International Exhibition which was opened at South Kensington on 1st May 1851. The Division was commanded by Superintendent Durkin who was seconded from 'F' Division. The division was disbanded in December 1862 when the exhibition was finally closed[41].

By the year 1875 the population had grown to such an extent that it was

Ealing Police Station. 1877 – 1966. 5 The High Street, Ealing W5

decided to erect a new and larger station. The estimated cost of the new station was put at £3,410. A freehold site was purchased at 5, The High Street, Ealing, W5., and building work commenced[42]. The new police station was opened in January 1877[43]. The construction of the new building was designed and supervised by John Butler, the Metropolitan Police Surveyor and was described as a red brick building with stone dressing and an attractive feature of the High Street. Carved in the stone lintel above the front door was the word 'POLICE' [44].The accommodation was for one married inspector and two married constables. At the same time the name of Hanwell Sub-Division was changed to Ealing Sub-Division.

In 1881 during the night of the census there were three police families living at the Police Station at 5, High Street, Ealing. Police Constable Thomas Paterson, his wife Emma and their young baby daughter. Also living there was Police Constable Carlos Jordon with his wife and two daughters. Finally the most senior officer living there was Police Inspector George Wills with his wife and son. Wills is an interesting person having been born on the island of St. Helena and was classified as a british subject and allowed to join the Force. In 1861 he had been a young constable at Stones End Police Station, Southwark[45].

In 1886 the police station in Ealing High Street was under the command of Inspector George Willis[46] and Superintendent Thomas Foinett was in charge

The rear yard and front gate to Ealing Police Station 1966 not pulled down until 1972

of 'X' Division. By 1894 the station was under the command of sub-Divisional Inspector Alfred Newnham and his superior was Superintendent James Cuthbert at Kilburn[47]. Above is a picture of Ealing Station yard. The station closed in July 1966.

A section house attached to Ealing, accommodating thirty single constables, was opened in August 1913[48]. The freehold for the land was purchased in 1911 and the address was 1 - 6 Baker's Lane, Ealing[49].

In 1911 'X' Division was one of the largest Divisions under the command of Superintendent James Olive. It consisted of four sub – divisional stations of Ealing, 5 High Street; Harlesden, Craven Park; Harrow and Uxbridge. There were six sectional stations at Acton. 250 High Street; Hanwell, 169 Uxbridge Road; Kilburn, 38 Salusbury Road; Southall, North Road; Willesden Green, High Road; and finally Wembley, Harrow Road[50].

In 1911 Sub-Divisional Inspector Henry Andrews was living at Ealing police station in five rooms with his wife Ellen and five children[51] He had taken over command from David Richards[52].

In 1912 the Ealing police were saddened at the sudden death of one of their officers. Inspector Alfred Edward Deeks collapsed and died after dispersing boys causing a nuisance outside a chapel in West Ealing[53].

In 1922 Ealing Police (as part of 'X' Division) along with many other police divisions undertook Ju Jitsu self-defence training to help combat the many injuries received on duty. This training took place under Capt. Leopold MacLagan. The successful class is shown in the picture below with their teacher.

The Ju Jitsu class of Capt. Leopold McLagan circa 1922

On 1st December 1933 a reorganisation of Divisions north of the Thames took place[54]. Ealing was transferred from 'X' to 'T' or Ealing Division and it became the divisional headquarters of that Division. At the same time a new sub-division was created which was known as Ealing sub-division with sectional stations at Southall and Norwood Green. Superintendent C. Adams was the officer in charge of the division[55]. The station was modernised in 1936 and [56] by 1937 Superintendent R.C. Hannaford was in charge.

During the Second World War many officers lost their lives on the streets of London. One such case was the death in 1940 of War Reserve Constable Arthur Wilfred White who was killed by the explosion of a bomb during an enemy air raid at Ealing[57].

After the war in 1949 another death occurred when Police Constable Albert Victor Hawkins was fatally injured while cycling to duty at Ealing Magistrates Court when he crashed in fog[58].

The Home Office authorised, in 1961, the purchase of the freehold interest of No's 67- 69 Uxbridge Road, Ealing, W.5, for the erection of a new station at the cost of £75,000.

Ealing Police Station. 1966 – present day.   67- 69 Uxbridge Road, Uxbridge, W5

Riding solo motor cycles was a dangerous affair at any time but more particularly at night. At Ealing in 1963 another police officer sadly died whilst on duty. Police Constable Brian Bernard Joseph Holden was fatally injured while on lightweight motorcycle patrol at night when struck by a car at Ealing[59].

These motorcycles were 200cc Velocettes known as 'noddy bikes' but were efficient in policing the streets of London. Co-author of this book, David Swinden, whilst a constable at West Ham Police Station in the 1960's rode these motor cycles over a number of years. Part of his beat covered the industrial and derelict area of Stratford now the transformed 2012 Olympic Park.

Police Constable Piara Singh Kenth a Sikh, was the first Indian officer appointed in the Metropolitan Police.

In 1965 the reorganisation of the police boundaries[60] to coincide with the new London Boroughs meant that Ealing once more became 'X' Division, with Acton as its sectional station both situated in the London borough of Ealing. The new station was built and opened on 4th July 1966[61]. At the same time the old police station and section house at 5, High Street, Ealing closed. This old station was not sold until 1970 and was used by the BBC on many occasions when filming location shots for the long running and very successful television series "Dixon of Dock Green".

In 1969 Ealing Police Station received the first Indian policeman in the Metropolitan Police. Police Constable Piara Singh Kenth, a Sikh was living in West Ealing[62].

In 1972 the old Ealing Police at High Street Ealing was pulled down after 166 years on that site. A car park replaced the police station until the site was incorporated into the new town centre redevelopment[63].

As far back as 2006 there were whispers that Ealing police station might close. In 2010 Ealing council also expressed concerns that the Metropolitan Police were still intending to sell or mothball Norwood Green Police station. However, just to show that the station at Ealing was still open they held an open day on 2nd October 2011 at two locations the Police Station, 67 Uxbridge Road, Ealing, W5 5SJ and Walpole Park, Mattock Lane, Ealing, W5 5EQ[64].

By 2012 the station closure was still under consideration[65] and still had not been resolved although in July the Mayor of London agreed that in principle Ealing was to be sold off[66].

Greenford Police Station

Prior to new cottages being built in 1896, it appears that a room in a sergeants house was used as a police office. Greenford is mentioned in Police Orders 11th January 1864 as designated as part of 'T' Division[67]. There were no cells in the accommodation but charges were taken there. The strength was one sergeant and nine constables, and the inspector at Hanwell was not posted for duty at a station but had to patrol and supervise Hanwell, Harrow and Greenford[68].

Greenford Police Station. 1896 present day. 21 Oldfield Road, Greenford, Middlesex UB6 9LQ

Mention was made in 1881 of Greenford Police Station –

> 'The police pay only a portion of the rent of a cottage in the village, which was occupied by an inspector'[69]

Due to the formation of three new Divisions 'W' or Clapham, 'X' or Paddington and 'Y' or Highgate, Greenford became annexed to the Exterior Districts of 'X' Division[70]. In 1872 there was a report from District Superintendent Robert Walker about Hanwell Sub-Division stating that there was a house to let at Greenford Green that was suitable for police purposes. This apparently was not taken up because in 1889 another mention is made that new premises were needed as the sergeant, whose house the room was used as a police office, had retired. Arising out of this, a portion of land was bought (freehold) from Mr Bishop for £300 in 1892, next door to the White Hart public house in Oldfield Lane.

Greenford Police Station garden being tended by Constable Norman Chatland

In 1894 constable Frederick Owen was the acting sergeant at Greenford police station[71].

Subsequently new cottages, at a cost of £1740, were taken into occupation for police on 12th October 1896[72]. The station was known as "The Police Station, Oldfield Lane". This was changed in 1936 to read 21, Oldfield Lane[73] later Oldfield Road.

In 1911 there were two police families living at Greenford Police Station. The first was Police Sergeant Peter Sherwood, his wife Eliza and their two sons. They occupied five rooms in the station. The other occupant was Police Constable William Bowler Lowe, his wife Harriet and their two children. They occupied four rooms[74]

Also in 1911 there was a James Hitchcock, an 83-year-old retired sergeant, living at Holly Cottage, Northolt Road, Greenford with his wife Jane Ann Hitchcock. When completing the census form he could only make his mark 'X' and he got Police Sergeant Sherwood, mentioned above to countersign his census form. One of the conditions required when joining the Metropolitan Police was that you were required to read and write. It maybe that James Hitchcock at 83 years old was too frail to sign the form himself. When he retired from the police in 1881 he was the publican of the White Public House, Greenford. He was born in Northolt in 1871 he had been living with his family in Kensington[75].

The London Government Act 1963 brought about an extensive revision of boundaries, aligning police to local government boundaries and was introduced 1st April 1965. Greenford (XG) was shown as a sub-divisional station but a footnote adds 'Pending re-building of Greenford sub-divisional Station, the sub-divisional Headquarters will be Southall'[76].

In 1974 the high quality of the garden at Greenford was recognised and it won an award under the annual police garden competition.

There was a revision of boundaries on 'X' Division and Greenford Police Station reverted to police office status[77]. Up until 2012 the station was one of four police stations in the London Borough of Ealing with opening hours of Monday to Friday 09:00 - 17:00 and closed 13:00 to 14:00[78].

Hanwell Police Station

In 1837 the village of Hanwell was recorded as having only 164 houses, but the population in the area had increased due to a number of workmen brought in to construct the Great Western Railway which passed through the village. An early mention of police in Hanwell is made in 1838 when an 'affray' took place at the Coach and Horses Public House between excavators and labourers employed in the construction of the railway. The constables and horse patrols were attacked with 'great violence' by men and women using pickaxe handles and shovels. Nine persons were arrested and each fined up to the sum of thirty shillings (£1.50) by the local magistrates[79].

Hanwell had a parish cage situated in the Halfacre. It was a small building about eight feet square and was contiguous to the old fire engine house. The building fell into disuse and became a resting place for the road labourers' tools. It was pulled down in 1844 and the materials used to build the west wall of the churchyard[80]

In the Metropolitan Police Surveyor's book of 1845 Hanwell was described as 'Horse Patrol Station No's 32 & 33'. Hanwell was the 4th Division of the horse patrol provided by the Bow Street Runners and was used as a base for the patrols. (See London Boroughs of Barnet and

Hanwell Police Station. 1868 – 1886. High Street, Hanwell.

Kingston (this publication) for more detail on these patrols). The building was 'a double brick tile and slate built house with two large gardens, two stables and a cellar for coals to each house'. Recorded in the book as 'given up'[81] with no date given, the exact location of the building was also not known.

A further entry in the Metropolitan Police Surveyor's book shows that a property was on a yearly tenancy from a Mr Hall of Kingsland. This property is described as 'a common built brick and slate house with small garden and two stall stables with loft over'. It contained four rooms and a scullery. Finally given up 24th December 1868[82] It appears that this second building is different from the first, and appears to be the first Metropolitan Police Station.

In 1847 it was reported that a train derailed near Southall and Inspector Luxton of Hanwell Police attended the scene and removed two corpses from the wreckage[83].

Records show that in 1866 plans were in hand to rebuild the police station at Hanwell but nothing happened[84]

A police funeral procession at Hanwell in the 1920s

By 1873 police lists show that the freehold of Hanwell Police Station at 169, High Street, Hanwell, was owned by the Receiver[85]. This having been purchased from Mr Joseph and Eliza Palmer for £1800 in 1872[86]. An Inspector was posted as the officer in charge.

In a Metropolitan Police Report of 1881 Hanwell Police Station was described as;

> 'Three old dilapidated cottages which have already been reported as totally unfit for the purpose of a police station. The sanitary conditions were very bad. These cottages should be replaced by a new station'

It was occupied at the time by one married inspector and two married constables[87].

The rebuilding of Hanwell Police Station on the same site took place between 1884 and 1885 at a cost of £3120 7s 5d (£3120. 27p)[88]. The new station opened on 26 January 1885[89]. In 1911 constable Charles Lewis Scammell lived in three rooms with his wife Francis and two children at the police

Hanwell Police Station. 1886 – 2012, 169 Uxbridge Road, Hanwell.

station at 169 Uxbridge Road, Hanwell.

Also living there was Police Inspector Albert Edward Sellars in four rooms with his wife Anne and three children[90].

The funeral above seems to be that of constable Percy Edwin Cook en route to Hanwell cemetery in January 1927. Cook bravely but unfortunately tried to rescue two workmen who become overcome by poisonous gases in a high tension chamber at Kensington. When both Cook and the workmen were found all had perished. In the foreground a Metropolitan Police band leads the hearse and entourage whilst many people look on.

Hanwell Police station was closed from 18th November 1933 as a police station but continued in use for other police purposes.

There was a full size police box was placed outside the station for public to have direct access to police as shown in the picture on the next page.

The building continued to be used for other police purposes.

By 2007 mention was made of selling the property but was not until 2012 that the property was cleared out and made ready to sell.

Norwood Green Police Station

In 1854 mention was made of there being a station at Heston on 'T' Division[91]. There is no information available as to where that station was situated or indeed what type of station it was.

However, on 9th October 1872 Superintendent W. Fisher 'T' Division reported on the availability of a nearly new house at 1, Harewood Villas, Frognal Green, Heston, suitable for a sectional police station. The premises were owned by a Henry Rowe of Norwood Green and were situated on the road from Southall to Heston and comprised six rooms. Water was supplied from a well on the premises and there was suitable accommodation available for a married sergeant. The rent of this house was £20 per annum.

The police surveyor inspected the premises on 1st November 1872 and reported them suitable for police purposes. Home Office sanctioned the lease of the house on 23rd November 1872 for a term of seven years commencing 24th June 1873 expiring 24th June 1880. In January 1874 Heston (Norwood Green) was ready to be opened for public business[92].

The weekly rent for the resident married sergeant was four shillings[93]. The premises were fairly small apart from the living accommodation it only allowed for a charge room and a reserve room.

On 15th July 1880 Home Office authorised the extension of the lease of the station for a further seven years at a rent of £22 per annum. The lease was further extended from 1887 until these premises were finally given up on 24 June 1890 when the new station opened.

In 1881 the police station at Norwood Green was described as a small cottage in the general line of the houses in the village, occupied by a police inspector. The report also stated that the premises were not fit for permanent occupation and that the frontage was too narrow[94]. In 1886 Inspector John Arnett was in charge[95].

Norwood Green Police circa 1890's

The Agent for the Earl of Jersey who owned the nearby Osterley Estate on 22nd November 1886 offered a piece of land opposite the station to the Receiver. The asking price was £215 freehold and this was purchased on 19th April 1888 with a view to the erection of a new station at some future date[96]. This piece of land was originally the site of Manor Farmhouse and occupied by Thomas Walton. It is not certain when the building was demolished prior to 1886[97].

A station, the present one, was built on the new site at a cost of £2714[98] and the new Station at Norwood Green was taken into occupation on 16th June 1890[99].

Norwood Green Police Station. 1890 – 2008. Norwood Road, Southall, Opposite Wimborne Avenue, Middlesex.

In 1894 Norwood Green was a sectional station on 'T' Division. Superintendent Charles Hunt was in charge of the Division[100].

In 1911 Police Sergeant Arthur Springthorpe was living in four rooms in Norwood Green Police Station with his wife Ada and their two sons[101].

You will note that on the roof of the station is one of the air raid sirens which were placed on police stations in the metropolis in preparation for the oncoming likelihood of war. It appeared that in May 1938 the Home Office placed the responsibility on the Commissioner of operating the public air raid warning system in London. To start with and to enable coverage across the Metropolitan Police District adequately and so that the sirens could be heard within a mile radius it was decided that 154 police stations should have a siren. Less powerful sirens which covered a half mile radius cover were to be placed on 227 Police Boxes. Work commenced in June 1939 and eventually the final figures were increased to 205 police stations and 246 police boxes[102].

As a result of experimental night closure of certain police stations in 1960 Norwood Green was one of those affected[103]. A telephone connected to the sub-divisional station was installed in a pillar in the front garden of the station. This was to allow members of the public to call police when the station was closed. The station remained closed at night until February 1968 when it re-opened at night[104]

With the reorganisation of the local authority boundaries in April 1965 Norwood Green police station was transferred from 'T' Division to 'X' Division as a sectional station on Southall Division situated in the London Borough of Ealing[105].

When Southall Police station was being rebuilt in 1973 Norwood Green Police station assumed sub-divisional status[106]. The senior officers and administration staff were transferred to Norwood Green and housed in a temporary building built in the station yard. However in December 1975 the new police station at Southall (XS) was ready for business and Norwood Green (XW) reverted to sectional status[107].

In 1972 police did consider rebuilding Norwood Green police station on the existing land which would have to be extended. A provisional date was set for April 1977 and the estimated cost to be about £150,000. The project was shelved[108].

By 2007 the police station was no longer considered viable and fit for purpose with the Metropolitan Police Asset Management Report suggesting that it should be sold in favour of a new building.

In 2008 all operational and administrative offices and staff were moved out of the station and the building boarded up.

In 2010 Simon Williams Commercial property consultants marketed and sold the old station[109] for development.

In 2012 the police in Norwood Green operate from two houses in Norwood Road, Southall, Middlesex located about 200 yards past Wimborne Road[110].

Southall Police Station

On 25th October 1905 the Commissioner sent a memorandum to the Receiver instructing him to purchase a property known as Elm Lodge, Southall for use as a Police Station. This property situated at 67, High Street was purchased early in 1906, freehold for the sum of £1,750. The premises were adapted for police purposes[111]. The temporary police station was opened on 17th August 1908[112].

In 1911 Southall Police Station was shown as in North Road with Sergeant Barnett in charge together with three other sergeants and fifteen constables there on the day of the census[113].

Southall Police Station. 1908 – 1927. North Road, Southall, Middlesex

In 1917 it was decided to build a custom-built station at Southall to replace the temporary station. Plans were drawn up and submitted to the Home Office for approval but because the 1914-18 Great War was still in progress it was temporarily shelved until its aftermath when the new station was completed in 1927.

It opened for business on 11th June 1927[114]. The new station was designed by Mackenzie Trench, the Metropolitan Chief Architect and Surveyor. The building covers an area of 51ft by 36ft. The new building was described as a fine building with;

'The entrance doors were in oak and when open reveal a neat lobby, the floor of which is mosaic and the walls are faced with monastic tiles. Another feature is the heavy moulded brick cornice which surrounds the building'.

Southall Police Station, 1927 – 1975. 250 High Street, Southall, Middlesex

The builders were Messrs' A. and B Hanson, Ltd., of Southall[115].

A reorganisation of Divisions in 1933 moved Southall as a sectional station on Ealing sub-division[116]. Then in 1965 a further reorganisation took place and the police boundaries of Southall (XS) found itself as a sectional station to Greenford sub-division within the London borough of Ealing.

In 1969 an additional freehold piece of land adjacent to the Station at 1 North Road was purchased for later development of the site. In 1970 plans were drawn up for the rebuilding of the Station. The old station was to be demolished and its personnel housed whilst re-building took place in temporary accommodation at the rear of the station, whilst the new station was to be erected on the site of the old one. The senior officers and the administration staff were moved to hutted accommodation at the rear of Norwood Green Police Station.

Work commenced on 1st October 1973 and the estimated completion date was 31 December 1975. The whole operation which in 1970 the Home Office said should cost no more that £204,725 eventually came to £640, 218[117]. The building was designed by Brewer, Smith and Brewer in association with J.

Southall police station. 1975 – present day. 67 High Street, Southall
UB1 3HG

Innes Elliot, the Metropolitan Police Chief Architect and Surveyor. It was built by Miller Buckley Construction. The five storey building is entirely brick-clad with a reinforced concrete frame[118].

The new Southall Police was opened for business on 8th December 1975 but formally opened in December 1976 by Sir Robert Mark, Commissioner of the Police of the Metropolis assisted by the Mayor and Mayoress of Ealing, councillor and Mrs John Wood. Leading representatives of the Indian, Sikh, Muslim and Pakistan communities were also present[119].

---

[1] www.met.police.uk/Site/ealing about us. Accessed on 28th September 2012
[2] Census 2001
[3] British History on-line accessed on 16th July 2012
[4] Pigots Directory of 1832
[5] Metropolitan Police Surveyors book 1845 p 143
[6] Weightman, G and Humphries, S. (1983) The making of Modern London. Sidgwick and Jackson, London p142
[7] Oates, J. Dr. *Policing the past*. London Borough of Ealing Library 2012
[8] Metropolitan Police Orders dated 11th January 1864
[9] www.met.police.uk/history/remembrance2 accessed on 28th September 2012
[10] J. Back archive circa 1975
[11] Metropolitan Police Orders dated 28th October 1865
[12] J. Back archive circa 1975
[13] Kelly's Directory for Middlesex 1878
[14] J. Back archive circa 1975
[15] Metropolitan Police Condition of police stations report 1881
[16] Kelly's Middlesex Directory 1886
[17] British History on-line accessed on 16th July 2012
[18] MP List of Police Stations 1912
[19] Oates, J. Dr. *Policing the past*. London Borough of Ealing Library 2012
[20] Metropolitan Police Orders dated 30th June 1894
[21] Oates, J. Dr. *Policing the past*. London Borough of Ealing Library 2012
[22] Kelly's Middlesex Directory 1894
[23] Kelly's Middlesex Directory 1911
[24] National Archives Census 1911
[25] Acton Gazette 14th December 1917
[26] www.met.police.uk/history/remembrance3. accessed on 28th September 2012
[27] Metropolitan Police Orders dated 28th November 1933
[28] J. Back archive
[29] Metropolitan Police Orders dated 6th August 1964
[30] Metropolitan Police Orders dated 7th July 1972
[31] J. Back archive
[32] Acton Gazette & Post 20th July 1972
[33] Acton Gazette & Post 21st September 1972
[34] www.met.police.uk/history/remembrance4. accessed 28th September 2012
[35] County Times and Gazette 4th February 1972
[36] J. Back archive circa 1975
[37] Metropolitan Police Surveyors Book 1845 p 145
[38] Metropolitan Police Orders dated 11th January 1864
[39] Metropolitan Police Orders dated 28th October 1865
[40] Metropolitan Police Orders dated 26th December 1865
[41] J. Back archive circa 1975
[42] J. Back archive circa 1975
[43] Metropolitan Police Orders dated 2nd January 1877

[44] County Times and Gazette 4th February 1972.
[45] National Archive Census 1861and 1881
[46] Kelly's directory of Middlesex 1886
[47] Kelly's Directory of Middlesex 1894
[48] Metropolitan Police Orders 30th July 1913
[49] MP List of Police stations 1912
[50] Kelly's Directory 1911
[51] National Archive Census 1911
[52] Kelly's Directory 1911
[53] www.met.police.uk/history/remembrance3 accessed on 28th September 2012
[54] Metropolitan Police Orders dated 28th November 1933
[55] Kelly's Directory 1933
[56] County Times and Gazette 4th February 1972
[57] www.met.police.uk/history/remembrance3. accessed on 28th September 2012
[58] ibid
[59] www.met.police.uk/history/remembrance4. accessed on 28th September 2012
[60] Metropolitan Police Orders dated 6th August 1964
[61] Metropolitan Police Orders dated 1st July 1966
[62] Middlesex County Times 31st October 1969
[63] County Times and Gazette 4th February 1972
[64] http://content.met.police.uk/Event/Ealing-Police-Open-Day accessed on 20th November 2012
[65] http://philtaylor.org.uk/2006/11/ealing-police-station-no-shock-shock/ accessed on 20th November 2012
[66] http://snipelondon.com/scoop/london-police-stations-to-be-sold-off-admits-boris accessed on 20th November 2012
[67] Metropolitan Police Orders 11th January 1864
[68] J. Back archive circa 1975
[69] Metropolitan Police Condition of police stations 1881
[70] Metropolitan Police Orders dated 28th October 1865
[71] Kelly's directory of Middlesex 1894
[72] Metropolitan Police Orders dated 10th October 1896
[73] J. Back archive circa 1975
[74] National Archives Census 1911
[75] National Archives Census 1871, 1881 and 1911
[76] Metropolitan Police Orders dated 6th August 1964
[77] Metropolitan Police Order dated 26th August 1977
[78] http://content.met.police.uk/PoliceStation/greenford accessed on 3th December 2012
[79] Sharpe. M. Sir Bygone Hanwell, General Calendar 1924 p 97
[80] Sharpe. M. Sir Bygone Hanwell, General Calendar 1924
[81] Metropolitan Police Surveyors Book as at 1845 p139
[82] Metropolitan Police Surveyors Book as at 1845 p141
[83] Oates, J. Dr. *Policing the past*. London Borough of Ealing Library 2012
[84] Charles Reeves, Metropolitan Police Surveyor letter to Sir Richard Mayne, Commissioner dated November 1866. MEPO File.
[85] Metropolitan Police List of police stations 1873
[86] Metropolitan Police Surveyors Register p.222
[87] Metropolitan Police Condition of Police Stations 1881
[88] Metropolitan Police Surveyors Register p 222
[89] Metropolitan Police Orders dated 24th January 1885
[90] National Archives Census 1911
[91] Metropolitan Police Order dated 11th January 1864
[92] Metropolitan Police Order dated 31th January 1874
[93] J. Back archive circa 1975
[94] Metropolitan Police Report Condition of Police Stations 1881
[95] Kelly's Directory 1886
[96] J. Back archive
[97] British History online accessed 16.7.2012 also Southall Boro' Library Norwood Valuations 1821
[98] Metropolitan Police Surveyors Register p 174
[99] Metropolitan Police Orders dated 28th June 1890

[100] Kelly's Directory of Middlesex 1894
[101] National Archives Census 1911
[102] Met Historical Collection
[103] Metropolitan Police Orders dated 5th August 1960
[104] Metropolitan Police Orders dated 30th April 1968
[105] Metropolitan Police Orders dated 6th August 1964
[106] Metropolitan Police Orders dated 20th March 1973
[107] Metropolitan Police Orders dated 5th December 1975
[108] J. Back archive
[109] http://www.sitesetserver2.co.uk/properties.php?site=swcpc accessed on 3rd December 2012
[110] Google maps accessed on 3rd December 2012
[111] J. Back archive
[112] Metropolitan Police Orders 22nd August 1908
[113] National Archives Census 1911
[114] Metropolitan Police Orders dated 8th June 1927
[115] The Times 1927
[116] Metropolitan Police Orders 28th November 1933
[117] J. Back Archive circa 1975
[118] Building Design 10th May 1974
[119] The Job dated 10th December 1976

Chapter 5

The London Borough of Hammersmith and Fulham

by David Swinden

Introduction

The London Borough of Hammersmith and Fulham is one of the smallest boroughs by area and forms part of Inner London. The borough was formed in 1965 by merging the Metropolitan Boroughs of Hammersmith and Fulham. Firstly, it was known as the London Borough of Hammersmith until it was changed in 1979. The two boroughs had been joined together previously as Fulham District from 1855 until 1886.

The new Metropolitan Police commenced responsibility for the policing of both Hammersmith and Fulham from May 1830.

There are three main police stations presently operating in the Borough namely Fulham, Hammersmith and Shepherds Bush. There are also sixteen Neighbourhood Units across the borough. In February 2011 the policing responsibility of the borough was given to the Commander, Chief Superintendent Lucy D'Orsi. Currently (2013) Shepherds Bush Police Station is under the threat of closure and on-going discussions with the community are taking place. Hammersmith is scheduled to have its front counter open to the public for 24 hours a day, whereas Fulham will only open during daytime[1].

Fulham Police Stations

Before looking at details of the police stations, it is worth mentioning that Fulham has been policed by two main police stations since the Metropolitan Police assumed the responsibility for policing the area in 1830.

Prior to 1862 the first police station was known as Walham Green Police Station. When the new police station was built in 1863 it became known as Fulham Police Station and the address was 520, Fulham Road, Walham Green. It became known as South Fulham Police Station in 1887 when North Fulham Police Station was opened. In the 1890s, after buying extra land, the police station was extended. A new police station opened in 1914 on a site opposite the old station with the address now being Heckfield Place. At this stage the name of the station was changed from South Fulham back to Walham Green. Then in 1960 the name was again changed back to Fulham Police Station. In 1992 the station was substantially extended.

The other police station was known as North Fulham and was built and opened in 1887 in Crown Road, where it joined with the junction of Lillie Road. It closed as a police station in 1944.

Fulham Police Station (Also known as Walham Green, South Fulham)

The first police building in Fulham was at Walham Green. It was described as a section house and many such places were often also used as police station houses. The first police station at Walham Green was situated in the corner of Lewis's Yard which was behind the George Inn in Fulham Road[2]. The owner of the property was a Mr Thornton of Walham Green. The building was described as a common brick and tile house with a yard at the back. It had a coal cellar, dust hole and water closet. It contained five rooms and had a scullery. This remained a rented building until the new police station, was built in 1863[3] when the premises were given up.

The inspector and the sergeants from Chelsea were required to patrol the section of Fulham on horseback. The station strength in 1861 was three sergeants, one acting sergeant and 24 police constables. There were six day beats and 16 night beats. Two sergeants were required to remain in the station at all times whilst one mounted sergeant and one section sergeant supervised and patrolled the station area[4]. The station was a sectional station to Chelsea on 'V' or Wandsworth Division.

The owner of the second Walham Green station was Captain Cotton of Fulham who leased the premises from 1862 for 60 years and charged an annual rent of £25. Even though the land was rented the building was erected by the Commissioner and technically was owned by the Metropolitan Police. Later the land was purchased either voluntarily or by compulsory purchase.

In June 1863, police were instructed to take charge and to occupy the new Station and Section House at 520, Fulham Road[5]; (at the junction that later became Heckfield Place). It was henceforth to be known as Fulham and not Walham Green as the previous station had been before June 1863, forming part of 'V' or Wandsworth Division[6]. The cost of the new building was £2116[7]. Then in 1864 Fulham is shown as being a station on 'V' Division[8]. With the formation in 1865 of the three new Divisions 'W', 'X' and 'Y', Fulham was transferred to the 'T' or Kensington Division [9].

In 1881 a report on Fulham Police Station stated that 'the station is somewhat arranged to the convenience of the married Police Inspector, who resides there'. At the time of the inspection the station was occupied by a married Police Inspector and six single Police Constables[10].

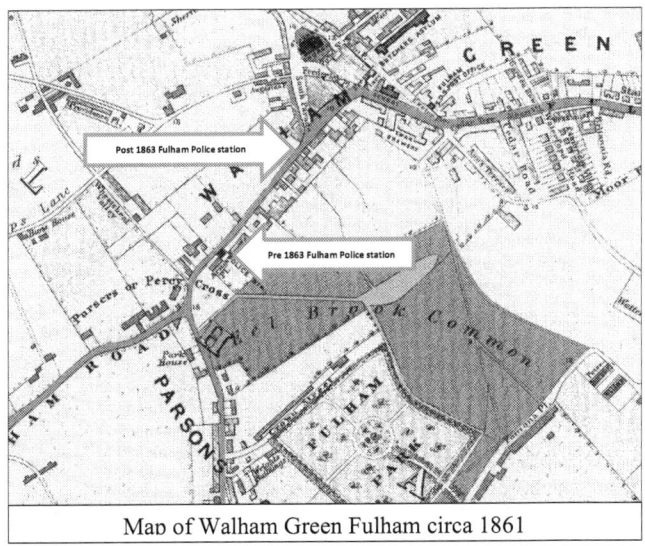

Map of Walham Green Fulham circa 1861

Fulham (Walham Green) Police Station. 1914 - 1992. Heckfield Place, Fulham SW6

In 1884 Fulham was a sub-divisional Station of 'T' Division[11]. In 1885, the police paid £350 for land at the rear of the station. An agreement was reached with the owners of the land on which the station was built that a further £900 was to be paid for the freehold of the property in 1890[12].

In 1887 there was the sad case of Constable Robert McGraw who unfortunately died from a fractured skull after being kicked by his police horse in Fulham police station stables[13].

When North Fulham police station opened in 1887 Fulham police station became known as South Fulham Police Station.

In 1909 there was a re-arrangement of the boundaries between 'T' and 'B' Divisions. The Fulham sub-division comprising the stations of North Fulham and South Fulham were transferred and became part of 'B' or Chelsea division[14].

The national census of 1911 shows the married quarters at South Fulham Police Station being occupied by a number of police families.

One of these was Sergeant Charles Francis Hancox at No. 5 Police Quarters.

He and his wife Lucy were living in four rooms with their two teenage children[15]. The station was described as having a section house and one set of married quarters. The picture below shows the line-up of South Fulham with their Sub-Divisional Inspector Frederick May (see Book 2 under Borough Police Station, Southwark for more on this officer) in the centre. This was taken in 1912 when the previous year's Coronation Medal was issued.

South Fulham contingent taken with SDI May in the centre in 1912.

During 1911 land at the rear of numbers 522-534, Fulham Road was purchased for the erection of a new police station, in Heckfield Place. This station was opened for business on 30th March 1914[16], and replaced the old station opposite, on the corner of Fulham Road and Heckfield Place.

There was no formal opening ceremony of the new station but Superintendent John B. Kitch escorted a number of local dignitaries around the station.

Chief Inspector (wt. no. 74004) George Shervington, Sub-Divisional Police Inspector Emerick (who took over from May) and Police Inspectors Reeves and Thursby were also in attendance[17]. The name of the station was changed at the express wish of the then Commissioner, Sir Edward Henry, from South Fulham to Walham Green[18].

The new station was five storeys, together with a basement, and was

Line-up of officers from South Fulham in greatcoats

built of red sand-faced bricks with a Portland stone dressing. It had oak front doors and large windows throughout the building. The building contractor for the building was Messrs John Garlick and Co. of Sloane Street, and was built to the designs of John Dixon Butler, Metropolitan Police Surveyor. At the time, this new building was considered to be one of the most modern police stations in London and was erected at the cost of £1200. The station now had accommodation for 38 single police officers under the charge of bachelor Sergeant Edhouse. At the rear of the station was a large yard, accessed although a large arched gateway. The yard contained a parade shed, and stables for up to six horses. The number of police officers operating from the new station in 1914 was two inspectors, four station sergeants, ten sergeants and 120 constables together with two mounted patrols[19].

By 1919 'B' Division was under the command of Superintendent Ernest Bacchus. At Fulham Police Station, Sub-Divisional Inspector George Wilcox was in charge, and was assisted by Inspectors G. Bonnyman and John Thursey[20]. In 1928 Walham Green Police Station was still shown on 'B' division and was at this time under the command of Superintendent William Crayfourd[21].

Superintendent Bacchus 'B' Division

The regulation of public carriage vehicles, including taxi cabs in London was passed to the Metropolitan Police in 1850.

The original Public Carriage Office (PCO) was situated in an annexe to New Scotland Yard called the Bungalow. It moved to 109, Lambeth Road in 1919. The PCO moved to 15, Penton Street, Islington in 1966 and then to Southwark in 2010. There were a number of 'Passing Stations' throughout the Metropolitan Police area for testing vehicles and drivers.

No 4 Passing Station of the PCO which had been at North Fulham Station was transferred to the old Fulham Police Station site in October 1938. It remained there until October 1966 when, with the other passing stations, it moved to Penton Street, Islington[22]. The PCO then moved to Southwark in 2010 and is now known as the London Taxi and Private Hire Office[23] as part of Transport for London.

A sad happening occurred in 1958 when Superintendent Thomas George James collapsed and died in the police car taking him to duty at Walham Green[24].

Once again there came a change of name for the station[25]. As from 1st January 1960 Walham Green Police Station became known as Fulham and the Telegraphic Code changed from 'BW' to 'BF'.

On a large scale revision of boundaries on the 1st April 1965 to match the local authority boundaries[26], Fulham changed Divisions yet again and this time became a sub-divisional Station of 'F' Division. A further revision of boundaries between Hammersmith and Fulham sub-divisions took place in 1975[27].

In May 1992 the Commissioner, Sir Peter Imbert, opened the refurbished Fulham Police Station. Work to extend and refurbish the building took almost four years to complete, at the cost of £4.5 million[28].

Also in 1992 ex-Constable Ken Walker was presented with a commendation, by Deputy Assistant Commissioner Alan Fry, to mark his retirement after 44 years' service at Fulham Police Station. He had joined the Police in September 1947 after four years in the Parachute Regiment, during which he took part in the Normandy invasion. During his service he had received two Commissioner's commendations and retired as a constable in 1960. He returned the following day to take up the post of Administrative Officer at the station[29].

In 1992 Heckfield Place was extended next to the station as the picture below shows. Its address is recorded as Heckfield Place, Fulham SW6 5NL.

Fulham Police Station. Built 1914 extended 1992 still in use today. Heckfield Place, Fulham SW6 5NL

Over the years, Fulham Police Station has been attached to a number of different Police Divisions:-

1830 – 1863 'V' Division (Wandsworth)

1863 – 1909 'T' Division (Kensington)

1909 – 1965 'B' Division (Chelsea)

1965 - 1979 'F' Division (Hammersmith) - this was when the new London Boroughs were created.

1979 – present day 'F' Division (Hammersmith and Fulham)

Fulham Police station code was (FF) in 1992 and was a Divisional Station under the charge of Chief Superintendent R. A. S. Johnson with Superintendent M. Schuck in support[30].

North Fulham Police Station

The land for North Fulham Police Station was purchased in September 1885 at the cost of £1350, and the new police station cost £2559[31] to build. It was situated at Crown Road at the junction of Lillie Road SW6. The new station was designed by John Butler, the Metropolitan Police Surveyor, and was opened in October 1887[32]. The police station was known locally as the 'Jubilee Police Station' because Queen Victoria celebrated her Diamond Jubilee that year.

In October 1893 a presentation took place at North Fulham police station. This was not to a retiring police officer, which was the normal practice, but to a member of the public. A handsome marble timepiece, subscribed for by the police of the sub-division, was made to Mr W. R. White, an employee of the London Road Car Company. It was for rendering assistance to Constable 121'T' Timpson when he was brutally assaulted by a number of 'roughs' in Lillie Road, Fulham on 18th July 1893[33].

In April 1894 two new cells were added to the existing three cells at a cost of £698[34].

In the national census of 1911 there were ten constables residing in North Fulham police station. The census form was completed and signed by Inspector William Bamsey, although he was living elsewhere with his family[35].

In 1928 the police station was a sectional station to Walham Green and the address was 353, Lillie Road, SW6[36].

On the 1st January 1938, at 6am, North Fulham Police Station in Lillie Road was closed and all business transferred to Walham Green[37]. The building was used for police purposes during the war years from 1939 until 1944 when it was closed[38].

Hammersmith Police Station

In 1832 Home Office authority was given to find a site for a new police station at Hammersmith. The station was sited at Brook Green, roughly where the M-O. Valve Co. (Hammersmith) works were. The property was owned by Mr. W. Bird and had been built on the site of the smith's old house[39]. The property was held on lease from 25th March 1833 for a period of 30 years. The lease required police to pay all rates and taxes, except land tax and sewer rate. The Receiver was also required to keep the premises in good repair, and paint the outside every three years and the inside every seven years. The building was a substantially built house of brick and slate with a small yard at the rear. There was a good coach house with copper boilers, three cells and stabling for eight horses. It was later agreed to rent the station and three double cottages plus one single cottage, (used as section house accommodation) for a further period of two years from Lady Day 1868 at a rent of £330 per annum. All were given up in 1870[40].

In 1842 The Reverend Edward Wakeham of Eagle House, Brook Green, Hammersmith, at the suggestion of Superintendent Williamson of 'T' Division, made a present of upwards of 100 well selected volumes of books to form the nucleus of a permanent library. The idea was to form a library at the station-houses for the instruction and amusement of the reserve part of the force, and when the men were off duty[41]. This was followed up in 1843 when the London City Mission presented about 50 volumes of books to each London police station for the use of the men attached to it. The works consisted of sacred writings, selected sermons, sound theological and moral works, together with the biographies and travels of good religious and moral men. The works could either be read at the station houses, or taken home by the constable, under certain restrictions[42]. Libraries were maintained at sub-divisional police stations well into the late 1960s.

Inspector James Morgan was shown in charge of the police station in 1845[43]. In 1864[44] Hammersmith was shown as a Station on 'T' Division.

In 1869[45] a new police station was built at the cost of £6415[46], on the site of Thatched Cottage, which was owned by two ladies. It was in Bridge Road which was later renamed Queen Street and is now known as Queen Caroline Street. It stood where the entrance to the District & Piccadilly Station (Queen Caroline Street entrance) stands now[47]. The land had been purchased at a cost of £3200[48] but there was an outcry at the time from the vicar and churchwardens of St. Paul's church as they thought it unseemly to have unsavoury characters such as drunks, etc., in the vicinity of the churchgoers[49]. The police station was probably designed by the Metropolitan Police Surveyor Thomas Sorby, but he left his position in 1868 and the deputy, Frederick Caiger would have finished supervising the building.

In 1879 Hammersmith police station was still shown as being on 'T' or Kensington Division. Superintendent William Fisher was in command of the Division[50].

The 'F' Division contingent at Earls Court for the 1904 Italian Exhibition.

In 1881 there was a report published which looked at the condition of each of the Metropolitan Police stations. Hammersmith was described as 'a nearly new station'. However the report was critical of the charge room and the distance it was from the cells. The station had a basement mess and a good stable in the yard. At the time of the inspection there were one married inspector, one single sergeant and 52 single constables living at the station[51].

In the year 1884 Hammersmith was shown as a sub-divisional station of 'T' Division, and then in 1888 there was an alteration in the boundaries of Hammersmith and Shepherds Bush sub-divisions with the opening of Ravenscourt Park, Hammersmith[52]. In 1889 part of 'T' or Hammersmith Division transferred to 'X' Division to provide better policing in the Ealing, Acton and Hanwell Districts[53].

In 1895 Chief Inspector P. Cronin of Hammersmith Police Station retired after 27 years' service. He had joined the Metropolitan Police in 1868 and had been posted to Stoke Newington. He was then specially selected for duty at the Exhibition of 1871 at South Kensington. He gained promotion and eventually came to Hammersmith as a Police Inspector in 1885. During the years between 1887 and 1890 he had the entire control of police arrangements at the exhibitions at Earls Court, the Paris Hippodrome and the great Barnam's Show at Olympia. He was promoted to Chief Inspector in 1892. He was a prominent and enthusiastic member of Hammersmith Police Rowing Club, and was police band inspector for a long time. He was also a prominent figure in the concerts and excursions of the District, which were promoted for the benefit of the police orphanage[54].

In January 1896 Hammersmith constable Harry Goddard returned to the station from Paris, France, where he had spent eighteen days at the Pasteur Institute being treated for a bite to his hand by a mad dog in the yard at the Hammersmith Police Station on Christmas Day 1895. Louis Pasteur had developed a vaccine for the treatment of rabies and the divisional surgeon felt it necessary to send the officer to France for treatment[55].

By 1896 'T' Division was commanded by Superintendent Charles Hunt with sub-divisional inspector James Boyle at Hammersmith Police Station assisted by Inspectors J. Lance, E. Harris, H. Ashwell, J. Scantlebury and T. Moffatt[56].

The rigours of police duty took its toll on the health of officers who died in service more frequently than in modern times. There were two such cases at Hammersmith Police Station in 1892 when Constable Ernest Ellis died from emphysema and pleurisy after 22 years service.

In 1900 this also happened to Constable Henry John Jiggins who died from thoracic aneurism. His widow received a pension of £15 per annum and £2 10s (£2.50p) was paid yearly to each of the five children until they reached 15 years of age[57].

The Navy and Military Tournament was the world's largest military tattoo and pageant, held by the British armed forces annually between 1880 and 1999. The venue was originally the Royal Agricultural Hall in Islington and latterly moved to Earls court as the former venue was too small. In its later years it also acted as a fundraising event for leading forces charities, such as The Royal British Legion. In the picture below Chief Inspector Shervington (centre seated), SDI Littlejohns (centre left seated), two inspectors, three sergeants and 31 constables were specially chosen to carry out supervision of the tournament buildings and to ensure the event was as trouble free as possible. Littlejohns had been trained well by his old boss SDI May who was an expert at policing exhibitions and large events like the Boat Race.

In 1909 'T' Division lost Fulham sub-division to 'B' or Chelsea Division in a revision of Divisional boundaries[58]. New married quarters and section house were taken into occupation in April 1911[59].

The Navy and Military Tournament Olympia circa 1907

The station was reconstructed at a cost of £5402[60] in 1913[61].

Local people showed great interest in May 1914, when 230 boys and girls from the Metropolitan and City Police Orphanage at Twickenham arrived in Hammersmith on special tramcars. Headed by their band and the orphanage banner they marched up Hammersmith Road to Olympia to watch a rehearsal performance of the Royal Naval and Military Tournament.

Children from the Orphanage together with SDI Littlejohns (seated 2nd left), Chief Inspector Shervington (centre) and others in the yard at Hammersmith Police Station

The children were described as smart and having a well cared-for appearance. The girls, who were mostly taller than the boys, were neatly attired in blue dresses, with black coats and straw hats, with blue and red ribbons, whilst the boys wore black suits with dark blue caps with red stripes.

After the performance the children, headed by the 'T' Divisional Band, and accompanied by Sub-Divisional Inspector (wt. no. 73375) Walter Littlejohns and Inspector Grosch, marched to Hammersmith

Police Station. They were received by Superintendent Powell and the children enjoyed tea and cakes set out for them in the station yard[62].

SDI Littlejohns

The Metropolitan Police Orphanage opened in 1870 with 20 dependent children of deceased policemen. In 1871 it was renamed to include the City of London Police and was granted Royal patronage the same year. Its original home was Fortescue House (long since demolished) in London Road, Twickenham. It had been the former home of Earl Fortescue. In 1874 the orphanage moved to Wellesley House, Hampton Road, Twickenham. The home closed in 1937 but the Metropolitan and City Police Orphans Fund continue to support the children of police officers[63] who had died or become unfit for duty. (For more on the Orphanage see London the Borough of Richmond)

In 1924 'T' Division was under the command of Superintendent William Newman. At Hammersmith Police Station, Sub-Divisional Inspector William Sergeant was in charge together with Detective Inspector William Gurney and Inspectors Charles Read, Thomas Taylor and George Harmon[64].

In 1928 the Superintendent in charge of 'T' Division was Thomas Coombs[65].

In the 1933 Re-organisation of the Divisions North of the Thames,

Hammersmith Police Station. 1940 - to present day. 226, Shepherds Bush Road, Hammersmith.

Hammersmith was transferred from 'T' to 'F' Division and became the main station of that Division[66].

In November 1939 the Section House at 3, Paddenswick Road, Hammersmith was taken into occupation after some reconstruction. It was now to be known as Ravenscourt House[67].

On 31st March 1940 Hammersmith Police Station at 1, Queen Caroline Street, W6 was closed and business was transferred to new premises at 19, Brook Green Road, W6. This road was then renamed and the police station address became 226, Shepherds Bush Road[68]. The police station had been built on the site of Messrs Rogers Garage premises at 19-27 Brook Green Road[69]. The site used to be a picturesque spot in Victorian days. Duckling's Nurseries with the adjoining Laurel Cottage and King's Forage Yard stood there for many years[70].

The new station took eighteen months to build and was designed by the London firm of architects, Messrs' Farquharson and McMorran. A local artist, Mr. G. Kruger Gray of Addison Cresent, Hammersmith designed the striking coat of arms over the main entrance. The walls of the entrance hall were covered with Portland stone and the ceiling was of silver-grey Indian wood. There were four cells

The front entrance to Hammersmith Police Station.

for male prisoners and four cells for females. Behind the main building was built a stable block for 20, with harness room, forage store, sick box and a blacksmith's forge. There was also a garage for 10 cars. Over the station there were married quarters for two resident officers[71]. Architectural comment has been made of the unusual placing of the attic windows which do not line up with the lower windows[72].

The old police station at Queen Street was sold on 5th April 1940 to Mr H. Salmon for £27,000[73].

During the Second World War there were a large number of fatalities in London by enemy aircraft during the air raids. Two War Reserve Constables at Hammersmith lost their lives. Simeon Oscar Glen and Arthur Needham Myers had both joined the Force in order to fill the gaps left at police stations when the regular policemen joined the armed forces. Both constables were killed by the explosion of a bomb during an enemy raid at Hammersmith[74].

The blue lamp outside Hammersmith Police station is over 100 years old as it had been taken from Whetstone Police Station when it was pulled down in 1963. It was placed outside the building in 1965 when some alterations were made to the station.

In 1965 divisional boundaries were altered to coincide with the new local authority boundaries. Hammersmith remained the divisional station of 'F' Division[75].

In 1975 Constable Stephen Andrew Tibble was riding his motorcycle off duty, and saw a man with a gun being chased by three plain clothes officers. Constable Tibble overtook him, dismounted, and approached, whereupon the suspect, an IRA terrorist, shot him three times at close range and killed him. Tibble was awarded posthumously the Queen's Police Medal which is only awarded for gallantry[76]. In May 1992, when the refurbished Fulham Police Station (all part of the London Borough of Hammersmith and Fulham) was reopened Pc Tibble's parents attended the ceremony and unveiled a new plaque in memory of their son in the front office of the new-look station[77].

The police have not escaped being the victims of crime themselves: in 1987 a massive 16 stone bench was stolen from Hammersmith Police Station's foyer. It seems that the eight feet long seat was carried out of the main entrance and along a busy road. The previous week two chairs were also stolen from the foyer[78]. Sadly this still happens at a number of police stations across the country. Police stations which are closed at night are particularly vulnerable in spite of sophisticated alarm systems.

Hammersmith Police Station is one of 40 police buildings that English Heritage has classified as a Grade II listed building. Of the 40 buildings 30 are police stations. There are many current and former Metropolitan Police stations being closed and the buildings sold to developers to either pull down or refurbish as private living accommodation. Local communities forming action groups to keep these police stations open, and to keep policing at a local level. They are also trying to keep the old buildings instead of new development. Many police buildings blend into the local area and buildings around them. English Heritage, and local authorities, take an interest in buildings which are at risk and need to be preserved for their architectural qualities.

However, whilst local residents fight for the preservation of their local police stations English Heritage point out that over 350 Metropolitan Police stations were built between 1842 and 1900 and several are included in the Heritage List of Grade II buildings. Buildings need to be exceptional examples of Victorian police stations, in terms of design, and with clear architectural quality. Having selected 30 police stations English Heritage feel that they have sufficient examples of London police stations on their list[79].

Shepherds Bush Police Station

Land in Askew Road, W12 was considered suitable for a police station and was purchased by the Receiver in June 1881 at a cost of £1107. The new station was built between 1883 and 1884. The building was designed by the Metropolitan Police Surveyor, John

Butler. The architectural plans are retained at the National Archives and are not available to the public. This is a policy laid down in respect of any police building still being used for police purposes[80].

In 1884 a new sub-division was formed on 'T' Division known as Shepherds Bush. At the same time a new police station was opened in February of that year[81]. The address of the new station was 142, Starch Green Road, but later in 1887 it was renamed 87, Askew Road, W.12. The cost of the land was £1457 and the construction of the building was £4589 giving a total cost of £6046[82].

By 1888 the boundaries of Hammersmith and Shepherds Bush Sub-Divisions were altered in consequence of the opening of Ravenscourt Park, Hammersmith[83].

Shepherds Bush Police Station. 1884 – 1963. 87 Askew Road, Shepherds Bush W6

In 1896 Inspector Thomas Neal was in charge of Shepherds Bush Police Station[84].

In 1924 Shepherds Bush was a sub-division under the command of the divisional commander, Superintendent William Newman at

Hammersmith. There were two inspectors, Edward Pinks and George Rhodes, based at Shepherds Bush[85].

In 1933 there was a reorganisation of divisions north of the Thames, and Shepherds Bush was transferred from 'T' to 'F' Division[86].

From 1937 onwards ideas were put forward to erect a new police station in the Shepherds Bush area to replace Notting Dale and Shepherds Bush police stations. Many sites in the Uxbridge Road were examined but were found to be unsuitable. The war years intervened and at last a suitable site was found. After protracted negotiations with the freeholder, construction got under way[87]. The new station at 252-258, Uxbridge Road, W.12 was completed and opened in July 1963[88]. At the same time the old station at Askew Road was closed and later sold to the London Borough of Hammersmith for re-development[89].

Once again there was a revision of police boundaries in 1965 to line them up with local authority boundaries, but Shepherds Bush police station remained on 'F' Division[90].

Shepherds Bush police station has had its share of police officers being fatally injured whilst on duty or travelling to or from duty. In 1930 Constable Henry Falshaw-Skelly died in a motorcycle accident whilst travelling to duty at the station. Then in 1993 Constable Noel Charles Frick was killed in a road accident whilst on motorcycle surveillance duty at Shepherds Bush. In 2002 Constable Nicholas Hill was also killed in a motorcycle accident at Barnes whilst travelling to duty at Shepherds Bush police station[91].

The most tragic case in recent times was the murder of three police officers in 1966 – known as the 'Shepherds Bush Murders'. Police Constable Geoffrey Roger Fox, Detective Sergeant Christopher Tippett Head and Temporary Detective Constable David Stanley Bertram Wombwell were all shot dead, without warning, as they were questioning three suspects in a van parked suspiciously outside Wormwood Scrubs Prison in Braybrook Street[92].

The outrage from the press and public over the shooting dead of the three police officers, in such a cold-blooded way, while they were carrying out their lawful duty, sparked calls for the re-instatement of the death penalty. The death penalty was never re-instated a matter which remains to this today.

As a result of these horrendous murders it should be remembered that Sir Billy Butlin, the holiday camp owner and philanthropist, immediately sent a cheque for £100,000 to the Commissioner, Sir Joseph Simpson, KBE. From that gesture, with the help of Lord Stonham, was born the Police Dependants' Trust[93]. The Trust, together with the National Police Fund, provides financial support to help ease some of the pressures that police families experience when a

Shepherds Bush Police Station. 1963 – Present day. 253 – 258 Uxbridge Road, London W12 7JB

police officer has been killed or injured on duty.

The Braybrook Suite at Hammersmith Police Station (FS) was named after the officers in 1996[94]. The station front counter and charging facilities were withdrawn in January 2013 however the station has been retained for other policing purposes and officers continue to patrol from the building[95].

---

[1] www.the Guardian.co.uk visited 9th January 2013
[2] A Potted History of Fulham and Hammersmith Police – Met Police Heritage collection
[3] Metropolitan Police Surveyors Book p 165
[4] Special Metropolitan Police Orders 1861
[5] Metropolitan Police Orders dated 20th June 1863
[6] John Back Archive circa 1975
[7] Metropolitan Police Surveyors Book
[8] Metropolitan Police Orders dated 11th January 1864
[9] Metropolitan Police Orders dated 28th October 1865
[10] Metropolitan Police Report on condition of Police Stations 1881
[11] Metropolitan Police Orders dated 22nd February 1884
[12] Metropolitan Police Surveyors Book
[13] Met.police.uk/history/remembrance2 visited 17th October 2012
[14] Metropolitan Police Orders dated 31st March 1909
[15] National Archives Census 1911
[16] Metropolitan Police Orders dated 21st March 1914
[17] Fulham Chronicle 3rd April 1914
[18] John Back Archive 1975
[19] Fulham Chronicle 3rd April 1914
[20] Kelly's West Kensington and Fulham Directory 1919
[21] Post Office Directory 1928
[22] John Back Archive circa 1975
[23] www.tfl.gov.uk visited January 2013
[24] Met.police.uk/history/remembrance2 accessed 17th October 2012
[25] Metropolitan Police Orders dated 29th December 1959
[26] Metropolitan Police Orders dated 6th August 1964
[27] Metropolitan Police Orders dated 24th October 1975
[28] The Job 29th May 1992
[29] ibid
[30] Police and Constabulary Almanac 1992
[31] Metropolitan Police Surveyors Book
[32] Metropolitan Police Orders dated 22nd October 1887
[33] Birmingham Daily Post – Gleanings. 27th October 1893. Issue 11031
[34] Metropolitan Police Surveyors Book
[35] National Archives Census 1911
[36] Post Office Directory 1928
[37] Metropolitan Police Orders dated 29th December 1937
[38] MEPO 2/6199
[39] Notes at Hammersmith & Fulham Archives 15.10.12
[40] Metropolitan Police Surveyors Book p.142
[41] Notes dated 1842 at Hammersmith & Fulham Archives 15th October 2012
[42] The Era (London) The Synopsis. 26 February 1843. Issue 231
[43] Kelly's Directory 1845
[44] Metropolitan Police Orders dated 11th January 1864
[45] Metropolitan Police Orders dated 15th November 1869
[46] Metropolitan Police Surveyors Book

[47] Notes at Hammersmith & Fulham Archives 15th October 2012
[48] Metropolitan Police Surveyors Book
[49] John Back Archive circa 1975
[50] Post Office Directory 1879
[51] Metropolitan Police Report on condition of Police Stations 1881
[52] Metropolitan Police Orders dated 7th June 1888
[53] Metropolitan Police Orders dated 28th December 1889
[54] West London Observer 6th April 1895
[55] Fulham Chronicle 24th January 1896
[56] Kelly's West Kensington & Hammersmith Directory 1896-7
[57] Met.police.uk/history/remembrance2 visited 17th October 2012
[58] Metropolitan Police Orders dated 31st March 1909
[59] Metropolitan Police Orders dated 26th April 1911
[60] Metropolitan Police Surveyors Book
[61] John Back Archive circa 1975
[62] Press Cutting at Hammersmith & Fulham Archives dated 15.5.1914. Visited 15th October 2012
[63] Met-City orphans.org.uk/history index2 visited 17th October 2012
[64] Kelly's Hammersmith & Shepherds Bush Directory 1924-5
[65] Post Office Directory 1928
[66] Metropolitan Police Orders dated 28th November 1933
[67] Metropolitan Police Orders dated 22nd November 1939
[68] Metropolitan Police Orders dated 28th March 1940
[69] Notes at Hammersmith & Fulham Archives 15th October 2012
[70] West London Observer 1940
[71] West London Observer 10th May 1940
[72] Cherry.B & Pevsner N. Buildings of England. 1991
[73] Metropolitan Police Surveyors Book
[74] Met.police.uk/history/remembrance2 accessed on 17th October 2012
[75] Metropolitan Police Orders dated 6th August 1964
[76] Fido M. & Skinner K. (1999) The Official Encyclopedia of Scotland Yard. Virgin, London
[77] The Job 29 May 1992
[78] The Sun Newspaper 27th October 1987
[79] English Heritage Letter dated 28th September 2011. Re Wanstead Police Station.
[80] National Archives MEPO 9/144
[81] Metropolitan Police Orders dated 22nd February 1884
[82] Metropolitan Police List of premises occupied at end of 1893
[83] Metropolitan Police Orders dated 7th June 1888
[84] Kelly's West Kensington and Hammersmith Directory 1896/7
[85] Kelly's Hammersmith and Shepherds Bush Directory 1924/5
[86] Metropolitan Police Orders dated 28th November 1933
[87] John Back Archive circa 1975
[88] Metropolitan Police Orders dated 5th July 1963
[89] John Back Archive circa 1975
[90] Metropolitan Police Orders dated 6th August 1964
[91] Met.police.uk/history/remembrance2 visited 17th October 2012
[92] Fido, M. & Skinner, K. (1999) The Official Encyclopedia of Scotland Yard. Virgin, London
[93] The Times 19th June 1980
[94] Fido M. & Skinner K. (1999) The Official Encyclopedia of Scotland Yard. Virgin, London

[95] http://shepherds-bush.blogspot.co.uk/2012/11/shepherds-bush-police-station-to-close.html accessed on 22nd October 2013

Chapter 6

The London Borough of Harrow

By Neil Watson

Introduction

In 1829, when the Metropolitan Police was founded by Sir Robert Peel, the area of Harrow was a rural outpost outside of London. The small villages of Pinner, Stanmore, Edgware and Harrow Weald were in the district whose only sizable settlement was Harrow on the Hill.

Harrow on the Hill had become notable due to the presence of the famous Harrow School which sits at the very top of the hill, looking south towards London. The school has been attended by hundreds of famous men since it was established in 1572 by John Lyon. Eight prime ministers are former Harrow pupils including Sir Winston Churchill and Sir Robert Peel.

In the early part of the 19th century, the area was patrolled by the 3rd Division of the Bow Street Horse Patrol which had been set up in 1805. The 'S' or Hampstead Division was extended in 1840 to include Edgware, where a station house was taken on the Edgware Road by the 8th mile stone adjoining the turnpike gate and this initially had 2 sergeants, fourteen constables and a horse patrol located there.

Over the last century the London Borough of Harrow has had four police stations to cover the policing needs of the district. They have been at Edgware, Pinner, Wealdstone and Harrow. West Street Police Station was the original 'Harrow Police Station' since Victorian times which was replaced in 1963 by the present Harrow Police Station although it was sold to Harrow School in 2011.

The district of Harrow grew with the coming of the railway which had the effect of killing off the coaching industry considering that Harrow was exactly one day's drive to Holborn. The London to Birmingham Railway from Euston cut through the borough with its first local station being at what is now Harrow & Wealdstone Station in 1837. Harrow was the first stop on the line out of Euston with a station at Hatch End being erected in 1844. Later still, the Metropolitan Line from London reached Harrow on the Hill in 1880 and progressed to Pinner in 1886.

Following the coming of the railway to Harrow, Pinner police station was closed and the policemen were moved to Harrow in 1842. By 1865 the increase in population saw the need for a police reorganisation and Harrow was to become part of the new 'X' or Paddington Division. Edgware police station remained in the 'S' or Hampstead Division.

In 1872/3 telegraph communication was being introduced across the Metropolitan Police and was installed at Edgware, which was given the code 'EG'. Soon after, the system was extended to include Harrow which became 'HW'. Pinner did not get its telegraph till the new station opened in 1899 and their designation became 'PI'.

London and its environs continued to grow steadily northwards towards Harrow and new rail lines and new stations sprang up into the first quarter of the 20th century. Industry began to develop in the area and Factories were built, especially large ones like Kodak's and particularly in Wealdstone which helped the area to grow. This also meant there was a considerable increase in the need for more police officers, as well as police buildings to cope with the building of new streets and houses as people migrated into the suburbs.

On 1st December 1933, Wealdstone Police station moved from 'S' or Hampstead Division to become part of 'X' or Kilburn Division.

On 1st April 1965 the old county of Middlesex was abolished and the GLC was formed creating the London Borough of Harrow. At the same time Edgware (QE) moved from 'S' Division to the new 'Q' or Wembley Division. Harrow (QA), Pinner (QP) and Wealdstone (QW) also moved to 'Q' Division. Today, Harrow Police Station is now the only 24 hour operational station in the borough.

This chapter includes the police station histories of Edgware, Pinner, Harrow, and Wealdstone.

Edgware Police Station

A police station existed in Edgware at 8 mile Stone in 1842. This was probably at the toll gate in Edgware road (known at the time as Watling Street). The station was part of 'S' or Hampstead Division under the charge of Superintendent John Carter. Prior to the building of the first Edgware Police Station, the area was policed by various local officials. In 1828 Great Stanmore had a single Parish constable, Francis Chapman who was assisted by four "headboroughs", (deputy constables) and the old system ran parallel with the introduction of the new police.

By 1829 they had printed notices cautioning boys from the parish from assembling in the town to the annoyance of the public and in breach of the public peace. A beadle was appointed in 1834 at 7 shillings a week and his role was to keep order and prosecute people for vagrancy as well as maintaining order in beer houses and preventing disorder on the Sabbath day.

The local stocks, which had been first mentioned in 1639 were moved to the workhouse yard in 1819. A cage built for imprisoning offenders was also situated at the Great Stanmore Workhouse. The Stanmore district became part of the Metropolitan Police District in 1842 though parish constables and headboroughs continued to be appointed till the 1860s.

Front entrance of the earlier, now demolished Edgware Police Station in Whitchurch Lane

Courts in the area were mostly held in Edgware from about 1551. They were usually held in a room of an inn such as The Crane, later renamed The Chandos Arms in Watling Street (later Edgware Road), or the Abercorn Arms on Stanmore Hill. The house next to the Chandos Arms belonging to the brewer Thomas Clutterbuck and joined to the inn by cellars and passageways became the first proper court of justices in 1850. By 1913 it was replaced by the new court in the Hyde, Hendon[1].

Land was sort on which to build a police station in Whitchurch Road, in the viilage of Edgware and Mr Andrew Jordan sold the Receiver John Wray a suitable plot for £80.

The first known police station in Edgware was built in Whitchurch Lane in 1848 at a cost of £582 for the building [2]. The building contained a charge room, three cells, three stall stable, two water closets and a coal shed. The station had one inspector, three sergeants and 21 constables and they were required to patrol

The building on the right is the court house in High Street, Edgware and to the left is the Chandos Arms Public House. The photo is thought to be a Victorian wedding party.

Bushey as well[3]. Edgware had a sergeant in charge until 1861 when it was considered important enough for an inspector to take over[4].

Edgware was originally part of 'S' or Hampstead Division and in 1889 it became part of Finchley sub division. In 1892 new land was acquired adjacent to the old station as there were plans to build to build a better and bigger purpose built station on site. A new station was built while the original building was converted into married quarters[5].

The station in Edgware (in the district of Little Stanmore) was opened for business on 19th May 1892 and immediately the building was occupied by a married inspector who paid 5/6 (28p) a week rent. More new land was acquired that cost

£250 for another building in 1889, while the alterations had cost an additional £1,693[6].

Edgware Police Station. 1848 – 1892. Whitchurch Lane, Edgware

In 1894 Edgware became a sub Divisional station with sectional stations at Bushey and Elstree. This meant the station and area was big enough for a sub divisional Inspector to take charge of the sub division[7]. The station was built with a waiting lobby, Inspector's office, charge room, two cells and an association cell (often referred to as the drunk tank). In the yard was a place to store oil lamps, two coal cellars, a three stall stable (with hay loft), ambulance store, parade shed and an inspectors store[8].

The area of Whitchurch Lane where the station was sited was known locally as 'Poor Lane'[9] especially as the alms houses were located there as well. In 1901 Sub Divisional Inspector (wt. no. 66383) Stephen W. T. Gifford (often misspelt Giffard) lived at the station with his wife and family. The station was small and he had recently been posted to Edgware where he was in overall charge[10]. Gifford from Kennington in London joined the police in 1882 remained in charge for six years until 1907 when his place was taken by Sub Divisional Inspector[11]. Gifford had been an Inspector on 'D' or Marylebone Division in 1891 when he was newly promoted residing in a block of flats at 54 Miles Buildings, Lintern Street Marylebone. Both Gifford, his wife and family must have been relieved to be moving out into the country from the smoky and built up conditions of Marylebone.

The area around the station had quite a narrow lane, as can be seen in the photograph above, and because of the main thoroughfare was restricted on 13th April 1927 the Receiver was served with a notice of compulsory requirement for the police station. This gave the receiver an opportunity to redevelop the station. The station was to be demolished due to road widening, and the Receiver was to be compensated with £2,000.

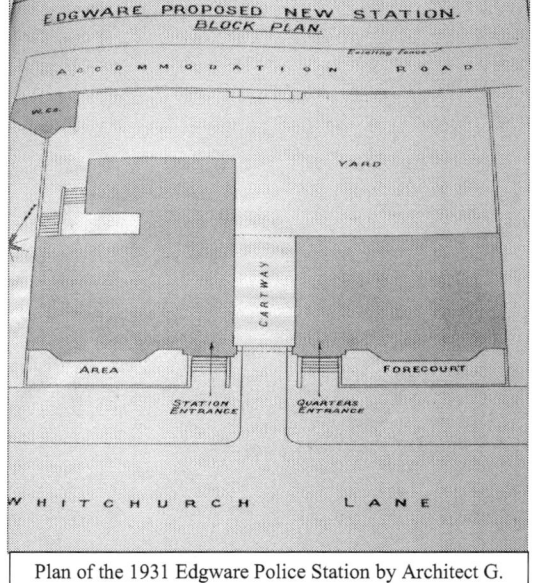

Plan of the 1931 Edgware Police Station by Architect G. MacKenzie French Esq., OBE, FRI, BA, FSI

An article in the Hendon and Finchley Times of 10th February 1928 gave an insight into the station's loss.

"No one, least of all the police, I imagine, will regret the news that the dismal old police station is to be pulled down. It is certainly a depressing place to visit, and must give the hump to those that work there.[12]"

Plan of the 1931 Edgware Police Station taken from the Met Police Architects drawings. The Architect was G. MacKenzie French Esq., OBE, FRI. The new station was constructed by Messrs Patman and Fotheringham.

1901 Census for Edgware Police Station, Whitchurch Lane[13]					
Name	Status	U/Married	Age	Occupation	Birthplace
Stephen Gifford	Head	Married	39 yrs	Police Inspector	Kennington, London
Rebecca Gifford	Wife	Married	41 yrs	-	Oxford
Percy Gifford	Son	Unmarried	13 yrs	-	Edgware Road, London
Lillian Gifford	Daughter	Unmarried	9 yrs	-	Edgware Road, London

Trench made sure that there were two separate entrances one into the station for business whilst the other enabled access to the living quarters both married and single officer's accommodation. Keeping these two areas separate was an essential feature of police station design.

Court Sergeant (wt. no. 67645) Hubert Hale from Gloucestershire retired in 1907 the same time as his Inspector[14]. Hale resided in the court House situated not far from the police station.

1901 Census for Edgware Court House, High Street, Edgware [15]					
Name	Status	U/Married	Age	Occupation	Birthplace
Hubert Hale	Head	Married	38yrs	Police Sergeant	East Dean, Glos
Ellen Hale	Wife	Married	38yrs	-	Monmouth, Pontypool
Edith Hale	Daughter	Unmarried	17yrs	Dressmaker	Rushdean, Glos
Margaret Hale	Daughter	Unmarried	6 mns	-	Little Stanmore

Also Edgware police station was built with three storeys and a basement. Most importantly it had a yard which could be accessed through a central arch. There was a back door to the yard which could be accessed on foot only. In the picture below the Sub divisional Inspector is flanked by his two colleagues

Edgware police line up circa 1920's

and the total strength of the station taken in about 1920. The new station was open for business on 6th June 1932.

By 1933 Edgware was given sub divisional status with Elstree and Bushey as sectional stations. In 1960 the station was located on 'S' Division and the sub

Division of Edgware had Superintendent A. J. Salter at its head. Its call sign was 'SE'.

Edgware Police Station. 1932 – present day. Whitchurch Lane, Edgware, Middlesex HA8 6LB.

On 1st April 1965, 'Q' Division was formed and Edgware moved from 'S' Division and given the station code of 'QE' [5].

By 1976 Sergeant Dennis Harris was in charge with 6 constables who patrolled the area. The station (QE) was reduced to office status with Pinner. The crime Prevention department was also located there with Constable John Rogers there.

In 2012 Edgware police station remained a police building but has been closed to the public for many years. It has been used as a base for the Child Protection Team. A recent report for Harrow Council described the Police Station as 'an imposing but appealing building, built in mock-Dutch style with modernist, angular details on an otherwise traditional form'[16].

Pinner Police Station

Pinner today is a fairly genteel and prosperous outer London, "Metroline" suburb. Going back in history however, Pinner was a small village 13 miles away from London[17]. A parish constable was responsible for early policing at least as far back as 1510. At that date the Manor Court Rolls show that Richard Rede was elected as constable of Pinner in place of John Clarke. One of their duties at that time was to ensure that all boys over the age of 12 years had bows and arrows[18].

In 1840, one sergeant and seven constables and a horse patrol were set up in Pinner, together with another four constables and a horse patrol in the town of Harrow. The area was part of an extended 'T' or Paddington Division. All charges at the two stations had their cases heard at Pinner.

In 1903 Pinner was a sectional station of Willesden. In the picture below taken in

Group outside Pinner Police Station, circa 1903   1 Waxwell Lane, Pinner,

1903 sub divisional Inspector Smith from Harrow Road, Willesden is seated in the centre being flanked to his right by the original inhabitant of the station, Station Sergeant 68 'X' John Moore (4 stripes on arms). Also located to the Inspectors left was Acting Sergeant 452 'X' Tooth (two stripes on arms). Other officers include Pc 557 'X' Barber to the left of door and Constable 160 'X' Thomas Westwood standing in the doorway to the right.

Standing to the right of the door are Constable 123 'X' Isaac Mitchell and the unfortunate horse patrol Constable 583 'X' William Batchelor who sports his riding boots and cutlass. He was later to be medically retired from the Force after one of the police horses in the stable bit off the thumb on his right hand in May 1902[19]. The stable block is shown to the far right of the photo.

By 1918, Constable Ivory Dean was in post and part of his duties included preventing the sale and setting off of fireworks. As Pinner grew in size in the 19th century, the need for a police station increased. Before the arrival of the police station birth, drunks, and disorderly prisoners were housed in a cage near the present Pinner Metropolitan Line Station. It's hard to say how needed the station was in those far off days but Pinner was, and still is one of London's quieter locations.

In a local case in 1893 held at the court it was pointed out to the Justice of the Peace (JP) by the defence that there had been no charges for being drunk for 10 years at Pinner. However, the local JP was quick to point out that this was mainly due to the fact that Pinner had no 'lock up'.

The 13 Mile post next to the 'police pub' the Oddfellows Arms opposite Pinner Police Station in 2012.

By 4th January 1892 a memo from the Commissioner's office stated;

> 'A Sergeants station with telegraphic communication is needed at Pinner where there are indications of a development of building operations. With a station on the Metropolitan Railway, an extensive suburb will doubtless grow up. At present there is no station nearer than Harrow and Ruislip, each over 3 miles distant'.

The locals had been petitioning for a police station for some time and in the spring 1898, The Harrow Gazette stated that;

> 'Thirty years ago the inhabitants of Pinner met in vestry and petitioned Scotland Yard for a police station. This requirement is about to be granted. The contractor's office and a quantity of bricks have been delivered on the site for the purpose[20]'.

It was reported to the Commissioner that there was no station nearer than Harrow and Ruislip, each about 3½ miles distant. A police station at Pinner was originally proposed in a Commissioner's Memorandum dated 4 January 1892 which noted housing development in the area and with a Station on the Metropolitan Railway an extensive suburb will doubtless grow up. On 30th March 1892 the Police Surveyor recommended purchase of a plot of land at the corner of the main Pinner Road and Waxwell Rise which was acquired for £250 on 29th September 1893.The plans by John Dixon Butler are dated August 1897 and were approved on 27th September[21].

The land on which the station now stands was eventually purchased on 29th September 1893 and the Home Office also kindly added £35 for the provision of a fence and gate to show the property's boundary. The freehold to land on which to build a police station was purchased by the Receiver of the Metropolitan Police for £250 on 29th September 1893 from a J. Healey Lea. The station was built between 1898 and 1899 by Fassnidge and Sons of Uxbridge, costing £3,165, 8 shillings and two pence to erect[22]. The station was originally shown as being at Waxwell Rise, High Road, Pinner, though it was later to be re numbered 1 Waxwell Lane on 13th March 1939. The building consisted of a lobby, waiting room, inspector's office, charge room, parade room and three cells. The stable had stalls for two horses and an attached ambulance shed. The Pinner Gas Company supplied the gas, and the Colne Valley Water Company supplied the water[23]. The site had previously been used as a penning area for stray animals which was called the Pinner Pound.

The building was described in a recent report by English Heritage;

> ...as a picturesque composition in the Domestic Revival manner, occupying a prominent corner site. The elevations have gables of different heights with deep eaves and bargeboards, some with decorative timber framing. Steep pitched roofs and tall stacks. Windows are mainly multi-pane timber sashes; those at ground floor within stone mullions, some with ogee carving to lintels. The front (south) elevation has a broad central gabled bay and a porch to the side with a moulded stone arch bearing a crenellated sign reading POLICE. There was an original plank door with cover fillets and brass furniture. Brick ramp and steps with metal railings are not of special interest. The east elevation has paired asymmetrical gables; the angle of the right-hand bay has a curved mullioned window above which is a deep moulded stone corbel. The single-storey cell block has a three-light mullioned window. The west elevation has paired asymmetrical gables and a single-storey WC block with a gablet; entrance to right (originally serving the married quarters) has ogee lintel and door similar to main entrance. The rear (north) elevation has a small tile-hung gable and full-width glazing to ground-floor parade room, with double doors. The roof has a steel platform, originally mounting a WWII air-raid siren. The

basement has metal ventilation grilles and stone steps down to the entrance. The rear (west) elevation of the cell block retains one original cell window with cast-iron frame, set high up in the wall; those to the other two bays have been enlarged. Small brick extension at north end is not of special interest[24].

As one enters the station through the glazed timber lobby, probably dating from the 1930s there are surviving features that include a simple stair with stick balusters

Pinner Police Station 1899- Waxwell Rise (later Waxwell Lane), High Road, Pinner, Middlesex

and chamfered newel posts, some doors and surrounds and a cell door. Glazed brick dados also survive in the parade room which have been painted over[25].

Outside there is a stable block consisting of a single storey with hayloft above, designed in similar style and materials to police station. The building exterior consisted of rendered gable to the front (east) elevation, chimney on the north and an outshut, originally a shed for a horse-drawn ambulance but now WCs, on the south side. The front elevation, which originally had a stable door to the right, has been re-modelled at ground floor level and now has paired sash windows and entrance to left[26]. This is now a canteen area.

Next to the stable is a brick boundary wall with a tall gate pier with pyramidal stone cap. Sections of perimeter fence to the east and west remain, with long and short close-boarding and timber piers. The small garden to the front elevation is enclosed by low stone bollards connected by a single iron rail; the western bollard has the original cast-iron police lamp-post and lantern. A signal lamp of uncertain date has been fixed to a pole mounted on the fence on Elm Park Road and another on the south-west corner of the building[27].

Police Orders show in the Buildings and Fixtures section the following announcement: -

> 'X (Division) The new Police Station at Pinner is to be taken into occupation by Police and business commenced therein 1st prox. The lodging assessment will be as follows; - 1 married sergeant at 4s per week.[28]"

The Pinner Gazette was happy to report the station finally open on 1st May 1899 under the headline "The New Police Station" writing thus, "The police authorities entered into occupation on Monday. The building is of prepossessing appearance and the interior arrangements have all been carried out with admirable circumspection. Station Sergeant Moore, who has for some months past been stationed at Harrow, is the officer in charge"[29].

Station Sergeant 68 'X' (wt. no. 62681) John Moore, was the first resident at Pinner police station in 1901. He was aged 43 years at the time, originally from Melton Mowbray in Leicestershire resided there with him were his wife Kate[30] aged 38 as well as the 3 children, John aged 14yrs. who was a railway parcels boy, Henry aged 9 yrs. and George aged 4yrs. Crime and punishment was in John's family, as his father Henry Moore was Superannuated Warder at Oakham Prison[31]. Sergeant Moore was fully six feet tall with grey eyes and dark, greying hair[32]. He retired to 22 Bedford Road, Kempston, Bedfordshire with a pension

Station Sergeant John Moore 68 'X'

of £69 11 shillings and 6 pence (£69.58p) in 1903. His pay at the end of his service in 1903 was £2-10-6 a (£2.53p) week plus his accommodation in the station.

Sergeant Moore's retirement was fully reported in the local press in 1903[33]. Inspector Smith made a speech on behalf of the Superintendent praising his efforts during the 'trials and difficulties that he had had to contend with'. He concluded that though 'there had not been much crime in the district,' Sergeant Moore's "promptitude had always been exerted with good result."

The ink on the front of Station Sergeant Moore's new Occurrence Book could hardly have been dry when the police station had its first 'customer' who was brought into the charge room on 11th May 1899. It arose from probably the most infamous public order outrages ever seen in leafy Pinner. The cause of the commotion was the Headstone Spring Races Riot. The incident was sensational news in the press for many weeks and it led directly to the cancellation of what had been a traditional event.

The Wealdstone Harrow and Wembley Observer reported the event with the headline "Riot at Headstone Races yesterday - Many Injured". The paper was scathing in its reporting on the behaviour of the race goers. It reported,

> 'There was a large gathering of persons at the Headstone Spring races yesterday, when a serious riot occurred in which many persons were badly injured. Unfortunately with the growth of the local races in popularity, the foreign and objectionable crowd from London has become each year in greater evidence, and yesterday it is safe to say that a more unruly, objectionable, and disgraceful mob has never been seen on any racecourse. Blackguards of the worst and lowest type, in fact the scum of civilisation came into the district. The police were totally inadequate to deal with the rough element[34]'.

Pinner police station lamp

Serious violence took place after a dispute of the result of one of the races and the event was stopped by the police. The race official, Mr. Drury had all the windows of his house smashed however he responded by threatening the "maddened crowd" with a gun. Only 9 police officers were on duty and they struggled to control a crowd of London roughnecks with 1,500 people attending the event.

The Harrow Gazette described the day as "Rampant ruffianism"[35] and that "organised gang of London scoundrels could do anything they wanted." Ginger beer bottles, poles and stones were being thrown around. The rioters then made their way back to Harrow Metropolitan Station. The mob sang ribald songs and swore at, and insulted passengers. The station book stall was over turned and scattered, a porter was cuffed and a lady had a watch taken from her breast.

One arrest was made on the day and it proved to be Pinner's first prisoner and later surrounded the case of Metropolitan Police v Charles Wilson (alias Williams). The same paper reported thus on the arrest. 'The First Charge'.

> 'This morning at Pinner Police Station, before Mr C.R. Nugent, the first police case was heard, and arose from the riot at Headstone races yesterday. Charles Wilson, who refused his address, was charged with attempting to pick pocket at the Headstone Races yesterday. Police evidence was given, and the prisoner was remanded to Edgware on Wednesday'[36].

At his subsequent trial, Mr. Wilson, who gave his address as Whitehorse Street, Stepney denied the charge but was convicted and sentenced to 6 weeks hard labour.

Police Constable 469 'X' Thomas Piner

The arresting officer Constable 384 'X', had had difficulty in effecting the arrest. He told the court that a large man in the road had tried to rescue the prisoner. He had managed to place Wilson in a trap which took him to Pinner. On the way to the station the prisoner threatened to throw the policeman out of the trap while the crowd threw sticks and stones at the police transport.

The appropriately named constable 469 'X' Thomas Piner[37] (at left) would have almost certainly been on duty on the day of the Pinner Races Riot. Constable Piner must have been quite a character. He was born on 11th March 1857 in Burnham, Bucks height a mere 5'8" tall and had joined the force at Great Scotland Yard on 5th February 1877 at the tender age of 19 years. He was tattooed on both arms with Britannia and crossed flags, and a ballad girl and crossed flags on his right arm and on his left was adorned with his initials, T.P. and the words "faith, hope and charity". He had been around a bit having transferred around the Metropolitan Police area frequently, serving on 'D', 'K', 'H', 'A' and 'X' Divisions, however his last 14 years were spent at Pinner. He lived at West End, Pinner with his wife Elizabeth and their 10 children[38]. Giving evidence at court must have been amusing as he would have taken the oath and described that he 'was Constable Pinner attached to Pinner Police station' which would have caused some amusement in court. Sometimes bored divisional clerks whose job it was to post officers from headquarters stations amused themselves with such antics.

The Harrow Gazette records constable Piner's retirement in 1902. He was presented with a 'handsome 8 day clock with barometer and thermometer combined' by Inspector Smith. He had been involved in a number of arrests over the years. In August 1899 together with Constable Batchelor he arrested 3 youths for robbing an orchard belonging to a Mr Elkington of Ruislip. He also felt George Halford's collar after catching him red handed pulling up a farmer's potatoes. The prisoner kicked Constable Piner in the leg and for this he was given seven days imprisonment for the theft but received one month imprisonment for assaulting Piner.

The Pinner Fair was first established in 1336 and has over the years caused no little upset to the peace and tranquility of the rural village of Pinner. Indeed the parishioners seemed to worry about the influx of undesirables into the area. It has always attracted a large police presence to see law and order upheld.

In 1879 the Fair was attended by 'several respectable people and a large number of roughs'[39].

Waxwell Lane entrance to the station c 1908. The scene is little changed today except that the lamps, the dog kennel and the washing have all been removed.

By 1908 Pinner was a sectional station to the newly created sub division of Harlesden and Sub Divisional Inspector Smith was still in charge[40].

A plan dated 1942 notes that the station was 'ameliorated in 1936' and showed alterations to the layout of the building with only the northern cell still in use with the other two now serving as a surgeon and matron's room and a detention room.

A telephone room was inserted between the parade room and Inspector's room incorporating what was originally a store room. Over the years the charge room and waiting room were reduced in size and an interview room added. Changes were also made to the layout of the entrance lobby and waiting room. On the upper floor the larder was converted to a third bedroom and a bicycle shed added to the rear of the cell block (subsequently converted to a generator room and later rebuilt). The stable has been converted to a canteen and the ambulance shed to WCs. The plan also shows the layout of the vegetable garden which once occupied the land to the west of the building.

Pinner Specials in 1918

The picture above shows 'X' Division specials in 1918, from Pinner receiving their long service medals which were presented by the Divisional Commandant seated second row from front and five from left. The Pinner first aid and ambulance section are seated at the front of the group with their stretchers. Special constables played a very significant part in Pinner as they did throughout the UK however in many ways their history has been largely forgotten.

Fairs attracted all sorts of people with Lady Northwick complaining in 1893 that the Fair was being attended by the people from Whitechapel. By the 1920's one correspondent claimed that the Fair attracted "every thief and ruffian for twenty miles." The police did record a number of thefts of purses wallets and cycles during Fair times. Things got really serious in 1906. A detective officer was brought into Pinner specially to guard against pick pockets however this unfortunate officer himself became a victim of some slippery fingered thief who relieved him of his watch and chain!

An affectionate artist's impression of Pinner Police Station

By 1942 the first floor corridor had been extended eastwards, the two northern rooms had been subdivided, the larder and scullery had been enlarged and several cupboards reconfigured. The partition in the north west room was later relocated to its present position. The basic original layout of two bedrooms to the north and a living room to the south flanked by a scullery and larder remains legible despite the later alterations. The ground floor layout remained as shown on the 1942 plan with some change of use of rooms and cells and the parade room has been encroached upon by the central store room and later subdivided into two irregular spaces, completely compromising its plan form and strongly affecting its character. 'the western outdoor lavatory has been converted into a modern interior one.

The lobby retains its original door and glazed entrance screen' the report notes that the 1897 plan shows an entrance screen with double doors rather than the present single door. While accepting that this may not have been as executed the report concludes that their date remains uncertain and from their character may date to the 1930s and relate to other alterations carried out in the lobby in 1936[41].

In 1962 a real bonus for the local constabulary arrived with the introduction to the event of the "Walkie Talkie" (better known now as personal radios), which were reported to have been a big success. Another success that year was the use of the interview Room at Pinner Police Station by a representative of Harrow Council and the Showman's Guild to arbitrate disputes. The cells ceased to be used in about 1964. Having served intermittently as offices since 1976, the police station reopened in July 2002 on a part time operational basis

The wheel really came off in 1964 when there were no less than 27 arrests[42] at the fair. There had been rumour's of 'Mods and Rockers' attending and 26 of the arrests were made for public order offences.

At the time of writing, Pinner Police Station houses two Safer Neighbourhood teams and is still open to the public though it's staffed by Volunteers. Pinner has over many years been a regular winner of the best kept police garden competition. In 2013 Pinner Police station became a grade 2 listed building.

Harrow (West Street) Police Station

West Street Police Station was the first police building in the borough of Harrow. In 1842 Harrow Police Station had been leased for an annual rent of £30[43]. Its exact location is unknown but it is thought to be near the bottom of the hill in West Street. A search of the 1851 census revealed the presence of a Sergeant James Cooper and four constables[44]. It's probable that Sergeant Cooper's first child, Arthur was born in the police station in 1850[45].

The police station was listed in the 1850 guide 'Handbook for Visitors to Harrow on the Hill'[46], as being at the bottom of the south side of West Street, next to a house in ruins, land and garden on land owned by George Beazley.

West Street Police Station, 76 West Street, Harrow on the Hill, Middlesex

In June 1866, the local Harrow Gazette was reporting under the heading 'Proposed New Police Station,' that a new site was being considered for a replacement police building. The Commissioner was considering spending £3,000 on a new station. A site in Crown Street had been offered and the paper suggested that the parish officers should make representations to headquarters before the final decision was taken. Despite this encouragement from the local paper, later the same year, the Receiver of the Metropolitan Police bought the freehold of West Street for £1,254[47].

Extract showing the 1851 Census record for West Street, Harrow on the Hill							
James J. Cooper	Head	Married	31	Sgt Met Police	Chelsea, Middx
Agnes S. Cooper	Wife	Married	23	-	Scotland
Arthur H. Cooper	Son	Unmarried	10 mths	-	Harrow, Middx
John Smith	Lodger	Unmarried	34	Police Constable	Kingston, Surrey
Edward Carston	Lodger	Unmarried	23	Police Constable	Marham, Norfolk
William Finlayson	Lodger	Unmarried	22	Police Constable	Scotland
William Rogers	Lodger	Unmarried	22	Police Constable	Shadwell, Middx

By 1869 the need for a new building appeared to be pressing. A letter to the editor of the Harrow Gazette complained as follows:

> 'Sir, permit me through the medium of your paper to draw the attention of our Nuisances Authorities to the badly constructed and unhealthy cells for the confinement of prisoners at the Harrow Police Station, with a view to their making representation to the Commissioner of Police of the unfitness of these cells for the most depraved of our creatures. I believe the Inspector of Nuisances has only to make an inspection of the cells for them to be at once condemned. I am sir, yours obediently, HUMANITAS'[48].

Relief was almost at hand when the Harrow Gazette reported action by the police in their report on 25th May 1872[49].

> 'We are glad to see that the Commissioners of police have at last pulled down and removed the dilapidated cottages near their station, and we trust that this work of demolition will soon be followed by the erection of a new and suitable police station. The present station is neither ample nor decent. Considering the large amount paid for Police Rates by the parish of Harrow, (nearly £1,900 a year), we think we should have a respectable looking building as we see in other parishes of less importance. If the Commissioners could add a room in which the magistrates could occasionally meet to transact business, it would be very desirable, for it would tend to lessen offences, and save the parish still further expenses, incurred by the police in conveying prisoners to Hammersmith and other police courts'.

On 9th November 1872, the Harrow Gazette reported more progress on the subject of the new station being erected 'above the cricket ground'[50]. It described the previous station as 'little better than a village cage'.

> The article went on, saying "The necessity for this building shows that Harrow is at least increasing in population, but, let us hope, not in crime."

West Street was finally finished in 1873[51]. Police Orders of 31st October reported that police business would commence on 1st November. The cost of the work was £2,271,[52] and was carried out by builders Messrs Fassnidge and Sons of Uxbridge. The same company was to build Pinner Police Station in 1899 and the building was designed by Mr R. H. Gager Esq[53].

The locals were pleased with their new station, so much so that a party to celebrate the opening was held in Crown Street in the room belonging to Mr J. Chapman. The Harrow Gazette reported in its 15th November 1873 edition that 70 guests attended the event[54]. Toasts were made to Inspector George Wills and Sergeant Arnold. The station was described as 'an ornament to that part of town'. The health of the clerk of works Mr Holloway and the foreman Mr Grace were also proposed.

The following week's edition of the local paper described the building in great detail[55]. The report mentioned the building being 'of classic design' with a frontage of 40 feet. Also that it was built of picked stock bricks with Doulton stone dressings. The building was 'entered by a portico of Doulton stone'. Three cells were present which were 'all warmed by Haydon's hot air apparatus'. The officers enjoyed a reading room and a bathroom with a hot air closet for drying the men's clothes. The first floor was the private apartment for the sergeant in charge, as well as the unmarried policemen. At the rear a two horse stable and an ambulance shed were erected. The only disappointment that the paper reported was that "No room has been provided for holding magistrates meetings in the new building, the present arrangements of taking cases to Edgware being both costly and inconvenient".

Harrow had originally been attached to 'T' or Kensington Division however in 1865 it transferred to 'X' or Paddington Division. Another change to 'X' Division was to follow in 1911, when Superintendent Olive submitted a report on 14th February suggesting that Harrow Sub Division comprised of Harrow, Pinner, Greenford and Northwood Police Stations. Harrow was to change for a final time in 1965 to become part of the newly formed 'Q' Division.

West Street was to close as the operational station for Harrow on 30th September 1963 having become too small[56]. The building remained in police ownership and has been used for various purposes since, such as Divisional

> **FATAL MOTOR CAR ACCIDENT.**
> On Saturday evening some gentlemen connected with Army and Navy stores were making an official trial of a waggonette motor car near Harrow. While the car was going down Grove Hill at a high speed the front wheels collapsed, and the occupants of the car were violently thrown out. A man named Sewell, who was driving the car, was killed, one gentleman being seriously injured, and four others received minor injuries. The car turned completely over, and was greatly damaged. The injured passengers were treated at the local hospital, but one of them, believed to be an army officer, is reported to be in a serious condition.
>
> Yorkshire Herald 27 February 1899

Offices, traffic wardens and the Harrow Town Team. Sadly, along with lots of other Victorian buildings, the Metropolitan Police Authority (MPA) have been selling off small cramped buildings not fit for 21st century policing and West Street was finally sold to Harrow School in 2011 to be used as offices[57].

West Street officers were to deal with the first fatal motor car accident in Britain. On 25th February 1899, Daimler representative Mr Edwin Sewell was demonstrating a 6HP Daimler Wagonette car to five people on a journey from Westminster[58]. After enjoying a lunch at the King's Head, Harrow, Mr Sewell was putting the car through its paces, in Grove Hill, Harrow, when a rear wheel rim collapsed causing the vehicle to crash. The 31-year-old engineer Mr Sewell died at the scene within minutes, while one of his passengers, Major James Ritcher, was thrown from the vehicle and suffered such serious injuries that he died four days later without gaining consciousness in hospital. The coroner's officer involved in this case, was West Street acting Sergeant James Walter Pearce[59]. The accident

Signpost in Grove Hill, Harrow where the fatality took place

The wheel's come off!
A West Street policeman surveys the damage and controls the crowds at Britain's first 'FATACC' involving a motor car passenger death.

attracted a great crowd and police from Harrow remained on scene to secure the vehicle once people had been conveyed to hospital. There was no traffic patrol to call on in those days and it wasn't until the 1930's that proper Traffic Units were introduced.

A very notable West Street police officer was Sergeant 32 'X' Charles Potter who retired on 21st April 1902 with a pension of £87, 16 shillings and 9 pence (£87.88p) [60]. He had a remarkable career and was involved in some infamous cases. The Harrow Gazette recorded details of Potters service as well as his retirement at Harrow after 26 years service [61]. He joined the Metropolitan Police on 17th April 1876. He came from a police family with his grandfather having been the parish constable in Chappell in Essex while his father had been a Superintendent in the Metropolitan Police. Three of his brothers were also policemen.

After arriving in London he was posted to Penge Police Station where his first charge was for four people who were connected with the murder of Harriett Staunton. All four were convicted and her husband and the husband's brother were sentenced to death. Both were later reprieved but were given life sentences. The method of killing Mrs Staunton was by keeping her locked up and starving her to death.

Sergeant Potter was present during the Trafalgar Square riots of 1887 as well as the Shipyard strikes of 1888. In 1890 he was posted to Notting Dale Police Station, 'In which rough district, was said to contain some of the worst characters in London". By 1895 Sergeant Potter was given his final posting to Harrow.

The other claim to fame that the good Sergeant could make was that he was the officer in charge of the only murder case where the defendant was a

Constable Potter was involved in the arrest of the four defendants. Harriet had been starved to death by the four accomplices

West Street Police Station Circa 1960's. Note the 'police' inscription above the main entrance which has now been removed.

serving policeman who was convicted at the Old Bailey and later hanged at Newgate. It was known as the Wormwood Scrubs Tragedy[62] and involved Constable 385 'X' (wt. no. 73717) George Samuel Cooke beating Maud Merton to death near the prison on 7th June 1893. Constable Cooke came from Ludham in Norfolk, joined the force aged 22 years on 22nd June 1888 and he was previously a fisherman.

The Old Bailey case report [63] gave details of the evidence on the case against constable Cooke. It recorded that he had served briefly on both 'L' and 'A' Division's before being posted to Bow Street as Constable 130 'E'. At about this time be became acquainted with Maud Merton who was a prostitute who frequented The Strand. She later complained about his behaviour towards her, to the station inspector and he was subsequently transferred to Notting Dale on 'X' Division. Maud Merton's body was found with severe head injuries in the area where Constable Cooke had been on night shift with witnesses reporting having seen Cooke with a female. On returning to his lodgings after his night shift Pc Cooke was seen burying something in the garden. When the inspector dug up the garden he found a truncheon which was marked 857 'A'. Constable Cooke was interviewed but denied the murder. He stated that he had bought the truncheon from 'Black Dick' for sixpence and that he had buried the truncheon as the truncheon was not his. Constable 857 'A' Henry Pomeroy told the court that he had been lodging at Westminster Section House at the same time as Constable Cooke when his truncheon had gone missing. Constable Cooke later confessed that he had not used the 'A' Division truncheon but had used his own 'X' Division issue one to strike Maud Merton. He told officers that Merton had been following him and was annoying him and that he 'was in misery'. He admitted hitting her three times with the truncheon and keeping his foot on her neck for five minutes.

An artists impressions of the forlorn looking constable Pc Cooke at West London Police Court

He said 'I felt nothing of killing her. I have been much happier since she has been dead'. Cooke did not call any witnesses at the trial although Cooke pleaded not guilty but after hearing the evidence the jury convicted him of murder. The jury strongly recommended to the Judge that Cooke should be shown mercy on the grounds of the provocation he received. The trial judge, Mr Justice Hawkins was clearly unimpressed for the call for mercy in sparing Cooke's life.

He told the prisoner that he would pass his plea for mercy to the Home Secretary. Mr Hawkins went on to describe the murder itself stating that 'a peculiar atrocity has been manifested'. He added that the act had been horribly cruel in response to her 'simply annoying him'. The blows to the head had been aggravated by his standing on her neck. He told Cooke 'It is my painful duty to sentence you to die'. As the sentence was passed by the black capped judge, a female in the gallery screamed out and then 'swooned'. The picture at left shows the constable at court in the Pall Mall magazine[64] during one of his hearings.

The Illustrated Police News[65] reported that Cooke and his sweetheart had arranged to marry in the October. She was unaware of the existence of Maud Merton and had discovered Cooke's arrest in the newspaper. She pawned her watch to bring comforts to her fiancé and visited him in prison every day.

Cooke wrote to a police comrade on 26th June where he lamented that he would no longer be able to share a half pint of 'bitter and Burton' and that he felt for his parents and for Nellie. He signed off, 'I remain your sincere friend, S. Cooke, HM Prison'.

The trial took place on 7th and 8th of July 1893. On 10th July he was dismissed from the Metropolitan Police. Cooke's sweetheart had tried to secure a reprieve for him but none was forthcoming. Cooke slept fitfully the night before the execution. In the morning he 'ate sparingly'. He expressed no sorrow for his crime, his only concern being that for his parents and sweetheart.

Though he looked haggard, he shook the hand of the chief warder and walked firmly to the scaffold where a five foot drop awaited him. Mr Billington performed the execution which took place without a struggle. A huge crowd had assembled outside Newgate on the morning on 25th July 1893 where Cooke met his death at 9am. A black flag was raised above the 'Debtors Door' to indicate the sentence had been carried out.

Police Orders[25] summed up Constable Cooke's demise as follows: Convicted of unlawful murder at the Central Criminal Court sessions and sentenced to death. NO PAY!

In the census details show that Potter and his wife, niece and four constables resided at the station in 1901[66]. These were Sergeant Charles Potter from Chappel in Essex, his wife Elenor, Florence Hull a book keeper and William Hall, Arthur Shepherd, John Eaton all constables.

Also retiring at the same time as Sgt Potter on 21st April 1902 was Acting Sergeant James Walter Pearce after 25 year's service. He also came from a police family having 3 brothers also in the force. After serving his first year at Carlton Terrace Station, Harrow Road, he transferred to Harrow where he spent the next 24 years. In 1887 he spent 3 months in plain clothes patrolling the grounds of Harrow School in an effort to prevent Irish terrorists blowing up the building.

The father of 10 children, Sergeant Pearce must have been a popular man. The local newspaper reported that arrangements were afoot for a collection to be made in the district to present a testimonial to both good sergeants on the day of the Coronation in 1902. It was said that a collector would be visiting every house in the district soliciting subscriptions[67]. He retired on an annual pension of £57 - 8 shillings and sixpence[68]. A prominent article in the local newspaper, the Harrow Gazette carried photographs of both the officers as well as a lengthy report of their service entitled 'The Police Retirements at Harrow'. The officers were both clearly well regarded.

The MSC played a significant part on 'X' Division and at Harrow during both World Wars. During World war one Harrow sustained the highest contingent of specials with 208.

Police sports days were a family event which allowed for some the chance to excel. Tug of war was a feat of combined strength and winners at these sport days were celebrated as the picture above shows. Widely believed to have been made famous in this country during the 16th century by Lord Elliott Simpson its origins date back to Egypt and China as part of rituals and ancient ceremonies. Teams of eight pull a rope measuring approximately 10 centimetres in circumference, in a weight class to ensure fairness. The rope has a white line was painted around the middle with two further markings either side at four metres distance. A centre line would be drawn on the ground and the centre of the rope would start from there. Teams positioned themselves at either end with an anchor man at the very end. The object is to pull the other team over the centre line. There are judges who ensure the rules are strictly adhered to e.g. sitting down is a foul. Tug of war was an Olympic sport from 1900 – 1920 when it was given up. The picture above shows the Harrow Division police winners in 1920 of the combined 'F' and 'X' Division Sports day. These were back row from (left to right) constables Hedges, Evans (res), Creed, Rush (res), Roots, Passmore, Sub Divisional Inspector Cosgrove. Front row, (left to right) constables Crabtree, Winters, Mansell (Captain), Savage and Greenfield.

Harrow Division Tug of War team winners 1920

West Street as it looked in November 2011 following its sale to Harrow School

At Harrow was a fire squad (a mixture of MSC and temporary Fire Brigade) which was formed with the co-operation of Captain Leader head of the Harrow Fire Brigade. The men were put through their drills and occasionally gave public displays. Numerous fires were attended by the Fire Squad but their biggest and most dangerous test was on 25th November 1918 when 500 tons of coke caught fire at the local gas works.

In 1957 Harrow was a station on 'X' with call sign 'XA'. It was a sub divisional station with Superintendent W. J. Poole was in charge with Pinner, Wembley and Wealdstone all being sectional stations. Poole was still in charge in 1962.

By 1965 Superintendent A. Flett DFC had taken over the sub division. With the amalgamations of the London boroughs of Ealing and Hillingdon Flett had been promoted to Chief Superintendent and placed in charge of 'X' Division.

The Boroughs of Harrow and Brent were now amalgamated on 'Q' Division and Harrow Police station had the call sign 'QA' with Superintendent A. C. Stanley in charge and Chief Inspector H. W. C. Howell was his deputy.

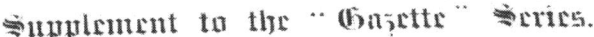

Station Sergeant Charles Potter and Acting Sergeant James Walter Pearce both retired on Coronation day 1902

Harrow had one sectional station – Pinner[69]. The station continued as 'QA' to 1989 where it was no longer a station taking charges and detaining prisoners for court.

Picture taken in 2003 outside West street Police Station

In 2011 the old station and grounds were sold to Harrow School for an undisclosed amount.

The word 'POLICE' has been removed from the plinth above the front entrance. In the picture below shows the line up outside West street Police Station West Street Police Station and officers in 2003 with Chief Superintendent Alex Fish of Harrow is seated front row 2nd from right.

Nicknames and police humour.

An amusing story involving the Chief Superintendent occurred before he retired. The author and another officer at Pinner were called by a resident of a small block of flats when water was seen coming from a flat above. They knocked on the door of the flat above but got no answer. The officers got into the flat and discovered what they first thought was that the tank housing some tropical fish was leaking as there was only 2 inches of water left.

This to the amusement of officers on the night duty at Pinner listening on the radio this incident became enshrined in Pinner folklore and rapidly became known as 'the tropical fish emergency'. On seeking advice the officers were told to take possession of the fish and remove them to London Zoo. However happy to oblige they found suitable container and placed the fish inside however due to a mix up by the Zoo staff the fish were placed in sea water and were later found dead. A complaint against the officers was made by the Zoo for bringing the fish to them in the first place. Fortunately the officers were found to be completely blameless but Harrow Police wrote to the Zoo and the letter informing them of the results of the inquiry was signed by 'A Fish'. Needless to say the author acquired the nickname 'Mr Fish'.

Harrow (Northolt Road) Police Station

The current Harrow Police Station is a relatively modern building in South Harrow which replaced the old West Street Police Station as the main station for the borough in the early 1960's. West Street was an old Victorian building in the oldest part of Harrow at the foot of Harrow on the Hill, right next to the cricket fields of the famous Harrow School. Less than half a mile away, the "new" Harrow Police Station became operational at 6am on 30th September 1963. The station was constructed by Messrs Dove Bros Ltd of Islington, with the work commencing on 24th April 1962[70]. Note the placement of the air raid siren on the roof and the old looking building next door to the police station was later replaced by an office block. That office now forms part of the "extended" police station.

In 1936 the Commissioner had asked for consideration to be given for the acquisition of a new site in Harrow "on which a station might be built in a few years time to replace the present one[71]. The old station in West Street was no longer suitable being very small and entirely inadequate to meet present day requirements".

Harrow Police Station under construction

The site in Northolt Road had in fact, originally been purchased in 1938 for the sum of £2,750 with plans for immediate building to commence. However, World War II was to halt the plans for a further 24 years. The site was let out to the G.P.O. from September 1950 to December 1961 as a garage for their vehicles and for storing their cable drums.

In 1963, 'Plato' from the local newspaper reported the new stations opening under the headline 'The Newcomers' [72]. It discovered an;

> 'air of gentle confusion. One detective entered a large office asking if anyone knew where the handcuffs were. It took several minutes to track them down'.

The reporter noted that the station was in possession of a full size billiards table and also that the building was fully up to date and imaginatively designed. The cost of the building was reported to be £120,000.

Harrow was later to be designated the divisional code 'QA' via Police Orders of 8th August 1964. The new telephone number for the station was **BYR**on 1113.

In recent years, Harrow Police Station has been struggling to cope with the demands of modern policing. The office building next door was incorporated into the station in the early 2000's. Extra 'portable' cells were also added. Plans for a new central police station has been discussed in recent years but is currently on hold[73].

Harrow Police Station 1963 – Present day. 74 Northolt Road, Harrow, Middlesex.

The present station in Northolt Road remains fully operational apart from the fact that there is no longer a front office. Members of the public who wish to report crimes, now have to visit the new police office a mile away in Peterborough Road, Harrow which opened in April 2010.

Wealdstone Police Station.

Wealdstone Police Station opened in 1909, but prior to this, the area was served by the Police Station at Edgware (Little Stanmore)[74]. In the 1880's, the London and North Western Railway was promoting a bill through Parliament for the construction of a railway line from Harrow to Stanmore. It was thought that a new line would attract a considerable amount of people to the area.

In the picture below Sergeant (wt. no. 83843) Fredrick Bolsover shown with flat cap back row 6th from left joined the police in April 1898 is taking part on the usual weekly pay parade. He went onto become a Station Sergeant and retired from 'X' Division in April 1923 after completing 25 years service[75].

Wealdstone and Stanmore Police Pay Parade (S Division)
1907

Also in the picture are; in the **Front row**: Constables Swan, Palethorpe, Alfred Wasp, Taylor, Sergeant Boyce, Sergeant Stewart, Constables William Chidgey, Howland. **Back row:** Parker, Chapman, William Larcombe, Turner, Albert Sands, Sergeant Bolsover, Constable Mills, Sergeants Pameter, Lanning, Constable Soper. Officers used to collect their pay at (Little) Stanmore on a wednesday.

Map taken from the Met Police Property records

In anticipation of greater numbers of people coming to the district, the Receiver of the Metropolitan Police bought an area of land opposite the Seven Balls Public House in Weald Lane at the junction with Hay Lane on 15th April 1887[76]. These roads are now renamed Kenton Lane and Gordon Avenue respectively. The site is now a car show room while the pub still survives.

In the map above shows the original site for Harrow Weald Police Station, opposite the Seven Balls Public House. The road 'from London' is now Kenton Lane at the junction with Gordon Avenue. Notice how this site is perfect for observation of all traffic coming up and down the London road.

By 1904 the proposed railway had never materialised, and the area around Stanmore remained as rural as ever. By this time, the population of Wealdstone had greatly increased due to several large factories being built in the area. With this in mind the Commissioner of police decided that the Harrow Weald site should be abandoned in favour of a new police station in Wealdstone[77]. The Harrow Weald site was eventually sold for £875 on 24th September 1934 to a Mr N.H. Sagar.

Front elevation plans for Wealdstone Police station

The site for the station was the four cottages called Mary's Place between the Board School and The Case Is Altered Public House. The cottages were purchased for £2,200 and then demolished[78]. The work on the new station began in late 1907 with the foundation stone being laid in 1908 and the station becoming fully operational on 22nd February 1909[79] at the cost of £7,768[80]. The first occupant of the station was Inspector Chapman who lived above the station and Sergeant Lanning was the first sergeant[81].

The picture above shows the site of the Wealdstone Police station in 1907. Once the old buildings were pulled down construction of a new station and court building commenced.

In the photograph of the buildings site shown below 'The Case is Altered Public House' is clearly visible on the right of the photograph.

The station, which is now a Grade II listed building[82] was built with an integral Magistrates Court and was described by the Scotland Yard architect J. Dixon Butler as "stone dressed in red brick with a central archway flanked by mullion bays." The right hand entrance was the Police Station, the left hand entrance, the Magistrates Court. The court comprised two court rooms, a Magistrates room, waiting room, Clerks office, strong room, women's waiting room, warrant office,

Site of the Wealdstone police station in 1907

solicitor's room and a store[83].

The court was operational until 25th June 1935 when court business transferred to the newly built Harrow Magistrates Court at Rosslyn Crescent Harrow. That court closed down in 2011.

When the court opened, the first sitting was reported by the local newspaper under the heading Wealdstone Petty Sessions - First Sitting. Mr Montague Sharpe of the Middlesex Quarter Sessions attended to officially declare the building open[84]. Twelve justices sat in the first session, among them Sir William Gilbert the famous composer of Gilbert and Sullivan fame who was a local JP. Also present was the local police chief, Superintendent T. Williams.

Wealdstone Police Station and Court Circa 1910

The very first case to be heard in the new court was a case of 65 year old Thomas Jeffs of Wembley who was charged with misconduct and using obscene language.

The Police station lamp

Constable 404 'X' told the court that Mr Jeffs had called him a 'Swede gnawer'. He had reacted violently to being arrested and was conveyed to the police station on a tram where he had to be held down. During the hearing, Jeffs clashed with his own solicitor. Later in the proceedings Mr Montague Sharpe observed that he was an excitable man but being as this was the first ever case at Wealdstone Court, a fine would suffice. After being fined five shillings, Mr Jeffs then swore at the chairman who increased the fine to one pound and fourteen shillings.

The police station section of the building comprised an inspectors office, charge room, waiting room, telegraph room, four cells, ambulance shed, store, coal room, heating and W.C's. Later in 1948 until 1964 the station shared the building with the Middlesex county Library[85].

In March 1909 the local newspaper[86] reported the playing of the annual Harrow Police v Harrow Firemen football match at Mr Atkins field. Terrible weather of rain and snow had affected the pitch which was in a 'shocking condition'. Having sold a large number of tickets for the match, the terrible weather restricted the size of the crowd to only 20 hardy souls. Six feet ten inch J.P., Mr Brian Piers Lascelles, the chairman of the local council, attended to kick off the match. The police led the game 2-0 with 5 minutes to play when the referee abandoned the match. The Fireman had put in a "plucky" performance though they had only been able to field 10 men.

The police team was Woodward; Saw & Gibson; Jackson, Lewendon & Rush; Moore, Windsor, Kessell, Tible (Captain) & Taschner with the secretary and linesman being Constable Thompson. The holders of the challenge cup were the Fire Brigade. The trophy was present at the match in the custody of fire chief, Captain Leader, but the report does not make clear whether it was actually awarded to the police due to the abandonment. The match was followed by a dinner with singing and speeches, which was attended by the Divisional Superintendent Olive, as well as Inspector McCondach. Much mutual respect was exchanged between the police and the Fire Brigade. It was said that 'Harrow Police are an excellent set of fellows'.

Wealdstone Police Station and Court building were appropriately situated right next to The Case is Altered Public House. This court replaced the courthouse located next to the Chandos Arms in Edgware.

In November 1933 Wealdstone was transferred from 'S' or Hampstead Division to 'X' or Kilburn division when it became a sectional station to Harrow. When the new courthouse opened in 1935 the police moved into the old court building and the CID took over some of the accommodation.

Another boundary change in 1964 saw Wealdstone become a sectional station to Edgware when it became part of 'Q' Division and took on the call sign 'QW'. Further re-organisation in 1976 saw 'QW' return to harrow and Pinner 'QP' and Edgware 'QE' revert to office status. A chief Inspector assisted by an inspector took charge.

The Wealdstone Train crash

The most momentous day in the history of Wealdstone Police Station was without question 8th October 1952 when the Harrow & Wealdstone Rail Disaster took place at Harrow & Wealdstone Station at 8.19am[87]. The Perth to Euston overnight sleeper crashed into the back of the stationary Tring to Euston train. Seconds later the London to Liverpool train collided with the first collision and 112 people died in Britain's second worst rail tragedy.

Aside from the 112 fatalities, there were an additional 167 taken to hospital and a further 183 people treated for injuries at the site. Casualties were taken to eight local hospitals. Edgware General Hospital had 40 doctors, 250 nurses and four operating theatres mobilised to help deal with the casualties. Police officers were drafted in from the surrounding area from Acton, Hampstead, Hendon, Hounslow, Golders Green, Ealing, Southall and Teddington Police Stations to help. Some 40 officers came from the Metropolitan Police Driving School from Hendon.

Police Sergeant 39 'X' Morgan witnessed the crash as he stepped off the number 30 bus outside the station. He ran 300 yards to Wealdstone Police Station to inform the station officer. By 9.05am Chief Superintendent David Illesley arrived from Harrow Road Police Station to take charge of the police operation at the scene and set up a control point on Platform 7. By 9.30am 137 police officers were on the scene as well as 18 police vehicles.

Wealdstone Police Station in 2012.

Chief Inspector Ivan Bray took charge of matters at Wealdstone Police Station.

The police mobile canteen finally arrived at the scene at 4pm, which was long after the US Air Force canteen from Ruislip had arrived at the station to help feed the rescue workers.

Wealdstone police station was overwhelmed by enquiries from relatives and a long queue formed outside the station. Extra phone lines had to be brought into the station to cope with the volume of calls. Overnight 100 officers continued to help with the police operation which continued for some days afterwards. Valuable lessons were learned by the police in dealing with major incidents as a result of the crash.

Wealdstone was originally part of 'S' Division, but on 28 November 1933, Police Orders noted that the station was to become part of 'X' Division. A further change was later announced by Police Orders dated 6 August 1965. The station then became part of 'Q' Division and was allocated the code 'QW'[88]. At the time of writing, the future of 'QW' remains uncertain. The building is still used by Harrow Police but is no longer open to the public, its front office having closed in 2010 however it is likely that the building will be sold off.

Acting Sergeant 713 'X' Eddie Phillips

There were originally 2 entrances to the building for the public. The rectangular stone above the door on the left of the gate was originally inscribed as 'Court House.' The right hand entrance was marked 'Police'. The stone above the court side is now blank, while the door to the police main entrance is now covered by the modern blue Met Police logo. The building is no longer open to the public.

In 1954 Acting sergeant 713 'X' Eddie Phillips was attached to the station. In the picture at left he is seen in the yard at Wealdstone in front of the wireless patrol car.

[1] Stanmore Past by Eileen M. Bowlt
[2] Metropolitan Police Property Register Page 154
[3] Edgware Police station history. Metropolitan Police Archives ESB London.
[4] Kellys directories 1861 -1900
[5] Harrow Highways Volume 8 by R S Brown 1978
[6] Metropolitan Police Surveyors Records p 154 ESB London.
[7] Kelly directory 1894
[8] Metropolitan Police Surveyors Records ESB London
[9] Harrow Division Athletic & Social Club Anniversary Souvenir Programme 1829 – 1979 Met Police 150th anniversary
[10] Kellys directory 1902
[11] Kellys directory 1908
[12] Harrow Division Athletic & Social Club Anniversary Souvenir Programme 1829 – 1979 Met Police 150th anniversary
[13] Census Records 1901
[14] Census Records 1901
[15] Census records 1901
[16] Edgware High Street Conservation Area Appraisal www.harrow.gov.uk
http://www2.harrow.gov.uk/documents/s15569/Edgware%20High%20Street%20Conservation%20Area%20-%20Appx.pdf
[17] Mile stone opposite Pinner Police Station which still stands outside the Oddfellows Arms states, "London 13 miles
[18] "Pinner in the Vale" by Edwin Ware's
[19] Harrow Gazette on 10th May 1902, article entitled "Sad Accident"
[20] The Harrow Gazette 7th May 1898
[21] Metropolitan Police Archives ESB London.
[22] Met Police Property Register for Pinner Police Station, page 218
[23] Ibid.
[24] English Heritage (2013) Letter confirming Listed building status of Pinner police station dated 25th January
[25] ibid
[26] ibid
[27] ibid
[28] Metropolitan Police Orders dated 29th April 1899
[29] The Pinner Gazette 6th May 1899
[30] 1901 Census for Pinner, RG13/1210, Folio 22, page 36, schedule 201
[31] 1881Census for St Martin's Leicester, RG11/3177 Folio 90, page 10, schedule 45 and also 1871 Census for Oakham, RG10/3300, Folio 70, page 32, schedule 138
[32] Metropolitan Police Pension record for Sgt John Moore
[33] Harrow Gazette 25th July 1903
[34] Wealdstone Harrow and Wembley Observer May 1899
[35] The Harrow Gazette 13th May 1899
[36] The Harrow Gazette 13th May 1899
[37] Metropolitan Police Pension records Constable Thomas Piner
[38] Census records 1891 and 1901
[39] Fairs Fair by Jim Golland
[40] Kellys directory 1908
[41] English Heritage (2013) Letter confirming Listed building status of Pinner police station dated 25th January.
[42] MEPO 2/7826 Metropolitan Police Pinner Fair records Public Record Office
[43] Harrow Division Athletic & Social Club Anniversary Souvenir Programme 1829 – 1979 Met Police 150th anniversary
[44] 1851 Census HO/107 /1700, page 42, schedule 160, folio 87
[45] Harrow - St Mary Parish Church Baptism Register for 1850, page 2, entry no 16. London Metropolitan Archives, ref DRO/003/01, Item 008
[46] T. Smith. Handbook for visitors to Harrow on the Hill
[47] Harrow Gazette, 1st June 1866 and Metropolitan Police Property Register sheet for West Street Police Station. Page 224
[48] Harrow Gazette, Page 4, January 1869
[49] Harrow Gazette, Page 4, January 1869
[50] Harrow Gazette, 9th Nov 1872

[51] Metropolitan Police Orders dated 31st October 1873
[52] Metropolitan Police Property Register sheet for West Street Police Station
[53] West Street Police Station 1st August 1970 (Harrow Civic Centre Archives, author unknown)
[54] Harrow Gazette, 15th November 1873
[55] Harrow Gazette, 22nd November 1873
[56] Harrow Police Station (Undated history deposited in Harrow Archives, author unknown)
[57] Harrow Observer, 2nd November 2011
[58] The Archive Photographs Series - Harrow by Brian Girling
[59] Harrow Gazette, 26th April 1902 "Acting Sergeant Pearce"
[60] Metropolitan Police pension records Met Police Archives ESB London
[61] The Harrow Gazette 7th May 1898
[62] The Peeler, No 14, 2010/11 "Fortunately the only one?" By Terry Stanford
[63] Old Bailey On Line http://www.oldbaileyonline.org Case reference T18930626-621. Page 957, Ninth Session 1892-3
[64] Pall mall Gazette 10th June 1893
[65] Illustrated Police News 15th July 1893
[66] Census records 1901
[67] Harrow Gazette 26th April 1902 "Acting Sergeant Pearce"
[68] Metropolitan Police pension records, Met Police Archives
[69] Police and Constabulary Almanacs 1965 - 1969
[70] Harrow Division Athletic & Social Club Anniversary Souvenir Programme 1829 – 1979 Met Police 150th anniversary
[71] Harrow Police Station (Met Police Archives, author unknown)
[72] Harrow Observer 3rd October 1963
[73] Harrow Observer 6th Jan 2009
[74] Wealdstone Police Station, A brief history (Stanmore & Harrow Historical Society newsletter), Autumn 1994 by Jean Linwood. (Harrow Archives)
[75] Metropolitan Police Pension Records ESB, London
[76] Metropolitan Police Property register and map for Harrow Weald, dated 15th April 1887, page 158
[77] Stanmore & Harrow Historical Society Newsletter, Autumn 1994 by Jean Linwood
[78] Metropolitan Police Property Register for Wealdstone, page 165
[79] Metropolitan Police Orders dated 20th February 1909
[80] Metropolitan Police Property Register for Wealdstone, page 165
[81] My Diary by Plato. Undated newspaper article held by Harrow Archives written after receiving an interesting letter from Mr Stanley Lanning of 110 College Road on policing in Wealdstone.
[82] English Heritage List, (Listed Buildings), entry Number: 1245418
[83] Metropolitan Police Property Register for Wealdstone, page 165
[84] Harrow Gazette 10th March 1909
[85] Wealdstone Police Station, A brief History (Stanmore & Harrow Historical Society newsletter), Autumn 1994 by Jean Linwood. (Harrow Archives)
[86] Harrow Gazette 10th March 1909
[87] Harrow & Wealdstone 50 years on. Clearing up the aftermath by Peter Tatlow
[88] Harrow Division Athletic & Social Club Anniversary Souvenir Programme 1829 – 1979 Met Police 150th anniversary

Chapter 7

The London Borough of Hillingdon

(incorporating Spelthorne & Heathrow Airport)

By David Swinden and Peter Kennison

Introduction

Originally set up in 1805 to patrol the radius of 16 miles around London the Bow Street Horse Patrol kept watch up and down the main highways to the West from London. Prior to the appearance of the 'New Police' as they were known, the area was described as 'the flattest and most bleakest in Middlesex', was the haunt of highwaymen who prayed upon the travellers on the main Exeter Mail Coach Road (the Staines Road) and would often rob the toll-house itself at Bedfont, near the Horse & Groom public-house[1].

The Staines road in the south of the parish was turnpiked in 1727[2]. There was a toll-house opposite the New Inn and also a side-bar at the end of the New Road and the Bedfont toll house was situated between the 15th and 16th Milestones, two of these stones (dated 1843) can still be seen today outside Bedfont Library (12 miles) and Bedfont Service station (13 Miles to Hyde Park Corner)[3].

Before the Bow Street patrols, highwaymen were sometimes pursued by soldiers from the cavalry barracks on Hounslow Heath. A Station was established at Bedfont as part of the 3rd division of the Bow Street Horse Patrol[4].

Before the railway came to Feltham in 1848 the village clustered around St. Dunstan's Church. Amongst the gravestones in the churchyard is that of William Wynne Ryland (d. 1783), a forger, a crime which was taken very seriously in those days. Ryland was one of the last criminals to be hanged on the public gallows at Tyburn (now Marble Arch)[5].

Feltham was a village and a parish in the Staines district of Middlesex. The village is located on the Richmond Extension railway, near the Longford river, 4¼ miles East by North of Staines. It has a station on the railway with telegraph, and a post office under the Hounslow postal district, London West; and is a pleasant rural place with many ornate dwellings. Feltham is situated 13 miles from London, two miles south of Heathrow Airport, close to the borders of Ashford and near the village of East Bedfont[6].

There is evidence of arrests being made by Bow Street Officers for murders and highway robberies as early as 1799 although one murder committed in 1802 wasn't solved until 1807[7].

Ashford and Ashford Police Cottages

In 1891 forty three year old Constable (wt. no. 49552) James Potterill lived at 3 Alpha Cottages, Ashford Middlesex with his wife Elizabeth and four children. Potterill had joined the London police in 1868 and he retired in 1893 from 'T' Division. In the same year Constable Henry Bassett (wt. no. 57060) and his family lived at York Cottages, Ashford. Bassett had joined in 1873 but resigned after only 20 years in 1893. Sergeant Edward Kemp, his wife and family lived in Staines Road, Ashford.

The freehold to the property in Feltham Road Ashford, Middlesex was purchased by the Receiver for a total of £305 in August 1903. This was not a police station but simply accommodation to house married officers and their families. These cottages were located on 'T' Division and included numbers 61 and 63 Feltham Road which were purchased together with plots of land at 39, 40, 41, 42, 43 and 44. The land formed part of the Chestnut Field estate whose owners included Mr. J. Collins and others. Situated also on the purchased land were some houses and cottages whose state of repair was unknown.

The site remained dormant for a while before authority was given for any police officers to make use of and cultivate the land before any building works commenced without paying any rates to the council. The Council adopted Chestnut Road in the meantime and the rates for no. 61 was £72. 19s 10d (£72.95p). Two further cottages were purchased in 1906 and cost £834 12s (£834.60p). The two cottages were occupied by two constables and their families and the rent was 7s 6d (38p) weekly. In 1934 the cottages were still being occupied by police families.

Harlington Police Station

The first police station at Harlington was a horse patrol station described as a house on a yearly tenancy of £30 from a Mrs Arabin Drayton[8] consisting of a durable brick and slate property with a stable for one horse and a garden at the rear. This station was given up in March 1870. Police then moved into another much larger property in Harlington owned by Mr William Hewett of Harlington however it was not only regarded as a police station but was also used as a section house for single constables[9]. Police occupied these premises from September 1870 until September 1873.

In 1886 police bought the freehold of a piece of land on the Bath Road for £350[10]. This land also included the mineral rights to Cranford St. John and Cranford Le Mote. Luckily for the landscape, the police officers were not mining prospectors[11].

It is not clear which premises, if any, police occupied until the new police station was built and occupied in September 1890. The police station cost £2,714 to build[12]. Accommodation at the new station allowed for the occupation of one married inspector at 5 shillings and 6 pence (28p) per week and one married

Harlington Police Station. 1890 – 1973. 75 Bath Road, Harlington

constable at three shillings (15p) a week living in the two adjoining police cottages[13]. The station also included an ambulance shed that housed the heavy wooden hand cart for the transfer of drunks, the sick or the dead.

In 1899 the police received notification from Lord Dawley, of nearby Dawley Manor, claiming that he had rights to the land and that police should vacate the police station. A stern letter from the Metropolitan Police Receiver to Lord Dawley, stating the police held the freehold interest, soon put an end to his claim, leaving him in no doubt who was the law in Harlington[14].

In 1911 Station Sergeant Fred Bristow, his wife Lilly and their two teenage children were living in the Police Cottages, Bath Road, Harlington[15].

In 1930 Harlington police station was described as one of the 'country stations' of the Metropolitan Police, and was situated about three miles short of Berkshire and Buckinghamshire boundaries.

In the early days of the station's existence, before public transport and the amenities of banks were available, the Superintendent would ride from Hammersmith, with an escort of three Police Constables (mounted) with the weekly pay for the officers at Harlington.

The rear entrance and yard of Harlington Police Station

Local inhabitants regarded this as a ceremonial occasion.

Invariably the Horse Guards on their way to Windsor would follow behind the Mounted Police[16].

The station closed at midnight and the constable, normally inside the station, would perform a short patrol in the vicinity. He carried the front door key to allow the patrolling station sergeant from Bedfont or sub-divisional inspector from Staines to sign the books, checking all was correct.

In 1951 the address of the station was changed to 75, Bath Road, Harlington[17], and it was situated on the perimeter of the expanding main London Heathrow Airport.

Harlington police station could not survive with all the changes being made to Heathrow Airport and the police station closed its doors on 8th November 1965. In 1967 the property was sold to the British Airport Authority who by then had become the owner of all the surrounding land and buildings. The police station was later demolished[18].

In 1972 a plaque entitled 'Metropolitan Police 1890' from the former Harlington police station was placed in the courtyard of West Drayton police station. West Drayton and the surrounding district had previously been policed from Harlington[19].

Harefield Police Station

A house in Rickmansworth Road, Harefield, owned by Mr Howe of Harefield, was acquired in 1842 on a 21-year lease at £16.10s.0d. (£16.50p) per year. It was a newly-built brick and slate building, with a large garden, good scullery, coal hole and water closets, a water supply from a well in the garden. The Receiver bought the freehold in October 1862 which included the adjoining cottage for £420.

The property was then converted at a cost of £410 to include an inspector's married quarters, two cells and two stall stables. The cottage nearby was occupied by a constable and his family[20]. In 1851 the two constables and their families living there were 29 year old George Broughton and his wife Matilda. Next door was Charles Paine and his wife Emma. George and Matilda remained there for a further 20 years[21]. In a police report from 1881 Harefield police station was described as being two small cottages in a village, with new stables. The water supply was

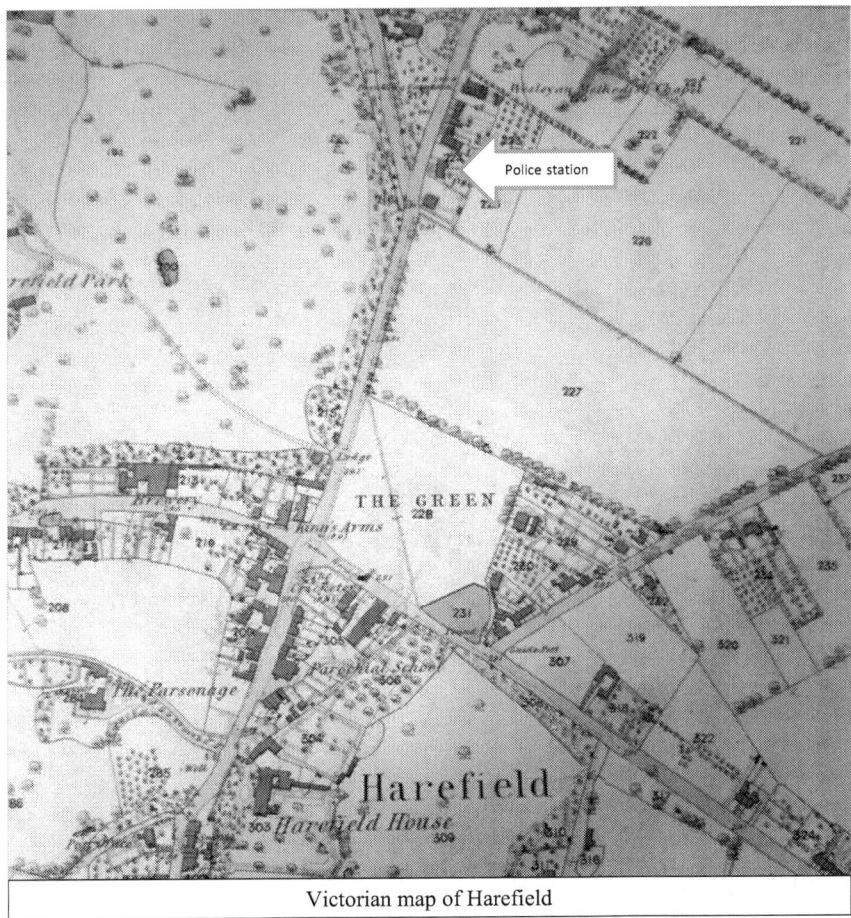

Victorian map of Harefield

polluted and there was difficulty in disposing of the sewage. At the time of the inspection the buildings were occupied by one married inspector and one married constable[22].

Harefield Police Station (cottages). 1862 – 1932. Rickmansworth Road, Harefield, Middlesex

In 1890 Harefield police station was on 'X' Division as a sectional station to Uxbridge, and was being policed by Sergeant William Filbee and eight constables[23]. Station Sergeant William Lay took charge before 1894 and he was assisted by one sergeant and eight police constables[24].

Harefield police cycle patrol circa 1908

In 1911 Police Sergeant George Grover, his wife Ellen and their three children were living in five rooms at the police station[25]. In the 1911 census, Constable John Albert Smith, his wife Agnes and their five children were living in five rooms in the Police Cottage, Harefield[26].

Harefield police station was closed in 1934 and the staff were transferred to Northwood and Ruislip police stations. After the station closed it was used as two sets of married quarters. These premises which were erected in 1842, apparently it had no proper foundations or damp-proof course, and during the last few years damp had started to seep in to the property. The house was demolished in 1957 and four new police flats were erected. These flats were opened in 1958 and then in October 1966 it was decided to build a police office. This was built at the side of the flats[27]. The address was 24, Rickmansworth Road, Harefield (XF)[28]. The police

Harefield Police Office. The Gate Office, Harefield Hospital, Hill End Road, Harefield.

office closed in 1974[29].

Currently there is a police office situated at the gate office of Harefield Hospital, in Hill End Road, Harefield and a Safer Neighbourhoods unit for Harefield.

Hayes and Gould's Green Police Stations

The original Hayes police station was a cottage on the Harlington Road just north of Gould's Green, and was in use in 1866 as shown on the Ordnance Survey Map of 1866[30]. It was actually called **Gould's Green Police Station.** The property was leased, first from W. F. de Salis, and later from Cecil de Salis both of Dawley Court, Uxbridge. The rental was £9 per annum[31].

A police report in 1881 described the property as 'a poor cottage, somewhat out of repair. The privy requires treatment'. The cottage was occupied by a married police constable[32]. In 1894 Constable (wt. no. 76106) Walter Selman (1890 – 1914) who had joined the police just four years before he occupied the cottage[33].

In 1898 constable John Christie appears to have been responsible for the policing of Gould's Green[34]. In the census of 1901 the officer is shown living with his wife Hannah and two children in Dawley Cottages, Gould's Green[35].

The Gould's Green Police Station was vacated in December 1902[36].

By 1864 a Hayes Police Station had not yet been mentioned, and nor was it

Early Victorian Map of Goulds Green

mentioned in 1865 when 'X' Division was formed. Yet a report from the Police Surveyor at that time pointing out the dilapidation of the Police Office (a Sergeant's cottage in Bag Lane, Hayes) stated that the property had been rented from a Mr. Gurney at a rent of £9 per annum for many years.

Hayes Police Station. 1870 - 1938. High Road, Hayes.

As a result of this report, property in High Road, Hayes was leased from Mr Tilbury for £400 in February 1870. An additional £480 was spent converting it into a police station. The premises consisted, on the ground floor, of a charge room, two cells, two stalls, coal cellar, coke cellar, W.C., Urinal and a dry earth store. Part of the first floor of the station was occupied by the adjoining owner an arrangement which had been in existence since 1871. The Home Office was aware of this unsatisfactory situation but continued to sanction this agreement as late as May 1892. The freehold of the property was later purchased in 1873.

Records confirm that the new Hayes police station was taken into occupation in September 1871[37] and later records in 1884 verify the address of the station as High Road, Hayes[38].

In 1878 Hayes police station was being supervised by Sergeant Samuel Dolphin and nine constables[39]. It was described in a police report in 1881 as a small cottage. A stable and cells had been built in the yard. The well was polluted by drains which passed quite close to it. At the time it was occupied by one married inspector[40]. In 1893 Hayes police station was held on an annual tenancy of £2 per annum[41].

The freehold of a new site for the present station site in Uxbridge Road at the corner of Morgan's Lane, Hayes, was purchased in 1911[42] from a Mr Phillips at a cost of £280, but the First World War delayed its building. When it did become operational on 19th June 1938 with one set of married quarters, it remained the

A rare view of the front office to Hayes Police Station

most modern station in Middlesex until long after the Second World War[43].

Meanwhile in July1912 an agreement was reached with Hayes Urban District Council for them to use the police station yard in High Road for the storage of fire appliances for a yearly rental of 5 Shillings (25p).

The agreement was terminated and the fire appliances removed in May 1928. Once the new station had been built, the property was sold to Middlesex County Council on 29th June 1938 for £2,400 in connection with the widening of Uxbridge Road[44].

The old police station was closed and all business was transferred to the new station in Uxbridge Road on 19th June 1938[45]. The old Hayes police station which

Hayes Police Station. 1938 – present day. 755 Uxbridge Road, Hayes. Middlesex UB4

was located on the north side of Uxbridge Road (formerly High Road, Hayes), opposite Angel Lane was later demolished.

In 1958 a notice from the then Hayes and Harlington Urban District Council required the station call sign (XY) to be numbered '755' Uxbridge Road[46].

In 1965 with the creation of the new London boroughs, Hayes became a Sub-Divisional Station in the new London Borough of Hillingdon. In 1966 freehold land adjoining the station at 1-5 Morgan's Lane was purchased by the Receiver.

With the formation of the Airport Division in 1974 the revision of police boundaries then placed Hayes as a sectional station to Ruislip sub-division.

In 1983 Police Constable John William Caplin died following the arrest of a violent shoplifter at Hayes during which he was punched in the chest. He collapsed at the police station and died later the same day from heart failure[47]. Once again the hazards of policing are shown in this tragic case. In 2013 the station was still open albeit with restricted opening hours for the station from Monday to Friday 9am until 9.30pm[48].

Hillingdon and Uxbridge Police Stations

In 1838, prior to the arrival of the Metropolitan Police, the Uxbridge Voluntary Police Force was set up in the town workhouse at Uxbridge[49]. For some months, it was supported by voluntary subscriptions, and after a satisfactory trial of its worth, the Force was permanently established on the 4th May in that same year, and placed under the directions of the Commissioner of Paving. The force comprised of Sergeant Superintendent William Winder, together with the following officers, William Servant, Robert Minchinton and John Simpson[50].

During the setting up of the Metropolitan Police in 1829 many of the London Parish Vestries strongly objected to the increase of rates payable for this new service. The old system of parish constables was less expensive for the Parish. Once the Force was established in the inner parts of London and seemed to be successful the outer parishes then wanted their share of the Metropolitan Police.

The Commissioner received a letter dated 18th September 1839 from the residents of Hillingdon and Uxbridge requesting that the Metropolitan Police be extended out to their part of London. The letter[51] addressed to the Home Secretary read as follows:-

> We, the undersigned Justices of the Peace acting for the division of Uxbridge in the county of Middlesex, also the undersigned inhabitants of the parish of Hillingdon and the town of Uxbridge and the vicinity, respectfully & earnestly beg your Lordship to be allowed to participate in the advantages and security offered by the recent Act of Parliament for the extension of the Metropolitan Police.
>
> *(signed) W. Wiseman J.P.*   B.P. Hodgson
>
> *T. Dagnall J.P.*   Curate of Hillingdon
>
> *Thomas T Clarke Jnr J.P.*
>
> *And others*

In January 1840 the Metropolitan Police extended cover to the outer areas of London, so Hillingdon and Uxbridge received their policemen.

A very substantial brick and slate house in Kingston Lane, Hillingdon was obtained on a 21-year lease from Michaelmas 1840 for use as a police station. The police station was known as Hillingdon and Uxbridge police station. The building had eight rooms, including a scullery, three cells, stables for three horses, coal shed, dung pit and yards at the front and rear. This was a inspector's station and remained so until 1871[52].

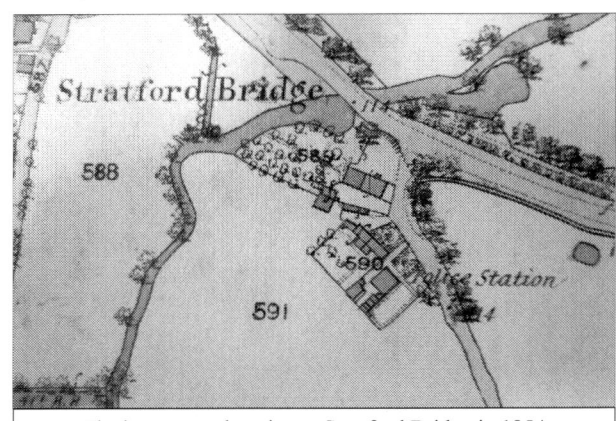

The horse patrol station at Stratford Bridge in 1854

In 1842 the 'T' Division was under the command of Superintendent David Williamson at Hammersmith, but Inspector Charles Otway was in charge of the Station House assisted by Police Sergeants R. Roadnight and L. Monaghan[53]. By 1843 Otways place was taken by Edward Cooke (wt. no.10679) who remained for some time until 1857. Otway had been transferred to 'A' or Whitehall Division. Cooke had joined in 1835 and promotion came early for him.

In 1851 Police Sergeant James Axley Turner, his wife Sarah and six single constables lived there. Also shown on the census record for that night are Police Inspector Charles Jeaks and Police Constable Joshua Turton, his wife Ann and four children. The address shown is the 'Police Station House', near the turnpike in Kingston Lane, Hillingdon[54]. Inspector Jeaks was still in charge of the Station in 1853[55].

On the map (shown above) of the Local Board of Health in 1854 the Police Station is shown as a horse patrol station. Today the station long since gone but the location is in present day Kingston Lane situated where Ivy Bridge Close now is. Stratford Bridge crosses the river at the point where Hillingdon Road meets Hillingdon Hill[56].

Since the 1840s policing in the area was from Hillingdon Police Station, there being no police station at Uxbridge. In 1864 Hillingdon was a station on 'T' or Kensington Division[57]. Then in 1865 a new Division (X) or Paddington Division was formed and Hillingdon was transferred from 'T' to 'X'[58].

In 1867 the 'X' Division was commanded by Superintendent Hugh Eccles who oversaw the purchase of the site in Uxbridge.

In 1866 a freehold plot of land owned by Mr George Baynham was purchased by the Receiver for £1500 at 49, Windsor Street, Uxbridge for the erection of a new police station. It then took a number of years before the new station was completed at a cost of £2870 and it was finally opened in September 1871 as Uxbridge Police Station[59]. Included in the station were two sets of married quarters.

The new police stations actual construction had taken just five months was taken possession of by Inspector John Eames and Acting Inspector Bullivent. The building was described in the local paper in 1871 as an imposing structure, brick built, with stone facings and ornamental coping. It contained, on the ground floor, a charge room, reserve room, reading room for the single men, store room and three cells. On the first floor were the quarters of the acting inspector, and sleeping accommodation for five single men. There was also a suite of apartments for the inspector. This was Inspector John Eames, his wife Jane and two children. Also living there was Police Constable Ames Smith and his wife Fanny[60]. The basement contained a mess room for the single men, cook's kitchen, bath and washing rooms and a drying closet. In the yard there was a four-stall stable[61].

In February 1871, an adjoining piece of land occupied by a stable and dung pits was bought again from Mr Baynham for £190[62].

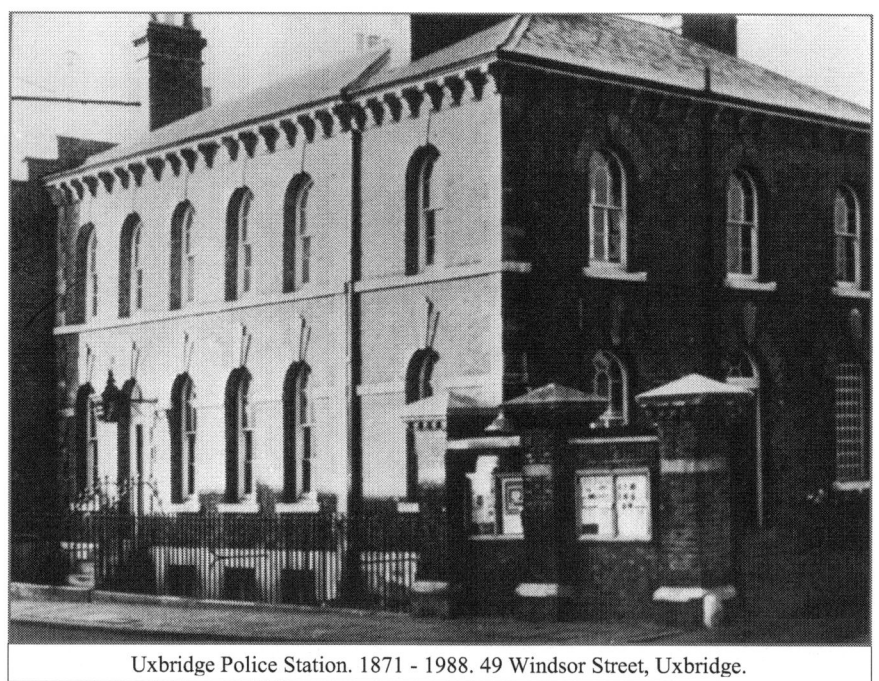

Uxbridge Police Station. 1871 - 1988. 49 Windsor Street, Uxbridge.

In 1881 a Metropolitan Police report stated that the Uxbridge site was limited, but the station had been specially constructed. The configuration of the accommodation needed revision as the married men and single men's quarters were mixed. They also found the basement was damp. Living there were two married inspectors and five single constables[63]. As a result of the above report, in 1882 one bed was taken away from the section house above the station to give every man 600 cubic feet of space. The water supply was from the Uxbridge Local Board, and was described as intermittent[64].

In the census of 1881 Inspector John Eames, his wife Jane and seven of their children were living at the police station. Inspector Joseph Capp and five constables were also there[65].

By 1887 the command of the Division was in the hands of Superintendent G. Skeats[66].

Sub Divisional Inspector Wade

In August 1889 William T. Wade, (wt. no. 52942) was promoted to Sub-Divisional Inspector and put in charge of Uxbridge Sub-Division. He was assisted by James Phillips and Charles Whitlock who were 3rd class Inspectors. There were also six sergeants and twenty eight constables[67].

William Wade had after two years in the Army had joined the City of London Police. In July 1870 he joined the Metropolitan Police and was posted to Bow Street police station. He then served at many different police stations in London as he rose through the ranks. He remained at Uxbridge for seven years until his retirement on 27th July 1896[68].

In 1893 at the police station described as in 'Ruislip Village', the following officers were stationed; Inspector Walter Weller and two constables William French and William Taylor (mounted)[69].

In 1903 Sub-Divisional Inspector Henry Brownscombe was in charge of Uxbridge sub–division and was medically retired from the Force as he had been partially blinded in an accidental shooting incident. He had been invited to a shoot on Lord Hillingdon's Estate and had incurred the injuries. His retirement presentations were performed by Lord Hillingdon himself who held himself responsible. He presented the officer with a gold watch and a cheque for £112. The inscription on the inner dome of the watch read:-

"Presented to H.P.Brownscombe by the inhabitants of Uxbridge and neighbourhood as a mark of their esteem and regard and an acknowledgement of his faithful service as Sub-Divisional Inspector of the Metropolitan Police. Nov., 1903"

The Inspector was also presented with a liqueur stand in an oak frame, mounted with silver, from the Captain and members of the Uxbridge Fire Brigade; an umbrella with ivory handle and travelling bag, from the Superintendent and Inspectors of 'X' Division, and a clock in an early English inlaid Chippendale case, from the Officers and men of the Uxbridge sub-division. The officer was obviously well liked and had drawn much sympathy from both inside and outside of the police service[70].

In April 1911 Inspector William Daniels and his wife Sarah were living in five rooms, and six single constables William O'Leary, George Thompson, Frederick Benner, George Sanderson, William Kentish and Robert Murton were living in five rooms in Uxbridge Police Station[71].

Uxbridge police station yard showing the old hand ambulance and new mode of transport the station van

The picture above taken in the 1930's shows the arrival of the new station van which replaced the hand ambulance on which drunks and sick or injured people would be transported. Dead bodies were also transported in this manner.

During the years 1937-39 talks were held with the Middlesex County Council and local Urban District Council on the question of building a new police station at Uxbridge.

There were plans for a new civic centre in the High Street with a police station forming part of it. The war intervened and plans had to be shelved for the duration. Discussions resumed in 1958-59 but by that time the situation had completely changed. The price of land and building costs had soared and so nothing happened.

A most unusual case that occurred in the area was that of the Russian master spies, Peter and Helen Kroger, who turned their bungalow at 45 Cranley Drive, Ruislip into the headquarters for a spy ring which included Gordon Lonsdale, Harry Houghton and Ethel Gee. The house was raided by police with some of Britain's top spy catchers in the late 1950s. The Krogers were jailed for 20 years at the Old Bailey in March 1961.

Sub Divisional Inspector Brownscombe

In 1969 they were exchanged in a deal with the Russians for Gerald Brooke. In 1977 local police went back to the bungalow to collect a radio transmitter, used by the spies, which had been dug up in the back garden by the family then living there[72].

In 1965 the new London boroughs were created and Uxbridge remained a Sub-Division Station on 'X' Division in the new London borough of Hillingdon[73].

Uxbridge Police Division was unaffected by the formation of the

The old police station now a public House – The Fig Tree

'Airport Division' in 1974[74].

302

In August 1978 a portakabin was placed into the yard of Uxbridge Police Station for use as a temporary police station prior to the station being closed for renovation and rewiring[75].

In 1983 Police Constable Frank Belienie was killed while on foot patrol when a car mounted the pavement and struck him at Hillingdon[76].

Planning permission was granted in 1984 for the building of a new police station at

Uxbridge Police Station. 1988 – until present day. Warwick place, Uxbridge.

the junction of Harefield Road and Warwick Place, Uxbridge. The new £3 million building was built and on 20th May 1988 the Home Secretary, Douglas Herd opened the new police station. The station is known as the Hillingdon Borough Headquarters at Uxbridge Police Station[77].

The old station closed in 1988 and was converted into The 'Fig Tree' - licensed premises. Whilst the outside of the buildings of the old station remain unaltered the inside has greatly changed. There is no sign of there having been a police presence inside, even the cells were converted into toilets. The property has been listed by the Local Authority as a building of architectural interest,

The plaque outside the old Uxbridge Police Station

In 1992, just five years after the new police station opened it was temporarily closed to install a divisional control room and to improve the custody suite. A 24 hour front counter service was available in portable offices next to the police station while the building work was in progress.

Northwood Police Station

At the turn of the 20th century Northwood, which until then had been just a village, began to expand. The arrival of the Metropolitan railway gave easier access to the capital and more residents were moving into the area. Northwood was sparsely policed and in 1905 Superintendent Olive 'X' Division sent a report to the Commissioner drawing his attention to the subject. This led directly to an increase in police strength at Ruislip police station of one sergeant and two constables[78] to patrol the Northwood area. There was no police station at Northwood at this stage[79].

A plot of freehold land in Northwood, situated at the corner of Murray and Maxwell Roads, was purchased from a Mr L.T.Simmons in December 1906 for £1000. This land had originally been part of the Eastbury Estate which had been split up and sold in plots for the building of houses. The Receiver had intended to erect four cottages for police officers to reside in on this site. However a letter, signed by four magistrates living in Northwood was received requesting that a police station with cell accommodation should be provided at Northwood and not just cottages[80].

Unfortunately the owners of the land and houses around and adjacent to the Receiver's site did not take kindly to there being a police station in their midst. In May 1908 they petitioned the Commissioner suggesting that the tone of the neighbourhood would be lowered and that the value of their property would drop considerably. They even suggested that the police station should be erected to the east of the railway in the poorer part of the town where it was most needed.

Nevertheless in spite of all objections a contract was signed on 7th September 1909 between the Receiver and a local builder, Mr Charles Keasley, for the erection of a new station at Northwood, including four sets of married quarters, for the sum of £4,793. The building was designed by the Metropolitan Police Surveyor, John Dixon Butler. The new station was built and ready for occupation in July 1911[81].

Northwood police station is one of only two stations in the whole of London that only have a white 'POLICE' light sign outside the building. The local authority would not allow a normal blue lamp. It may have been due to the pressure of local residents who did not want the police station in the first place. The other police station was, Bow Street, opposite the Royal Opera House in Bow Street, London. Queen Victoria, on a visit to the Opera House, objected to the blue lamp. Two stories are told as to why she objected, the first was that the blue lamp spoilt the 'ambience' of the area, and secondly that she objected to the blue of the lamp as

Northwood Police Station. 1911 – to present day. 2 Murray Road, Northwood.

her husband, Prince Albert, died in the Blue Room at Windsor Castle.

The citizens of Northwood had not ceased in their fight against the new police station and several actions for damages were instituted against the Receiver. In fact two actually reached the King's Bench Division in the High Court. On counsel's advice minimal costs for damages were paid to the plaintiffs and there the matter finally ended, and the presence of the police station was accepted by one and all[82].

In 1911 Police Constable William Munday and his wife Ellen and two teenage children were living in four rooms at the police station[83].

There are rumours of a ghost in the police station. Apparently a sergeant hanged himself in the married quarters in the 1920s and is said that his ghost occasionally walks from the cells to the station office[84].

In October 1927 the local Council informed police that the postal address of the station would be 2, Murray Road as the entrance was in that road, and that the married quarters should be shown in Maxwell Road as it was a corner site[85].

In the reorganisation of police boundaries, as a result of the creation of new London boroughs with effect from 1st April 1965, the Northwood Police Station became a section station of Uxbridge sub-division in the new London Borough of Hillingdon[86].

In 1973 Inspector George Rowland was in charge of the station.

Special constables leaving the station on patrol in the 1920's

In 2008 Northwood police station was designated a British listed building, Grade II, under the English Heritage System[87]. The principal reasons for listing the building were:

There was special architectural interest as a notable example of a police station by John Dixon Butler, Metropolitan Police Surveyor and Architect, in an old English style, a response to the particularities of the location. Also the style was subtly expressed and the building is equal in architectural quality to the best of the domestic suburban development with which it sought to be in keeping.

Lastly it was in a good state of preservation with interior and subsidiary features of interest including front doors, vestibule screen, front desk, staircase, post lamp and 1930s police call box.

Ruislip Police Station

In the 1840s when the Metropolitan Police took over Ruislip they moved into an old cottage on the Ruislip Park Estate in Ickenham Road near the junction of Clark Avenue, Ruislip[88].

The cottage was held on a £10 yearly tenancy from a Mr Clark. The cottage was later owned by Mr J. Spinks. It was a brick and tiled property with a large garden, scullery and two stables. The sergeant living in the quarters paid rent and taxes for the use of the garden[89]. The cottage of the horse patrol shown in the map below is the north side of what is now called King Edwards Road about 100 yards from

Church Avenue Ruislip. It is likely the horse patrol station was given up in 1869 when the new Ruislip police station became operational at 17 High Street, Ruislip.

Police records in 1864 show that Ruislip was a police station on 'T' or Kensington Division, but it was premises without cells or a charge room[90]. Then in 1865 with the formation of three new divisions, Ruislip transferred to the newly formed 'X'

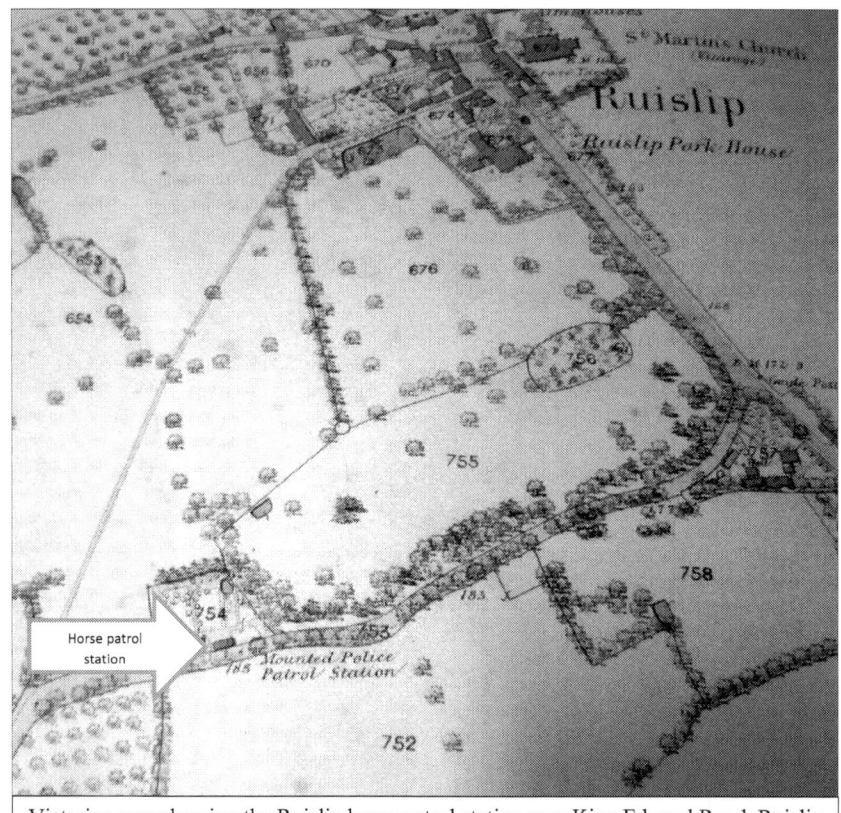

Victorian map showing the Ruislip horse patrol station now King Edward Road, Ruislip

or Paddington Division[91].

The Police Surveyor reported in May 1869 on the dilapidated condition of the station and suggested that it should be given up as soon as more suitable premises could be found.

Superintendent Hugh Eccles of 'X' Division also reported in June 1869 on the dangerous state of the existing police station. He further reported on a seven roomed house at 17, High Street, Ruislip, belonging to a Mr. Richard Ewer of Hill

Farm, Ruislip as being ideal for the purpose. The Surveyor inspected the premises and reported there would be accommodation available for a married sergeant and constable and a room could be appropriated as a charge room. It would require stabling and cells to be provided. The property could be leased at a rent of £20 per annum[92]. The lease was for 21 years from Michaelmas 1869 to Michaelmas 1890 with the option to purchase for £500 within three years. The Receiver was responsible for repairs and paying the taxes and insurance[93]. Police eventually purchased the freehold of the property in 1873[94].

In December 1869 the Surveyor reported that the newly leased premises were ready for occupation by Police[95]. The first floor and parts of the ground floor were occupied as police quarters until 1935 when the Sergeant, who lived there with his family, retired and moved out allowing the whole of the building to be converted for police use[96]. The ground floor rooms were altered to become the front office,

Ruislip Police Station. 1869 – 1961. 17 High Street, Ruislip.

charge room and communication room. The upstairs rooms became the canteen and C.I.D. office. A room above the stables became the Special Constabulary office. The station had its own water well in the yard. The cells were used as a decontamination centre and were never again used for prisoners. From that date until 1961 Ruislip was without cells and prisoners were conveyed to Uxbridge[97]. The Receiver purchased the freehold of the property in 1873[98].

The police station sandbagged up during the 2nd World War.

When police moved out of the old police station cottage into the new property in 1869, the old cottage was converted into tea rooms. However, in the 1911 census[99] there is reference to an address of 'Old Police Station Ruislip' where we find John Weatherly a bricklayer and builder, living with his wife Grace, and seven children. The cottage was probably the old police station which was vacated by police in 1869. The building was eventually demolished in 1926.

A police report in 1881 described the property acquired in 1869 with one married inspector in occupation but showing that it was 'an ordinary dwelling in a small village with cells and stables added'[100].

By 1902 Ruislip police station was often referred to as Ruislip Village police station[101]. A freehold piece of land and shop, opposite the station, was acquired late in 1906 for £850 by the Receiver with a view to one day erecting a new station[102]. The shop was let at 15 shillings and 6d (78p) per week including rates and taxes[103].

In 1908 Police Constable George Rolfe was fatally injured when he accidentally collided with a man while cycling to work at Ruislip[104].

In 1911 Police Sergeant John Dunford, his wife Eliza and two children were living in four rooms at the police station[105].

Superintendent Olive of 'X' Division reported in May 1912 that some 6,000 acres of land lying between Ruislip and Northwood were to be converted into a Garden City. The increase in the population would mean an increase in the number of police at Ruislip and a new police station would need to be built. Plans were drawn up for the new station but the outbreak of the 1914-18 War stopped any further building[106].

Ruislip station following judging for the garden competition

In 1924 the address of Ruislip Police Station, together with one set of married quarters, was shown as 1 West End Road, Ruislip[107]. In March 1928 a strip of the frontage outside Ruislip Police Station was sold to Middlesex County Council for £72.12s.0d[108].

In 1934 a property called 'The Oaks' was purchased at a cost of £4,500. The site was next to the undeveloped site previously bought by police in 1906. Parts of this property were sold off as surplus to requirements. Once again war intervened this time the 1939-45 conflict. Building was very slow after the War but eventually five sets of married quarters and a new Ruislip police station were built on the site[109].

The new sectional police station at The Oaks, Manor Road, Ruislip was opened for business 30th October 1961. At the same time the existing station at 17, High Street, Ruislip was closed[110]. The old station with its beautiful little front garden adding colour to the High Street was sold in 1963 and demolished to make way for offices and shops[111], and the builders had great trouble filling in the well at the rear[112]. Up until about 1935 the well was in full use pumping up

Ruislip Police Station. 1961 – present day. The Oaks, Manor Road, Ruislip

clear water[113].

At the beginning of the Second World War in 1940 two War Reserve Constables Alexander Bruce and Thomas Oswald Bell Cockburn were killed in a bomb explosion during an enemy raid at Ruislip[114].

In 1965 Ruislip became a section station of Uxbridge sub-division when the new London Borough of Hillingdon was created[115]. In 1968 further changes enhanced the status of Ruislip when it became a sub division and Uxbridge and Northwood were sectional stations on the division[116].

In 1993 Police Constable Michael Robert Perry was unfortunately killed when his patrol car crashed into a tree while responding to an emergency call at Ruislip[117].

Silver Jubilee celebrations at Ruislip in 1977

The new Ruislip police station was opened and occupied on 31st October 1961[118].

Staines Police Station (and Spelthorne)

In the 1830's, the parishioners of Staines requested that a corps of the Metropolitan Police be placed on permanent duty in the town. The fame of the force largely composed of former Bow Street horse patrol and dismounted Bow Street patrols and military men, was spreading outwards from London to the suburbs, where residents felt the need for effective policing.

Bounty hunters in the style of the Wild West would, it appears, have been encouraged to aid law and order. Following the incident in January 1819 when postman James Harris, conveying mail between Chertsey and Staines was 'feloniously stopped in the highway and robbed of his watch, and was also cruelly beaten by the robber or robbers', the General Post Office in London offered a £20 reward to 'whoever shall apprehend the person or persons guilty of the said robbery'[119].

As early as 1805 the men of the Bow Street horse patrols had set up horse patrol stations on the Staines Road at Hounslow Heath, at Bedfont and on the Bath Road at Colnbrook in Berkshire. These original horse-patrols were absorbed into the Metropolitan Police in 1839 and in January 1840 the 'New Police' established station houses in the parishes of Staines and Sunbury. Staines was placed under the 'T' or Kensington Division (Brentford sub-division) whose complement of three Sergeants and 15 constables patrolled the parishes of Staines (Population 2486), Stanwell, (population 1386 with Colnbrook), Ashford (population 4518), Bedfont, West Bedfont, Hatton, Laleham, Littleton, Shepperton (Population 847) and Upper Halliford[120].

> The old 'parish cage' - probably little more than a single brick built cell with a solid door and barred window - stood on the junction of the High Street and Thames Street in Staines. It was demolished in 1830[121].

Night time foot patrols were introduced, followed by horse patrols which operated on main roads within a 16 mile radius of central London. Until the 1830's, the Bow Street Runners had a station in London Road, Staines, at the junction with Swinburn Lane, now non-existent, which led to Stanwell Moor. The station was manned by a Captain, a corporal and five troopers or townsmen. One of their jobs was to control the local and farm traffic along the London and Kingston Roads, and along the High Street towards Staines Bridge, so that the streets were clear when the fast mail coaches were due through.

The Runners had already disbanded by 1839 when two constables and four headboroughs', nominated by the 'leet jury and sworn in before the Lord of the Manor at his court leet' were tasked with keeping the peace. The Metropolitan Police took over the area a few years later. In 1829, Parliament passed the Metropolitan Police Improvement (MPI) Act. This provided for the establishment of a new force, the headquarters of which was to be at the old Royal Palace of Whitehall - Scotland Yard. The Bow Street runners were not disbanded for about ten years, and worked in parallel with the new force, but many of them joined the Metropolitan Police.

A number were fairly quickly sacked, however, as they were not used to the sort of discipline now being imposed on constables and many were rather too fond of a drink on duty. Three officers in Spelthorne alone were fined and dismissed for drunkenness in 1840. One got 21 days hard labour for trying to stab a sergeant!

The whole of Middlesex - including Spelthorne which became known as 'T'

Staines Police Station. 1872 – 1999. London Road, Staines, Surrey.

Division - eventually came under the authority of the new force.

In 1841 a substantial brick and slate building in Staines containing seven rooms with a yard was rented by the Receiver from Mr South of Staines on an annual rent of £33. The station was shown as part of 'T' Division. There was a kitchen, charge room and cells on the ground floor. The agreement was that the police would have it painted regularly and the station was whitened usually every four years. Records show in 1868 and 1871 that this was done. When surveyed in 1845 the station was said to be in a good, clean condition with plenty of water and good ventilation[122].

Thames Division, operated patrol boats as far as Staines Bridge. The Marine police had been financed by the West India Company in the 1790s, when numerous rogues were stealing from ships on the Thames. The marine police set up their base at Wapping and Thames division still has its headquarters there to this day.

The officers in charge at Staines in 1851 (the year Surrey Constabulary was formed) was an Inspector George Bailey and a Sergeant Walter Lee. The nearest railway station to Staines was at West Drayton, opened by the Great Western Railway (G.W.R.) in June 1838 from which incidentally a branch line ran to Staines by way of Colnbrook between 1885-1965. A decade later in August 1848 the London and South Western Railway extended their Richmond branch to Datchet with stations at Staines and Ashford, the latter for some years carrying the suffix (Middlesex) to differentiate its namesake in Kent[123]. In 1861 Constables Henry Ing, Patrick Roche, Richard Williams, Joseph Burbridge, and Charles Brill were resident in the section house at the station. Sergeant Charles Simpkins, his wife and three children who were resident at the station. Sergeant William Atter, Constables Charles Brooks and William Prideaux also lived at the station then.

Staines Police Station Yard and rear entrance to the building

The old station survived until November 1998 when it was replaced by the present modern building in Kingston Road. Sunbury was transferred from 'V division to 'T' division in October 1865 and ever since then Staines and Sunbury have been closely associated. The latter was served by the Thames Valley Railway from November 1864 as part of the Shepperton Branch, Upper Halliford however only dates from 1944 when it was opened for war workers[124].

Despite Staines now being within the jurisdiction of the Metropolitan Police District (MPD) one Jasper Adams still held the ancient office of High Constable. The Sunbury section, then part of the 'V or Wandsworth Division was within the vast Kingston sub-division and was located at No. 19 Thames Street. Four Sergeants and 21 constables were responsible for the parishes of Sunbury (population 1863), Teddington, Hampton Court, Hampton Wick, Feltham and Hanworth[125].

The old two cell Staines police-station dating from 1841 in London Road was replaced in 1872, at a cost of £3,932. The new station had four cells and four stalls for the horse patrols. The town now had a population of 3,469, while the parish itself numbered 3,659 souls[126].

Women were first appointed in 1919 following the First World War. When there was a proposal to disband the group of a hundred 'patrols' and their ten sergeants less than four years later, there was an outcry, Many of them were later sworn in as constables but it was to be another fifty years - in 1973 - before they got equal pay, and the same training and promotion prospects as their male colleagues.

The old Bow Street patrol office was the first building to be occupied in Staines by the Metropolitan Police. Then in 1865, a building almost opposite was taken over, the site of the candle factory. It soon became clear that a purpose-built station was required, and for the sum of £500, Nightingale's Field was purchased. The new station, built at a cost of over £4,000 and opened in 1876, served Staines for over 100 years. Meanwhile, during its construction a temporary move into yet another building was deemed necessary. This was where Kingston Road School was later built. Spelthorne's new police Station is on the same site[127].

The rear yard of Staines Police station circa 1908 showing gardening plot

Under the Summary Jurisdiction Act 1879 the old station was used as an Occasional Court house until January 1883 when this function passed to the new station[128].

Although Staines was a nearly new police station there were problems with sanitation and design. In 1881 an inspection of the station found the well in the yard was contaminated with sewage, and instructions were given to isolate the cesspool and dig a new well to provide drinking water. The station contained the inspector and sergeant with their respective families although these rooms were not considered sufficiently private enough and they were not self contained. The men would parade inside the station in the charge room but this was no longer workable as numbers of officers on parade often interfered with the station inspector or sergeant dealing with prisoners. It was recommended that a suitably sized parade shed was constructed in the yard for this purpose[129].

An amusing story is told about the Victorian building. One of the men working on the construction of the cells was brick layer 'Socky' Bolton. At their completion he celebrated in time honoured manner, and was then arrested for being drunk, thus becoming the first ever occupant of the cells. The next day he had to walk to Bedfont for the Petty Sessions alongside a mounted police officer, where he was

Staines Police Station celebrations for the 1911 Coronation

fined a shilling, plus a shilling costs (a total of 10 pence (4p). He then had to walk home again[130].

Both Ashford and Stanwell were apparently not large enough communities to warrant their own police stations, although not too far away there was a station at Bedfont, which was then a sub-division of Staines.

Staines in 1890 had a resident inspector, two other inspectors, three sergeants and twenty constables. Sunbury had two inspectors, two sergeants and seventeen constables[131].

In 1894 the various parishes were placed under the jurisdiction of Urban Districts. Sunbury U.D.C. took in an area of 2,659 acres which in 1911 had a population of

4,606, while Staines U.D.C. with a population of 6,756 covered an area of 1918 acres. In addition a Staines Rural District was also created, comprising a vast 17,964 acres with a population of 21,932 stretching as far north as Harlington including a detached portion at Hanworth[132].

Awards ceremony at Staines circa early 1930's

Prior to the Great War the Staines section had been part of the Bedfont sub-division but in January 1917 assumed sub-divisional status to include Bedfont, Harlington and Sunbury sections. In 1926, the year of the General Strike, Staines was under the charge of Sub Divisional Inspector Alfred Harwood who had under him ten Sergeants and 32 constables. The old Rural District Council ceased to exist after 1929 leaving just the two Urban districts, Littleton parish passing from Sunbury to Staines U.D.C[133].

Retired Staines police officer Fred Lipscombe, who was spoken to when he was aged 92, clearly remembered 1932 when he was posted to Staines once his probation finished. As an East-ender he felt it was a punishment to be sent out into the country but he married a local girl and stayed. The six-footer with army experience was considered an excellent candidate for the Met, which only recruited physically fit, disciplined men of at least 5'10" in height. In those days, the whole eight hour shift had to be spent on the beat. Constables ate their sandwiches sitting in a police box, after booking off by phone. They were not allowed back to the station except for necessary reports and at some point, even in the middle of the night, a sergeant would make sure they were still on the beat, whatever the weather.

> 'Decent people weren't out at night in those days...So anyone abroad after midnight was probably up to no good! On the 11 pm to 7am beat, officers were expected to pass lengths of black cotton over doorways and alleyways, and check before they booked off that the thread was intact, to ensure no-one had been that way. If the cotton was broken, the building was checked out'[134].

Fred was one of the first Metropolitan Police radio telegraphy (RT) operators in the new patrol cars, known as 'Bean' cars[135]. They were little more than a framework with an engine and transparent screens to keep the weather out, said Fred. He had learned morse code in the army, and after brushing up his skills, went out with the drivers on the division. Later during the war he also accompanied an Assistant Commissioner around London as his personal operator[136].

Other memories of the War include arresting Canadian soldiers, one a huge Red Indian, billeted in Windsor Great Park, who came to Staines to get drunk. He also has memories of the 'razor gangs' who got into bloody fights after a boozy day at the Kempton Park races.

The 1930s saw a major upheaval of police boundaries resulting in the closure of both Bedfont and Sunbury police-stations in June 1932, followed in December 1933 by Hampton being transferred from Twickenham sub-division to Staines in lieu of Hounslow[137].

A deputation was made to Scotland Yard by members of Sunbury-on-Thames Urban District Council concerned over the closure of their police station but the Home Secretary decided that there was adequate policing in the area. In July 1936 a Dr. Who Tardis type police box was installed in front of the closed station. A plan was mooted for a new police station at Feltham which was deferred due to the war and a temporary station opened in November 1953 as a part replacement for Bedfont under the jurisdiction of the Staines sub-division[138].

In April 1965 with the creation of the G.L.C. a further revision of Staines boundaries occurred when Feltham passed to the Hounslow sub-division while Staines was once again reduced to a mere sectional station on Twickenham Sub-Division along with Hampton, upon the closure of Harlington. Up until this date the Thames Division had only patrolled upstream as far as Teddington Lock hut (although in the early 1800's the Marine police had patrolled to Staines Bridge), were now authorised to patrol up to Staines Bridge, new moorings and a police station being taken into use at Shepperton Lock[139].

As Staines and Sunbury were beyond the G.L.C. the urban districts were now administered by Surrey Council instead of Middlesex. In November 1974 the Metropolitan Police assumed responsibility for the former British Airports Authority police at Heathrow. The new division now included Staines, and from October 1980 also Sunbury (having reopened in January 1966) both stations returning to what was then 'T' District in December 1984[140].

An unusual anomaly occurred in May 1988 when a small section of Felix Lane, Shepperton was handed over to the Metropolitan Police from the Surrey Police. At least a mile into the MPD the area had traditionally been patrolled by Surrey but with realignment of the Thames tributaries over the years it gradually found itself on the Middlesex side of the river. In January 1989 the Staines and Sunbury sections were amalgamated as the Spelthorne Division taking its name from the ancient Hundred. Instead of wearing the divisional letters 'TW' (Twickenham) on officers shoulders, they now use the letters 'TG' (Staines). One might ask why the letters 'TS' were not used. 'TS' was in fact the station code for Staines up until 1946 when it was adopted for the new Training School Division, although this went out of use in 1993[141].

With the introduction of sector policing in 1992/1993 two new sector offices were opened in Shepperton and Ashford. In April 1995 however part of the latter sector was reduced in size when Poyle and Colnbrook in Middlesex were taken over by Berkshire County Council and policing passed to the Thames Valley force[142].

Late in 1998, the long awaited new station on the site of the former Kingston Road School, opened its doors to police and civil staff. The official opening ceremony, conducted by the Metropolitan Police Commissioner, Sir Paul Condon, was planned for April 24th, 1999. In recent years, new police office's had been opened for the convenience of Shepperton and Ashford residents. Officers could quickly call on various specialist units not too far away to ensure effective policing - there was a traffic unit at Hampton, dog patrols based at West Drayton and Teddington, a fully equipped helicopter with heat searching equipment based at Fairoaks airport, and the Thames Division at Shepperton. Large numbers of officers could be called in from surrounding divisions in an emergency - and Spelthorne also sends officers all over the Metropolitan Police area to help when required[143].

Spelthorne had its own scenes of crime officer (SOCO), crime prevention officer (CPO) and schools officers on division. Staines had a dedicated officer looks after vulnerable people with problems of a domestic, racist or homophobic nature. Partnership schemes with the local council and businesses sought to reduce crime.

Staines Police Station 1998 to present day. 22 Kingston Road, Staines Middlesex.

In the year 2,000, boundary changes which were discussed as long ago as the 1960s, came into force and from April 2000 the entire Spelthorne division was placed under the jurisdiction of the Surrey Police, albeit officially still part of Middlesex. The white 'coal-posts' bearing the City of London crest will no longer mark the boundary between the County Constabulary and the MPD whose jurisdiction ended after 160 years. The transfer occurred a year after the new super station and area headquarters was built at Staines so the Surrey Constabulary were gifted a modern state of the art purpose built station and headquarters[144].

Shepperton Lock Police Station.

Following the extension of River Police patrols to Staines authority was given to take from the Thames Conservancy in September 1965 a lease for 21 years of a piece of land at a nominal rent of £1 per annum. The intention was to erect a small hut and landing stage to provide Thames Division with a new station at Shepperton Lock[145].

A new sectional station for Shepperton Lock was introduced into service at 6 am on Monday, 4th April. The station would be open from 6 am to 10 pm daily and the

Shepperton Lock Police Office. 1965 - 1992

telephone number will be Walton-on-Thames 29281 or by police line through Hampton (TM), and the telegraphic code being (UP)[146].

A mutual arrangement with the lock keeper enabled one patrol boat during the summer months to occupy a berth just above the lock alongside the river wall. This arrangement was regularised with the Thames Conservancy Board with an agreement to run as from 1st November 1972 for a permanent mooring above the lock for a Thames launch.

The advantage of having permanent berths available below and above Shepperton Lock has proved most valuable. It obviated the need for duty boats passing through the lock at the beginning and end of a patrol, an operation which takes at least 15 minutes in each direction. The time saved over the years in not having to 'lock through' may well have resulted in the saving of life or the prevention of injury to persons or damage to property. In 1967 Hampton station was opened on the river island known as Platts Eyot (pronounced eight and sometimes spelt 'eit')[147].

Hampton was shut in 1978 and Shepperton Lock in 1992. There are just mooring facilities located there today.

Stanwell Police Station

The parish of St. Marys together with its church and churchyard at Stanwell is famous featuring contains many notable burials. Several houses are listed, including Dunmore House on the village green built in 1719 by John, Earl of Dunmore. This is a very fine building with a galleried hall and a worthy accompaniment to any village. Arundel House at the east end of the village was originally a police station in the middle of the 19th century. The building originated between 1620-40 but extensive alterations leave little of the original features visible. These never included glazed windows but some of the interior walls contain bricks larger than normal which were an answer to the brick tax instituted to finance the Napoleonic wars[148].

In 1845 an additional police-station (in fact the sergeant's house) was established in Stanwell Village which was rented yearly at a cost of £14. 14s (£14.70p) from Mr W. Hall of Kingsland. This was a common brick and slate house in good condition with a small garden. In the yard was a two stall stable with hay loft. Also at the station was a scullery and accommodation consisting of four rooms rented at a cost of 2/6d (13p) per week.

Sergeant George Bigarlsford, his wife and family lived at the station in 1851. The police station was still there in 1866. Living in Stanwell having retired was pensioner ex-Metropolitan Police Superintendent William Durkin aged 53 and his wife aged 33 who lived on the village green.

The police officers from the horse patrol were housed there and there was a cupboard originally with an exterior entrance which used to house drunken prisoners overnight. On one occasion a prisoner was found to have suffocated after a very hot night, later ventilation holes were drilled over the interior door and they are still visible today[149]. This horse patrol station was later given up on Christmas Eve 1868 along with Colnbrook when the new Bedfont police station opened[150].

In 1901 35-year-old Sergeant Harry England from Radlett in Hertfordshire and his wife Annie and five children lived at Stanwell Moor to the north west of the station.

Sunbury Police Station

The Metropolitan Police Force was extended to its present limits by virtue of the Metropolitan Police Act 1839. No 10 Thames Street, Sunbury (previously called Belle View) was acquired from Monday 13th January 1840 as a sectional police station under the Kingston sub-division as part of the 'V' or Wandsworth Division. The station, held on a yearly tenancy from a Mr Roe of Brentford, was described as a brick and tile built house with a two stall stable, two cells, small rear garden, and eight rooms in all. The landlord was responsible for all rates and taxes[151].

There were 21 constables and four sergeants worked from Sunbury and were deployed as follows: three constables in Teddington, (housed privately), three constables in Hampton (housed in section house), two constables in Hampton Court (housed privately), two constables in Hampton Wick (housed privately), three constables in Feltham and Feltham Hill (housed privately), one constable at Hanworth (housed privately) one constable in Ashford (housed privately)[152].

There were two sergeants, six constables and two horse patrol sergeants housed in the section house at Sunbury police station, Thames Street who patrolled Sunbury and Upper Halliford. The early police constables were former parish constables and were not used to the discipline of the 'New Police'. Many were dismissed from the force; 22nd February 1840 - Constable Daniel Brian 'for being drunk and assaulting Mr J Turner Esq of Sunbury and other misconduct; 30th March 1840 - Constable Charles Smith and Constable Thomas Yates - 'for being in *The Goat* public house Upper Halliford at 2am and tossing for gin and water when on duty' In August 1840 - Constable Francis Masters was 'convicted by the Staines magistrates and committed for 21 days hard labour for attempting to stab his sergeant when drunk'[153]. The sergeant was likely to have been 31-year-old Robert Graham McIntyre from Perthshire who resided at the station with his wife, a local lady from Sunbury, and three children in 1851[154].

The police station at Sunbury is shown in 1842 as being part of 'V' or Wandsworth Division[155] and by 1844 it was designated a sergeant station[156].

The distribution of the Force in Police Orders 11th January 1864 again shows Sunbury as a Station of 'V' or Wandsworth Division however due to the formation of three new Division's, Sunbury wan transferred to 'T' or Kensington Division[157].

The house had been altered to provide two cells, two stables, eight rooms and a small back garden. Officers based there covered Teddington, all the Hamptons, Feltham and Hanworth.

This was not a suitable arrangement as the premises were cramped and unsuitable. Records show that in 1861 30 year old Sergeant Charles Simpkins from Walton on Thames, his wife and three children resided at Sunbury Police station. Five

Sunbury Police Station. 1880 - 1998. 189 Staines Road Sunbury, Surrey

unmarried constables, all under 23 years old also resided at the station[158]. In 1864 a sergeant was in charge with three constables by day whilst during the hours of darkness an acting sergeant and twelve constables patrolled[159].

At Christmas 1875 the station was taken on a five year lease from the landlord, who was now a Mr E. R. Fisher Esq of Farncombe, Guildford, at £35 per annum. The Receiver of the Metropolitan Police had to pay all rates, taxes and repairs[160].

In 1881 an inspection of Sunbury stated that it was a dilapidated station and in urgent need of replacement although plans were already underway to find a site on which to build a purpose-built police station in the area.

In June 1880 Home Office approval was given for the purchase of a site at 189, Staines Road for the sum of £300 from a Mr. Baker. The new station was taken into use accordingly[161] and immediately upgraded to an inspector supervised station[162].

In the meantime the old building was used as an occasional court house for some time after the present Sunbury police station in Staines Road East opened at Christmas, 1882[163].

Police officers were housed in rented accommodation all over the areas covered by the sections and sub-divisions, and there would be little doubt that much of their work was done from home as they could hardly be expected to walk to and from their stations every day.

A building in the rear yard of the station

There were only a couple of horses available in each area - a stables with a flat above were built at the Victorian Staines police station which was later turned into stores and canteen and can still be seen by the rear gates. A stable building in the rear yard (shown above) at Sunbury was demolished when horses were phased out and room was needed for vehicles to drive in and out. In the nineteenth century and into the early years of the twentieth, a sergeant - possibly an inspector – lived in at the police station, together with a few constables. They and their families had just two rooms, if they were lucky. The constables wives were expected to do all the cleaning and chores, and allotments were provided at the rear to provide fresh vegetables. Water had to be carried from the yard, and the toilets were of course outside.

The well and parade shed in the yard at Sunbury

In 1891 Constable Jabez Lamb and his family lived at the police station. Also resident at the same time were constable James Watson and family. The officer in charge was Irishman Inspector James Donnolly who also lived there in 1891 with his wife Kate and two children.

Sunbury Police Station strength celebrating the end of the War in 1919

In 1894 Maurice Elms was an inspector at Sunbury and responsible to the Sub Divisional Inspector at Hampton, Thomas Neal. Constable James Watson and family, Constable Edward Rudge and family lived at Sunbury Police Station in 1901. In 1911 alterations were made to the station.

At the end of WW1 a commemoration photograph was taken outside Sunbury police station to mark the end of hostilities. At the back from left to right are constables Newman, Fry, Baker and Judd. Next row forward (L-R) are constables Hitchcock, Newnham, Smith, Archer, Axleton, Strutt, George and Adams. The next row forward Constable Cookie, Acting Sergeant (APS) Porter, an unidentified sergeant, Sergeant Muggeridge, Station Sergeants Newman and Barnard, Sergeant Bligh, APS Clapham, Constable Proops. Seated on the ground (L-R) constables Chambleton, Titheridge, Kennough and Budmead.

In 1921 the premises next door at 187 Staines Road was purchased with a large area of land. Two sets of quarters were built to accommodate married officers and

Sunbury Police Tug of War team

their families. Further land was purchased freehold in 1936.

In due course the Commissioner announced certain police station closures often an unpopular move. Accordingly Bedfont and Sunbury Stations were closed at 6am on Wednesday 1st June 1932 and all business transferred to Harlington and Staines Stations respectively[164]. This caused a furious outrage, members of Sunbury-on-Thames Urban District Council made representations on 25th April 1932 to the Deputy Commissioner, the Hon. Sir Trevor Bigham at Scotland Yard. A further deputation from the Council was seen by the Commissioner Air Vice Marshall Sir Philip Game on 15th July 1937. Questions were asked in the House of Commons by the local Member of Parliament, Sir Reginald Blaker, on the 15th April 1932 regarding the closure of Sunbury Police Station with the Home Secretary replying that the area as far as he was aware, was adequately policed[165]. In 1934 the address of the station was 189 Staines Road, Sunbury Middlesex.

The station was later altered into two sets of married quarters (from three) with one dwelling on the first floor for an inspector and one on the ground floor for a constable.

A retirement group at Sunbury circa 1910

Although the station was closed to the public for business, certain rooms to the rear were used by the local police for parading and refreshment purposes. Office accommodation was also used by members of the Special Constabulary. A police box was erected in the front entrance lobby of the station for the use by the public.

In 1965 the two sets of married quarters were taken out of use altogether. Alterations were made to the interior plus an extension was built on the side of the station at the cost of £14,000. The station was re-opened for police business as a sectional station on 11th January 1966. The station remained in use until after 1992 but shut before 1998. It was transferred to the Surrey Constabulary in 2000.

West Drayton Police Station

In 1959 the Commissioner approved the search for land in West Drayton on which to build a police station. Initially the council declined approval of land found by the Surveyors to the north and along Bath Road in1961 on the grounds that this was green belt land and subject to restrictions.

This refusal delayed any planning and construction but despite the obstruction the Commissioner went ahead and with Home Office approval, purchased some land originally part of Drayton Hall for the sum of £12,500.

This site and plans for a station were given approval and in January 1964 the Home Office approved expenditure of initially £83, 500 but later upgraded to £87,500 to build the police station at West Drayton. In the meantime representations were made to the Commissioner over the delay in the building of the much-needed station because vandalism and hooliganism had greatly increased in the area. Plans were drawn up and contractors hired to build the station which was completed in 1965.

West Drayton Police Station. 1965 – 2011. Station Road West Drayton, Middlesex UB7 7JQ.

When the station at Harlington was closed in 1965 the policing of the area was transferred to the newly opened West Drayton. Because of the changes in borough boundaries within the Greater London Council Hillingdon Borough included West Drayton[166]. The 'police' sign made of stone from the portico at Harlington was removed from the building when it was closed and taken to West Drayton where it was placed in the driveway.

Records show that the police station was located in Station Road, West Drayton, Middlesex, UB7 7JQ. The station was incomplete when built as it was not supplied with the traditional police blue lamp to the front of the building. In 1969 Yiewsley Tenants Association wrote to the police complaining about the lack of a lamp which they stated 'would show passers by that here was a police station'. When the Airport Division was introduced in July 1970 this sectional station came under the control of Heathrow.

In 2000 West Drayton station ('XE') was a temporary station with limited opening hours on Hillingdon Borough. It was still open in 2009 again with restricted opening times and had no charging facilities as prisoners were taken to Uxbridge for detention and charging.

In 2013 the police station at West Drayton was no longer open to the public. A Safer Neighbourhood Team was located in the town in private premises. The police headquarters for this area is located at Uxbridge.

Heathrow airport police station is also situated in West Drayton. A new purpose built custody facility opened in 2011 located at Unit 3, Polar Park, Bath Rd, Sipson, West Drayton, Middlesex UB7 0DG.

Heathrow Airport Division SO18 (by David Little and Peter Kennison)

Introduction

Heathrow Airport is situated on the south end of the London Borough of Hillingdon on a parcel of land that is designated part of the Metropolitan Green Belt. The airport is surrounded by the built-up areas of Harlington, Harmondsworth, Longford and Cranford to the north and by Hounslow and Hatton to the east. To the south lie East Bedfont and Stanwell while to the west Heathrow is separated from Colnbrook in Berkshire by the M25 motorway.

Heathrow Airport is located within the London Borough of Hillingdon. Strangely, Heathrow Airport is not currently incorporated into one of the MPS Boroughs but sits independently as an entity of its own - as SO18 Aviation Security since 2007. SO18 are responsible for both Heathrow and London City Airport.

Heathrow is an airport owned by the British Aviation Authority (BAA) and currently handles in excess of 68 million passengers and 450,000 aircraft movements per year. There are over 80,000 staff working within the airport (The town of Wigan in Northern England has a population of just over 80,000). Additionally, over 12 million other visitors and more than 20 million vehicles travel through the airport each year. Terminal 5 was opened in March 2008, after the longest Public Inquiry that sat for 524 days and concluded eight years after the initial application for Government approval. The Inquiry cost £80m, heard 700 witnesses and generated 100,000 pages of transcripts[167].

Originally, Heathrow was a hamlet in the parish of Harmondsworth and consisted of a small number of cottages on the edge of Hounslow Heath.

> 'Hounslow Heath was once an oak forest that spread its green boughs from Staines to Brentford, and there is an old tradition that the last wolf in England, killed centuries ago, was hunted down at Perry Oaks in that neighbourhood'[168].

Prior to the existence of any police station in the area, there was still a need for the forces of law and order to maintain peace on Hounslow Heath. Once part of the extensive Forest of Middlesex, and now largely buried beneath the runways of London Airport, Hounslow Heath was for more than 200 years the most dangerous place in Britain. Between the 17th and early 19th centuries, the heath occupied perhaps 25 square miles. No one was really certain where its boundaries lay, and no one cared, for it was a tract of country to be crossed as quickly as possible. Though Hounslow itself was not large, it was, after London, the most important of coaching centres. Across the heath ran the Bath Road and the Exeter Road, along which travelled wealthy visitors to West Country resorts and courtiers travelling to Windsor. All provided rich pickings for highwaymen lurking in copses bordering the lonely ways. Claude Duval (Du Val, Duvall or Duvail) was a highwayman who had been born in France in 1643 but moved to England in 1660 to pursue his 'career' as a highwayman. Duval was eventually captured and executed in 1670 for his crimes but was remembered for his success at seducing his female victims as much as the notoriety of his crimes. He was known as a 'true gentleman of the road'. He stopped a woman's coach on Hounslow Heath in which there was a booty of four hundred pounds but only took one hundred, allowing 'the fair owner to ransom the rest by dancing 'a coranto' with him on the Heath[169].'

The hamlet of Heathrow was beset by highwaymen and in 1805, the Bow Street horse patrols were introduced for 'the suppression of highwaymen, footpads and housebreakers'. Horse patrols station were established at Bedfont, Hounslow, Harlington Corner and Colnbrook and these were integrated into the Metropolitan Police in 1837[170].

The Metropolitan Police area was extending further out from the centre of London. The hamlet of Heath Row became part of the Metropolitan Police District in 1840 as the old 'T' or Paddington Division was extended from the boundary set at Brentford in 1830 to Staines. By 1849 a sectional police station had been opened in Stanwell village to police the local area. In 1857, another station was opened on the Staines Road at Bedfont and took over from the nearby horse patrol station. In 1865, Hattons Road, Harlington was chosen as the site for a new station which was moved to a new site on the Bath Road in 1890[171].

In 1919, the first commercial flight from London to France left Hounslow Aerodrome, a former First World War aerodrome. At that time the first record occurred of police officers being stationed at Hounslow Aerodrome, an increase in the complement of 'T' District by one sergeant and nine constables, was noted whose presence was commensurate with the use of aircraft. However, Hounslow Aerodrome was closed in 1920, as operations were moved to the London Croydon Airport.

In 1925 a Royal Air Force pilot, Norman MacMillan was forced to land his plane on a piece of flat land in the area. His appraisal of the land as being suitable for an airfield was noted by Fairey Aviation. In 1929/30, Fairey Aviation bought several plots of land. British aero engineer and aircraft builder Richard Fairey paid the Vicar of Harmondsworth £15,000 for a 150-acre plot to build a private airport to assemble and test aircraft. Complete with a single grass runway and a handful of hastily-erected buildings, Fairey's Great West Aerodrome was created from humble beginnings[172].

During World War II the government requisitioned land in and around the ancient agricultural village of Heath Row, including Fairey's Great West Aerodrome, to build RAF Heston, a base for long-range troop-carrying aircraft bound for the Far East. An RAF-type control tower was constructed and a 'Star of David' pattern of runways laid, the longest of which was 3,000 yards long and 100 yards wide[173]. In 1944, the hamlet of Heath Row was demolished to make way for the new airport as part of the war effort. As the airport (known then as the Great Western Aerodrome) began to expand, the families who lived in the area were relocated.

Ministry of Civil Aviation Constabulary Helmet Plate Badge

During the war the Air Ministry Constabulary were responsible for airports and stations. At the conclusion of the war, the RAF no longer needed the airport so the site was transferred to the Ministry of Civil Aviation and the airport was officially opened for commercial operations in May 1946. The first aircraft to take off from Heathrow after the war was a Starlight (a converted Lancaster) which flew to Buenos Aires. The early passenger terminals were primitive indeed and consisted of;

> 'ex-military marquees which formed a tented village along the Bath Road. The terminals were primitive but comfortable, equipped with floral-patterned armchairs, settees and small tables containing vases of fresh flowers. To reach aircraft parked on the apron, passengers walked over wooden duckboards to protect their footwear from the muddy airfield. There was no heating in the marquees, which meant that during winter it could be bitterly cold, but in summer when the sun shone, the marquee walls were removed to allow a cool breeze to blow through'[174].

The policing of Heathrow fell to the Ministry of Civil Aviation Constabulary from 1948 – two years after flights commenced - although during any major incident the Metropolitan Police always took overall command. By 1954 the name changed again to the Ministry of Transport and Civil Aviation Constabulary, although uniform buttons still contained the initials MCA. All this just meant that tunics and coats remained the same but headgear badges and plates were changed.

The British Airports Authority was established in 1965 by the Airport Authority Act 1965, and on 1 April 1966 the new British Airports Authority Constabulary took on responsibility for operating London Heathrow, London Gatwick and London Stansted airports[175]. This occurred at the same time as Terminal 3 was built with Terminal 2 having been constructed in 1955. The change of administration was seen as an opportunity to partially reform old working methods, and then-novel innovations were introduced, such as report forms with tick-boxes, an index card system and dictation machines for detectives[176]. In December of that year, the strength of the force stood at 201[177].

Ministry of Civil Aviation Constabulary Inspector cap badge

In 1965, at the formation of the Greater London Council (GLC), Heathrow ceased to be part of Middlesex and was incorporated into the GLC. It is now part of the London Borough of Hillingdon although the postal address is in Hounslow. In 1969 the Chief Constable, Major W. Ronnie, was awarded the Queen's Police Medal[178]. The police strength at the time stood at 326, of which 28 were women[179].

British Airports Authority Constabulary Cap badge

BAAC constables were sworn in under section 10 of the Airport Authority Act 1965 [180]. They were all attested before a justice of the peace (or a sheriff in Scotland), and had "the powers and privileges and [were] liable to the duties and responsibilities of a constable" on all the aerodromes owned or managed by BAA[181]. They also enjoyed their powers when following (pursuing) a person from such an aerodrome, if they could have arrested them on the aerodrome[182] although they were not a Home Office force and subject to their supervision. BAA had the power to sack or suspend constables, and were vicariously liable for their actions whilst on duty. In April 1971, R. M. Carson was appointed as Chief Constable of the BAAC[183].

The policing of Heathrow by the constabulary ceased in 1974, when with the exception of the Chief Constable and his deputy the remainder transferred into the Metropolitan Police – the same thing had happened with the Dockyard officers of Chatham, Portsmouth, Devonport and Pembroke when the Metropolitan police took control of them in the 1860's and the old dockyard officers merged with the Metropolitan Police.

Heathrow Airport Police Station (ID)

The area of Heathrow airport holds an important yet significant secret which effect's all of us today. In 1783 General Roy, a Scottish Engineer, realised the military importance of knowing precisely where things were. In order to do so, he required a baseline and chose Hounslow Heath – the current location of Heathrow Airport. General Roy's men painstakingly measured out a distance of 27404.01 feet using rods and iron bars. Their measurement subsequently proved to be accurate to within two inches.

This baseline was to become the Ordnance Survey in 1791, used to this day[184] on every single map surveyed and reproduced for them.

General Roys ordnance survey baseline

On the 17th November 1967, a plaque was unveiled at Heathrow police station commemorating General Roy's first Ordnance Survey baseline in 1783. The plaque now stands immediately above the road tunnel that emerges from the middle of Terminal Island.

Terrorism

The biggest policing requirement in recent times at Heathrow has been the fight against terrorism. As one of the world's biggest transport hubs, Heathrow has in excess of 80 million visitors passing through each year. This number not only lends itself to an ideal opportunity for terrorists to pass through but also creates an attractive target for terrorists, 'Due to the large amounts of civilian visitors and the sheer number of access points to control they are still generally very vulnerable'.

Government concern around security at Heathrow Airport included the fact that this function was carried out by a non-Home Office police force. There were serious concerns whether they could cope and keep up-to-date with current firearms in the same way as the Metropolitan Police had done. It was the Metropolitan Police which was at the forefront of firearms training and policy and in fact the BAA police received their training and reclassification from them. In August 1967 the American Embassy in London had been machine-gunned. Nine months later the Spanish Embassy and the American Officers' club in Lancaster Gate were both bombed. During the following year eight more bomb attacks - one at Heathrow airport, another at the home of the Attorney-General, followed. The reign of bombings continued throughout 1971 until members of what became known as the 'Angry Brigade' were arrested and convicted. In September 1972 the Arab terrorist organisation 'Black

British Airports Authority Constabulary Helmet Plate Badge

September' launched its letter bombing campaign in London, despatching 43 bombs over a four month period. The same month, in front of the world's media, members of that organisation had attacked Israel's Olympic team taking several hostages at the close of the Munich Olympic Games. Following an unsuccessful rescue attempt by the West German police, all nine hostages were killed. A year earlier, the IRA had launched its Christmas 1971 bombing campaign in Ulster and the following month saw British para-troopers fire upon a crowd of unarmed demonstrators in Northern Ireland, killing 14 people. Amidst a growing profile of international terrorist activity, the IRA turned its attention to London, launching a bombing campaign there in March 1973. Mainland bombings continued throughout 1974, notably in Birmingham, Manchester and Guildford[185]. In 1969-1970 a number of incidents occurred involving the hijacking of commercial aircraft by terrorists such as Leila Khaled.

On the 29th April 1974, it was announced in Parliament that;

> '... the Metropolitan Police should assume responsibility for the policing of London Airport – Heathrow ... following the escalation of terrorist activity against civil aviation'

The Home Secretary, Mr Roy Jenkins, stated

> 'dealing with terrorism could not satisfactorily be divided from other police work and the course suggested by the BAAC of making the Metropolitan Police responsible for dealing

Heathrow Police Station 1974 -2011. East Ramp, Heathrow Airport, Hounslow TW6 2DJ with terrorism while (sic) the BAAC retained responsibility for other Police functions was in the opinion of Ministers and the Metropolitan Commissioner unworkable'[186].

In 1974 as a result of the Policing of Airports Act the Metropolitan Police assumed the responsibility. Police Notice of 31st October 1974, Item 11 (Joined the Force) lists the officers who transferred from the British Airports Authority. On Friday 1st November 1974, the new Airport Division of the Metropolitan Police came into being.

Police Orders published on 31st October 1974 contained the entry;

> '... in consequence of the above Orders, the Metropolitan Police will assume responsibility for the policing of Heathrow Airport..." Two Chief Superintendents, six Chief Inspectors, 12 Inspectors, 47 Sergeants and 262 Constables (including CID officers) transferred from the BAAC to the MPS. Initially, the new Division also incorporated Staines and West Drayton, increasing in size in 1980 to include Sunbury'[187].

Airport District was formed as a 'single-Division District: District Code I, Heathrow Station ID ... the staff levels remained almost the same' albeit they traded their old uniforms, hats, helmets and accoutrements with Metropolitan police issue. It also stated that 'Probationers will not be posted to Heathrow' – an indication of the specialised nature of policing at the airport[188].

On January 13th 1986, police officers patrolling Heathrow Airport became routinely armed with Heckler and Koch machine guns.

The Metropolitan Police's internal newspaper, The Job, reported that, prior to the opening of Terminal Four, the Airport District – 'the Force's only one-station district' had launched 'a recruitment campaign to bring the number of officers up to the establishment of 330'. It also stated that officers based at Heathrow received more training than any others in the Metropolitan Police in order to deal with the diverse incidents that they might be called upon to deal with. The article went on to describe the 'state of art' telephonic computer system originally designed for the Stock Exchange that had been fitted into the Communications and Major Incident Rooms. The system replaced telephones and directories and enabled greater speed and efficiency when dealing with any incidents[189].

There was concern that the division was somewhat top heavy as far as senior officers were concerned. By 1991 the complement at Heathrow had changed to one chief superintendent (reduced by one), one superintendent, four chief inspectors (decreased by two), 14 inspectors (increased by two), 56 sergeants (increased by nine) and 365 constables (including CID Officers and increased by 97). They were augmented by 14 Specials, 64 traffic wardens and 54 civilians. From these officers, each terminal had a team of permanent beat officers[190].

In 2007 Heathrow became an Operational Command Unit in its own right as Aviation Security SO18. Airports, since the attack on New York's Trade Centre on 11th September 2001 have become terrorist targets, following the example and as early as 1939, of the Irish Republican Army (IRA) launched a campaign of bombing and sabotage against the civil, economic, and military infrastructure of the United Kingdom. In earlier years the main transport hubs were railways stations. As air transportation became more affordable for the masses the airports became more viable targets[191].

Sisters Dolores and Marion Price and nine others placed four car bombs in London on 8 March 1973. Ten of the team were apprehended as they attempted to leave Heathrow and two bombs were defused[192].

On December 21, 1988 at about 6.25pm just four days before Christmas, Pan-Am Flight 103 departed from Heathrow Airport with 243 passengers and 16 crew members. Just as they were preparing themselves for a relatively long flight to New York the plane blew up over the town of Lockerbie at about 7.03pm killing all on board. This incident was to change the way that policing at a UK Airport was undertaken for all time.

In March 1994, the IRA launched a series of mortar attacks on Heathrow airport, partially paralysing the capital's main airport. During the first attack five mortars were fired into the airport grounds but none detonated. The second attack, two days later, involved the firing of four mortars. Once again the mortars failed to detonate. The headlines in *The Independent* on 11th March 1994 read 'Heathrow Bombing: IRA exposes airport's vulnerability: Perimeter protection 'almost impossible'. Four mortars from a stolen red Nissan Micra car, registration number A274 TGK, had been fired from the car park, over Heathrow police station and the perimeter fence and landed on a 20-metre wide apron at the edge of the 45-metre wide north runway. None exploded, although traces of high explosive, including Semtex, found later indicate that the damage could have been extensive[193].

The third, and final, attack on Sunday 13th March 1994 caused the airport to close between 0800 and 1340 hours despite the mortars failing to detonate yet again. The airport was again closed that evening after further coded warnings. The rationale for the Metropolitan Police

Both Police and Military at Heathrow Airport in 2003

taking over the policing of Heathrow in 1974 was being vindicated.

In February 2003, British troops were again deployed at Heathrow in support of the Metropolitan Police - not as a result of an IRA threat on this occasion but in response to an heightened threat level from Islamic terrorists. "The British Prime Minister, Tony Blair personally authorised the use of 450 troops, with armoured vehicles, to back up more than 1,300 police officers. A suspected Islamist plot to fire a missile at an airliner prompted the largest security operation at Heathrow for a decade[194].

In 1998 the address of Heathrow police station was shown as East Ramp, Heathrow Airport, Hounslow TW6 2DJ with OCU commander Superintendent I. Hutcheson in charge. His deputy was Superintendent M. Calaminus[195]. The station opening times in 2002-3 were 6am until 10pm[196]. By 2007 the OCU Commander of Heathrow Airport was Chief Superintendent Jerry Savill and his deputy was Superintendent Leigh Orwin[197]. The East Ramp Police station was decommissioned in 2011 and ceased to be used by police with the completion of the Polar Park complex.

Heathrow Police Station, Polar Park

The newest police station within the Metropolitan Police Service (MPS) opened on the 7th July 2011 at Polar Park, West Drayton the new headquarters of Heathrow's Specialist Operations Aviation Command policing Heathrow Airport. Its opening hours were from 7am until 10pm daily. The station was opened by Commissioner Sir Paul Stephenson and Graham Speed, Independent member of the Metropolitan Police Authority with the responsibility for estates issues. The station was part of Specialist Operations Aviation Command SO18.

The station is designed to accommodate all of the specialist teams working at the airport, including baggage crime, human smuggling and all airport related crime. It contains 30 custody cells together with ancillary rooms for interviewing, medical examination and a 'state of the art' control room for dealing with major incidents. The station also boasts a 'silver suite' capable of co-ordinating and managing major incidents.

The commander of Heathrow who took over the new station was Chief Superintendent Bert Moore who was very pleased with the new building having been five years in the planning and construction.

A Safer Neighbourhoods Team, Heathrow Villages, formed to offer a 'community and bespoke aviation policing (experience)' provides policing for the Terminals, much as Neighbourhood Policing Teams do for geographical boroughs elsewhere in the Metropolitan Police Service[198].

In 2011 the National Police Improvement Agency in conjunction with the Association of Chief Police officers together with others has developed a reference handbook on the guidance on the policing of airports following a risk assessment. This was led by the Policing and Crime Act 2009 (enacted in 2010) on a security planning framework and has provided a proper contingency on the protection of airports.

Heathrow Police Station 2011 – present day. Polar Park, West Drayton

The last major air accident involving Heathrow was BEA flight 548 which crashed near Staines on 18th June 1972, soon after take-off but there have been numerous emergencies and less serious incidents since which have served to reaffirm the importance of good contingency planning and exercises.

---

[1] Brown, B. (1997) Policing Old Feltham. Metropolitan Police Museum
[2] Act for repairing road from Hounslow Heath to Basingstone, I Geo. II, Stat. ii, c. 6.
[3] Brown, B. (1997) Policing Old Feltham. Metropolitan Police Museum
[4] Brown, B. (1997) Policing Old Feltham. Metropolitan Police Museum
[5] http://www.hounslow.info/libraries/local-history-archives/discover-hounslow/#fel accessed 24th December 2012
[6] ibid
[7] The Job dated 14th January 1983 p13
[8] Metropolitan Police Surveyors Book p.150
[9] Metropolitan Police surveyors Book p.150
[10] Hillingdon Mirror 19th June 1979
[11] West Drayton and District Local Historian. September 1972 p.10
[12] Metropolitan Police Station List 1893
[13] Metropolitan Police Orders dated 26th September 1890
[14] West Drayton and District Local Historian. September 1972 p.10

[15] National Archives Census 1911
[16] Metropolitan Police Heritage Centre Archive
[17] Metropolitan Police Orders dated 3rd August 1951
[18] Uxbridge Gazette 5th May 1983
[19] West Drayton and District Local Historian. September 1972 p.10
[20] Hillingdon Mirror - date unknown and Met Police Surveyors Book.p158
[21] Census records 1851, 1861, 1871
[22] Metropolitan Police – Condition of Police Stations 1881
[23] Kelly's Middlesex Directory 1890
[24] Kellys Middlesex Directory 1894
[25] Census records 1911
[26] Census records 1911
[27] Jephcote. J. Histories of Police Stations in Hillingdon 1969
[28] Metropolitan Police Orders dated 30th September 1966
[29] Metropolitan Police Orders dated 23rd August 1974
[30] Ordnance Survey Map 1/25000 Middx. Xiv 8, 12, 1866
[31] Metropolitan Police Surveyors Book p.225
[32] Metropolitan Police Report - Condition of Police Stations 1881
[33] Kellys directory Middlesex 1894
[34] Kelly's Directory Middlesex 1898
[35] National Archives Census 1901
[36] Metropolitan Police Orders dated 5th February 1903
[37] Metropolitan Police Orders dated 15th September 1871
[38] Metropolitan Police Orders dated 20th June 1884
[39] Post Directory Middlesex 1878
[40] Metropolitan Police- Condition of Police Stations 1881
[41] Metropolitan Police Station List 1893
[42] 'X' Division List of Police Stations 1924
[43] Hillingdon Mirror – date unknown
[44] Metropolitan Police Surveyors Book
[45] Metropolitan Police Orders dated 14th June 1938
[46] 'X' Divisional Report – date unknown
[47] Metropolitan Police Book of Remembrance
[48] http://content.met.police.uk/PoliceStation/hayes accesed on 3rd March 2013.
[49] British History Online – Hutsons Recollections. – visited 18th February 2013
[50] Lakes Uxbridge Appendix to the Almanacs 1840
[51] Letter dated 18 September 1839 – Met Police Heritage centre
[52] Met Police Heritage Centre Archives
[53] Lakes Uxbridge Appendix to the Almanacs 1842
[54] National Archives Census 1851
[55] Uxbridge Appendix to the Almanacs 1853
[56] Google maps
[57] Metropolitan Police Orders dated 11th January 1864
[58] Divisional Plan 'X' District. 'XR' Ruislip Division (undated).
[59] Metropolitan Police Orders dated 29th September 1871
[60] Census Records 1871
[61] Middlesex and Bucks Advertiser 30th September 1871
[62] Jephcote J. Histories of Police stations in Hillingdon. 1969
[63] Metropolitan Police - Condition of Police Stations 1881
[64] Jephcote J. Histories of Police stations in Hillingdon. 1969
[65] Census Records 1881
[66] Illustrated Uxbridge Almanac 1887
[67] Kelly's Directory 1890
[68] The Police Review and Parade and Gossip- date unknown.
[69] King's Uxbridge 'Gazette' Almanac 1893
[70] The Police Review and Parade Gossip 11th Dec 1903
[71] Census records 1911
[72] Hillingdon Mirror 19th June 1979
[73] Metropolitan Police Orders dated 6th August 1964

[74] Metropolitan Police Orders dated 31st October 1974
[75] Uxbridge Gazette 31st August 1978
[76] Metropolitan Police Book of Remembrance
[77] Uxbridge Gazette 18th May 1988
[78] Metropolitan Police Orders dated 12th February 1906
[79] John Back Archive circa 1975
[80] John Back Archive circa 1975
[81] Metropolitan Police Orders dated 29th July 1911
[82] John Back Archive circa 1975.
[83] National Archives Census 1911
[84] Metropolitan Police Heritage Archives
[85] John Back Archive circa 1975
[86] Metropolitan Police Orders dated 6th August 1964
[87] www.britishlistedbuildings.co.uk visited 21st December 2010
[88] Hillingdon Mirror 19th June 1979
[89] Metropolitan Police Heritage Centre Archives
[90] Metropolitan Police Orders dated 11th January 1864
[91] Metropolitan Police Orders dated 28th October 1865
[92] John Back Archives circa 1975
[93] List of Police Station 1873. MEPO4/234
[94] X Division Surveyors List 1924
[95] Commissioner's Annual Report 1870
[96] Hillingdon Mirror 19th June 1979
[97] Metropolitan Police Heritage Centre Archives
[98] 'X' Division Surveyors List 1924
[99] National Archives Census 1911
[100] Metropolitan Police Report – Condition of Police Stations 1881
[101] Post Office London Directory 1902
[102] John Back Archives circa 1975
[103] 'X' Division Surveyors List 1924
[104] Metropolitan Police Book of Remembrance
[105] National Archives Census 1911
[106] John Back Archives 1975
[107] 'X' Division Surveyors List 1924
[108] John Back Archives circa 1975
[109] John Back Archives circa 1975
[110] Metropolitan Police Orders dated 27th October 1961
[111] Jephcote, J. Histories of Police Stations in Hillingdon 1969
[112] Hillingdon Mirror 19th June 1979
[113] Metropolitan Police Heritage Centre Archives .
[114] Metropolitan Police Book of Remembrance
[115] Metropolitan Police Orders dated 6th August 1964
[116] Metropolitan Police Orders dated 6th December 1968
[117] Metropolitan Police Book of Remembrance
[118] Jephcote, J. Histories of Police Stations in Hillingdon 1969
[119] Whitling, D. (1999)'A History of Policing in Spelthorne' Metropolitan Police London
[120] Brown, B. (1989) Policing old Spelthorne. ESB London
[121] Whitling, D. (1999) 'A History of Policing in Spelthorne' Metropolitan Police, London
[122] Metropolitan Police Surveyors Records ESB London
[123] Brown, B. (1989) Policing old Spelthorne. ESB London
[124] Spelthorne History sheet. ESB London author unknown
[125] Brown, B. (1989) Policing old Spelthorne. ESB London
[126] ibid
[127] Whitling, D. (1999) 'A History of Policing in Spelthorne' Metropolitan Police, London
[128] Brown, B. (1989) Policing old Spelthorne. ESB London
[129] Condition of Police Stations 1881
[130] Whitling, D. (1999) 'A History of Policing in Spelthorne' Metropolitan Police, London
[131] ibid
[132] Brown, B. (1989) Policing old Spelthorne. ESB London

[133] Brown, B. (1989) Policing old Spelthorne. ESB London
[134] Whitling, D. (1999)'A History of Policing in Spelthorne' Metropolitan Police, London
[135] Bean Cars were made in factories in Dudley, Worcestershire, and Coseley, Staffordshire, England, between 1919 and 1929. For a few years in the early 1920s Bean outsold Austin and Morris although their success was not sustainable (source Wikipedia accessed 23rd October 2013).
[136] Whitling, D. (1999)'A History of Policing in Spelthorne' Metropolitan Police, London
[137] Brown, B. (1989) Policing old Spelthorne. ESB London
[138] ibid
[139] ibid
[140] ibid
[141] ibid
[142] ibid
[143] Whitling, D. (1999)'A History of Policing in Spelthorne' Metropolitan Police, London
[144] Brown, B. (1989) Policing old Spelthorne. ESB London
[145] Shepperton Lock Police Station History. John Back Archive. ESB London
[146] Metropolitan Police Orders dated 1st April 1966
[147] Budworth, G. (1997) The River Beat.
[148] Grigg, F. C. (date unknown) Stanwell the village that would not die. Copy Hounslow Library
[149] ibid
[150] Brown, B. (1989) Policing old Spelthorne. ESB London
[151] Brown, B. (1987) Private correspondence to Mr Hayes architect of 10 Thames Street (The old police station)
[152] ibid
[153] ibid
[154] Census records 1851
[155] Kellys Directory 1842 p1042
[156] Kellys directory 1844 p1373
[157] Metropolitan Police Orders dated 28th October 1865 and Sunbury Station history – John back archive ESB London
[158] Census records 1861
[159] Metropolitan Police Special Police Orders 1st January 1864
[160] Metropolitan Police Orders dated 28th October 1865 and Sunbury Station history – John back archive ESB London
[161] Metropolitan Police Orders dated 23rd December 1882
[162] Kellys Directory 1881 p1909
[163] Whitling, D. (1999) ' A History of Policing in Spelthorne' Metropolitan Police, London
[164] Metropolitan Police 0rders dated 30th May 1932
[165] Sunbury Station history – John back archive ESB London
[166] Metropolitan Police Orders dated 8th November 1965
[167] guardian.co.uk dated 22nd May 2007
[168] All the Year Round 1868
[169] www.flageolets.com/biographies/duval accessed 20.3.12, and www.stand-and-deliver.org.uk/highwaymen/claude_duval. htm accessed 20th March 2012
[170] http://www.scribd.com/doc/57482167/Heathrow-The-Lost-Hamlet
[171] John Back Archive. (1972) ESB London
[172] http://www.heathrowairport.com/about-us/company-news-and-information/company-information/our-history accessed on 24th February 2013
[173] http://www.heathrowairport.com/about-us/company-news-and-information/company-information/our-history accessed on 25th February 2013
[174] http://www.heathrowairport.com/about-us/company-news-and-information/company-information/our-history accessed on 24th February 2013
[175] http://en.wikipedia.org/wiki/Airport_policing_in_the_United_Kingdom accessed on 2nd May 2012
[176] Crime and security at British airports". *Flight International*. 15th April 1971. Retrieved 27th May 2011
[177] ibid
[178] "In the Birthday Honours list". *Flight International*. 26th June 1969. Retrieved 26th May 2011
[179] Crime and security at British airports". *Flight International*. 15th April 1971. Retrieved 27th May
[180] Airports Authority Act 1965
[181] ibid
[182] ibid

[183] British Airports Authority. Flight International. 8th April 1971. Retrieved 27th May 2011.
[184] Map Addict Mike Parker 30th April 2009.
[185] Squires, P and Kennison, P. (2010) 'Shooting to kill? Policing, firearms and armed response'. Wiley Blackwell. Chichester
[186] Police Review of 3rd May 1974
[187] Metropolitan Police Orders dated 31st October 1974
[188] Special Police Notice of 28th November 1984
[189] The Job – February 1986
[190] The Job (1991)
[191] http://historyofwar.org/articles/concepts_terrortargets.htlm
[192] BBC 4th March 2001 accessed at http://news.bbc.co.uk/1/hi/uk/1201738.stm
[193] The Independent 11th March 1994 located at http://www.independent.co.uk/news/uk/heathrow-bombing-ira-exposes-airports-vulnerability-perimeter-protection-almost-impossible--delay-in-closing-runway-defended-1428295.html).
[194] The Telegraph 12th February 2003 accessed at http://www.telegraph.co.uk/education/3307672/Troops-in-Heathrow-terror-alert.html
[195] Police and Constabulary Almanac 1998 p39
[196] Metropolitan Police Phone directory 2002 and 2003 located at http://www.met.police.uk/contact/phone.htm accessed 2th October 2003
[197] Police and Constabulary Almanac 2007 p33
[198] (http://content.met.police.uk/News/New-police-station-at Heathrownveiled/1260269186481/1257246745756 accessed 22nd March 2012

Chapter 8

The London Borough of Hounslow

by Peter Kennison

Introduction

The name Hounslow first appeared in the Domesday Book as '*Honeslauu*, a combination of the Old English words for hounds and hill. A year before the signing of the Magna Carta the Friars founded the Priory of Holy Trinity in Hounslow, their first permanent home in England. They built a hospice for travellers and the sick, and a chapel. The chapel survived the transition to lay ownership at the Dissolution until it was replaced by the new Holy Trinity Church in the 19th century. The ownership of the manor and the estate passed through many hands, though from 1704 till 1820 it was held by the Bulstrode family[1].

By 1650 there were 120 houses in the town and many of them were either inns or alehouses catering for travellers. The development of regular coach services in the 18th century benefitted the town – it was usually the first stop from, or the last stop to, London. At the turn of the 19th century there were stables for 800 horses, and 150 coaches passed through the town each day. In a town so dependent on coach traffic the opening of the railways in the 1830s and 1840s caused a depression, though the arrival of the suburban line in 1850 encouraged the development of South Hounslow as a high-class residential area[2].

For most of its history the town has been divided between the parishes of Isleworth and Heston – the parish boundary was the middle of the main road. The two vestries found it hard to agree on improvements to the town so in the 19th century a body of local philanthropists – including Dr Frogley the surgeon, Dr Benson the curate of the chapel, Mr Henry Pownall, Mr Farnell of the Isleworth Brewery, Dr Joseph Banks and James Clitherow – took it upon themselves to raise money for a new chapel, the town school and the town hall. Since Heston and Isleworth united in an Urban Sanitary District in 1875 with Hounslow as its centre the area has developed through an Urban District Council and Borough Council to the present London Borough of Hounslow[3].

Edward Fitt Superintendent. 'T' Division

On 10th May 1830 the 16th Company of the newly-formed Metropolitan Police came into existence when men of Kensington or 'T' Division matched into the parishes of Chiswick and Brentford. Station houses were established at Front Street, Old Brentford and Market Place[4].

In November 1912 (wt. no. 72486) William Edward Fitt, before he transferred to 'T' Division became Superintendent of 'J' Division. And it was here that he formed a close relationship with Major Manners as Commander and later Deputy Commander Jerborough-Bonsey the 'J' Division Metropolitan Police Special Constabulary(MSC) Commander.

William Edward Fitt (signature)	The signature of William Fitt when he signed the Police attestation registers on joining the regular police.

As seen in in both our previous publications the help given to the police in the UK but particularly the Metropolitan Police by the MSC from 1914 through the war years and then later as the MSC Reserve from 1919 onwards progressing into the 1920s and 30s cannot be underestimated.

Fitt was transferred to 'T' Division in November 1916 where he remained in charge until April 1919, when he retired on pension. William Fitts son Percy, as we shall see also had an association with the MSC on both 'J' and 'T' Divisions as later he became the 'T' Division full-time paid staff officer Sub Inspector at Hammersmith. Superintendent Fitt and his MSC head Commander W. C. E. Gibson and later Commander George Gentry OBE were located at Hammersmith and worked together regarding the day-to-day running of the division. Gentry from Isleworth had joined the MSC as a constable but quickly, because of his connections came to the attention of the Home Office. Gentry was a very wealthy coal merchant and secretary of the Coal Merchants Federation of Great Britain. He co-ordinated with the Home Office, became advisor to the various Government officials and coal controllers who dealt with the distribution side of the coal trade throughout the country, until the de-control of the trade. Because of his managerial ability he quickly gained promotion so that he became Assistant Commander of 'T' division by 1919. Inspector Percy Fitt worked to Commandant (wt. no. 011905) McAdam who was taken on full pay in

Commander George Gentry OBE

September 1939 when the war started. He was assisted by Commander Roe who also went on pay at the same time as his colleague.

This chapter deals with the police stations of Brentford, Chiswick, Feltham, Hounslow and Isleworth.

Bedfont Police Station.

In 1807 the parish constable was Edmund Betts who was low born as he could not read or write but would serve summonses at 4d (2p) a time[5]. Parish constables were usually appointed yearly but those who did not want the job would sub-contract the employment, often to the cheapest bidder. By 1834 the parish constable had changed to a school teacher whose responsibility was to ensure that the cage at Feltham had enough straw on the floor and he was required to purchase 'a truss of straw' and claim the cost of 10d (5p) it back from the vestry[6].

The local court heard some cases from Bedfont. In 1837 for instance, during the Ascot Races two men took over the Toll house refusing to pay the toll and locking the toll keeper up. He remained there for a while until the horse patrol arrived and set him free. When one of the assailants appeared on his return from the races he was identified to the police, arrested and prosecuted[7].

In 1872 a man who was begging in High Road Feltham had been given a sovereign by the magistrate but continued to beg and was brought before the justice and sentenced to one month's hard labour[8]. A regular occurrence (and often a dangerous one) along the main Staines road was that drivers of small carts would fall asleep at the reins. For this, a man was fined 10 shillings (50p). Most accidents that occurred on the roads were caused by the drivers of small carts and their reckless or irresponsible use. A driver falling asleep meant that a horse could be spooked by other vehicles or people and runaway carriages were a fairly frequent and dangerous occurrence.

A man arrested at the Railway Arms public house for drunk and disorderly was being taken back to the station when his friend tried to rescue his mate from custody. The friend even resorted to throwing stones at the officer's helmet. Both were sentenced to 14 days imprisonment[9].

The pair of cottages of the Bedfont horse patrol station

On 13th January 1840 the parish of Feltham became part of the 'T' Division (or 16th company) policed from Staines, although the Bow Street horse patrols, (now part of the Metropolitan Police) continued to have a station at Bedfont until Lady Day 1887 separate from the police station. The horse patrol station situated in the Staines Road, Bedfont was rented from Mr Francis Newborn of Bedfont for the annual sum of £28. There were three sets of married quarters there where constables would live and they each paid one shilling (5p) a week rent[10]. The horse patrol station acted as the principal police station in the area until the new one was built in 1866. The horse patrol station was still in use in 1881 and was described as 'two semi-detached cottages on the roadside' which were occupied by two constables and their families. Regular complaints were made from them as the cesspool leaked, providing unhygienic odours in the yard at the rear[11]. The horses were housed to the side of each building and had a hay loft for the storage of equipment and fodder.

Not all the new recruits were of the calibre desired, such as Constable John Moore, who in January 1842 was dismissed 'for entering the police service under an assumed Christian name, having been previously in custody for pot-stealing'[12].

The parish of Feltham then comprised of 2,620 acres and population in 1851 consisted of 1,109 people but ten years later it was 1,837 spread throughout some 306 homes. The increase of population arose partly from the facilities of railway communication with London, and partly from the establishment of industrial and Welsh schools[13]. In 1854 an industrial school was built in Feltham and opened in 1859 as the more respectable sounding Middlesex Industrial School, but was in fact a Reformatory for 1,000 boys aged between 7-14 years connected with crime sentenced from 1-3 years in lieu of transportation. In 1910 this became the second borstal in the UK and today it is a prison and young offenders institution.

A line up of the Bedfont police in the 1880's

In 1861 Constable Joseph Davidson his wife and family lived at the station.

Land on which to build Bedfont police station had been purchased by the Receiver from Mr George Daws for £360 in June 1866. Construction of a new purpose built police station commenced later the same year and was completed for occupation on Christmas Eve 1868. The new station was erected adjoining the Load of Hay public house, at a cost of £2,185[14]. It had a charge room, three cells and was an inspector designated station with an inspectors office situated on the ground floor. There was also a general wash house on the ground floor store and three coal cellars. In the yard was a three stall stable with hay loft. The inspector was allowed five rooms to rent at the station which cost him 6s and 6d (33p) a week. There was a slight revision of the sub-divisional boundary upon the opening of a new station at Hatton(s) Road, Harlington in September 1870[15]. There were three horses located at Bedfont in the stables[16] and they had to patrol the 22 square miles of the sub division.

Living at Bedfont police station in 1871 was Hackney born 37 year old constable William Andrews, his wife Susan and family. Andrews had recently witnessed a change of senior officer in charge at Bedfont Police station and Inspector George Bush became the officer in charge of the sub division although he did not live at the police station. Instead he lived at no. 57 with his wife and three children. By 1878 Bush was no longer there and most likely had retired from the service. Next door was Sergeant John Laver with his wife and three children. The police wives (family) were a close community and helped each other out with chores or when there were problems. Further along the road at 117 was Sergeant Charles Salter who lived with his wife and family. Constable Fredrick Farley from Mile End who was widowed lived at 116 with his four children with his 16-year-old niece helping out looking after the children[17]. The police officers and their wives would have given advice rendered help when necessary and looked after children when necessary.

By December 1872 Bedfont was considered to be important enough to be connected to the new telegraph system and was given the identification station code letters 'BE'[18] . The telegraph enabled quick communication between Scotland Yard and the station. Sergeants were trained to use the telegraph initially but later reserve constables took over the task. The address was shown as Staines Road, Bedfont and along this road lived other police officers and their families.

Inspector Barrett of Bedfont from 1881 – 1894 on his horse patrol

In 1881 Warwickshire born Joseph Hughes (wt. no. 46722) was the inspector in charge of Bedfont police station where he lived above the station with his wife Ann and two children. The address was shown as 66 Staines Road, Bedfont and also resident were two married constables, Joseph Webb with his wife and two children together with John Bluekwill and his wife[19]. Tragedy struck Hughes who was a busy officer and held in high esteem whilst returning from Sunbury court when he was thrown from his horse and killed in 1882[20]. There were no witnesses to the accident and the startled horse was grazing nearby[21]. His police service funeral was attended by most of the station and members of the whole of 'T' Division were

Bedfont Police Station. 1868 – 1932. Staines Road, Bedfont.

present and Hughes was buried in the churchyard at St. Mary's Church, Bedfont. A headstone was purchased by the police of 'T' Division as a mark of the respect and esteem in which that Inspector Hughes was held. The inspector's quarters at the station were vacated within a short while rendering the family not only fatherless but homeless. Ann would have received a lump sum of money from the insurance scheme her husband had paid into together with a gratuity from the police which would tide her over.

Even at the newly built Bedfont the station's well in the yard was found to be polluted and this was meant to supply fresh drinking water to the inspector and two constables and their families. Instructions were given to sink a new well to provide suitable drinking water[22]. At this time the police in general were constantly aware that drunkenness was a problem amongst the constables and they often chose to drink 'fermented near beer' which provided a suitable and safer alternative to polluted water.

Coronation celebrations at Bedfont Police Station in 1902

Also living at Bedfont in 1881 was 38 year old Inspector William Barrett from Sidmouth with his wife Sarah and three children[23]. Barrett is shown above on his horse above whilst on his patrol. He remained there for some time and left Bedfont in 1894 on retirement.

In 1884 there was room for one married inspector and two married constables reside at the station although this was rather cramped. The surveyors replaced the polluted well by having pipes laid by the local water company for the supply of fresh water[24].

In 1892 Sub Divisional Inspector (wt. no. 49647) James Morsley was the officer in charge of the station which had a strength of four sergeants and 20 constables[25]. Morsley resigned on pension in May 1894[26]. Taking over from Morsley was Sub Divisional Inspector 55187 Fredrick Foster who only remained for a short while until May 1898. Foster, from Deal in Kent, had been posted to 'T' division and lived had in Hammersmith in 1891 with his wife and two children. He had already been stationed at Bedfont for some time as an inspector and received promotion on Morsleys resignation. In due course Foster's position was taken by Sub Divisional

Inspector 65779 Henry Herwin. Herwin lived at the station with his wife Caroline and their son and four daughters. Herwin remained for ten years retiring on pension in July 1907 and is shown in the centre of the group pictured above.

Sub Divisional Inspector Herwin

Sergeant John Neville and his wife and family lived in Victoria Road, Staines in 1901. Sergeant George Sallows and his wife and seven children lived in George Street Staines in the same year. At the same time Sergeant Richard Chamberlain, his wife and four children lived in London Road Staines. In the same year Station Sergeant Edward Hagarty, his wife and family lived nearby in Argyle Cottages where a number of other police families were resident like Sergeant Albert Kidd who lived near the station with his wife Jane and four children.

As the areas of Staines, Feltham, Ashford and Bedfont were rapidly expanding due to the influx of people and the building of houses it was necessary to re-organise policing arrangements for the Spelthorne area. As such in January 1907 Bedfont subdivision was renamed the Staines sub-division, with the unfortunate Inspector Mott being dismounted upon his transfer to the latter station. At that time the urban district of Feltham consisted of 1,790 acres and now had a population of 5,315. In 1908 Harry Smith took over as Sub Divisional Inspector of the new Staines sub division even though he was located at Bedfont. Bedfont had two sectional stations located at London Road, Staines and Bath Road, Harlington.

There were 150 men and nine horses attached to the sub division. The pay for the stations was brought on a Wednesday by the Sub Divisional Inspector on a horse but later this was replaced by a pony and trap. When motor cycle combinations were introduced the sub divisional inspector would carry out the same duty using a motor cycle and the divisional clerk would use the side car.

One police officer out on patrol recalled that he saw his inspector out riding his horse and saw him ride up the steps to the Hounds Public House (now the Bull Dog at Ashford), order and drink his pint of beer whilst still astride the horse and then reverse down the steps and continue his patrol. The hours for an inspector were long and arduous.

A police telephone box was installed in 1904 between Bedfont police station and the fixed point at the junction of Hanworth Road/High Street, Feltham, here a constable was stationed continuously day and night in all weathers, until replaced by the new DR WHO type 'TARDIS' which appeared during the 1930s[27]. There were five such police boxes in Feltham at the following locations: -

BOX NO. LOCATION

T 8 Hatton Cross, Great South West Road/Hatton Road
T 9 Staines Road/Hounslow Road
T 10 Hanworth Road, Front of Urban District Council Offices
T 11 Staines Road, Old Bedfont Police Station
T 12 Ashford Road/Lower Sunbury Road. Lower Feltham

Up until 1908 Bedfont was a sub division without responsibility for any other areas however it acquired Harlington and Staines as sectional stations by 1910[28]. In 1908 Sub Divisional Inspector Harry Smith was in charge of the sub division until 1915[29]. The following is a small extract from the writings of Inspector Smith, on his posting to Bedfont in 1908.

Sub Divisional Inspector Smith

'After a course of equitation I was in 1908 appointed as Sub Divisional Inspector (mounted) in charge of what is known as Staines Sub Division. This comprised an area of some 40 square miles with three stations, over 100 men, and nine horses and with occasional charge of the adjoining Sub Division of Hampton with four stations and 150 men. This entailed long and arduous hours of duty '

Inspector SMITH stayed at Bedfont until 1915 when he retired on doctor's advice and joined the Volunteer Home Defence. It was whilst serving with them that he was awarded the bronze medal of the Royal Society for the Protection of Life from Fire and also the Meritorious Service Medal for saving the life of a flying officer from his crashed and burning plane whereby he himself sustained injury. It was about this period that the large Feltham marshalling yards were built, mainly by prisoners of war[30].

Hanworth Park House originally the home of Lord Lafone, was used as a hospital for injured troops returning from the war and many local ladies helped out at the hospital during this time. St. Anthony's Catholic Orphanage was at Bedfont and St. Theresa's was a home for inebriate women near the Crown and Sceptre. Ashford hospital was at this time a workhouse and this was in fact what it was originally built for.

In 1931 the districts of Bedfont and Feltham were being policed from Harlington police station.

The town's Magistrate's Court was built as a town hall in 1903 when the growing town of Feltham when it became separated from the Rural District of Staines to become an Urban District in its own right.

Constable Jimmy Payne at Bedfont in 1921 recalled;

> 'There were two beats at the Station at this time and they were set 12 hour beats designed to be covered in a regular way, but as the officers only did an 8 hour day they had to be covered as best they could. One should remember that a lot of the roads were long and only lead to a single farm. Also at this time there were only four or five men on the street at one time, one of these was posted to a fixed post at the High Street, junction with Bedfont Lane. There were no Police Cars at this time in this area. There were some police boxes however, one of these was in the High Street near Wilton Parade. Communications were a little old fashioned by today's standards. Bedfont had a direct (telephone) line to Staines and communication with Harlington was by way of Telegraph. Internal despatches were carried by the mounted men until about 1925 when the good old bikes took over'[31].

In 1930 the neighbouring villages of Bedfont and Hanworth were incorporated into the Urban District of Feltham[32].

Dead bodies were dealt with and removed by Police using a hand-ambulance and this was sometimes also used to convey persons from as far as Stanwell to Hounslow hospital[33].

Oil lamps were carried by the Police during the hours of darkness and these were covered by a shutter when not in use, in rainy weather. When the cape was being worn one can imagine the smell that came from the uniforms. Refreshments were taken out on the street wherever you happened to be at the appointed time, tea was carried in a small container with a meths burner underneath and brewed up on the roadside. There was no refreshment period for men on night duty. It is remembered by several officers that when walking out to Bedfont they found that the walking was very hard, with many tracks and unmade roads to walk along.

Houses in the Bedfont area could be brought from about £400 and there are several ex-officers who took the plunge in buying their own house often not in the capability of many families who had to rely on rented accommodation. Pay at this time had increased to about £3 per week which apparently was not too bad for the time[34]. Also at this time you could see the Southall gasometer quite clearly from Bedfont.

In the early 1920s there was a footpath, known as Lovers Lane across the High Street at the junction of Manor Lane which ran to the airpark opposite. This was closed to the public when the War Department built the houses on what is now the junction of Elmwood Avenue. This caused an uproar amongst the residents and a local business man named Parker supplied a very large crowd with pieces of wood and iron. The result in the breaking down of the wall, and once opened the road stayed like it.

Receiving gratuities from local business-men in line with instructions needed to be reported to the Commissioner and whilst it was accepted that local people wanted to show their appreciation this should be done by supporting a charity like the orphanage at Twickenham. In line with this policy in 1932 the then Commissioner Viscount Byng stopped the Bedfont Police from receiving an annual gift from Mr. David Waring of either tea or tobacco at Christmas time.

At 6am on Monday 16th November 1932 the Police facilities at Bedfont old Station were withdrawn and transferred to Feltham which would be a Sectional Station of Staines Sub-Division. However this produced a local outcry and calls for the station to be re-instated. As soon as war was declared Bedfont opened again.

Just prior to the war in Uxbridge Road, constable Walter Woods at Bedfont was awarded the Kings Police Medal for bravery for rescuing two men from a fume filled sewer. At the outbreak of the war a further four Sergeants and 56 Constables, who were either Specials or War Reserves, reported for duty but the numbers soon dwindled as many were called up for active service. At this time serving regular officers could only volunteer as air crew[35].

In Hatton Road recreation ground during the war an anti aircraft unit (AAU) had been built consisting of four 3.7AA guns and later a Bofors gun was added. This is well remembered by everyone in the area especially when they opened up on the enemy above. Several land mines were reported to have landed in the area during the war and a 'doodle-bug' landed in Florence Road. The only bomb to land on the Allied Estate in Lower Feltham fell right outside the house of a police officer[36].

Police officers whether they were re-engaged pensioners, War Reserve or full time paid special Constables would be called out to unexploded bombs when they were reported, and one consequence of having an AAU nearby was occasionally their shells failed to explode and returned to earth, often providing fatal consequences to inquisitive young boys seeking mementoes from the aerial battles overhead.

The station was pulled down in 1952 to make way for a block of police flats. In the revision of boundaries which took place on the 1st April 1965[37], Feltham, which took over the policing of Bedfont was shown then as a sectional station of Hounslow sub-division.

In 1973 a new sectional police station for Feltham and this replaced Bedfont. The old temporary station at Feltham was replaced with a new but very cube like unimaginative building that became operational at 6am on Monday 8th October, the postal address being, 34 Hanworth Road[38]. With the formation of Airport Division certain other boundary changes took place with 'T' Division.

In 2013 a Safer neighbourhoods unit, based at operated in Bedfont.

Brentford Police Station

New Brentford was a narrow strip of land between the River Brent and Half Acre and research into the history crime of Brentford taken from ledgers shows some intriguing entries. A somewhat unusual one appears in the record for 1634:

> 'Paid Robert Warden (a smith by trade) the Constable which he dispurs'd for conveying away the witches 11s. 0d[39].

Brentford had long been associated with witches. Falstaff, in the Merry Wives of

Brentford Market square circa early 1800s

Windsor, disguised himself as the old fortune-telling Fat Woman of Brentford, whom Master Ford swore was a witch. However, the witches taken away by Robert Warden were no doubt of more humble origin. Typically such women were old and poor and the victims of the gossiping slander of neighbours who accused them of bringing sickness to both men and beasts[40].

The ripples of the Industrial Revolution reached Brentford in the early 19th century with the opening of the Grand Junction Canal. Breweries, mills and other industries began to displace the previous agricultural economy. The coming of the railways, the opening of Brentford Dock, the waterworks, gas works and factories increased noise and pollution, changing the character of New Brentford. With the development of more sophisticated forms of transport Brentford grew into a thriving market town and became the county town of Middlesex, now no longer a county.

Land at New Brentford for a cage, stocks, and whipping post was sought in 1720. A cage was to be built or rebuilt in 1753; a watch box for the beadle was to be set up near the market house and a new stocks provided in 1787 [41].

At Brentford the cage stood on the corner of Ferry Lane and High Street in 1839[42].

Brentford Police Station. 1813 – 1830 (1897) 60 High Street (previously front Street), Old Brentford, Middlesex.

The first Brentford police station was situated on the eastern corner of Town Meadow.

> 'The building was early C18, with 3 bays and consisted of house, stable and yard. Prior to its use by the Police, Lawrence Rowe, who ran a local soap works business, bought this property (complete with its own wharf) in 1799[43].

A report in *The Times* of 19th July 1831 stated that a constable of the 'T' Division stopped two boys in possession of an ass which they confessed they had stolen in the neighbourhood of Oxford and had travelled all that distance without being stopped despite the presence of Bow Street horse patrols which had been set up in 1805 and were based in Hounslow[44]. Although rural in nature, Chiswick and Brentford suffered with traffic congestion with no fewer than 50 stage coaches which passed though the towns daily en route to the southwest.

In the tythe map of Front Street, Brentford[45] above the police station marked 36 is a short distance to no. 49 – the lock up house or cage where prisoners were

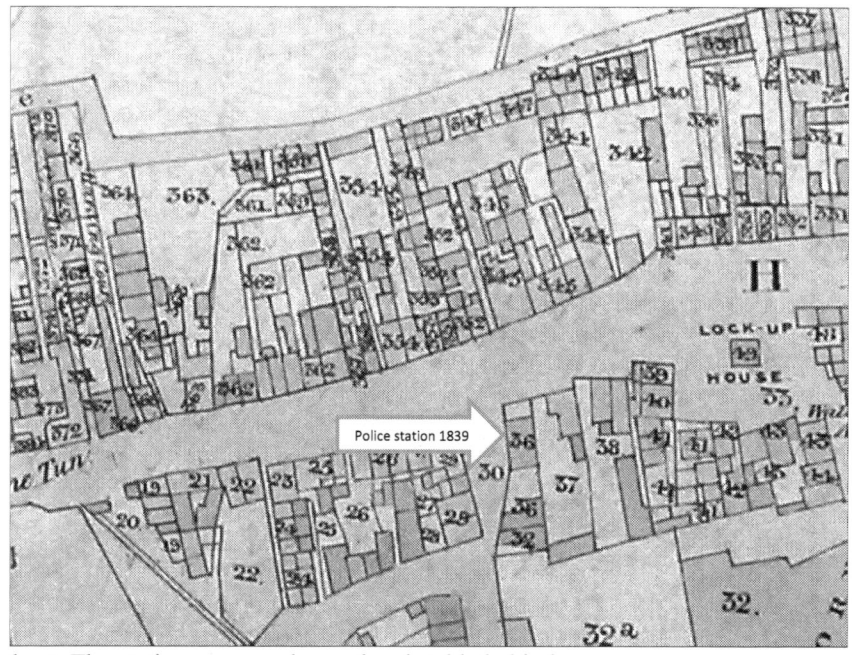

kept. The station possessed a yard and stable behind.

On 13th January 1840 'T' or Kensington division was extended west of Brentford up to the Buckinghamshire county boundary. All arrests made in the parishes of Isleworth, Hounslow, Heston, Hanwell, Greenford, Perivale, Norwood and Alperton were taken to Brentford police station[46].

The station address in 1836 was Front Street, Old Brentford near the cage and was a station on 'T' or Kensington Division under Superintendent David Williamson[47]. In the 1839/41 tithe return (mentioned above) the owner Thomas and L. Rowe is recorded as renting a 'house, stable & yard'[48] to the Metropolitan Police as a station house. Access to a yard was a fundamental requirement for police officers as it was essential to house horses for transport and to patrol the main routes.

And so the Metropolitan Police moved into the Brentford area. When the first Brentford police station was built here in 1830 the main thoroughfare was called 'Front Street' rather than 'High Street' its later name. The station also had a covered passage way, washhouse at extreme rear, a water closet; three store sheds at rear; side gateway entrance, and a cellar in the basement[49]. The cells for holding prisoners were also located in the basement[50].

In due course the station address became 60 High Street, Old Brentford and in 1841 Inspector Cortney Henry Marquard and five constables lived there, two having small families living with them. Marquard had joined as a constable in April 1830 with promotion to inspector in 1834. He was recognised for his leadership skills in Brentford by the Commissioners who in 1845 promoted him to Superintendent of the 'K' or Stepney Division. One wonders how impressed he was being posted from a semi-rural location into the depths of the East End of London where he stayed until 1852[51]. The East End was the most difficult area to police in London with its levels of crime and assaults on police officers. Marquard was discharged by the Medical Officer as being 'used up' (a term later replaced with 'worn out'), with a gratuity of £150 having only completed 22 years. He had not completed the usual 25 years' service[52] which would have qualified him for a pension. By 1844 Brentford had become 'an inspector station' meaning that the highest rank supervising the police station area of Brentford was an Inspector[53] with Marquard being its first incumbent. In 1841 Marquard was assisted by 30-year old police Sergeant James Levy who lived at the station with his wife and two children[54]. Constable John Duckett and his family also lived there[55].

William Brown was the inspector in charge in 1851 and resided there with two sergeants and three constables. In 1853 Thomas Bristow was sergeant of police living in Brookshot Road, Old Brentford, with sergeant James Oxley Turner living in Orchard Road[56]. Charles Cox started working there in 1862. The station moved to 42 High Street in 1869. In 1987 the cells were still evident in the building and by 2003 the station had become a solicitor's office. Constable Joseph Jacobs who resided in Ealing Lane was also attached to the station in 1851.

In July 1861 there are complaints to the vestry of the 'annoyance to which the inhabitants are subjected by persons standing about in the streets and obstructing the footpaths thereof and by the obscene, blasphemous and immoral language which are so shamefully and indecently prevalent in the streets of the township at all hours of the day and night.' Sergeant 42 'T' Charles Blake from Southwold in Suffolk, his wife Mary and two sons and a daughter lived at the police station in 1861. Blake was ten years older than his wife whom he had met locally, but displayed a lack of ability as a sergeant and had been reported a number of times to the Superintendent. He was placed on report but it was decided by the Commissioner that he had taken sufficient steps to come up to standard. But things did not go well for Charles in 1868 as he had by then been demoted to onstable and sent to urban Stepney from rural Brentford as punishment. By 1872 he had been medically retired as being 'worn out' by the police doctor. Constables Edward Hitchcock and Fredrick Forman were also stationed at Brentford at the time[57].

Brentford Police Station. 1830 – 1869. 60 High Street, Brentford, Middlesex.

The Brentford Vestry minutes in 1863 recorded that;

'During the 19th century powers had been stripped away from the vestry and given to a variety of elected boards and councils. Policing had become the responsibility of police commissioners in 1829 and an Act of 1839 allowed JPs to create a county force of chief and petty constables. The rough and ready systems that had proved adequate in the past were being transformed into a modern industry'[58].

Police Orders show that Brentford was a station of 'T' Division in 1864.

Originally built in 1850 as a town hall when Queen Victoria was only 31, the building which became the court building and stands in Market Place off London Road was used for Brentford's first library and other Victorian social gatherings such as vegetable shows. By 1891 the building was fully bought out by Middlesex County Council to be used full-time as a magistrate's court. The police officers of the district were frequent visitors often taking their prisoners there to appear before the magistrate. This was never used as a police station although it did have a police room.

Brentford Magistrates Court. 1850 – 2011. Market Place, Brentford, Middlesex.

Brentford Magistrates court shut in 2011 after 161 years[59] and is likely to become a public house.

Inspector Tarling lived at the police station with his wife Anne and five children. The conditions were cramped and space at a premium. Constable Charles Pontin and his wife, constable John Bucks and his wife, constable Philip Vaughn and his wife and 15 single constables all resided there. In July 1867 the Police Surveyor recommended purchase of the site and the Home Office approved the transaction in August 1867[60]. By 1881 Tarling had retired and become the licensee of the Red Lion public house situated opposite the police station at 318 High Street.

The duties of all officers of the police were published in 1868. At Brentford there was only one inspector at this time (Tarling) who was responsible for patrolling only. His job specifically excluded him from duty at the police station and he was to supervise on horseback the sections of Hounslow, Staines, Isleworth, Heston and Stanwell section - where there was no police station. The beats were split into two sections – the day beats and the night beats. There were two sergeants at the station. One sergeant and six constables covered the days beats whilst the other sergeant and 12 constables patrolled by night. There were two horses stabled at Brentford, one for use by the Inspector and the other for a constable to patrol on[61].

On 21st January 1867, Superintendent 'T' Division Robert Beckerson reported that Inspector James Tarling had found a suitable site for a new station in Main Street near the Church at the township of New Brentford close to the town hall. Main street was later named High street. A new three-storey police station with basement was built in 1869 at a cost of £5,674. 44p (£7,000 including land) and be occupied on 28th September[62] and the police of 'T' Division moved to the new Station at Brentford on this day. The station had six cells and the building is no longer standing. The boundaries of Bedfont, Brentford and Hampton Sub-Divisions were altered in 1890[63]. Brentford became one of nine new purpose built police stations to have been built in the two years prior to 1870[64]. The population of Brentford at the time was 11,091.

Early in the 20th century Mrs Mary Ann Cox (1869-1954) was matron at the police station and employed to search female prisoners. In 1894 she married Charles William Cox (1869-1950) at St. Paul's Church. He worked as a potter in the Bull Lane Pottery, Pottery Road, making chimney pots. Mary and family lived in New Road and then at several addresses in Ealing Road not far from the station. There were several members of the Cox family living on Brentford High Street from 1841, including a John Cox from Northamptonshire at the police station in 1891 where he was a police sergeant [65]. Charles Cox joined Brentford police force (constable 187 'T' Division) and lived with his wife and family in Town Meadow Road. This was convenient since, Brentford police station (where he served) was then situated at 60 High Street at the junction with Town Meadow, Brentford. Cox died at Kew bridge in 1870 when he accidentally drowned[66].

The numbering of the High Street took place in 1876 and the police station was allocated no. 42. However there appears to be an extra property between the police station and the George IV public house at no. 50 which may account for later

Brentford Police Station. 1869 – 1966. 42 High Street, Brentford, Middlesex.

references to no. 43a and no. 45a[67]. These may have been used as police living accommodation[68]. In 1881 Sub Divisional Inspector (wt. no. 47987) John Rowling was the officer in charge and he resided at the station with his wife Mary Ann and their two children. Rowling, an ardent Cornishman from St. Columb, joined the police in January 1867 and retired in March 1892. They were still resident at the station in 1891 but Rowling had died by 1901 and his wife had moved back to

Cornwall in the meantime. His place was taken by inspector (wt. no. 54453) John Oran Mumford. Mumford, born 1851 in London, joined the Metropolitan Police in 1871 and took over at Brentford from March 1892 until 1897 when he was retired on pension. He lived in the married quarters at the station with his wife Catherine and Minnie his daughter. On retirement he moved to 14, Lateward Road, Brentford[69].

The following report appeared in the 'Police Review' in 1897;

> "RETIREMENT OF AN INSPECTOR.- Having completed upwards of twenty-five years' service in the Metropolitan Police Force, Sub-divisional Inspector Mumford has retired on a pension. Mr. Mumford came to Brentford in 1891, on the retirement of Sub-divisional Inspector ROWLING, his immediately preceding appointment having been at Albany Street in the 'S' Division. During his residence in Brentford, Inspector Mumford has gained the respect and esteem of the general body of the residents alike by his genial and kindly bearing and by the efficiency with which he has discharged the onerous duties of his position. Mr. Mumford intends, we understand, to enter into business in Brentford."

In fact Mumford did indeed stay in Brentford once he retired because he took over the George IV Public House situated at 50 High Street, on the corner of Goat Wharf until 1899 when he died in Brentford Cottage Hospital. As licensee he would be well aware of his responsibilities as he would have closely supervised all the licensed establishments in his area when he was the inspector. In the 1913 directory a Mrs C. Mumford is listed at the George IV although her daughter then aged 20 had pre-deceased her in 1905[70]. Joseph B. Hart had taken over by 1920. The public house was situated right near the police station and was a place that off duty police officers would go to and be in comfortable surroundings with the ex-police inspector and his wife in charge.

From 1897 until 1908 Sub Divisional Inspector Edwin Digby was in charge of the station and lived there with his wife Emily and their two sons. Digby had been promoted from 'E' or Holborn Division in 1896. Also resident at the station were Constable William Clayden with his wife and family, Constable John Seaman and his wife and in the section house were 20 single officers. These were Constables Charles Anderson, Goodman Proops, Ernest Wachter, Thomas Rimmington, Frank Potter, Herbert Cottage, George Smith, William Hope, William Farrer and Henry Rudling, Arthur Rickens and Charles Gaylor, Fred Burchell, Wallace Sturrock, James Willie, Joseph Harwood, Henry Nock, James Duguid, Edward Smith, and David Thomas, [71].

In the same year Digby was assisted by nine sergeants and 34 constables. Brentford was the sub-divisional station with Hounslow, Isleworth, and Norwood Green all sectional stations. Digby had retired to the local area and moved to 70 Hamilton

Road, Brentford where he resided with his wife, his two sons and daughter[72]. In 1908 Sub Divisional Inspector Richard Wallis[73] took his place and in turn his place was taken in 1914 by Charles Richardson[74].

Brentford Police station was a one of a number of places designated under the Royal Humane Society for the receiving of dead bodies, apparently drowned, where drags and other apparatus were kept. Other storage locations included the public houses in Brentford[75].

There were problems with the drainage at the station in early 1903 which caused some discomfort and complaint by the inhabitants. Works were carried out by the Surveyors who not only improved the sanitary conditions but in the single men's accommodation partitions were set up between the beds giving some degree of privacy on the part of the occupants[76].

In 1910 the police station at no. 42 was owned by the Receiver of the Metropolitan

Brentford police station yard and a retirement celebration circa 1906

Police and valued at £4,410. Richard Wallis, in 1910, and Thomas Faulkner, in 1913 were the sub-divisional inspector at the police station.

The picture above shows an officer wearing plain clothes without a hat receiving his ornamental time piece for completing 25 years' service. Sub Divisional Inspector Digby - in charge of Brentford is sat on his horse to the back left of the group facing away from the camera. Divisional Superintendent James Powell is seated in the front row wearing plain clothes and a bowler hat. Powell as the chief officer of the division would often officiate at retirement celebrations where it would be incumbent on him to 'say a few words' about the outgoing officer's service and contribution.

Police Orders dated 30th December 1916 stated that the Sub-Division would comprise of the stations of Brentford and Chiswick, with Brentford the sub-divisional station. Brentford did not escape enemy action World War One; bombs fell on 29th January 1918 demolishing a house in White Star Road and the houses either side being severely damaged. Eight people were also killed at Brentford water works. Special constable P. Bentley tried to rescue people from a partly demolished building, removing a dead body and won a commendation for his actions[77].

Special constable Fredrick Tickner

Fredrick Tickner, a local boat builder and foreman joined the Metropolitan Police Special Constabulary at the start of the war to supplement the regular police officers being called up and was posted to Brentford police station. He is seen at left standing in front of the bricks at Goat Wharf. Research shows the cap badge is that of the Metropolitan Special Constabulary and this suggests he volunteered to be a Special Constable during World War One. Special Constables often had no uniform provided but were issued with armlets, whistles and truncheons, and later on, badges. Fredrick recalled some of his experiences whilst a special constable. He saw a German Zeppelin follow the river up to Brentford and bombed the town, the damage being most severe in Green Dragon Lane and Walnut Tree Road. He also wrote that the Vestry Hall Brentford was used as a County Court until the new building in Alexandra Road was built[78]. Once the war was finished the area returned to normality but there was a feeling that a permanent reserve of Special Constables should remain after 1919.

The stables at the rear of the station were converted into a District Traffic Garage and re-occupied in 1932. In 1937 a site on which to build a police station was purchased freehold in Ealing Road, Brentford. Because of the impending situation in Europe and the likelihood of war plans were temporarily shelved and the site was rented out to Alpha Romeo Co. Ltd for 21 years commencing in 1944 on an annual rent of £100[79]. In the same year Brentford was classified as a sectional station to Acton sub division, call sign TB.

It was not long before preparations were being made to go to war again and the police special constabulary reserves were increased to support local policing. However this time the methods of wreaking havoc changed with the delivery of bombs not only coming from heavy bombers but also via new remote technology, Rocket, flying bomb and bombing raids severely affected Brentford during the World War Two a V1 Rocket hit 63 Clayponds Avenue, Brentford at 15.20 hours on the 12th July 1944 causing considerable damage including some houses in Ealing Road. The blast resulted in George Forgan and his sister being trapped in the rubble, but luckily they were pulled out quickly and not harmed[80]. Police were quickly on the scene of any bombing or damage caused from aerial bombardment. They would quickly secure the area, rescue victims, recover bodies and search for unexploded munitions. Any of the injured would be conveyed to the medical stations or hospitals for treatment. Dead bodies would be conveyed to the mortuary. Until families were informed of the damage, police would remain on scene to protect property from looters.

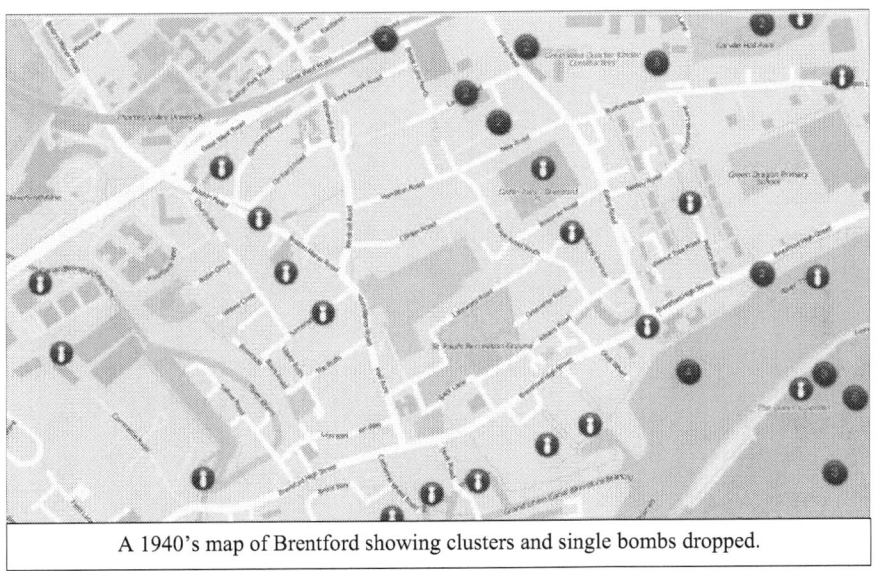

A 1940's map of Brentford showing clusters and single bombs dropped.

Brentford's fortunes were rather mixed when it came to bombs falling during German air raids between 7th October 1940 and 6th June 1941. Two bombs fell in Brentford High Street, one quite close to the police station. Also Syon Lane, Beech Avenue, Somerset Road, Barnhurst Road were hit causing damage and injury but six fell harmlessly into the Thames[81].

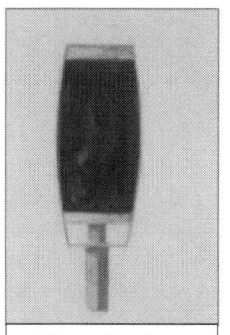

A revision of boundaries took place on the 1st April 1965 to align with local authorities and Brentford was shown as a sectional station to Chiswick as the sub-divisional station. Later, until 1963 when the re-building of Chiswick was completed, Brentford became the sub-divisional headquarters[82]. The vestry hall was on the Half Acre corner with St Paul's Road and was demolished in the 1960s to make way for a new police station.

The design of the station lamp shown at left is that for Brentford.

The station lamp

The *Police Review* of 1st July 1966 reported that the £400,000 new station would comprise police station and section house within the eleven floor tower block with

Brentford Police Station. 1967 – present day. The Half Acre, St. Pauls Road, Brentford Middlesex TW8 8BH.

accommodation for 98 single officers, each with their own room. The station would replace the existing Brentford police station in the High Street reverting to a sectional station with the opening of the new Chiswick sub-divisional station on 27th March 1972. The old station was shut for day- to-day policing in 1967 after the new station became operational. The public were directed to the new station whilst the Metropolitan Police retained the old building for use as administrative offices.

In December 1969 the old station was pulled down and workmen found several artefacts of interest such as an 1865 warrant and a badly made counterfeit half sovereign believed to have belonged to a prisoner who hid it in the cell where he was kept[83].

The plush new sub-Divisional Police Station for Brentford on 'T' Division was built at The Half Acre, Brentford was taken into operational use at 6am on 4th July 1967[84]. In 2012 Brentford police station St Paul's Road, Half Acre Brentford, TW8 8BH was open Monday - Friday 9am to 5pm and closed on bank holidays and also Saturdays and Sundays[85].

Chiswick Police Station

Hounslow Heath to the west of Brentford became a natural training ground for the military, and its proximity led to the development of Brentford and Chiswick. The increased traffic in and out of the capital both by road and river brought an increase in population to the area along the routes, not always of the most desirable kind since highwaymen and women were a common hazard to the newly-developing stage coach service. The Star and Garter Inn at Kew Bridge became one of many coaching inns along the way. Chiswick, Isleworth and Osterley were the sites of some of the most magnificent house building together with estates consisting of parkland and formal gardens. In the present day they are open to the public, preserving a very necessary green area. The region prospered and the villages expanded with small family housing for the estate workers and the small retail shops stretching along the increasingly busy roads[86].

This general trend to expansion and merging of boundaries continued and the region continued comfortably and unspectacularly. Roads were steadily improved, the railway arrived, horse-drawn trams gave way to trolley buses. There were some Victorian terrace house developments in common with most other areas, but despite the innovations the essential character of the four original communities was retained[87].

Although the river traffic and associated commerce has declined since World War Two, the water front retains its importance in the life and development of this part of Hounslow borough as it is the leisure and recreational aspects of this oldest asset which is ripe for exploitation and can only serve to enhance the reputation of Brentford and Chiswick as a desirable place to live and work - something it seems it has always enjoyed[88].

Chiswick did not possess a police station at that time and was policed from Hammersmith and Shepherds Bush although there were stables at Turnham Green for the Bow Street horse patrol. Brentford was to be the western extent of the Metropolitan Police District (MPD) until about 1840. Although somewhat rural in nature Chiswick and Brentford had its traffic problems even then, as no fewer than 50 stage-coaches passed through the towns daily, to the South-West, nine coaches a day to Bristol alone, with the Star and Garter Hotel at Kew Bridge being an important coaching hostelry[89].

Toll gates were erected at Brentford and Isleworth near Busch Corner which added to the congestion but were finally removed in July 1872. Prosperity came to Brentford, in the form of the Grand Junction Canal which opened in November 1794 as far as Uxbridge[90].

In 1840 further development commenced with the coming of the London and South Western Railway who opened a line from Waterloo with stations at Chiswick, Kew Bridge and Brentford. In January 1869 the company opened stations at Bedford Park (now Turnham Green) and Brentford Road (now Gunnersbury) while the Great Western Railway had opened a branch to Brentford from the Southall direction in May 1860. This closed during the last war. Like the canal companies the railways had their own police forces. The London & South Western Railway became part of the Southern Railway Police in 1923, both companies coming under the British Transport Commission Police in 1948. The British Transport Police were formed in1962. Finally the District Railway opened a station called Acton Green (now Chiswick Park) in July 1879 bringing yet another police force[91].

Chiswick and Brentford were stations both connected to the telegraph system in December 1872, the identification codes being 'CK' and 'BR' respectively.

The first horse-trams appeared on the streets in March 1882 running between Shepherds Bush and Young's Corner, owned by the West Metropolitan Tramway Co. and were extended to Kew Bridge in December that year. They were replaced by electric trams in April 1901 and extended through Brentford to Hounslow that July[92].

In Police Orders of l864 Chiswick was shown as a station of 'T' or the Kensington Division. In November 1869 a report by Superintendent Fisher spoke of a piece of land for sale which was suitable on which to build a police station near The Windmill Public House on the South side of Great Western Road, Chiswick High Road at the corner of Windmill Lane[93]. A second Police station opened in January 1870 replacing the original 1850's structure at Chiswick field Road, Turnham Green, an area which was to become London's first garden suburb in 1876. This building was a temporary measure pending the opening of a purpose built station in the High Street in December 1872[94].

In February 1884 following the creation of a new Shepherds Bush sub-division the Chiswick sub-divisional boundary was revised, the strength at the at time being three Inspectors, five Sergeants and 61 constables.

Home Office approval was received in June 1870 for the purchase of a site at Turnham Green. Police Orders in January 1870 shows a new Station being brought into use. The entry reads,

> 'The Commissioner approves of the temporary police station in Chester Terrace, Chiswick Field Road, Turnham Road, being occupied by police from the 25th inclusive'.

Police Orders of 20th December 1884 recorded that a portion of the new police station at Chiswick which is required for police purposes and was ready for use was occupied on 'T' division and that possession of the old Station was given up. Chiswick was shown as a Sub-Divisional Station of 'T' Division in Police Orders of 22nd February 1884[95].

One of the more notable senior officers to take charge of Chiswick sub division was sub divisional Inspector (wt. no. 55889) David Rawlings who transferred there in 1888 where he remained until he retired in 1898. A rare pen picture of Rawlings highlights his special leadership and detective qualities. In 1867 Rawlings, a native of Danbury in Essex went to sea and travelled all over the world. On his return in 1872 he joined the police and once the preparatory class was finished he was sent to Old Street Police station on 'G' or Shoreditch Division. After only 8 months he was transferred to Rochester Row on 'B' or Chelsea division where he soon came into favour of his superiors being seconded to special duties at the Army and Navy stores in Victoria Street, Westminster. With this special duty he was promoted to 1st class constable on the top rate of pay.

Sub Divisional Inspector David Rawlings

In 1879 he was promoted to sergeant and transferred to Souhwark on 'M' Division where he only remained for a short time as his seniors on 'B' Division wanted him back. Whist there he was rewarded with another special duty and was placed in charge of the police staff at the Fisheries Exhibition at South Kensington. Such was the success of this exhibition and police arrangements that he was rewarded with a purse of money which the Commissioner allowed him to keep. Again he was placed in charge of another exhibition in 1884 and on its successful conclusion Rawlings was promoted to Inspector and sent to Fulham Police station on 'T' Division. It was whilst at Fulham that he investigated and arrested a man named Tucker who had murdered his wife. Tucker was sentenced to death and Rawlings was commended by the trial judge Mr Justice Hawkins. A fire occurred at Favart Road where a family was trapped, Rawlings without thought to his own safety entered the building and, one by one, brought the family to safety. For this act of bravery and selflessness he was rewarded with a certificate on vellum from the Society for the Protection of Life from Fire and two guineas (£2. 2 shillings or £2.20p), also receiving a reward of one guinea from the Commissioner for his promptitude. In 1888 he was again recognised for his leadership skills and example when he was further promoted to sub divisional inspector and moved to Chiswick.

At Chiswick he brought a notable burglar to justice, supervised and also featured prominently in a case of manslaughter in the district. Apart from his normal duties and other cases he took charge of the police arrangements at an industrial dispute at the Thorneycroft factory in 1897. Through his leadership and guidance he was able to defuse the tensions in the strike which passed off peacefully. He was also considered popular amongst the local population, possessing firmness and even temper. He was also well liked and respected amongst his men and especially the younger constables who would often receive guidance and advice for their future careers.

Rawlings also favoured sporting activities, where he became involved in charitable activities between the police and the Fire Brigade donating monies raised to local and other good causes. On retirement he received a 1st class certificate of service plus an annual pension of £126 6s 8d (£126. 33p). Chiswick local tradesmen presented him with an illuminated address on vellum, a purse containing £110 and a gold watch. His wife Mary also was included and she received a purse of money as well. His colleagues presented him with a silver cruet set, and the sergeants and constables gave him a liqueur stand[96]. Rawlings, then aged 48 years old could not have been in particular good health as his wife Mary was widowed in 1901, living on her own means and without any children in Glebe Street, Chiswick.

When Rawlings retired his replacement was Sub Divisional Inspector (wt. no. 66050) William Cheyney who was promoted from 'A' or Whitehall Division. Cheyney resided at the Chiswick police station with his wife Barbara and their three children[97]. Cheyney remained at Chiswick until 1907 when he retired on pension.

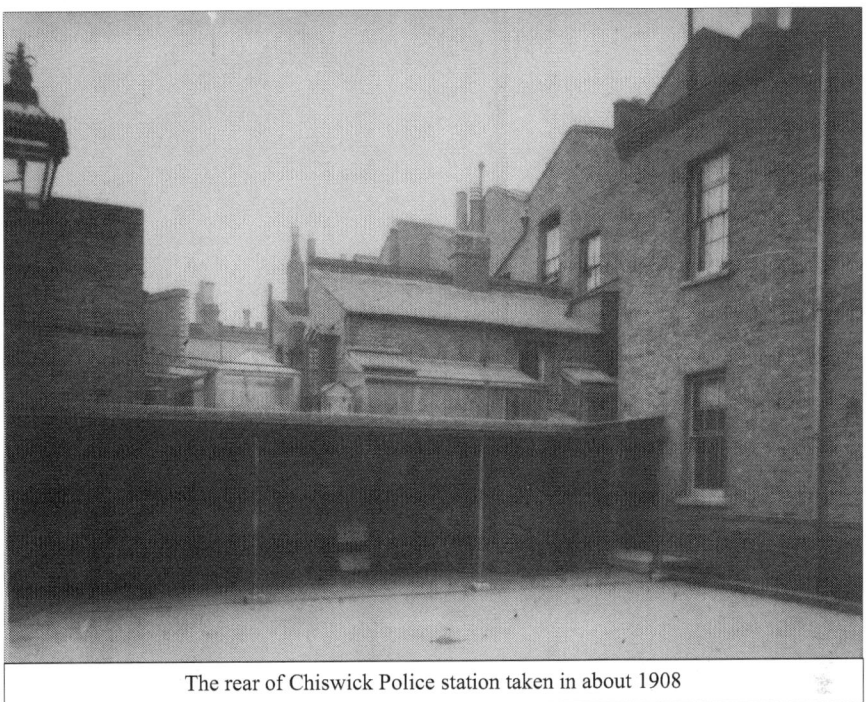

The rear of Chiswick Police station taken in about 1908

Sub Divisional Inspector (wt. no. 75231) Arthur Copping from Suffolk was in charge in 1911 and resided at the station with his wife Louisa and their son and three daughters[98]. Also present and living at the station were six single constables living in the section house. Coppping remained there until 1917 when he retired from 'T' Division.

In 1912 there was a fixed point box situated in Grove Park, Chiswick on land owned by Chiswick Urban District council. These were to be manned for 24 hours a day and could be a place for a member of the public to find a constable should the need arise. These are not to be confused with the Dr Who TARDIS-type police box which were introduced later in the 1920s and 1930s.

The introduction of the 'T' Division Specials saw a large contingent being enrolled at Chiswick where Chief Inspector G. Gentry worked together with SDI Copping to cover the stations duties[99]. There were at least 250 specials posted to Chiswick perhaps the largest and keenest group in the division.

During the Great War, in 1917, Chiswick became a mere sectional station to Brentford and was supplemented by a contingent of 'T' Division Special Constabulary made up of employees of the London General Omnibus Co. from Turnham Green depot in Belmont Road.

During the same year postal code numbers were introduced e.g. Chiswick W4[100]. Three bombs dropped on Chiswick High Road on the night of 29th January 1918 injuring five people and causing damage to surrounding properties but also smashing the gas and water mains[101]. This was part of a raid that also did substantial damage to Brentford and Isleworth on the same night. Chiswick specials were good at first aid and some 94 held first aid certificates. This prompted the senior officers to make arrangements with the District Council for an ambulance station where the man-power was provided by the police and the lorry and equipment by the council. Over 700 regulars from 'T' division were sent to the armed services[102].

The narrow streets of Brentford were at last by-passed in 1924 by the opening of the Great West Road, however the section between, South Ealing Road and Boston

Chiswick Police Station in 1919 dressed up in celebration of the ending of WW1.

Road was not completed until June 1926 and its extension over the Chiswick flyover much later in September 1959. Up until June 1931 a police station existed at Isleworth and when it closed in the same year Chiswick became a sub-division again with Shepherds Bush as a section to it. Brentford meanwhile became a sectional station of Hounslow sub-division together with Norwood Green, at the same time temporary workshops were opened at Brentford to ease the workload at Barnes Garage but closed in December 1939. In July 1931 a new railway station

Chiswick Police Station. 1884 – 1963. 210 High Road, Chiswick, Middlesex

opened, at Syon Lane due to a new housing development[103].

An entry in Police Orders of 28th May 1931 read;

> 'The following re-arrangement of Sub-Divisions will take effect on the 1st June. Chiswick Sub- Division to be comprised of Chiswick as the Sub-Divisional Station and Shepherds Bush as its Sectional Station'.

In the re-oganisation of the divisions North of the Thames on 1st December 1933[104] Chiswick was transferred from 'T' to 'F' Division.

The police station is said to be haunted by the ghost of Mrs Abercrombie who was murdered by her son-in-law in 1792. When not pacing about the ground floor she is apparently seen on the upper floors[105]. The station was located at 210 High Road, Chiswick in 1931 and was a sectional station of Brentford sub division on 'T' Division[106].

A rather amusing speeding case was heard at Brentford Magistrates Court during this period when evidence was given in defence to the effect that the new traffic patrols had lured drivers into speeding by causing them to overtake the slow-moving police vehicle which was disguised as a fruiterer from the vast Brentford fruit market, displaying a large board to the rear reading 'BANANAS 3 for 2d'[107].

Police Box in Chiswick Road circa 1950's

Chiswick ceased to be part of 'T' division in December 1933 (the same year that Chiswick Bridge opened) and passed to 'F' division where it was to remain for over 30 years[108].

In Police Orders of 5th July 1933 mention is made of a new Sub-Divisional Station to be opened on the 8th July at Shepherds Bush. Chiswick is to become a sectional station and form part of the new Shepherds Bush sub-division[109].

London Transport had its own police force from 1933 but is now part of the British Transport Police.

The division has public order commitments within its own boundary with the presence of Brentford Football Club established in 1889, and the annual boat race run over the present stretch of the Thames since 1864. Between 1923 -1928, a police sports day was a regular local event and was held at the Polytechnic Sports Ground in Cavendish Road, Brentford. These events were very popular with the public and the local bus route 55 (now E3) was specially extended from Chiswick railway station to cater for the crowds[110].

During the large-scale revision of boundaries in 1965 Chiswick returned to 'T' Division as a sub-divisional Station with Brentford as its sectional station[111]. Pending the re-building of Chiswick, Brentford became the sub-divisional Station and headquarters of the sub-division. The site for the new Chiswick police station was found on the site of the (old) fire station, at 209/211, Chiswick High Road, and purchased on 16th March 1967.

In Police Orders in March 1972 a paragraph read,

> 'A new sub-divisional station for Chiswick (TC) at 205/211, Chiswick High Road will be taken into operational use at 6am on Monday 27th March when the existing Chiswick Station will be closed and Brentford (TB) will revert to sectional status'.

In 1972 a new purpose built police station was opened at Chiswick. In Police Orders of 5th July 1963 mention is made of a new sub-divisional station to be opened on the 8th July at Shepherds Bush. Chiswick is to become a sectional station and form part of the new Shepherds Bush sub-division[112].

Chiswick (FC) returned to 'T' division in 1965 as a sub-divisional station, it had only been a sectional station since July 1963 when the present Shepherds Bush

Chiswick police station. 1963 – present day. 205 -211 High Road, Chiswick.

opened and now once again had Brentford as a section which hitherto had been part of Acton sub-division. On 1st April 1965 the G.L.C. came into existence and created the new London Borough of Hounslow replacing the old borough of Brentford and Chiswick and at this point Middlesex ceased to be a county.

When the Metropolitan Police abolished Districts in April 1986 'T' district as it had been known since 1980 ceased to exist and Chiswick became a division which included Brentford as part of a new No.5 or South West Area[113].

It is now over 160 years since the 'New Police first extended to Chiswick and Brentford but the Metropolitan Police continue to give service to the community. In 2012 Chiswick police station is open 24 hours a day 7 days a week and detains and charges prisoners for court[114]. In 2012 consultations between the local police and public have indicated that because of cutbacks Chiswick police station was likely to close[115] in favour of a more user friendly shop front or office at the Town Hall. The fate of the station will be discussed in 2013.

Feltham Police Station.

In 1932 the Chief Constable in charge of D2 branch, Mr. G. ABBISS, later to become Sir George ABBISS, reported that he was doubtful whether it was politic at that time to close down the police stations of Bedfont and Sunbury without providing a suitable replacement in the area. He commented that as Staines sub-division was one of the largest in No.1 District and that Staines station itself was situated on the extreme western boundary of the Metropolitan Police District, it would not be a wise move. He suggested that if the stations were closed then a new police station should be found in the Feltham area. The two stations were closed on the 1st June 1932 as a measure of re-organisation and economy but a room remained open for public visits until a replacement was found. In the meantime, Bedfont was not sold and remained as living quarters for police officers and their families[116] although an office was manned by a local constable who lived at the station.

Frequent representations were made by the two local authorities -

Feltham Police Station. 1952 -1971. 34 Hanworth Road, Feltham, Middlesex.

Sunbury and Feltham Urban District Councils that a station should be provided in the area. The Commissioner considered the matter in 1937 and came to the conclusion that it was indeed desirable to build a station at Feltham[117].

Prior to the World War Two plans were made by the police to locate a police station in Feltham and many sites were examined. Eventually two parcels of land were purchased in 1939 and 1940 at 'Auckland House', 34 Hanworth Road and a frontage to Ashfield Avenue[118] on which to build a purpose-built station on the site used during the war as the headquarters of the local Home Guard unit. However because of the war and the general lack of funds, immediate plans were shelved. In the meantime policing of Feltham continued to take place from nearby Bedfont.

In September 1951 a single storey temporary pre-fabricated building previously used as a canteen for the Festival of Britain – the South Bank Exhibition was purchased by the Receiver and re-used from 1952 as the first Feltham police station (until 1971)[119].

The garden at the front of the temporary Feltham police station being lovingly tended

With the ending of hostilities and the restriction on new building in the post war years the site was not developed until 1952 with the closing of the Police room at the old Bedfont police station. The situation had by now become serious and the Commissioner asked for accommodation to transact essential police business at Feltham[120].

The picture above shows Feltham as a temporary office in 1953 with its prize garden being carefully tended.

In the meantime the nearby Heathrow Airport continued to expand and plans were made to build a purpose-built new modern station in Feltham. There was a further revision of the Feltham boundary in November 1974 when Staines was transferred to the new Heathrow Airport sub-division.

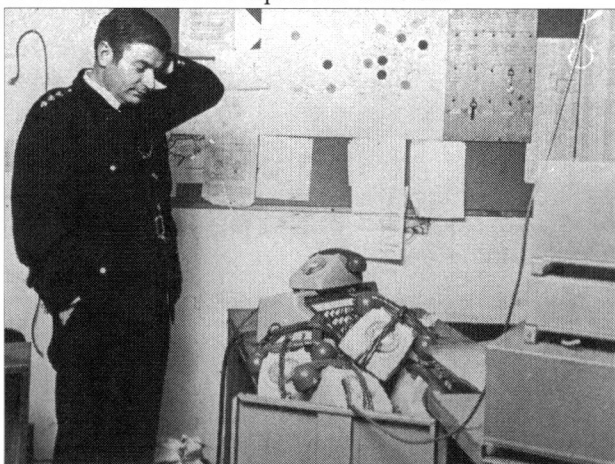

Felthams' Chief Inspector prepares himself with the task of moving to the new station.

In 1955 Feltham was 'TF' on Staines sub division with the address of Ashfield Avenue, Feltham. In 1957 Feltham station was (TG) and was a sectional station, together with both Hampton and Harlington, part of Staines sub division on 'T' Division. In 1971 a three-storey flat- roofed police station was erected on the site and the pre-fabricated building removed.

In the revision of boundaries in conjunction with the local authorities and the setting up of the G.L.C. on the 1st April 1965, Feltham is shown as a sectional station of Hounslow sub-division[121]. In 1965 Feltham continued as a sectional station to Hounslow sub division and Chief Inspector Hudson took responsibility for the station. In the picture the Chief Inspector surveys the mountain of equipment needed to move to the new station.

At 6am on Monday 8th October 1973 the new sectional police station at Feltham was opened and became fully operational, the postal address being, 34, Hanworth Road, Feltham[122].

With the formation of the new Airport Division in 1975 certain boundary changes took place within 'T' Division and these were covered by Metropolitan Police Orders dated 31st October 1974 and 1st July 1975.

Feltham's green and pond still provide a focal point for the High Street today. The Old Red Lion public house stands beside the green, a fortunate survivor of the redevelopment of the town that occurred in the mid-1960s.

Under the borough based policing policy of the 1990s Chiswick and Hounslow Divisions with the exception of Spelthorne but including Feltham were amalgamated thereby returning virtually to the former 'T' District system in use since 1829[123].

Feltham's Centre was rebuilt during 2005 and 2006 as a mixed development including flats; a hotel; new shops; a new library and medical centre; and an Asda superstore. Proximity to Heathrow Airport makes Feltham an important interchange for West London's bus and rail networks and a hotel chain has taken over and converted one of Feltham's prominent 1960s office blocks for use as a hotel[124].

In 2012 the police station situated at 34 Hanworth Road, Feltham TW13 5BD shut its front counter and any public inquiries were being diverted to Chiswick police station. The station was retained as part of a patrol base[125].

Hounslow Police Station

There is evidence of settlement in the borough which pre-dates Roman Britain

Feltham Police Station 1971- present day. 34 Hanworth Road, Feltham, TW13 5BD.

more particularly at the eastern end, at the confluence of the Thames and the River Brent. Historically Hounslow and Hounslow Heath have always been associated with the Army and things military. In medieval and Reformation times armies were bivouacked on the heath prior to battle. The area gradually evolved into a training ground with more substantial barracks being built. Until comparatively recent times the present Hounslow West Station was known as Hounslow Barracks, when it formed part of the old District railway. Two such barracks are still occupied by the army, in the form of the 10th Royal Signals Regiment and 1st Battalion Grenadier Guards.

Quite naturally, industries associated with the military grew up in the area and Hounslow once had a wide reputation for the quality of its sword making. In addition there was a gun powder mill in Hanworth for over two hundred years, which did not cease trading as such until 1925.

There is still a road in Hanworth called Powder Mill Lane, for obvious reasons. Other industries have gradually taken hold in the borough and many of these became the targets for bombing in both world wars. Norwood had extensive brickworks, with acres of brick cooling fields. Agriculture was quite important in the area, with extensive acreage given over to the production of wheat and fruit. It

Hounslow Police Station. 1887 – 1965. Montague Road, Hounslow.

was not until 1955 that the last local orchards were ploughed under to provide more housing.

The beginnings of the aircraft industry are associated with the borough. Fighter aircraft were produced locally during the First World War and there was a small commercial aerodrome at Heston. It is the place where Neville Chamberlain landed on his return from Germany, with his historic 'piece of paper'. Light to medium industry still flourished in the borough, much of it associated with servicing the

The rear yard of the station in circa 1908

nearby Heathrow Airport. Part of the reason is that the area is well served by major trunk roads and motorways with such household names as Gillette, Thorn - E.M.I., and Del Monte foods all having extensive premises in the borough.

In 1864 Police Orders show Hounslow as being a station on 'T' Division. A letter from the Home Office dated March 1885 was received authorising the purchase of a plot of land suitable for the site on which to construct a purpose built new police station. In the meantime plans were made and contracts advertised for builders to present their quotes to the police surveyors for the task. The building job got under way once a suitable piece of land in Montague Road, Hounslow was bought in 1885. An entry in Police Orders read that the new station at Hounslow would be ready for occupation about the 15th March 1887^{126}. The front of the police station was actually in York Road.

In 1915 Inspector William Bingham was in charge at Hounslow and he was responsible for the operational running of the station and its area to Sub Divisional Inspector Charles Richardson at Brentford[127]. Hounslow was a sectional station to Twickenham[128] and remained so for some time. There were a large number of vulnerable points to be protected on the division during war time. These included reservoirs, water works and gun powder mills. These potential targets would wreak havoc to the infrastructure if anything was to happen to them.

The senior officers and sergeants of 'T' Division receive their Coronation medals and certificates at Hounslow in 1937

The following changes were made in 1916 to Sub-Divisions from the 1st January - Brentford sub-division would comprise the stations of Brentford and Chiswick; Hounslow sub-division the stations of Hounslow, Isleworth and Norwood Green, with the sub-divisional stations being Brentford and Hounslow respectively[129].

Isleworth Station was closed at 6am on Monday 1st June 1931 and all business transacted at that station was transferred to Hounslow police station[130].

There was a strong contingent of Metropolitan Police Special Constabulary at Hounslow since the First World War and as previously mentioned one of them was Percy the son of the 'T' division Superintendent Edward Fitt who took his full part in the challenges of policing at the time[131].

Staff Officer Sub Inspector Percy Fitt (shown right) at Hammersmith

In the picture on the previous page Percy Fitt is shown extreme left and has just helped distribute the 1937 Coronation medals to the Hounslow sergeants and inspectors of the sub divisions MSC who were on duty for the occasion. Hounslow continued to be a sectional station on Twickenham sub division.

Percy Fitt (wt. no. 003750H) continued his service. In 1934 Commandants of Division were allowed to formalise their administration and Fitt was put forward as a suitable candidate for the role of Staff Officer Inspector. Following a rigorous interview on police duty subjects successful candidates awaited their promotion. These were salaried staff who held an equivalent Civil Service post but without any opportunity to transfer across to the police service. His role was;

> 'to act for and on behalf of the Commandant and in accordance with his directions....he should have an intimate knowledge of his commandant's mind and ideas in general that he would be able to perform accurate judgement on what the commandant would do if present... and so issue such instruction as may be necessary[132]'

George V MSC Long Service Medal

In 1937 he was a Staff Officer Sub Inspector to the officer in charge and later Fitt became a full Inspector in 1939 at the outbreak of the 2nd World War when staff officer roles were suspended[133]. In the picture above Percy Fitt who is displaying his MSC Long service medal is shown on the right together with his two senior officers. The MSC medal is awarded for nine years' continuous service. In times of war each year counted as double for awarding purposes. Notice that on Sub Inspector Fitt's forearm is also a star. This denotes that he joined the MSC in 1914 and the star was issued in recognition of the fact he was an early joiner. His two comrades do not have this because they had joined the armed services and many of their medals show they had a distinguished service in the 1st World War. Extra bars can be added to the long service medal for further service or for recognition during war time. Inspector Fitt also has 'gorget patches' either side on his collar to show his status and rank. These patches originate from the British army and consist of silver thread on a black background rather similar to those worn by ACPO ranks of the police. No other member of the MSC has this distinction.

Hounslow Police Station. 1965 – present day. 5, Montague Road, Hounslow, TW3
1LB

With the formation of the G.L.C. on 1st April 1965, and the revision of police boundaries to coincide with those of the local authorities, Hounslow remained on 'T' Division[134] but with a brand new police station at 5, Montague Road which was taken into operational use at 6am on 1st March 1965[135]. On that date Hounslow became sub-divisional headquarters and divisional headquarters for 'T' Division[136]. The officer in charge of the sub division in 1965 was Superintendent C. Clarke and the call sign for Hounslow station was 'TD'.

As a result of the formation of the Airport Division in 1974 certain boundary changes within 'T' and 'X' Divisions took place[137]. Hounslow sub-division became Hounslow and Feltham sections. A further revision of boundaries took place between Airport and 'T' Divisions[138]. In 2012 the station was open 7 days a week 24 hours a day. There were five Safer neighbourhoods teams operating in Hounslow[139].

Isleworth Police station

'The village of Isleworth is situated on the banks of the Thames, at the distance of eight miles and a half from Hyde Park Corner. It lies within the hundred, to which it gives name. The parish is bounded on the south by the river Thames; on the east, north, and west, principally by Brentford, Heston, Twickenham, and Feltham. It touches also in some parts (upon Hounslow-heath) Bedfont, and Hanworth'[140].

The main route in London covers many communities. In Kensington it is 'High Street', in Hammersmith 'King Street', in Chiswick it's the 'High Road', in Brentford it's the 'High Street', and as Isleworth's 'London Road' and as it passes into Hounslow it again becomes 'High Street'. Previously this formed part of the 'King's Highway' to Windsor[141] and is still an important thoroughfare today.

The local police gather outside Isleworth Police Station circa 1887

In 1845 a police section house was brought into service in Isleworth. This was a constable's station house and did not have any facilities for detaining prisoners or charging suspects for crimes. The house was owned by Mr George Wiles and Mrs Salways of Richmond on a yearly renewable rent of £17 (later increased to £20). It was a small single storey brick and tile house which had been painted some two years before. There were three rooms with a kitchen and scullery but one room was used for police business as a reserve room. There were also some premises in the rear which were in a poor state of repair and needed renovation[142]. A constable paid one shilling (5p) a week to rent the rooms at the house. The buildings in the rear were probably for stabling a horse for use by the constable on his patrols.

By 1862 a proper, much larger station house was being rented in Isleworth where charges were taken but prisoners had to be conveyed to nearby station of Staines because there were no cell facilities. This was a police station and section house rented from Mr James Hugh Wiles of Ickenham Road, Isleworth on three yearly contracts for £40 per year. The accommodation consisted of a charge room, reserve room and kitchen with cooking facilities. Outside there were our coal vaults to store fuel. There were a further six rooms for residential purposes. This was now a sergeant supervised police station[143]. The contract was renewed in 1870 for three years whilst surveyors considered purchasing a piece of land on which to build a proper station.

Isleworth Police Station. 1873 - 1931 . Worple Road, Isleworth.

The inspector from Brentford would patrol not only his own section on horseback but also go as far as Staines, visiting Heston, Hounslow, Stanwell and Isleworth.

Isleworth was a station on 'T' or Kensington Division and had one sergeant and eight constables posted there with two constables who worked the day shift and six on night duty[144]. The old station had space for two married officers and their families to live and was probably a horse patrol station with stables in a rear yard.

There were two sets of married quarters with one being slightly larger than the other. The larger accommodation was occupied by the sergeant and the weekly rent was five shillings (25p) and four shillings (20p) respectively[145]. The rather old picture above shows the police of Isleworth with their inspector who is seated front centre outside their station in the 1880s. Land was purchased in Worple Road, Isleworth in 1869 and it is likely that it was the result of a compulsory purchase. The address of the old station is unknown and it is unlikely to have been on the same site since the old station was given up by the police in order to occupy the new station later. Plans were drawn up and the front of the station would face Byfield Road.

The building consisted of a purpose-built police station with one set of married quarters. It also had a charge room, store, kitchen, scullery, drying room, four coal cellars and three cells. There was sufficient space for three sets of married quarters, one for the station sergeant and two others for married constables and their families. The new police station was built on land purchased as freehold and the above station came into service in 1873[146].

The address of the station in Police Orders of 20th June 1884 was shown as Worple Road, Isleworth[147]. Isleworth together with Hounslow were sectional stations to Brentford and in 1914 Station Sergeant J. Blake, three sergeants and 30 constables were located there[148]. Isleworth became an important station during both world wars when a contingent of the MSC was formed in 1914 and stationed there. An office and changing room was made available for them to arrange duties and parade in.

Side aspect of Isleworth Police station circa 1906

In the picture left the side and rear view of the station can be seen. Its shows that access to the rear of the station can made be through the yard gate, and access into the residential part of the station is through the small side door where the cycle is situated.

The station closed at 6 a.m. Monday 1st June 1931 and all business was transferred to Hounslow Police Station. The building was later sold privately and is still in its original location today.

---

[1] http://brentfordandchiswicklhs.org.uk/local-history/places/the-history-of-hounslow-town/ accessed on 15th December 2012

[2] http://brentfordandchiswicklhs.org.uk/local-history/places/the-history-of-hounslow-town/ accessed on 15th December 2012
[3] http://brentfordandchiswicklhs.org.uk/local-history/places/the-history-of-hounslow-town/ accessed on 15th December 2012
[4] http://www.bhsproject.co.uk/section4.shtml#60 accessed on 15th December 2012
[5] The Job dated 14th January 1983 p13
[6] ibid
[7] ibid
[8] ibid
[9] ibid
[10] Metropolitan Police Surveyors Records ESB, London
[11] Condition of Police Stations 1881
[12] Brown, B. (1997) Policing Old Feltham. Metropolitan Police Museum
[13] John Marius Wilson (1870-72) Imperial Gazetteer of England and Wales
[14] Metropolitan Police Surveyors Records ESB, London
[15] Brown, B. (1997) Policing Old Feltham. Metropolitan Police Museum
[16] Metropolitan Police Surveyors Records ESB, London
[17] Census records 1871
[18] Brown, B. (1997) Policing Old Feltham. Metropolitan Police Museum
[19] Census records 1881
[20] http://www.rollofhonour.org/forces/england/metropolitan/metropolitan_roll_1829-1899.htm accessed on 5th January 2013
[21] Pall Mall Gazette 28th November 1882
[22] Condition of stations 1881.
[23] Census records 1881
[24] Condition of stations survey 1884.
[25] Kellys Hertfordshire and Middlesex directory 1894
[26] Kellys Hertfordshire and Middlesex directory 1894
[27] Brown, B. (1997) Policing Old Feltham. Metropolitan Police Museum
[28] Kellys directory 1910
[29] ibid
[30] Local history of Police –Bedfont and Feltham (date and author unknown) ESB London
[31] ibid
[32] http://www.hounslow.info/libraries/local-history-archives/discover-hounslow/#fel accessed 24th December 2012
[33] Local history of Police –Bedfont and Feltham (date and author unknown) ESB London
[34] ibid
[35] ibid
[36] ibid
[37] Metropolitan Police Orders dated 6th August 1964
[38] Metropolitan Police Orders dated 5th October 1973
[39] http://brentfordandchiswicklhs.org.uk/publications/the-journal/journal-8-1999/law-and-order-in-new-brentford/ accessed on 15th December 2012
[40] http://brentfordandchiswicklhs.org.uk/publications/the-journal/journal-8-1999/law-and-order-in-new-brentford/ accessed on 15th December 2012
[41] Baker et al (1982) The History of the county of Middlesex Vol 7.
[42] ibid
[43] Baker et al (1982) The History of the county of Middlesex Vol. 7.
[44] http://www.chiswickw4.com/default.asp?section=info&link=police/history.htm accessed on 18th December 2012.
[45] Courtesy of the London Metropolitan Archives.
[46] http://www.chiswickw4.com/default.asp?section=info&link=police/history.htm accessed on 18th December 2012.
[47] Kelly directory 1836
[48] http://www.bhsproject.co.uk/section4.shtml#60 accessed on 15th December 2012
[49] ibid
[50] ibid
[51] Kellys directory 1845 - 1851
[52] Metropolitan Police pension registers 1840 - 1848

[53] Kelly directory 1844
[54] Census records 1841
[55] Census records 1841
[56] Masons Court Guide for Brentford 1853
[57] Census records 1861
[58] http://brentfordandchiswicklhs.org.uk/publications/the-journal/journal-8-1999/law-and-order-in-new-brentford/ Law and Order in New Brentford by David Shavreen accessed on 15th December 2012
[59] http://www.hounslowchronicle.co.uk/west-london-news/local-hounslow-news/2011/12/14/brentford-s-historic-court-could-become-a-pub-109642-29952587/ accessed on 18th December 2012
[60] John Back Archive circa 1975
[61] Metropolitan Police Special Police Order 1868
[62] Metropolitan Police Orders dated 28 September 1870
[63] Metropolitan Police Orders dated 18th July 1890.
[64] Metropolitan Police Commissioners Annual Report 1870
[65] http://www.bhsproject.co.uk/families_cox.shtml accessed on 15th December 2012
[66] Metropolitan Police Commissioners Annual Report 1870
[67] http://www.bhsproject.co.uk/section4.shtml#60 accessed on 15th December 2012
[68] Ibid
[69] http://www.bhsproject.co.uk/families_mumford.shtml accessed on 22nd December 2012
[70] ibid
[71] Census records 1901
[72] Census records 1911
[73] Kellys Ealing Hanwell, Brentford and Hounslow directory 1911
[74] Kellys Ealing Hanwell, Brentford and Hounslow directory 1914
[75] ibid
[76] The Report of the Commissioner of the Metropolis of the year 1904.
[77] Reay, W. T. (1919) The Specials. How they served London. Heineman, London
[78] http://www.bhsproject.co.uk/memories_fatickner.shtm accessed on 10th January 2013
[79] Police Property list 1947
[80] http://www.bhsproject.co.uk/mem_gforgan.shtml accessed on 23rd December 2012
[81] http://bombsight.org/#15/51.4830/-0.3038 accessed on 23rd December 2012
[82] Metropolitan Police Orders dated 6th August 1964.
[83] Brentford and Chiswick Times 23rd December 1969
[84] Metropolitan Police Orders dated 1st July 1967
[85] http://www.hounslow.gov.uk/police_stations accessed on 19th December 2012
[86] John Back Archive 1975
[87] Brown, B. (1991) A brief History of Brentford and Chiswick. (unpublished monograph)
[88] ibid
[89] ibid
[90] John Back Archive circa 1975
[91] John Back Archive circa 1975
[92] John Back Archive circa 1975
[93] Brown, B. (1991) A brief History of Brentford and Chiswick. (unpublished monograph)
[94] Brown, B. (1991) A brief History of Brentford and Chiswick. (unpublished monograph)
[95] Brown, B. (1991) A brief History of Brentford and Chiswick. (unpublished monograph)
[96] The Police Review and Parade Gossip 14th April 1899
[97] Kellys directory 1891 - 1901
[98] Census records 1911
[99] Reay, W. (1919) The Specials, Heineman, London p86
[100] Brown, B. (1991) A brief History of Brentford and Chiswick. (unpublished monograph)
[101] Reay, W. T. (1919) The Specials. How they served London. Heineman, London
[102] ibid
[103] John Back Archive circa 1975
[104] Metropolitan Police Orders dated 28/11/1933
[105] http://www.paranormaldatabase.com/hotspots/W4.php accessed on 22nd December.12.12
[106] Kirchners Police Index 1931
[107] Brown, B. (1991) A brief History of Brentford and Chiswick. (unpublished monograph)
[108] ibid
[109] ibid

[110] ibid
[111] Metropolitan Police Orders dated 6th August 1964
[112] John Back Archive circa 1975
[113] Brown, B. (1991) A brief History of Brentford and Chiswick. (unpublished monograph)
[114] http://www.hounslow.gov.uk/police_stations accessed 23.12.12
[115] http://www.hounslowchronicle.co.uk/west-london-news/local-hounslow-news/2012/12/21/sham-consultation-about-chiswick-police-station-closure-criticised-109642-32475108/ accessed on 28th December 2012
[116] Brown, B. (1997) Policing Old Feltham. Metropolitan Police Museum
[117] ibid
[118] The Police List 1947
[119] http://www.metpolicehistory.co.uk/1946-to-date.html accessed on 23rd December 2012
[120] Brown, B. (1997) Policing Old Feltham. Metropolitan Police Museum
[121] Metropolitan Police Orders dated 6th August 1960
[122] Metropolitan Police Orders dated 5th October 1973
[123] Brown, B. (1997) Policing Old Feltham. Metropolitan Police Museum
[124] http://www.hounslow.info/libraries/local-history-archives/discover-hounslow/#fel accessed 24th December 2012
[125] Hounslow, Heston and Witton Chronicle 'Brentwood and Feltham closed for good this weekend'. 28th August 2013
[126] Metropolitan Police Orders dated 29th December 1886
[127] Kellys Hertfordshire and Middlesex directory 1915
[128] Metropolitan Police List 1925
[129] Metropolitan Police Orders dated 30th December 1916
[130] Metropolitan Police Orders dated 28th May 1931
[131] Reay, W. (1919) The Specials, Heineman, London
[132] Pullen, H. G. (1981) A brief History of the Metropolitan Special Constabulary
[133] Metropolitan Police Special Constabulary Orders dated 02/09/1939
[134] Metropolitan Police Orders dated 6th August 1965
[135] Metropolitan Police Orders dated 26th February 1965
[136] Metropolitan Police Orders dated 26th March 1965
[137] Metropolitan Police Orders dated 31th October 1974
[138] Metropolitan Police Orders dated 1st July 1975
[139] http://content.met.police.uk/Borough/Hounslow/Contact accessed on 18th January 2013
[140] http://www.british-history.ac.uk/report.aspx?compid=45433 accessed 8th January 2013
[141] http://en.wikipedia.org/wiki/Isleworth accessed on 8th January 2013
[142] Metropolitan Police Surveyors Records – The Met Collection, ESB, London.
[143] Metropolitan Police Surveyors Records – The Met Collection, ESB, London.
[144] The Metropolitan Special Police Order 1862
[145] Metropolitan Police Orders dated 4th February 1871
[146] Metropolitan Police Orders dated 26th March 1873
[147] Metropolitan Police Orders dated 28th July 1870
[148] Kellys Hertfordshire and Middlesex directory 1915

Chapter 9

The Royal Borough of Kensington and Chelsea

by Alan Moss

Introduction

The area within the current boundaries of this London Borough has been policed by a number of Divisions over the years, the various re-organisations taking place as London has changed and developed. When the Metropolitan Police was first formed in September 1829, the second of the six companies formed 'B' (then Westminster) Division and policed part of the parish of St Luke's Chelsea. It formed, for a few months, the external boundary of the Metropolitan Police District until 'T' (Kensington) and 'V' (Wandsworth) Divisions were formed on 13th May 1830. In those early years, the World's End part of Chelsea was policed by 'V' (Wandsworth) Division. Gradually with the influx of people from the country, urbanisation took place which saw the boundary pushed further out from the centre of London.

It was not until 1st April 1886, when many of the inner London Divisions were re-aligned, that 'B' Division became known as Chelsea Division. The new 'B' Division headquarters were then taken over from 'T' (Kensington) whilst 'B' Division's Rochester Row police station passed to 'A' (first Whitehall, then Westminster) Division. In the early days of 'T' Division the Commissioner's residence was located in Old Brompton Road so this provided an extra pressure for the Divisional Superintendent.

Fixed points had been introduced throughout London in 1871 not only to provide help unblock some of the more congested roads but also to give the public a dedicated location where they could find a police officer most times of the day and night. On 'T' or Kensington Division these were located (usually at junctions) at Hammersmith Road outside West Kensington Gardens, Holland Road at the junction with Holland Villas, Fulham High Street, and Tregunter Road[1].

Notting Hill, Notting Dale and Kensington stations were transferred from 'F' to 'B' Division under the Local Government reorganisation of April 1965 when Gerald Road was transferred to 'A' Division. Fulham (formerly Walham Green) went to 'F' Division[2]. In 2012 there were three stations that served the borough, are Chelsea, Kensington, and Notting Hill[3].

Chelsea Police Station

An early section house stood at 4 Union Place, Chelsea, which may have had an earlier life as a watch house before 1829. The Metropolitan Police took over the old watch house and by 1833 was responsible for its upkeep and maintenance. It was brick and tile built, with 10 rooms and a yard at the back that was shared, along with a solitary WC, with the neighbouring house. Another section house existed at Exeter Buildings, Brompton, but it was given up in 1851.

In 1832, a police station existed in Worlds' End at Milman's Row, later Milman's Street as a station on 'V' or Wandsworth Division. This road, where the former Gorges House once stood, ran from King's Road down to the river. Milman's Row was built up on its East side with rows of terraced cottages in 1836. On the West side were two brick and tile built houses at numbers 1 – 2 which served as the police station and section house. They were rented, and described as being old in 1845, but there were 11 rooms on the first floor, a yard to the rear, and two cells.

In 1844 Inspector James Shepherd who had been promoted from sergeant in 1837 was the officer in charge of the station[4]. Shepherd was born in 1796, lived at the police station and resided on the east side of the building with his wife Louisa who was 15 years his junior. They had no children. By 1851 Thomas Drake had taken his place, was the Inspector in charge and resided at the station with his wife Charlotte, daughter Isabelle and son Edwin. Drake was happy here and remained at the station for the next 15 years and only retired when Chelsea was transferred from 'V' or Wandsworth to 'T' or Kensington. Constable William Walker and his wife also resided at the station in the other married quarters and living on the same floor in a number of rooms were 10 single constables who resided in what was called the section house[5]. Constable Samuel Cutts and his wife also lived at the police station[6] like the Walkers'.

One of the officers living at Milman's Row in 1846 was 30-year-old constable 54 'V' Robert Woolgar. He had been born in the Isle of Wight, had 9 years' service, and lived above the police station with his dressmaker wife Ann and their 5-year-old son. One May Saturday afternoon he was called to a dreadful incident on Battersea Bridge when 24-year-old Eliza Clark had walked to the middle of the bridge and thrown her three children into the river. The officer was in time to stop the mother jumping in after her children, but only one child was rescued alive. The incident had occurred at about 3pm, and, in a reflection of the rapid speed of justice of the day, by 5pm Mrs Clark was in Westminster police court. She had been subject to domestic violence from her husband, a journeyman painter, and later told the court that he had been a good husband and father, when sober. She had been obliged to pawn her petticoat and sell other clothing to buy food when he had been out of work. Eliza Clark was charged with the murder of her daughter who had hit her head on the river bottom and drowned, but the jury at the Old Bailey found that she was not mentally responsible for her actions and she was detained 'during Her Majesty's pleasure'[7].

Chelsea Police Station. 1852 – 1897 (added to). Milmans Row j/w Kings Road, Chelsea.

A plot of land was leased from Lord Cadogan in Strewan Place, Chelsea, from Christmas 1850. Strewan Place was effectively part of the adjoining King's Road at the junction with Millman's Row and the Receiver thereby gained control of a useful corner plot. Chelsea police station and section house was built for £1,500 in 1852 as a station on 'V' or Wandsworth Division. This was described as a substantial brick and slate building with a day room, charge room and 3 cells. Built with three floors it was a typical design for police stations of the time. The station also had a basement side entrance, station yard and stables.

In the picture above the Old Victorian station is seen however later in 1897 a completely new purpose built police station was added to it on the left.

London was increasing in size rapidly at that time, and World's End was beginning to lose the validity of its name. The Metropolitan Police was conscious of the risk of its patrolling strength being diminished by increased demands, and in 1855 a 'B' Division report indicated that since 1849 some 44 streets, four squares, and 1860 houses had been added to the Division, with another 199 in the process of construction. The average length of their night duty beats had increased from 1100 yards to 2000 yards in that time, despite 15 new beats being formed. Arguments over the adequacy of resources are not new. The Superintendent estimated that four extra Sergeants and 20 Constables would be needed to keep up the level of protection that had been given in 1849[8]. Some of the 'B' Division beats were covered by the Reserve Force, which had been established with six Inspectors, 30 Sergeants and 300 Constables on 24th August 1848 (although a Metropolitan Police-wide Reserve was established in 1871). This body of officers were selected to be ready to deal with public order problems and ceremonial events. Sergeants and Constables would display the letter 'R' on their uniform after the letter of their Division (eg BR) and for some periods, these officers received extra pay. Chelsea watch house was given up in April in 1858 having been in service since 1825[9].

The amount of property in police possession in World's End increased when

Chelsea police station. 1897 – 1939. 385 Kings Road. SW10 (demolished 1984)

Earl Cadogan's estate leased premises to the Receiver at 389 King's Road. Adjoining houses at 383 – 7 were then also purchased and the freehold bought in 1892 for £2,750. Enlargement works were undertaken at a cost of £7,352 and the resulting new police station, covering the entire corner plot, was taken into use on 9th August 1897. The picture above shows the distinctly Victorian old station to the right and its much larger extension on the left.

The 1939 Chelsea police station was closed when the new 'B' Division headquarters were taken into use at 2 Lucan Place SW3 3PB at 6am on Sunday 6th August 1939.

The outbreak of the Second World War in 1939 ensured that the station and its officers were kept at full stretch. Within the Metropolitan Police District there were 1900 cases of war damage to police stations, 124 of them being regarded as 'serious'. 'B' Division was hit by 24 V1 flying bombs and one V2 rocket during the war. A total of 5000 members of the Special Constabulary enrolled for war service as full time officers at the beginning of the war, and of those who did not enrol, 6000 joined the Armed Forces.

The strength was supplemented by re-engaged police pensioners and war reserve officers but thousands of regular officers were released to the Armed Forces, and part-time Specials were used extensively, often after they had performed a full day's work at their normal jobs[10]. The value of having a substantial body of relatively experienced officers available for emergencies was thereby plainly demonstrated.

Chelsea Police Station, 1939 – present day. 2 Lucan Place, SW3 3PB

The case of Gunther Padola

One traumatic event to occur at Chelsea involved the arrest of Günther Podola in 1959. Podola had been a member of the Hitler Youth movement, and escaped to Canada from East Berlin in 1952. He was deported to West Germany in 1958 after being sentenced to prison for burglary in Canada, and later came to England with the intention of promoting himself as a gangster. On 7th July 1959 he broke into a flat in Roland Gardens, South Kensington, stole money and some passports, and then wrote to the victim in an attempt to blackmail her. These cases have always been difficult to investigate, but in due course, when Podola telephoned her, using an alias, to make arrangements for a payment of $500 to be made, the victim cleverly kept Podola on the telephone for long enough for the call to be traced. Detective Sergeant Sandford from Chelsea rushed to a telephone box in Thurloe Street near South Kensington Underground station with his colleague DS Raymond Purdy to arrest Podola whilst the suspect was still talking on the telephone.

Podola broke away and escaped to a block of flats in Onslow Square where the officers caught up with him in the entrance hall. Suddenly the situation escalated. John Sandford saw Podola pull out a gun, shoot Raymond Purdy at point blank range, and then run off. Despite his desire to catch the suspect, John Sandford remained to give what assistance he could to his dying colleague, and telephoned Chelsea for assistance. Detective Superintendent David Hislop and Detective Chief Inspector Bob Acott rushed to the scene and a full scale murder hunt ensued.

Raymond Purdy's widow had been given her dead husband's personal possessions, but within these there was an address book that she did not recognise. This appeared to belong to the suspect, and it provided the clue to his identification. One of the addresses belonged to 'Little Jack', the owner of a shop where, a few days earlier, Podola had attempted to sell a stolen tape recorder, and had been stopped and questioned by two 'aides to CID'. Because the tape recorder had not then been recorded as stolen, the officers had, reasonably, not arrested Podola, but the details they had recorded in their pocket books enabled the investigating team to identify him as having been in Canada, and they obtained a copy of his photograph and fingerprints.

Podola was then traced to the Claremont House hotel in Kensington. When the officers tried to enter his room, they thought they heard the click of a gun being cocked the other side of the door, but nevertheless charged the door open, knocking Podola across the other side of the room in the process. After a trial at the Old Bailey, Podola was executed on 5 November 1959[11].

In 1965 the officer in charge at Chelsea (BK) was Superintendent R. F. Hinxmann and Chief Inspector S. G. O'Brian[12]. Lucan Place was also the Divisional Headquarters with Chief Superintendent D. F. Lightwood in charge[13].

Kensington Police Station

The first police station appears to have been located at 1 Church Court, Kensington (shown as 1 Church Street in 1832[14]) where the rate book shows the police station for 1830.

It was perhaps linked to premises at 1-2 High Street, where a lease was taken out for 21 years from September 1838 from the landlord, a Mr T. Cade of Marchmont Street, Brunswick Square. The freehold was bought for £670 in 1855. It became a substantial brick and slate built house with its own yard, and four cells[15]. This was a station shown on 'T' or Kensington Division and in 1844 Inspector Thomas B. Smith was in charge having been promoted in 1838[16]. As the map of the area shows, the station was located between the Vestry Hall and St. Mary Abbotts church.

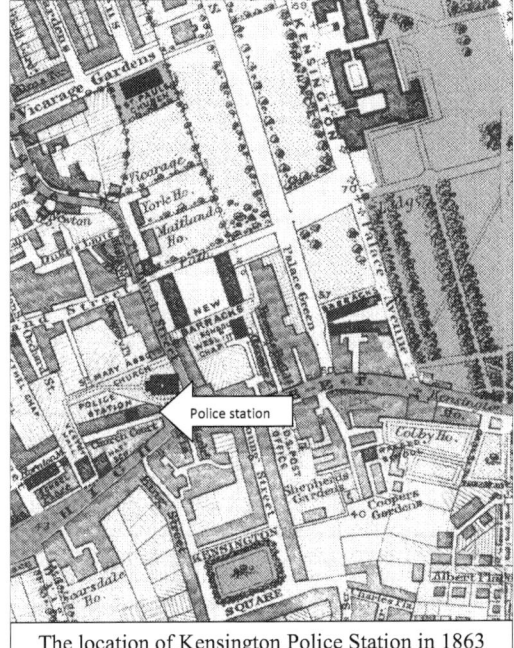

The location of Kensington Police Station in 1863

The unfortunate and tragic events of a Kensington Superintendent.

Edward Tarlton was born in Ireland in 1812. He applied to join the Metropolitan Police and was accepted in 1836 with wt. no. 11677. Some ten years later he married Louisa Hannah Purdie from Islington. Louisa was very attached to her parents who resided at 17 Upper Park Street, Islington and visited them often. In 1851 he was living with his wife and children at 7 Upper Crown Street, Westminster and travelled to Stoke Newington each day for his duty as an Inspector after being a sergeant on 'A' Division. He finally moved his wife and five daughters to Hackney in 1851. Tarlton was a hardworking and conscientious police officer who attracted attention from his superiors that marked him out for further promotion.

Within a short period he was rewarded with further promotion. By 1857 he had had been promoted to Superintendent where he took charge of 'T' Division or Kensington Division. His time at Hackney saw his wife give birth to a son in 1853 whom he called Edward Pitt Tarlton, named after his younger brother Pitt a 'V' Division Inspector attached to Chelsea Police Station.

Tarlton was a strong family man and his only son was the apple of his father's eye. The family had moved to the Superintendent's quarters at 152 Hammersmith Bridge Road a fine house suitable for a Superintendent of this busy Division and his family. As the Divisional Superintendent he was heading alleged murder investigations, dealing with suspicious deaths or taking control of fires using reserves of police from the section house. He appeared before the local courts frequently and was a well-known and respected senior police officer in the neighbourhood.

Tarlton and his family then experienced a series of tragic events that spelled disaster for the whole family. In December 1860 his wife Louisa (then aged just 41 years) had returned to Upper Park Street, Islington to nurse her sick mother Hannah (aged 59) when tragically and mysteriously both mother and daughter died within the same hour.

This tragedy left him to bring up his children Ann (21) Susannah (19) Emily (12), Louisa (14) and son Edward Pitt (8), and it fell to the eldest, Ann, to help her father, together with a house servant, to bring up the rest of the family.

In early November 1862 Inspector Searle of 'T' Division submitted a bill for expenses to Tarlton which the Superintendent failed to sign that he had seen and agreed its payment. Instead the bill was forwarded to the Commissioner Sir Richard Mayne accidentally. Mayne was not best pleased and immediately called for the Inspector to appear before him at Scotland Yard. On hearing the Inspector's evidence he found that Searle had spoken truthfully about the circumstances but recommended to Tarlton that Searle should be transferred to another station as soon as a position became available.

It appears that word had got back to the Commissioner about the running of the division, as within a month Captain Labalmondiere had stipulated that he wanted to inspect the division. He duly arrived on the 1st December and whilst it is unknown what he discovered within 4 days Tarlton had been placed on leave and his deputy Inspector John Mitchell was put in charge. Tarlton's daughter Susannah had died on 5th December and his son Edward also became seriously ill with little chance of survival. Two weeks later on the 19th December 1862 Tarlton became worse and on medical advice given was prescribed bed rest. Superintendent Tarlton was then placed on sick leave and Police Orders confirmed that Inspector Mitchell was temporarily in charge of 'T' or Kensington Division. This series of events had left Tarlton severely depressed and confined to bed. In fact so serious was the situation that Inspector Mitchell's wife went to help out at the Tarlton family home in Bridge Road.

Mary Ball had been resident in the house at 38 Bridge Road for about three months helping out as the house keeper. Tarlton and the house keeper had helped to look after his ailing daughter during her long illness. It was at this point the house keeper noticed how much of a depressed state Tarlton was in and disclosed that he was despondent and heartbroken at the loss of his wife and daughter.

At about 7pm on 2nd January 1863 the house keeper left Tarlton in his room in bed and returned after a short while. When she entered the room she cried out as she found that Tarlton had cut his throat with a razor blade left in the drawer of the wash basin and he was bleeding profusely. She called on Tarlton's brother Pitt who was downstairs at the time, to come to the room and he also witnessed the events.

Tarlton died having, according to police records, taken his own life with the bland comment in police orders explaining that Tarlton had 'committed suicide' with the reference in other documents that his police account had 'insufficient funds'. An inquest took place on Saturday evening at the Sussex Arms Public House, Bridge Road. Mr Alfred Bird the Coroner had known Tarlton extremely well. So upset were Bird and other witnesses in viewing the body that evening, which had been kept in the cool cellar of the public house that proceedings had to be delayed in order that those who were distressed could compose themselves. During the inquest, evidence was heard from the doctor in attendance that Tarlton was suffering from an inflamed stomach and chronic bronchitis from which he could not recover, also adding that 'he wanted to be put at the bottom of a pond'. The jugular had been severed and this was the cause of his demise leaving the Coroner to record a verdict of 'death due to temporary insanity'. A verdict of suicide would have amounted to a criminal offence in those days. His son Edward died a short while later.

Kensington police station 1873 – 1956. 78 Kensington High Street, London

Superintendent Tarlton held a contingent account which was used for paying the men under his command and for other financial matters. His clerk sergeant and the man who organised the finances for the Division was Sergeant 2 'T' Thomas Hindes from Beccles in Suffolk (joined in 1853). Hindes would travel with his superintendent on a Wednesday to Scotland Yard to collect the cheque paid into the Bank of England as cash.

On 7th January as a consequence of checking the accounts prior to a new Superintendent being transferred to the Division, the Receiver's Office found these accounts to be incorrect and seized them. Sergeant Hindes was immediately suspended from duty 'as a consequence of the errors found in the late Superintendent's accounts' and his pay was stopped. Checking and re-checking these accounts took some considerable time.

In the meantime Sir Richard Mayne decided to move a substantive superintendent into 'T' Division and Beckerson was duly transferred from 'L' Division on 19th January.

Sergeant Hindes was called before the Commissioner to explain himself but it was not until 23rd April that he was finally dealt with. All this time was spent at home with his wife Eliza and his large family worrying about his likely fate. During his suspension there would have been concerns that this would end in the criminal courts as this was viewed very dimly indeed. The mis-appropriation of police funds was a very serious matter and so this fact was reflected in the punishment given to Hindes. Fining the sergeant one month's pay (on top of losing 11 weeks' pay on suspension anyway) the Commissioner stated;

> 'The sergeant was I believe unconscious of the very serious nature of the offence he was committing, and was certainly acting under the express orders of his superintendent at the time'.

But after all this tragedy and misfortune there was some fair play in the end when this matter was not held against him and Hindes was promoted to Inspector in January 1864 and transferred to 'D' Division. By 1879 he had become Divisional Superintendent at Woolwich Dockyard (and arsenal) and in March 1889 he retired on pension and remained in Plumstead. In the meantime Tarlton's family had to vacate the house probably by 19th January 1863 and were scattered around London with the remaining daughters all finding suitors and having their own families.

Chief Inspector Thomas Bocking

The Metropolitan Police also swore in constables who needed to undertake special duties. A constable was sworn in 1866 to help keep order at Kensington workhouse. He was issued with a warrant from the Commissioner which was returned when not needed.

When Chief Inspector Thomas Bocking from Kensington retired in 1873 it was a year of change in policing the area. One development was the demolition of Jennings' Buildings, a wooden-built 'rookery' slum housing 1000 poor families, whose inhabitants had kept Mr Bocking and his officers busy for many years. One local magistrate said 'Jenning's Buildings was a lawless neighbourhood and the police were compelled to use a great deal of severity'[17].

The local newspaper commented about Mr Bocking that 'he was not only respected by the inhabitants [of Kensington], but by the roughs themselves'. Jennings Buildings was near Kensington Palace and the parish church, so one can imagine the animosity that might be felt towards the residents of the block by the better-off residents of Kensington.

But another event that year was the opening of a new police station, the address now being recorded as 78 Kensington High Street, adjacent to St Mary Abbott Church, Kensington Church Street, at a total cost of £11,000. The building work was delayed by legal issues, and the Receiver eventually made an undertaking to Kensington parish that there would be strict compliance with the design of the building as set out by the famous Victorian architect Sir Gilbert Scott who lived locally in Courtfield Gardens, South Kensington.

Adam and Eve Mews

There were Inspectors' married quarters in nearby Adam and Eve Stables, on the south side of Kensington High Street, from 1888 until 1933. From 1887 to 1919, Adam & Eve Mews was also the location of a reserve stables for new police horses (remounts) and officers being trained for Mounted Branch. The stables had been opened by Captain Dean and were an improvement in training for the Mounted Branch over the previous informal arrangements at Rochester Row[18]. 1919 was an important year for the Mounted Branch, which was revitalised by Colonel Sir Percy Laurie who bought 43 horses that were surplus to army requirements, acquired Imber Court for a training base, and encouraged the traditional cavalry spirit of grooming and care.[19]

In 1901 a section house for single officers was built at the rear of the premises at Kensington Church Court, accommodating 30 single officers.

Constable Charles Riseboro and a special award

Charles William Riseboro was born at Sherringham in Norfolk in 1894. He was employed as a porter for the Metropolitan and Great Northern Railway and later joined the Metropolitan Police (wt. no. 104874) in February 1915. At nearly 5ft

Constable Riseboro receives his Distinguished Flying Medal at Kensington Police Station from the Commissioner in 1920

11inches tall he commanded a solid presence and so was initially posted to 'F' Division where he stayed until 1929 when he was transferred to 'X' as a detective.

During the war men of a certain age including police officers were expected to join the colour's, in fact women would openly castigate young police officers who had not joined up. Riseboro put in an application to fight for King and country and in January 1917 he transferred to H.M. Forces being posted to Palestine. No.187480 C. W. Riseboro was a Sergeant Mechanic in the newly formed Royal Air Force (RAF). What happened next saw Riseboro as an NCO display courage and devotion to duty whilst flying on active operations against the enemy. Accordingly, it was whilst an observer flying dangerous missions over enemy territory that he was awarded the Distinguished Flying Medal

(DFM) for service in Palestine - a particularly rare event. Of the 104 DFM's awarded during 1918 -19, this was the only one identified as being awarded for service in Palestine. His award was announced in the London Gazette on 3rd June 1919. In the picture above he is receiving his medal together with other war veterans of various police divisions who displayed meritorious and courageous service by the Commissioner Brig. General Sir William Horwood at Kensington Police Station. The canteen had been prepared for the award ceremony and the Divisional Superintendent J. Cameron was also present.

The medal (both sides of which are displayed below) was established on 3rd June 1918. It was the other ranks equivalent to the Distinguished Flying Cross which was awarded to commissioned officers and warrant officers (WOs could also be awarded the DFM), although it ranked below the DFC in order of precedence, between the Military Medal and the Air Force Medal. Recipients of the Distinguished Flying Medal were allowed to use "DFM". In 1993 the DFM was discontinued, and since then the Distinguished Flying Cross has been awarded to personnel of all ranks. Constable Riseboro's medal group of DFM, British War and Victory Medals were sold at auction on 29th March 2000 for £1650[20].

The Distinguished Flying medal

Riseboro, married around the same time as his award and had two children. He was an active police officer although he did not get on well initially with learning first aid as he failed his examination four times during his service. On the other hand he passed his Educational exams 2nd class in 1921, the technical equivalent and in July 1922 the following year was promoted to sergeant, staying on 'F' Division. He was well thought of by his superior officers and was not involved in any disciplinary matters. In 1929 he transferred as a Detective sergeant 2nd class to 'X' Division and later 1st Detective sergeant in March 1936. He failed his 1st Class educational examinations which meant he was precluded from Inspector rank. He had 16 commendations with one involving a case of murder in 1937. He retired in March 1942 after just over 27 years' service aged 47 years old on a pension of £208 14s per year. He was awarded an Exemplary certificate of conduct from the Commissioner for his service. He died aged 63 years in February 1958.

In 1942 the section house was converted for use as offices, and after a period of being rented out, they were taken back into police use in 1969 as a Traffic Wardens' centre and, in due course, a base for the Diplomatic Protection Group.

A new police station at 72 Earls Court Road was opened on 14 September 1956, boasting double windows to combat traffic noise. It had been built on a site purchased for £10,250 before the Second World War and construction was delayed because of hostilities and post-war austerity. The total cost eventually reached £230,000, and housed a new District headquarters and, with its own separate entrance, a section house for 67 officers. The section house featured a billiards room, common rooms, a library, a hobbies room and a residents' dining room. The District headquarters had previously been at Great Scotland Yard, and the new premises provided offices for the District Commander, with the District Detective Chief Superintendent, the District Superintendents of the Women Police, Mounted Branch and Traffic Division, a map room and a conference room.[21]

In an exemplary initiative to improve public relations and understanding of police work, a public open day at the station was hosted by Commander Gordon Maggs in August 1970. Guests included Prince Richard of Gloucester, who opened the event, and Jack Warner, the actor who played PC George Dixon in the TV series *Dixon of Dock Green.* The Metropolitan Police band was present, playing under the direction of their Director of Music, Major Williams.

Kensington Police Station, 1956 – present day. 72 Earls Court Road, Kensington W8.

It was on Kensington's ground in 1973 that an incident occurred which resulted in the award of a George Medal to constable Peter Slimon. There have been 138 George Medals awarded to Metropolitan Police officers since the medal's inception in 1940, 59% of them in connection with war time activities. In constable Slimon's case he witnessed an armed bank robbery taking place, and, having possession of a police firearm himself because of his Diplomatic Protection Group duties, he challenged the robbers, and was wounded in the subsequent exchange of gunfire which resulted in the death of one of the robbers. Constable Slimon's citation published in the *London Gazette* mentions his 'outstanding resolution, devotion to duty, and courage of a very high order'[22].

Inexplicably, the most recent award of the George Medal to a Metropolitan Police officer was back in 1992, despite the undoubted bravery shown by police officers on the streets of modern day London. The incident also reminds us of the courage required to challenge armed and dangerous criminals, notwithstanding the fact of the officer himself being armed. The death of criminals engaged in their unlawful activities must surely be regarded as an occupational hazard for them, despite the obligation to refer such cases, without further comment, to the Independent Police Complaints Commission.

A section house in Gore Lane, Kensington was in use from 1836 until 1857.

Notting Dale Police Station

The current police station, at 58 Sirdar Road (known as St Clement's Road before 1897) was taken into use on 14th October 1968, replacing an earlier station on the site that had opened in 1876 and had cost £4,881 to build. New cells were added 10 years later in 1886. At the official opening of the new station in 1968, one of the guests was 87-year-old retired Constable Richard Jago who had joined the Metropolitan Police in 1919 and remembered living in the earlier police station. Constable Jago had been brought up to London as a servant in the household of a wealthy family from his native Cornwall, enlisted in the Duke of Cornwall's Light Infantry for the First World War, and then joined the Metropolitan Police, where he described the training as 'making sure that you could read and write'. The uniform consisted of a thick serge jacket with a stiff collar, rather than any shirt and tie, and this became very hot in the summer. Crime was low, and arrests were mainly drunks, who were transported to the station by means of a hand barrow. Transport consisted of three horses, and twenty officers would parade for night duty. The old Notting Dale was described by Mr Jago as hardly a prestige building. 'It was a terrible place. We lived in little boxes at the top, and the basement where we ate was dark and damp'. [23]

The architect's plan of Notting Dale, opened 1868

The Potteries District of Notting Dale had been described in the *Daily News* of January 1893 under the title 'A West End Avernus' (a mythical entrance to the underworld). The reporter used lurid language to describe the social conditions there, concluding that he had 'never seen anything in London more hopelessly degraded and abandoned in life than these wretched places'[24].

There were 11 common lodging houses there, accommodating 723 people. The death rate in 1896 was found by a Dr Dudfield to be 42.6 per 1000 living population, dramatically higher than the London average of the time. The lodging houses were inspected twice per week by the police.

Mary Osbourne (born 1928) lived nearby and described life in her childhood for *The Story of Notting Dale*. She said;

> 'We had an area what got flooded and ratty through the summer. We had so many bugs you'd be glad to come out in the summer and sit on the step to get away from them. They'd be crawling up the walls everywhere and them times you had that thick brown paper and inside you could see the larvae. You'd have bets on what one was going to reach the top first. The bugs were in abundance and you would paraffin the bed. They were always buying stuff to get rid of the bugs but you never did.'

She described how the Local Authority had, despite the protests of her father, a totter, insisted on fumigating their furniture when they were being re-housed from Windsor House, Sirdar Road as late as 1951. They had also lived in Bangor Street where;

Notting Dale Police Station, 1968 – present day. 58 Sirdar Road, Notting Hill.

' ... people helped one another. If you were ill they would order the food. They'd order the food, take it to the family and then go out and collect it, and their first stop used to be Notting Dale Police Station. They had a basin and everybody would drop in.'

Street betting was also something that the police there had to deal with;

'We'd get the gamblers at night and then the police would come. We'd have the gamblers standing around the lamppost and there would be a boy there and he'd clap the clapper. My brother done it one night and as he clapped the clapper the policeman got hold of my brother and slapped his face. So me mum come out of the house and she, down she went, took my brother away, my Jim it was, and she's hit the copper back and she had to run and the police chased her. She couldn't come out for about a week because every time he was there and they asked the kids 'do you know that lady?' and they'd say no. If they asked anybody they'd say she only just moved there, we don't know her. They used to call the policeman Lightning because he was quick, so she said to him 'you're not like lightning today are you? You're more like bleedin' thunder' and she smacked his face and ran' [25].

When the new Notting Dale was opened in October 1968, in addition to Constables, the establishment included three Station Sergeants, six Section Sergeants for patrolling, a Detective Inspector and CID officers. It was a good example of the scheme for extended responsibility for local policing that was a policy of the time.

Community relations of a different perspective were represented by the later location of the Community Liaison Officer and Juvenile Bureau at Notting Dale.

Notting Hill police station

In the early 19th century, the clay of the Notting Hill area made it a centre for brick making and potteries in the area that later became the Norlands Estate. Pig farming came to the area in the 1820s.

A police station and section house for then 'T' Division was erected in 1854 at a cost of £1,425 at 69 Ladbroke Road, W11 on land leased for 50 years from June that year. The building boasted a reserve room, library, charge room, mess, four cells, two WCs, a urinal, and 'pits for dung and dust' [26]. When the current station at 101 Ladbroke Road W11 was opened in 1906, the former police station was converted into married quarters and was used as such from 1907 until 1939.

Kensington and Notting Hill were amalgamated into the Kensington Sub Division of 'F' Division on 20th August 1939.

The Notting Hill police station shut for operational purposes in 1906 however it became married quarters until 1939.

Later the larger houses in the area became multi-occupied and Notting Hill eventually became one of the centres for Afro- Caribbean settlement in London after the Second World War. Tensions between white racist youths and the immigrant community resulted in perceptions that the police were not taking racist assaults seriously, and protests about the situation led up to the Notting Hill Race Riots on 1958.

A series of attacks on black people led to the arrest of 10 white youths immediately before the riots erupted, and their trial, that took place after the riots, led to exemplary sentences of 5 years' imprisonment to act as a deterrent.

The following year, 1959, saw the start of Notting Hill Carnival, intended by Claudia Jones as a positive celebration of black culture. This event gradually increased in size to become the largest regular public order commitment for the Metropolitan Police, attracting over one million people to the streets of Notting Hill on the last Sunday and Monday of each August.

Notting Hill Police Station 1854 – 1906. Ladbroke Road j/w Ladbroke Grove W11

Rioting after the 1976 carnival saw police officers trying to protect themselves with dustbin lids, prior to the introduction of public order shields and protective uniform and equipment.

In 1985 the moving music floats were persuaded to adopt a set route rather than adopting random and sometimes conflicting paths through narrow streets. Greater control over the static sound systems, street trading, close-down times and alcohol sales have gradually made the event more manageable and attractive to sponsors. Public safety and street crime remain important issues in terms of policing the event, so that exuberant enjoyment can take place, but with some ability to control things when the need arises. The scale of the

Notting Hill Police Station. 1906 – present day. 101 Ladbroke Road W11.

event has long since been taken over by the Metropolitan Police as a whole rather than managed by the local Division.

Walton Street police station

Walton Street police station was added to 'B' Division in 1851, the same year when the major development of creating Victoria Street was implemented. There was a lease from a Mr W. Delferier from Michaelmas 1849[27]. It was connected to the Metropolitan Police telegraph network with the code WS in December 1871[28].

Walton Street was seen as a good location for a police station. It was just to the south of Brompton Road and its rear yard could be accessed from Yeoman's Row, a cul-de-sac that ran south from Brompton Road that ended in the alleyway (Glynde Mews) that connected to Walton Street itself. The police commitment to the area was confirmed with the purchase of the freehold of the site at 60-62 Walton Street on 31st May 1894. Plans were started for a new police station.

The files relating to the development are an interesting reflection of how the police operated in those days. The Receiver would write formal letters to the Commissioner about relatively small details. At times the Receiver's office acted almost as if it were a separate organisation. Letters were exchanged about giving access to the roof for police families, and running a pipe from the kitchen so that they might have hot water for a bath. The Receiver stated that the plumbing cost of £20 would need to be referred to the Secretary of State, that the police officers should pay an extra 6d (2.5p) in rent for the extra facility, and that it would be important that washing should not be hung out within the view of the well-kept garden of a highly rented house in Egerton Terrace. Rent details had already been published, and perhaps waiting deliberately, the Commissioner then suggested that the Receiver might not wish to undertake the extra administrative effort and submissions to have the rent changed again for the sake of the extra 6d (2.5p) per week.

Yeoman's Row, showing the rear of Walton Street (left background)

The local Division were not given access to the plans, but they made up a sketch plan on the basis of which they made their representations. They thought that it would be desirable for the Surgeon's Room to be big enough to accommodate a [hand] ambulance. Superintendent Isaac objected to plans for the detention room to be practically in the charge room because a detention room was;

'intended for the occupation of persons of the better class who …should not be treated as the ordinary prisoner and …subject to the vile language used by low class prisoners waiting to be charged, which is sometimes of a shocking nature'.

By October 1907 the Commissioner was writing to the Receiver about the delay, stating that he would 'be greatly obliged if consideration of the plans were dealt with a pressing matter' [29].

The basements of the police station and section house were connected by means of a passageway running underneath the police station yard.

One part of the development was completed on 18th December 1895 and the next stage was ready for occupation in April 1911. The first floor accommodated offices for the Superintendent, a Chief Inspector, the Divisional Clerks and the CID. On the ground floor were the Inspectors' office, the charge room, six cells and an association cell. In the yard was an ambulance shed for the hand ambulances that were used by the police officers of the day for taking people to hospital, or drunks to the station.

In the days when the rank of Sub Divisional Inspector existed, quarters were provided (April 1905 until 1910) for him at 47 Ovingdon Street, Chelsea. A

Walton Street Police Station. 1894 – 2009. 60-62 Walton Street, Brompton SW3.

new section house at Yeoman's Row was taken into use on 14th February 1910.

Walton Street became absorbed into one Sub Division when Chelsea was opened at Lucan Place in 1939. More recently it had been used as a base for the Diplomatic Protection Group and was put up for sale and disposed of with 64 Yeoman's Row in March 2009.

---

[1] Commissioners Annual report for the Metropolitan Police 1871
[2] Bernard Brown (1987) *The Job* 15th May.
[3] http://content.met.police.uk/Borough/Kensington/Contact accessed on 18th September 2012
[4] The Police and Constabulary List 1844
[5] Census records 1851
[6] ditto
[7] http://www.woolgar.org/timespdf/times072.pdf
[8] National Archives MEPO 2/26.
[9] http://www.metpolicehistory.co.uk/1829-1899.html?page=6 accessed on 24th September 2012
[10] H. M. Howgrave-Graham. (1947) .*The Metropolitan Police At War* HMSO
[11] Kirby, D. (2012) *Death on the Beat*, Pen and Sword.
[12] The Police List 1955
[13] ditto
[14] Return of Mops allowed to clean stations (1832) MPS. London
[15] Metropolitan Police Property Register ESB London
[16] The Police and Constabulary List 1844
[17] Jennifer Davis (1986) *Policing of the Poor* in Police Review 7th February.
[18] Chris Forester *Police History Society Newsletter* No 78, August 2012.
[19] Fido, M. and Skinner, K. (1999) *The Official Encyclopaedia of Scotland Yard.* Virgin, London.
[20] Private correspondence with Richard Hayes.
[21] *Police Review* 31 August 1956.
[22] Supplement to the *London Gazette* 18th September 1973
[23] *All Change at the Dale,* newspaper item by Simon Frodsham, Metropolitan Police Heritage Centre.
[24] *Survey of London* p 346.
[25] *Notting Dale Urban Studies.* Interview of Mary Osbourne by Sharon Whetlor for *The Story of Notting Dale* ref:ND-INT/11/01 KCCHG oral history interview.
http://www.historytalk.org/Notting%20Dale/nd%20maryosbourne.pdf
[26] Metropolitan Police Property Register
[27] National Archives – List of Metropolitan Police stations 1873 MEPO 4/234.
[28] Bernard Brown (1987) *The Job* 15th May
[29] National Archives ref: MEPO 2/726

Chapter 11

The Royal Borough of Kingston on Thames

by Peter Kennison

Introduction

The second division of the Bow Street horse patrol was responsible for Kingston in 1827[1]. Originally set up in 1805 to patrol a radius of 16 miles around London to combat the frequency of highway robberies, the officers patrolled North Cheam, Croydon, Sutton, Merton, Wimbledon, Robin Hood Hill, Kingston and Ditton Marsh which were all far beyond the MPD at that time. The horse patrol stations were situated on Robin Hood Hill, Kingston Market and Ditton Marsh, and by October 1836 had been under the jurisdiction of the Metropolitan Police as part of 'V' or Wandsworth Division. The policing of the Kingston area before 1820s was carried out and supervised by the various vestries and parish authorities.

There was a fairly efficient police within the Surrey parishes and these consisted of sworn constables (including those of the Bow Street horse patrol), beadles and head-boroughs who would patrol during the day and night by rota.

Bow Street Horse Patrol circa 1812

Qualification for appointment into the horse patrol included previous horse experience often in the cavalry regiments. Men should be aged over 35 years and at least 5ft 5 inches tall. They were paid four shillings (20p) a day and had to be in uniform at all times when out on duty. The horse patrol was well armed with a truncheon, cutlass and belt with a certain number of them carrying pistols[2].

The area was not included within the Metropolitan Police until 1839 when Kingston, Hook and Chessington formed part of the inner district of 'V' or Wandsworth Division[3]. As the boundary of the MPD was extended the mounted officers, under Inspector Dowsett then became full time members of 'V' Division. In January 1840 these areas came under the jurisdiction of the Metropolitan Police when the force boundary was extended to its present limits. Another 13 sergeants and 101 constables were added to the division, new 'V' division stations being opened at Kingston, Epsom, Hampton, Sunbury and Richmond (the Surrey Constabulary not coming into existence for another decade)[4].

The division also took in Epsom, Hampton, Sunbury, Princes Street, Richmond and Sigh Street, Mortlake[5] where there were police stations or houses.

Further extensions to the Metropolitan Police area occurred in 1865 when a number of new divisions 'W', 'X' and 'Y' were formed and others re-organised. The new division called the 'W' or Clapham division was formed with its HQ at Brixton police station. No fewer than two inspectors, eight sergeants and 71 constables were transferred to the new division from 'V' Division along with Tooting and Clapham police stations[6]. Superintendent Edward Butt who was then in charge at Wandsworth, oversaw the decrease when Chelsea (and Inspector Pitt Tarlton) was transferred from 'W' to 'T' division; and Clapham (and Inspector William Bushnell) transferred from 'V' to 'W' division. The five inspector stations on 'V' were now reduced to three these being Wandsworth, Kingston and Richmond. All the stations in Middlesex — Sunbury, Hampton, Twickenham, Chelsea and Fulham — were transferred from 'V' or Wandsworth Division to the 'T' or Kensington Division[7]. These stations, excepting Kingston were closed to the public when sergeants or acting Sergeants were patrolling.

Special duties included one sergeant as Divisional Clerk, one sergeant and three constables in charge of the police van and horses, one Constable as Superintendents groom, two Constables at Wandsworth Police Court, one constable at Cremorne Gardens, three Constables at Kew Gardens, one constable at Strawberry Hill House, and six constables at Hampton Court Palace[8].

The policing of the division evolved, expanded and become more complex as greater numbers of people moved into the suburbs to find work. Gradually, as travel and transport became easier and cheaper, sleepy villages soon became overwhelmed with traffic, people and crime.

Furthermore an electricity supply was created in Kingston in 1893 and Victoria Hospital was built in 1897. By 1841 Kingston upon Thames had a population of over 8,000 people. Meanwhile in 1838 the railway reached Kingston. The railway led to the rapid growth of the Kingston area. By 1901 the population of Kingston was 37,000. In the early 19th century Surbiton was a little hamlet, then it boomed. By the 1880s Surbiton had over 10,000 people[9].

Kingston upon Thames was made an urban district council in 1894 and the Borough of Kingston was formed in 1936. The Guildhall was built in 1935.

Meanwhile, from 1875 horse-drawn buses and from 1906, electric trams ran in the streets of Kingston. Buses replaced them in 1931. Meanwhile Kingston by-pass was built in 1927. Eden Walk Shopping Centre first opened in 1979. The Bentall Centre was built in 1987-1992. In 2011 the population of Surbiton, Ewell, Epsom and Kingston upon Thames was 147,000[10].

In 2011 the Borough of Kingston was served by four police stations one central station at 5-7 High Street Kingston, New Malden Police Community Office and Millbank Police Community Office. There are also sixteen Safer Neighbourhoods Teams who are there to prevent crime and deal with community problems. Response teams were available 24 hours a day to deal with the emergency calls; CID officers and forensic teams investigated crimes and brought criminals before the court.

In the following histories only the police stations of Epsom, Ewell, New Malden, Kingston and Surbiton will be covered.

Ewell Police Station

Although there was an intention to build a police station in Ewell village which led to the purchase of the freehold title to land shown as a vacant site in London Road in 1907, the start of building procedures upset the local people and led to disquiet and resistance. By 1912 the project met with significant local resistance resulting in a covenant being placed on the title deeds that a wall not less than 4ft 6ins tall should be erected on the SW and NW of the site. This led to police surveyors rethinking the proposed building and deciding to abandon the idea. A station was not built and in 1927 detailed negotiations occurred to sell the site to Major Vernon for £500, the final sale being completed in 1930.

Kingston Police Station

In 1777 the Corporation of Kingston was granted permission to raise money to build watch houses and to recruit 14 constables[11] who also lit the street lamps. In 1835 the Corporation applied for the Metropolitan Police boundary to extend to Kingston at this stage it was declined. From 13th January 1840, the MPD was extended out to Kingston parish and beyond. The new Kingston sub-division, under an Inspector, comprised three Sergeants and 16 constables who were responsible for the town, together with the hamlet of Hook and Chessington parish. Two constables were deployed in Long Ditton, Thames Ditton and West Mousley (as spelt), while a solitary constable patrolled East or Upper Mousley parish and another in the hamlet of Claygate[12].

When the Metropolitan Police Act extended the boundaries to Kingston, initially the first police inspector in Kingston occupied an office located in the town hall until new premises were found elsewhere.

A building was rented in London Road, Kingston in 1840, belonging to Mr William Walker at £50 per year for a period of 21 years[13] as a station on 'V' or Wandsworth Division.

Of the three sergeants posted with the inspector two sergeants were mounted patrols and lodged in the section house[14]. The watch house in Kingston was returned to the parish authorities on 7th April 1840 as it was no longer required.

Inspector Richard Dowsett had been appointed as Inspector in 1814 for the horse patrol and was incorporated into the division as the Inspector in charge of Kingston in 1844. He was an experienced officer and remained in charge until retirement in 1850[15]. Pension records show that Dowsett was 60 years old having completed 35 years service when he retired and was classified as being 'worn out'. His annual pension was £95 per year (when a constable's typical pension was £27 per year)[16].

Crime in Kingston

On 6th July 1840 at the Central Criminal Court Thomas John Simms was tried for simple larceny at the Bird in Hand public house at Hampton (Wick). The crime involved stealing three spoons value 12 shillings, silver sugar tongs value 3 shillings, a broach valued at three shillings and a one shilling coin the property of James Atkins. William George Worfall Sergeant 23 'V' was on duty as station officer at Kingston when the prisoner was brought in and property handed over. Simms was found guilty and sentenced to seven years transportation[17].

Thomas Bicknell the Divisional Superintendent, was stationed at Waterside, Wandsworth and had been in charge of the Division since 1840. He remained there until 1855 when he retired on pension of £166 pa with 24 years service suffering with vertigo. In 1851 Septimus Fenn (who had been a constable at Deptford in 1841) replaced Dowsett (the ex horse patrol inspector) as the Inspector in charge of the station which was shown as located in Norbiton Street. Fenn remained there until 1855 when he was promoted to Divisional Superintendent replacing Bicknell. In turn, his place was taken by Inspector James Rapsey in the same year who remained the officer in charge until 1861[18]. Whilst doing duty at Kingston the unfortunate Rapsey now aged 41 years, received a serious chest injury whilst on duty and was quickly pensioned off[19]. After retirement he moved to Brixton and was cared for by his wife and family but sadly died of his injuries shortly afterwards - times were harsh.

Whilst there would have been remuneration for Mrs Rapsey this was by no means a forgone conclusion since she needed to apply to the Commissioner for an annual award which needed to be sanctioned by the Home Department. This was an annual figure usually about £40. By 1871 Eliza Rapsey had moved away from Brixton and was residing with her 24 year old daughter in Hackney without her other five children[20].

In 1862 a report was sent to the Commissioner Sir Richard Mayne concerning the condition of the police station at Kingston which had been badly damaged by fire, recommending an urgent need for new premises. Land in London Street belonging to Mr Edward Ward of Claremont Square, Pentonville was leased from 1863 for 100 years at an annual rental of £30. This land was suitable[21] for a purpose-built police station and the metropolitan police surveyor Charles Reeves set about arranging the plans, building works and their organisation.

During the 1860s there was an augmentation of personnel generally and this was reflected with additional staff for Kingston who increased to one inspector, five sergeants and 31 Constables[22].

In 1861 Inspector Joseph Armstrong replaced pensioned Inspector Rapsey as the inspector in charge of Kingston. Originally from Brighton, Armstrong was ably assisted by Sergeant John Ayre from Devon. Armstrong remained there until 1870 when he retired to Kingston on pension and died in 1902 aged 95[23]. Ayre resided with his wife in Albert Road just a few doors away from his Inspector who lived at number 159[24]. Clearly Inspector Armstrong thought a lot of Sergeant Ayre, whom on his recommendation was promoted to inspector in 1863 allowing Ayre to remain on 'V' Division until 1871 when he himself retired to live in Sunbury[25].

The photograph at left was taken in Kingston in 1868 and shows a local police officer who is on duty. It was common in those days to wear whiskers – but this caused a problem with identifying the police officer from his collar number in case of complaint by a

An early Kingston Police officer taken in 1868

member of the public. This was rectified as the collar number was also shown in the centre of the helmet plate as well as on each side of the officer's collar.

The Inspector's task was not an easy one and at Kingston he did not undertake any station duty, this being was left to the station sergeants. Instead he had to patrol on horseback visiting the Kingston, Ditton, Epsom, Hampton and Sunbury areas. There were four sergeants at the station who assisted him. One sergeant with one acting sergeant performed day duty with nine constables who covered the foot beats in the town area. There was also one sergeant and one acting sergeant, together with 20 constables who covered the night beats.

The inspector had to visit each police station in the area and sign the occurrence book to ensure that all was running well. Additionally, two

Kingston Police Station. 1864 - 1968. London Road Kingston, Surrey

sergeants at Kingston were required also to patrol both 9 and 12 hour tours of duty alternately every night from 9pm. Instructions were given that the sergeants should 'take care of their horse' as it could be an arduous and difficult duty[26]. In all there were five horses stabled at the station and two constables per shift would cover the main highways on horseback in and out of Kingston. One horse each belonged to the Inspector and the two sergeants. In addition to other duties one constable was designated 'the groom' and it was his job to ensure the horses were properly fed and looked after. It was important that each of the constables and sergeants employed on mounted patrol were able to be drilled in proper horsemanship. One of the sergeants at Kingston in 1870 was George Robbins who was practising mounted drill on the drill ground in accordance with regulations and whilst maintaining his horse he was killed instantly when he was kicked in the chest[27].

The station area boundary commenced at;

> 'Kingston Vale immediately West of the 'Robin Hood Public House' by right of Kingston Hill to Warren road, thence in a straight line to the bridge over the London and South Western Railway (Kingston Branch) by Dickerage Lane, and right of same to Kingston Head, thence in a straight line to the London and South Western Main Line, and then by centre of Hoggsmill Stream to Uwell Road (sic), 'by centre of same to Park Avenue by right to London road, by right to High Street, south west , by right of same to Mongers Lane, by right of same to Reigate Road, to Fir Tree Road, by right of same to Tattenham Corner, then by Metropolitan Police District Boundary to Headley Road and Epsom Common to Ashstead Woods, by northeast side of same to Telegraph Hill to Star Lane, continuing by Metropolitan Police District Boundary to River Thames at West Molesey, by centre of same to Half Mile Tree at Lower Ham Road, thence following the boundary of the Parish of Ham eastward to starting point (taking the centre of Molesey and Kingston Bridges'[28].

A magnificent new and substantial station was designed by Charles Reeves Metropolitan Police Surveyor on the land rented from Edward Ward and brought into service in London Road, Kingston in June 1864. It included section house accommodation for single officers[29] and also one set of married quarters[30] for the inspector in charge. However when this station came to the end of its serviceable life, it will be seen there were great hurdles to overcome and a sequence of unfortunate events which led to delays in securing a suitable new police station site in Kingston.

Whilst stationed at Kingston in 1881 constable Fred Atkins (wt. no. 61462) disturbed a burglar in a house on Kingston Hill. These were dangerous times for a constable on his own as Atkins found out because the burglar was armed and he fired at the officer a number of times trying to escape.

Rear Yard aspect of Kingston Police station

423

The officer fell dead having been shot three times and the burglar made good his escape[31].

In 1881 a review of all Metropolitan Police accommodation for the Secretary of State showed that Kingston was a well-built tenement however the Inspector and his family occupied two quarters. The station cell space was inadequate since they could hold few prisoners when on Derby day they could expect to hold at least 26 prisoners. There were 13 single constables who occupied the section house but there were no locks on door between the inspector's rooms and the section house. Recommendations included separating both the married and single quarters, building in a toilet on the upper floor, placing better lighting to the cells area and putting in buzzers into each cell[32].

Kingston on Thames police station was a main station and Sub Divisional Inspector (wt. no. 49827) Alfred Rushbridge was in charge in 1891. He was supported by four inspectors, five sergeants and 60 constables[33]. Rushbridge did not reside at the station but lived at May Cottage Avenue Road, Kingston. He remained in charge until 1894 when he retired having joined the force in 1868, a total 26 years service [34]. Inspector (wt. no. 63063) Henry Trott had joined 'V' Division in 1893 however just a year later he was promoted to Sub Divisional Inspector in charge of Kingston Sub Division[35].

Kingston sub division was responsible for hosting the 14th Annual Garden Party and Sports day in 1895, held in Woodbines Park, with funds going to the Metropolitan Police and City Orphanage at Twickenham. This event was attended by the divisional senior officers including Superintendent David Saines whose responsibility was to give out the prizes to the winners at the end, and Chief Inspector Pryke who was a judge seeing to fair play. This was a heavy responsibility which fell to Inspector Trott who arranged for the club secretary Sergeant Collins to help. The garden party was a well-attended event with the police officers, their wives and children taking the

The rear entrance to the station taken in 1906

day off to be present. On this Monday it rained, but this did not stop the enjoyment and fun of the participants and the races going ahead. In the tug of war the Kingston and Surbiton Fire Brigade beat the Kingston team. There was a balloon race during the day, the divisional police band was in attendance and after dark, once dancing had finished, there was a firework display[36].

Sub Divisional Inspector Trott retired in 1897 after completing 25 years' service[37], and his place was taken by Sub Divisional Inspector (wt. no. 63737) Edward West who remained until 1902. West was promoted to Chief Inspector and transferred to 'K' or Bow division north of the River Thames in the East End. West eventually became a respected superintendent and took charge of 'W' Division[38]. Also residing with West was his wife Emma and five children. The section house also had eight single constables in residence in 1901.

The weather was getting worse, especially for the patrolling police officers. In 1890 it was recorded as the coldest December in 150 years. By 1894 the centre of Kingston was flooded in November followed by a very severe winter. The wet weather made drying the police boots and shoes a problem since those not living at the station (where there was a drying room) often did not have facilities for keeping their footwear dry. In such extreme inclement weather supervising sergeants would give orders for the patrolling police officers to remain in the station and they would only go out in an emergency.

One of the acute problems police face in their daily work, was (and still is) the

Retirement through injury at Kingston circa 1908

risk of injury which they receive in the execution of their duty. In October 1895 Station Sergeant (wt. no. 59515) William Mace at Kingston was dealing with a prisoner in the charge room when he was violently assaulted by him. Once the prisoner was restrained and placed in a cell Mace was seen by the divisional surgeon who placed him on the sick list. His injuries were so severe that the police medical officer decided that Mace could not carry on as a police officer and retired him after 22 years' police service. This was very disappointing for Mace as it was likely he could have been further promoted but such was the esteem the local townsfolk had in the officer a collection was made on his behalf. A quantity of gold and silver coin was presented to the officer together with an engraved pocket watch. There was a presentation at the station for Mace who heard tributes from his colleagues and from Mr Greenwood who represented the Kingston Committee[39].

The picture above shows a retirement on 'V' division around 1908 of an officer invalided out of the service as denoted by the crutches and the pensioned officer with his wife to the right of the clock. To the left of the clock is the mayor, divisional Superintendent Robinson and Chief Inspector James Smith[40].

There were many police officers who were recruited from the army before they joined. This often meant that they remained part of the military reserve. Henry Edwin Flack joined 'V' or Wandsworth Division in August 1896 as Constable 155 'V' wt. no. 81488 where he remained for three years until he applied to return to the military and join the Boer War campaign in South Africa. He left his Irish wife Martha and ten-year-old son and returned to the colours. Fortunately he survived this harsh war. On his return in 1902 he became constable 406 'V' division and saw service at Kingston Police station. He saw all his entire service on 'V' or Wandsworth division. Flack lived at 126 Clifton Road, Kingston and retired in August 1921 (his army service counting towards his police service) after 25 years. Aged 47 he was entitled to an annual pension of £153. 13s.5d.

One of the principle policing problems in Kingston was the Cattle Fair held once a year in November. There was also a weekly fair held on Wednesdays, Thursdays and Saturdays[41].

The picture below shows a very early car accident on Kingston Hill in 1903. These were still a rare thing to see but their speed often caused accidents and Kingston Hill posed its difficulties, especially in stopping or braking. Because of the rarity of such an event the cameras were soon on scene and people, including the police constable, posed for the picture.

Motor Car accident on Kingston Hill in 1903

The photograph below shows the rear aspect of the station including a high protective wall and the rear entrance door through which all police officers with a key would be able to pass through.

On the top floor of the main building one can see where the station inspector and his family lived. Children could often be seen playing in the station yard. A rather strange case arose at Kingston in 1904 when a Metropolitan Police sergeant residing at the police station with his family applied to the Kingston Board of Guardians for assistance in paying nearly 16 shillings (80p) a week for the detention of his wife who was an invalid and in the County Asylum at Brookwood. The sergeant's take home pay was a mere £2 per week and from this he had to employ a house keeper to

Rear aspect of Kingston Police Station in 1908

look after the children. During a hearing where the sergeant was questioned regarding every detail of his expenditure down to the last penny the Board made recommendation that the sergeant should pay eight shillings per week and they would pay the remainder.

Sergeant 5 VR Brooks stationed at Kingston

The case of rent allowance was also being considered in Parliament at the time especially poignant when the wages were so low[42].

In the picture at left is Sergeant 5 'VR' Brooks stationed at Kingston smartly dressed in his double breasted greatcoat with whistle chain hanging from the 2nd button down and also showing his cape which is draped over the fence behind.

Another retirement occurred in 1904 when a very popular officer, Inspector Challingsworth of Kingston police station, completed his service. Challingsworth who was the court inspector was received by the mayor who on behalf of the Justices presented him with a gold Albert (fob watch) and medallion. There were speeches and also the presentation of a certificate of appreciation for services given to them during his service on the sub division[43]. A short time later another presentation took place, this time by Mr Sticklands of the Esher bus conductors and drivers, who expressed his gratitude and gave him an ebony walking stick in appreciation of his 25 year's police service[44].

Inspector William Bryce took charge of the sub division in West's place until 1910 when his place was taken by Sub Divisional Inspector David Thompson[45]. David Thompson, who had been a respected and hard working inspector on 'W' or Clapham Division was recommended for and had passed all the necessary examinations (including a medical) to the rank of Sub Divisional Inspector. On promotion Thompson transferred to 'V' Division and was posted in charge of Kingston, however this was not to be for long. Northumberland-born David Thompson, his wife Alice from Norfolk, their three sons and four daughters resided in the cramped and unsanitary police station accommodation at Kingston living above the police station itself. Their children ranged between 14 years and one year old[46].

By 1912 the station was proving to be inadequate for police purposes it being too small for current use and even the divisional surgeon recorded that the sanitary conditions were appalling. The Commissioner sent a request to the Receiver to search for a new plot of land and a site was found in Richmond Road. Purchased in June 1914 the land was not developed, probably because of the commencement of World War One. Yet when war finished and what with the post war depression, even this land was considered too small to be of use. In August 1914 the boundaries of Wandsworth, Battersea, Wimbledon and Kingston sub divisions were re-drawn. This re-organisation created the Earlsfield Sub Division[47].

By 1913 after only a short time, Thompsons place was taken by Race Thomas Hooper (wt. no. 78043) as the Sub Divisional Inspector in charge of the station. Unlike in Victorian times where he might have been assisted by sergeants, these places were taken by junior inspectors who were Inspectors Henry

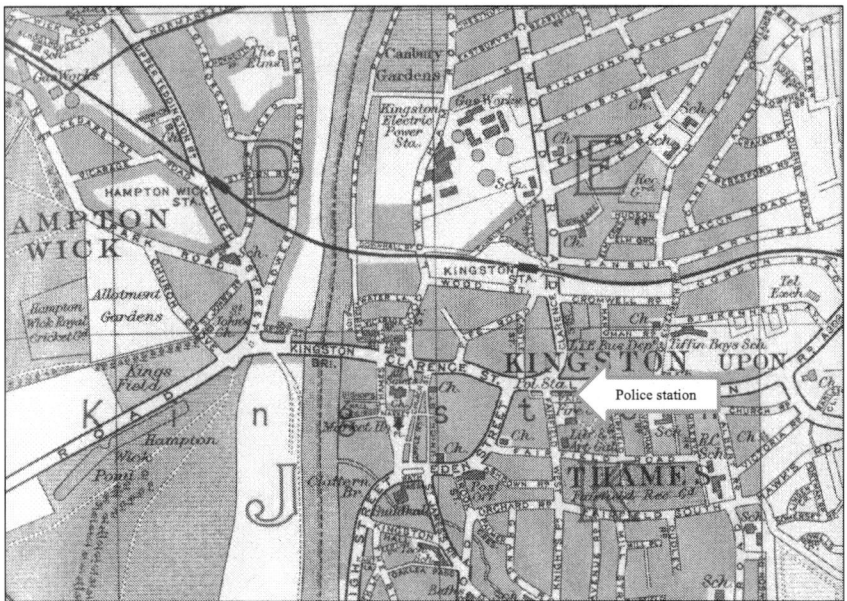

Winter and William Grimmett. They would deal with the day-to-day workings of the station and its ground rather than the whole sub division of Kingston, Ditton, Epsom, Surbiton and East Molesey. Also in support were two station

sergeants, nine section sergeants and 76 constables. There was also one detective sergeant and two detective constables attached to the station[48]. Hooper remained in charge until 1921 when he retired on pension[49]. The sub divisional inspectors at Kingston, Richmond and Wimbledon were the only SDIs on the 'V' Division who were authorised as mounted officers and each was allocated a horse for that purpose[50].

During 1915 Constable 2 'VR' Welton retired from Kingston after 25 years service. Welton had made his name stopping speeding motorists and in ten years had dealt with 2,000 cases which had raised £2,000 in fines imposed. Some of his most notable 'captures' were Prince Henry of Battenburg, the Duke of Westminster, Earl Lonsdale, Viscount Curzon and Winston Churchill MP[51].

In the same year sergeant Kempster and constable Freeman of Kingston were investigating a theft in the town centre by two guardsmen. They scoured the area and saw both men cross Home Park. They gave chase on their pedal cycles on seeing the two suspects who had now crossed the river. A search took place and they were both found hiding in the undergrowth and were arrested[52].

Another serious incident occurred later in 1915 when Constable Fredrick Daniel Kennett who was on his patrol in Kingston stopped two men who he wished to speak to. Soon both men started to escape and in the process seriously assaulted the officer. Kennet hung onto one of his assailants who was continually striking him whilst the other one made off, pleading for help from passers-by, Miss Gladys Avis ran to the officer and not being able to help much pulled out his whistle and blew it as hard as she could. This attracted a number of people including other police officers at the police station. A soldier came over together with a retired naval officer and helped the constable who lapsed into unconsciousness as they held the prisoner before the police arrived. Kennett was placed on the sick list after seeing the Divisional surgeon who sent him home. At Kingston magistrates court Kennett and all the people who came to the officers aid where thanked for their courage and helpfulness[53].

On February 2nd 1929 'V' division was chosen for an experiment using new police boxes on the Richmond sub-division (which also included Barnes and Kew), soon to be a familiar sight all over London until the 1960s. A later generation knew them only as Dr Who's Tardis. 'Time travel' was soon extended to the rest of 'V' division in October 1930 (Wimbledon), March 1931 (Kingston) and in April 1931 (Wandsworth)[54].

After the war a review was undertaken and it was decided that 'V' or Wandsworth division would be increased in size with the transfer of Esher sub-division which included stations at Cobham, and Oxshott from the Surrey Constabulary on April 1, 1947. Oxshott however was not used operationally by the Metropolitan Police[55].

An opportunity arose to exchange the purchased land with another available site called 'Meadowland', Berrylands Road, Surbiton on which a section house could be built but this did not happen as after World War 2 it was developed as Married quarters instead[56]. Attempts were made to purchase another site on which a station could be built in St. James Road, behind the Guildhall however the onset of World War Two prevented completion of the sale[57]. On 23rd September 1940 the station suffered a near miss when a stick of bombs fell near with one high incendiary bomb demolishing some shops on the same side of the road[58].

Once the war had finished fresh attempts were made to re-start the purchase of the Fairfield West site but town planning proposals made it unacceptable for the corporation. Instead, co-operation with the corporation secured a site in Thames Street for the police[59] and the freehold was purchased July 1955[60]. As the development of the Thames Street site was nearing its final stages the corporation again intervened and a revised town plan meant the new proposals for the station became unacceptable. An exchange of lands were finally agreed in 1964 and freehold purchased in 1965 enabling a new station to be built.

At Kingston Superintendent T. E. Thomas and Chief Inspector F. L. Sharp were in charge of the sub division in 1965[61].

The Local Government Act 1963 (introduced in 1965) caused the Metropolitan police to revise its divisional boundaries in line with those of the new local authorities. The intention was that Kingston be designated as the Divisional Headquarters however during the planning, development and building stage, which would take a further three years, Putney police station became the temporary divisional HQ until Wimbledon became available[62].

The divisional staff included senior officers moved between these two stations until the new station became occupied in April 1968. The new station, designed by J. Innes Elliott in association with Kingston Architects Brewer, Smith and Brewer, was built on the banks of the Hogsmill at Clatern Bridge.

It was an architectural challenge, being built adjoining the Guildhall and the Coronation stone on really poor wet land that needed 50 ft deep piles from the basement in order to support the structure.

Kingston Police Station (VD) 1968 – present day. 5-7 High Street, Kingston, Surrey.

The Hogsmill river was often liable to flooding and precautions had to be taken to ensure that flooding in the basement was kept to a minimum. The building, fronted in Portland stone, cost £254,503 to build[63].

The details of the station stated Kingston (VD) was now located at 5-7 High Street Kingston and the existing station at 22 London Road (VK) was closed[64].

In 1980 Kingston and Esher divisions were amalgamated making one of the largest divisions in the Metropolitan police District. The new division incorporated New Malden, Esher, Cobham, Surbiton and East Molesey into Kingston sub division on 'V' Division[65].

The old station was quickly rented as offices to a local company who took possession of the building. Kingston division covers a highly developed residential area with a smattering of light industry. Kingston is famous for its Hawker Sidley factory where the famous first vertical take-off jump jets were built. Kingston is the original home of British wine making. Kingston market attracts large crowds and with them come pick-pockets and shop-lifters. Kingston Bridge over the Thames is the second busiest river crossing but the recently built A3 Kingston bypass saves the Town from very severe congestion where personal injury accidents were fairly high.

Chief Superintendent Peter Jackson was in charge of the newly-built Kingston Police Station with Chief Inspector Bill Stevens as his deputy in 1968. Crime problems for the division included cycle thefts, underage drinking, drug offences which the Chief Inspector stated 'comes from the hippies which exist in encampments along the Thames'. There was a new Chief Inspector's suite, a new modern collator's office and a juvenile bureau at the station which also boasted a social club, volunteer cadet scheme and sea cadets squad located on the training ship HMS Trafalgar moored on the Thames.

In 2000 the only station open 24 hours a day on Kingston Borough[66] was Kingston itself which also was the centre for detaining, processing and charging of prisoners for court.

In 1986 the old police station in London Road which had been listed as of special architectural interest was put up for sale by the police and purchased by Garfunkels restaurant[67].

Surbiton (Tolworth) Police Station

The Portsmouth Road, which had been turn-piked by the Surrey & Sussex Trust in 1718, boasted no fewer than six stage-coach services on the Portsmouth to London route serving Kingston, bearing such colourful names as 'The Independent', 'The Economist', 'The Rocket', 'The Regulator', 'The Nelson' and of course 'The Royal Mail'.

Although, Kingston parish was beyond the Metropolitan Police District until 1840, the area had, since 1805, been patrolled by the Bow Street horse-patrols, who had stations situated on Robin Hood Hill, Kingston Market and Ditton Marsh. These were placed under the jurisdiction of the Metropolitan Police as part of 'V' division in October 1836.

The horse patrol constables were each paid four shillings daily. They wore a uniform consisting of blue trousers with blue double-breasted greatcoat bearing yellow metal buttons over a scarlet waistcoat, wellington boots with steel spurs and tall black leather hat. To complete the uniform the protective leather stocks were available as a guard against garrotting. Not all of the uniform was provided free. The spurs, greatcoat and hats had to be paid for out of the patrolmen's wages. The horse harness and loaded pistol completed the equipment. Although the pistol was supplied no officially sanctioned means of carrying spare ammunition was available until pouches were added to the saddles from December 1852[68].

The parish constable of Kingston at that time was Mr. R.W. Cooke[69].

When the 'V' or Wandsworth Division of the Metropolitan Police was formed in May 1830, it came no nearer to Kingston-upon-Thames than the parish boundary on Putney Heath. The old stage-coaches gradually dwindled after the opening of the London & Southampton Railway from Nine Elms to Woking Common on 21 May 1838, with intermediate stations at Esher and Kingston. The latter was in fact, some distance from Kingston-upon-Thames in the hamlet of Surbiton and was renamed Surbiton & Kingston station in July 1863, after Kingston received its own branch the same year. A further branch, at first horse-drawn, opened to Hampton Court serving Thames Ditton in 1849.

The 'V' Division stretched at that time as far east as Vauxhall Bridge until cut back to Battersea in October 1865, the whole of which was at that time in the parish of Surrey. The roads through Surbiton prior to the introduction of Turnpike Trusts were, for most of the winter months, virtually impassable. The first road to be turn-piked west of Kingston was built by the Great Kingston Trust to Petersfield in 1749, who erected a toll-gate at Sandown Farm[70].

This was followed by the Epsom Trust in 1755, who erected a toll-gate at Talworth Court (as spelt) and finally in 1811, The Leatherhead Trust erected a toll-gate in Hook Road at its junction with Ditton Road by 'The Maypole' public house. In order to stop the evasion of tolls, the Epsom Trust erected a new toll-house and gate on the corner of Ewell Road/Ditton Road. After the turnpike system was given up in 1883, the site was purchased by the Metropolitan Police on 22nd May 1886.

A communication dated 15 December 1885 was received from the Secretary of State for the Home Department authorising the Receiver to purchase a freehold plot of land in the Ewell Road, Surbiton from Mr. M. Bryant, for the sum of £640, for the site of a police station. The freehold title to land was obtained by the Receiver and the transaction was completed on 22nd May 1886. In the meantime plans were drawn up for the new police station and when built cost £3,107. 15s. 5d (£3,107. 77p)[71]. The station finally opened on 7th December 1888, its telegraphic station code being (SA), Kingston was (KT) and Ditton was (DT). The new station was a station on 'V' or Wandsworth Division and was ready for occupation about the 28th August [72] however there was a delay in the building since it was not occupied for police purposes until 10th December. As was usual, the Receiver stipulated what rent was due to the Commissioner by the occupants of the accommodation in order that this would be taken from their weekly pay. The married inspector was charged 5s. 6d (28p) whilst the married constable paid just 3s (13p). The station was built on the site at 1 Ditton Road, Tolworth together with two sets of married quarters[73].

In 1891 Inspector Robert McFadden was in charge of Tolworth police station as it was then called. He was supported by another Inspector, William Pickett, three sergeants and 19 constables[74].

The 1907 Kelly's directory of Surrey shows that Surbiton had three Station

Surbiton Police Station. 1888 – 1974. 1 Ditton Road, Tolworth, Surrey.

Sergeants, four Sergeants and 30 constables but unfortunately does not name the officers in charge, as it does at Winters Bridge, Ditton which was in the charge of Station Sergeant Willie Tilby, who had three Sergeants and 20 P.C.s under him. Included as part of the Kingston sub-division was Molseley (opened as (MY) in September 1902) and Epsom (EM), the latter being transferred to 'W' Division in February 1921, when 'Z' Division was formed.

The new Kingston-by-pass road, now known as the A3 opened through Tolworth and Hook in 1929, bringing with it suburban development. New railway stations served the new communities at Hinchley Wood (1930), Berrylands (1933), Tolworth (1939) and Chessington North and South (1939). There was a fixed point box located at Surbiton railway station on land owned by the Surbiton Urban District Council[75].

This was replaced in December 1930 by a telephone box and located inside the station yard. Southern Railway did not insist on any rent to be paid by the police for the purpose. Surbiton finally became a separate borough in 1936, the same time as neighbouring Malden and Coombe.

Police boxes were introduced throughout Kingston sub-division in March

Rear aspect of Tolworth (Surbiton) Police Station circa 1908

1931, and this more efficient means of communication finally led to the closure of Ditton police station two years later. Kingston had been the 'V' Division HQ but in July 1935, this was moved to Putney.

The Surrey Constabulary had only been formed in 1851. In that year white coal posts had been erected about 16 miles around the Metropolis bearing the City of London arms which were re-sited at the MPD boundary a decade later.

One of these posts at the former turnpike at Sandown Park, part of a series extending from the Thames at Sunbury over to the MPD boundary on Erith Marshes in Kent, ceased to be the extent of 'V' Division in April 1947, when the Esher and Cobham sections were transferred to the Metropolitan Police from Surrey. The former urban district has, since 1974, been part of Elmbridge and since 1980, been part of the Kingston Sub-Division.

Police officers and their families still lived at the station up until the 1950's. Constable David Osborne and his wife Barbara resided there for nine years in

1954. Their daughter aged two years moved in with them and in 1959 their son Richard was born there. They lived on the top floor. Constable Osborne worked at the station in the administration unit for a while but also worked at Esher and Kingston – not moving far[76].

One notable officer who was stationed at Surbiton was Detective Sergeant Ray Purdy who was killed on duty in the 1950s by Gunter Podola a burglar who he had arrested for blackmail. It was a note book which Purdy had taken from Podola that eventually led to his arrest, conviction (See Chapter 10 and Chelsea Police Station for more on this case) Constable Osborne and his family knew Ray Purdy well and it was a shocking event to happen for all police officers as many of them face danger and sometimes pay the ultimate price. Podola was sentenced to death and was hanged at Wandsworth in 1959. Purdy was given a service funeral paid for by the police. Purdy's widow lived at Berrylands Road, Subiton and there was a call to grant Mrs Purdy a special grant in recognition of the price paid by her husband in the line of duty. She was awarded £10 10s. 8d (£10.53p) per week and this included a special allowance for her two children who had lost their father[77].

On 9th May 1962, Surbiton saw the very last trolleybus route to operate in London. This route, the 601 from Twickenham to Tolworth had a direct replacement in the present bus route 281.

In 1965 there was a revision of boundaries within the Metropolitan Police District because of the municipal boundary changes – where the Secretary of State authorised a re-organisation of the Force designed to relate police boundaries to the new local authority boundaries created by the London Government Act, 1963. The new local authority and police boundaries were implemented on 1 April 1965. Surbiton (VS) was designated a sub-divisional station with East Molesey (VE), Esher (VH)and Cobham (VC) as its sectional stations situated in Esher (Surrey)[78].

In April 1968, Surbiton acquired its own traffic garage in Hollyfield Road, although 'V' District had been the first to be abolished in 1985 when the area was split between the two divisions of Kingston and Wimbledon. Surbiton then became part of the new No. 5 (South West) Area on Kingston Division, which changed its code letters from 'VD' to 'VK'. Surbiton will then reach its 100th birthday. Discussions had taken place during the 1970s as to the urgency of rebuilding Surbiton Police Station however difficulties were being encountered in acquiring adjacent properties or land to the existing station. The plan was to build a much bigger police station with all the equipment necessary for policing such as computerisation. There was a lack of suitable space where a much larger new sub-divisional Station could be built.

Surbiton Police Station. 1977 – 2012. 299 Ewell Road, Surbiton, Surrey.

In 1974 because of financial cutbacks the project was shelved and temporary accommodation was sought in the vicinity of the existing station. In the meantime the freehold of Old St Matthews School, 299 Ewell Road, Surbiton was obtained in July 1974 which was about 100 yards away from the old station. Building works to adapt the school house for police purposes was started costing £120, 000[79] although this took longer than anticipated and the new station was not opened until the end of December 1977 with a police order that stated;

> 'On 19th December, a new (temporary) sectional Police Station will be opened at Surbiton (VS). The address of the new Station is 299 Ewell Road Surbiton, Telephone numbers will remain unaltered'.[80]

The station was much bigger with plenty of space although it had been a purpose built school.

In 1980 there were further re-organisations to 'V District - which reduced the divisions from three to two when Kingston and Esher Divisions were amalgamated. The new division became known as Kingston division and incorporated New Malden, Esher, Cobham, Surbiton and East Molesey sub-divisions. There was no change to the sub-divisional boundaries or the contact telephone numbers[81].

From 2000 Surbiton was subject to restricted opening hours under a review by the Metropolitan Police Authority of police station opening times[82]. These opening times lasted until 2012 where Surbiton was open Mondays to Fridays from 10am until 6pm being closed on Saturdays and Sundays[83]. The station was shut in 2012 and the building put up for sale[84]. A police office in Ewell Road has been opened instead.

New Malden Police Station

On 30 July 1886 Superintendent, 'V' or Wandsworth Division reported that a Mr. J. King of Cromwell House, Maiden Road, New Malden, Surrey, has a plot of land for sale on the corner of Maiden and Burlington Roads. The asking price was £600 and was well situated for a police station, 'exactly in the position required'. It is near the railway station and in the most central position. It was a fast growing neighbourhood and in the course of a few years became a populous area. The Police Surveyor recommended the purchase of the site in August 1886 and in the October Home Office approval was received for negotiations to be entered into with the vendor. The freehold site was purchased on 28th January 1887 for the sum of £550. Plans were drawn up and a builder obtained to construct the new police station. The cost of erecting the new station was £3,306. 3s. 10 (£3,306.19p).

The new Station on 'V' or Wandsworth Division at New Malden was occupied by the police and business started there on 1st August 1881. The premises were built with two sets of married quarters which were rented to police officers who were married with children. The lodging assessment was one married Inspector at 5s. 6d. (28p) per week and one married Constable at 3s. (15p) per week[85].

Sergeant (wt. no. 66554) William Ough aged 40 years resided at the station with his wife Jane and two sons in 1901. Ough had joined the police in 1882 and resigned on pension in 1907. There was also another family living at the station. This was Constable Thomas Adams (who was the same age as Ough), his wife Elizabeth and their two children[86].

A communication was received at the station dated 28th March 1911 from the Maldens and Coombe Urban District Council decreeing that the number 128

New Malden Police Station. 1881 – 1998. 128 Malden Road, New Malden Surrey.

should be marked on the premises. The address of the station became 128 Malden Road, New Malden, Surrey. The Secretary of State authorised a reorganisation of the Force designed to relate police boundaries to the new local authority boundaries created by the London Government Act 1963.

The new local authority and police boundaries were introduced on 1st April 1965. New Malden (VN) was designated a sectional station of Kingston (VD) sub-division situated in the new London Borough of Kingston-upon-Thames[87].

In February 1980 there were further boundary changes on 'V' District with a reduction of divisions from three to two when Kingston and Esher Divisions were amalgamated. The new division was named Kingston Division and incorporated New Malden, Esher, Cobham, Surbiton and East Molesey sub-

Rear aspect to New Malden Police station circa 1908

divisions. There was no change to the sub-divisional Boundaries[88].

The photograph above shows the rear aspect to the station. To the right is the cell block with iron bars on the windows. Behind the block (where the coal bunker can be seen) was a large charge room where the station sergeant would take and record all prisoners brought in. He would remove and itemise all their personal items of property and place them safely in paper envelopes which were methodically sealed for safe keeping until the prisoner was taken to court or given bail.

The station was shut in 1998 and boarded up, but after a while it was sold to J. D. Weatherspoons who have turned the old station into a public house named the 'Watchman'[89].

A new police community office was opened soon after the police station was shut. This was located at the CI Tower – St Georges Square, High Street, New Malden KT3 3HH. The hours of opening in 2012 were Monday to Friday 1230 - 1730, Saturday 1030 – 1530[90]. The office or shop front is situated on the ground floor with the entrance in Dukes Avenue and is the base for the Safer Neighbourhoods Team as well[91]. This area is police by the Beverley Safer Neighbourhoods team (under Sergeant Ellis in 2011).

---

[1] MEPO2/25
[2] Wade, J. (1829) A Treatise on the Police and the Crimes of the Metropolis. Patterson Smith New York (reprinted 1972)
[3] MEPO 2/76
[4] Tim Lambert (2011) A Brief History of Kingston upon Thames http://www.localhistories.org/kingston.html accessed on 25th January 2011
[5] Kellys Directory 1841
[6] Brown, B. (1985) When Victor Bowed out. Police Review 29th October.
[7] Ibid
[8] Ibid
[9] Tim Lambert (2011) A Brief History of Kingston upon Thames http://www.localhistories.org/kingston.html accessed on 25th January 2011
[10] Tim Lambert (2011) A Brief History of Kingston upon Thames http://www.localhistories.org/kingston.html accessed on 25th January 2011
[11] The Job 13th August 1971
[12] Metropolitan Police Correspondence ESB London
[13] MEPO 5/3 (10/44)
[14] MEPO 2/76
[15] Kellys directory 1851
[16] Pension Records 1840 - 1858
[17] *Old Bailey Proceedings Online* (www.oldbaileyonline.org, version 6.0, 14th February 2012), July 1840, trial of THOMAS JOHN SIMMS (t18400706-1881).
[18] Kellys directories 1855 - 1860
[19] The Metropolitan Police Roll of Honour www.policememorial.org.uk accessed on 12th March 2002
[20] Census records 1861 and 1871
[21] MEPO 5/51
[22] Metropolitan Police Orders dated 11th January 1864
[23] The Police Review and Parade gossip 20th June 1902
[24] Census Records 1861
[25] Census records 1871
[26] Metropolitan Police Orders dated 11th January 1864
[27] The Metropolitan Police Roll of Honour www.policememorial.org.uk accessed on 12.3.2002
[28] The Police and Constabulary list 1871
[29] Metropolitan Police Orders dated 21st September 1864
[30] Metropolitan Police Surveyors Records 1924
[31] The Metropolitan Police Roll of Honour www.policememorial.org.uk accessed on 12.3.2002
[32] Condition of station 1881
[33] Kellys directory 1891
[34] Kellys directory 1894 p2203
[35] Ibid and Kellys directory 1895
[36] The Police Review and Parade Gossip dated 16th August 1895

[37] MEPO 3/340
[38] MEPO 4/346
[39] The Police Review and Parade Gossip 25th October 1895
[40] Kellys directory 1908
[41] Kellys directory 1913
[42] The Police Review and Parade Gossip 12th August 1904 p386
[43] The Police Review and Parade Gossip 1st July 1904 p323
[44] The Police Review and Parade Gossip 8th July 1904 p335
[45] Census records 1911
[46] Census records 1911
[47] Metropolitan Police Orders dated 27th August 1914
[48] Kellys directory 1913
[49] MEPO 4/346
[50] Metropolitan Police Orders dated 27th September 1919
[51] The Police Chronicle 30th April 1915
[52] The Police Chronicle 3rd September 1915
[53] The Police Chronicle 10th September 1915
[54] Brown, B. (1985) When Victor Bowed out. Police Review 29th October.
[55] ibid
[56] Back, J. (1975) Kingston Police Station. Metropolitan Police Collection ESB, London
[57] Ibid.
[58] Kingston Library resources http://www.rbksch.org/museum/map_large.asp?mapid=1 accessed on the 9.2.12
[59] LB 660/67/1
[60] LB660/-/0 Part 2
[61] Metropolitan Police Stations 1965
[62] Metropolitan Police Orders dated 6th August 1964
[63] The June Sampson Feature. Surrey Comet. March 1998
[64] Metropolitan Police Orders dated 29th March 1968
[65] Metropolitan Police Orders dated 4th February 1980
[66] Metropolitan Police Authority (2000) Police Station opening hours Committee; MPA Reports 9th November
[67] The June Sampson Feature. Surrey Comet. March 1998
[68] http://www.eppingforestdc.gov.uk/Library/Leisure/MUSEUM/collections/PEELERSPROGRESS.pdf accessed on 9.2.12
[69] Ibid
[70] Metropolitan Police Correspondence, ESB London
[71] Back, J. (1975) Surbiton Police Station. The Metropolitan Police Collection. ESB London
[72] Police Orders 23 August 1888)
[73] Metropolitan Police Surveyors Records 1924
[74] Kellys directory 1891
[75] Metropolitan Police Surveyors Records 1924
[76] London Police pensioner No. 114 dated September 2004
[77] http://hansard.millbanksystems.com/written_answers/1959/jul/23/detective-sergeant-r-purdy accessed on 27.4.12
[78] Back, J. (1975) Surbiton Police Station. The Metropolitan Police Collection. ESB London
[79] The Job (1978) 'New Home Opens' 6th January
[80] Metropolitan Police Orders dated 16th December 1977
[81] Metropolitan Police Orders dated 1st February 1980
[82] Metropolitan Police Authority (2000) Police Station opening hours Committee; MPA Reports 9th November
[83] http://www.allinlondon.co.uk/directory/1252/101922.php accessed on 14.2.2012
[84] http://www.surbitonpeople.co.uk/Surbiton-Police-Station-grabs/story-13312500-detail/story.html accessed on 14.2.2012
[85] Metropolitan Police Orders dated 31st August 1881
[86] Census records 1901
[87] Metropolitan Police Orders dated 6th August 1964
[88] Metropolitan Police Orders dated 1st February 1980

[89] http://www.newmaldenpeople.co.uk/New-Weatherspoon-pub-New-Malden/story-15122381-detail/story.html accessed on 14th February 2012
[90] http://content.met.police.uk/PoliceStation/newmalden accessed on 20.4.2012
[91] ibid

Chapter 12

The London Borough of Richmond-upon-Thames and Elmbridge

by Peter Kennison

Introduction

Mounted patrols were introduced by John Fielding the Bow Street magistrate to deal with the plague of highwaymen infesting the metropolitan area's turnpikes. The plan was so successful that the original horse patrol of eight men was strengthened to more than 50 in 1805. The Bow Street horse patrol could then provide protection on all main roads within 20 miles of Charing Cross. Their scarlet waistcoats, blue greatcoats and trousers and black leather hats and stocks, were the first uniform issued to any police force in the world[1].

The second division of the Bow Street horse patrol was responsible for Kingston in 1827[2]. The area was not included within the Metropolitan Police until 1839 when Kingston, Hook and Chessington formed part of the inner district of 'V' Division[3]. When the Metropolitan Police boundary was extended to cover the Richmond area in 1840 the responsibility for supervision fell to the senior officers of Metropolitan Police of 'V' or Wandsworth Division. The extension of the Metropolitan Police for the division also took in Epsom, Hampton, Sunbury, Princes Street, Kingston; and High Street, Mortlake[4].

In 1837 the second division of the Bow Street horse patrol, under the command of Inspector Dowsett, was amalgamated with the Metropolitan Police as part of the Mounted Branch attached to 'V' division. But in January 1840 these geographical areas also came under the jurisdiction of the Metropolitan Police when the force boundary was extended to its present limits. Another 13 sergeants and 101 constables were added to the division, new 'V' Division stations being opened at Kingston, Epsom, Hampton, Sunbury and Richmond (the Surrey Constabulary not coming in existence for another decade).

Further extensions to the Metropolitan Police area occurred in 1865 when a number of new divisions 'W', 'X' and 'Y' were formed and others re-organised[5]. This affected Superintendent Edward Butt at Wandsworth – the divisional headquarters' significantly when Chelsea (with Inspector Pitt Tarlton) was removed to 'T' Division, and Clapham (and Inspector William Bushnell) to 'W' Division. The five Inspector stations were now reduced to three these being Wandsworth, Kingston and Richmond. All the stations in Middlesex — Sunbury, Hampton, Twickenham, Chelsea and Fulham — were transferred from 'V' to the 'T' or Kensington Division[6]. These stations excepting Kingston, were closed when sergeants or acting sergeants were patrolling. Special duties included one sergeant as divisional clerk, one sergeant and three constables in charge of the police van and horses, one constable as Superintendent's Groom, two constables at Wandsworth Police Court, one constable at Crermorne Gardens, three constables at Kew Gardens, one constable at Strawberry Hill House, and six constables at Hampton Court Palace[7].

The Municipal Borough of Richmond was incorporated by Royal Charter in 1890. In 1892 its boundaries were enlarged to include the parishes of Kew, Petersham, and a portion of Mortlake, and again in 1933 by addition of Ham Common and village[8].

In 1965 the borough of Richmond was merged with the Municipal Borough of Twickenham, on the other side of the Thames and previously in Middlesex, to form the new London Borough of Richmond[9].

In 2011 the Borough of Richmond on Thames was served by three police stations, Twickenham, Richmond and Teddington. There are also eighteen Safer Neighbourhoods Teams who are there to prevent crime and deal with community problems. Response teams are available 24 hours a day to deal with the emergency calls; CID officers and forensic teams investigate crimes and bring criminals before the court. All this work is undertaken for the residents of the borough of Richmond with the express aim of keeping the borough one of the safest in London. The following histories include the police stations at Barnes, Cobham, Ditton, East Molesey, Esher, Ham, Hampton, Kew, Long Ditton, Richmond, Twickenham and Teddington but also the Police Orphanage at Strawberry Hill, Twickenham.

Barnes Police Station

Barnes Police station was shown as a station on 'V' or Wandsworth Division in 1841. At Barnes there were no charging facilities and no space for cells at the cottage brought into use for police purposes. There was one sergeant, one acting sergeant and 15 constables. There were four day beats and 10 night beats. There were also no stabling facilities for horses. The inspector at Richmond was expected to patrol the area and to visit each station to see that everything was in good order[10].

In 1878 a cottage belonging to W. Lowther MP was rented for £25 per year for the purposes of a police station. The freehold to land was purchased by the police in 1887 for £575 and a station was re-built, at a cost of £4,038, on the site. This consisted of a police station and one set of married quarters which, although the station building was not completed until march and the section house was finished by may 1892. The section house can be seen on the next page with the coal bunker leaning against it. This was a station of 'V' or Wandsworth Division situated in the Borough of Barnes.

The inspector's office was on the ground floor with a charge room, waiting room, store and two cells. There was also a larger association cell (often used for drunks) and a parade shed outside in the yard. On the first floor was a mess room, recreation room, bathroom, lavatory and a locker place where the private property of police officers could be secured. At the back of the station also on the ground floor was a kitchen, scullery, boot room, drying room, clothes room, brushing room and a place to store paraffin lamps. In the basement was a coal cellar, coke cellar, seven water closets and a urinal. In the section house lived eight single constables who paid one shilling (5p) a week rent. This was deducted from their weekly pay.

Barnes Police Station. 1892 – 1976. 371 Lonsdale Road, Barnes SW13

In 1887 the Receiver sold a strip of land for £100 at the front of the station to the Mortlake District Highways Board for the purposes of road widening. There was a condition that the Board would make good the road and footways in an area known as 'The Jews Garden'. In 1900 neighbours overlooking the station gave up their right to light to the Receiver providing one shilling (5p) a year was paid to them.

One of the notable inspectors at Barnes was Sub Inspector (wt. no. 54066) William Feaver who by the time he retired in 1896 had spent over eight years at Barnes. His leaving celebration, held at the Bulls Head, Barnes, was attended by friends and colleagues including the police band with Mr C. E. Morley making the presentation of a substantial cheque for £55 18s. 2d (£55.91). Mr Morley gave a short speech indicating this was a pleasant duty for him and that he hoped the Inspector would have many more years of life to enjoy his retirement. The inspector responded with thanks to those who contributed to this handsome present[11].

Rear access to Barnes Police station circa 1908

In 1898 a strange incident occurred to a constable at Barnes who was patrolling near Kew Bridge which clearly demonstrates the dangers of police work. Constable 411 'V' Wear was walking his beat between Kew and Mortlake just before midnight in August when he detected a man in the bushes. He aimed a gun at him and shot the officer in the chest. The assailant made off, leaving the officer bleeding profusely on the ground. The bullet had passed through the body to the left of the heart, and once he was discovered he was rushed to Richmond hospital where he was critically ill. It was believed that Wear had discovered a potential burglar who was in the process of breaking into one of the isolated houses nearby. There was no real description of the suspect as this happened so quickly and no one was ever arrested for these crimes. However, later in the year, Constable Wear was presented with a testimonial in the shape of a silver cruet set by the Pioneer Sick and Provident Society (Mortlake) to commemorate his recovery[12].

In 1907 the Conservators of the River Thames gave the Receiver permission to build a mooring above Barnes Bridge to take a police launch for a nominal amount of one shilling annually[13].

Barnes Police station yard showing the dog kennel and parade room circa 1908

In 1924 the address of the station was shown as 371 Lonsdale Road, SW13[14]. There was correspondence in 1927 asking the Receiver if there were any objections to an advertisement noticeboard being placed on the flank wall of an adjoining building – the Bulls Head Public House. No objection was raised and the boarding was erected[15].

A property was also used in Barnes High Street for the purposes of repairing police motor vehicles and rented from Sir Henry Lowther. The premises had originally been rented for £143 per annum from 1920 but were purchased from the owner in 1930 for £3,593. 15 shillings[16] (£3,593 75p) and its use as a police garage continued.

In May 1976 the New Barnes Police Station was opened.

The old Barnes police station was put up for sale by the police and eventually sold for redevelopment. In 2004 work was completed on the site which now consists of a mixture of commercial and residential properties estimated to be

Barnes Police Station. 1976 – present day. 92- 102 Station Road, Barnes SW13 0NG

worth in excess of £1,800M[17].

Barnes police station is no longer an operational police station and does not take charges or prisoners.

Kingston, Merton and Wandsworth Child Protection Team operate from Barnes Police station[18] 92 to 102 Station Road, Barnes SW13 0NG.

Cobham Police Station

Cobham is a village about 4 miles south-east of Weybridge and the same distance south-west of Esher. The parish is bounded on the north by Walton, Esher, Thames Ditton, and a corner of Kingston; on the south-east by Stoke D'Abernon; on the south by Little Bookham, Effingham and East Horsley; on the south-west by Ockham; on the west by a corner of Wisley and by Walton— thus touching ten other parishes[19].

It was usual in rural villages to have parish lock ups, cage or stocks where drunken or violent individuals needed on occasions to be placed temporarily, however Cobham seemed to go against the trend. In 1824 the overseers of Cobham parish were fined by the Court-Leet for not having a cage or stocks for the detention of prisoners. It was agreed that a cage be built at the south end of the village, near the alms houses on The Tilt. It was not proceeded with however and a further resolution adopted for a building of an octagon plan with a domed ceiling to be built on the old common, near the Royal Oak Tavern[20] instead.

The lord of the manor had view of frankpledge. Constables and tithing-men were elected for the tithings of Street Cobham, Church Cobham, and Downeside, together with one pinder and one ale-taster [21]. There was a paid Surrey Constabulary constable residing in Cobham in the 1850s[22].

During the summer of 1859 Constable Allen Mason aged 30, who had been stationed at Cobham for some years, sustained a ruptured blood vessel in the lungs caused during a violent assault by a deserter whom he was trying to arrest and died as a result of his injuries. *The Surrey Comet* newspaper commented that Constable Mason was 'greatly respected both by the inhabitants and the members of the Force'[23]. His funeral was attended by many police officers, like typical official police funerals. Surrey Police Force records of 1859 stated:

> 'I regret to have to report the death of Police Constable Allen Mason, an old and efficient officer of this Force, which took place on 29th ultimo. The deceased had a ruptured blood vessel a few weeks ago, and attributed his previous reduced state of health to a violent assault committed upon him by a Deserter in July last ...'

The road through Cobham (now the main A3) was becoming busy and there were reports in 1896 regarding the furious riding by light locomotives and motor cars. Calls from police reported that all vehicles should be fixed with some identifying features like an index mark. Also reports of reckless cycling at Pains Hill and Hartar Hill, Cobham were made to the Chief Constable who ordered Sergeant Fletcher from Esher to investigate. Later the sergeant was knocked down and seriously injured in trying to prevent the furious riding of bicycles[24].

During the 1920s the Metropolitan Police had introduced police (Dr Who type) telephone boxes and telephone posts across London. When Cobham came into the Metropolitan Police District arrangements were made for police call box V71 to be situated in the village. This took place on 1st December 1948 and the box was sited at the junction of Fairmile Lane (on the east side) and Green Lane Cobham. The box was removed on 21st October 1970. This box contained a telephone but did not have an air raid warning siren[25].

In 1931 Cobham was a sectional station of Hersham division of the Surrey Constabulary with a sergeant in charge[26].

In 1937 Cobham which was a sergeant station was part of Woking Division

Cobham Police station. 1947 – 2000. 91-93 Portsmouth Road, Cobham, Surrey, KT11 1JJ.

with Superintendent J. H. White in charge[27].

In 1947 there were boundary changes and Cobham (VC) joined the Metropolitan Police on 'V' or Wandsworth Division and was a sub divisional station of Kingston. In 1955 Superintendent D. C. Horsley at Kingston was in charge of the sub division[28] with Surbiton, East Molesey and Esher. In 1960 he had been replaced by Superintendent E. J. E Tickle[29]. By 1965 the station had limited opening times and was shut from 10pm until 6am daily although this was soon to change.

Daily life at Cobham in the 1970's.

Experienced Sergeant Desmond Randall who had served at Barnes, Esher and Epsom was the officer in charge of the station in 1971. He had been posted there in 1964 when the station reverted from being open 16 hours a day as a section of Epsom. He was responsible for supervising 14 constables and records show that Cobham was open to the public 24 hours a day seven days a week[30]. The home beat system of policing was also introduced in 1971.

Cobham was responsible for four Surrey villages, Cobham, Downside, Oxshott and Stoke D' Abernon. Constable John Wallace covered Stoke D'Abernon whilst and Constable Patrick Lynch patrolled Oxshott. Both the constables lived in their villages and were known as 'residentials'. Constable Jenner who reitired on ill health grounds in 1968 and was the residential for Oxshott before constable Lynch was an experienced and well-respected officer who was greatly appreciated by the community. So much so that when he retired he was presented with a gift of £714 raised for his retirement fund by the local people[31]. Advertisement's for a station cleaner were placed in a number of papers and the job was given to a local lady. These ladies and sometimes gentlemen (who would also be telephone exchange operators at bigger stations) often formed the backbone of the station and remained in the local area when others police officers had moved on. In Cobham's case it was Florence Bundy[32] who ensured the station was kept clean and tidy. She also from time to time would make the tea, answer enquiries by members of the public at the front counter when the station officer was temporarily engaged, and cook a fried breakfast for the station staff. They were a consistent feature of the 'nick' being much valued and part of the police family. Many a new young recruit miles away from home and coming to London would seek advice from such ladies. It was a sad day when computerisation and the outsourcing of cleaning services made them redundant.

Constable Bob Powell was Cobham's dog handler in 1971. His dog Kim71 was a very good police dog and had won the Frederika Shield in the Metropolitan Police dog trials in the same year[33]. Constable Powell also lived in the community and lived with his family in purpose-built police house. The back garden also housed the dog kennel and whilst this was a working dog they were often part of the family when 'off duty'. Dog handlers had a dog van which they kept at home when not on duty if no other dog handler was patrolling for use in an emergency call out. If near a police station they would keep the van at the station instead. The dog handler had to ensure the fitness of his/her dog at all times which meant daily exercise and training. The dog had to be fed in accordance with police regulations where a mixture of biscuit and tinned meat was measured out daily for the animal. Handlers were often called out to search premises or land where people had been seen committing crime and making off.

Detective Sergeant Harold (Ben) Dover was in charge of the crime books and was responsible for supervising and investigating the offences reported to police at Cobham[34]. Because Cobham was a good class residential area burglary was (and probably still is) a problem in Cobham and it was his job to ensure that offenders were caught and brought before the courts. The main A3 ran through Cobham and at Fairmile the road was treacherous to motorists becoming known as 'Murder mile'. Although planned in 1938, the main Esher and Cobham bypass was not built until the 1970's and the planned re-routing would ease traffic problems in the area.

Cobham Police station was located at 91-93 Portsmouth Road, Cobham, Surrey, KT11 1JJ. Up until the year 2000 it was open on Tuesday, Thursday and Friday between 10am-12 noon and closed Mondays, weekends and bank holidays. In 1998 Cobham (VC) was a station which was located on 5 Area and did not have authorised cell space so it could not detain prisoners or operate as a charging station because it was not a Police and Criminal Evidence Act 1984 (PACE) designated station. The officer in charge was Borough Commander Superintendent W. Wilson[35].

In 1965 Cobham (VC) was a sectional station of Esher (VH)[36]. In 2000 under new boundary revisions between the Metropolitan Police and Surrey Constabulary Cobham Police station was returned to Surrey.

In 2004, under the auspices of the Surrey Police, a team of 20 volunteers kept the front desk of the station open for four days a week. Whilst in the control of the Metropolitan Police the station had been shut but now in the hands of the Surrey Constabulary it had remained open. An evaluation into police buildings and establishment considered Cobham as unsuitable for its purpose and decided to sell the building. In 2009 discussions commenced over the likely sale of Cobham Police station by Surrey Police Authority who have re-considered its ageing estate. Front counter services ceased in April 2011 and a mobile police station replaced services usually administered from the old police station[37].

In 2012 the preferred bidder for the station was the Cobham Free school who it was hoped would take over the old police station for educational purposes.

Ditton Police Station (also known as Thames Ditton and Long Ditton)

Thames Ditton is situated on a busy thoroughfare of the Portsmouth Road some two miles south-west of Kingston. The area was developing and there was a need for a police station in the area. The Metropolitan Police purchased the freehold title to a site in Ferry Road, Thames Ditton in 1855[38], for £350 from Mr Clarkson and Mr Avery[39]. Surveyors drew up plans to build a police station and suitable builders were employed for the purpose. The purpose-built station cost £978. 7s. (£978 35p) to construct in 1856 at Winters Bridge, Long Ditton (DT) and had three cells and two stables. Sergeant Robert Mittall was placed in charge of the station and lived upstairs[40] with his family. Although closed since December 1933 this fine building still stands in Ferry Road.

Two single constables lived on the first floor in a large room, two more lived on the second floor and a further two on the third floor for which they paid one shilling (5p) each per week. On the ground floor there was an inspector's office, lobby, charge room, parade room and three cells. There was also a three stall stable and loft in the yard. Also on the ground floor was a store, mess room, kitchen and pantry, whilst on the first floor there was a library[41] where off duty police officers could rest, read and smoke. In 1891 the status of the

Thames Ditton Police Station. 1855 -1933. Ferry Road, Thames Ditton

station had been upgraded and an Inspector was placed in charge. Inspector William Aldridge was the first such officer in charge and he was supported by two sergeants and 20 constables[42].

In 1910 the single men vacated the section house and were relocated elsewhere while the rooms were set aside for a married family to occupy at a rather expensive cost of 6/6d (33p) per week. The station address changed to Long

Ditton by 1924 and consisted of a station and one set of married quarters situated above[43].

A police call telephone Box V51 was erected on 16th March 1931 at the junction with Weston Green Road and Ember Court Road, Thames Ditton in the centre of the road on the double pier of the railway bridge. The box provided a refuge for a patrolling constable either to phone into the station, take meal or smoke break. It was removed on 23rd October 1970[44]. Box V69 with air raid warning sirens was also erected at Portsmouth Road, south-east side 20 yards west of Thorkhill Road Thames Ditton. It was removed on 16th October 1970[45]. Thames Ditton was a sub-division of Kingston in 1931.

During the First World War an army light bi-plane made a forced landing and came down at Thames Ditton. Special Constable George John Wiley went to assist from the station but the officer collapsed and died whilst trying to help[46].

The rear yard and dog kennels at Thames Ditton in 1908

A review of police station stock under Lord Trenchard suggested that the station was no longer considered suitable for its original purpose so Ditton was closed as a station in December 1933[47]. In November 1933 instructions were issued that all police business previously undertaken at Ditton was now to be transferred to Kingston whilst all details of telegraph codes for the station were to be deleted from the manuals.

The photograph below shows the station's rear yard and garden. It was usual for the occupant, whether it was the constable, sergeant or inspector and family to cultivate the garden in order to provide fresh vegetables for the kitchen. The picture was taken in about 1906 and as we see, the senior officer who was in residence was keen on his runner beans. Sometimes if the land was not used, the reserve constable would tend the garden and grow produce for the benefit of all.

Thames Ditton Police Station Garden in 1908

It was often the vogue and not against Force orders to dress the station with ivy as we see above to cover the bare London brick face of the walls. To the right of the main building one can see the cell block area which has bars added to prevent prisoners escaping.

Ditton was put up for sale and in September 1936 sold to Mr. Fredrick Vernon Worthy for £1,200. On the side of the old building Surrey County Council have placed a plaque marking Ditton out as a building of special interest.

East Molesey Police Station

Premises were found at 1 and 2 Rothsay Villas, East Molesey which would be suitable as a police station but because it was not purpose-built was in need of being adapted. Because the buildings were owned by Mr Bowers on a mortgage and No. 2 had an occupant with an interest (believed to be a sitting tenant) careful negotiations were undertaken by surveyors for the purchase. In 1900 these cottages, now located in Bridge Road, were purchased for £550. Additional land adjacent was also purchased for £1500 whilst the sitting

East Molesey Police Station . 1902 – 2000. 1 Walton Road, East Molesey, Surrey.

tenant's interest was purchased for £70. A covenant attached to the deeds established that the minimum worth of any houses to be erected on the site was £200, or £300 for a pair of buildings, so Surveyors had to be mindful to build a substantial station.

The freehold title to premises at 1 Walton Road, East Molesey, Surrey was purchased in 1900 by the Receiver and a police station was built in 1903 together with two sets of married quarters[48] at a cost of £3,334. In August 1902 the rental costs for the married quarters were assessed. A married constable and his family occupied the married quarters on the ground floor at a cost of three shillings (15p) per week. A married sergeant lived in the married quarters which were rooms on the ground and first floor would pay four shillings (20p) a week rent.

In 1908 the lodging assessment was raised to 3/6d (18p) and 4/6d (23p) respectively. Originally Mr Bowers the previous owner had negotiated with Messrs Kerrison and Sons for an advertising hoarding to be erected on the side of the building at an annual cost of £12. Permission was granted in 1913 by the Receiver to East Molesey Urban District Council for a fire alarm box connected to the fire station to be fitted to the railings of the station.

A Police call telephone Box V51 with air raid warning siren was erected on 16th March 1931 at the junction with Walton Road (south side) and Langton Road, East Molesey. It was removed on 23rd October 1970[49]. East Molesey is shown as being a sub-division of Kingston in 1931. By 1957 there was only one set of married quarters in use at the station whilst the other rooms were used for administrative purposes. The call sign for the station was Victor Echo (VE).

In 2000 East Molesey became a station which was transferred to Surrey Constabulary[50] as the area reverted to the Surrey police area.

Esher Police Station

When the Metropolitan Police District was extended from its original seven mile radius in January 1840 this part of the 'V or Wandsworth Division included only the parishes of Long Ditton, Thames Ditton, East and West Mousley (sic), together with the hamlets of Ember, Weston and Cleygate (sic). the latter having been enclosed two years earlier and creating an ecclesiastical parish in 1841 separated from the civil parish of Thames Ditton[51].

The Surrey County Constabulary had still a decade to wait before it came into being and, like most of the county, each parish had its own constables (normally unpaid). Parish constables continued in their office as late as 1872. Both Cobham and Esher were important stops on the route of the Southampton stage coaches as they were on the Portsmouth turnpike road, a system that was soon to fall into decline after the opening in May 1838 of the London and Southampton Railway between Nine Elms and Woking Common with intermediate stops at Kingston (now Surbiton) and at Ditton Marsh (now Esher)[52].

The Bow Street horse patrols had established a station at the latter described as being 'Near Esher' in a small double cottage taken on a yearly lease under the charge of Inspector David Cornwell (wt. no. 15498). Cornwell had been a patrol since 1822 and retired from the Metropolitan Police in October 1852 after they had been absorbed into the London force[53].

The location of the former Metropolitan/Surrey force boundary between 1851-1947 can be found by the former toll-house at Kempton (Farm) Park and elsewhere in the form of a white coal-post bearing the City of London crest[54].

The Metropolitan Police stations were under the command of Station Sergeant (SPS) James Whitmore (East Molesley) and Station Sergeant Willie Tilby. (Ditton), who wore four chevrons instead of the Sergeants three until these were replaced in 1921 by three chevrons and a crown[55].

Two notable events in 1929 were the opening of the Metropolitan Police Sports Club at Imber Court and the opening of the Kingston by pass. An important piece of legislation passed between the wars was the Surrey Review Order 1933 whereby Esher and Dittons U.D. was renamed Esher Urban District, and enlarged to include The Molesleys, the Dittons, Stoke and Cobham.

On 1st April 1947 Esher Police Station was in the Surrey Joint Police Force Area, but under Section 16 of the Police Act 1964, deferred by WWII, the parishes of Esher, Stoke D'Abernon and Cobham, all in Esher Urban District Council, were transferred into the Metropolitan Police District. The area acquired from the Surrey Police approximately 18 square miles. The change-over took place at 6am on 1 April 1947 and Esher and Cobham became Metropolitan Police Stations. The area served by Esher (VH) and Cobham (VC) Stations became the Esher Section of Kingston Sub-Division, 'V' Division[56].

The Surrey Police also allowed officers who served at the stations to remain and transfer into the London force if they wished. As a result 10 sergeants, 34 constables, one detective sergeant and a detective constable transferred. In October that year Dr. J. Stanley Whitton Sandcroft of The Green, Esher was appointed by the Metropolitan Police as the first dedicated divisional surgeon for Cobham and Esher[57].

The county police station at Oxshott was not used operationally by the Met and to compensate a DR WHO-type police telephone box (No V70) was erected in the High Street, more familiar on the streets of London than in rural Surrey.

The station call sign was (VE) in 1957. Between August and December 1960 both Cobham and Esher were closed at night as an experiment, only to be re-opened 24 hours a day in April 1965. Esher was replaced by the present modern looking building in December that year, which until January 1980, along with East Molesley, was placed under the Surbiton sub-division in lieu of Kingston[58].

In December 1964 a new sectional police station opened at Esher (VH) replacing the old Surrey Constabulary station acquired in 1947.

The old Esher U.D. was replaced by the present Borough of Elmbridge in April 1974 but still part of the MPD.

Estates Branch, in a memorandum to the Receiver in December 1959 stated that Esher which is a Sectional Station of Kingston sub-division was transferred to the Receiver by the Surrey Standing Joint Committee in 1947.

Esher Police Station. 1960 – 2000. 113 High Street, Esher, Surrey.

The present station, which was originally a public house, was likely to be scheduled for demolition to enable Esher High Street to be widened. It was suggested that a new site be found and, in any case owing to the inadequacy of the existing premises, a new station would be necessary whether the High Street was to be widened or not. One of Dixon Committee (Surrey Police Authority Review of police station stock) proposals was that Esher should remain a sectional station. The inter-departmental committee, which has recently concluded a review of police stations, recommended that Esher station should be scheduled for rebuilding during the years 1961/63 and was included in the provisional building programme for 1962/63.

Freehold premises adjacent to the existing station known as Belvedere House, High Street, Esher were purchased as a site for a new station on 13 July 1960 for the sum of £11,000. The Secretary of State had authorised a re-organisation of the Force designed to relate police boundaries to the new local authority boundaries created by the London Government Act, 1963. The new local authority and police boundaries were introduced on 1st April 1965. Esher (VH) was designated a sectional station of Surbiton (VS) sub-division situated in the local authority Area of Esher, Surrey.

> 'A new Sectional Police Station for Esher, 'V' Division, at 113 High Street, Esher, will be taken into operational use at 6am on 7th December (1967). The telephone numbers will remain unchanged[59].

From 1st February 1980, 'V' District was reduced from three to two Divisions when Kingston and Esher Divisions will be amalgamated. The new division of Kingston incorporated New Malden, Esher, Cobham, Surbiton and East Molesey Sub-Divisions and there was no change to the Sub-Divisional Boundaries[60]. In 2000 Esher became a station subject to boundary changes and was transferred to the Surrey Constabulary[61].

Ham Police Station (Office)

On 2nd December 1929 a police telephone call box was erected in Ham on the north-west corner of Ham Street and Lock Road. There was no police station in Ham at the time and the box was the only connection with police in the area. Members of the public could contact Richmond police station by going to the box and making a call. Police officers out on patrol would make a pre-arranged call from the box on their rounds. Many were on cycles in these rural beats.

In the early 1970s the area of Ham needed a police office or station and a site for the office in the grounds of Ham Clinic, Ashburnham Road was purchased by surveyors in November 1971.

An entry in Police Orders of the 26th April 1972 reads;

> 'On Monday 29th April, a Police Office to be known as Ham Police Office will be opened at 18, Ashburnham Road, Ham, Richmond, Surrey. Its station code was (TH)'.

In the late 1990s the office was only open for an hour in the morning and evening but due to staff shortages it frequently did not open at all.

In 1998 it was announced that the station was to close. The local community of Petersham and Ham were concerned at the removal of their station/office and a campaign was introduced to try and prevent its closure. In the eyes of the local population the presence of a station adds to the notion of community in the same way as a school, railway station or hospital are closed. The police station, even if only open part-time, was a visible reassurance to the community. The community had been assured that the police presence locally, both on foot and in cars, would be kept up. Concerned that their nearest station was Richmond or Twickenham, it was suggested that it would take a considerable time to get to these places by car, particularly in the rush hour. The campaign consisted of public meetings and even included a petition which collected many signatures and was handed in to Richmond police station to help prevent the shutting of

Ham Police Office. 1972 – 1999. 18, Ashburnham Road, Ham, Richmond, Surrey

the station. This campaign was in vain since in October 1999 the office and land came up for auction and was sold at Allsops who were then the Receiver's agents for the disposal of police buildings and property.

Hampton Police Station

A horse patrol station was taken over by the Metropolitan Police from 1841 which was rented from Mr Kent of Castle House, Hampton and designated a station on 'V' or Wandsworth Division. It consisted of a brick and tile house which cost £16. 16s (316.80p) per year to rent. Hampton was also designated a sergeant station and as this officer was originally from the horse patrol, his family also resided there with him. In the remaining part of the building three constables resided paying 1 shilling (5p) a week rent each. In general use was a kitchen, scullery and a stable in the yard. The building was given up and vacated in 1848[62] when it was no longer suitable.

On the 1st December 1846 Home Office approved the building of a police station at Hampton[63]. Hampton was shown as being a station of 'V' or Wandsworth Division. In the 1865 alteration of the Exterior Divisions formation of three new Divisions took place with Hampton being transferred to 'T' or Kensington Division[64].

There were alterations in the boundaries relating to the sub-divisions of 'F' Division in 1890 and these were the Sub-Divisions of Bedfont, Brentford and

Hampton Police Station. 1848 – 1901. 1 New Street (now 12 Station Road) Hampton, Middlesex

Hampton[65]. As a result a police station was put into use in New Street, Hampton from June 1847. Land on which to build a police station was rented for 60 years from Mrs E. Sawyers of Bushey Park on an annual rent of £10. The surveyors undertook to design a new station on the site which cost £879. 2s. 5d (£879 13p) and was finished in 1848. The substantial property consisted of an inspectors office, charge room, two cells and a reading room. Outside there was a hand ambulance shed, urinals, and coal cellar, with a two stall stable and hay loft. Because of a lack of running water, earth closets were also installed[66].

Upstairs there was accommodation for the married inspector and his family who occupied five rooms which included bedrooms, for sleeping together with a kitchen and scullery[67]. The weekly rent for the inspector was 6/6d (33p) but this was reduced by one shilling in 1896 to 5/6d (28p) weekly. In 1853 it was cleaned and repainted something which would be completed every three years until it was given up.

Policing Victorian Hampton.

Policing in the area was not necessarily very quiet. When trouble broke out there needed to be a firm hand. The beer houses, some of which in course of time were to become our public houses, were far from being the orderly places they appear today, and there were far too many reports of drunken fights breaking out.

In May 1864, Edward Danes, water bailiff of the Queen's River, Bushy Park, who lodged at the Star beer house made an attempt on his own life by cutting his throat. He was unsuccessful and the wound was not serious but the incident could scarcely have helped the already dubious reputation of the village.

In July, 1864, there was a quarrel which developed into a full-scale riot between the Irish labourers, who were engaged in laying down the railway, and the locals. The trouble started in the Duke of Wellington, when, after refusing to pay for their beer, the Irish broke stools and windows. Mr Austin, the landlord, remonstrated with them and was knocked down and jumped on by four men who assaulted him badly and he made a complaint to the magistrate. More fighting broke out and the Irish called reinforcements from their encampment which was close by. About twenty of them, armed with sticks and loaded with stones, set about the villagers and there was a full scale fight which lasted about half-an-hour. The unfortunate Mr Austin was again knocked down with half a brick, dragged into a ditch and brutally beaten with the butt end of a gun. Six policemen arrived, accompanied by Dr Holberton, and after tending the wounded, marched at the head of about fifty civilians to the encampment of the Irish in a field, belonging to Mr Deacon, in Burton's Lane, to detain them but they had already gone. What was left behind was immediately levelled to the ground and set fire to. A great search ensued and four men were captured hiding behind hay ricks in Mr Deacon's farmyard. They were all injured and had to be carried to the police station in a cart. A further search of tents in Mr Brice's meadows at Rectory Farm was to no avail and the crowd dispersed. At the petty sessions one of the prisoners was still so seriously hurt that he had to be carried to the bench and the *Surrey Comet* reported that,

> 'the case created a great sensation in court as it was quite a sight to see the bandages and plasters which had been applied to the wounds'[68].

In 1866 the landlord at The Star was charged with keeping a disorderly house after a brawl on his premises. Previous convictions of keeping a disorderly house, being open at unlawful hours and of assault were also mentioned. The constable who made the charge in this instance, doubtless incensed by having been told 'that no b—y policemen' were wanted on the scene, described how a crowd of eight or ten persons, male and female, were fighting. The landlord was said to have used 'the most disgusting language' and to have slammed the door in the constable's face. Despite the former's aggrieved declaration that he was in bed at the time in question and that his house was a well conducted one, the landlord, Charles Digby by name, was fined £4 with 14 shillings (70p) costs.

In 1868 Robert Rolfe, beer house keeper, was summoned for having his house open at 11 a.m. on a Sunday. His house backed on to the park and access via a ladder was easy and presumably not obvious to passers-by in the road[69].

By 1867 re-organisation of the divisions saw Hampton transfer to 'T' or Kensington Division, still as a sergeant station[70]. However by 1873 Hampton became an inspector-designated station for the first time since it came into being. Inspector George Steed took charge but he did not live at the station. Steed, aged 31 years old, resided with his wife and three daughters in Hammersmith. Steed remained in charge until 1877 when he was promoted to Chief Inspector and sent to 'K' or Bow Division. Inspector Edward Bullivent took over from Steed at Hampton, living not far away from the station in New Hampton, a short walk away. In 1881 Bullivent and his wife lived at 2 Pantile Close, Hampton[71] which seemed to be a favoured road for the occupation of police officers and their families. Bullivent remained there until about 1885 as Sub Divisional Inspector when he retired. He later died at Kingston in 1899[72].

In 1898 Sub Divisional Inspector (wt. no. 59080) Edwin Carter Unsted was in charge of Hampton sub division and remained there until 1905 when he retired on pension and was replaced. Unsted, originally from Falmer near Brighton in Sussex had joined the Metropolitan Police in 1875. In 1901 he resided at Castle Mail Cottage, Tudor Road, Hampton with his wife and seven children. Police Constable Mackintosh was on the sub-division at the time and he became ill, falling blind and being partially paralysed. He was made to retire and received a small annual grant in addition to a reduced pension. It fell to Unsted and his colleagues to look after Mackintosh, and as a result an appeal was made to the officers of the sub-division who raised £80. Unsted presented the money to Constable Mackintosh at a ceremony at Hampton[73].

Hampton Police Station. 1901 – 2013. Station Road, Hampton Middlesex.

The lease to the old station was surrendered in January 1906.

In February 1901 the approval was given by the Home Office for building a new police station at Hampton. Hampton was at this time a sectional station of Kingston, a position it shared with Sunbury and Epsom.

The freehold to a new site in Station Road, Hampton was purchased for £512.15s (£512 75p) in 1901. The new purpose-built police station also comprised of a section house for single

The aspect of Hampton police station circa 1908

constables and one set of married quarters. The administrative portion of the new police station at Hampton was taken into occupation by the police, and business commenced therein on 16th October 1905[74].

The photograph above shows the rear aspect of the station and the huge amount of space purchased with the sale of this building plot. To the left is the stable block, complete with hay loft situated away from the station. Since often in older stations families of police officers occasionally lived above the stables this was a welcomed beginning in situating stables away from main buildings where the odours were less offensive.

In 1907 Inspector (wt. no. 72741) John Henry Kempin was the Sub Divisional Inspector at Hampton police station. He resided at the station with his wife Alice. No children lived with them. In the section house were nine single constables[75]. Kempin joined the service in 1887 but remained in charge at

Hampton Police Station dressed for the 1911 Coronation

Hampton until 1912 when he retired on pension[76].

In 1924 Hampton was shown as a station on 'T' or Hammersmith Division.

Station Beats

Each station area is split into beats which were either patrolled on foot, on a bicycle or by car. The beats at Hampton which in 1932 was a station on 'T'

Division and a sub-divisional station of Twickenham were patrolled by both constables and special constables (when available). Special constables would not patrol a regular officers assigned beat. There were 3 priority patrol beats, 4 ordinary beats and 3 extra patrols.

The three priority beats were patrolled from 7am - 3pm, 3pm – 11pm and 7pm creating an geographical overlap with ordinary beats. The constable was meant to patrol at a standard speed of about 2 and a half miles an hour, with beat patrol one being two miles and 440yds long and set to take 54 minutes to complete.

Rear aspect and stable views circa 1908

On the ordinary beats the 2nd and 4th beats were cycle patrols. No. one beat was 6 miles 661 yds long and was patrolled from 6am – 2pm, 2pm – 10pm and 10pm until 6am. No 2 beat was a cycle beat 8 miles and 807 yds long, No 3 beat was 11 miles and 1026 yds long. Refreshment times were staggered throughout the beats at Hampton and details shown in the beat book. It was the responsibility of the section sergeants to complete the daily duty state which would show everyone at work and the duty to which they were assigned.

The inspector would sign at the bottom of the duty state when it was completed and checked by him. Refreshments times were just half an hour in those days and were taken either at a police box or back at the police station.

The officer would either phone in from the box or report to the reserve officer that they were in the station/box for refreshments. If out on patrol the constable would take sandwiches with him. The details of each beat were recorded in the beat book which was kept in the station office for anyone who needed to familiarise themselves with the beats. From here newly-posted constables, sergeants and inspectors would write out details of beats as the beat book held the latest instructions and changes.

A revision of boundaries took place on the 1st April 1965 in conjunction with the local authorities and the formation of the Greater London Council (GLC)

Hampton was designated as a sectional station of Twickenham sub-division[77]. In 1965 the call sign for the station was Tango Romeo (TR) and had Superintendent Mulcahy MM in charge with Chief Inspector A. G. Meapham as his deputy[78]. Hampton was a sub divisional station with Barnes being its sectional station.

In 1968 the existing station area of was incorporated into Teddington (TT) Section and Hampton police station will revert to the status of a police office

Hampton Police Station yard circa 1970's

on Monday 4th November[79]. Hampton was shut in 2013[80].

Kew Police Station

The freehold title to a vacant site was purchased at 96 North Road, Kew in 1912 when a station and two sets of married quarters were built[81]. Originally, when it was brought into service in 1914[82] Kew like Barnes was a sectional station on 'V' or Wandsworth Division to Richmond.

It remained a station on 'V' Division until 1932.

In 1929 a police call box V6 was erected on the south-west corner of North Road and High Park Avenue on the forecourt of the now closed police station.

The box was taken down in 1960[83]. There was another box, V8, situated in Kew at the southeast corner of the junction with Kew Road and the Avenue, Kew and that was removed in July 1959[84].

Kew Police Station. 1914 – 1933. 96 North Road, Kew

This station was shut as a police station in April 1933 as part of police re-organisation under the new commissioner Lord Trenchard, but it was retained for other police purpsoes by the Receiver.

Richmond Police Station

From early mediaeval times until the 19th century, the maintenance of law and order in Richmond was largely the responsibility of the Lord of the Manor through his Court Leet. The Court Leet was presided over by the Steward of the Manor or his deputy. The Steward was the judge, with all administrative matters such as the empanelling of the jury and the election of officials being handled by the bailiff[85].

The elected officials of the court were the constable, headborough (chief of the ten men who made up the jury of frankpledge) and the aleconner who was the forerunner of the present day Public Protection Officer, responsible for the quality of the ale and beer, and also for ensuring that they were sold to the proper weight and measure. Richmond, Ham and Kew each had their own officials. The constable was responsible for supervising the "Watch and Ward" under the Statute of Westminster 1285. This was the forerunner of our police service, the "Ward" being daytime patrols and the "Watch", night time ones. The constable was also responsible for inspecting alehouses and suppressing gaming houses, the apprenticing of poor children, the supervising of the settlement or removal of vagrants and beggars, the welfare of the poor, the collecting of taxes, the supervision of military arms supply and military training, and ensuring the upkeep of the local means of punishment. In other words, he was the equivalent of the local council and the police. It was a considerable undertaking and a highly unpopular job[86].

In 1631, Edward Monday 'obstinately refused to perform his office'. The court records show that the constable was not exempt from being brought before the Steward for failing to carry out his duties and was subject to punishment. In Richmond those duties relating to the poor were dealt with by the parish constable[87]. The law and order situation was somewhat confused in Richmond by the fact that the manor covered three parishes, each with their own vestry that had the duty to elect constables and maintain law and order. Presumably there was a working agreement as to the duties that were undertaken by the manor constables and those by the parish constables. In practice it appears that the parish constable was responsible for the 'social' and 'military' aspects of the work. In 1651 the constable presented to the vestry certain strangers and inmates who had crept into the parish and were likely to be a charge on the parish. In July 1654

> 'several persons were ordered to remove tenants out of their houses, or give a bond to the Churchwardens, to save the Parish against expenses to be incurred for their relief'

and Thomas Raymond was ordered;

> 'to remove his wife's mother out of the parish within a fortnight'[88].

A small watch house and lock-up can be seen in the 'Prospect of Richmond' map of 1726, standing in the wide part of George Street near the junction with Duke Street. By 1730, there was a new watch house with;

> 'a convenient house…to contain the two fire engines adjacent to it[89].

In 1768, the Parish Trustees appointed two able-bodied men to watch and patrol the streets, by 1772 there were six men on regular watch and that number was doubled in 1783. In 1785 saw the introduction of a 'nightly watch' within the said parish.'[90]

It appears not to have been a success because in 1785 a further Act was passed

> 'for making new provisions for the relief of the poor...and watching the streets...'

and the trustees were replaced by Vestrymen. This was a much better system and the first meeting of the newly-constituted body was held at The Greyhound Inn in George Street. Thereafter they met at the Parish Room in the churchyard [91]. New offices were built and the first meeting held at the corner of Vineyard Passage and Paradise Road took place, on 11th April 1791.

The time of the Vestry was largely taken up by the relief of the poor and by provision of a new workhouse on Pest House Common in Queens Road to replace the one in Petersham Road. The old workhouse occupied Rump Hall in Petersham Road (then Lower Road) which the vestry had leased for some 30 years. However, they also had a duty to maintain law and order in the town and one of their first acts in this direction was on 24 April 1786 when they ordered;

> 'that the surveyor give notice to the inhabitants who leave out carriages... in the streets, highways...that if they cause such obstructions in future this Vestry must be obliged to levy the penalties upon them for their neglect'.

In 1787 the beadles were sent to remove the stage of a mountebank and threatened to prosecute him, while Robert Tasker was let off with a caution for allowing his swine to roam the streets[92].

In 1793 the Vestry had to deal with problems caused by an influx of emigrants from France. There was a;

> 'complaint...that some idle and disorderly persons have of late made a practice of assaulting and grossly abusing several of the foreigners resident in the town without cause... it is ordered that the beadles be particularly attentive in the discovery of such persons'

These people would then be taken before the magistrates. The magistrates were appointed by the county, and the two resident in Richmond had a seat on the Vestry. Offenders were taken before one of them sitting in his own home - throughout the latter part of the 18th century there is frequent mention of offenders being taken before Sir William Richardson at his home on Richmond Hill (later known as Doughty House)[93].

In 1794 John Thatcher, apprehended by the Sergeant of the Night for stealing malt from Edward Collins' brewery, was taken before the magistrate and later sentenced at the Guildford Assizes to seven years transportation. Offenders were generally sent by the magistrates to Southwark Jail to await the Assize – which could be held in one of several different towns in Surrey including Reigate, Dorking and Guildford. Sentences included transportation for stealing and hanging for murder. The vestry was empowered to send men to Bridewell Jail for failing to maintain their wives and families and to the House of Correction at Kingston for embezzlement and assault. The vestry did not punish blindly as Edward Brown and George Barley discovered in 1829 when, having expressed their regret at having obstructed and assaulted one of the watchmen and made a public acknowledgement of their misdemeanour by circulating a handbill, all further proceedings against them were suspended[94].

One of the first tasks of the reorganised vestry in 1785 had been to order the erection of a watch house. On 30th December 1793, it adopted Mr. Justice Bonding's system of watching and laid down a rota of 'beats' to be walked by the watchmen[95].

Originally set up in 1805 to patrol the local area up to 16 miles around London, the new 'V' division horse patrols were stationed at North Cheam, Croydon, Sutton, Merton, Wimbledon, Robin Hood Hill, Kingston and Ditton Marsh which were all far beyond the MPD when it was first established.

By 1829 the watch was in its final years. Barnes had been the only part of the present borough to come within the Metropolitan Police area when Wandsworth or 'V' Division was formed in 1830. But Richmond was added to the MPD on 13th January 1840 and the Vestry was relieved of its duty in that direction, other than collecting the Police Levy. They did not completely give up their responsibilities however, and warned the police in February 1840;

> 'to suppress the nuisances which occur on Shrove Tuesday in every year occasioned by a football being kicked through the public streets and thoroughfares of this parish to the great annoyance of all persons desirous of passing quietly through the same and to the detriment of the shopkeepers in Richmond'[96].

In 1849 the Vestry Hall was enlarged and the police (magistrates) court was added. The watch house had been closed in 1841 when the police station, in two converted cottages in Princes Street (the cottages were demolished in 1966 to make way for Waitrose's supermarket in Sheen Road), was opened. At the station in 1851 and residing in one of the cottages (the section house for single police officers) was Constable Michael Madigan from Ireland who lived there with Constables Henry Upton, Edward Bourke, and Merrick Perfse. In the other cottage was Constable John Jukes and his wife Elizabeth. Tragically the

30-year-old Madigan fell into the Thames whilst out on his patrol, got into difficulties and drowned[97].

Richmond Police Station. 1871 – 1912. 35 George Street, Richmond, Surrey

The station was later moved to a new building at 35 George Street. The land had been purchased in 1867 for £3,300 from Mr Vialls and the new large purpose built police station built at a cost of £3,884. 4s 2d (£3884 21p), was opened in 1871. The station ground floor consisted of a charge room, inspector's office, four cells, drying room, mess room, library and smoking room. Outside was Parade shed, ambulance shed and a four stall stable with loft. In the basement there was a clothes room, recreation room, kitchen, lavatory, and bathroom. One married inspector and his family occupied six rooms at a weekly rent of 6/6d (33p). Ten single constables also resided upstairs at the station and they paid 1 shilling (5p) a week rent which was stopped from their pay.

In 1864 a re-organisation of the Metropolitan Police divisions took place with Richmond being authorised as an Inspector station. To assist the inspector were three sergeants and 30 constables split into a day and night shift whose sole responsibility was for the area of Richmond. The Inspector was also responsible for Twickenham and Barnes and he was instructed not to do

Rear aspect of Richmond Police Station with officers by the scullery

station duty as that would be done by one of the sergeants. The inspector's duty was continual patrolling in all weathers and at all times. Inspectors could choose their patrol times as they saw fit which would overlap shift changes.

The rear gate and yard of Richmond Police station.

The Divisional Superintendent often made unannounced visits which could catch the inspector out if he was not careful. There were two horses, one for the Inspector and the other for the mounted sergeant who would patrol the sub-division but not go beyond Richmond[98]. The two pictures show the rear of the police station at Richmond. The picture above shows two officers enjoying the sunshine during their meal break outside what was probably their mess room. It was important for all police stations to have a rear access through which prisoners could be transported on foot or in a prison van in and out of the station out of the view of the public.

There were two inspectors at the station and one was more senior than the other. In 1878 John Pearman became inspector in charge of Richmond police station and he was assisted a year later by Inspector William Jones. In 1891 Inspector Charles Pearn (wt. no 64842) from Cornwall, with only after 11 years service became a Sub Divisional Inspector and took over charge of the station at Richmond. This was still a station on 'V' Division and he was assisted by a strength of three sergeants and 22 constables[99]. Pearn was destined for far higher rank and by 1901 was a Chief Inspector at Stoke Newington. In 1907 had become Divisional Superintendent of 'J' or Bethnal Green Division from where he retired in 1910[100].

The Richmond murder mystery.

In October 2010 a human skull was found in the garden of Sir Richard Attenborough in Park Road, Richmond which was later linked to a most notorious Richmond murder that took place in March 1879[101]. This was the second time police at Richmond station were asked to investigate this alleged murder. The Richmond mystery started when a box had been seen floating in the Thames near Barnes Bridge settled along the foreshore. A man named Wheatley kicked it, only to discover there were bones, flesh and body parts inside. A passing man by the name of Kennison (a distant relative of one of the authors) was asked to mind the box whilst the finder went to the police station to report the matter, but Mr Kennison himself summoned a local constable before the finder returned. Sergeant 5'V' Childs had been summoned by Mr Kennison who verified the contents of the box as being body parts before removing them to the Mortuary and referring to the coroner. There was no clue as to whose remains these were at that time. Other body parts had been hidden in an allotment not far away and in other places[102].

Mrs Thomas the murder victim

However on Saturday 22nd March 1879 a Mr Porter, Mr Church and Mr Hughes, a solicitor, went to Richmond police station and saw Inspector

Pearman to report Mrs Julia Martha Thomas who lived at 2 Vine Cottages, Richmond Surrey, missing. Inspector Pearman and the men went immediately to 2 Vine Cottages and when no one answered the door the Inspector broke in. Mr Porter had unknowingly helped to dispose of stolen property. This was property that had come into the hands of Catherine Webster whom he knew and who had told him an aunt had died and left the property to her[103]. In truth Webster a 29-year-old maid, had been employed by the missing Mrs Thomas and had pushed her down the stairs and strangled her. She then disposed of the body by cutting it up, burning some of it in the grate of the fire and then placing some of the parts in a box which she threw into the Thames off Barnes Bridge[104].

Inspector Creswell Wells (later a famous Superintendent of 'K' and 'A' divisions) gave evidence at Websters Old Bailey trial regarding plans he had drawn for the Treasury Counsel conducting the prosecution. Wells was an expert in this regard. Although he was not shown as an Inspector on 'V' Division he may have been attached to Scotland Yard. Inspector John Dowdell, a Scotland Yard detective had travelled to Wexford in Ireland where Webster was believed to be and had arrested her for murder and theft of property. On the journey back, she made a statement incriminating Mr Church in the murder, an allegation she repeated at Richmond police station in front of Inspectors William Jones and John Pearman the next day. Inspector Pearman had found a carpet bag in the basement of the cottage containing a variety of body parts, a razor and blood-stained clothing. In the fire grate he also discovered a chopper, charred bones and other body materials[105].

Webster the murderess

At the end of her trial at the Old Bailey Webster was found guilty of murder. She pleaded that she was pregnant to escape punishment. A panel of medical experts was convened and they examined Webster, reporting back to the judge that she was not 'with child'. She was sentenced to death and executed, only telling the priest shortly beforehand that it was her and no one else who killed Mrs Thomas[106]. Only in 2010 did the riddle regarding the whereabouts of the victims head get solved.

In 1935 the address changed to 8 Red Lion Street[107]. Richmond council sought permission in 1894 to place a telephone at the station.

The tragic and suspicious death of Sub Divisional Inspector George Henry Dixon

Fifty-year-old Sub Divisional Inspector from Richmond George Henry Dixon, (wt. no. 52444) was found drowned in a few inches of water of the River Thames after going missing on duty in suspicious circumstances at Hampton Court in 1893. Foul play was suspected and an inquiry was launched by detectives. The investigation revealed that the inspector came on duty on 2nd March 1893 arriving at Richmond from Hampton station. He made his customary round of the sub division on his horse, calling at Bedfont, Twickenham and Teddington arriving at Hampton at 10pm, although he soon found that he had lost some disciplinary papers relating to an officer at Twickenham. He remained at the station for a further hour, and on telling Station Sergeant George Smith he would return in an hour – he left the station. He was last seen hurriedly making his way to Hampton Court Palace where he would have had to pass the recreation ground next to the Thames – the place where he was found two days later.

The officer never reached the Palace. Dixon was a keen police officer and prior to his disappearance he had an altercation with navvies working on an adjacent water works. At the inquest held at the Red Lion Public house, one witness who lived near the recreation ground stated that she had 'heard a man's scream in some distress' coming from the recreation ground at 11.15pm which also woke her house keeper. No further cries were heard although heavy footsteps came past the house from the direction of the recreation ground soon afterwards. Dixon was found 2-3 feet from the bank and in 16 inches of water lying face down with his cap over his face and arms embedded in the mud. The inquest concluded that he did not commit suicide[108].

Dixons funeral took place on the 11th March when his coffin was carried by men of the division. A large body of men were in attendance at Hampton cemetery where he was buried. Dixon was born and bred in the East End of London – in St. Georges. In the 1891 census he was resident at 11 Smith Street, Mile End Old Town where he resided with his wife Louisa Ann and five children. Dixon had been an Inspector on 'Y' Division but had come to 'V' Division from 'H' or Whitechapel Division. Dixon had joined the Metropolitan Police in February 1870 He remained only for a very short period in Whitechapel from 1888 until 1891 from where he had been promoted to Sub Divisional Inspector and transferred to Richmond. Dixon was present in the East End of London during the Jack the Ripper murders and may have had more than a suspicion on the likely suspects.

In 1891 there were seven Inspectors attached to Richmond section with Dixons predecessor Sub Divisional Inspector John Pryke in charge of the area. He was supported by Inspectors Richard Feaver and Arthur How who were in charge of the station and together with three sergeants, three acting sergeants and 38 constables[109] dealt with the day to day running of the station and neighbourhood. The Divisional surgeon appointed for Richmond police station was James Adams MD who resided at 3 The Terrace[110].

Constable James Frank Dellar (wt. no. 78885) who was constable 1169 'V'

The photograph left shows Constable James Frank Dellar (wt. no. 78885) who was constable 1169 'V' born Homerton, East London. He joined the Metropolitan Police at Richmond in 1893 but a year later was transferred to 'A' or Westminster Division. However within a year of that he was again transferred but this time to 'S' or Highgate Division but returned to 'V' or Wandsworth Division in March 1901 where he stayed until 1920 serving at Kingston until he retired. Dellar resided with his wife, son and daughter at 106 Elm Road Kingston[111]. By 1911 the family had moved to bigger premises and a further son and daughter had been born in the meantime[112]. The photograph taken on his return to 'V' Division shows him with three medals, the 1897 Queen's Jubilee medal, the 1902 Coronation medal and the 1911 Coronation medal.

In 1895 the old Vestry Hall, which in 1859 had witnessed the enquiry of the Coroner into the poisoning of Isabella Bankes and, on 31st March 1879, the beginning of the prosecution of the arch-murderess Kate Webster, having outlived its usefulness and been replaced for all except its magisterial duties by the new Town Hall in Hill Street (Richmond became a borough in 1890), was pulled down and replaced by a new magistrates court and mortuary which opened in October 1896. This building was greeted with mixed feelings. According to one local paper;

> 'the universal opinion (that) the exterior…is not exactly calculated to inspire respect mingled with admiration, (whilst) the interior is very well adapted to for its purpose. …No money (has been spent on its outside) ornamentation'.

In 1903 it was decided to improve the cell area of the station by providing better drainage and heating for the prisoners who were detained there. These alterations cost £963. 18s (3963 90p).

A well-known police officer on Richmond sub division retired in March 1904 and to mark the occasion there was the ceremonial leaving party. Police Sergeant (wt. no. 63381) Henry Burrows was entertained at the station where Divisional Superintendent Saines presented him with a marble clock and made a speech[113]. These arrangements would have normally taken place on a Wednesday after 2pm when the men had been paid. Afterwards there was a party where the divisional band played music and food and drink was available.

By 1905 it was felt that the single officers residing in the section house should get more privacy, so cubicles were erected around each bed space at a cost of £67[114].

The present home in Red Lion Street was a site acquired by the Council in 1912 for £1,625. The land situated at 8 Red Lion Street, Richmond was purchased from the council in the same year and the police set to work to build

Royal Flying Corps verses Richmond Police station teams raise money for the British Sportsman's Ambulance Fund

a station, section house and two sets of married quarters[115]. The picture above is an historic one and shows the Royal Flying Corps (RFC) and Richmond Police football teams in November 1916 who played a game in aid of the

British Sportsman's Ambulance Fund. The RFC won 6-1. The game was played in Old Deer Park, Richmond at the back of the police station in the recreation ground and was kicked off by the Solicitor General Sir George Cave. The event was also attended by many spectators and dignitaries.

Robert Ward, one-time contender for a seat on Richmond Council, asked

> 'Who are the people to be hanged...for inflicting on Richmond that disgraceful building of the new Court House'.

This building was replaced by the new court house opened in Parkshot, on the site previously occupied by Parkshot Rooms and the swimming baths, in 1975[116]. In 1919 the sub divisional station of Richmond (VR) was a station on

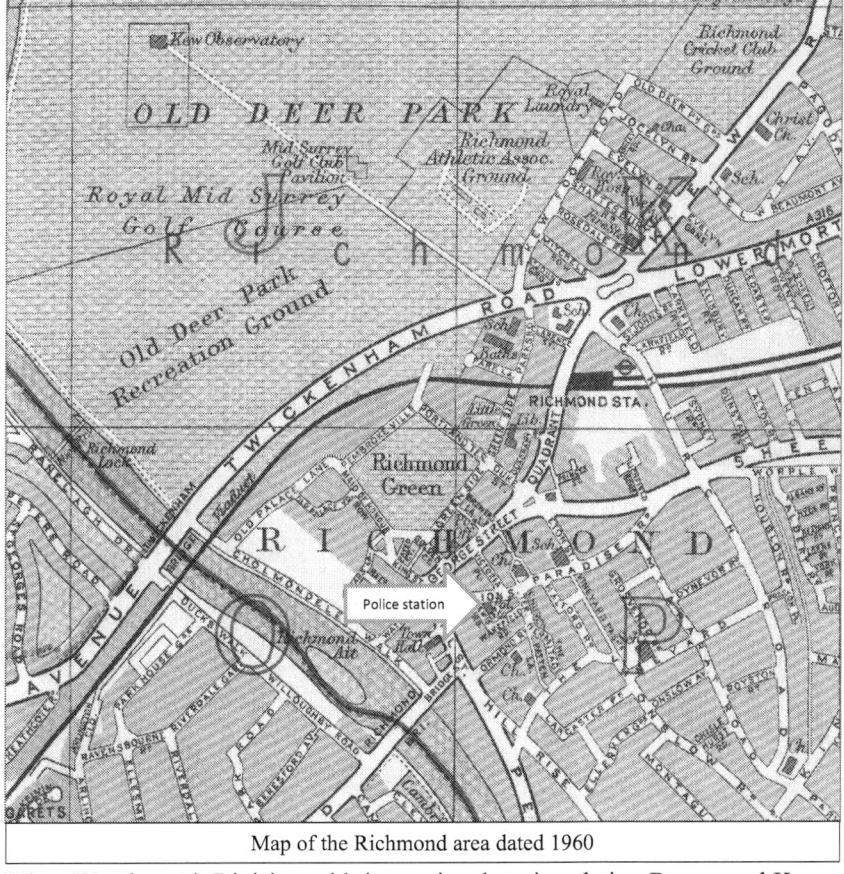

Map of the Richmond area dated 1960

'V' or Wandsworth Division with its sectional stations being Barnes and Kew.

Inspectors were still in charge of the station. In 1924 the old police station at 35 George Street, Richmond was sold to Express Dairies for £12,000[117].

Kew closed as a police station in 1932 although the area was still policed from Richmond. Between 1955 and 1960 Superintendent Rawlings was in charge of the sub-division. His place was taken by Superintendent Mulchay MM.

Richmond Police Station. 1912 – present day. 8 Red Lion Street, Richmond, Surrey.

In 1965 Richmond became a sub-division on 'T' Division as police divisions started to match the boundaries of local authorities. The call sign for the station altered to (TR). Within 'T' Division were the London Boroughs of Richmond upon Thames, Hounslow and the Urban Districts of Staines and Sunbury on Thames. The divisional headquarters changed to Hounslow situated at 5 Montague Road, Hounslow. By 1969 Superintendent R. H. Anning was in charge of the station and his deputy was Chief Inspector F. J. Attwood[118]. The sub-division remained on 'T' Division throughout the 1980s.

In 1989 the Richmond and Twickenham Police divisions amalgamated to form the Richmond upon Thames division. A review of police station opening times saw the station open Mondays to Fridays from 9am until 5pm[119]. In the meantime Richmond police station still remained in the ownership of the Metropolitan police however by 2011 its opening times were extended to 8am until 8pm.

In 2012 a new police office opened at Sovereign Gate, 18-20 Kew Road Richmond Surrey TW9 2NA. The front counter at a new police base – Sovereign Gate – officially opened to the public on Wednesday 8th February 2012 and replaced the front counter at Richmond Police Station.

To reflect the needs of the public, Sovereign Gate's front counter operates from 8am to 8pm every day. Members of the public who need to report crimes outside of these hours were encouraged to go to Twickenham Police Station, open 24 hours a day, or by calling 101 for non-emergencies and 999 for emergencies.

Sovereign Gate is also the new base for South Richmond Safer Neighbourhoods Team (SNT) and Kew SNT, both formerly situated at Richmond Police Station. Additionally, it is a Regional Learning Centre, where officers from the borough and other areas of south west London will receive training in matters such as emergency life support.

Richmond Police Station continues to operate as a base for some of the borough's other police departments, including CID.

The then Borough Commander, Chief Superintendent Clive Chalk, said:

> 'I am pleased to announce the opening of Sovereign Gate's front counter which, with its external lift, split-level counters and hearing loops, is much more modern and accessible to the public than Richmond Police Station was'[120].

Instead of going to Richmond Police Station, anyone who needs help or who wants to report a crime in person should now go to Sovereign Gate which, being a two minute walk from Richmond British Rail and London Underground Station, should prove more convenient to get to.

It was felt that Sovereign Gate would prove to be a better base for Kew and South Richmond Safer Neighbourhoods Teams. It was designed to bring Kew SNT closer to their ward and the front yard area – which Richmond Police Station lacked, and is an ideal place for South Richmond SNT to hold crime prevention and awareness events for residents[121].

Teddington Police station

In 1873 at station was situated at Teddington and was designated a police station on 'T' or Kensington division and Sergeant Edward Wilkins was in charge[122]. Teddington remained a sergeant station until the late 1870s when an

Teddington Police Station. 1881 – 1998. Church Road, Teddington. Surrey

Inspector was placed in charge.

A new larger station at Church Road, Teddington was built in 1881 and with the promotion of more sergeants to inspector rank, every station on 'T' or Kensington Division including Teddington became an Inspector station[123]. Upstairs was accommodation for the family of the inspector in charge of the station. The photograph below shows the rear of the station including a garden where the inspector and his family were allowed to grow their own vegetables etc. Another photograph at left shows another aspect of the station which included a rounded elevated wall to the left of the station which was put in place to afford protection to the occupants either from Fenian bomb attacks or provide additional security.

Teddington Police station rear aspect taken in about 1908

In 1894 Teddington, together with Sunbury and Twickenham were sectional stations to Hampton sub-division[124].

In 1924 Teddington Police Station was shown as a station on 'T' or Hammersmith Division. It was located at 52 Church Road, Teddington at the junction of Luther Road, and the freehold to the site had been purchased in 1880. The station had been built with two sets of married quarters but a re-allocation of space meant that only one set was acceptable[125].

The call sign of the station was (TT) from 1960 until at least the mid 1980s.

A police call telephone Box T28 without air raid warning siren was erected on 20th July 1936 at the junction with Kingston Road (west side) 30 yards south of Bushey Park Road, Teddington. It was removed in March 1970[126].

Teddington's protective wall against bombs

The photograph below shows a retirement of two police officers from Teddington police station. Each have been awarded two expensive ornate mantle clocks which would have been purchased from contributions made by the officers and men of the sub division. The Sub-Divisional Inspector for Hampton John Kempin whose sub-divisional station was Teddington presided over the retirement arrangements. Here he is seen with is flat cap standing behind the clock in the centre of the picture behind the two police officers who were retiring. Arrangements would have included the taking of this ceremonial photograph which would have been presented to the officers later, together with the station band who would have played music. In the canteen area food would have been prepared by the wives and daughters of the men to mark the

Teddington Police station retirement celebrations circa 1910

occasion with the likelihood beer would have been consumed.

In 1932 Teddington became a sectional station to Twickenham together with a down-graded Hampton which also lost its sub-divisional status[127]. After WW2 the headquarters of 'T' Division became Ealing, and Teddington (TT) remained under the supervision of Superintendent A. R. Thomas[128].

A site had been purchased in 1950 at Park Road and Park Lane on which there was an old building called Teddington Lodge which was demolished to make way for the new police station[129].

A new modern police station at 18 Park Road, Teddington TW11 0AQ was built at Teddington and in 1998 was situated on 5 Area. This was a fully

Teddington Police Station. 1998 – present day. 18 Park Road, Teddington TW11 0AQ

operational station with charging facilities under the Police and Criminal Evidence Act. No longer was Teddington and station on 'T' Division but was now located within the new Borough Occupational Command Unit of Richmond on Thames. It was now sub divisional-station to Twickenham (the Borough Headquarters) where Borough Commander Chief Superintendent J. Hurst was in charge[130].

In 2000 Teddington was subject of a review of police station opening times which were restricted to Monday to Friday 9am until 5pm[131]. By 2012 the opening hours of the station had been varied to 10am – 5pm Monday to Friday and 11am – 2pm on Saturdays[132].

Twickenham Police station

Land and a property in Twickenham was rented from Miss Ward of Disraeli Road, Ealing by the Receiver in 1854 on a ground rent of £17 per annum. The rental agreement was for 94½ years with the rates, taxes, insurance and repairs being borne by the Receiver.

In 1858 a purpose-built police station was built on the site which cost

Twickenham Police Station. 1858 – 1947 (demolished and rebuilt) 41 (previously 45) London Road, Twickenham, Surrey

£1230.00. The station consisted of a ground floor with an Inspector's office, three cells, urinal, coal cellars, a library, mess room, kitchen, lavatory and boot room. Upstairs on the first floor was a section house which consisted of single room in which five single constables lived. They paid a weekly rent of 1 shilling (5p) up until at least 1911 which was deducted from their pay.

Also residing in four rooms upstairs originally was the station sergeant and his family however later his place was taken by the inspector and his family. The inspector paid 4 shillings (20p) a week for these rooms which also included a scullery[133].

Rear aspect to the station circa 1908

In 1864 Twickenham police station was originally situated at 45 London Road, Twickenham, but this was later changed to no. 41 and shown as a station on 'V' or Wandsworth Division sectional station together with Barnes police station to Richmond. The Inspector at Richmond was instructed not to do station duty but his purpose was to patrol for supervisory purposes.

Contractors were paid to re-paint the outside of the station in 1869 and in 1872 the inside of the station was white-washed[134].

Twickenham had two sergeants, one for day duty and the other for night duty, and 14 constables. There were four day beats and nine night beats covered by the constables[135]. The extra constable was the reserve and required to a variety of extra jobs like covering for a constable who had made an arrest.

The Commissioner suggested that when the sergeants were on patrol then the station could be closed. Twickenham had facilities for charging prisoners and holding them in cells[136]. In 1873 Twickenham was a station of 'T' or Kensington Division and a sergeant was designated as in charge[137].

Parade shed and station year circa 1908

The freehold to the property was purchased in 1902 by the police for £550[138].

Twickenham Police station rear yard circa 1908

Twickenham Police station was now situated at 41 London Road, Twickenham and included a section house for single police officers although this accommodation was converted and given up in favour of one set of married quarters in 1924[139].

In 1920 the freehold to a site at 60 – 88 Grosvenor Road, Twickenham, at the rear of the old police station, was purchased by the Receiver. The site also fronted onto the High Street with the purchase of 41-45 (odd no's) London Road, Twickenham in 1929. The police station is shown in London Road, Twickenham just opposite Katherine Road with rear access into the yard at the back through Grosvenor Road with the purchase also of Caroline Cottages[140].

In 1936 the Metropolitan Police introduced police boxes on to 'T' Division and box T32 was erected on the 20th July. The police call box was situated at the Green (Staines Road), south side, 10 yards west of Knowle Road, Twickenham. The box was removed in March 1970[141]. In 1939 an air raid warning dedicated telephone was installed (and later removed when no longer needed) in the station the cost being borne by Twickenham Borough council[142].

Twickenham Police Station 1947 – present day. 41 London Road Twickenham TW1 3SY

In 1965 Twickenham (TW) was a sub divisional station with Superintendent Brough in charge[143].

Two officers from Twickenham who lost their lives whilst on duty were Constable Matthew John Allen, who died in a crash in Twickenham, while responding to an emergency call in 1992 and Constable Kulwant Singh Sidhu, who was killed when he fell through a glass skylight pursuing suspects across a roof in Twickenham in 1999[144]. It was this last case that brought the Commissioner at the time Sir John Stevens to face trial at the Old Bailey on charges relating to health and safety. In a prosecution considered by many to be at best pedantic, but a reflection of the Health and Safety Executives policies, the Commissioner was acquitted. Later the law was changed to remove a Chief Officers' personal liability for health and safety law infringements.

In 2000, Twickenham became the subject of a review by the Metropolitan Police Authority and was designated a station to remain open 24 hours a day. Also it was a charging station within the terms of the Police and Criminal Evidence Act where officers could detain, process and charge prisoners for court[145].

The Metropolitan and City Police Orphanage, Strawberry Hill Twickenham.

Lt. Col. Sir Edmund Y.W. Henderson, K.C.B., Commissioner of Police of the Metropolis from 1869 to 1886, was widely known as the founding father of the charity we know today as the Metropolitan and City Police Orphans Fund. Established in 1870, the fund can be safely attributed to his reputed kindness, sympathy and understanding. After all, Henderson himself knew the conditions of service of the 8,800 constables and sergeants serving in London in 1870. He would appreciate, too, that if a Constable died from injuries received in the course of duty, his widow received an annuity of £15 plus £2.10s.0d (£2.50p) for each child and that in any other case she received a gratuity of £31 and nothing else. He also knew that any police accommodation would need to be vacated, often with indecent haste, rendering the situation even more desperate[146].

This was not the first home which catered for the dependent children of deceased policemen as unofficial premises existed at the Home for Destitute Orphans of Police which had been established at Brighton. Privately owned, it relied on subscriptions from both inside and outside the Police Service. By 1870, of the 28 children accommodated in the Home, 17 were from the London area[147].

The Metropolitan Police Orphanage was opened in October 1870 with 20 children however by 1871 it was renamed to include the City of London Police and granted Royal Patronage the same year[148].

Metropolitan and City Police Orphanage, Twickenham.   The Main Entrance.

Its original home was Fortescue House, London Road, Twickenham (long since demolished) the former home of Earl Fortescue. Admission was confined to children orphaned after 1st January, 1870 and was limited to two from each family. However the number of orphaned children rose rapidly, and to cater for these ever-increasing numbers, Bath House, London Road, (opposite Fortescue House and since demolished) was taken on lease to accommodate 40 of the younger children. Yet this was not enough. Within three years there were 115

Metropolitan and City Police Orphanage, Twickenham.   Group of the Children.

orphans eligible for accommodation. In 1874 Wellesley House, Hampton Road, Twickenham, was also purchased. With accommodation for at least 200 children, later extended to house a further 60, Wellesley House was occupied on 25th September, 1874 where the Orphanage was to remain for the next 63 years[149].

During the 67 years of its existence 2,807 boys and girls passed through the Institution as it became known under the rules.

By 1878, however, there were 1,000 orphaned children, only 200 of who could be given Orphanage accommodation. It was clear the Institution could not fulfil its purpose and a new dimension was necessary. Thus, in 1883 a compassionate allowance at the rate of £2 12s.0d (£2.60p) per child per annum became payable for children for whom there was no accommodation, and between that year and 31st December 1969 £1,369,320 had been paid to 5,243 widows in respect of 10,728 orphaned children. So in the course of 100 years, benefit in kind or in cash has been bestowed on 13,535 children. But this new dimension demanded increased income. Raising money for the charity was always difficult because where do you draw the line between many destitute police families who are deserving of relief from poverty especially when the circumstances of their situation were not their fault[150].

A boat race on the Thames in 1871 from Putney Bridge to Barnes Bridge between crews from 'T' and 'TA' Divisions and a collection on the towpath which yielded £4 1s.7d £4.08p) is typical of several Herculean fund raising efforts. The Police Minstrels, who raised over £200,000 before being disbanded in 1933, were by far the biggest benefactors. But periods of recurring adversity added aggravations. Six hundred-and-nine children were orphaned in the two world wars, 283 in the first and 326 in the second and a further 170 through the influenza epidemic of 1919. In 1919, 1,275 children received benefit the highest annual total in the history of the charity[151].

In 1874 the Baroness Burdett Coutts made an interest-free loan of £3,000 to build a new wing to house 60 additional children. It was opened in 1882 by H.R.H. the Prince of Wales, later King Edward VII, and named the Burdett

Metropolitan and City Police Orphanage, Twickenham. The Dining Hall.

Coutts Wing.

The late Henry Whiting, founder of the Police Relief Fund, afterwards the Bow Street Reward Fund and the Metropolitan and City Police Relief Fund gave generously during his lifetime. In his death in 1895 his widow and daughter erected a striking clock to his memory in the Orphanage overlooking the grounds. It still survives, as does a wall-plaque beneath, commemorating the occasion[152]. The late Alexander Mann of Richmond, Surrey, who died in 1917, bequeathed the residue of his estate to the Orphanage. His memory is permanently enshrined in the Alexander Mann Bequest which appears in the annual balance sheet, as does the Twells Memorial Fund founded in 1880 by the late Mrs G. Twells of Enfield with a donation of £500 in memory of her

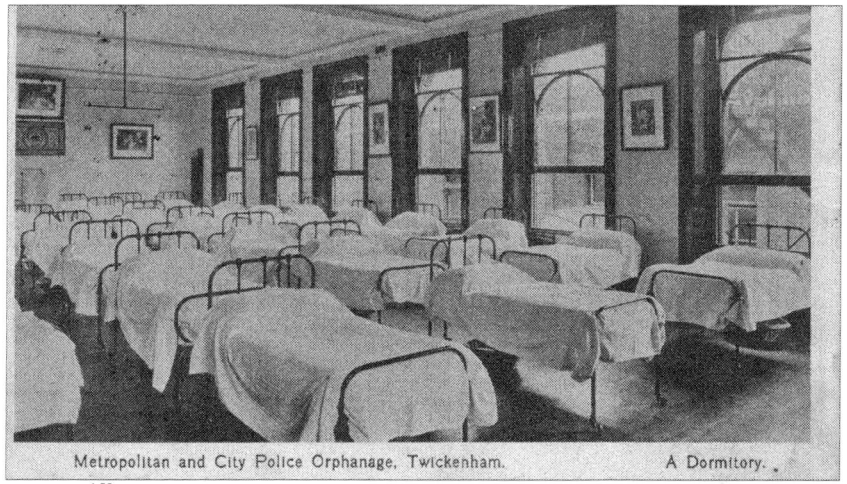

Metropolitan and City Police Orphanage, Twickenham. A Dormitory.

husband[153].

The Orphanage's War Memorial Hospital that was built in the grounds of the Orphanage on subscriptions from members of the two Forces in memory of 387 colleagues who gave their lives in the First World War, still exists and functions as a hospital. It was opened in 1923 by H.R.H. the Prince of Wales, subsequently the Duke of Windsor[154]. The introduction of the 1921 Police Pensions Act probably hastened the closure of the Orphange as it gave the widow of a constable and sergeant who had completed at least five year's service an annual pension and an allowance per child to stay at home. The numbers dwindled and following a vote of the trustees the Orphange shut in July 1937. On closure the Fund was set up and today it is a registered charity.

Since that time there have been small increases whenever possible, and, following a further increase in the minimum rate of police subscriptions from three pence to five pence weekly from January 1963, the allowance has gradually been increased to £168 per child per annum, the amount payable at 31st December, 1969. During 1969 a total of 357 children received benefit and at 1st January, 1970, 303 children were in receipt of monthly allowances[155].

The charity supports the children of serving or former police officers from the Metropolitan and City Police who contributed to the fund and are now either deceased or retired on pension and are so incapacitated that they are unable to contribute materially to the family upkeep. Applicants can apply to the fund for compassionate allowance etc. and each case is considered on merit by the management board. (If you would like to donate please see how to do this at http://www.met-cityorphans.org.uk/support.phpse)

Imber Court   By Chris Forester

Metropolitan Police Orders announced the appointment of Lt. Colonel Percy Robert Laurie, DSO to the post of Deputy Assistant Commissioner. His duties were stated;

> to 'act generally as assistant to the Assistant Commissioner of 'A' Department in the work of supervision of the Metropolitan Police Administration and to take direct charge of the Mounted Branch of the force '[156].

The appointment of an officer of this rank to control and direct the Mounted Police was to transform the duties and operations of the Branch and consolidate its role as a principal and specialised agency to deal with public order, thus ensuring its survival to the present day. Laurie's remit was also to help raise the morale of the force as there had been strikes by the workforce in 1918 and 1919. The then 39 years old Percy Laurie (later Sir Percy Laurie) was eminently qualified to undertake the all the tasks required of him and had been strongly recommended to the Home Office for the post by no less a personage than Brigadier General Sir William Horwood, his most recent military Commanding officer and soon to be the incumbent Commissioner.

An early mounted police officer

Percy Laurie's most recent military posting had been as Provost Marshal in Germany and responsible for policing a now destroyed and bankrupt city. His experiences were to aid him in his new post. As a long serving cavalryman in the prestigious Royal Scots Greys Regiment he would be expert in organising a large body of men such as the Mounted Branch. This part of the police had for some years been in decline, both men and horses were all in need of retraining and in many cases retirement! After making several much needed changes to routine stable and operational patrol work he turned his attention to training, both of horses (remounts) and men. Until 1887 remounts and recruits to the Mounted Branch had been trained 'On the job' from Rochester Row Police Stables; This training commitment had impeded the day to day operational work of the Branch and under the auspices of an earlier innovator, Captain George H. Dean the Adam & Eve Mews site at Kensington High Street had been opened. This location had been opened to enable a reserve section to be created to concentrate on just training and dealing with sick or injured horses. By 1919 Adam & Eve Mews had become untenable due to increasing traffic on the surrounding roads and a lack of turn out facilities for the sick horses.

The choice of Imber Court as the new training centre may have been suggested by Major W. H. Smith who had run the Munitions and Inventions Department (MID) on this site from 1915 to 1919. The MID had been a secret testing ground for many weird and wonderful inventions, one of which was an embryo helicopter. At the cessation of hostilities the shrewd and far sighted Major had purchased the whole estate from the owner Lord Michaelham. The old manor house at Imber Court had now fallen down and after its demolition Smith created a new trading and housing estate and sold the residue –some 38 acres to the Metropolitan Police in 1920 as a mounted training establishment, headquarters and later in 1929 an MPAA Sports ground.

From 1919 Imber Court was purpose built as a Mounted Branch training

The opening of the Clubhouse at Imber Court in June 1929

establishment for both horses and men. It was also to become the headquarters of the Mounted Branch. Utilising some existing buildings a headquarters building, stabling, garaging, four sets of married quarters, a section house, an entrance lodge, a pavilion and grounds man's cottage were constructed or renovated[157]. The police architect G. Mackenzie Trench designed the Imber Court Sports Club.

Laurie spared no expense in equipping the site with all the latest innovative aids. An electric grooming machine (based on a Hoover) was purchased and found to

Final rehearsal at Imber Court of the combined Mounted Branch and Traffic patrol display for the international Horse show

be of limited use. Proper saddle soap was brought in along with redesigned saddles and the adoption of the 'Universal Reversible Port Mouthpiece' bit. This bit was that standard military bit designed to fit virtually any animal that could be ridden or harnessed, from Llamas to Camels, Mules and Horses. The stables themselves were built of Major Smith's invention, The Triangular Brick'. The brick was based on moulding triangular bricks on site and the whole stable was built with them. Whilst extremely strong in construction as many builders will testify after trying to drill into them their basic flaw was that they were hollow and damp could track right up to the roof. Smith's company was named 'TRIANCO' and after the failure of the Triangular Brick it went on to pioneer central heating boilers. The Mounted Branch had been run down during the war as most of its own horses had been requisitioned for the war effort and there was now a dire need to replenish the stock. Laurie wasted no time in purchasing 43 horses from the army which were surplus to requirements.

He personally selected the horses himself making journeys to studs in Yorkshire to view and make purchases[158].

During the 1930s Colonel Laurie again took advantage of the opportunity to purchase what were known as the Glebe lands or 40 acres for horse gallops. This area too changed when the new river was pushed through in 1980 to 1983.

As the years passed the training regime became routine, much of which endures to this day. From 1971 women were introduced to the Mounted Branch and during the mid 1980s civilian trainers and grooms were to supplant the serving remount training officers at Imber Court. Apart from the recruit instructors and supervisory staff the Mounted Training Establishment is now virtually completely civilianised.

In 1923 Laurie was to create another institution that lasted until the 1990s; that of the annual horse show at Imber Court. This spectacle was to be attended by royalty downwards. The cream of society would attend and participate in Coaching and Jumping events whilst police forces from all over Great Britain would compete for a variety of cups donated by scions of industry. This show was financed and arranged by the shrewd Colonel Laurie and his myriad of society contacts. Seating and tentage was loaned free by a local tent manufacturer, flowers would be borrowed from the Royal Parks Nurseries. The Catering and bars would be done by various local people and ground and gate staffing by officers and their families who 'Volunteered'. Stabling for the many horses and men would be within the Imber Court site or at nearby Hampton Court stables. These last were literally unchanged from Henry VIII days. This show whilst never making a great profit always broke even. The event acted a showpiece for the Metropolitan Police Service and enabled its Commissioner to invite many influential guests. For the men of the Branch it also acted as a bonding exercise with many advantages for training horses and officers in the skills required on the street.

But what of the Sports and Social Club? After the General Strike in 1926 the Daily Mail set up the Police Fund in thanks for the work done by the Police in keeping London going during the Strike.

This fund was to finance the building of the Clubhouse designed by Mackenzie Trench the Police architect. The original MPAA clubhouse had been established in the 'Eagle Hut' in Trafalgar Square. This had been built as a social centre for Canadian troops during the first war. At the end the MPAA had taken it over as their office. The new Clubhouse had been built and was opened on 11th June 1929 when the MPAA held the opening ceremony which was attended by Percy Laurie who with his many contacts managed to get Prince George (later King George VI) as guest of honour.

The Clubhouse in 2013 at Imber Court originally designed by G. Mackenzie Trench

Originally it was possible to stay overnight in the clubhouse and over the next few years the Clubhouse would be extended and improved. In the 1970s major improvements took place and a new frontage was put on the old lodge house and entrance were demolished with the car park now fully covered. More upgrading took place in 1998 when the interior of the Club was gutted and enhanced with new bars and meeting rooms.

In 2000 Esher, Thames Ditton and Molesey became part of the Surrey Police area and Imber Court became isolated from the MPD. Thirteen years on and in spite of the attentions of avaricious developers it is still part of the Metropolitan Police.

---

[1] http://www.met.police.uk/mountedbranch/history.htm accessed on 22nd February 2012
[2] MEPO2/25
[3] MEPO 2/76
[4] Kellys Directory 1841
[5] Brown, B. (1985) 'When Victor Bowed out'. Police Review 29th October.
[6] Ibid
[7] Ibid
[8] http://library.wellcome.ac.uk/assets/wtl039768.pdf accessed on 31st January 2012
[9] http://library.wellcome.ac.uk/assets/wtl039768.pdf accessed on 31st January 2012
[10] Metropolitan Police Special Police Orders 1864
[11] The Police Review and Parade gossip 24th July 1896
[12] The Police Review and Parade Gossip August 19th and December 23rd 1898
[13] Surveyors Records ESB
[14] Metropolitan Police Surveyors Records 1924
[15] Metropolitan Police Surveyors Registers ESB
[16] Metropolitan Police Surveyors Records 1924
[17] http://www.goddardmanton.com/projects/selected_projects.php?title=Barnes%20Police%20Station accessed on 16th February 2012
[18] http://www.met.police.uk/scd/specialist_units/child_abuse_investigation_teams.htm accessed on 16.2.2012
[19] http://www.british-history.ac.uk accessed on 2nd March 2012
[20] Brown, B. (1999) Policing Old Esher ESB
[21] Ct. R. of Cobham.

[22] 1851 – 1951 A short Centenary History of the Surrey Constabulary, Biddles Guildford.
[23] http://blog.old-and-bold.info//?s=cobham accessed on 2nd March 2012
[24] ibid
[25] Site Locations for Metropolitan Police Telephone boxes and telephone posts for 'V' Division. ESB, London
[26] Kirchners Guide 1931
[27] Police and Constabulary Almanac 1937
[28] Police and Constabulary Almanac 1955
[29] Police and Constabulary Almanac 1960
[30] The Job, 1st January 1971
[31] ibid
[32] ibid
[33] ibid
[34] ibid
[35] Police and Constabulary Almanac 1998
[36] Metropolitan Police Stations 1965
[37] http://www.elmbridgeguardian.co.uk/news accessed on 2nd March 2012
[38] Metropolitan Police Surveyors records 1912
[39] Metropolitan Police Surveyors Registers ESB
[40] Kellys directory for Surrey 1855
[41] Metropolitan Police Surveyors Records ESB London
[42] Kellys Directory 1891
[43] Metropolitan Police Surveyors Records 1924
[44] Site Locations for Metropolitan Police Telephone boxes and telephone posts for 'V' Division. ESB, London
[45] ibid
[46] The Metropolitan Police Roll of Honour www.policememorial.org.uk accessed on 12th March 2002
[47] Metropolitan Police Surveyors Records 1924
[48] Metropolitan Police Surveyors Records 1924
[49] Site Locations for Metropolitan Police Telephone boxes and telephone posts for V Division. ESB, London
[50] Metropolitan Police Authority (2000) Police Station opening hours Committee; MPA Reports 9th November
[51] Brown, B. (1999) Policing Old Esher ESB
[52] ibid
[53] ibid
[54] Ibid p4
[55] Ibid
[56] Metropolitan Police Orders dated 14th March 1947
[57] Brown, B. (1999) Policing Old Esher ESB
[58] ibid
[59] Metropolitan Police Orders dated 4th December 1967
[60] Metropolitan Police Orders dated 1st February 1980
[61] Metropolitan Police Authority (2000) Police Station opening hours Committee; MPA Reports 9th November
[62] Metropolitan Police Surveyors Registers ESB London
[63] Metropolitan Police Orders dated 11th January 1864
[64] Metropolitan Police Orders dated 28th October 1865
[65] Metropolitan Police Orders dated 18th July 1890
[66] Metropolitan Police Surveyors Registers ESB London
[67] ibid
[68] http://www.stjames-hamptonhill.org.uk/History/B&G/1ChFace.htm accessed on16th February 2012
[69] http://www.stjames-hamptonhill.org.uk/History/B&G/1ChFace.htm accessed on 16th February 2012
[70] Kellys Directory 1867
[71] Census records 1881
[72] Census Records of Death
[73] Police Review and Parade Gossip 27th February 1903
[74] Metropolitan Police Orders dated 16th October 1905
[75] Census records 1911

[76] Kellys directory 1912
[77] Metropolitan Police Orders dated 6th August 1964
[78] Districts and Divisions 1965
[79] Metropolitan Police Orders dated 29th October 1968
[80] http://www.flickr.com/photos/61129021@N06/8250957130/ accessed on26th October 2013
[81] Metropolitan Police Surveyors Records 1924
[82] Kellys Directory 1914
[83] Site Locations for Metropolitan Police Telephone boxes and telephone posts for 'V' Division. ESB, London
[84] ibid
[85] http://www.richmond.gov.uk/home/leisure_and_culture/local_history_and_heritage/local_studies_collection/local_history_notes/law_and_order_in_richmond.htm accessed on 31st January 2012
[86] ibid
[87] http://www.richmond.gov.uk/local_history_and_heritage/law_and_order_in_richmond.htm accessed on 31st January 2012
[88] ibid
[89] ibid
[90] ibid
[91] ibid
[92] ibid
[93] ibid
[94] ibid
[95] ibid
[96] ibid
[97] Metropolitan Police Roll of Honour www.policememorial.org.uk accessed on 12th March 02
[98] Metropolitan Police Special Police Orders 1864
[99] Kellys Directory 1891
[100] Kellys Directory 1907 and Census records 1901
[101] http://www.thisislocallondon.co.uk/news/8484943.Murder_mystery/ accessed on 14th February 2012
[102] www.oldbaileyonline.org/browse.jsp?id=t18790630-653&div=t18790630-653&terms accessed on 14th February 2012
[103] www.oldbaileyonline.org/browse.jsp?id=t18790630-653&div=t18790630-653&terms accessed on 14th February 2012
[104] http://www.thisislocallondon.co.uk/news/8484943.Murder_mystery/ accessed on 14th February 2012
[105] www.oldbaileyonline.org/browse.jsp?id=t18790630-653&div=t18790630-653&terms accessed on 14th February 2012
[106] http://www.thisislocallondon.co.uk/news/8484943.Murder_mystery/ accessed on 14th February 2012
[107] Metropolitan Police Surveyors Records 1924
[108] The Police Review and Parade Gossip 9th October 1893
[109] Kellys Directory 1891
[110] ibid
[111] Census records 1901
[112] Census records 1911
[113] The Police Review and Parade Gossip 6th May 1904
[114] Metropolitan Police Surveyors Records ESB London.
[115] Metropolitan Police Surveyors Records 1924
[116] http://www.richmond.gov.uk/local_history_and_heritage/law_and_order_in_richmond.htm accessed on 31st January 2012
[117] Metropolitan Police Surveyors Records 1924
[118] Police and Constabulary Almanac 1969
[119] Metropolitan Police Authority (2000) Police Station opening hours Committee; MPA Reports 9th November
119 http://content.met.police.uk/News/Sovereign-Gates-Front-Counter-Officially-Opens/1400006512411/1257246745756 accessed on 9th December 2012
[121] ibid
[122] Kellys directory 1873
[123] Kellys Directory 1881
[124] Kellys Directory 1894
[125] Metropolitan Police Surveyors Records 1924

[126] Site Locations for Metropolitan Police Telephone boxes and telephone posts for V Division. ESB, London
[127] Kellys Directory 1932 p744
[128] The Police and Constabulary Almanac 1946 p93
[129] http://www.twickenham-museum.org.uk/tour_detail.asp?TourID=60 accessed on 30.3.12
[130] Police and Constabulary Almanac 1998
[131] Metropolitan Police Authority (2000) Police Station opening hours Committee; MPA Reports 9th November
[132] http://www.totallyrichmond.co.uk/RichmondUponThames.html accessed on 30th March 2012
[133] Metropolitan Police Surveyors registers ESB London
[134] ibid
[135] Metropolitan Police Special Police Orders 1864
[136] Metropolitan Police Special Police Orders 1864
[137] Metropolitan Police General Orders 1873
[138] Metropolitan Police Surveyors Registers ESB, London.
[139] Metropolitan Police Surveyors records 1924
[140] The Police List 1947
[141] Site Locations for Metropolitan Police Telephone boxes and telephone posts for 'V' Division. ESB, London
[142] Metropolitan Police Surveyors registers ESB, London.
[143] Metropolitan Police Stations 1965
[144] Metropolitan Police Roll of Honour www.policememorial.org.uk accessed on 12th March 2012
[145] Metropolitan Police Authority (2000) Police Station opening hours Committee; MPA Reports 9th November
[146] http://www.met-cityorphans.org.uk/history/index3.php accessed on 30th March 2012
[147] ibid
[148] ibid
[149] ibid
[150] ibid
[151] ibid
[152] ibid
[153] ibid
[154] ibid
[155] http://www.met-cityorphans.org.uk/history/index6.php accessed on 6th November 2013
[156] Metropolitan Police Orders dated 17th February 1919
[157] Metropolitan Police property Schedule 1924
[158] Fido, M. and Skinner, K. (1999) The Official History of Scotland yard. Virgin Books London. P170-174

Metropolitan Police Officers mentioned in the Book				
NAME	RANK	DATE	STATION	LONDON BOROUGH
ABBIS George Sir	Assistant Commissioner	1966	Peel House (Training)	City of Westminster
ABBIS George Sir	Chief Constable	1932	Feltham	Hounslow
ACOTT Bob	Detective Chief Inspector	1959	Chelsea	Kensington & Chelsea
ADAMS	Constable	1919	Sunbury	Hillingdon
ADAMS C.	Superintendent	1933	Ealing	Ealing
Adams Thomas	Constable	1907	New Malden	Kingston
ALDERTON	MSC Sub Inspector	1917	Finchley	Barnet
ALDRIDGE William	Inspector	1891	Ditton	Richmond
ALLEN Mary	Constable	1914	Harlesden	Brent
ALLEN Matthew John	Constable	1992	Twickenham	Richmond
ALLINSON Tom	Station Sergeant	1914	Bushey	Barnet
ANDERSON Charles	Constable	1911	Brentford	Hounslow
ANDREWS Henry	Sub-Divisional Inspector	1911	Ealing	Ealing
ANDREWS William	Constable	1871	Bedfont	Hillingdon
ANNING Raymond. H.	Superintendent	1969	Richmond	Richmond
ANNIS Arthur	Superintendent	1933	Golders Green	Barnet
ARCHER	Constable	1919	Sunbury	Hillingdon
ARMSTRONG Joseph	Inspector	1861	Kingston	Kingston
ARNETT John	Inspector	1881	Norwood Green	Ealing
ARNOLD	Sergeant	1873	Harrow	Harrow
ARTHURTON William	Constable	1911	Barnet	Barnet
ASHWELL H.	Inspector	1896	Hammersmith	Hammersmith & Fulham
ATKINS Fred	Constable	1881	Kingston	Kingston
ATTER William	Sergeant	1861	Staines	Hillingdon
ATTWOOD F.J.	Chief Inspector	1969	Richmond	Richmond
AXLETON	Constable	1919	Sunbury	Hillingdon
AYRE John	Sergeant	1861	Kingston	Kingston
BACCHUS Ernest	Superintendent	1919	Fulham	Hammersmith & Fulham
BAILEY Bill	Sergeant	1968	Hendon	Barnet
BAILEY George	Inspector	1851	Staines	Hillingdon
BAKER	Constable	1919	Sunbury	Hillingdon
BAKER William	Station Sergeant	1912	South Mimms	Barnet
BALDOCK	Inspector	1893	Westminster	City of Westminster
BALDRY Jim	Constable	1947	Hendon	Barnet
BALM L.R.	Chief Superintendent	1966	Golders Green	Barnet
BAMSEY William	Inspector	1911	North Fulham	Hammersmith & Fulham

Name	Rank	Year	Location	Borough
BARBER	Constable	1903	Pinner	Harrow
BARNARD	Station Sergeant	1919	Sunbury	Hillingdon
BARNETT George	Inspector	1915	Harlesden	Brent
BARRETT William	Inspector	1881	Bedfont	Hillingdon
BARRETT T.	D/Chief Superintendent	1958	Hendon	Barnet
BARTON Henry	A/Sergeants	1914	East Barnet	Barnet
BASSETT Henry	Constable	1891	Ashford	Hillingdon
BATCHELOR William	Constable	1903	Pinner	Harrow
BATHER Elizabeth	Chief Superintendent	1946	Badges of Office and Uniforms	
BEARD	Superintendent	1893	Westminster	City of Westminster
BECKERSON	Superintendent	1864	Kensington	Kensington & Chelsea
BECKERSON Robert	Superintendent	1867	Brentford	Hounslow
BEDI Pirthi Ralpal Singh	Constable	2004	Wembley	Brent
BELIENIE Frank	Constable	1983	Hillingdon and Uxbridge	Hillingdon
BELL William	Inspector	1895	Harrow Road	City of Westminster
BELL William	Inspector	1898	Kilburn	Brent
BENNER Frederick	Constable	1911	Hillingdon and Uxbridge	Hillingdon
BENTLEY P.	Special Constable	1918	Brentford	Hounslow
BICKNELL Thomas	Divisional Superintendent	1840	Kingston	Kingston
BIGARLSFORD George	Sergeant	1851	Staines	Hillingdon
BIGHAM Trevor Sir	Deputy Commissioner	1932	Sunbury	Hillingdon
BILLERS George	Inspector	1845	Barnet	Barnet
BINGHAM William	Inspector	1915	Hounslow	Hounslow
BISSETT Thomas	Inspector	1888	Whetstone	Barnet
BLACKWELL William Henry	Station Sergeant	1960	Hendon	Barnet
BLAKE Charles	Sergeant	1861	Brentford	Hounslow
BLAKE J.	Station Sergeant	1914	Isleworth	Hounslow
BLIGH	Sergeant	1919	Sunbury	Hillingdon
BLUEKWILL John	Constable	1881	Bedfont	Hillingdon
BOBYER Sackville	Constable	1901	Shenley	Barnet
BOCKING Thomas	Chief Inspector	1873	Kensington	Kensington & Chelsea
BOLSOVER Frederick	Sergeant	1907	Wealdstone	Harrow
BONNYMAN G.	Inspector	1919	Fulham	Hammersmith & Fulham
BORHAM George	War Reserve Constable	1940	Kilburn	Brent
BOWES Leonard	War Reserve Constable	1940	Kilburn	Brent
BOYCE	Sergeant	1907	Wealdstone	Harrow
BOYLE James	Sub-Divisional Inspector	1896	Hammersmith	Hammersmith & Fulham
BRACEY Ivan	Constable	1960	Elstree	Barnet

Name	Rank	Year	Location	Area
BRADSTOCK Daniel	Inspector	1864	Westminster	City of Westminster
BRAIN Thomas	Inspector	1918	Kilburn	Brent
BRAY Ivan	Chief Inspector	1952	Wealdstone	Harrow
BRENHAM	Inspector	1917	Acton	Ealing
BRIAN Daniel	Constable	1840	Sunbury	Hillingdon
BRIDGEN George	Sub-Divisional Inspector	1895	Kilburn	Brent
BRILL Charles	Constable	1861	Staines	Hillingdon
BRISTOW Fred	Station Sergeant	1911	Harlington	Hillingdon
BRISTOW Thomas	Sergeant	1853	Brentford	Hounslow
BROAD P.R.	Chief Superintendent	1955	New Scotland Yard	City of Westminster
BROKENSHIRE F	Chief Inspector	1966	Barnet	Barnet
BROOKS	Sergeant	1907	Kingston	Kingston
BROOKS Charles	Constable	1861	Staines	Hillingdon
BROUGH	Superintendent	1965	Twickenham	Richmond
BROUGHTON George	Constable	1851	Harefield	Hillingdon
BROWING Thomas	Inspector	1901	Barnet	Barnet
BROWN	Station Sergeant	1917	Acton	Ealing
BROWN Charles	Inspector	1909	Harrow Road	City of Westminster
BROWN John	Constable	1940	Kilburn	Brent
BROWN William	Inspector	1851	Brentford	Hounslow
BROWNING George	Chief Inspector	1879	Harlesden	Brent
BROWNSCOMBE Henry	Sub-Divisional Inspector	1903	Hillingdon and Uxbridge	Hillingdon
BRUCE Alexander	War Reserve Constable	1940	Ruislip	Hillingdon
BRYCE William	Inspector	1902	Kingston	Kingston
BUCHANAN A.	Superintendent	1955	Peel House (Training)	City of Westminster
BUCKS John	Constable	1863	Brentford	Hounslow
BUDMEAD	Constable	1919	Sunbury	Hillingdon
BULLIVENT	A/Inspector	1871	Hillingdon and Uxbridge	Hillingdon
BULLIVENT Edward	Inspector	1877	Hampton	Richmond
BUNDOCK A.M.F	Superintendent	1966	Barnet	Barnet
BURBRIDGE Joseph	Constable	1861	Staines	Hillingdon
BURCHELL Fred	Constable	1911	Brentford	Hounslow
BURROWS Henry	Sergeant	1904	Richmond	Richmond
BUSH George	Inspector	1871	Bedfont	Hillingdon
BUSHNELL William	Inspector	1865	Intro	Kingston
BUSHNELL William	Inspector	1865	Intro	Richmond
BUTT Charles	Station Sergeant	1911	Acton	Ealing
BUTT Edward	Superintendent	1865	Intro	Kingston
BUTT Edward	Superintendent	1865	Intro	Richmond
BUTT Thomas	Superintendent	1881	Badges of Office and Uniforms	

Name	Rank	Year	Station	Borough
BYRNE M.J.	Superintendent	1965	Finchley	Barnet
BYRNE M.J.	Superintendent	1966	Golders Green	Barnet
CALAMINUS M	Superintendent	1998	Heathrow	Hillingdon
CAPLIN John William	Constable	1983	Hayes and Gould's Green	Hillingdon
CAPP Joseph	Inspector	1881	Hillingdon and Uxbridge	Hillingdon
Carr George	Superintendent	1890	Kilburn	Brent
CARSTON Edward	Constable	1851	Harrow	Harrow
CARTER John	Divisional Superintendent	1841	Barnet	Barnet
CARTER John	Superintendent	1842	Edgware	Harrow
CAWDWELL	Constable	1965	Bow Street	City of Westminster
CHALLINGSWORTH	Inspector	1904	Kingston	Kingston
CHAMBERLAIN Richard	Sergeant	1901	Bedfont	Hillingdon
CHAMBERS S	Constable	1914	Harlesden	Brent
CHAMBLETON	Constable	1919	Sunbury	Hillingdon
CHANDLER William	Constable	1901	Potters Bar	Barnet
CHAPMAN	Constable	1907	Wealdstone	Harrow
CHAPMAN	Inspector	1909	Wealdstone	Harrow
CHAPMAN	Inspector	1909	Wealdstone	Harrow
CHEESEMAN Thomas King	Sergeant	1911	Acton	Ealing
CHENNELL William	Constable	1881	Whetstone	Barnet
CHEYNEY William	Sub-Divisional Inspector	1898	Chiswick	Hounslow
CHIDGEY William	Constable	1907	Wealdstone	Harrow
CHILDS	Sergeant	1879	Richmond	Richmond
CHRISTIE John	Constable	1898	Hayes and Gould's Green	Hillingdon
CHURCH Stephen	A/Sergeant	1925	Potters Bar	Barnet
CLAPHAM	A/Sergeant	1919	Sunbury	Hillingdon
CLARKE C.	Superintendent	1965	Hounslow	Hounslow
CLAYDEN William	Constable	1911	Brentford	Hounslow
CLELLAND	Chief Inspector	1965	Finchley	Barnet
CLELLAND D.	Chief Inspector	1966	Golders Green	Barnet
CLOUGHTON Arthur	Constable	1911	Barnet	Barnet
COBBAN Jock	Constable	1956	Hendon	Barnet
COCKBURN Thomas Oswald Bell	War Reserve Constable	1940	Ruislip	Hillingdon
COE Thomas	War Reserve Constable	1940	Kilburn	Brent
COLE Thomas	Inspector	1881	Barnet	Barnet
COLE William	Constable	1885	House of Parliament	City of Westminster
COLE William George	Inspector	1918	Willesden Green	Brent
CONDON Paul Sir	Commissioner	1999	Staines	Hillingdon
COOK Edward	Inspector	1843	Hillingdon and	Hillingdon

				Uxbridge	
COOK Percy Edwin	Constable	1927	Hanwell	Ealing	
COOK Percy Edwin	Constable	1927	Hanwell	Ealing	
COOKE George Samuel	Constable	1893	Harrow	Harrow	
COOKIE	Constable	1919	Sunbury	Hillingdon	
COOMBS Thomas	Superintendent	1928	Hammersmith	Hammersmith & Fulham	
COOPER Ellis	Constable	1911	Barnet	Barnet	
COOPER James J.	Sergeant	1851	Harrow	Harrow	
COOPER Joseph	Inspector	1896	Harlesden	Brent	
COOPER Joseph W.	Inspector	1890	Kilburn	Brent	
COPPING Arthur	Sub-Divisional Inspector	1911	Chiswick	Hounslow	
CORDEN Alfred	Sergeant	1957	Hendon	Barnet	
CORNISH George	Detecive Chief Inspector	1927	Charing Cross	City of Westminster	
CORNWALL David	Inspector	1852	Esher	Richmond	
COTTAGE Herbert	Constable	1911	Brentford	Hounslow	
COUSINS	Sub-Divisional Inspector	1893	King Street	City of Westminster	
Cox Charles	Constable	1862	Brentford	Hounslow	
COX John	Sergeant	1891	Brentford	Hounslow	
CRANEY	Constable	1893	Kilburn	Brent	
CRAVEN Thomas	War Reserve Constable	1940	Kilburn	Brent	
CRAYFOURD William	Superintendent	1928	Fulham	Hammersmith & Fulham	
CRONIN P.	Chief Inspector	1895	Hammersmith	Hammersmith & Fulham	
CROSS	MSC Chief Inspector	1926	Finchley	Barnet	
CRYAN James	A/Sergeant	1925	Potters Bar	Barnet	
CUNDELL John	Sub-Divisional Inspector	1907	Finchley	Barnet	
CURL	Constable	1965	Hendon	Barnet	
CUTHBERT James	Superintendent	1893	Kilburn	Brent	
CUTHBERT James	Superintendent	1894	Ealing	Ealing	
CUTTS Samuel	Constable	1851	Chelsea	Kensington & Chelsea	
DACE C.J.	Superintendent	1962	Golders Green	Barnet	
DANIELS William	Inspector	1911	Hillingdon and Uxbridge	Hillingdon	
DAVIDSON Joseph	Constable	1861	Bedfont	Hillingdon	
DAVIES Clifford	Constable	1940	Kilburn	Brent	
DAVIES Llewellyn	War Reserve Constable	1940	Kilburn	Brent	
DAVY William John	Constable	1863	Acton	Ealing	
DAWSON Margaret D	Constable	1914	Harlesden	Brent	
DAY Ashley	Constable	1990	Acton	Ealing	
DEAN Ivory	Constable	1918	Pinner	Harrow	

DEEKS Alfred Edward	Inspector	1912	Ealing	Ealing	
DELLAR James Frank	Constable	1901	Richmond	Richmond	
DIGBY Edwin	Sub-Divisional Inspector	1897	Brentford	Hounslow	
DINGLE William	Inspector	1911	Harlesden	Brent	
DIXON George Henry	Sub-Divisional Inspector	1893	Richmond	Richmond	
DODD	Superintendent	1905	Finchley	Barnet	
DOLPHIN Samuel	Sergeant	1878	Hayes and Gould's Green	Hillingdon	
DONNOLLY James	Inspector	1891	Sunbury	Hillingdon	
D'ORSI Lucy	Chief Superintendent	2013	Hammersmith	Hammersmith & Fulham	
DOVER Harold	Detective Sergeant	1971	Cobham	Richmond	
DOWDELL John	Detective Inspector	1879	Richmond	Richmond	
DOWSETT	Inspector	1837	Intro	Kingston	
Dowsett	Inspector	1837	Intro	Richmond	
DOWSETT Richard	Inspector	1844	Kingston	Kingston	
DOWSETT Richard	Inspector	1844	Kingston	Kingston	
DRAKE Thomas	Inspector	1851	Chelsea	Kensington & Chelsea	
DUCKETT John	Constable	1841	Brentford	Hounslow	
DUGUID James	Constable	1911	Brentford	Hounslow	
DUNFORD John	Sergeant	1911	Ruislip	Hillingdon	
DURKIN	Superintendent	1851	Ealing	Ealing	
DURKIN William	Superintendent	1851	Stanwell	Hillingdon	
EAMES John	Inspector	1871	Hillingdon and Uxbridge	Hillingdon	
EATON John	Constable	1901	Harrow	Harrow	
ECCLES	A/Superintendent	1865	Acton	Ealing	
ECCLES Hugh	Superintendent	1879	Harlesden	Brent	
ECCLES Hugh	Superintendent	1867	Hillingdon and Uxbridge	Hillingdon	
ECCLES Hugh	Superintendent	1869	Ruislip	Hillingdon	
EDGAR Nat	Constable	1948	Harrow Road	City of Westminster	
EDHOUSE	Sergeant	1914	Fulham	Hammersmith & Fulham	
ELLIS	Sergeant	2011	New Malden	Kingston	
ELLIS Benjamin	Inspector	1881	Finchley	Barnet	
ELLIS Ernest	Constable	1892	Hammersmith	Hammersmith & Fulham	
ELLIS Truman	Constable	1891	Barnet	Barnet	
ELLISON William	Inspector	1886	Acton	Ealing	
ELMS Maurice	Inspector	1894	Sunbury	Hillingdon	
EMERICK	Sub-Divisional Inspector	1914	Fulham	Hammersmith & Fulham	
ENDICOTT Bowden	Constable	1887	Great Marleborough Street	City of Westminster	
ENGLAND Harry	Sergeant	1901	Stanwell	Hillingdon	

Name	Rank	Year	Location	Area
EVANS Samuel	Superintendent	1841	Barnet	Barnet
FABIAN Robert	Detective Inspector	1940	Cannon Row	City of Westminster
FALSHAW-SKELLY Henry	Constable	1930	Shepherds Bush	Hammersmith & Fulham
FARLEY Frederick	Constable	1871	Bedfont	Hillingdon
FARRER William	Constable	1911	Brentford	Hounslow
FAULKNER Thomas	Sub-Divisional Inspector	1913	Brentford	Hounslow
FEAVER Richard	Inspector	1891	Richmond	Richmond
FEAVER William	Inspector	1896	Barnes	Richmond
FENN Septimus	Divisional Superintendent	1855	Kingston	Kingston
FILBEE William	Sergeant	1890	Harefield	Hillingdon
FINLAYSON William	Constable	1851	Harrow	Harrow
FISH Alex	Chief Superintendent	2003	Harrow	Harrow
FISHER	Superintendent	1869	Chiswick	Hounslow
FISHER W.	Superintendent	1872	Norwood Green	Ealing
FISHER William	Superintendent	1879	Hammersmith	Hammersmith & Fulham
FITT Percy	MSC Inspector	1919	Intro	Hounslow
FITT William Edward	Chief Inspector	1912	Hendon	Barnet
FITT William Edward	Superintendent	1912	Intro	Hounslow
FLACK Henry Edwin	Constable	1896	Kingston	Kingston
FLETCHER	Sergeant	1896	Cobham	Richmond
FLETCHER Yvonne	Constable	1984	Bow Street	City of Westminster
FLETT A. DFC	Superintendent	1965	Harrow	Harrow
FLOYD William	Sergeant	1851	Shenley	Barnet
FOINETT Thomas	Superintendent	1886	Ealing	Ealing
FORDHAM Reuben	Constable	1901	Shenley	Barnet
FOREMAN	Constable	1914	Vine Street	City of Westminster
FORMAN Frederick	Constable	1872	Brentford	Hounslow
FOSSKET George	Constable	1871	Potters Bar	Barnet
FOSTER Frederick	Sub-Divisional Inspector	1894	Bedfont	Hillingdon
FOWLES	Constable	1934	Hendon	Barnet
FOX Geoffrey Roger	Constable	1966	Shepherds Bush	Hammersmith & Fulham
FREEMAN	Constable	1915	Kingston	Kingston
FRENCH William	Constable	1893	Hillingdon and Uxbridge	Hillingdon
FRICK Noel Charles	Constable	1993	Shepherds Bush	Hammersmith & Fulham
FRY	Constable	1919	Sunbury	Hillingdon
FRY Alan	D/ Assistant Commissioner	1992	Fulham	Hammersmith & Fulham
FRY Len	Constable	1939	Hendon	Barnet
Game Philip Sir	Commissioner	1937	Sunbury	Hillingdon
GANE William George	War Reserve Constable	1911	Harlesden	Brent

Name	Rank	Year	Station	Borough
GARDNER Matthew	Chief Superintendent	2012	Wembley	Brent
GAVIN	Sub-Divisional Inspector	1941	Tottenham Court Road	City of Wsetminster
GAYLOR Charles	Constable	1911	Brentford	Hounslow
GEATER John	Inspector	1891	Potters Bar	Barnet
GENTRY	MSC Chief Inspector	1915	Chiswick	Hounslow
GENTRY George	MSC Commander	1919	Intro	Hounslow
GEORGE	Constable	1919	Sunbury	Hillingdon
GERMAN	Inspector		Westminster	City of Westminster
GIBSON	Constable	1909	Wealdstone	Harrow
GIBSON W.C.E.	MSC Commander	1919	Intro	Hounslow
GIFFORD Stephen W.T.	Sub-Divisional Inspector	1901	Edgware	Harrow
GIRLING William	Sub Inspector	1891	Shenley	Barnet
GLASBY H.S	Sub-Divisional Inspector	1927	Peel House (Training)	City of Westminster
GLEN Simeon Oscar	War Reserve Constable		Hammersmith	Hammersmith & Fulham
GODDARD George	Sergeant	1921	West End Cenral	City of Westminster
GODDARD Harry	Constable	1896	Hammersmith	Hammersmith & Fulham
GOOD	Inspector	1998	Finchley	Barnet
GORDON	Constable	1977	Hendon	Barnet
GORE	Special Inspector	1941	Hendon	Barnet
GRACE Herbert	Sub-Divisional Inspector	1914	Barnet	Barnet
GRAY William	Constable	1901	Finchley	Barnet
GRIMMETT William	Inspector	1913	Kingston	Kingston
GRIMMETT William Gilbert	Sub- Divisional Inspector	1915	Harlesden	Brent
GROSCH	Inspector	1914	Hammersmith	Hammersmith & Fulham
GROVER George	Sergeant	1911	Harefield	Hillingdon
GUMBS (ROBERTS) Norwell	Constable	1967	Bow Street	City of Westminster
GURNEY William	Detective Inspector	1924	Hammersmith	Hammersmith & Fulham
HAGARTY Edward	Sergeant	1901	Bedfont	Hillingdon
HAINES Charles	Sergeant	1925	South Mimms	Barnet
HALE Hubert	Sergeant	1907	Edgware	Harrow
HALL William	Constable	1901	Harrow	Harrow
HANCOX Charles Francis	Sergeant	1911	Fulham	Hammersmith & Fulham
HANNAFORD R.C.	Superintendent	1937	Ealing	Ealing
HARMON George	Inspector	1924	Hammersmith	Hammersmith & Fulham
HARPER William John	Constable	1900	Harrow Road	City of Westminster
HARRIS Dennis	Sergeant	1976	Edgware	Harrow
HARRIS E.	Inspector	1896	Hammersmith	Hammersmith & Fulham
HARRIS Thomas Henry	Sergeant	1914	Shenley	Barnet

Name	Rank	Year	Location	Borough
HARROD James	Constable	1851	Potters Bar	Barnet
HARVEY Gerald	War Reserve Constable	1940	Kilburn	Brent
HARWOOD Alfred	Sub-Divisional Inspector	1926	Staines	Hillingdon
HARWOOD Joseph	Constable	1911	Brentford	Hounslow
HATTON Albert	Constable	1890	Whetstone	Barnet
HAWKINS Albert Victor	Constable	1949	Ealing	Ealing
HAYERS	Sub-Divisional Inspector	1901	Bow Street	City of Westminster
HAYERS	Sub-Divisional Inspector	1901	Charing Cross	City of Westminster
HEAD Christopher Tippett	Detective Sergeant	1966	Shepherds Bush	Hammersmith & Fulham
HEASMAN Ernest Edward	Constable	1881	Westminster	City of Westminster
HENRY Edward	Commissioner	1917	A' Division	City of Westminster
HENRY Edward Sir	Commissioner	1914	Fulham	Hammersmith & Fulham
HERBERT Gray	Constable	1911	Barnet	Barnet
HERWIN Henry	Sub-Divisional Inspector	1897	Bedfont	Hillingdon
HILL Nicholas	Constable	2002	Shepherds Bush	Hammersmith & Fulham
HILLIER Fred	Sergeant	1919	Tottenham Court Road	City of Westminster
HINDES Thomas	Sergeant	1863	Kensington	Kensington & Chelsea
HINXMAN	Chief Superintendent		Hendon	Barnet
HINXMANN R.F.	Superintendent	1965	Chelsea	Kensington & Chelsea
HISLOP David	Detective Superintendent	1959	Chelsea	Kensington & Chelsea
HITCHCOCK	Constable	1919	Sunbury	Hillingdon
HITCHCOCK Edward	Constable	1872	Brentford	Hounslow
HITCHCOCK James	Retired Sergeant	1911	Greenford	Ealing
HITE	Special Constable	1941	Hendon	Barnet
HOBDEN	Inspector	1893	Westminster	City of Westminster
HODDER George	Inspector	1993	Kilburn	Brent
HODDER George Robert	Inspector	1896	Harlesden	Brent
HOLDEN Brian Bernard Joseph	Constable	1963	Ealing	Ealing
HOLLIER Zachariah	Sergeant	1855	Bushey	Barnet
HOLMES Albert	Constable	1891	Barnet	Barnet
HOOPER Race Thomas	Sub-Divisional Inspector	1913	Kingston	Kingston
HOPE William	Constable	1911	Brentford	Hounslow
HORSLEY	Chief Inspector	1893	House of Commons	City of Westminster
HORSLEY D.C.	Superintendent	1955	Cobham	Richmond
HOUNDSOME John	Constable	1891	Barnet	Barnet
HOUNDSOME John	Constable	1901	Shenley	Barnet
HOW Arthur	Inspector	1891	Richmond	Richmond

Name	Rank	Year	Location	Borough
HOWARD	Constable	1907	Wealdstone	Harrow
HOWARD Johnny	Constable	1956	Hendon	Barnet
HOWELL H.W.C.	Chief Inspector	1965	Harrow	Harrow
HUDSON	Chief Inspector	1965	Feltham	Hounslow
HUGHES Samuel	Superintendent	1865	Harrow Road	City of Westminster
HUGHES Joseph	Inspector	1881	Bedfont	Hillingdon
HUMPHREY Simon	Superintendent	1998	Finchley	Barnet
HUNT Charles	Superintendent	1884	Norwood Green	Ealing
HUNT Charles	Superintendent	1896	Hammersmith	Hammersmith & Fulham
HUNT T.B.	Chief Inspector	1966	West Hendon	Barnet
HURST J.	Chief Superintendent	1998	Teddington	Richmond
HUTCHESON Ian	Superintendent	1998	Heathrow	Hillingdon
HUTCHINS	Station Sergeant	1917	Acton	Ealing
HUXLEY	Constable	1949	Hyde Park	City of Westminster
ILLESLEY David	Chief Superintendent	1952	Wealdstone	Harrow
IMBERT Peter Sir	Commissioner	1992	Fulham	Hammersmith & Fulham
ING Henry	Constable	1861	Staines	Hillingdon
INSTANCE Frederick	Inspector	1911	Acton	Ealing
ISAAC	Superintendent	1894	Notting Hill	Kensington & Chelsea
JABBAL Harbans Singh	Constable	1970	Badges of Office and Uniforms	
JACKSON	Constable	1909	Wealdstone	Harrow
JACKSON Peter	Chief Superintendent	1968	Kingston	Kingston
JACOBS Joseph	Constable	1851	Brentford	Hounslow
JAGO Richard	Constable	1968	Notting Dale	Kensington & Chelsea
JAMES Thomas George	Superintendent	1958	Fulham	Hammersmith & Fulham
JARDINE Frederick	Sergeant	1925	South Mimms	Barnet
JASPER Thomas	Constable	1911	Barnet	Barnet
JEAKS Charles	Inspector	1851	Hillingdon and Uxbridge	Hillingdon
JENKINS Charles	Constable	1911	Barnet	Barnet
JENNER	Constable	1968	Cobham	Richmond
JERBOROUGH-BONSEY	MSC Deputy Commander	1914	Intro	Hounslow
JEWELL George	Station Sergeant	1894	East Barnet	Barnet
JIGGINS John	Constable	1900	Hammersmith	Hammersmith & Fulham
JOHNSON R.A.S.	Chief Superintendent	1992	Fulham	Hammersmith & Fulham
JONES William	Constable	1901	Shenley	Barnet
JONES William	Inspector	1889	Richmond	Richmond
JORDON	Constable	1934	Hendon	Barnet
JORDON Carlos	Constable	1881	Ealing	Ealing
JOSLING Horace	Sergeant	1921	West End Cenral	City of Westminster

JUDD	Constable	1919	Sunbury	Hillingdon	
KELLY James	Constable	1920	Acton	Ealing	
KEMP Edward	Sergeant	1891	Ashford	Hillingdon	
KEMPIN John	Sub-Divisional Inspector	1907	Teddington	Richmond	
KEMPIN John Henry	Inspector	1907	Hampton	Richmond	
KEMPSTER	Sergeant	1915	Kingston	Kingston	
KENNETT Frederick Daniel	Constable	1915	Kingston	Kingston	
KENNOUGH	Constable	1919	Sunbury	Hillingdon	
KENTH Piara Singh	Constable	1969	Ealing	Ealing	
KENTISH William	Constable	1911	Hillingdon and Uxbridge	Hillingdon	
KESSELL	Constable	1909	Wealdstone	Harrow	
KIDD Albert	Sergeant	1901	Bedfont	Hillingdon	
KING	Inspector	1934	Hendon	Barnet	
KING A.T.	Chief Inspector	1935	Hendon	Barnet	
KIRKER Ralph	Constable	1941	West End Cenral	City of Westminster	
KITCH John B.	Superintendent	1914	Fulham	Hammersmith & Fulham	
KNELL George	Detective Constable	1914	Finchley	Barnet	
LABALMONDIERE	Deputy Commissioner	1862	Kensington	Kensington & Chelsea	
LAMB Jabez	Constable	1891	Sunbury	Hillingdon	
LANCASTER William	Constable	1901	Shenley	Barnet	
LANCE J.	Inspector	1896	Hammersmith	Hammersmith & Fulham	
LANNING	Sergeant	1907	Wealdstone	Harrow	
LARCOMBE William	Constable	1907	Wealdstone	Harrow	
LAVER John	Sergeant	1871	Bedfont	Hillingdon	
LAY William	Station Sergeant	1894	Harefield	Hillingdon	
LEE Walter	Sergeant	1851	Staines	Hillingdon	
LEECH	Sub-Divisional Inspector	1905	Finchley	Barnet	
LEGGATT Frederick	Inspector	1901	South Mimms	Barnet	
LEVY James	Sergeant	1841	Brentford	Hounslow	
LEWENDON	Constable	1909	Wealdstone	Harrow	
LEWIS Henry	Station Sergeant	1914	Elstree	Barnet	
LIGHT Don	Constable	1940	Kilburn	Brent	
LIGHTWOOD D.F.	Chief Superintendent	1965	Chelsea	Kensington & Chelsea	
LINDBERN	Constable	1957	Hendon	Barnet	
LINGE R.	Superintendent	1955	Harlesden	Brent	
LIPSCOMBE Fred	Constable	1932	Staines	Hillingdon	
LITTLEJOHNS	Sub-Divisional Inspector	1914	Hammersmith	Hammersmith & Fulham	
LLOYD Samuel	Sergeant	1832	Acton	Ealing	
LOWE	Inspector		Westminster	City of Westminster	

Name	Rank	Year	Location	Area
LOWE William Bowler	Constable	1911	Greenford	Ealing
LOXTON	Superintendent	1865	Barnet	Barnet
JUKES John	Constable	1851	Richmond	Richmond
LUSCOMBE Samuel Henry	Constable	1928	Hendon	Barnet
LUXTON	Inspector	1847	Hanwell	Ealing
LYNCH Patrick	Constable	1971	Cobham	Richmond
MACDONALD D.C.	Deputy Commander	1964	Hendon	Barnet
MACE William	Station Sergeant	1895	Kingston	Kingston
MACER Arthur	Inspector	1918	Kilburn	Brent
MacINNES Charles	Constable	1940	Kilburn	Brent
MACKINTOSH	Constable	1903	Hampton	Richmond
MACMILLAN William	Sub- Divisional Inspector	1915	Harlesden	Brent
MAGGS Gordon	Commander	1970	Kensington	Kensington & Chelsea
MAINE Richard	Commisssioner	1862	Kensington	Kensington & Chelsea
MALLIN Henry William	Sergeant	1969	Peel House (Training)	City of Westminster
MANNERS	MSC Commander	1914	Intro	Hounslow
MANSFIELD N.	Inspector	1890	Kilburn	Brent
MARK Robert Sir	Commissioner	1976	Southall	Ealing
MARQUARD Cortney Henry	Inspector	1841	Brentford	Hounslow
MARRIOTT J.F.	Chief Inspector	1966	West Hendon	Barnet
MARSHALL	Constable	1973	Hendon	Barnet
MARTIN A.	Sergeant	1941	Wembley	Brent
MARTIN A.	Sergeant	1941	Wembley	Brent
MASON Allen	Constable	1859	Cobham	Richmond
MASTERS Francis	Constable	1840	Sunbury	Hillingdon
MATTHEWS Annie	Constable	1950	Badges of Office and Uniforms	
MATTHEWS Terrence	Inspector	1990	Golders Green	Barnet
MAY Frederick	Sub-Divisional Inspector	1912	Fulham	Hammersmith & Fulham
MAY John	Superintendent	1829	A' Division	City of Westminster
MAYNE Richard	Commissioner	1829	Scotland Yard	City of Westminster
MAYNE Richard	Commissioner	1855	Hyde Park	City of Westminster
MAYNE Richard Sir	Commissioner	1866	Finchley	Barnet
MAYNE Richard Sir	Commissioner	1862	Kingston	Kingston
McADAM	MSC Commandant	1919	Intro	Hounslow
McCLOSKEY Ronan	Constable	1978	Willesden Green	Brent
McCLOSKEY Ronan	Constable	1978	Willesden Green	Brent
McCONDACH	Inspector	1909	Wealdstone	Harrow
McCULLOCK	Constable	1934	Hendon	Barnet
McCULLOCK Percy	Station Sergeant	1911	Acton	Ealing
McDONALD A.	Inspector	1890	Kilburn	Brent
McFADDEN Robert	Inspector	1891	Surbiton	Kingston

Name	Rank	Year	Location	Borough
McGRAW Robert	Constable	1887	Fulham	Hammersmith & Fulham
McINTYRE Robert Graham	Sergeant	1840	Sunbury	Hillingdon
McNEE Sir David	Commissioner	1980	Kilburn	Brent
McNee David Sir	Commissioner	1977	Barnet	Barnet
MEADON Arthur	Constable	1911	Barnet	Barnet
MEAPHAM A.G.	Chief Inspector	1965	Hampton	Richmond
MEASURES John	Sergeant	1867	King Street	City of Westminster
MILLARD Oliver	Inspector	1916	Harlesden	Brent
MILLER J.J.	Chief Superintendent	1963	Peel House (Training)	City of Westminster
MILLER J.J.	Chief Superintendent	1963	Hendon	Barnet
MILLS	Constable	1907	Wealdstone	Harrow
MILNER Ernest	Detective Constable	1914	East Barnet	Barnet
MITCHELL Frederick	Sub-Divisional Inspector	1885	Harrow Road	City of Westminster
MITCHELL Isaac	Constable	1903	Pinner	Harrow
MITCHELL John	Inspector	1862	Kensington	Kensington & Chelsea
MITTALL Robert	Sergeant	1856	Ditton	Richmond
MOBLEY John	Inspector	1885	Harrow Road	City of Westminster
MOFFATT T.	Inspector	1896	Hammersmith	Hammersmith & Fulham
MONAGHAN L	Sergeant	1842	Hillingdon and Uxbridge	Hillingdon
MOORE	Constable	1909	Wealdstone	Harrow
MOORE Bert	Chief Superintendent	2011	Heathrow	Hillingdon
MOORE Charles	Constable	1891	Potters Bar	Barnet
MOORE John	Station Sergeant	1903	Pinner	Harrow
MOORE John	Constable	1842	Bedfont	Hillingdon
MOORE John	Station Sergeant	1899	Pinner	Harrow
MOORE John	Station Sergeant	1899	Pinner	Harrow
MORGAN	Sergeant	1952	Wealdstone	Harrow
MORGAN James	Inspector	1845	Hammersmith	Hammersmith & Fulham
MORSLEY James	Sub-Divisional Inspector	1892	Bedfont	Hillingdon
MUGGERIDGE	Sergeant	1919	Sunbury	Hillingdon
MULCAHY MM	Superintendent	1965	Hampton	Richmond
MULCAHY MM	Superintendent	1960	Richmond	Richmond
MULES Thomas	Inspector	1886	Acton	Ealing
MUMFORD John Oran	Sub-Divisional Inspector	1901	Brentford	Hounslow
MUNDAY William	Constable	1911	Northwood	Hillingdon
MURPHY Daniel	Constable	1901	Shenley	Barnet
MURTON Robert	Constable	1911	Hillingdon and Uxbridge	Hillingdon
MYERS Arthur Needham	War Reserve	1940	Hammersmith	Hammersmith & Fulham

	Constable				
NEAL	Constable	1967	Shenley	Barnet	
NEAL Thomas	Inspector	1896	Shepherds Bush	Hammersmith & Fulham	
NEAL Thomas	Sub-Divisional Inspector	1894	Sunbury	Hillingdon	
NEVILLE John	Sergeant	1901	Bedfont	Hillingdon	
NEWLANDS Hugh	Reserve Inspector	1885	Harrow Road	City of Westminster	
NEWMAN	Constable	1919	Sunbury	Hillingdon	
NEWMAN	Station Sergeant	1919	Sunbury	Hillingdon	
NEWMAN William	Superintendent	1924	Hammersmith	Hammersmith & Fulham	
NEWMAN William	Superintendent	1924	Shepherds Bush	Hammersmith & Fulham	
NEWNHAM	Constable	1919	Sunbury	Hillingdon	
NEWNHAM Alfred	Sub-Inspector	1894	Acton	Ealing	
NEWNHAM Alfred	Sub-Divisional Inspector	1894	Ealing	Ealing	
NOCK Henry	Constable	1911	Brentford	Hounslow	
NORMAN Ralph	Sergeant	1855	Whetstone	Barnet	
NORRIS William	Sergeant	1914	East Barnet	Barnet	
NUTT Robert	Sub-Divisional Inspector	1890	Barnet	Barnet	
O'BRIAN S.G.	Chief Inspector	1965	Chelsea	Kensington & Chelsea	
OGDEN S.M.	Sub -Divisional Inspector	1927	Peel House (Training)	City of Westminster	
O'LEARY William	Constable	1911	Hillingdon and Uxbridge	Hillingdon	
OLIVE	Superintendent	1905	Northwood	Hillingdon	
OLIVE James	Superintendent	1915	Westminster	City of Westminster	
OLIVE James	Superintendent	1917	Acton	Ealing	
OLIVE James	Superintendent	1911	Harrow	Harrow	
OLIVE James William	Superintendent	1918	Kilburn	Brent	
OLIVE James William	Superintendent	1918	Willesden Green	Brent	
OLIVER	Station Sergeant	1946	Hendon	Barnet	
OLIVER John	Chief Inspector	1998	Finchley	Barnet	
ORR	Sub Inspector	1941	Hendon	Barnet	
ORWIN Leigh	Superintendent	2007	Heathrow	Hillingdon	
OSBORNE David	Constable	1950	Surbiton	Kingston	
OSBOURNE	Sub -Divisional Inspector	1941	Tottenham Court Road	City of Westminster	
OTWAY Charles	Inspector	1842	Hillingdon and Uxbridge	Hillingdon	
OUGH William	Sergeant	1901	New Malden	Kingston	
OWEN Frederick	A/Sergeant	1894	Greenford	Ealing	
PAGE Tom Alec	War Reserve Constable	1943	Finchley	Barnet	
PAINE Charles	Constable	1852	Harefield	Hillingdon	
PALETHORPE	Constable	1907	Wealdstone	Harrow	

Name	Rank	Year	Location	Borough
PAMETER	Sergeant	1907	Wealdstone	Harrow
PARISH William	Constable	1825	Potters Bar	Barnet
PARKER	Constable	1907	Wealdstone	Harrow
PARTNER David	Station Sergeant	1925	Potters Bar	Barnet
PASHLEY	Reserve Inspector	1893	King Street	City of Westminster
PATERSON Thomas	Constable	1881	Ealing	Ealing
PAYNE G.F.	Sub-Divisional Inspector	1941	Hendon	Barnet
PAYNE Jimmy	Constable	1921	Bedfont	Hillingdon
PEARCE James Walter	A/Sergeant	1899	Harrow	Harrow
PEARCE Nicholas	Detective Inspector	1842	Gardiner's Lane	City of Westminster
PEARMAN John	Inspector	1878	Richmond	Richmond
PEARN Charles	Sub-Divisional Inspector	1891	Richmond	Richmond
PEEL Robert Sir	Commissioner	1829	Intro	Harrow
PERRY Michael Robert	Constable	1993	Ruislip	Hillingdon
PERRY William	Inspector	1911	Harlesden	Brent
PETO	Superintendent	1930	Peel House (Training)	City of Westminster
PHILLIPS Phillip	A/Sergeant	1925	Potters Bar	Barnet
PHILLIPS Eddie	A/Sergeant	1954	Wealdstone	Harrow
PICKETT William	Inspector	1891	Surbiton	Kingston
PIKE Francis	Detective Sergeant	1905	Finchley	Barnet
PINER Thomas	Constable	1899	Pinner	Harrow
PINER Thomas	Constable	1889	Pinner	Harrow
PINER Thomas	Constable	1889	Pinner	Harrow
PINKS Edward	Inspector	1924	Shepherds Bush	Hammersmith & Fulham
PLUMB G.R.	Constable	1949	Hyde Park	City of Westminster
POMEROY Henry	Constable	1893	Harrow	Harrow
PONTIN Charles	Constable	1867	Brentford	Hounslow
POOLE W.J.	Superintendent	1957	Harrow	Harrow
PORTER	A/Sergeant	1919	Sunbury	Hillingdon
PORTER Hubert	Sergeant	1925	Potters Bar	Barnet
POTTER Charles	Sergeant	1902	Harrow	Harrow
POTTER Frank	Constable	1911	Brentford	Hounslow
POTTERILL James	Constable	1891	Ashford	Hillingdon
POWELL	Superintendent	1914	Hammersmith	Hammersmith & Fulham
POWELL James	Superintendent	1919	Cannon Row	City of Westminster
POWELL Bob	Constable	1971	Cobham	Richmond
POWELL James	Divisional Superintendent	1906	Brentford	Hounslow
PRIDEAUX William	Constable	1861	Staines	Hillingdon
PROOPS	Constable	1919	Sunbury	Hillingdon
PROOPS Goodman	Constable	1911	Brentford	Hounslow
PRYKE	Chief Inspector	1895	Kingston	Kingston
PRYKE John	Inspector	1891	Richmond	Richmond

Name	Rank	Year	Location	Borough
PURDY Raymond	Detective Sergeant	1959	Chelsea	Kensington & Chelsea
RACEY Henry	Constable	1911	Barnet	Barnet
RAISHBROOK	Station Sergeant	1958	Hendon	Barnet
RANDALL Desmond	Sergeant	1971	Cobham	Richmond
RANDALL Ernest	Constable	1891	Barnet	Barnet
RAPSEY James	Inspector	1855	Kingston	Kingston
RAWLINGS	Superintendent	1960	Richmond	Richmond
RAWLINGS David	Sub-Divisional Inspector	1888	Chiswick	Hounslow
READ Charles	Inspector	1924	Hammersmith	Hammersmith & Fulham
REDSTONE W.	Inspector	1890	Kilburn	Brent
REES W.L.	Superintendent	1966	West Hendon	Barnet
REEVES	Inspector	1914	Fulham	Hammersmith & Fulham
RHODES George	Inspector	1924	Shepherds Bush	Hammersmith & Fulham
RICHARDS David	Sub-Divisional Inspector	1911	Ealing	Ealing
RICHARDSON Charles	Sub-Divisional Inspector	1914	Brentford	Hounslow
RICKENS Arthur	Constable	1911	Brentford	Hounslow
RIMMINGTON Thomas	Constable	1911	Brentford	Hounslow
RIVETT Frederick	Chief Inspector	1916	Cannon Row	City of Westminster
ROADNIGHT R	Sergeant	1842	Hillingdon and Uxbridge	Hillingdon
ROBBINS Edwin	Constable	1891	Barnet	Barnet
ROBBINS George	Sergeant	1870	Kingston	Kingston
ROBINSON	Chief Inspector	1893	Westminster	City of Westminster
ROBINSON	Divisional Superintendent	1908	Kingston	Kingston
ROCHE Patrick	Constable	1861	Staines	Hillingdon
ROE	MSC Commander	1939	Intro	Hounslow
ROGERS John	Constable	1976	Edgware	Harrow
ROGERS R.E. MBE	Commader	1963	Golders Green	Barnet
ROGERS William	Constable	1851	Harrow	Harrow
ROLFE George	Constable	1908	Ruislip	Hillingdon
ROSE	Chief Inspector	1893	Westminster	City of Westminster
ROWAN Charles	Commissioner	1829	Scotland Yard	City of Westminster
ROWELL Andy	Chief Superintendent	2011	Ealing	Ealing
ROWLAND George	Inspector	1973	Northwood	Hillingdon
ROWLING John	Sub-Divisional Inspector	1881	Brentford	Hounslow
RUDGE Edward	Constable	1901	Sunbury	Hillingdon
RUDLING Henry	Constable	1911	Brentford	Hounslow
RUFF Robert	Inspector	1907	Finchley	Barnet
RUSH	Constable	1909	Wealdstone	Harrow
RUSHBRIDGE Alfred	Sub-Divisional	1891	Kingston	Kingston

Name	Rank	Year	Location	Borough
SAINES	Divisional Superintendent Inspector	1904	Richmond	Richmond
SAINES David	Superintendent	1895	Kingston	Kingston
SALLOWS George	Sergeant	1901	Bedfont	Hillingdon
SALTER A.J.	Superintendent	1933	Edgware	Harrow
SALTER Charles	Sergeant	1871	Bedfont	Hillingdon
SANDERSON George	Constable	1911	Hillingdon and Uxbridge	Hillingdon
SANDFORD John	Detective Sergeant	1959	Chelsea	Kensington & Chelsea
SANDS Albert	Constable	1907	Wealdstone	Harrow
SAVAGE Frederick	Sergeant	1878	Acton	Ealing
SAVILL Jerry	Chief Superintendent	2007	Heathrow	Hillingdon
SAW	Constable	1909	Wealdstone	Harrow
SCAMMELL Charles Lewis	Constable	1911	Hanwell	Ealing
SCANTLEBURY	Inspector	1893	Westminster	City of Westminster
SCANTLEBURY J.	Inspector	1896	Hammersmith	Hammersmith & Fulham
SCHUCK M.	Superintendent	1992	Fulham	Hammersmith & Fulham
SCOREY George	Constable	1923	Wembley	Brent
SCOTT Harold Sir	Commissioner	1948	Harrow Road	City of Westminster
SEAMAN John	Constable	1911	Brentford	Hounslow
SEARLE	Inspector	1862	Kensington	Kensington & Chelsea
SELLARS Albert Edward	Inspector	1911	Hanwell	Ealing
SERGEANT William	Sub-Divisional Inspector	1924	Hammersmith	Hammersmith & Fulham
SEWELL Beryl	Constable	1954	Hendon	Barnet
SHAPLIN George	A/Sergeants	1914	East Barnet	Barnet
SHARP F.L	Chief Inspector	1965	Kingston	Kingston
SHEPHERD Arthur	Constable	1901	Harrow	Harrow
SHEPHERD James	Inspector	1844	Chelsea	Kensington & Chelsea
SHERVINGTON	Chief Inspector	1914	Fulham	Hammersmith & Fulham
SHERVINGTON	Chief Inspector	1907	Hammersmith	Hammersmith & Fulham
SHERWOOD Peter	Sergeant	1911	Greenford	Ealing
SHORT Joseph	Chief Inspector	1916	Cannon Row	City of Westminster
SIDHU Kulwant Singh	Constable	1999	Twickenham	Richmond
SIMPKINS Charles	Sergeant	1861	Staines	Hillingdon
SIMPKINS Charles	Sergeant	1861	Sunbury	Hillingdon
SIMPSON Joseph	Commissioner	1959	Hendon	Barnet
SIMPSON Joseph, KBE	Commissioner	1966	Shepherds Bush	Hammersmith & Fulham
SKEATS G	Superintendent	1887	Hillingdon and Uxbridge	Hillingdon
SKEATS Lewis	Sub Inspector	1891	South Mimms	Barnet
SKEGGS	Constable	1934	Hendon	Barnet
SLIMON Peter	Constable	1973	Kensington	Kensington & Chelsea
SMITH	Inspector	1903	Pinner	Harrow

SMITH	Constable	1919	Sunbury	Hillingdon
SMITH Ames	Constable	1871	Hillingdon and Uxbridge	Hillingdon
SMITH Charles	Constable	1840	Sunbury	Hillingdon
SMITH Edward	Constable	1911	Brentford	Hounslow
SMITH F.	Superintendent	1927	Peel House (Training)	City of Westminster
SMITH George	War Reserve Constable	1940	Kilburn	Brent
SMITH George	Constable	1911	Brentford	Hounslow
SMITH George	Station Sergeant	1893	Richmond	Richmond
SMITH Harry	Sub-Divisional Inspector	1908	Bedfont	Hillingdon
SMITH James	Chief Inspector	1908	Kingston	Kingston
SMITH Jesse	Sergeant	1878	Acton	Ealing
SMITH John	Constable	1851	Harrow	Harrow
SMITH John Albert	Constable	1911	Harefield	Hillingdon
SMITH Sydney	Inspector	1899	Harlesden	Brent
SMITH Thomas B.	Inspector	1844	Kensington	Kensington & Chelsea
SMITH William	Superintendent	1910	Badges of Office and Uniforms	
SMITHERAM Arthur	Inspector	1914	Barnet	Barnet
SOPER	Constable	1907	Wealdstone	Harrow
SPRINGTHORPE Arthur	Sergeant	1911	Norwood Green	Ealing
SPRUCES	Inspector	1930	Finchley	Barnet
SQUIRE Stan	Commander	1977	Barnet	Barnet
STANLEY A.C.	Superintendent	1965	Harrow	Harrow
STEED George	Inspector	1873	Hampton	Richmond
STEELE	Constable	1934	Hendon	Barnet
STEPHENSON Paul Sir	Commissioner	2011	Heathrow	Hillingdon
STEVENS Bill	Chief Inspector	1968	Kingston	Kingston
STEVENS John Sir	Commissioner	1999	Twickenham	Richmond
STEWART	Sergeant	1907	Wealdstone	Harrow
STRATTON	Inspector	1893	Westminster	City of Westminster
STRUTT	Constable	1919	Sunbury	Hillingdon
STURROCK Wallace	Constable	1911	Brentford	Hounslow
SUMMERS Charlie	Constable	1940	Kilburn	Brent
SUTHERLAND A	Station Sergeant	1905	Finchley	Barnet
SWAINE James W.	Constable	1894	Harlesden	Brent
SWAN	Constable	1907	Wealdstone	Harrow
SWINDEN David	Constable	1961	Hendon	Barnet
SWINDEN David	Constable	1961	Ealing	Ealing
SWINDEN James	Sergeant	1863	King Street	City of Westminster
SYME	Inspector	1918	Vine Street	City of Westminster
SYME John	Inspector	1908	Gerald Road	City of Westminster
TARLING James	Inspector	1867	Brentford	Hounslow

TARLTON Edward	Superintendent	1857	Kensington	Kensington & Chelsea
TARLTON Pitt	Inspector	1857	Kensington	Kensington & Chelsea
TARLTON Pitt	Inspector	1865	Intro	Kingston
TARLTON Pitt	Inspector	1865	Intro	Richmond
TASCHNER	Constable	1909	Wealdstone	Harrow
TAYLOR	Chief Superintendent	1946	Hendon	Barnet
TAYLOR	Constable	1907	Wealdstone	Harrow
TAYLOR Charles	Inspector	1910	Kilburn	Brent
TAYLOR Charles	Inspector	1918	Kilburn	Brent
TAYLOR Thomas	Inspector	1924	Hammersmith	Hammersmith & Fulham
TAYLOR W.M.	Chief Superintendent	1945	Hendon	Barnet
TAYLOR William	Constable	1893	Hillingdon and Uxbridge	Hillingdon
THOMAS	Superintendent	1893	Bow street	City of Westminster
THOMAS	Constable	1934	Hendon	Barnet
THOMAS A.R.	Superintendent	1946	Teddington	Richmond
THOMAS David	Constable	1911	Brentford	Hounslow
THOMAS T.E.	Superintendent	1965	Kingston	Kingston
THOMPSON	Constable	1909	Wealdstone	Harrow
THOMPSON David	Sub-Divisional Inspector	1910	Kingston	Kingston
THOMPSON George	Constable	1911	Hillingdon and Uxbridge	Hillingdon
THOMPSON Joseph	Station Sergeant	1914	East Barnet	Barnet
THOMSON James	Superintendent	1880	Badges of Office and Uniforms	
THOMSON James Warrender	Constable	1936	Barnet	Barnet
THURSBY	Inspector	1914	Fulham	Hammersmith & Fulham
THURSEY John	Inspector	1919	Fulham	Hammersmith & Fulham
TIBBLE Stephen Andrew	Constable	1976	Hammersmith	Hammersmith & Fulham
TIBLE	Constable	1909	Wealdstone	Harrow
TICKLE E.J.E.	Superintendent	1960	Cobham	Richmond
TICKNER Frederick	Special Constable	1915	Brentford	Hounslow
TILBY Willie	Station Sergeant	1907	Surbiton	Kingston
TILBY Willie	Station Sergeant		Esher	Richmond
TIMPSON	Constable	1893	North Fulham	Hammersmith & Fulham
TITHERIDGE	Constable	1919	Sunbury	Hillingdon
TODD William	Constable	1891	Barnet	Barnet
TOOTH	A/Sergeant	1903	Pinner	Harrow
Trenchard Lord	Commissioner	1934	Harrow Road	City of Westminster
TRENCHARD Lord	Commissioner	1935	Hendon	Barnet
TRENCHARD Lord	Commissioner	1933	Kew	Richmond
TROTT Henry	Inspector	1893	Kingston	Kingston

Name	Rank	Year	Station	Borough
TROTT Thomas George	Sub-Divisional Inspector	1926	Finchley	Barnet
TROUNCE Willian	Constable	1842	Gardiner's Lane	City of Westminster
TUCKWELL Alfred	Sergeant	1871	Barnet	Barnet
TURNER	Constable	1907	Wealdstone	Harrow
TURNER James Axley	Sergeant	1851	Hillingdon and Uxbridge	Hillingdon
TURNER James Oxley	Sergeant	1853	Brentford	Hounslow
TURNER William	Constable	1891	Barnet	Barnet
TURTON Joshus	Constable	1851	Hillingdon and Uxbridge	Hillingdon
UNSTED Edwin Carter	Sub-Divisional Inspector	1898	Hampton	Richmond
VAUGHN Philip ???	Constable	1863	Brentford	Hounslow
WACHTER Ernest	Constable	1911	Brentford	Hounslow
WADE William T	Sub-Divisional Inspector	1889	Hillingdon and Uxbridge	Hillingdon
WALKER	Superintendent	1864	Westminster	City of Westminster
WALKER Ken	Constable	1992	Fulham	Hammersmith & Fulham
WALKER Robert	Disitrict Superintendent	1872	Greenford	Ealing
WALKER William	Constable	1851	Chelsea	Kensington & Chelsea
WALL Thomas	Superintendent	1955	Peel House (Training)	City of Westminster
WALLACE John	Constable	1971	Cobham	Richmond
WALLIS George	War Reserve Constable	1940	Kilburn	Brent
Wallis Richard	Sub-Divisional Inspector	1908	Brentford	Hounslow
WALTER	Constable	1894	Hayes and Gould's Green	Hillingdon
WARNE J	Station Sergeant	1905	Finchley	Barnet
WARREN	Constable	1956	Hendon	Barnet
WARREN Charles Sir	Commissioner	1887	Great Marleborough Street	City of Westminster
WASP Alfred	Constable	1907	Wealdstone	Harrow
WATSON Archibald	Inspector	1911	Acton	Ealing
WATSON James	Constable	1891	Sunbury	Hillingdon
WATSON James	Constable	1901	Sunbury	Hillingdon
WATSON William	Station Sergeant	1980	Wembley	Brent
WAY A.G.P	Assistant Commissioner	1964	Hendon	Barnet
WEAR	Constable	1898	Barnes	Richmond
WEBB Joseph	Constable	1881	Bedfont	Hillingdon
WEBB O	Sub-Divisional Inspector	1925	Barnet	Barnet
WEBB Thomas	Constable	1829	Barnet	Barnet
WEBBER Tom	Constable	1891	Barnet	Barnet

WELLER Walter	Inspector	1893	Hillingdon and Uxbridge	Hillingdon
WELLS Cresswell	Inspector	1879	Richmond	Richmond
WELLS Creswell	Superintendent	1907	A' Division	City of Westminster
WELLS Sidney George	Constable	1914	Bow Street	City of Westminster
WELTON	Constable	1915	Kingston	Kingston
WENSLEY Frederick	Chief Constable	1921	West End Cenral	City of Westminster
WEST Edward	Sub-Divisional Inspector	1897	Kingston	Kingston
WESTWOOD Thomas	Constable	1903	Pinner	Harrow
WHEATON Walter	Sergeant	1924	Wembley	Brent
WHELLAMS	Constable	1941	Hendon	Barnet
WHELLER James	Station Sergeant	1899	South Mimms	Barnet
WHITE Arthur Wilfred	War Reserve Constable	1940	Ealing	Ealing
WHITE J.H.	Superintendent	1931	Cobham	Richmond
WHITING Michael	Constable	1973	Bow Street	City of Westminster
WHITMORE James	Station Sergeant	1920	Esher	Richmond
WHYTE	Constable	1959	Hendon	Barnet
WIGGINS William	Inspector	1841	Paddington	City of Westminster
WILCOX George	Sub-Divisional Inspector	1919	Fulham	Hammersmith & Fulham
WILEY George John	Special Constable	1951	Ditton	Richmond
WILKINS Edward	Sergeant	1873	Teddington	Richmond
WILKINSON Tom Albert	Sub-Divisional Inspector	1911	Barnet	Barnet
WILLIAMS	Superintendent	1910	Golders Green	Barnet
WILLIAMS Richard	Constable	1861	Staines	Hillingdon
WILLIAMS T	Superintendent	1907	Wealdstone	Harrow
WILLIAMS T	Superintendent	1907	Wealdstone	Harrow
WILLIAMS Thomas	Superintendent	1910	Barnet	Barnet
WILLIAMSON	Superintendent	1842	Hammersmith	Hammersmith & Fulham
WILLIAMSON David	Superintendent	1836	Brentford	Hounslow
WILLIAMSON David	Superintendent	1842	Hillingdon and Uxbridge	Hillingdon
WILLIE James	Constable	1911	Brentford	Hounslow
WILLS George	Inspector	1881	Ealing	Ealing
WILLS George	Inspector	1873	Harrow	Harrow
WILSON Eleanor	Constable	1954	Hendon	Barnet
WILSON W	Superintendent	1998	Cobham	Richmond
WINDSOR	Constable	1909	Wealdstone	Harrow
WINKLER	Chief Inspector	1893	Marlborough Street Court	City of Westminster
WINTER Henry	Inspector	1913	Kingston	Kingston
WINTERFLOOD	Constable	1947	Hendon	Barnet
WISE George	Chief	1980	Kilburn	Brent

		Superintendent			
WOMBWELL David Stanley Bertram		Detective Constable	1966	Shepherds Bush	Hammersmith & Fulham
WOODS Walter		Constable	1939	Bedfont	Hillingdon
WOODWARD		Constable	1909	Wealdstone	Harrow
WOOLARD G.H.K.		Superintendent	1966	West Hendon	Barnet
WOOLGAR Robert		Constable	1846	Chelsea	Kensington & Chelsea
WOOLMORE Arthur		Constable	1891	Barnet	Barnet
WORFALL William George		Sergeant	1840	Kingston	Kingston
WORTH Leonard		Sergeant	1925	South Mimms	Barnet
WREN John		Constable	1954	Hendon	Barnet
WYLES Lilian		Detective Inspector	1950	Badges of Office and Uniforms	
YALLOP Charles		Constable	1911	Barnet	Barnet
YATES Thomas		Constable	1840	Sunbury	Hillingdon
YOUNG Richmond		Station Sergeant	1901	Shenley	Barnet

Appendix 2

Balham / Cavendish Road Police Station

Land was sought on which to build a police station in Balham in the late 1880's because there was a demand for police as there had been a growth in population. A sectional station was built and occupied for operational purposes in August 1891 and attached to the divisional station, which was situated at Brixton at the

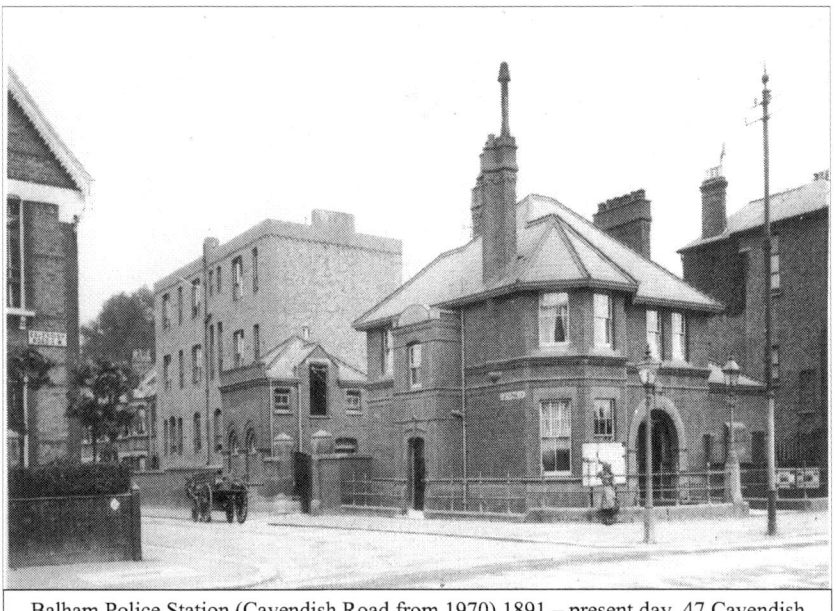

Balham Police Station (Cavendish Road from 1970) 1891 – present day. 47 Cavendish Road, SW12.

time. It was designed by John Dixon Butler, Metropolitan Police Surveyor. Balham also had a section house for single police office situated at the rear[1]. The section house is the two storey building behind the cart in the yard of the station. The rear access gate provided the entrance into the station yard. What can also be observed from the picture above between the section house and the station are the stables which were a separate building with hay loft and arched windows to the front. The bowed front office window to the front of the building also afforded a good observation point to see who was coming up and down the main road. The call sign for telegraphic purposed was Bravo (BB) in 1893.

In 1912 Balham police station was situated on 'W' division and situated at 47 Cavendish Road SW, the freehold having been purchased in 1888. An ambulance shelter had been built in Station Road[2] with a hand cart referred to as a hand ambulance. The hand ambulance was not only used for the transportation of sick or injured people but also for drunken prisoners as well who could be strapped to the cart. This allowed for proper security of a prisoner who might escape or prevent from further injury to themselves.

Balham and Battersea Park Road police stations were both sectional station of Clapham which was the sub divisional station. In the 1880's there had been an increase in funding from the government due in part to help the police cope with the influx of people into the metropolis. The police sought to recruit more police officers and with increases in constable numbers resulting in additional sergeants and Inspectors as well. For example an inspector was placed in charge of each police station and a sub divisional inspector located at the Sub Divisional stations. The Clapham Sub Divisional Inspector was James Janes who was a frequent visitor to Balham checking duty states, ledgers, charge sheets, the refused charge book, lost and cab property returns and all other books.

In the 1920's the station also had a set of married quarters above the station however when Brixton was removed to 'L' Division and Balham became the Divisional headquarters these rooms became administrative offices[3]. The accommodation above the stables was also converted for administrative functions. The station was reconditioned in 1939 and the address became 47 Cavendish Road, SW12[4].

By the 1930's the chart below shows the station of 'W' or Clapham Division.

W or Clapham	Brixton	367 Brixton Rd, SW9
	Earlsfield	Garratt Lane, Earlsfield, SW17
	Wandsworth Con	76 Trinity Rd, Upper Tooting SW17
	Balham	47 Cavendish Rd, Balham, SW12
	Streatham	101 High Rd, Streatham, SW16
	Mitcham	The Causeway, Lower Grn, Surrey
	South Tooting	204 Mitcham Rd, SW17
	Sutton	Carshalton Rd, Sutton, Surrey
	Wallington	Stafford Rd, Wallington, Surrey
	Banstead	High Street Banstead, Suuer
	Epsom	Ashley Rd, Epsom, Surrey

By 1937 Cavendish Road was the principle station of the new and reformed 'W' or Tooting Division with Superintendent Ballantyne in charge[5].The station transferred its Divisional function, administration and staff moved to the new station in Mitcham Road SW17 in 1939.

Balham was a station situated on 'W' or Tooting Division in 1960 and was a sub divisional station call sign Whiskey Hotel (WH) with Superintendent F. C. Brown in charge[6]. The station was shut from 1976 to 1984[7].

In 1970 the station became known as Cavendish Road. The station closed in June 1973 and became a traffic warden centre. The station was then closed operationally between May 1975 and May 1984. In 1977 local residents tried to have the station reopened with a small number of police officers operating from it but this effort failed[8]. In 1984 the station reopened and in January 1996 it reverted to a police office[9].

By 2001 Cavandish Road had moved and was situated within the London Borough of Lambeth part of 'L' Division with call sign Lima Charlie (LC). The station was supervised by Superintendent C. Jarrett from Clapham (LM). It became a non charging station where no prisoners were housed but this station was still in operation in 2001 housing administrative offices for various divisional functions[10]. The headquarters station was located at Brixton where in 2000 the now famous Borough Commander was Brian Paddick, later Liberal candidate for Mayor of London.

In 2007 the station front counter was open Monday to Friday from 10am – 6pm. It is the base for three Safer Neighbourhood Teams but the future use of the police station is the subject of on-going discussion[11].

In 2013 the station was still open and subject to the following opening times Wednesday 7-8pm, Thursday 7-8pm, Saturday 2-3pm[12].

---

[1] Metropolitan Police Surveyors records 1912
[2] ibid
[3] Metropolitan Police Surveyors records 1924
[4] ibid
[5] Police and Constabulary Almanac 1937
[6] Police and Constabulary Almanac 1960
[7] South London Press 3rd July 1984
[8] South London Press 11 March 1977
[9] B Brown A Brief history of Vauxhall Division. July 1997
[10] Police and Constabulary Almanac 2001
[11] Met.Police Estate. Asset Management Plan Nov.2007
[12] http://content.met.police.uk/Borough/Lambeth/Contact#CavendishRoadPoliceStation accessed on 7th November 2013